The C++ Standard Library

A Tutorial and Reference

The C++ Standard Library

A Tutorial and Reference

Nicolai M. Josuttis

ADDISON–WESLEY

Boston • San Francisco • New York • Toronto • Montreal
London • Munich • Paris • Madrid
Capetown • Sydney • Tokyo • Singapore • Mexico City

The publisher offers discounts on this book when ordered in quantity for special sales. For more information, please contact:

Pearson Education Corporate Sales Division
201 W. 103rd Street
Indianapolis, IN 46290
(800) 428-5331
corpsales@pearsoned.com

Visit AW on the Web: www.awprofessional.com

Library of Congress Cataloging-in-Publication Data

Josuttis, Nicolai M.
   The C++ standard library: a tutorial and reference / Nicolai M. Josuttis.
      p.   cm.
   Includes bibliographical references and index.
   ISBN 0-201-37926-0
      1. C++ (Computer program language)   I. Title.
   QA76.73.C153J69   1999
   005.13'3--dc21   99-24977
                                                                  CIP

Text printed in the United States on recycled paper at Courier in Westford, Massachusetts.

ISBN 0-201-37926-0

Text printed in the United States on recycled paper at Courier Westford in Westford, Massachusetts.

21st Printing   January 2008

Contents

Preface   **xvii**

Acknowledgments   **xix**

1 About this Book   **1**

  1.1 Why this Book   1

  1.2 What You Should Know Before Reading this Book   2

  1.3 Style and Structure of the Book   2

  1.4 How to Read this Book   4

  1.5 State of the Art   5

  1.6 Example Code and Additional Information   5

  1.7 Feedback   5

2 Introduction to C++ and the Standard Library   **7**

  2.1 History   7

  2.2 New Language Features   9

    2.2.1 Templates   9

    2.2.2 Explicit Initialization for Fundamental Types 14

    2.2.3 Exception Handling 15

    2.2.4 Namespaces 16

    2.2.5 Type `bool` 18

    2.2.6 Keyword `explicit` 18

    2.2.7 New Operators for Type Conversion 19

    2.2.8 Initialization of Constant Static Members 20

    2.2.9 Definition of `main()` 21

  2.3 Complexity and the Big-O Notation 21

3 General Concepts   **23**

   3.1   Namespace `std` 23

   3.2   Header Files 24

   3.3   Error and Exception Handling 25

        3.3.1   Standard Exception Classes 25

        3.3.2   Members of Exception Classes 28

        3.3.3   Throwing Standard Exceptions 29

        3.3.4   Deriving from Standard Exception Classes 30

   3.4   Allocators 31

4 Utilities   **33**

   4.1   Pairs 33

        4.1.1   Convenience Function `make_pair()` 36

        4.1.2   Examples of Pair Usage 37

   4.2   Class `auto_ptr` 38

        4.2.1   Motivation of Class `auto_ptr` 38

        4.2.2   Transfer of Ownership by `auto_ptr` 40

        4.2.3   `auto_ptrs` as Members 44

        4.2.4   Misusing `auto_ptrs` 46

        4.2.5   `auto_ptr` Examples 47

        4.2.6   Class `auto_ptr` in Detail 51

   4.3   Numeric Limits 59

   4.4   Auxiliary Functions 66

        4.4.1   Processing the Minimum and Maximum 66

        4.4.2   Swapping Two Values 67

   4.5   Supplementary Comparison Operators 69

   4.6   Header Files `<cstddef>` and `<cstdlib>` 71

        4.6.1   Definitions in `<cstddef>` 71

        4.6.2   Definitions in `<cstdlib>` 71

5 The Standard Template Library   **73**

   5.1   STL Components 73

   5.2   Containers 75

        5.2.1   Sequence Containers 76

        5.2.2   Associative Containers 81

        5.2.3   Container Adapters 82

5.3   Iterators 83

     5.3.1   Examples of Using Associative Containers 86

     5.3.2   Iterator Categories 93

5.4   Algorithms 94

     5.4.1   Ranges 97

     5.4.2   Handling Multiple Ranges 101

5.5   Iterator Adapters 104

     5.5.1   Insert Iterators 104

     5.5.2   Stream Iterators 107

     5.5.3   Reverse Iterators 109

5.6   Manipulating Algorithms 111

     5.6.1   "Removing" Elements 111

     5.6.2   Manipulating Algorithms and Associative Containers 115

     5.6.3   Algorithms versus Member Functions 116

5.7   User-Defined Generic Functions 117

5.8   Functions as Algorithm Arguments 119

     5.8.1   Examples of Using Functions as Algorithm Arguments 119

     5.8.2   Predicates 121

5.9   Function Objects 124

     5.9.1   What Are Function Objects? 124

     5.9.2   Predefined Function Objects 131

5.10   Container Elements 134

     5.10.1   Requirements for Container Elements 134

     5.10.2   Value Semantics or Reference Semantics 135

5.11   Errors and Exceptions Inside the STL 136

     5.11.1   Error Handling 137

     5.11.2   Exception Handling 139

5.12   Extending the STL 141

6   STL Containers   **143**

6.1   Common Container Abilities and Operations 144

     6.1.1   Common Container Abilities 144

     6.1.2   Common Container Operations 144

6.2   Vectors 148

     6.2.1   Abilities of Vectors 148

     6.2.2   Vector Operations 150

6.2.3   Using Vectors as Ordinary Arrays 155

6.2.4   Exception Handling 155

6.2.5   Examples of Using Vectors 156

6.2.6   Class `vector<bool>` 158

6.3   Deques 160

6.3.1   Abilities of Deques 161

6.3.2   Deque Operations 162

6.3.3   Exception Handling 164

6.3.4   Examples of Using Deques 164

6.4   Lists 166

6.4.1   Abilities of Lists 166

6.4.2   List Operations 167

6.4.3   Exception Handling 172

6.4.4   Examples of Using Lists 172

6.5   Sets and Multisets 175

6.5.1   Abilities of Sets and Multisets 176

6.5.2   Set and Multiset Operations 177

6.5.3   Exception Handling 185

6.5.4   Examples of Using Sets and Multisets 186

6.5.5   Example of Specifying the Sorting Criterion at Runtime 191

6.6   Maps and Multimaps 194

6.6.1   Abilities of Maps and Multimaps 195

6.6.2   Map and Multimap Operations 196

6.6.3   Using Maps as Associative Arrays 205

6.6.4   Exception Handling 207

6.6.5   Examples of Using Maps and Multimaps 207

6.6.6   Example with Maps, Strings, and Sorting Criterion at Runtime 213

6.7   Other STL Containers 217

6.7.1   Strings as STL Containers 217

6.7.2   Ordinary Arrays as STL Containers 218

6.7.3   Hash Tables 221

6.8   Implementing Reference Semantics 222

6.9   When to Use which Container 226

6.10   Container Types and Members in Detail 230

6.10.1   Type Definitions 230

6.10.2   Create, Copy, and Destroy Operations 231

6.10.3 Nonmodifying Operations 233

6.10.4 Assignments 236

6.10.5 Direct Element Access 237

6.10.6 Operations to Generate Iterators 239

6.10.7 Inserting and Removing Elements 240

6.10.8 Special Member Functions for Lists 244

6.10.9 Allocator Support 246

6.10.10 Overview of Exception Handling in STL Containers 248

7 STL Iterators   **251**

7.1 Header Files for Iterators 251

7.2 Iterator Categories 251

7.2.1 Input Iterators 252

7.2.2 Output Iterators 253

7.2.3 Forward Iterators 254

7.2.4 Bidirectional Iterators 255

7.2.5 Random Access Iterators 255

7.2.6 The Increment and Decrement Problem of Vector Iterators 258

7.3 Auxiliary Iterator Functions 259

7.3.1 Stepping Iterators Using `advance()` 259

7.3.2 Processing Iterator Distance Using `distance()` 261

7.3.3 Swapping Iterator Values Using `iter_swap()` 263

7.4 Iterator Adapters 264

7.4.1 Reverse Iterators 264

7.4.2 Insert Iterators 271

7.4.3 Stream Iterators 277

7.5 Iterator Traits 283

7.5.1 Writing Generic Functions for Iterators 285

7.5.2 User-Defined Iterators 288

8 STL Function Objects   **293**

8.1 The Concept of Function Objects 293

8.1.1 Function Objects as Sorting Criteria 294

8.1.2 Function Objects with Internal State 296

8.1.3 The Return Value of `for_each()` 300

8.1.4 Predicates versus Function Objects 302

8.2   Predefined Function Objects 305
     8.2.1   Function Adapters 306
     8.2.2   Function Adapters for Member Functions 307
     8.2.3   Function Adapters for Ordinary Functions 309
     8.2.4   User-Defined Function Objects for Function Adapters 310
8.3   Supplementary Composing Function Objects 313
     8.3.1   Unary Compose Function Object Adapters 314
     8.3.2   Binary Compose Function Object Adapters 318

9   STL Algorithms   321

9.1   Algorithm Header Files 321
9.2   Algorithm Overview 322
     9.2.1   A Brief Introduction 322
     9.2.2   Classification of Algorithms 323
9.3   Auxiliary Functions 332
9.4   The `for_each()` Algorithm 334
9.5   Nonmodifying Algorithms 338
     9.5.1   Counting Elements 338
     9.5.2   Minimum and Maximum 339
     9.5.3   Searching Elements 341
     9.5.4   Comparing Ranges 356
9.6   Modifying Algorithms 363
     9.6.1   Copying Elements 363
     9.6.2   Transforming and Combining Elements 366
     9.6.3   Swapping Elements 370
     9.6.4   Assigning New Values 372
     9.6.5   Replacing Elements 375
9.7   Removing Algorithms 378
     9.7.1   Removing Certain Values 378
     9.7.2   Removing Duplicates 381
9.8   Mutating Algorithms 386
     9.8.1   Reversing the Order of Elements 386
     9.8.2   Rotating Elements 388
     9.8.3   Permuting Elements 391
     9.8.4   Shuffling Elements 393
     9.8.5   Moving Elements to the Front 395

    9.9   Sorting Algorithms 397
        9.9.1   Sorting All Elements 397
        9.9.2   Partial Sorting 400
        9.9.3   Sorting According to the *n*th Element 404
        9.9.4   Heap Algorithms 406
    9.10   Sorted Range Algorithms 409
        9.10.1   Searching Elements 410
        9.10.2   Merging Elements 416
    9.11   Numeric Algorithms 425
        9.11.1   Processing Results 425
        9.11.2   Converting Relative and Absolute Values 429

10 Special Containers   **435**
    10.1   Stacks 435
        10.1.1   The Core Interface 436
        10.1.2   Example of Using Stacks 437
        10.1.3   Class `stack<>` in Detail 438
        10.1.4   A User-Defined Stack Class 441
    10.2   Queues 444
        10.2.1   The Core Interface 445
        10.2.2   Example of Using Queues 446
        10.2.3   Class `queue<>` in Detail 447
        10.2.4   A User-Defined Queue Class 450
    10.3   Priority Queues 453
        10.3.1   The Core Interface 455
        10.3.2   Example of Using Priority Queues 455
        10.3.3   Class `priority_queue<>` in Detail 456
    10.4   Bitsets 460
        10.4.1   Examples of Using Bitsets 460
        10.4.2   Class `bitset` in Detail 463

11 Strings   **471**
    11.1   Motivation 471
        11.1.1   A First Example: Extracting a Temporary File Name 472
        11.1.2   A Second Example: Extracting Words and Printing Them Backward 476
    11.2   Description of the String Classes 479
        11.2.1   String Types 479

11.2.2 Operation Overview 481
11.2.3 Constructors and Destructors 483
11.2.4 Strings and C-Strings 484
11.2.5 Size and Capacity 485
11.2.6 Element Access 487
11.2.7 Comparisons 488
11.2.8 Modifiers 489
11.2.9 Substrings and String Concatenation 492
11.2.10 Input/Output Operators 492
11.2.11 Searching and Finding 493
11.2.12 The Value npos 495
11.2.13 Iterator Support for Strings 497
11.2.14 Internationalization 503
11.2.15 Performance 506
11.2.16 Strings and Vectors 506
11.3 String Class in Detail 507
11.3.1 Type Definitions and Static Values 507
11.3.2 Create, Copy, and Destroy Operations 508
11.3.3 Operations for Size and Capacity 510
11.3.4 Comparisons 511
11.3.5 Character Access 512
11.3.6 Generating C-Strings and Character Arrays 513
11.3.7 Modifying Operations 514
11.3.8 Searching and Finding 520
11.3.9 Substrings and String Concatenation 524
11.3.10 Input/Output Functions 524
11.3.11 Generating Iterators 525
11.3.12 Allocator Support 526

12 Numerics 529
12.1 Complex Numbers 529
12.1.1 Examples Using Class Complex 530
12.1.2 Operations for Complex Numbers 533
12.1.3 Class complex<> in Detail 541
12.2 Valarrays 547
12.2.1 Getting to Know Valarrays 547
12.2.2 Valarray Subsets 553

	12.2.3	Class `valarray` in Detail	569
	12.2.4	Valarray Subset Classes in Detail	575
12.3		Global Numeric Functions	581

13 Input/Output Using Stream Classes   **583**

13.1		Common Background of I/O Streams	584
	13.1.1	Stream Objects	584
	13.1.2	Stream Classes	584
	13.1.3	Global Stream Objects	585
	13.1.4	Stream Operators	586
	13.1.5	Manipulators	586
	13.1.6	A Simple Example	587
13.2		Fundamental Stream Classes and Objects	588
	13.2.1	Classes and Class Hierarchy	588
	13.2.2	Global Stream Objects	591
	13.2.3	Header Files	592
13.3		Standard Stream Operators << and >>	593
	13.3.1	Output Operator <<	593
	13.3.2	Input Operator >>	594
	13.3.3	Input/Output of Special Types	595
13.4		State of Streams	597
	13.4.1	Constants for the State of Streams	597
	13.4.2	Member Functions Accessing the State of Streams	598
	13.4.3	Stream State and Boolean Conditions	600
	13.4.4	Stream State and Exceptions	602
13.5		Standard Input/Output Functions	607
	13.5.1	Member Functions for Input	607
	13.5.2	Member Functions for Output	610
	13.5.3	Example Uses	611
13.6		Manipulators	612
	13.6.1	How Manipulators Work	612
	13.6.2	User-Defined Manipulators	614
13.7		Formatting	615
	13.7.1	Format Flags	615
	13.7.2	Input/Output Format of Boolean Values	617
	13.7.3	Field Width, Fill Character, and Adjustment	618

   13.7.4 Positive Sign and Uppercase Letters 620

   13.7.5 Numeric Base 621

   13.7.6 Floating-Point Notation 623

   13.7.7 General Formatting Definitions 625

  13.8 Internationalization 625

  13.9 File Access 627

   13.9.1 File Flags 631

   13.9.2 Random Access 634

   13.9.3 Using File Descriptors 637

  13.10 Connecting Input and Output Streams 637

   13.10.1 Loose Coupling Using `tie()` 637

   13.10.2 Tight Coupling Using Stream Buffers 638

   13.10.3 Redirecting Standard Streams 641

   13.10.4 Streams for Reading and Writing 643

  13.11 Stream Classes for Strings 645

   13.11.1 String Stream Classes 645

   13.11.2 `char*` Stream Classes 649

  13.12 Input/Output Operators for User-Defined Types 652

   13.12.1 Implementing Output Operators 652

   13.12.2 Implementing Input Operators 654

   13.12.3 Input/Output Using Auxiliary Functions 656

   13.12.4 User-Defined Operators Using Unformatted Functions 658

   13.12.5 User-Defined Format Flags 659

   13.12.6 Conventions for User-Defined Input/Output Operators 662

  13.13 The Stream Buffer Classes 663

   13.13.1 User's View of Stream Buffers 663

   13.13.2 Stream Buffer Iterators 665

   13.13.3 User-Defined Stream Buffers 668

  13.14 Performance Issues 681

   13.14.1 Synchronization with C's Standard Streams 682

   13.14.2 Buffering in Stream Buffers 682

   13.14.3 Using Stream Buffers Directly 683

14 Internationalization   **685**

  14.1 Different Character Encodings 686

   14.1.1 Wide-Character and Multibyte Text 686

        14.1.2   Character Traits 687
        14.1.3   Internationalization of Special Characters 691
    14.2 The Concept of Locales 692
        14.2.1   Using Locales 693
        14.2.2   Locale Facets 698
    14.3 Locales in Detail 700
    14.4 Facets in Detail 704
        14.4.1   Numeric Formatting 705
        14.4.2   Time and Date Formatting 708
        14.4.3   Monetary Formatting 711
        14.4.4   Character Classification and Conversion 715
        14.4.5   String Collation 724
        14.4.6   Internationalized Messages 725

15 Allocators   **727**
    15.1 Using Allocators as an Application Programmer 727
    15.2 Using Allocators as a Library Programmer 728
    15.3 The Default Allocator 732
    15.4 A User-Defined Allocator 735
    15.5 Allocators in Detail 737
        15.5.1   Type Definitions 737
        15.5.2   Operations 739
    15.6 Utilities for Uninitialized Memory in Detail 740

Internet Resources   **743**

Bibliography   **745**

Index   **747**

Preface

In the beginning, I only planned to write a small German book (400 pages or so) about the C++ standard library. That was in 1993. Now, in 1999 you see the result — an English book with more than 800 pages of facts, figures, and examples. My goal is to describe the C++ standard library so that all (or almost all) your programming questions are answered before you think of the question. Note, however, that this is not a complete description of all aspects of the C++ standard library. Instead, I present the most important topics necessary for learning and programming in C++ by using its standard library.

Each topic is described based on the general concepts; this discussion then leads to the specific details needed to support every-day programming tasks. Specific code examples are provided to help you understand the concepts and the details.

That's it — in a nutshell. I hope you get as much pleasure from reading this book as I did from writing it. Enjoy!

Acknowledgments

This book presents ideas, concepts, solutions, and examples from many sources. In a way it does not seem fair that my name is the only name on the cover. Thus, I'd like to thank all the people and companies who helped and supported me during the past few years.

First, I'd like to thank Dietmar Kühl. Dietmar is an expert on C++, especially on input/output streams and internationalization (he implemented an I/O stream library just for fun). He not only translated major parts of this book from German to English, he also wrote sections of this book using his expertise. In addition, he provided me with invaluable feedback over the years.

Second, I'd like to thank all the reviewers and everyone else who gave me their opinion. These people endow the book with a quality it would never have had without their input. (Because the list is extensive, please forgive me for any oversight.) The reviewers for the English version of this book included Chuck Allison, Greg Comeau, James A. Crotinger, Gabriel Dos Reis, Alan Ezust, Nathan Myers, Werner Mossner, Todd Veldhuizen, Chichiang Wan, Judy Ward, and Thomas Wikehult. The German reviewers included Ralf Boecker, Dirk Herrmann, Dietmar Kühl, Edda Lörke, Herbert Scheubner, Dominik Strasser, and Martin Weitzel. Additional input was provided by Matt Austern, Valentin Bonnard, Greg Colvin, Beman Dawes, Bill Gibbons, Lois Goldthwaite, Andrew Koenig, Steve Rumsby, Bjarne Stroustrup, and David Vandevoorde.

Special thanks to Dave Abrahams, Janet Cocker, Catherine Ohala, and Maureen Willard who reviewed and edited the whole book very carefully. Their feedback was an incredible contribution to the quality of this book.

A special thanks goes to my "personal living dictionary" — Herb Sutter — the author of the famous "Guru of the Week" (a regular series of C++ programming problems that is published on the `comp.lang.c++.moderated` Internet newsgroup).

I'd also like to thank all the people and companies who gave me the opportunity to test my examples on different platforms with different compilers. Many thanks to Steve Adamczyk, Mike Anderson, and John Spicer from EDG for their great compiler and their support. It was a big help during the standardization process and the writing of this book. Many thanks to P. J. Plauger and Dinkumware, Ltd, for their early standard-conforming implementation of the C++ standard library. Many thanks to Andreas Hommel and Metrowerks for an evaluative version of their CodeWarrior Programming Environment. Many thanks to all the developers of the free GNU and egcs compilers. Many thanks to Microsoft for an evaluative version of Visual C++. Many thanks to Roland Hartinger from Siemens Nixdorf Informations Systems AG for a test version of their C++ compiler. Many thanks to Topjects GmbH for an evaluative version of the ObjectSpace library implementation.

Many thanks to everyone from Addison Wesley Longman who worked with me. Among others this includes Janet Cocker, Mike Hendrickson, Debbie Lafferty, Marina Lang, Chanda Leary, Catherine Ohala, Marty Rabinowitz, Susanne Spitzer, and Maureen Willard. It was fun.

In addition, I'd like to thank the people at BREDEX GmbH and all the people in the C++ community, particularly those involved with the standardization process, for their support and patience (sometimes I ask really silly questions).

Last but not least, many thanks and kisses for my family: Ulli, Lucas, Anica, and Frederic. I definitely did not have enough time for them due to the writing of this book.

Have fun and be human!

Chapter 1

About this Book

1.1 Why this Book

Soon after its introduction, C++ became a de facto standard in object-oriented programming. This led to the goal of standardization. Only by having a standard, could programs be written that would run on different platforms — from PCs to mainframes. Furthermore, a standard *library* would enable programmers to use general components and a higher level of abstraction without losing portability, rather than having to develop all code from scratch.

The standardization process was started in 1989 by an international ANSI/ISO committee. It developed the standard based on Bjarne Stroustrup's books *The C++ Programming Language* and *The Annotated C++ Reference Manual*. After the standard was completed in 1997, several formal motions by different countries made it an international ISO and ANSI standard in 1998. The standardization process included the development of a C++ standard library. The library extends the core language to provide some general components. By using C++'s ability to program new abstract and generic types, the library provides a set of common classes and interfaces. This gives programmers a higher level of abstraction. The library provides the ability to use

- String types
- Different data structures (such as dynamic arrays, linked lists, and binary trees)
- Different algorithms (such as different sorting algorithms)
- Numeric classes
- Input/output (I/O) classes
- Classes for internationalization support

All of these are supported by a fairly simple programming interface. These components are very important for many programs. These days, data processing often means inputting, computing, processing, and outputting large amounts of data, which are often strings.

The library is not self-explanatory. To use these components and to benefit from their power, you need a good introduction that explains the concepts and the important details instead of simply listing the classes and their functions. This book is written exactly for that purpose. First, it introduces the library and all of its components from a conceptional point of view. Next, it describes the details needed for practical programming. Examples are included to demonstrate the exact usage of the components. Thus, this book is a detailed introduction to the C++ library for both the beginner and the practical programmer. Armed with the data provided herein, you should be able to take full advantage of the C++ standard library.

Caveat: I don't promise that everything described is easy and self-explanatory. The library provides a lot of flexibility, but flexibility for nontrivial purposes has a price. Beware that the library has traps and pitfalls, which I point out when we encounter them and suggest ways of avoiding them.

1.2   What You Should Know Before Reading this Book

To get the most from this book you should already know C++. (The book describes the standard components of C++, but not the language itself.) You should be familiar with the concepts of classes, inheritance, templates, and exception handling. However, you don't have to know all of the minor details about the language. The important details are described in the book (the minor details about the language are more important for people who want to implement the library rather than use it). Note that the language has changed during the standardization process, so your knowledge might not be up to date. Section 2.2, page 9, provides a brief overview and introduction of the latest language features that are important for using the library. You should read this section if you are not sure whether you know all the new features of C++ (such as the keyword `typename` and the concept of namespaces).

1.3   Style and Structure of the Book

The C++ standard library provides different components that are somewhat but not totally independent of each other, so there is no easy way to describe each part without mentioning others. I considered several different approaches for presenting the contents of this book. One was on the order of the C++ standard. However, this is not the best way to explain the components of the C++ standard library from scratch. Another was to start with an overview of all components followed by chapters that provided more details. Alternatively, I could have sorted the components, trying to find an order that had a minimum of cross-references to other sections. My solution was to use a mixture of all three approaches. I start with a brief introduction of the general concepts and the utilities that are used by the library. Then, I describe all the components, each in one or more chapters. The first component is the standard template library (STL). There is no doubt that the STL is the most powerful, most complex, and most exciting part of the library. Its design influences other components heavily. Then I describe the more self-explanatory components, such as special containers, strings, and numeric classes. The next component discussed is one you probably know and use already: the IOStream library. It is followed by a discussion of internationalization, which had some influence on the IOStream library.

Each component description begins with the component's purpose, design, and some examples. Next, a detailed description follows that begins with different ways to use the component, as well as any traps and pitfalls associated with it. The description usually ends with a reference section, in which you can find the exact signature and definition of a component's classes and its functions.

The following is a description of the book's contents. The first four chapters introduce this book and the C++ standard library in general:

- **Chapter 1: About this Book**
  This chapter (which you are reading right now) introduces the book's subject and describes its contents.

- **Chapter 2: Introduction to C++ and the Standard Library**
  This chapter provides a brief overview of the history of the C++ standard library and the context of its standardization. It also contains some general hints regarding the technical background for this book and the library, such as new language features and the concept of complexity.

- **Chapter 3: General Concepts**
  This chapter describes the fundamental concepts of the library that you need to understand to work with all the components. In particular, it introduces the namespace `std`, the format of header files, and the general support of error and exception handling.

- **Chapter 4: Utilities**
  This chapter describes several small utilities provided for the user of the library and for the library itself. In particular, it describes auxiliary functions such as `max()`, `min()`, and `swap()`, types `pair` and `auto_ptr`, as well as `numeric_limits`, which provide more information about implementation-specific details of numeric data types.

Chapters 5 through 9 describe all aspects of the STL:

- **Chapter 5: The Standard Template Library**
  This chapter presents a detailed introduction to the concept of the STL, which provides container classes and algorithms that are used to process collections of data. It explains step-by-step the concept, the problems, and the special programming techniques of the STL, as well as the roles of its parts.

- **Chapter 6: STL Containers**
  This chapter explains the concepts and describes the abilities of the STL's container classes. First it describes the differences between vectors, deques, lists, sets, and maps, then their common abilities, and all with typical examples. Lastly it lists and describes all container functions in form of a handy reference.

- **Chapter 7: STL Iterators**
  This chapter deals in detail with the STL's iterator classes. In particular, it explains the different iterator categories, the auxiliary functions for iterators, and the iterator adapters, such as stream iterators, reverse iterators, and insert iterators.

- **Chapter 8: STL Function Objects**
  This chapter details the STL's function object classes.

- **Chapter 9: STL Algorithms**
  This chapter lists and describes the STL's algorithms. After a brief introduction and comparison of the algorithms, each algorithm is described in detail followed by one or more example programs.

Chapters 10 through 12 describe "simple" individual standard classes:

- **Chapter 10: Special Containers**

  This chapter describes the different special container classes of the C++ standard library. It covers the container adapters for queues and stacks, as well as the class `bitset`, which manages a bitfield with an arbitrary number of bits or flags.

- **Chapter 11: Strings**

  This chapter describes the string types of the C++ standard library (yes, there are more than one). The standard provides strings as kind of "self-explanatory" fundamental data types with the ability to use different types of characters.

- **Chapter 12: Numerics**

  This chapter describes the numeric components of the C++ standard library. In particular, it covers types for complex numbers and classes for the processing of arrays of numeric values (the latter may be used for matrices, vectors, and equations).

Chapters 13 and 14 deal with I/O and internationalization (two closely related subjects):

- **Chapter 13: Input/Output Using Stream Classes**

  This chapter covers the I/O component of C++. This component is the standardized form of the commonly known IOStream library. The chapter also describes details that may be important to programmers but are typically not so well known. For example, it describes the correct way to define and integrate special I/O channels, which are often implemented incorrectly in practice.

- **Chapter 14: Internationalization**

  This chapter covers the concepts and classes for the internationalization of programs. In particular, it describes the handling of different character sets, as well as the use of different formats for such values as floating-point numbers and dates.

The rest of the book contains:

- **Chapter 15: Allocators**

  This chapter describes the concept of different memory models in the C++ standard library.

- An **appendix** with
  - **Internet Resources**
  - **Bibliography**
  - **Index**

1.4   How to Read this Book

This book is a mix of introductory user's guide and structured reference manual regarding the C++ standard library. The individual components of the C++ standard library are independent of each other, to some extent, so after reading Chapters 2 through 4 you could read the chapters that discuss the individual components in any order. Bear in mind, that Chapter 5 through Chapter 9 all describe the same component. To understand the other STL chapters, you should start with the introduction to the STL in Chapter 5.

If you are a C++ programmer who wants to know, in general, the concepts and all parts of the library, you could simply read the book from the beginning to the end. However, you should skip the reference sections. To program with certain components of the C++ standard library, the best way to find something is to use the index. I have tried to make the index very comprehensive to save you time when you are looking for something.

In my experience, the best way to learn something new is to look at examples. Therefore, you'll find a lot of examples throughout the book. They may be a few lines of code or complete programs. In the latter case, you'll find the name of the file containing the program as the first comment line. You can find the files on the Internet at my Web site at `http://www.josuttis.com/libbook/`.

1.5 State of the Art

While I was writing this book, the C++ standard was completed. Please bear in mind that some compilers might not yet conform to it. This will most likely change in the near future. As a consequence, you might discover that not all things covered in this book work as described on your system, and you may have to change example programs to fit your specific environment. I can compile almost all example programs with version 2.8 or higher of the EGCS compiler, which is free for almost all platforms and available on the Internet (see `http://egcs.cygnus.com/`) and on several software CDs.

1.6 Example Code and Additional Information

You can access all example programs and acquire more informations about this book and the C++ standard library from my Web site at `http://www.josuttis.com/libbook/`. Also, you can find a lot of additional information about this topic on the Internet. See Internet Resources on page 743 for details.

1.7 Feedback

I welcome your feedback (good and bad) on this book. I tried to prepare it carefully; however, I'm human, and at some time I have to stop writing and tweaking. So, you may find some errors, inconsistencies, or subjects that could be described better. Your feedback will give me the chance to improve later editions. The best way to reach me is by Email:

`libbook@josuttis.com`

You can also reach me by phone, fax, or "snail" mail:

> Nicolai M. Josuttis
> Berggarten 9
> D–38108 Braunschweig
> Germany
>
> Phone: +49 5309 5747
> Fax: +49 5309 5774

Many thanks.

Chapter 2

Introduction to C++ and the Standard Library

2.1 History

The standardization of C++ was started in 1989 and finished at the end of 1997, although some formal motions delayed the final publication until September 1998. The result was a reference manual with approximately 750 pages, published by the International Organization for Standardization (ISO). The standard has the title "*Information Technology — Programming Languages — C++.*" Its document number is ISO/IEC 14882-1998, and it is distributed by the national bodies of the ISO, such as the ANSI in the United States.[1]

The standard was an important milestone for C++. Because it defines the exact contents and behavior of C++, it makes it easier to teach C++, to use C++ in applications, and to port C++ programs to different platforms. It also gives users greater freedom of choice regarding different C++ implementations. Its stability and portability help library providers and tool providers as well as implementers. Thus, the standard helps C++ application developers build better applications faster, and maintain them with less cost and effort.

Part of the standard is a standard library. This library provides core components for I/O, strings, containers (data structures), algorithms (such as sort, search, and merge), support for numeric computation, and (as could be expected from an international standard) support for internationalization (such as different character sets).

You may wonder why the standardization process took almost 10 years, and if you know some details about the standard you might wonder why after all this time it is still not perfect. Ten years, in fact, was not enough time! Although, according to the history and the context of the standardization

---

[1] At the time this book was written, you could get the C++ standard at the ANSI Electronics Standard Store for $18.00 (US; see http://www.ansi.org/).

process, a lot was accomplished. The result is usable in practice, but it is not perfect (nothing ever is).

The standard is not the result of a company with a big budget and a lot of time. Standards organizations pay nothing or almost nothing to the people who work on developing standards. So, if a participant doesn't work for a company that has a special interest in the standard, the work is done for fun. Thank goodness there were a lot of dedicated people who had the time and the money to do just that.

The C++ standard was not developed from scratch. It was based on the language as described by Bjarne Stroustrup, the creator of C++. The standard library, however, was not based on a book or on an existing library. Instead, different, existing classes were integrated.[2] Thus, the result is not very homogeneous. You will find different design principles for different components. A good example is the difference between the string class and the STL, which is a framework for data structures and algorithms:

- String classes are designed as a safe and convenient component. Thus, they provide an almost self-explanatory interface and check for many errors in the interface.
- The STL was designed to combine different data structures with different algorithms while achieving the best performance. Thus, the STL is not very convenient and it is not required to check for many logical errors. To benefit from the powerful framework and great performance of the STL, you must know the concepts and apply them carefully.

Both of these components are part of the same library. They were harmonized a bit, but they still follow their individual, fundamental design philosophies.

One component of the library existed as a de facto standard before standardization began: the IOStream library. Developed in 1984, it was reimplemented and partially redesigned in 1989. Because many programs were using it already, the general concept of the IOStream library was not changed, thus keeping it backward compatible.

In general, the whole standard (language and library) is the result of a lot of discussions and influence from hundreds of people all over the world. For example, the Japanese came up with important support for internationalization. Of course, mistakes were made, minds were changed, and people had different opinions. Then, in 1994, when people thought the standard was close to being finished, the STL was incorporated, which changed the whole library radically. However, to get finished, the thinking about major extensions was eventually stopped, regardless of how useful the extension would be. Thus, hash tables are not part of the standard, although they should be a part of the STL as a common data structure.

The current standard is not the end of the road. There will be fixes of bugs and inconsistencies, and there likely will be a next version of the standard in five years or so. However for the next few years, C++ programmers have a standard and the chance to write powerful code that is portable to very different platforms.

---

[2] You may wonder why the standardization process did not design a new library from scratch. The major purpose of standardization is not to invent or to develop something; it is to harmonize an existing practice.

2.2   New Language Features

The core language and the library of C++ were standardized in parallel. In this way, the library could benefit from improvements in the language and the language could benefit from experiences of library implementation. In fact, during the standardization process the library often used special language features that were not yet available.

C++ is not the same language it was five years ago. If you didn't follow its evolution, you may be surprised with the new language features used by the library. This section gives you a brief overview of those new features. For details, refer to books on the language in question.

While I was writing this book (in 1998), not all compilers were able to provide all of the new language features. I hope (and expect) that this will change very soon (most compiler vendors were part of the standardization process). Thus, you may be restricted in your use of the library. Portable implementations of the library typically consider whether features are present in the environment they use (they usually have some test programs to check which language features are present, and then set preprocessor directives according to the result of the check). I'll mention any restrictions that are typical and important throughout the book by using footnotes.

The following subsections describe the most important new language features that are relevant for the C++ standard library.

2.2.1   Templates

Almost all parts of the library are written as templates. Without template support, you can't use the standard library. Moreover, the library needed new special template features, which I introduce after a short overview of templates.

Templates are functions or classes that are written for one or more types not yet specified. When you use a template, you pass the types as arguments, explicitly or implicitly. The following is a typical example — a function that returns the maximum of two values:

```
template <class T>
inline const T& max (const T& a, const T& b)
{
    // if a < b then use b else use a
    return  a < b ? b : a;
}
```

Here, the first line defines T as an arbitrary data type that is specified by the caller when the caller calls the function. You can use any identifier as a parameter name, but using T is very common, if not a de facto convention. The type is classified by `class`, although it does not have to be a class. You can use any data type as long as it provides the operations that the template uses.[3]

---

[3] `class` was used here to avoid the introduction of a new keyword when templates were introduced. However, now there is a new keyword, `typename`, that you can also use here (see page 11).

Following the same principle, you can "parameterize" classes on arbitrary types. This is useful for container classes. You can implement the container operations for an arbitrary element type. The C++ standard library provides many template container classes (for example, see Chapter 6 or Chapter 10). It also uses template classes for many other reasons. For example, the string classes are parameterized on the type of the characters and the properties of the character set (see Chapter 11).

A template is not compiled once to generate code usable for any type; instead, it is compiled for each type or combination of types for which it is used. This leads to an important problem in the handling of templates in practice: You must have the implementation of a template function available when you call it, so that you can compile the function for your specific type. Therefore, the only portable way of using templates at the moment is to implement them in header files by using inline functions.[4]

The full functionality of the C++ standard library requires not only the support of templates in general, but also many new standardized template features, including those discussed in the following paragraphs.

Nontype Template Parameters

In addition to type parameters, it is also possible to use nontype parameters. A nontype parameter is then considered as part of the type. For example, for the standard class `bitset<>` (class `bitset<>` is introduced in Section 10.4, page 460) you can pass the number of bits as the template argument. The following statements define two bitfields, one with 32 bits and one with 50 bits:

```
bitset<32> flags32;      // bitset with 32 bits
bitset<50> flags50;      // bitset with 50 bits
```

These bitsets have different types because they use different template arguments. Thus, you can't assign or compare them (except if a corresponding type conversion is provided).

Default Template Parameters

Template classes may have default arguments. For example, the following declaration allows one to declare objects of class `MyClass` with one or two template arguments[5]:

```
template <class T, class container = vector<T> >
class MyClass;
```

If you pass only one argument, the default parameter is used as second argument:

```
MyClass<int> x1;          // equivalent to: MyClass<int,vector<int> >
```

Note that default template arguments may be defined in terms of previous arguments.

---

[4] To avoid the problem of templates having to be present in header files, the standard introduced a *template compilation model* with the keyword `export`. However, I have not seen it implemented yet.

[5] Note that you have to put a space between the two ">" characters. ">>" would be parsed as shift operator, which would result in a syntax error.

Keyword `typename`

The keyword `typename` was introduced to specify that the identifier that follows is a type. Consider the following example:

```
template <class T>
class MyClass {
    typename T::SubType * ptr;
    ...
};
```

Here, `typename` is used to clarify that `SubType` is a type of class `T`. Thus, `ptr` is a pointer to the type `T::SubType`. Without `typename`, `SubType` would be considered a static member. Thus

```
T::SubType * ptr
```

would be a multiplication of value `SubType` of type `T` with `ptr`.

According to the qualification of `SubType` being a type, any type that is used in place of `T` must provide an inner type `SubType`. For example, the use of type `Q` as a template argument

```
MyClass<Q> x;
```

is possible only if type `Q` has an inner type definition such as the following:

```
class Q {
    typedef int SubType;
    ...
};
```

In this case, the `ptr` member of `MyClass<Q>` would be a pointer to type `int`. However, the subtype could also be an abstract data type (such as a class):

```
class Q {
    class SubType;
    ...
};
```

Note that `typename` is always necessary to qualify an identifier of a template as being a type, even if an interpretation that is not a type would make no sense. Thus, the general rule in C++ is that any identifier of a template is considered to be a value, except if it is qualified by `typename`.

Apart from this, `typename` can also be used instead of `class` in a template declaration:

```
template <typename T> class MyClass;
```

Member Templates

Member functions of classes may be templates. However, member templates may not be virtual, nor may they have default parameters. For example:

```
class MyClass {
    ...
    template <class T>
    void f(T);
};
```

Here, `MyClass::f` declares a set of member functions for parameters of any type. You can pass any argument as long as its type provides all operations used by `f()`.

This feature is often used to support automatic type conversions for members in template classes. For example, in the following definition the argument x of `assign()` must have exactly the same type as the object it is called for:

```
template <class T>
class MyClass {
  private:
    T value;
  public:
    void assign (const MyClass<T>& x) { // x must have same type as *this
        value = x.value;
    }
    ...
};
```

It would be an error to use different template types for the objects of the `assign()` operation even if an automatic type conversion from one type to the other is provided:

```
void f()
{
    MyClass<double> d;
    MyClass<int> i;

    d.assign(d);    // OK
    d.assign(i);    // ERROR: i is MyClass<int>
                    //        but MyClass<double> is required
}
```

By providing a different template type for the member function, you relax the rule of exact match. The member template function argument may have any template type then, as long as the types are assignable:

```
template <class T>
class MyClass {
  private:
    T value;
```

```
public:
  template <class X>                    // member template
  void assign (const MyClass<X>& x) {   // allows different template types
      value = x.getValue();
  }
  T getValue () const {
      return value;
  }
  ...
};

void f()
{
    MyClass<double> d;
    MyClass<int> i;

    d.assign(d);    // OK
    d.assign(i);    // OK (int is assignable to double)
}
```

Note that the argument x of `assign()` now differs from the type of `*this`. Thus, you can't access private and protected members of `MyClass<>` directly. Instead, you have to use something like `getValue()` in this example.

A special form of a member template is a *template constructor.* Template constructors are usually provided to enable implicit type conversions when objects are copied. Note that a template constructor does not hide the implicit copy constructor. If the type matches exactly, the implicit copy constructor is generated and called. For example:

```
template <class T>
class MyClass {
  public:
    // copy constructor with implicit type conversion
    // - does not hide implicit copy constructor
    template <class U>
    MyClass (const MyClass<U>& x);
    ...
};

void f()
{
    MyClass<double> xd;
```

```
    ...
    MyClass<double> xd2(xd);      // calls built-in copy constructor
    MyClass<int> xi(xd);          // calls template constructor
    ...
}
```

Here, the type of xd2 is the same as the type of xd, so it is initialized via the built-in copy constructor. The type of xi differs from the type of xd, so it is initialized by using the template constructor. Thus, if you write a template constructor, don't forget to provide a copy constructor, if the default copy constructor does not fit your needs. See Section 4.1, page 33, for another example of member templates.

Nested Template Classes

Nested classes may also be templates:

```
template <class T>
class MyClass {
    ...
    template <class T2>
    class NestedClass;
    ...
};
```

2.2.2 Explicit Initialization for Fundamental Types

If you use the syntax of an explicit constructor call without arguments, fundamental types are initialized with zero:

```
int i1;                // undefined value
int i2 = int();        // initialized with zero
```

This feature is provided to enable you to write template code that ensures that values of any type have a certain default value. For example, in the following function the initialization guarantees that x is initialized with zero for fundamental types:

```
template <class T>
void f()
{
    T x = T();
    ...
}
```

2.2.3   Exception Handling

The C++ standard library uses exception handling. Using this feature, you can handle exceptions without "polluting" your function interfaces: arguments and return values. If you encounter an unexpected situation, you can stop the usual data processing by "throwing an exception":

```
class Error;

void f()
{
    ...
    if (exception-condition) {
        throw Error();   // create object of class Error and throw it as exception
    }
    ...
}
```

The `throw` statement starts a process called *stack unwinding*; that is, any block or function is left as if there was a `return` statement. However, the program does not jump anywhere. For all local objects that are declared in the blocks that the program leaves due to the exception their destructors are called. Stack unwinding continues until `main()` is left, which ends the program, or until a `catch` clause "catches" and handles the exception:

```
int main()
{
    try {
        ...
        f();
        ...
    }
    catch (const Error&) {
        ... // handle exception
    }
    ...
}
```

Here, any exception of type `Error` in the `try` block is handled in the `catch` clause.[6]

---

[6] Exceptions end a call of the function, where you find the exception, with the ability to pass an object as argument back to the caller. However, this is not a function call back in the opposite direction (from the bottom where the problem was found to the top where the problem is solved or handled). You can't process the exception and continue from where you found the exception. In this regard, exception handling is completely different from signal handling.

Exception objects are ordinary objects that are described in ordinary classes or ordinary fundamental types. Thus, you can use `ints`, strings, or template classes that are part of a class hierarchy. Usually you design (a hierarchy of) special error classes. You can use their state to pass any information you want from the point of error detection to the point of error handling.

Note that the concept is called *exception handling* not *error handling*. The two are not necessarily the same. For example, in many circumstances bad user input is not an exception; it typically happens. So it is often a good idea to handle wrong user input locally using the usual error-handling techniques.

You can specify which set of exceptions a function might throw by writing an *exception specification*:

```
void f() throw(bad_alloc);   // f() may only throw bad_alloc exceptions
```

You can specify that a function does not throw an exception by declaring an empty set of exceptions:

```
void f() throw();              // f() does not throw
```

A violation of an exception specification causes special behavior to occur. See the description of the exception class `bad_exception` on page 26 for details.

The C++ standard library provides some general features for exception handling, such as the standard exception classes and class `auto_ptr` (see Section 3.3, page 25, and Section 4.2, page 38, for details).

2.2.4 Namespaces

As more and more software is written as libraries, modules, or components, the combination of these different parts might result in a name clash. Namespaces solve this problem.

A *namespace* groups different identifiers in a named scope. By defining all identifiers in a namespace, the name of the namespace is the only global identifier that might conflict with other global symbols. Similar to the handling of classes, you have to qualify a symbol in a namespace by preceding the identifier with the name of the namespace, separated by the operator : : as follows:

```
// defining identifiers in namespace josuttis
namespace josuttis {
    class File;
    void myGlobalFunc();
    ...
}
...


// using a namespace identifier
josuttis::File obj;
...
josuttis::myGlobalFunc();
```

Unlike classes, namespaces are open for definitions and extensions in different modules. Thus you can use namespaces to define modules, libraries, or components even by using multiple files. A namespace defines logical modules instead of physical modules (in UML and other modeling notations, a module is also called a *package*).

You don't have to qualify the namespace for functions if one or more argument types are defined in the namespace of the function. This rule is called *Koenig lookup*. For example:

```
// defining identifiers in namespace josuttis
namespace josuttis {
    class File;
    void myGlobalFunc(const File&);
    ...
}
...

josuttis::File obj;
...
myGlobalFunc(obj);      // OK, lookup finds josuttis::myGlobalFunc()
```

By using a *using declaration*, you can avoid the (remaining) tedious, repeated qualification of the namespace scope. For example, the declaration

```
using josuttis::File;
```

makes File a local synonym in the current scope that stands for josuttis::File.

A *using directive* makes all names of a namespace available, because they would have been declared outside their namespace. However, the usual name conflicts may arise. For example, the directive

```
using namespace josuttis;
```

makes File and myGlobalFunc() global in the current scope. The compiler will report an ambiguity if there also exists an identifier File or myGlobalFunc() in the global scope and the user uses the name without qualification.

Note that you should never use a using directive when the context is not clear (such as in header files, modules, or libraries). The directive might change the scope of identifiers of a namespace, so you might get different behavior than the one expected because you included or used your code in another module. In fact, using directives in header files is really bad design.

The C++ standard library defines all identifiers in namespace std. See Section 3.1, page 23, for details.

2.2.5 Type `bool`

To provide better support for Boolean values, type `bool` was introduced. Using `bool` increases readability and allows you to overload behavior for Boolean values. The literals `true` and `false` were introduced as Boolean values. Automatic type conversions to and from integral values are provided. The value 0 is equivalent to `false`. Any other value is equivalent to `true`.

2.2.6 Keyword `explicit`

By using the keyword `explicit`, you can prohibit a single argument constructor from defining an automatic type conversion. A typical example of the need for this feature is in a collection class in which you can pass the initial size as constructor argument. For example, you could declare a constructor that has an argument for the initial size of a stack:

```
class Stack {
    explicit Stack(int size);     // create stack with initial size
    ...
};
```

Here, the use of `explicit` is rather important. Without `explicit` this constructor would define an automatic type conversion from `int` to `Stack`. If this happens, you could assign an `int` to a `Stack`:

```
Stack s;
...
s = 40;     // Oops, creates a new Stack for 40 elements and assigns it to s
```

The automatic type conversion would convert the 40 to a stack with 40 elements and then assign it to s. This is probably not what was intended. By declaring the `int` constructor as `explicit`, such an assignment results in an error at compile time.

Note that `explicit` also rules out the initialization with type conversion by using the assignment syntax:

```
Stack s1(40);     // OK
Stack s2 = 40;     // ERROR
```

This is because there is a minor difference between

```
X x;
Y y(x);     // explicit conversion
```

and

```
X x;
Y y = x;     // implicit conversion
```

The former creates a new object of type Y by using an explicit conversion from type X, whereas the latter creates a new object of type Y by using an implicit conversion.

2.2.7 New Operators for Type Conversion

To enable you to clarify the meaning of an explicit type conversion for one argument, the following four new operators were introduced:

1. `static_cast`

   This operator converts a value logically. It can be considered a creation of a temporary object that is initialized by the value that gets converted. The conversion is allowed only if a type conversion is defined (either as a built-in conversion rule or via a defined conversion operation). For example:

   ```
   float x;
   ...
   cout << static_cast<int>(x);        // print x as int
   ...
   f(static_cast<string>("hello"));  // call f() for string instead of char*
   ```

2. `dynamic_cast`

   This operator enables you to downcast a polymorphic type to its real static type. This is the only cast that is checked at runtime. Thus, you could also use it to check the type of a polymorphic value. For example:

   ```
   class Car;        // abstract base class (has at least one virtual function)

   class Cabriolet : public Car {
       ...
   };

   class Limousine : public Car {
       ...
   };

   void f(Car* cp)
   {
       Cabriolet* p = dynamic_cast<Cabriolet*>(cp);
       if (p == NULL) {
           // cp did not refer to an object of type Cabriolet
           ...
       }
   }
   ```

   In this example, `f()` contains a special behavior for objects that have the real static type `Cabriolet`. When the argument is a reference and the type conversion fails, `dynamic_cast` throws a `bad_cast` exception (`bad_cast` is described on page 26). Note that from a design point of view, it is always better to avoid such type-dependent statements when you program with polymorphic types.

3. `const_cast`

   This operator adds or removes the `const`ness of a type. In addition, you can remove a `volatile` qualification. Any other change of the type is not allowed.

4. `reinterpret_cast`

   The behavior of this operator is implementation defined. It may reinterpret bits, but it is not required to do so. Using this cast is usually not portable.

These operators replace the old cast techniques that use parentheses. They have the advantage of clarifying the intention of the conversion. The old casts with parentheses could be used for any of these type conversions except for `dynamic_cast`, so when they were used you could not formulate the exact reason for the conversion. The new operators enable the compiler to receive more information regarding the reason for the conversion and to report an error if the conversion does more than it should.

Note that these operators are provided for only *one* argument. Consider the following example:

```
static_cast<Fraction>(15,100)      // Oops, creates Fraction(100)
```

This example does not do what you might expect. Instead of initializing a temporary fraction with numerator 15 and denominator 100, it initializes a temporary fraction only with the single value 100. The comma is not an argument separator here. Instead, it is the comma operator that combines two expressions into one expression and yields the second. The correct way to "convert" values 15 and 100 into a fraction is still

```
Fraction(15,100)                   // fine, creates Fraction(15,100)
```

2.2.8   Initialization of Constant Static Members

It is now possible to initialize integral constant static members inside the class structure. This is useful when the constant is used in the class structure after the initialization. For example:

```
class MyClass {
    static const int num = 100;
    int elems[num];
    ...
};
```

Note that you still have to define space for a constant static member that is initialized within a class definition:

```
const int MyClass::num;      // no initialization here
```

2.2.9   Definition of `main()`

I'd also like to clarify an important, often misunderstood, aspect of the core language — namely, the only correct and portable versions of `main()`. According to the C++ standard, only two definitions of `main()` are portable:

```
int main()
{
    ...
}
```

and

```
int main (int argc, char* argv[])
{
    ...
}
```

where `argv` (the array of command-line arguments) might also be defined as `char**`. Note that the return type `int` is required because the implicit `int` is deprecated.

You may, but are not required to, end `main()` with a `return` statement. Unlike C, C++ defines an implicit

```
return 0;
```

at the end of `main()`. This means that every program that leaves `main()` without a `return` statement is successful (any value other than 0 represents a kind of failure). Because of this, my examples in this book have no `return` statement at the end of `main()`. Note that some compilers might print a warning message regarding this or even handle it as error. Well, that's life before the standard.

2.3   Complexity and the Big-O Notation

For certain parts of the C++ standard library (especially for the STL), the performance of algorithms and member functions was considered carefully. Thus, the standard requires a certain "complexity" of them. Computer scientists use a specialized notation to compare the relative complexity of an algorithm. Using this measure, one can categorize quickly the relative runtime of an algorithm as well as perform qualitative comparisons between algorithms. This measure is called *Big-O notation*.

The Big-O notation expresses the runtime of an algorithm as a function of a given input of size n. For example, if the runtime grows linearly with the number of elements (doubling the input doubles the runtime) the complexity is $O(n)$. If the runtime is independent of the input, the complexity is $O(1)$. Table 2.1 lists typical values of complexity and their Big-O notation.

It is important to observe that the Big-O notation hides factors with smaller exponents (such as constant factors). In particular, it doesn't matter how long an algorithm takes. Any two linear algorithms are considered equally acceptable by this measure. There even may be some situations in which the constant is so huge in a linear algorithm that even an exponential algorithm with a small

Type	Notation	Meaning
Constant	O(1)	The runtime is independent of the number of elements.
Logarithmic	O($log(n)$)	The runtime grows logarithmically with respect to the number of elements.
Linear	O(n)	The runtime grows linearly (with the same factor) as the number of elements grows.
n-log-n	O($n * log(n)$)	The runtime grows as a product of linear and logarithmic complexity.
Quadratic	O(n^2)	The runtime grows quadratically with respect to the number of elements.

Table 2.1. Typical Values of Complexity

constant would be preferable in practice. This is a valid criticism of the Big-O notation. Just be aware that it is only a rule of thumb; the algorithm with optimal complexity is not necessarily the best one.

Table 2.2 lists all the categories of complexity with a certain number of elements to give you a feel of how fast the runtime grows with respect to the number of elements. As you can see, with a small number of elements the runtimes don't differ much. Here, constant factors that are hidden by the Big-O notation may have a big influence. However, the more elements you have, the bigger the differences in the runtimes, so constant factors become meaningless. Remember to "think big" when you consider complexity.

Complexity		No. of Elements						
Type	Notation	1	2	5	10	50	100	1000
Constant	O(1)	1	1	1	1	1	1	1
Logarithmic	O($log(n)$)	1	2	3	4	6	7	10
Linear	O(n)	1	2	5	10	50	100	1,000
n-log-n	O($n * log(n)$)	1	4	15	40	300	700	10,000
Quadratic	O(n^2)	1	4	25	100	2,500	10,000	1,000,000

Table 2.2. Runtime with Respect to the Complexity and the Number of Elements

Some complexity definitions in the C++ reference manual are specified as *amortized*. This means that the operations *in the long term* behave as described. However, a single operation may take longer than specified. For example, if you append elements to a dynamic array, the runtime depends on whether the array has enough memory for one more element. If there is enough memory, the complexity is constant because inserting a new last element always takes the same time. However, if there is not enough memory, the complexity is linear. This is because, depending on the actual number of elements, you have to allocate new memory and copy all elements. Reallocations are rather rare, so any sufficiently long sequence of that operation behaves as if each operation has constant complexity. Thus, the complexity of the insertion is "amortized" constant time.

Chapter 3
General Concepts

This chapter describes the fundamental concepts of the C++ standard library that you need to work with all or most components:

- The namespace `std`
- The names and formats of header files
- The general concept of error and exception handling
- A brief introduction to allocators

3.1 Namespace `std`

If you use different modules and/or libraries, you always have the potential for name clashes. This is because modules and libraries might use the same identifier for different things. This problem was solved by the introduction of *namespaces* into C++ (see Section 2.2.4, page 16, for an introduction to the concept of namespaces). A namespace is a certain scope for identifiers. Unlike a class, it is open for extensions that might occur at any source. Thus, you could use a namespace to define components that are distributed over several physical modules. A typical example of such a component is the C++ standard library, so it follows that it uses a namespace. In fact, all identifiers of the C++ standard library are defined in a namespace called `std`.

According to the concept of namespaces, you have three options when using an identifier of the C++ standard library:

1. You can qualify the identifier directly. For example, you can write `std::ostream` instead of `ostream`. A complete statement might look like this:

   ```
   std::cout << std::hex << 3.4 << std::endl;
   ```

2. You can use a *using declaration* (see page 17). For example, the following code fragment introduces the local ability to skip `std::` for `cout` and `endl`.

   ```
   using std::cout;
   using std::endl;
   ```

Thus the example in option 1 could be written like this:

```
cout << std::hex << 3.4 << endl;
```

3. You can use a *using directive* (see page 17). This is the easiest option. By using a using directive for namespace `std`, all identifiers of the namespace `std` are available as if they had been declared globally. Thus, the statement

```
using namespace std;
```

allows you to write

```
cout << hex << 3.4 << endl;
```

Note that in complex code this might lead to accidental name clashes or, worse, to different behavior due to some obscure overloading rules. You should never use a using directive when the context is not clear (such as in header files, modules, or libraries).

The examples in this book are quite small, so for my own convenience, I usually use the last option throughout this book in complete example programs.

3.2 Header Files

The use of namespace `std` for all identifiers of the C++ standard library was introduced during the standardization process. This change is not backward compatible to old header files, in which identifiers of the C++ standard library are declared in the global scope. In addition, some interfaces of classes changed during the standardization process (however, the goal was to stay backward compatible if possible). So, a new style for the names of standard header files was introduced. This allows vendors to stay backward compatible by providing the old header files.

The definition of new names for the standard header files was a good opportunity to standardize the extensions of header files. Previously, several extensions for header files were used; for example, `.h`, `.hpp`, and `.hxx`. However, the new standard extension for header files might be a surprise: Standard headers no longer have extensions. Hence, `include` statements for standard header files look like this:

```
#include <iostream>
#include <string>
```

This also applies to header files assumed from the C standard. C header files now have the new prefix c instead of the old extension `.h`:

```
#include <cstdlib>        // was: <stdlib.h>
#include <cstring>        // was: <string.h>
```

Inside these header files, all identifiers are declared in namespace `std`.

One advantage of this naming scheme is that you can distinguish the old string header for `char*` C functions from the new string header for the standard C++ class `string`:

```
#include <string>         // C++ class string
#include <cstring>        // char* functions from C
```

Note that the new naming scheme of header files does not necessarily mean that the file names of standard header files have no extensions from the point of view of the operating system. How `include` statements for standard header files are handled is implementation defined. C++ systems might add an extension or even use built-in declarations without reading a file. However, in practice, most systems simply include the header from a file that has exactly the same name that is used in the `include` statement. So, in most systems, C++ standard header files simply have no extension. Note that this requirement for no extension applies only to *standard* header files. In general, it is still a good idea to use a certain extension for your own header files to help identify them in a file system.

To maintain compatibility with C, the "old" standard C header files are still available. So if necessary you can still use, for example,

```
#include <stdlib.h>
```

In this case, the identifiers are declared in both the global scope and in namespace `std`. In fact, these headers behave as if they declare all identifiers in namespace `std` followed by an explicit using declaration (see page 17).

For the C++ header files in the "old" format, such as `<iostream.h>`, there is no specification in the standard (this changed more than once during the standardization process). Hence, they are not supported. In practice, most vendors will probably provide them to enable backward compatibility. Note that there were more changes in the headers than just the introduction of namespace `std`. So in general you should either use the old names of header files or switch to the new standardized names.

3.3   Error and Exception Handling

The C++ standard library is heterogeneous. It contains software from very different sources that have different styles of design and implementation. Error and exception handling is a typical example of these differences. Parts of the library, such as string classes, support detailed error handling. They check for every possible problem that might occur and throw an exception if there is an error. Other parts, such as the STL (the standard template library) and valarrays, prefer speed over safety, so they rarely check for logical errors and throw exceptions only if runtime errors occur.

3.3.1   Standard Exception Classes

All exceptions thrown from the language or the library are derived from the base class `exception`. This class is the root of several standard exception classes that form a hierarchy, as shown in Figure 3.1. These standard exception classes can be divided into three groups:

1. Exceptions for language support
2. Exceptions for the C++ standard library
3. Exceptions for errors outside the scope of a program

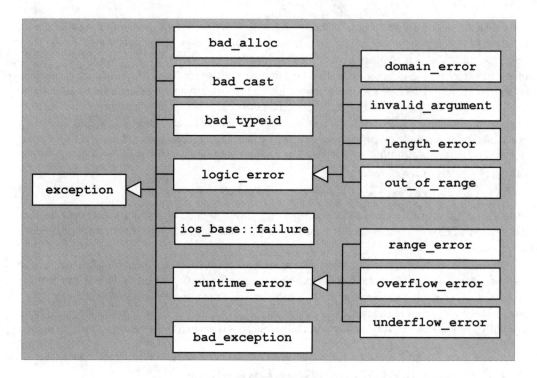

Figure 3.1. Hierarchy of Standard Exceptions

Exception Classes for Language Support

Exceptions for language support are used by language features. So in a way they are part of the core language rather than the library. These exceptions are thrown when the following operations fail.

- An exception of class `bad_alloc` is thrown whenever the global operator `new` fails (except when the `nothrow` version of `new` is used). This is probably the most important exception because it might occur at any time in any nontrivial program.

- An exception of class `bad_cast` is thrown by the `dynamic_cast` operator if a type conversion on a reference fails at runtime. The `dynamic_cast` operator is described on page 19.

- An exception of class `bad_typeid` is thrown by the `typeid` operator for runtime type identification. If the argument to `typeid` is zero or the null pointer, this exception gets thrown.

- An exception of class `bad_exception` is used to handle unexpected exceptions. It does this by using the function `unexpected()`. `unexpected()` is called if a function throws an exception that is not listed in an exception specification (exception specifications are introduced on page 16). For example:

```
class E1;
class E2;
```

```
void f() throw(E1)        // throws only exceptions of type E1
{
    ...
    throw E1();           // throws exception of type E1
    ...
    throw E2();           // calls unexpected(), which calls terminate()
}
```

The throw of an exception of type E2 in f() violates the exception specification. In this case, the function unexpected() gets called, which usually calls terminate() to terminate the program. However, if class bad_exception is part of the exception specification, then unexpected() usually rethrows an exception of this type:

```
class E1;
class E2;

void f() throw(E1,std::bad_exception)
                          // throws exception of type E1 or
                          // bad_exception for any other exception type
{
    ...
    throw E1();           // throws exception of type E1
    ...
    throw E2();           // calls unexpected(), which throws bad_exception
}
```

Thus, if an exception specification includes the class bad_exception, then any exception not part of the specification may be replaced by bad_exception within the function unexpected().[1]

Exception Classes for the Standard Library

Exception classes for the C++ standard library are usually derived from class logic_error. Logic errors are errors that, at least in theory, could be avoided by the program; for example, by performing additional tests of function arguments. Examples of such errors are a violation of logical preconditions or a class invariant. The C++ standard library provides the following classes for logic errors:

- An exception of class invalid_argument is used to report invalid arguments, such as when a bitset (array of bits) is initialized with a char other than '0' or '1'.
- An exception of class length_error is used to report an attempt to do something that exceeds a maximum allowable size, such as appending too many characters to a string.

---

[1] You can modify the exact behavior of unexpected(). However, a function never throws exceptions other than those stated in its exception specification (if any).

- An exception of class `out_of_range` is used to report that an argument value is not in the expected range, such as when a wrong index is used in an array-like collection or string.
- An exception of class `domain_error` is used to report a domain error.

In addition, for the I/O part of the library, a special exception class called `ios_base::failure` is provided. It may be thrown when a stream changes its state due to an error or end-of-file. The exact behavior of this exception class is described in Section 13.4.4, page 602.

Exception Classes for Errors Outside the Scope of a Program

Exceptions derived from `runtime_error` are provided to report events that are beyond the scope of a program and are not easily avoidable. The C++ standard library provides the following classes for runtime errors:

- An exception of class `range_error` is used to report a range error in internal computations.
- An exception of class `overflow_error` is used to report an arithmetic overflow.
- An exception of class `underflow_error` is used to report an arithmetic underflow.

Exceptions Thrown by the Standard Library

The C++ standard library itself can produce exceptions of classes `range_error`, `out_of_range`, and `invalid_argument`. However, because language features as well as user code are used by the library, their functions might throw any exception indirectly. In particular, `bad_alloc` exceptions can be thrown whenever storage is allocated.

Any implementation of the standard library might offer additional exception classes (either as siblings or as derived classes). However, the use of these nonstandard classes makes code non-portable because you could not use another implementation of the standard library without breaking your code. So, you should always use only the standard exception classes.

Header Files for Exception Classes

The base class `exception` and class `bad_exception` are defined in `<exception>`. Class `bad_alloc` is defined in `<new>`. Classes `bad_cast` and `bad_typeid` are defined in `<typeinfo>`. Class `ios_base::failure` is defined in `<ios>`. All other classes are defined in `<stdexcept>`.

3.3.2   Members of Exception Classes

To handle an exception in a `catch` clause, you may use the exception interface. The interface of all standard exceptions classes contains only one member that can be used to get additional information besides the type itself: the member function `what()`, which returns a null-terminated byte string:

```
namespace std {
    class exception {
      public:
```

```
        virtual const char* what() const throw();
        ...
    };
}
```

The content of the string is implementation defined. It most likely (but not necessarily) determines the level of help and detail of such information. Note that the string might be a null-terminated multibyte string that is suitable to convert and display as `wstring` (`wstring`s are introduced in Section 11.2.1, page 480). The C-string returned by `what()` is valid until the exception object from which it is obtained gets destroyed.[2]

The remaining members of the standard exception classes create, copy, assign, and destroy exception objects. Note that besides `what()` there is no additional member for any of the standard exception classes that describes the kind of exception. For example, there is no portable way to find out the context of an exception or the faulty index of a range error. Thus, a portable evaluation of an exception could only print the message returned from `what()`:

```
try {
    ...
}
catch (const std::exception& error) {
    // print implementation-defined error message
    std::cerr << error.what() << std::endl;
    ...
}
```

The only other possible evaluation might be an interpretation of the exact type of the exception. For example, when a `bad_alloc` exception is thrown a program might try to get more memory.

3.3.3 Throwing Standard Exceptions

You can throw standard exceptions inside your own library or program. All standard exception classes that enable you to do this have only one parameter to create the exception: a `string` (class `string` is described in Chapter 11) that will become the description returned by `what()`. For example, the class `logic_error` is defined as follows:

```
namespace std {
    class logic_error : public exception {
      public:
        explicit logic_error (const string& whatString);
    };
}
```

---

[2] The lifetime of the return value of `what()` is not specified in the original standard. However, this is the proposed resolution to fix this problem.

The set of standard exceptions that provide this ability contains class `logic_error` and its derived classes, class `runtime_error` and its derived classes, as well as class `ios_base::failure`. Thus, you can't throw exceptions of the base class `exception` and any exception class that is provided for language support.

To throw a standard exception, you simply create a string that describes the exception and use it to initialize the thrown exception object:

```
std::string s;
...
throw std::out_of_range(s);
```

Implicit conversions from `char*` to `string` exist, so you can also use a string literal directly:

```
throw std::out_of_range("out_of_range (somewhere, somehow)");
```

3.3.4 Deriving from Standard Exception Classes

Another possibility for using the standard exception classes in your code is to define a special exception class derived directly or indirectly from class `exception`. To do this, you must ensure that the `what()` mechanism works.

The member function `what()` is virtual. So, one way to provide `what()` is to write your own implementation of `what()`:

```
namespace MyLib {
    /* user-defined exception class
     * derived from a standard class for exceptions
     */
    class MyProblem : public std::exception {
      public:
        ...
        MyProblem(...) {                              // special constructor
        }

        virtual const char* what() const throw() {   // what() function
            ...
        }
    };
    ...

    void f() {
        ...
        // create an exception object and throw it
```

```
        throw MyProblem(...);
        ...
    }
}
```

Another way to provide the `what()` function is to derive your exception class from one of the classes that have a string constructor for the `what()` argument:

```
namespace MyLib {
    /* user-defined exception class
     * - derived from a standard class for exceptions
     *   that has a constructor for the what() argument
     */
    class MyRangeProblem : public std::out_of_range {
      public:
        MyRangeProblem (const string& whatString)
         : out_of_range(whatString) {
        }
    };
    ...

    void f() {
        ...
        // create an exception object by using a string constructor and throw it
        throw MyRangeProblem("here is my special range problem");
        ...
    }
}
```

For examples that are part of a complete program, see class `Stack` on page 441 and class `Queue` on page 450.

3.4 Allocators

The C++ standard library uses in several places special objects to handle the allocation and deallocation of memory. Such objects are called *allocators*. An allocator represents a special memory model. It is used as abstraction to translate the *need* to use memory into a raw *call* for memory. The use of different allocator objects at the same time allows you to use different memory models in a program.

Allocators originally were introduced as part of the STL to handle the nasty problem of different pointer types on PCs (such as near, far, and huge pointers). They now serve as a base for technical solutions that use certain memory models, such as shared memory, garbage collection, and object-oriented databases, without changing the interfaces. However, this use is relatively new and not yet widely adopted (this will probably change).

The C++ standard library defines a *default allocator* as follows:

```
namespace std {
    template <class T>
    class allocator;
}
```

The default allocator is used as the default value everywhere an allocator can be used as an argument. It does the usual calls for memory allocation and deallocation; that is, it calls the `new` and `delete` operators. However, when or how often these operators are called is unspecified. Thus, an implementation of the default allocator might, for example, cache the allocated memory internally.

The default allocator is used in most programs. However, sometimes other libraries provide allocators to fit certain needs. In such cases you simply must pass them as arguments. Only occasionally does it make sense to program allocators. In practice, typically the default allocator is used. So the discussion of allocators is deferred until Chapter 15, which covers in detail not only allocators, but also their interfaces.

Chapter 4

Utilities

This chapter describes the general utilities of the C++ standard library. These utilities are:
- Small, simple classes and functions that perform often-needed tasks
- Several general types
- Some important C functions
- Numeric limits[1]

Most, but not all, of these utilities are described in clause 20, "General Utilities," of the C++ Standard, and their definitions can be found in the `<utility>` header. The rest are described along with more major components of the library either because they are used primarily with that particular component or due to historical reasons. For example, some general auxiliary functions are defined as part of the `<algorithm>` header, although they are not algorithms in the sense of the STL (which is described in Chapter 5).

Several of these utilities are also used within the C++ standard library. In particular, the type `pair` is used whenever two values need to be treated as single unit (for example, if a function has to return two values).

4.1 Pairs

The class `pair` is provided to treat two values as a single unit. It is used in several places within the C++ standard library. In particular, the container classes `map` and `multimap` use `pairs` to manage their elements, which are key/value pairs (see Section 6.6, page 194). Another example of the usage of `pairs` is functions that return two values.

---

[1] One could argue that numeric limits should be part of Chapter 12, which covers numerics, but these numeric limits are used in some other parts of the library, so I decided to describe them here.

The structure pair is defined in <utility> as follows:

```cpp
namespace std {
    template <class T1, class T2>
    struct pair {
        // type names for the values
        typedef T1 first_type;
        typedef T2 second_type;

        // member
        T1 first;
        T2 second;

        /* default constructor
         * - T1() and T2() force initialization for built-in types
         */
        pair()
          : first(T1()), second(T2()) {
        }

        // constructor for two values
        pair(const T1& a, const T2& b)
          : first(a), second(b) {
        }

        // copy constructor with implicit conversions
        template<class U, class V>
        pair(const pair<U,V>& p)
          : first(p.first), second(p.second) {
        }
    };

    // comparisons
    template <class T1, class T2>
    bool operator== (const pair<T1,T2>&, const pair<T1,T2>&);
    template <class T1, class T2>
    bool operator< (const pair<T1,T2>&, const pair<T1,T2>&);
    ... // similar: !=, <=, >, >=
```

```
        // convenience function to create a pair
        template <class T1, class T2>
        pair<T1,T2> make_pair (const T1&, const T2&);
    }
```

Note that the type is declared as struct instead of class so that all members are public. Thus, for any value pair, direct access to the individual values is possible.

The default constructor creates a value pair with values that are initialized by the default constructor of their type. Because of language rules, an explicit call of a default constructor also initializes fundamental data types such as int. Thus, the declaration

```
    std::pair<int,float> p;    // initialize p.first and p.second with zero
```

initializes the values of p by using int() and float(), which yield zero in both cases. See page 14 for a description of the rules for explicit initialization for fundamental types.

The template version of a copy constructor provided here is used when implicit type conversions are necessary. If an object of type pair gets copied, the normal implicitly generated default copy constructor is called.[2] For example:

```
    void f(std::pair<int,const char*>);
    void g(std::pair<const int,std::string>);
    ...
    void foo() {
        std::pair<int,const char*> p(42,"hello");
        f(p);    // OK: calls built-in default copy constructor
        g(p);    // OK: calls template constructor
    }
```

Pair Comparisons

For the comparison of two pairs, the C++ standard library provides the usual comparison operators. Two value pairs are equal if both values are equal:

```
    namespace std {
        template <class T1, class T2>
        bool operator== (const pair<T1,T2>& x, const pair<T1,T2>& y) {
            return x.first == y.first && x.second == y.second;
        }
    }
```

---

[2] A template constructor does not hide the implicitly generated default constructor. See page 13 for more details about this topic.

In a comparison of pairs, the first value has higher priority. Thus, if the first values of two pairs differ, the result of their comparison is used as the result of the comparison of the whole pairs. If the first values are equal, the comparison of the second values yields the result:

```
namespace std {
    template <class T1, class T2>
    bool operator< (const pair<T1,T2>& x, const pair<T1,T2>& y) {
        return x.first < y.first ||
                (!(y.first < x.first) && x.second < y.second);
    }
}
```

The other comparison operators are defined accordingly.

4.1.1   Convenience Function `make_pair()`

The `make_pair()` template function enables you to create a value pair without writing the types explicitly[3]:

```
namespace std {
    // create value pair only by providing the values
    template <class T1, class T2>
    pair<T1,T2> make_pair (const T1& x, const T2& y) {
        return pair<T1,T2>(x, y);
    }
}
```

For example, by using `make_pair()` you can write

```
std::make_pair(42,'@')
```

instead of

```
std::pair<int,char>(42,'@')
```

In particular, the `make_pair()` function makes it convenient to pass two values of a pair directly to a function that requires a `pair` as its argument. Consider the following example:

```
void f(std::pair<int,const char*>);
void g(std::pair<const int,std::string>);
...
void foo() {
    f(std::make_pair(42,"hello"));      // pass two values as pair
```

---

[3] Using `make_pair()` should cost no runtime. The compiler should always optimize any implied overhead.

```
    g(std::make_pair(42,"hello"));    // pass two values as pair
                                      //  with type conversions
}
```

As the example shows, `make_pair()` makes it rather easy to pass two values as one `pair` argument. It works even when the types do not match exactly because the template constructor provides implicit type conversion. When you program by using maps or multimaps, you often need this ability (see page 203).

Note that an expression that has the explicit type description has an advantage because the resulting type of the pair is clearly defined. For example, the expression

```
std::pair<int,float>(42,7.77)
```

does *not* yield the same as

```
std::make_pair(42,7.77)
```

The latter creates a pair that has `double` as the type for the second value (unqualified floating literals have type `double`). The exact type may be important when overloaded functions or templates are used. These functions or templates might, for example, provide versions for both `float` and `double` to improve efficiency.

4.1.2 Examples of Pair Usage

The C++ standard library uses pairs a lot. For example, the map and multimap containers use `pair` as a type to manage their elements, which are key/value pairs. See Section 6.6, page 194, for a general description of maps and multimaps, and in particular page 91 for an example that shows the usage of type `pair`. Objects of type `pair` are also used inside the C++ standard library in functions that return two values (see page 183 for an example).

4.2   Class `auto_ptr`

This section covers the `auto_ptr` type. The `auto_ptr` type is provided by the C++ standard library as a kind of a smart pointer that helps to avoid resource leaks when exceptions are thrown. Note that I wrote "a kind of a smart pointer." There are several useful smart pointer types. This class is smart with respect to only one certain kind of problem. For other kinds of problems, type `auto_ptr` does not help. So, be careful and read the following subsections.

4.2.1   Motivation of Class `auto_ptr`

Functions often operate in the following way[4]:

1. Acquire some resources.
2. Perform some operations.
3. Free the acquired resources.

If the resources acquired on entry are bound to local objects, they get freed automatically on function exit because the destructors of those local objects are called. But if resources are acquired explicitly and are not bound to any object, they must be freed explicitly. Resources are typically managed explicitly when pointers are used.

A typical example of using pointers in this way is the use of `new` and `delete` to create and destroy an object:

```
void f()
{
    ClassA* ptr = new ClassA;      // create an object explicitly
    ...                            // perform some operations
    delete ptr;                    // clean up (destroy the object explicitly)
}
```

This function is a source of trouble. One obvious problem is that the deletion of the object might be forgotten (especially if you have `return` statements inside the function). There also is a not-so-obvious danger that an exception might occur. Such an exception would exit the function immediately without calling the `delete` statement at the end of the function. The result would be a memory leak or, more generally, a resource leak. Avoiding such a resource leak usually requires that a function catches all exceptions. For example:

---

[4] This motivation of class `auto_ptr` is based, with permission, partly on Scott Meyers' book *More Effective C++*. The general technique was originally presented by Bjarne Stroustrup as the "resource allocation is initialization" in his books *The C++ Programming Language*, 2nd edition and *The Design and Evolution of C++*. `auto_ptr` was added to the standard specifically to support this technique.

```
void f()
{
    ClassA* ptr = new ClassA;        // create an object explicitly

    try {
        ...                          // perform some operations
    }
    catch (...) {                    // for any exception
        delete ptr;                  // - clean up
        throw;                       // - rethrow the exception
    }

    delete ptr;                      // clean up on normal end
}
```

To handle the deletion of this object properly in the event of an exception, the code gets more complicated and redundant. If a second object is handled in this way, or if more than one catch clause is used, the problem gets worse. This is bad programming style and should be avoided because it is complex and error prone.

A kind of smart pointer can help here. The smart pointer can free the data to which it points whenever the pointer itself gets destroyed. Furthermore, because the pointer is a local variable, it gets destroyed automatically when the function is exited regardless of whether the exit is normal or is due to an exception. The class auto_ptr was designed to be such a kind of smart pointer.

An auto_ptr is a pointer that serves as *owner* of the object to which it refers (if any). As a result, an object gets destroyed automatically when its auto_ptr gets destroyed. A requirement of an auto_ptr is that its object has only one owner.

Here is the previous example rewritten to use an auto_ptr:

```
// header file for auto_ptr
#include <memory>

void f()
{
    // create and initialize an auto_ptr
    std::auto_ptr<ClassA> ptr(new ClassA);

    ...                              // perform some operations
}
```

The delete statement and the catch clause are no longer necessary. An auto_ptr has much the same interface as an ordinary pointer; that is, operator * dereferences the object to which it points, whereas operator -> provides access to a member if the object is a class or a structure. However, any pointer arithmetic (such as ++) is not defined (this might be an advantage, because pointer arithmetic is a source of trouble).

Note that class auto_ptr<> does not allow you to initialize an object with an ordinary pointer by using the assignment syntax. Thus, you must initialize the auto_ptr directly by using its value[5]:

```
std::auto_ptr<ClassA> ptr1(new ClassA);        // OK
std::auto_ptr<ClassA> ptr2 = new ClassA;       // ERROR
```

4.2.2   Transfer of Ownership by auto_ptr

An auto_ptr provides the semantics of strict ownership. This means that because an auto_ptr deletes the object to which it points, the object should not be "owned" by any other objects. Two or more auto_ptrs must not own the same object at the same time. Unfortunately, it might happen that two auto_ptrs own the same object (for example, if you initialize two auto_ptrs with the same object). Making sure this doesn't happen is up to the programmer.

This leads to the question of how the copy constructor and the assignment operator of auto_ptrs operate. The usual behavior of these operations would be to copy the data of one auto_ptr to the other. However, this behavior would result in the situation, in which two auto_ptrs own the same object. The solution is simple, but it has important consequences: The copy constructor and assignment operator of auto_ptrs "transfer ownership" of the objects to which they refer.

Consider, for example, the following use of the copy constructor:

```
// initialize an auto_ptr with a new object
std::auto_ptr<ClassA> ptr1(new ClassA);
```

```
// copy the auto_ptr
// - transfers ownership from ptr1 to ptr2
std::auto_ptr<ClassA> ptr2(ptr1);
```

After the first statement, ptr1 owns the object that was created with the new operator. The second statement transfers ownership from ptr1 to ptr2. So after the second statement, ptr2 owns the

---

[5] There is a minor difference between

```
X x;
Y y(x);  // explicit conversion
```
and
```
X x;
Y y = x;  // implicit conversion
```
The former creates a new object of type Y by using an explicit conversion from type X, whereas the latter creates a new object of type Y by using an implicit conversion.

object created with `new`, and `ptr1` no longer owns the object. The object created by `new ClassA` gets deleted exactly once — when `ptr2` gets destroyed.

The assignment operator behaves similarly:

```
// initialize an auto_ptr with a new object
std::auto_ptr<ClassA> ptr1(new ClassA);
std::auto_ptr<ClassA> ptr2;         // create another auto_ptr

ptr2 = ptr1;                        // assign the auto_ptr
                                    // - transfers ownership from ptr1 to ptr2
```

Here, the assignment transfers ownership from `ptr1` to `ptr2`. As a result, `ptr2` owns the object that was previously owned by `ptr1`.

If `ptr2` owned an object before an assignment, `delete` is called for that object:

```
// initialize an auto_ptr with a new object
std::auto_ptr<ClassA> ptr1(new ClassA);
// initialize another auto_ptr with a new object
std::auto_ptr<ClassA> ptr2(new ClassA);

ptr2 = ptr1;                        // assign the auto_ptr
                                    // - delete object owned by ptr2
                                    // - transfers ownership from ptr1 to ptr2
```

Note that a transfer of ownership means that the value is *not* simply copied. In all cases of ownership transfer, the previous owner (`ptr1` in the previous examples) loses its ownership. As a consequence the previous owner has the null pointer as its value after the transfer. This is a significant violation of the general behavior of initializations and assignments in programming languages. Here, the copy constructor *modifies* the object that is used to initialize the new object, and the assignment operator *modifies* the right-hand side of the assignment. It is up to the programmer to ensure that an `auto_ptr` that lost ownership and got the null pointer as value is no longer dereferenced.

To assign a new value to an `auto_ptr`, this new value must be an `auto_ptr`. You can't assign an ordinary pointer:

```
std::auto_ptr<ClassA> ptr;                        // create an auto_ptr

ptr = new ClassA;                                 // ERROR
ptr = std::auto_ptr<ClassA>(new ClassA);          // OK, delete old object
                                                  //     and own new
```

Source and Sink

The transfer of ownership implies a special use for `auto_ptrs`; that is, functions can use them to transfer ownership to other functions. This can occur in two different ways:

1. A function can behave as a *sink* of data. This happens if an `auto_ptr` is passed as an argument to the function by value. In this case, the parameter of the called function gets ownership of the `auto_ptr`. Thus, if the function does not transfer it again, the object gets deleted on function exit:

```
void sink(std::auto_ptr<ClassA>);      // sink() gets ownership
```

2. A function can behave as a *source* of data. When an `auto_ptr` is returned, ownership of the returned value gets transferred to the calling function. The following example shows this technique:

```
std::auto_ptr<ClassA> f()
{
    std::auto_ptr<ClassA> ptr(new ClassA); // ptr owns the new object
    ...
    return ptr;              // transfer ownership to calling function
}

void g()
{
    std::auto_ptr<ClassA> p;

    for (int i=0; i<10; ++i) {
        p = f();             // p gets ownership of the returned object
                             // (previously returned object of f() gets deleted)
        ...
    }
}                            // last-owned object of p gets deleted
```

Each time `f()` is called, it creates an object with `new` and returns the object, along with its ownership, to the caller. The assignment of the return value to p transfers ownership to p. In the second and additional passes through the loop, the assignment to p deletes the object that p owned previously. Leaving `g()`, and thus destroying p, results in the destruction of the last object owned by p. In any case, no resource leak is possible. Even if an exception is thrown, any `auto_ptr` that owns data ensures that this data is deleted.

Caveat

The semantics of `auto_ptr` always include ownership, so don't use `auto_ptr`s in a parameter list or as a return value if you don't mean to transfer ownership. Consider, for example, the following naive implementation of a function that prints the object to which an `auto_ptr` refers. Using it would be a disaster.

```
// this is a bad example
template <class T>
void bad_print(std::auto_ptr<T> p)      // p gets ownership of passed argument
{
```

```
// does p own an object ?
if (p.get() == NULL) {
    std::cout << "NULL";
}
else {
    std::cout << *p;
}
}               // Oops, exiting deletes the object to which p refers
```

Whenever an `auto_ptr` is passed to this implementation of `bad_print()`, the objects it owns (if any) are deleted. This is because the ownership of the `auto_ptr` that is passed as an argument is passed to the parameter p, and p deletes the object it owns on function exit. This is probably not the programmer's intention and would result in fatal runtime errors:

```
std::auto_ptr<int> p(new int);
*p = 42;            // change value to which p refers
bad_print(p);       // Oops, deletes the memory to which p refers
*p = 18;            // RUNTIME ERROR
```

You might think about passing `auto_ptrs` by reference instead. However, passing `auto_ptrs` by reference confuses the concept of ownership. A function that gets an `auto_ptr` by reference might or might not transfer ownership. Allowing an `auto_ptr` to pass by reference is very bad design and you should always avoid it.

According to the concept of `auto_ptrs`, it is possible to transfer ownership into a function by using a constant reference. This is very dangerous because people usually expect that an object won't get modified when you pass it as a constant reference. Fortunately, there was a late design decision that made `auto_ptrs` less dangerous. By some tricky implementation techniques, transfer of ownership is not possible with constant references. In fact, you can't change the ownership of any constant `auto_ptr`:

```
const std::auto_ptr<int> p(new int);
*p = 42;            // change value to which p refers
bad_print(p);       // COMPILE-TIME ERROR
*p = 18;            // OK
```

This solution makes `auto_ptrs` safer than they were before. Many interfaces use constant references to get values that they copy internally. In fact, all container classes (see Chapter 6 or Chapter 10 for examples) of the C++ standard library behave this way, which might look like the following:

```
template <class T>
void container::insert (const T& value)
{
    ...
    x = value;      // assign or copy value internally
    ...
}
```

If such an assignment was possible for `auto_ptrs`, the assignment would transfer ownership into the container. However, because of the actual design of `auto_ptrs`, this call results in an error at compile time:

```
container<std::auto_ptr<int> > c;
const std::auto_ptr<int> p(new int);

...

c.insert(p);        // ERROR

...
```

All in all, constant `auto_ptrs` reduce the danger of an unintended transfer of ownership. Whenever an object is passed via an `auto_ptr`, you can use a constant `auto_ptr` to signal the end of the chain.

The `const` does not mean that you can't change the value of the object the `auto_ptr` owns (if any). You can't change the *ownership* of a constant `auto_ptr`; however, you can change the *value* of the object to which it refers. For example:

```
std::auto_ptr<int> f()
{
    const std::auto_ptr<int> p(new int);   // no ownership transfer possible
    std::auto_ptr<int> q(new int);         // ownership transfer possible

    *p = 42;          // OK, change value to which p refers
    bad_print(p);     // COMPILE-TIME ERROR
    *p = *q;          // OK, change value to which p refers
    p = q;            // COMPILE-TIME ERROR
    return p;         // COMPILE-TIME ERROR
}
```

Whenever the `const auto_ptr` is passed or returned as an argument, any attempt to assign a new object results in a compile-time error. With respect to the `constness`, a `const auto_ptr` behaves like a constant pointer (`T* const p`) and not like a pointer that refers to a constant (`const T* p`); although the syntax looks the other way around.

4.2.3   `auto_ptrs` as Members

By using `auto_ptrs` within a class you can also avoid resource leaks. If you use an `auto_ptr` instead of an ordinary pointer, you no longer need a destructor because the object gets deleted with the deletion of the member. In addition, an `auto_ptr` helps to avoid resource leaks that are caused by exceptions that are thrown during the initialization of an object. Note that destructors are called only if any construction is completed. So, if an exception occurs inside a constructor, destructors are only called for objects that have been fully constructed. This will result in a resource leak if the first `new` was successful but the second was not. For example:

```
class ClassB {
  private:
    ClassA* ptr1;          // pointer members
    ClassA* ptr2;
  public:
    // constructor that initializes the pointers
    // - will cause resource leak if second new throws
    ClassB (const ClassA& val1, const ClassA& val2)
      : ptr1(new ClassA(val1)), ptr2(new ClassA(val2)) {
    }

    // copy constructor
    // - might cause resource leak if second new throws
    ClassB (const ClassB& x)
      : ptr1(new ClassA(*x.ptr1)), ptr2(new ClassA(*x.ptr2)) {
    }

    // assignment operator
    const ClassB& operator= (const ClassB& x) {
        *ptr1 = *x.ptr1;
        *ptr2 = *x.ptr2;
        return *this;
    }

    ~ClassB () {
        delete ptr1;
        delete ptr2;
    }
    ...
};
```

To avoid such a possible resource leak, you can simply use auto_ptrs:

```
class ClassB {
  private:
    const std::auto_ptr<ClassA> ptr1;        // auto_ptr members
    const std::auto_ptr<ClassA> ptr2;
  public:
    // constructor that initializes the auto_ptrs
    // - no resource leak possible
```

```
ClassB (ClassA val1, ClassA val2)
 : ptr1(new ClassA(val1)), ptr2(new ClassA(val2)) {
}

// copy constructor
// - no resource leak possible
ClassB (const ClassB& x)
 : ptr1(new ClassA(*x.ptr1)), ptr2(new ClassA(*x.ptr2)) {
}

// assignment operator
const ClassB& operator= (const ClassB& x) {
    *ptr1 = *x.ptr1;
    *ptr2 = *x.ptr2;
    return *this;
}

// no destructor necessary
// (default destructor lets ptr1 and ptr2 delete their objects)
    ...
};
```

Note, however, that although you can skip the destructor, you still have to program the copy constructor and the assignment operator. By default, both would try to transfer ownership, which is probably not the intention. In addition, and as mentioned on page 42, to avoid an unintended transfer of ownership you should use constant `auto_ptr`s here if the `auto_ptr` should not change the object to which it refers throughout its lifetime.

4.2.4 Misusing `auto_ptrs`

`auto_ptrs` satisfy a certain need; namely, to avoid resource leaks when exception handling is used. Unfortunately, the exact behavior of `auto_ptrs` changed in the past and no other kind of smart pointers are provided in the C++ standard library, so people tend to misuse `auto_ptrs`. Here are some hints to help you use them correctly:

1. **`auto_ptrs` cannot share ownership.**
   An `auto_ptr` must *not* refer to an object that is owned by another `auto_ptr` (or other object). Otherwise, if the first pointer deletes the object, the other pointer suddenly refers to a destroyed object, and any further read or write access may result in disaster.

2. **`auto_ptrs` are not provided for arrays.**

   An `auto_ptr` is *not* allowed to refer to arrays. This is because an `auto_ptr` calls `delete` instead of `delete[]` for the object it owns. Note that there is no equivalent class in the C++ standard library that has the `auto_ptr` semantics for arrays. Instead, the library provides several container classes to handle collections of data (see Chapter 5).

3. **`auto_ptrs` are not "universal smart pointers."**

   An `auto_ptr` is *not* designed to solve other problems for which smart pointers might be useful. In particular, they are not pointers for reference counting. (Pointers for reference counting ensure that an object gets deleted only if the last of several smart pointers that refer to that object gets destroyed.)

4. **`auto_ptrs` don't meet the requirements for container elements.**

   An `auto_ptr` does *not* meet one of the most fundamental requirements for elements of standard containers. That is, after a copy or an assignment of an `auto_ptr`, source and sink are not equivalent. In fact, when an `auto_ptr` is assigned or copied, the source `auto_ptr` gets modified because it transfers its value rather than copying it. So you should not use an `auto_ptr` as an element of a standard container. Fortunately, the design of the language and library prevents this misuse from compiling in a standard-conforming environment.

Unfortunately, sometimes the misuse of an `auto_ptr` works. Regarding this, using nonconstant `auto_ptrs` is no safer than using ordinary pointers. You might call it luck if the misuse doesn't result in a crash, but in fact you are unlucky because you don't realize that you made a mistake.

See Section 5.10.2, page 135, for a discussion and Section 6.8, page 222, for an implementation of a smart pointer for reference counting. This pointer is useful when sharing elements in different containers.

4.2.5 `auto_ptr` Examples

The first example shows how `auto_ptrs` behave regarding the transfer of ownership:

```
// util/autoptr1.cpp

#include <iostream>
#include <memory>
using namespace std;

/* define output operator for auto_ptr
 * - print object value or NULL
 */
template <class T>
ostream& operator<< (ostream& strm, const auto_ptr<T>& p)
{
    // does p own an object ?
    if (p.get() == NULL) {
```

```
        strm << "NULL";              // NO: print NULL
    }
    else {
        strm << *p;                  // YES: print the object
    }
    return strm;
}

int main()
{
    auto_ptr<int> p(new int(42));
    auto_ptr<int> q;

    cout << "after initialization:" << endl;
    cout << " p: " << p << endl;
    cout << " q: " << q << endl;

    q = p;
    cout << "after assigning auto pointers:" << endl;
    cout << " p: " << p << endl;
    cout << " q: " << q << endl;

    *q += 13;                        // change value of the object q owns
    p = q;
    cout << "after change and reassignment:" << endl;
    cout << " p: " << p << endl;
    cout << " q: " << q << endl;
}
```

The output of the program is as follows:

```
after initialization:
 p: 42
 q: NULL
after assigning auto pointers:
 p: NULL
 q: 42
after change and reassignment:
 p: 55
 q: NULL
```

Note that the second parameter of the output operator function is a constant reference. So it uses `auto_ptrs` without any transfer of ownership.

As mentioned on page 40, bear in mind that you can't initialize an `auto_ptr` by using the assignment syntax or assign an ordinary pointer:

```
std::auto_ptr<int> p(new int(42));    // OK
std::auto_ptr<int> p = new int(42);   // ERROR

p = std::auto_ptr<int>(new int(42));  // OK
p = new int(42);                      // ERROR
```

This is because the constructor to create an `auto_ptr` from an ordinary pointer is declared as `explicit` (see Section 2.2.6, page 18, for an introduction of `explicit`).

The following example shows how constant `auto_ptrs` behave:

```
// util/autoptr2.cpp

#include <iostream>
#include <memory>
using namespace std;

/* define output operator for auto_ptr
 * - print object value or NULL
 */
template <class T>
ostream& operator<< (ostream& strm, const auto_ptr<T>& p)
{
    // does p own an object ?
    if (p.get() == NULL) {
        strm << "NULL";              // NO: print NULL
    }
    else {
        strm << *p;                  // YES: print the object
    }
    return strm;
}

int main()
{
    const auto_ptr<int> p(new int(42));
    const auto_ptr<int> q(new int(0));
    const auto_ptr<int> r;
```

```
        cout << "after initialization:" << endl;
        cout << " p: " << p << endl;
        cout << " q: " << q << endl;
        cout << " r: " << r << endl;

        *q = *p;
//      *r = *p;        // ERROR: undefined behavior
        *p = -77;
        cout << "after assigning values:" << endl;
        cout << " p: " << p << endl;
        cout << " q: " << q << endl;
        cout << " r: " << r << endl;

//      q = p;          // ERROR at compile time
//      r = p;          // ERROR at compile time
    }
```

Here, the output of the program is as follows:

```
    after initialization:
     p: 42
     q: 0
     r: NULL
    after assigning values:
     p: -77
     q: 42
     r: NULL
```

This example defines an output operator for `auto_ptrs`. To do this, it passes an `auto_ptr` as a constant reference. According to the discussion on page 43, you should usually not pass an `auto_ptr` in any form. This function is an exception to this rule.

Note that the assignment

```
    *r = *p;
```

is an error. It dereferences an `auto_ptr` that refers to no object. According to the standard, this results in undefined behavior; for example, a crash. As you can see, you can manipulate the objects to which constant `auto_ptrs` refer, but you can't change which objects they own. Even if `r` was nonconstant, the last statement would not be possible because it would change the constant p.

4.2.6   Class `auto_ptr` in Detail

Class auto_ptr is declared in <memory>:

```
#include <memory>
```

It provides auto_ptr as a template class for any types in namespace std. The following is the exact declaration of the class auto_ptr:[6]

```
namespace std {
    // auxiliary type to enable copies and assignments
    template <class Y> struct auto_ptr_ref {};

    template<class T>
    class auto_ptr {
      public:
        // type names for the value
        typedef T element_type;

        // constructor
        explicit auto_ptr(T* ptr = 0) throw();

        // copy constructors (with implicit conversion)
        // - note: nonconstant parameter
        auto_ptr(auto_ptr&) throw();
        template<class U> auto_ptr(auto_ptr<U>&) throw();

        // assignments (with implicit conversion)
        // - note: nonconstant parameter
        auto_ptr& operator= (auto_ptr&) throw();
        template<class U>
            auto_ptr& operator= (auto_ptr<U>&) throw();

        // destructor
        ~auto_ptr() throw();

        // value access
```

---

[6] This is a slightly improved version that fixes some minor problems of the version in the C++ standard (auto_ptr_ref is global now and there is an assignment operator from auto_ptr_ref to auto_ptr; see page 55).

```
T* get() const throw();
T& operator*() const throw();
T* operator->() const throw();

// release ownership
T* release() throw();

// reset value
void reset(T* ptr = 0) throw();

    // special conversions to enable copies and assignments
    public:
        auto_ptr(auto_ptr_ref<T>) throw();
        auto_ptr& operator= (auto_ptr_ref<T> rhs) throw();
        template<class U> operator auto_ptr_ref<U>() throw();
        template<class U> operator auto_ptr<U>() throw();
    };
}
```

The individual members are described in detail in the following sections, in which *auto_ptr* is an abbreviation for auto_ptr<T>. A complete sample implementation of class auto_ptr is located on page 56.

Type Definitions

auto_ptr::**element_type**
- The type of the object that the auto_ptr owns.

Constructors, Assignments, and Destructors

auto_ptr::**auto_ptr** () throw()
- The default constructor.
- Creates an auto_ptr that does not own an object.
- Initializes the value of the auto_ptr with zero.

explicit *auto_ptr*::**auto_ptr** (T* *ptr*) throw()
- Creates an auto_ptr that owns and points to the object to which ptr refers.
- After the call, *this is the owner of the object to which *ptr* refers. There must be no other owner.

- If *ptr* is not the null pointer, it must be a value returned by `new` because the destructor of the `auto_ptr` calls `delete` automatically for the object it owns.
- It is not correct to pass the return value of a new array that was created by `new[]`. (For arrays, the STL container classes, which are introduced in Section 5.2, page 75, should be used.)

auto_ptr::**auto_ptr** (auto_ptr& *ap*) throw()

template<class U> *auto_ptr*::**auto_ptr** (auto_ptr<U>& *ap*) throw()

- The copy constructor (for nonconstant values).
- Creates an `auto_ptr` that adopts the ownership of the object *ap* owned on entry. The ownership of an object to which *ap* referred on entry (if any) is transferred to *this.
- After the operation, *ap* no longer owns an object. Its value becomes the null pointer. Thus, in contrast to the usual implementation of a copy constructor, the source object gets modified.
- Note that this function is overloaded with a member template (see page 11 for an introduction to member templates). This enables automatic type conversions from the type of *ap* to the type of the created `auto_ptr`; for example, to convert an `auto_ptr` to an object of a derived class into an `auto_ptr` to an object of a base class.
- See Section 4.2.2, page 40, for a discussion of the transfer of ownership.

auto_ptr& *auto_ptr*::**operator =** (auto_ptr& *ap*) throw()

template<class U> *auto_ptr*& *auto_ptr*::**operator =** (auto_ptr<U>& *ap*) throw()

- The assignment operator (for nonconstant values).
- Deletes the object it owns on entry (if any) and adopts the ownership of the object that *ap* owned on entry. Thus, the ownership of an object to which *ap* referred on entry (if any) is transferred to *this.
- After the operation, *ap* no longer owns an object. Its value becomes the null pointer. Thus, in contrast to the usual implementation of an assignment operator, the source object gets modified.
- The object to which the `auto_ptr` on the left-hand side of the assignment (*this) refers is deleted by calling `delete` for it.
- Note that this function is overloaded with a member template (see page 11 for an introduction to member templates). This enables automatic type conversions from the type of *ap* to the type of *this; for example, to convert an `auto_ptr` to an object of a derived class into an `auto_ptr` to an object of a base class.
- See Section 4.2.2, page 40, for a discussion about the transfer of ownership.

auto_ptr::~**auto_ptr** () throw()

- The destructor.
- If the `auto_ptr` owns an object on entry, it calls `delete` for it.

Value Access

T* *auto_ptr*::**get** () const throw()

- Returns the address of the object that the auto_ptr owns (if any).
- Returns the null pointer if the auto_ptr does not own an object.
- This call does not change the ownership. Thus, on exit the auto_ptr still owns the object that it owned on entry (if any).

T& *auto_ptr*::**operator *** () const throw()

- The dereferencing operator.
- Returns the object that the auto_ptr owns.
- If the auto_ptr does not own an object, the call results in undefined behavior (which may result in a crash).

T* *auto_ptr*::**operator ->** () const throw()

- The operator for member access.
- Returns a member of the object that the auto_ptr owns.
- If the auto_ptr does not own an object, the call results in undefined behavior (which may result in a crash).

Value Manipulation

T* *auto_ptr*::**release** () throw()

- Releases the ownership of the object that the auto_ptr owns.
- Sets the value of the auto_ptr to zero.
- Returns the address of the object that the auto_ptr owned on entry (if any).
- Returns the null pointer if the auto_ptr does not own an object on entry.

void *auto_ptr*::**reset** (T* *ptr* = 0) throw()

- Reinitializes the auto_ptr with *ptr*.
- deletes the object that the auto_ptr owns on entry (if any).
- After the call, *this is the owner of the object to which *ptr* refers. There should be no other owner.
- If *ptr* is not the null pointer it should be a value returned by new because the destructor of the auto_ptr automatically calls delete for the object it owns.
- Note that it is not correct to pass the return value of a new array that was creates by new[]. (For arrays, the STL container classes, which are introduced in Section 5.2, page 75, should be used.)

Conversions

The rest of the class `auto_ptr` (auxiliary type `auto_ptr_ref` and functions using it) consists of rather tricky conversions that enable you to use copy and assignment operations for nonconstant `auto_ptrs` but not for constant `auto_ptrs` (see page 44 for details). The following is a quick explanation.[7] We have the following two requirements:

1. It should be possible to pass `auto_ptrs` to and from functions as rvalues.[8] Because `auto_ptr` is a class, this must be done using a constructor.
2. When an `auto_ptr` is copied, it is important that the source pointer gives up ownership. This requires that the copy modifies the source `auto_ptr`.

An ordinary copy constructor can copy an rvalue, but to do so it must declare its parameter as a reference to a `const` object. To use an ordinary constructor to copy an `auto_ptr` we would have to declare the data member containing the real pointer `mutable` so that it could be modified in the copy constructor. But this would allow you to write code that copies `auto_ptr` objects that were actually declared `const`, transferring their ownership in contradiction to their constant status.

The alternative is to find a mechanism to enable an rvalue to be converted to an lvalue. A simple operator conversion function to reference type does not work because an operator conversion function is never called to convert an object to its own type (remember that the reference attribute is not part of the type). Thus, the `auto_ptr_ref` class was introduced to provide this convert-to-lvalue mechanism. The mechanism relies on a slight difference between the overloading and template argument deduction rules. This difference is too subtle to be of use as a general programming tool, but it is sufficient to enable the `auto_ptr` class to work correctly.

Don't be surprised if your compiler doesn't support the distinction between nonconstant and constant `auto_ptrs` yet. And be aware that if your compiler does not yet implement this distinction, your `auto_ptr` interface is more dangerous. In this case, it is rather easy to transfer ownership by accident.

---

[7] Thanks to Bill Gibbons for pointing this out.

[8] The names *rvalue* and *lvalue* come originally from the assignment expression *expr1* = *expr2*, in which the left operand *expr1* must be a (modifiable) lvalue. However, an lvalue is perhaps better considered as representing an object *locator value*. Thus, it is an expression that designates an object by name or address (pointer or reference). Lvalues need not be modifiable. For example, the name of a constant object is a nonmodifiable lvalue. All expressions that are not lvalues are rvalues. In particular, temporary objects created explicitly (`T()`) or as the result of a function call are rvalues.

Sample Implementation of Class `auto_ptr`

The following code contains a sample implementation of a standard-conforming `auto_ptr` class[9]:

```
// util/autoptr.hpp

/* class auto_ptr
 * - improved standard conforming implementation
 */
namespace std {
    // auxiliary type to enable copies and assignments (now global)
    template<class Y>
    struct auto_ptr_ref {
        Y* yp;
        auto_ptr_ref (Y* rhs)
         : yp(rhs) {
        }
    };

    template<class T>
    class auto_ptr {
      private:
        T* ap;      // refers to the actual owned object (if any)
      public:
        typedef T element_type;

        // constructor
        explicit auto_ptr (T* ptr = 0) throw()
         : ap(ptr) {
        }

        // copy constructors (with implicit conversion)
        // - note: nonconstant parameter
        auto_ptr (auto_ptr& rhs) throw()
         : ap(rhs.release()) {
        }
```

---

[9] Thanks to Greg Colvin for this implementation of `auto_ptr`. Note that it does not conform exactly to the standard. It turned out that the specification in the standard is still not correct regarding the special conversions encountered using `auto_ptr_ref`. The version presented in this book, hopefully, fixes all the problems. However, at the writing of this book, there was still ongoing discussion.

```
template<class Y>
auto_ptr (auto_ptr<Y>& rhs) throw()
 : ap(rhs.release()) {
}

// assignments (with implicit conversion)
// - note: nonconstant parameter
auto_ptr& operator= (auto_ptr& rhs) throw() {
    reset(rhs.release());
    return *this;
}
template<class Y>
auto_ptr& operator= (auto_ptr<Y>& rhs) throw() {
    reset(rhs.release());
    return *this;
}

// destructor
~auto_ptr() throw() {
    delete ap;
}

// value access
T* get() const throw() {
    return ap;
}
T& operator*() const throw() {
    return *ap;
}
T* operator->() const throw() {
    return ap;
}

// release ownership
T* release() throw() {
    T* tmp(ap);
    ap = 0;
    return tmp;
}
```

```
// reset value
void reset (T* ptr=0) throw() {
    if (ap != ptr) {
        delete ap;
        ap = ptr;
    }
}

/* special conversions with auxiliary type to enable copies and assignments
 */
auto_ptr(auto_ptr_ref<T> rhs) throw()
 : ap(rhs.yp) {
}
auto_ptr& operator= (auto_ptr_ref<T> rhs) throw() {   // new
    reset(rhs.yp);
    return *this;
}
template<class Y>
operator auto_ptr_ref<Y>() throw() {
    return auto_ptr_ref<Y>(release());
}
template<class Y>
operator auto_ptr<Y>() throw() {
    return auto_ptr<Y>(release());
}
};
}
```

4.3   Numeric Limits

Numeric types in general have platform-dependent limits. The C++ standard library provides these limits in the template `numeric_limits`. These numeric limits replace and supplement the ordinary preprocessor constants of C. These constants are still available for integer types in `<climits>` and `<limits.h>`, and for floating-point types in `<cfloat>` and `<float.h>`. The new concept of numeric limits has two advantages: First, it offers more type safety. Second, it enables a programmer to write templates that evaluate these limits.

The numeric limits are discussed in the rest of this section. Note, however, that it is always better to write platform-independent code by using the minimum guaranteed precision of the types. These minimum values are provided in Table 4.1.

Type	Minimum Size
`char`	1 byte (8 bits)
`short int`	2 bytes
`int`	2 bytes
`long int`	4 bytes
`float`	4 bytes
`double`	8 bytes
`long double`	8 bytes

Table 4.1. Minimum Size of Built-in Types

Class `numeric_limits<>`

Usually you use templates to implement something once for any type. However, you can also use templates to provide a common interface that is implemented for each type, where it is useful. You can do this by providing specialization of a general template. `numeric_limits` is a typical example of this technique, which works as follows:

- A general template provides the default numeric values for any type:

```
namespace std {
    /* general numeric limits as default for any type
     */
    template <class T>
    class numeric_limits {
      public:
        // no specialization for numeric limits exist
        static const bool is_specialized = false;

        ...    // other members that are meaningless for the general numeric limits
    };
}
```

This general template of the numeric limits says simply that there are no numeric limits available for type T. This is done by setting the member is_specialized to false.

- Specializations of the template define the numeric limits for each numeric type as follows:

```
namespace std {
    /* numeric limits for int
     * - implementation defined
     */
    template<> class numeric_limits<int> {
      public:
        // yes, a specialization for numeric limits of int does exist
        static const bool is_specialized = true;

        static int min() throw() {
            return -2147483648;
        }
        static int max() throw() {
            return 2147483647;
        }
        static const int digits = 31;
        ...
    };
}
```

Here, is_specialized is set to true, and all other members have the values of the numeric limits for the particular type.

The general numeric_limits template and its standard specializations are provided in the header file <limits>. The specializations are provided for any fundamental type that can represent numeric values: bool, char, signed char, unsigned char, wchar_t, short, unsigned short, int, unsigned int, long, unsigned long, float, double, and long double. They can be supplemented easily for user-defined numeric types.

Table 4.2 and Table 4.3 list all members of the class numeric_limits<> and their meanings. Applicable corresponding C constants for these members are given in the right column of the tables (they are defined in <climits>, <limits.h>, <cfloat>, and <float.h>).

Member	Meaning	C Constants
`is_specialized`	Type has specialization for numeric limits	
`is_signed`	Type is signed	
`is_integer`	Type is integer	
`is_exact`	Calculations produce no rounding errors (`true` for all integer types)	
`is_bounded`	The set of values representable is finite (`true` for all built-in types)	
`is_modulo`	Adding two positive numbers may wrap to a lesser result	
`is_iec559`	Conforms to standards IEC 559 and IEEE 754	
`min()`	Minimum finite value (minimum positive normalized value for floating-point types with denormalization; meaningful if `is_bounded||!is_signed`)	`INT_MIN,FLT_MIN,` `CHAR_MIN,...`
`max()`	Maximum finite value (meaningful if `is_bounded`)	`INT_MAX,FLT_MAX,...`
`digits`	Character,Integer: number of nonsigned bits (binary digits)	`CHAR_BIT`
	Floating point: number of `radix` digits (see below) in the mantissa	`FLT_MANT_DIG,...`
`digits10`	Number of decimal digits (meaningful if `is_bounded`)	`FLT_DIG,...`
`radix`	Integer: base of the representation (almost always two)	
	Floating point: base of the exponent representation	`FLT_RADIX`
`min_exponent`	Minimum negative integer exponent for base `radix`	`FLT_MIN_EXP,...`
`max_exponent`	Maximum positive integer exponent for base `radix`	`FLT_MAX_EXP,...`
`min_exponent10`	Minimum negative integer exponent for base 10	`FLT_MIN_10_EXP,...`
`max_exponent10`	Maximum positive integer exponent for base 10	`FLT_MAX_10_EXP,...`
`epsilon()`	Difference of one and least value greater than one	`FLT_EPSILON,...`
`round_style`	Rounding style (see page 63)	
`round_error()`	Measure of the maximum rounding error (according to standard ISO/IEC 10967-1)	
`has_infinity`	Type has representation for positive infinity	
`infinity()`	Representation of positive infinity if available	
`has_quiet_NaN`	Type has representation for nonsignaling "Not a Number"	
`quiet_NaN()`	Representation of quiet "Not a Number" if available	
`has_signaling_NaN`	Type has representation for signaling "Not a Number"	
`signaling_NaN()`	Representation of signaling "Not a Number" if available	

Table 4.2. Members of Class `numeric_limits<>`, *Part 1*

Member	Meaning	C Constants
`has_denorm`	Whether type allows denormalized values (variable numbers of exponent bits, see page 63)	
`has_denorm_loss`	Loss of accuracy is detected as a denormalization loss rather than as an inexact result	
`denorm_min()`	Minimum positive denormalized value	
`traps`	Trapping is implemented	
`tinyness_before`	Tinyness is detected before rounding	

Table 4.3. Members of Class `numeric_limits<>`, *Part 2*

The following is a possible full specialization of the numeric limits for type `float`, which is platform dependent. It also shows the exact signatures of the members:

```
namespace std {
    template<> class numeric_limits<float> {
      public:
        // yes, a specialization for numeric limits of float does exist
        static const bool is_specialized = true;

        inline static float min() throw() {
            return 1.17549435E-38F;
        }
        inline static float max() throw() {
            return 3.40282347E+38F;
        }

        static const int digits = 24;
        static const int digits10 = 6;

        static const bool is_signed = true;
        static const bool is_integer = false;
        static const bool is_exact = false;
        static const bool is_bounded = true;
        static const bool is_modulo = false;
        static const bool is_iec559 = true;

        static const int radix = 2;

        inline static float epsilon() throw() {
```

```
        return 1.19209290E-07F;
    }

    static const float_round_style round_style
        = round_to_nearest;
    inline static float round_error() throw() {
        return 0.5F;
    }

    static const int min_exponent = -125;
    static const int max_exponent = +128;
    static const int min_exponent10 = -37;
    static const int max_exponent10 = +38;

    static const bool has_infinity = true;
    inline static float infinity() throw() { return ...; }
    static const bool has_quiet_NaN = true;
    inline static float quiet_NaN() throw() { return ...; }
    static const bool has_signaling_NaN = true;
    inline static float signaling_NaN() throw() { return ...; }
    static const float_denorm_style has_denorm = denorm_absent;
    static const bool has_denorm_loss = false;
    inline static float denorm_min() throw() { return min(); }

    static const bool traps = true;
    static const bool tinyness_before = true;
    };
}
```

Note that all nonfunction members are constant and static so that their values can be determined at compile time. For members that are defined by functions, the value might not be defined clearly at compile time on some implementations. For example, the same object code may run on different processors and may have different values for floating values.

The values of round_style are shown in Table 4.4. The values of has_denorm are shown in Table 4.5. Unfortunately, the member has_denorm is not called denorm_style. This happened because during the standardization process there was a late change from a Boolean to an enumerative value. However, you can use the has_denorm member as a Boolean value because the standard guarantees that denorm_absent is 0, which is equivalent to false, whereas denorm_present is 1 and denorm_indeterminate is -1, both of which are equivalent to true. Thus, you can consider has_denorm a Boolean indication of whether the type may allow denormalized values.

Round Style	Meaning
`round_toward_zero`	Rounds toward zero
`round_to_nearest`	Rounds to the nearest representable value
`round_toward_infinity`	Rounds toward positive infinity
`round_toward_neg_infinity`	Rounds toward negative infinity
`round_indeterminate`	Indeterminable

Table 4.4. Round Style of `numeric_limits<>`

Denorm Style	Meaning
`denorm_absent`	The type does not allow denormalized values
`denorm_present`	The type does allow denormalized values to the nearest representable value
`denorm_indeterminate`	Indeterminable

Table 4.5. Denormalization Style of `numeric_limits<>`

Example of Using `numeric_limits<>`

The following example shows possible uses of some numeric limits, such as the maximum values for certain types and determining whether `char` is signed.

```
// util/limits1.cpp

#include <iostream>
#include <limits>
#include <string>
using namespace std;

int main()
{
    // use textual representation for bool
    cout << boolalpha;

    // print maximum of integral types
    cout << "max(short): " << numeric_limits<short>::max() << endl;
    cout << "max(int):   " << numeric_limits<int>::max() << endl;
    cout << "max(long):  " << numeric_limits<long>::max() << endl;
    cout << endl;
```

```
// print maximum of floating-point types
cout << "max(float):        "
     << numeric_limits<float>::max() << endl;
cout << "max(double):       "
     << numeric_limits<double>::max() << endl;
cout << "max(long double): "
     << numeric_limits<long double>::max() << endl;
cout << endl;

// print whether char is signed
cout << "is_signed(char): "
     << numeric_limits<char>::is_signed << endl;
cout << endl;

// print whether numeric limits for type string exist
cout << "is_specialized(string): "
     << numeric_limits<string>::is_specialized << endl;
}
```

The output of this program is platform dependent. Here is a possible output of the program:

```
max(short):  32767
max(int):    2147483647
max(long):   2147483647

max(float):        3.40282e+38
max(double):       1.79769e+308
max(long double): 1.79769e+308

is_signed(char): false

is_specialized(string): false
```

The last line shows that there are no numeric limits defined for the type string. This makes sense because strings are not numeric values. However, this example shows that you can query for any arbitrary type whether or not it has numeric limits defined.

4.4   Auxiliary Functions

The algorithm library (header file `<algorithm>`) includes three auxiliary functions, one each for the
selection of the minimum and maximum of two values and one for the swapping of two values.

4.4.1   Processing the Minimum and Maximum

The functions to process the minimum and the maximum of two values are defined in `<algorithm>`
as follows:

```
namespace std {
    template <class T>
    inline const T& min (const T& a, const T& b) {
        return  b < a ? b : a;
    }

    template <class T>
    inline const T& max (const T& a, const T& b) {
        return  a < b ? b : a;
    }
}
```

If both values are equal, generally the first element gets returned. However, it is not good programming style to rely on this.

Both functions are also provided with the comparison criterion as an additional argument:

```
namespace std {
    template <class T, class Compare>
    inline const T& min (const T& a, const T& b, Compare comp) {
        return comp(b,a) ? b : a;
    }

    template <class T, class Compare>
    inline const T& max (const T& a, const T& b, Compare comp) {
        return comp(a,b) ? b : a;
    }
}
```

The comparison argument might be a function or a function object that compares both arguments
and returns whether the first is less than the second in some particular order (function objects are
introduced in Section 5.9, page 124).

The following example shows how to use the maximum function by passing a special comparison
function as an argument:

```
// util/minmax1.cpp

#include <algorithm>
using namespace std;

/* function that compares two pointers by comparing the values to which they point
 */
bool int_ptr_less (int* a, int* b)
{
    return *a < *b;
}

int main()
{
    int x = 17;
    int y = 42;
    int* px = &x;
    int* py = &y;
    int* pmax;

    // call max() with special comparison function
    pmax = max (px, py, int_ptr_less);
    ...
}
```

Note that the definition of `min()` and `max()` require that both types match. Thus, you can't call them for objects of different types:

```
int i;
long l;
...
l = std::max(i,l);        // ERROR: argument types don't match
```

However, you could qualify explicitly the type of your arguments (and thus the return type):

```
l = std::max<long>(i,l);   // OK
```

4.4.2 Swapping Two Values

The function `swap()` is provided to swap the values of two objects. The general implementation of `swap()` is defined in `<algorithm>` as follows:

```
namespace std {
    template<class T>
    inline void swap(T& a, T& b) {
        T tmp(a);
        a = b;
        b = tmp;
    }
}
```

By using this function you can have two arbitrary variables x and y swap their values by calling

```
std::swap(x,y);
```

Of course, this call is possible only if the copy constructions and assignments inside the `swap()` function are possible.

The big advantage of using `swap()` is that it enables to provide special implementations for more complex types by using template specialization or function overloading. These special implementations might save time by swapping internal members rather than by assigning the objects. This is the case, for example, for all standard containers (Section 6.1.2, page 147) and strings (Section 11.2.8, page 490). For example, a `swap()` implementation for a simple container that has only an array and the number of elements as members could look like this:

```
class MyContainer {
  private:
    int* elems;        // dynamic array of elements
    int  numElems;     // number of elements
  public:
    ...
    // implementation of swap()
    void swap(MyContainer& x) {
        std::swap(elems,x.elems);
        std::swap(numElems,x.numElems);
    }
    ...
};


// overloaded global swap() for this type
inline void swap (MyContainer& c1, MyContainer& c2)
{
    c1.swap(c2);       // calls implementation of swap()
}
```

So, calling `swap()` instead of swapping the values directly might result in substantial performance improvements. You should always offer a specialization of `swap()` for your own types if doing so has performance advantages.

4.5   Supplementary Comparison Operators

Four template functions define the comparison operators !=, >, <=, and >= by calling the operators == and <. These functions are defined in `<utility>` as follows:

```
namespace std {
    namespace rel_ops {
        template <class T>
        inline bool operator!= (const T& x, const T& y) {
            return !(x == y);
        }

        template <class T>
        inline bool operator> (const T& x, const T& y) {
            return y < x;
        }

        template <class T>
        inline bool operator<= (const T& x, const T& y) {
            return !(y < x);
        }

        template <class T>
        inline bool operator>= (const T& x, const T& y) {
            return !(x < y);
        }
    }
}
```

To use them, you only need to define operators < and ==. By using namespace `std::rel_ops`, the other comparison operators are defined automatically. For example:

```
#include <utility>

class X {
    ...
  public:
```

```
        bool operator== (const X& x) const;
        bool operator< (const X& x) const;
        ...
};

void foo()
{
    using namespace std::rel_ops;        // make !=, >, etc., available
    X x1, x2;
    ...

    if (x1 != x2) {
        ...
    }
    ...

    if (x1 > x2) {
        ...
    }
    ...
}
```

Note that these operators are defined in a subnamespace of std, called rel_ops. The reason that
they are in a separate namespace is so that users who define their own relational operators in the
global namespace won't clash even if they made all identifiers of namespace std global by using a
general using directive:

```
    using namespace std;                 // operators are not in global scope
```

On the other hand, users who want to get their hands on them explicitly can implement the following
without having to rely on lookup rules to find them implicitly:

```
    using namespace std::rel_ops;     // operators are in global scope
```

Some implementations define the previous templates by using two different argument types:

```
    namespace std {
        template <class T1, class T2>
        inline bool operator!=(const T1& x, const T2& y) {
            return !(x == y);
        }
        ...
    }
```

The advantage of such an implementation is that the types of the operands may differ (provided the types are comparable). But, note that this kind of implementation is not provided by the C++ standard library. Thus, taking advantage of it makes code nonportable.

4.6 Header Files `<cstddef>` and `<cstdlib>`

Two header files compatible with C are often used in C++ programs: `<cstddef>` and `<cstdlib>`. They are the new versions of the C header files `<stddef.h>` and `<stdlib.h>`, and they define some common constants, macros, types, and functions.

4.6.1 Definitions in `<cstddef>`

Table 4.6 shows the definitions of the `<cstddef>` header file. `NULL` is often used to indicate that a pointer points to nothing. It is simply the value 0 (either as an `int` or as a `long`). Note that in C, `NULL` often is defined as `(void*)0`. This is incorrect in C++ because there the type of `NULL` must be an integer type. Otherwise, you could not assign `NULL` to a pointer. This is because in C++ there is no automatic conversion from `void*` to any other type.[10] Note that `NULL` is also defined in the header files `<cstdio>`, `<cstdlib>`, `<cstring>`, `<ctime>`, `<cwchar>`, and `<clocale>`.

Identifier	Meaning
`NULL`	Pointer value for "not defined" or "no value"
`size_t`	Unsigned type for size units (such as number of elements)
`ptrdiff_t`	Signed type for differences of pointer
`offsetof()`	Offset of a member in a structure or union

Table 4.6. Definitions in `<cstddef>`

4.6.2 Definitions in `<cstdlib>`

Table 4.7 shows the most important definitions of the `<cstdlib>` header file. The two constants `EXIT_SUCCESS` and `EXIT_FAILURE` are defined as arguments for `exit()`. They can also be used as a return value in `main()`.

The functions that are registered by `atexit()` are called at normal program termination in reverse order of their registration. It doesn't matter whether the program exits due to a call of `exit()` or the end of `main()`. No arguments are passed.

---

[10] Due to the mess with the type of `NULL`, several people and style guides recommend not using `NULL` in C++. Instead, 0 or a special user-defined constant such as `NIL` might work better. However, I use it, so you will find it in my examples in this book.

Definition	Meaning
`exit (int status)`	Exit program (cleans up static objects)
`EXIT_SUCCESS`	Indicates a normal end of the program
`EXIT_FAILURE`	Indicates an abnormal end of the program
`abort()`	Abort program (might force a crash on some systems)
`atexit (void (*function)())`	Call *function* on exit

Table 4.7. Definitions in `<cstdlib>`

The `exit()` and `abort()` functions are provided to terminate a program in any function without going back to `main()`:

- `exit()` destroys all static objects, flushes all buffers, closes all I/O channels, and terminates the program (including calling `atexit()` functions). If functions passed to `atexit()` throw exceptions, `terminate()` is called.
- `abort()` terminates a program immediately with no clean up.

None of these functions destroys local objects because no stack unwinding occurs. To ensure that the destructors of all local objects are called, you should use exceptions or the ordinary return mechanism to return to and exit `main()`.

Chapter 5

The Standard Template Library

The heart of the C++ standard library, the part that influenced its overall architecture, is the *standard template library* (*STL*). The STL is a generic library that provides solutions to managing collections of data with modern and efficient algorithms. It allows programmers to benefit from innovations in the area of data structures and algorithms without needing to learn how they work.

From the programmer's point of view, the STL provides a bunch of collection classes that meet different needs, together with several algorithms that operate on them. All components of the STL are templates, so they can be used for arbitrary element types. But the STL does even more: It provides a framework for supplying other collection classes or algorithms for which existing collection classes and algorithms work. All in all, the STL gives C++ a new level of abstraction. Forget programming dynamic arrays, linked lists, and binary trees; forget programming different search algorithms. To use the appropriate kind of collection, you simply define the appropriate container and call the member functions and algorithms to process the data.

The STL's flexibility, however, has a price, chief of which is that it is not self-explanatory. Therefore, the subject of the STL fills several chapters in this book. This chapter introduces the general concept of the STL and explains the programming techniques needed to use it. The first examples show how to use the STL and what to consider while doing so. Chapters 6 through 9 discuss the components of the STL (containers, iterators, function objects, and algorithms) in detail and present several more examples.

5.1 STL Components

The STL is based on the cooperation of different well-structured components, key of which are containers, iterators, and algorithms:

- **Containers** are used to manage collections of objects of a certain kind. Every kind of container has its own advantages and disadvantages, so having different container types reflects different requirements for collections in programs. The containers may be implemented as arrays or as linked lists, or they may have a special key for every element.

- **Iterators** are used to step through the elements of collections of objects. These collections may be containers or subsets of containers. The major advantage of iterators is that they offer a small but common interface for any arbitrary container type. For example, one operation of this interface lets the iterator step to the next element in the collection. This is done independently of the internal structure of the collection. Regardless of whether the collection is an array or a tree, it works. This is because every container class provides its own iterator type that simply "does the right thing" because it knows the internal structure of its container.

  The interface for iterators is almost the same as for ordinary pointers. To increment an iterator you call operator ++. To access the value of an iterator you use operator *. So, you might consider an iterator a kind of a smart pointer that translates the call "go to the next element" into whatever is appropriate.

- **Algorithms** are used to process the elements of collections. For example, they can search, sort, modify, or simply use the elements for different purposes. Algorithms use iterators. Thus, an algorithm has to be written only once to work with arbitrary containers because the iterator interface for iterators is common for all container types.

  To give algorithms more flexibility you can supply certain auxiliary functions called by the algorithms. Thus, you can use a general algorithm to suit your needs even if that need is very special or complex. For example, you can provide your own search criterion or a special operation to combine elements.

The concept of the STL is based on a separation of data and operations. The data is managed by container classes, and the operations are defined by configurable algorithms. Iterators are the glue between these two components. They let any algorithm interact with any container (Figure 5.1).

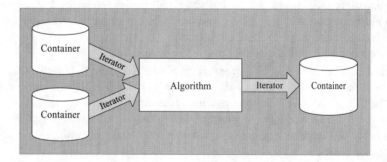

Figure 5.1. STL Components

In a way, the STL concept contradicts the original idea of object-oriented programming: The STL *separates* data and algorithms rather than combining them. However, the reason for doing so is very important. In principle, you can combine every kind of container with every kind of algorithm, so the result is a very flexible but still rather small framework.

One fundamental aspect of the STL is that all components work with arbitrary types. As the name "standard template library" indicates, all components are templates for any type (provided the type is able to perform the required operations). Thus the STL is a good example of the concept of *generic programming*. Containers and algorithms are generic for arbitrary types and classes respectively.

The STL provides even more generic components. By using certain *adapters* and *function objects* (or *functors*) you can supplement, constrain, or configure the algorithms and the interfaces for special needs. However, I'm jumping the gun. First, I want to explain the concept step-by-step by using examples. This is probably the best way to understand and become familiar with the STL.

5.2   Containers

Container classes, or *containers* for short, manage a collection of elements. To meet different needs, the STL provides different kinds of containers, as shown in Figure 5.2.

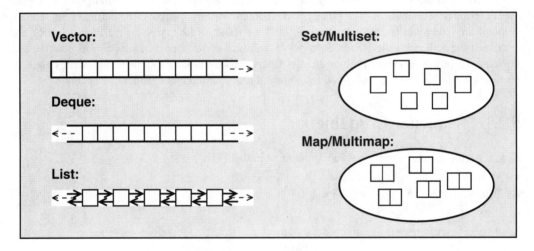

Figure 5.2. STL Container Types

There are two general kinds of containers:

1. **Sequence containers** are *ordered collections* in which every element has a certain position. This position depends on the time and place of the insertion, but it is independent of the value of the element. For example, if you put six elements into a collection by appending each element at the end of the actual collection, these elements are in the exact order in which you put them. The STL contains three predefined sequence container classes: `vector`, `deque`, and `list`.

2. **Associative containers** are *sorted collections* in which the actual position of an element depends on its value due to a certain sorting criterion. If you put six elements into a collection, their order depends only on their value. The order of insertion doesn't matter. The STL contains four predefined associative container classes: `set`, `multiset`, `map`, and `multimap`.

An associative container can be considered a special kind of sequence container because sorted collections are ordered according to a sorting criterion. You might expect this especially if you have used other libraries of collection classes like those in Smalltalk or the NIHCL,[1] in which sorted collections are derived from ordered collections. However, note that the STL collection types are completely distinct from each other. They have different implementations that are not derived from each other.

The automatic sorting of elements in associative containers does *not* mean that those containers are especially designed for sorting elements. You can also sort the elements of a sequence container. The key advantage of automatic sorting is better performance when you search elements. In particular, you can always use a binary search, which results in logarithmic complexity rather than linear complexity. For example, this means that for a search in a collection of 1,000 elements you need, on average, only 10 instead of 500 comparisons (see Section 2.3, page 21). Thus, automatic sorting is only a (useful) "side effect" of the implementation of an associative container, designed to enable better performance.

The following subsections discuss the different container classes in detail. Among other aspects, they describe how containers are typically implemented. Strictly speaking, the particular implementation of any container is not defined inside the C++ standard library. However, the behavior and complexity specified by the standard do not leave much room for variation. So, in practice, the implementations differ only in minor details. Chapter 6 covers the exact behavior of the container classes. It describes their common and individual abilities, and member functions in detail.

5.2.1   Sequence Containers

The following sequence containers are predefined in the STL:
- Vectors
- Deques
- Lists

In addition you can use strings and ordinary arrays as a (kind of) sequence container.

Vectors

A vector manages its elements in a dynamic array. It enables random access, which means you can access each element directly with the corresponding index. Appending and removing elements at the end of the array is very fast.[2] However, inserting an element in the middle or at the beginning of the array takes time because all the following elements have to be moved to make room for it while maintaining the order.

---

[1] The National Institute of Health's Class Library was one of the first class libraries in C++.

[2] Strictly speaking, appending elements is *amortized* very fast. An individual append may be slow, when a vector has to reallocate new memory and to copy existing elements into the new memory. However, because such reallocations are rather rare, the operation is very fast in the long term. See page 22 for a discussion of complexity.

The following example defines a vector for integer values, inserts six elements, and prints the elements of the vector:

```
// stl/vector1.cpp

#include <iostream>
#include <vector>
using namespace std;

int main()
{
    vector<int> coll;      // vector container for integer elements

    // append elements with values 1 to 6
    for (int i=1; i<=6; ++i) {
        coll.push_back(i);
    }

    // print all elements followed by a space
    for (int i=0; i<coll.size(); ++i) {
        cout << coll[i] << ' ';
    }
    cout << endl;
}
```

With

```
#include <vector>
```

the header file for vectors is included.

The declaration

```
vector<int> coll;
```

creates a vector for elements of type int. The vector is not initialized by any value, so the default constructor creates it as an empty collection.

The push_back() function appends an element to the container:

```
coll.push_back(i);
```

This member function is provided for all sequence containers.

The size() member function returns the number of elements of a container:

```
for (int i=0; i<coll.size(); ++i) {
    ...
}
```

This function is provided for any container class.

By using the subscript operator [ ], you can access a single element of a vector:

```
cout << coll[i] << ' ';
```

Here the elements are written to the standard output, so the output of the whole program is as follows:

```
1 2 3 4 5 6
```

Deques

The term *deque* (it rhymes with "check"[3]) is an abbreviation for "double-ended queue." It is a dynamic array that is implemented so that it can grow in both directions. Thus, inserting elements at the end *and* at the beginning is fast. However, inserting elements in the middle takes time because elements must be moved.

The following example declares a deque for floating-point values, inserts elements from 1.1 to 6.6 at the front of the container, and prints all elements of the deque:

```
// stl/deque1.cpp

#include <iostream>
#include <deque>
using namespace std;

int main()
{
    deque<float> coll;        // deque container for floating-point elements

    // insert elements from 1.1 to 6.6 each at the front
    for (int i=1; i<=6; ++i) {
        coll.push_front(i*1.1);        // insert at the front
    }

    // print all elements followed by a space
    for (int i=0; i<coll.size(); ++i) {
        cout << coll[i] << ' ';
    }
    cout << endl;
}
```

---

[3] It is only a mere accident that "deque" also sounds like "hack" :-) .

In this example, with

```
#include <deque>
```

the header file for deques is included.

The declaration

```
deque<float> coll;
```

creates an empty collection of floating-point values.

The `push_front()` function is used to insert elements:

```
coll.push_front(i*1.1);
```

`push_front()` inserts an element at the front of the collection. Note that this kind of insertion results in a reverse order of the elements because each element gets inserted in front of the previous inserted elements. Thus, the output of the program is as follows:

```
6.6 5.5 4.4 3.3 2.2 1.1
```

You could also insert elements in a deque by using the `push_back()` member function. The `push_front()` function, however, is not provided for vectors because it would have a bad runtime for vectors (if you insert an element at the front of a vector, all elements have to be moved). Usually, the STL containers provide only those special member functions that in general have "good" timing ("good" timing normally means constant or logarithmic complexity). This prevents a programmer from calling a function that might cause bad performance.

Lists

A `list` is implemented as a doubly linked list of elements. This means each element in a list has its own segment of memory and refers to its predecessor and its successor. Lists do not provide random access. For example, to access the tenth element, you must navigate the first nine elements by following the chain of their links. However, a step to the next or previous element is possible in constant time. Thus, the general access to an arbitrary element takes linear time (the average distance is proportional to the number of elements). This is a lot worse than the amortized constant time provided by vectors and deques.

The advantage of a list is that the insertion or removal of an element is fast at any position. Only the links must be changed. This implies that moving an element in the middle of a list is very fast compared with moving an element in a vector or a deque.

The following example creates an empty list of characters, inserts all characters from 'a' to 'z', and prints all elements by using a loop that actually prints and removes the first element of the collection:

```
// stl/list1.cpp

#include <iostream>
#include <list>
using namespace std;
```

```
int main()
{
    list<char> coll;           // list container for character elements

    // append elements from 'a' to 'z'
    for (char c='a'; c<='z'; ++c) {
        coll.push_back(c);
    }

    /* print all elements
     * - while there are elements
     * - print and remove the first element
     */
    while (! coll.empty()) {
        cout << coll.front() << ' ';
        coll.pop_front();
    }
    cout << endl;
}
```

As usual, the header file for lists, `<list>`, is used to define a collection of type `list` for character values:

```
list<char> coll;
```

The `empty()` member function returns whether the container has no elements. The loop continues as long as it returns `false` (that is, the container contains elements):

```
while (! coll.empty()) {
    ...
}
```

Inside the loop, the `front()` member function returns the first element:

```
cout << coll.front() << ' ';
```

The `pop_front()` function removes the first element:

```
coll.pop_front();
```

Note that `pop_front()` does not return the element it removed. Thus, you can't combine the previous two statements into one.

The output of the program depends on the character set in use. For the ASCII character set, it is as follows[4]:

```
a b c d e f g h i j k l m n o p q r s t u v w x y z
```

Of course it is very strange to "print" the elements of a list by a loop that outputs and removes the first element. Usually, you would iterate over all elements. However, direct element access by using operator [ ] is not provided for lists. This is because lists don't provide random access, and thus using operator [ ] would cause bad performance. There is another way to loop over the elements and print them by using iterators. After their introduction I will give an example (if you can't wait, go to page 84).

Strings

You can also use strings as STL containers. By *strings* I mean objects of the C++ string classes (basic_string<>, string, and wstring), which are introduced in Chapter 11. Strings are similar to vectors except that their elements are characters. Section 11.2.13, page 497, provides details.

Ordinary Arrays

Another kind of container is a type of the core C and C++ language rather than a class: an ordinary array that has static or dynamic size. However, ordinary arrays are not STL containers because they don't provide member functions such as size() and empty(). Nevertheless, the STL's design allows you to call algorithms for these ordinary arrays. This is especially useful when you process static arrays of values as an initializer list.

The usage of ordinary arrays is nothing new. What is new is using algorithms for them. This is explained in Section 6.7.2, page 218.

Note that in C++ it is no longer necessary to program dynamic arrays directly. Vectors provide all properties of dynamic arrays with a safer and more convenient interface. See Section 6.2.3, page 155, for details.

5.2.2 Associative Containers

Associative containers sort their elements automatically according to a certain ordering criterion. This criterion takes the form of a function that compares either the value or a special key that is defined for the value. By default, the containers compare the elements or the keys with operator <. However, you can supply your own comparison function to define another ordering criterion.

Associative containers are typically implemented as binary trees. Thus, every element (every node) has one parent and two children. All ancestors to the left have lesser values; all ancestors to

---

[4] For other character sets the output may contain characters that aren't letters or it may even be empty (if 'z' is not greater than 'a').

the right have greater values. The associative containers differ in the kind of elements they support and how they handle duplicates.

The following associative containers are predefined in the STL. Because you need iterators to access their elements, I do not provide examples until page 87, where I discuss iterators.

- **Sets**

  A set is a collection in which elements are sorted according to their own values. Each element may occur only once, thus duplicates are not allowed.

- **Multisets**

  A multiset is the same as a set except that duplicates are allowed. Thus, a multiset may contain multiple elements that have the same value.

- **Maps**

  A map contains elements that are key/value pairs. Each element has a key that is the basis for the sorting criterion and a value. Each key may occur only once, thus duplicate keys are not allowed. A map can also be used as an *associative array*, which is an array that has an arbitrary index type (see page 91 for details).

- **Multimaps**

  A multimap is the same as a map except that duplicates are allowed. Thus, a multimap may contain multiple elements that have the same key. A multimap can also be used as *dictionary*. See page 209 for an example.

All of these associative container classes have an optional template argument for the sorting criterion. The default sorting criterion is the operator <. The sorting criterion is also used as the test for equality; that is, two elements are equal if neither is less than the other.

You can consider a set as a special kind of map, in which the value is identical to the key. In fact, all of these associative container types are usually implemented by using the same basic implementation of a binary tree.

5.2.3   Container Adapters

In addition to the fundamental container classes, the C++ standard library provides special predefined container adapters that meet special needs. These are implemented by using the fundamental containers classes. The predefined container adapters are as follows:

- **Stacks**

  The name says it all. A stack is a container that manages its elements by the LIFO (last-in-first-out) policy.

- **Queues**

  A queue is a container that manages its elements by the FIFO (first-in-first-out) policy. That is, it is an ordinary buffer.

- **Priority Queues**

  A priority queue is a container in which the elements may have different priorities. The priority is based on a sorting criterion that the programmer may provide (by default, operator < is used). A priority queue is, in effect, a buffer in which the next element is always the element that has the highest priority inside the queue. If more than one element has the highest priority, the order of these elements is undefined.

Container adapters are historically part of the STL. However, from a programmer's view point, they are just special containers that use the general framework of the containers, iterators, and algorithms provided by the STL. Therefore, container adapters are described apart from the STL in Chapter 10.

5.3 Iterators

An iterator is an object that can "iterate" (navigate) over elements. These elements may be all or part of the elements of an STL container. An iterator represents a certain position in a container. The following fundamental operations define the behavior of an iterator:

- **Operator ***
  Returns the element of the current position. If the elements have members, you can use operator -> to access those members directly from the iterator.[5]

- **Operator ++**
  Lets the iterator step forward to the next element. Most iterators also allow stepping backward by using operator --.

- **Operators == and !=**
  Return whether two iterators represent the same position.

- **Operator =**
  Assigns an iterator (the position of the element to which it refers).

These operations are exactly the interface of ordinary pointers in C and C++ when they are used to iterate over the elements of an array. The difference is that iterators may be *smart pointers* — pointers that iterate over more complicated data structures of containers. The internal behavior of iterators depends on the data structure over which they iterate. Hence, each container type supplies its own kind of iterator. In fact, each container class defines its iterator type as a nested class. As a result, iterators share the same interface but have different types. This leads directly to the concept of generic programming: Operations use the same interface but different types, so you can use templates to formulate generic operations that work with arbitrary types that satisfy the interface.

All container classes provide the same basic member functions that enable them to use iterators to navigate over their elements. The most important of these functions are as follows:

- **begin()**
  Returns an iterator that represents the beginning of the elements in the container. The beginning is the position of the first element (if any).

- **end()**
  Returns an iterator that represents the end of the elements in the container. The end is the position *behind* the last element. Such an iterator is also called a *past-the-end iterator*.

---

[5] In some older environments, operator -> might not work yet for iterators.

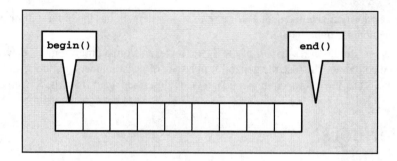

Figure 5.3. `begin()` *and* `end()` *for Containers*

Thus, `begin()` and `end()` define a *half-open range* that includes the first element but excludes the last (Figure 5.3). A half-open range has two advantages:

1. You have a simple end criterion for loops that iterate over the elements: They simply continue as long as `end()` is not reached.

2. It avoids special handling for empty ranges. For empty ranges, `begin()` is equal to `end()`.

Here is an example demonstrating the use of iterators. It prints all elements of a list container (it is the promised enhanced version of the first list example on page 79).

```
// stl/list2.cpp

#include <iostream>
#include <list>
using namespace std;

int main()
{
    list<char> coll;          // list container for character elements

    // append elements from 'a' to 'z'
    for (char c='a'; c<='z'; ++c) {
        coll.push_back(c);
    }

    /* print all elements
     * - iterate over all elements
     */
    list<char>::const_iterator pos;
    for (pos = coll.begin(); pos != coll.end(); ++pos) {
        cout << *pos << ' ';
```

```
    }
    cout << endl;
}
```

After the list is created and filled with the characters 'a' through 'z', all elements are printed within
a for loop:

```
list<char>::const_iterator pos;
for (pos = coll.begin(); pos != coll.end(); ++pos) {
    cout << *pos << ' ';
}
```

The iterator pos is declared just before the loop. Its type is the iterator type for constant element
access of its container class:

```
list<char>::const_iterator pos;
```

Every container defines two iterator types:

1. *container*::iterator
   is provided to iterate over elements in read/write mode.
2. *container*::const_iterator
   is provided to iterate over elements in read-only mode.

For example, in class list the definitions might look like the following:

```
namespace std {
    template <class T>
    class list {
      public:
        typedef ... iterator;
        typedef ... const_iterator;
        ...
    };
}
```

The exact type of iterator and const_iterator is implementation defined.

Inside the for loop, the iterator pos first gets initialized with the position of the first element:

```
pos = coll.begin()
```

The loop continues as long as pos has not reached the end of the container elements:

```
pos != coll.end()
```

Here, pos is compared with the past-the-end iterator. While the loop runs the increment operator,
++pos navigates the iterator pos to the next element.

All in all, `pos` iterates from the first element, element-by-element, until it reaches the end (Figure 5.4). If the container has no elements, the loop does not run because `coll.begin()` would equal `coll.end()`.

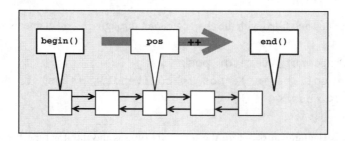

Figure 5.4. Iterator `pos` *Iterating Over Elements of a List*

In the body of the loop, the expression `*pos` represents the actual element. In this example, it is written followed by a space character. You can't modify the elements because a `const_iterator` is used. Thus, from the iterator's point of view the elements are constant. However, if you use a nonconstant iterator and the type of the elements is nonconstant, you can change the values. For example:

```
// make all characters in the list uppercase
list<char>::iterator pos;
for (pos = coll.begin(); pos != coll.end(); ++pos) {
    *pos = toupper(*pos);
}
```

Note that the preincrement operator (prefix ++) is used here. This is because it might have better performance than the postincrement operator. The latter involves a temporary object because it must return the old position of the iterator. For this reason, it generally is best to prefer ++pos over pos++. Thus, you should avoid the following version:

```
for (pos = coll.begin(); pos != coll.end(); pos++) {
                                        ^^^^^     // OK, but slower

    ...
}
```

For this reason, I recommend using the preincrement and pre-decrement operators in general.

5.3.1 Examples of Using Associative Containers

The iterator loop in the previous example could be used for any container. You only have to adjust the iterator type. Now you can print elements of associative containers. The following are some examples of the use of associative containers.

Examples of Using Sets and Multisets

The first example shows how to insert elements into a set and to use iterators to print them:

```cpp
// stl/set1.cpp

#include <iostream>
#include <set>

int main()
{
    // type of the collection
    typedef std::set<int> IntSet;

    IntSet coll;            // set container for int values

    /* insert elements from 1 to 6 in arbitrary order
     * - value 1 gets inserted twice
     */
    coll.insert(3);
    coll.insert(1);
    coll.insert(5);
    coll.insert(4);
    coll.insert(1);
    coll.insert(6);
    coll.insert(2);

    /* print all elements
     * - iterate over all elements
     */
    IntSet::const_iterator pos;
    for (pos = coll.begin(); pos != coll.end(); ++pos) {
        std::cout << *pos << ' ';
    }
    std::cout << std::endl;
}
```

As usual, the `include` directive

```cpp
#include <set>
```

defines all necessary types and operations of sets.

The type of the container is used in several places, so first a shorter type name gets defined:

```
typedef set<int> IntSet;
```

This statement defines type `IntSet` as a set for elements of type `int`. This type uses the default sorting criterion, which sorts the elements by using operator `<`. This means the elements are sorted in ascending order. To sort in descending order or use a completely different sorting criterion, you can pass it as a second template parameter. For example, the following statement defines a set type that sorts the elements in descending order[6]:

```
typedef set<int,greater<int> > IntSet;
```

`greater<>` is a predefined function object that is discussed in Section 5.9.2, page 131. For a sorting criterion that uses only a part of the data of an object (such as the ID) see Section 8.1.1, page 294.

All associative containers provide an `insert()` member function to insert a new element:

```
coll.insert(3);
coll.insert(1);
...
```

The new element receives the correct position automatically according to the sorting criterion. You can't use the `push_back()` or `push_front()` functions provided for sequence containers. They make no sense here because you can't specify the position of the new element.

After all values are inserted in any order, the state of the container is as shown in Figure 5.5. The elements are sorted into the internal tree structure of the container so that the value of the left child of an element is always less (with respect to the actual sorting criterion) and the value of the right child of an element is always greater. Duplicates are not allowed in a set, so the container contains the value 1 only once.

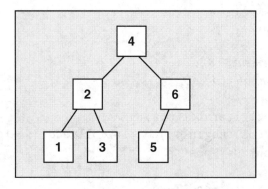

Figure 5.5. A Set that Has Six Elements

---

[6] Note that you have to put a space between the two ">" characters. ">>" would be parsed as shift operator, which would result in a syntax error.

To print the elements of the container, you use the same loop as in the previous list example. An iterator iterates over all elements and prints them:

```
IntSet::const_iterator pos;
for (pos = coll.begin(); pos != coll.end(); ++pos) {
    cout << *pos << ' ';
}
```

Again, because the iterator is defined by the container, it does the right thing, even if the internal structure of the container is more complicated. For example, if the iterator refers to the third element, operator **++** moves to the fourth element at the top. After the next call of operator **++** the iterator refers to the fifth element at the bottom (Figure 5.6).

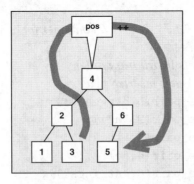

Figure 5.6. Iterator pos *Iterating over Elements of a Set*

The output of the program is as follows:

```
1 2 3 4 5 6
```

If you want to use a multiset rather than a set, you need only change the type of the container (the header file remains the same):

```
typedef multiset<int> IntSet;
```

A multiset allows duplicates, so it would contain two elements that have value 1. Thus, the output of the program would change to the following:

```
1 1 2 3 4 5 6
```

Examples of Using Maps and Multimaps

The elements of maps and multimaps are key/value pairs. Thus, the declaration, the insertion, and the access to elements are a bit different. Here is an example of using a multimap:

```cpp
// stl/mmap1.cpp

#include <iostream>
#include <map>
#include <string>
using namespace std;

int main()
{
    // type of the collection
    typedef multimap<int,string> IntStringMMap;

    IntStringMMap coll;          // container for int/string values

    // insert some elements in arbitrary order
    // - a value with key 1 gets inserted twice
    coll.insert(make_pair(5,"tagged"));
    coll.insert(make_pair(2,"a"));
    coll.insert(make_pair(1,"this"));
    coll.insert(make_pair(4,"of"));
    coll.insert(make_pair(6,"strings"));
    coll.insert(make_pair(1,"is"));
    coll.insert(make_pair(3,"multimap"));

    /* print all element values
     * - iterate over all elements
     * - element member second is the value
     */
    IntStringMMap::iterator pos;
    for (pos = coll.begin(); pos != coll.end(); ++pos) {
        cout << pos->second << ' ';
    }
    cout << endl;
}
```

The program may have the following output:

```
this is a multimap of tagged strings
```

However, because "this" and "is" have the same key, their order might be the other way around.

When you compare this example with the set example on page 87, you can see the following two differences:

1. The elements are key/value pairs, so you must create such a pair to insert it into the collection. The auxiliary function `make_pair()` is provided for this purpose. See page 203 for more details and other possible ways to insert a value.
2. The iterators refer to key/value pairs. Therefore, you can't just print them as a whole. Instead, you must access the members of the `pair` structure, which are called `first` and `second` (type `pair` is introduced in Section 4.1, page 33). Thus, the expression

```
pos->second
```

yields the second part of the key/value pair, which is the value of the multimap element. As with ordinary pointers, the expression is defined as an abbreviation for[7]

```
(*pos).second
```

Similarly, the expression

```
pos->first
```

yields the first part of the key/value pair, which is the key of the multimap element.

Multimaps can also be used as *dictionaries*. See page 209 for an example.

Maps as Associative Arrays

In the previous example, if you replace type `multimap` with `map` you would get the output without duplicate keys (the values might still be the same). However, a collection of key/value pairs with unique keys could also be thought of as an *associative array*. Consider the following example:

```
// stl/map1.cpp

#include <iostream>
#include <map>
#include <string>
using namespace std;

int main()
{
    /* type of the container:
     * - map: elements key/value pairs
     * - string: keys have type string
     * - float: values have type float
     */
    typedef map<string,float> StringFloatMap;
```

---

[7] In some older environments, operator `->` might not work yet for iterators. In this case, you must use the second version.

```
StringFloatMap coll;

// insert some elements into the collection
coll["VAT"] = 0.15;
coll["Pi"] = 3.1415;
coll["an arbitrary number"] = 4983.223;
coll["Null"] = 0;

/* print all elements
 * - iterate over all elements
 * - element member first is the key
 * - element member second is the value
 */
StringFloatMap::iterator pos;
for (pos = coll.begin(); pos != coll.end(); ++pos) {
    cout << "key: \"" << pos->first << "\" "
         << "value: " << pos->second << endl;
}
}
```

The declaration of the container type must specify both the type of the key and the type of the value:

```
typedef map<string,float> StringFloatMap;
```

Maps enable you to insert elements by using the subscript operator [ ]:

```
coll["VAT"] = 0.15;
coll["Pi"] = 3.1415;
coll["an arbitrary number"] = 4983.223;
coll["Null"] = 0;
```

Here, the index is used as the key and may have any type. This is the interface of an *associative array*. An associative array is an array in which the index may be of an arbitrary type.

Note that the subscript operator behaves differently than the usual subscript operator for arrays: Not having an element for an index is *not* an error. A new index (or key) is taken as a reason to create and to insert a new element of the map that has the index as the key. Thus, you can't have a wrong index. Therefore, in this example in the statement

```
coll["Null"] = 0;
```

the expression

```
coll["Null"]
```

creates a new element that has the key "Null". The assignment operator assigns 0 (which gets converted into float) as the value. Section 6.6.3, page 205 discusses maps as associative arrays in more detail.

You can't use the subscript operator for multimaps. Multimaps allow multiple elements that have the same key, so the subscript operator makes no sense because it can handle only one value. As shown on page 90, you must create key/value pairs to insert elements into a multimap. You can do the same with maps. See page 202 for details.

Similar to multimaps, for maps to access the key and the value of an element you have to use the first and second members of the pair structure. The output of the program is as follows:

```
key: "Null" value: 0
key: "Pi" value: 3.1415
key: "VAT" value: 0.15
key: "an arbitrary number" value: 4983.22
```

5.3.2 Iterator Categories

Iterators can have capabilities in addition to their fundamental operations. The additional abilities depend on the internal structure of the container type. As usual, the STL provides only those operations that have good performance. For example, if containers have random access (such as vectors or deques) their iterators are also able to perform random access operations (for example, positioning the iterator directly at the fifth element).

Iterators are subdivided into different *categories* that are based on their general abilities. The iterators of the predefined container classes belong to one of the following two categories:

1. **Bidirectional iterator**

   As the name indicates, bidirectional iterators are able to iterate in two directions: forward, by using the increment operator, and backward, by using the decrement operator. The iterators of the container classes list, set, multiset, map, and multimap are bidirectional iterators.

2. **Random access iterator**

   Random access iterators have all the properties of bidirectional iterators. In addition, they can perform random access. In particular, they provide operators for "iterator arithmetic" (in accordance with "pointer arithmetic" of an ordinary pointer). You can add and subtract offsets, process differences, and compare iterators by using relational operators such as < and >. The iterators of the container classes vector and deque, and iterators of strings are random access iterators.

Other iterator categories are discussed in Section 7.2, page 251.

To write generic code that is as independent of the container type as possible, you should not use special operations for random access iterators. For example, the following loop works with any container:

```
for (pos = coll.begin(); pos != coll.end(); ++pos) {
    ...
}
```

```
      /* find position of element with value 3
       * - there is none, so pos gets coll.end()
       */
      pos = find (coll.begin(), coll.end(),      // range
                   3);                           // value


      /* reverse the order of elements between found element and the end
       * - because pos is coll.end() it reverses an empty range
       */
      reverse (pos, coll.end());


      // find positions of values 25 and 35
      list<int>::iterator pos25, pos35;
      pos25 = find (coll.begin(), coll.end(),   // range
                     25);                        // value
      pos35 = find (coll.begin(), coll.end(),   // range
                     35);                        // value


      /* print the maximum of the corresponding range
       * - note: including pos25 but excluding pos35
       */
      cout << "max: " << *max_element (pos25, pos35) << endl;


      // process the elements including the last position
      cout << "max: " << *max_element (pos25, ++pos35) << endl;
  }
```

In this example, the collection is initialized with integral values from 20 to 40. When the search for an element with the value 3 fails, find() returns the end of the processed range (coll.end() in this example) and assigns it to pos. Using that return value as the beginning of the range in the following call of reverse() poses no problem because it results in the following call:

```
      reverse (coll.end(), coll.end());
```

This is simply a call to reverse an empty range. Thus, it is an operation that has no effect (a so-called "no-op").

However, if find() is used to find the first and the last elements of a subset, you should consider that passing these iterator positions as a range will exclude the last element. So, the first call of max_element()

```
      max_element (pos25, pos35)
```

finds 34 and not 35:

```
      max: 34
```

To process the last element, you have to pass the position that is one past the last element:

```
max_element (pos25, ++pos35)
```

Doing this yields the correct result:

```
max: 35
```

Note that this example uses a list as the container. Thus, you must use operator ++ to get the position that is behind pos35. If you have random access iterators, as with vectors and deques, you also could use the expression pos35 + 1. This is because random access iterators allow "iterator arithmetic" (see Section 2, page 93, and Section 7.2.5, page 255, for details).

Of course, you could use pos25 and pos35 to find something in that subrange. Again, to search including pos35 you have to pass the position after pos35. For example:

```
// increment pos35 to search with its value included
++pos35;
pos30 = find(pos25,pos35,      // range
             30);              // value
if (pos30 == pos35) {
    cout << "30 is NOT in the subrange" << endl;
}
else {
    cout << "30 is in the subrange" << endl;
}
```

All the examples in this section work only because you know that pos25 is in front of pos35. Otherwise, [pos25,pos35) would not be a valid range. If you are not sure which element is in front, things get more complicated and undefined behavior may occur.

Suppose you don't know whether the element that has value 25 is in front of the element that has value 35. It might even be possible that one or both values are not present. By using random access iterators, you can call operator < to check this:

```
if (pos25 < pos35) {
    // only [pos25,pos35) is valid

    ...

}
else if (pos35 < pos25) {
    // only [pos35,pos25) is valid

    ...

}
else {
    // both are equal, so both must be end()

    ...

}
```

However, without random access iterators you have no simple, fast way to find out which iterator is in front. You can only search for one iterator in the range of the beginning to the other iterator or in the range of the other iterator to the end. In this case, you should change your algorithm as follows: Instead of searching for both values in the whole source range, you should try to find out, while searching for them, which value comes first. For example:

```
pos25 = find (coll.begin(), coll.end(),    // range
              25);                         // value
pos35 = find (coll.begin(), pos25,         // range
              35);                         // value
if (pos25 != coll.end() && pos35 != pos25) {
    /* pos35 is in front of pos25
     * so, only [pos35,pos25) is valid
     */
    ...
}
else {
    pos35 = find (pos25, coll.end(),       // range
                  35);                     // value
    if (pos35 != coll.end()) {
        /* pos25 is in front of pos35
         * so, only [pos25,pos35) is valid
         */
        ...
    }
    else {
        // 25 and/or 35 not found
        ...
    }
}
```

In contrast to the previous version, here you don't search for 35 in the full range of all elements of coll. Instead, you first search for it from the beginning to pos25. Then, if it's not found, you search for it in the part that contains the remaining elements after pos25. As a result you know which iterator position comes first and which subrange is valid.

This implementation is not very efficient. A more efficient way to find the first element that either has value 25 or value 35 is to search exactly for that. You could do this by using some abilities of the STL that are not introduced yet as follows:

```
pos = find_if (coll.begin(), coll.end(),              // range
               compose_f_gx_hx(logical_or<bool>(),    // criterion
                        bind2nd(equal_to<int>(),25),
                        bind2nd(equal_to<int>(),35)));
```

```
if (pos == coll.end()) {
    // no element with value 25 or 35 found
    ...
    break;
}
else if (*pos == 25) {
  case 25:
    // element with value 25 comes first
    pos25 = pos;
    pos35 = find (++pos, coll.end(),      // range
                  35);                    // value
    ...
}
else {
    // element with value 35 comes first
    pos35 = pos;
    pos25 = find (++pos, coll.end(),      // range
                  25);                    // value
    ...
}
```

Here, a special expression is used as a sorting criterion that allows a search of the first element that has either value 25 or value 35. The expression is a combination of several predefined function objects, which are introduced in Section 5.9.2, page 131, and Section 8.2, page 305, and a supplementary function object compose_f_gx_hx, which is introduced in Section 8.3.1, page 316.

5.4.2   Handling Multiple Ranges

Several algorithms process more than one range. In this case you usually must define both the beginning and the end only for the first range. For all other ranges you need to pass only their beginnings. The ends of the other ranges follow from the number of elements of the first range. For example, the following call of equal() compares all elements of the collection coll1 element-by-element with the elements of coll2 beginning with its first element:

```
if (equal (coll1.begin(), coll1.end(),
           coll2.begin())) {
    ...
}
```

Thus, the number of elements of coll2 that are compared with the elements of coll1 is specified indirectly by the number of elements in coll1.

This leads to an important consequence: When you call algorithms for multiple ranges, make sure the second and additional ranges have at least as many elements as the first range. In particular, make sure that destination ranges are big enough for algorithms that write to collections!

Consider the following program:

```
// stl/copy1.cpp

#include <iostream>
#include <vector>
#include <list>
#include <algorithm>
using namespace std;

int main()
{
    list<int>   coll1;
    vector<int> coll2;

    // insert elements from 1 to 9
    for (int i=1; i<=9; ++i) {
        coll1.push_back(i);
    }

    // RUNTIME ERROR:
    // - overwrites nonexisting elements in the destination
    copy (coll1.begin(), coll1.end(),      // source
          coll2.begin());                  // destination
    ...
}
```

Here, the `copy()` algorithm is called. It simply copies all elements of the first range into the destination range. As usual, for the first range, the beginning and the end are defined, whereas for the second range, only the beginning is specified. However, the algorithm overwrites rather than inserts. So, the algorithm *requires* that the destination has enough elements to be overwritten. If there is not enough room, as in this case, the result is undefined behavior. In practice, this often means that you overwrite whatever comes after the `coll2.end()`. If you're in luck, you'll get a crash; at least then you'll know that you did something wrong. However, you can force your luck by using a safe version of the STL for which the undefined behavior is defined as leading to a certain error handling procedure (see Section 5.11.1, page 138).

To avoid these errors, you can (1) ensure that the destination has enough elements on entry, or (2) use *insert iterators*. Insert iterators are covered in Section 5.5.1, page 104. I'll first explain how to modify the destination so that it is big enough on entry.

To make the destination big enough, you must either create it with the correct size or change its size explicitly. Both alternatives apply only to sequence containers (vectors, deques, and lists). This is not really a problem because associative containers cannot be used as a destination for purposes for overwriting algorithms (Section 5.6.2, page 115, explains why). The following program shows how to increase the size of containers:

```
// stl/copy2.cpp

#include <iostream>
#include <vector>
#include <list>
#include <deque>
#include <algorithm>
using namespace std;

int main()
{
    list<int>   coll1;
    vector<int> coll2;

    // insert elements from 1 to 9
    for (int i=1; i<=9; ++i) {
        coll1.push_back(i);
    }

    // resize destination to have enough room for the overwriting algorithm
    coll2.resize (coll1.size());

    /* copy elements from first into second collection
     * - overwrites existing elements in destination
     */
    copy (coll1.begin(), coll1.end(),      // source
          coll2.begin());                  // destination

    /* create third collection with enough room
     * - initial size is passed as parameter
     */
    deque<int> coll3(coll1.size());
```

```
        // copy elements from first into third collection
    copy (coll1.begin(), coll1.end(),      // source
          coll3.begin());                  // destination
}
```

Here, `resize()` is used to change the number of elements in the existing container `coll2`:

```
coll2.resize (coll1.size());
```

`coll3` is initialized with a special initial size so that it has enough room for all elements of `coll1`:

```
deque<int> coll3(coll1.size());
```

Note that both resizing and initializing the size create new elements. These elements are initialized by their default constructor because no arguments are passed to them. You can pass an additional argument both for the constructor and for `resize()` to initialize the new elements.

5.5   Iterator Adapters

Iterators are *pure abstractions*: Anything that *behaves* like an iterator *is* an iterator. For this reason, you can write classes that have the interface of iterators but do something (completely) different. The C++ standard library provides several predefined special iterators: *iterator adapters*. They are more than auxiliary classes; they give the whole concept a lot more power.

The following subsections introduce three iterator adapters:

1. Insert iterators
2. Stream iterators
3. Reverse iterators

Section 7.4, page 264, will cover them in detail.

5.5.1   Insert Iterators

The first example of iterator adapters are *insert iterators*, or *inserters*. Inserters are used to let algorithms operate in insert mode rather than in overwrite mode. In particular, they solve the problem of algorithms that write to a destination that does not have enough room: They let the destination grow accordingly.

Insert iterators redefine their interface internally as follows:

*   If you assign a value to their actual element, they insert that value into the collection to which they belong. Three different insert iterators have different abilities with regard to where the elements are inserted — at the front, at the end, or at a given position.

*   A call to step forward is a no-op.

Consider the following example:

```
// stl/copy3.cpp

#include <iostream>
#include <vector>
#include <list>
#include <deque>
#include <set>
#include <algorithm>
using namespace std;

int main()
{
    list<int> coll1;

    // insert elements from 1 to 9 into the first collection
    for (int i=1; i<=9; ++i) {
        coll1.push_back(i);
    }

    // copy the elements of coll1 into coll2 by appending them
    vector<int> coll2;
    copy (coll1.begin(), coll1.end(),      // source
          back_inserter(coll2));            // destination

    // copy the elements of coll1 into coll3 by inserting them at the front
    // - reverses the order of the elements
    deque<int> coll3;
    copy (coll1.begin(), coll1.end(),      // source
          front_inserter(coll3));           // destination

    // copy elements of coll1 into coll4
    // - only inserter that works for associative collections
    set<int> coll4;
    copy (coll1.begin(), coll1.end(),      // source
          inserter(coll4,coll4.begin()));   // destination
}
```

This example uses all three predefined insert iterators:

1. **Back inserters**

   Back inserters insert the elements at the back of their container (appends them) by calling `push_back()`. For example, with the following statement, all elements of `coll1` are appended into `coll2`:

   ```
   copy (coll1.begin(), coll1.end(),    // source
         back_inserter(coll2));         // destination
   ```

   Of course, back inserters can be used only for containers that provide `push_back()` as a member function. In the C++ standard library, these containers are `vector`, `deque`, and `list`.

2. **Front inserters**

   Front inserters insert the elements at the front of their container by calling `push_front()`. For example, with the following statement, all elements of `coll1` are inserted into `coll3`:

   ```
   copy (coll1.begin(), coll1.end(),    // source
         front_inserter(coll3));        // destination
   ```

   Note that this kind of insertion reverses the order of the inserted elements. If you insert 1 at the front and then 2 at the front, the 1 is after the 2.

   Front inserters can be used only for containers that provide `push_front()` as a member function. In the C++ standard library, these containers are `deque` and `list`.

3. **General inserters**

   A general inserter, also called simply an *inserter*, inserts elements directly in front of the position that is passed as the second argument of its initialization. It calls the `insert()` member function with the new value and the new position as arguments. Note that all predefined containers have such an `insert()` member function. This is the only predefined inserter for associative containers.

   But wait a moment. I said that you can't specify the position of a new element in an associative container because the positions of the elements depend on their values. The solution is simple: For associative containers, the position is taken as a *hint* to start the search for the correct position. If the position is not correct, however, the timing may be worse than if there was no hint. Section 7.5.2, page 288, describes a user-defined inserter that is more useful for associative containers.

Table 5.1 lists the functionality of insert iterators. Additional details are described in Section 7.4.2, page 271.

Expression	Kind of Inserter
`back_inserter(`*container*`)`	Appends in the same order by using `push_back()`
`front_inserter(`*container*`)`	Inserts at the front in reverse order by using `push_front()`
`inserter(`*container*`,`*pos*`)`	Inserts at *pos* (in the same order) by using `insert()`

Table 5.1. Predefined Insert Iterators

5.5.2 Stream Iterators

Another very helpful kind of iterator adapter is a *stream iterator*. Stream iterators are iterators that read from and write to a stream.[8] Thus, they provide an abstraction that lets the input from the keyboard behave as a collection, from which you can read. Similarly you can redirect the output of an algorithm directly into a file or onto the screen.

Consider the following example. It is a typical example of the power of the whole STL. Compared with ordinary C or C++, it does a lot of complex processing by using only a few statements:

```
// stl/ioiter1.cpp

#include <iostream>
#include <vector>
#include <string>
#include <algorithm>
#include <iterator>
using namespace std;

int main()
{
    vector<string> coll;

    /* read all words from the standard input
     * - source: all strings until end-of-file (or error)
     * - destination: coll (inserting)
     */
    copy (istream_iterator<string>(cin),        // start of source
          istream_iterator<string>(),           // end of source
          back_inserter(coll));                 // destination

    // sort elements
    sort (coll.begin(), coll.end());

    /* print all elements without duplicates
     * - source: coll
     * - destination: standard output (with newline between elements)
     */
    unique_copy (coll.begin(), coll.end(),              // source
                 ostream_iterator<string>(cout,"\n"));  // destination
}
```

---

[8] A stream is an object that represents I/O channels (see Chapter 13).

The program has only three statements that read all words from the standard input and print a sorted list of them. Let's consider the three statements step-by-step. In the statement

```
copy (istream_iterator<string>(cin),
      istream_iterator<string>(),
      back_inserter(coll));
```

two input stream iterators are used:

1. The expression

```
    istream_iterator<string>(cin)
```

creates a stream iterator that reads from the standard input stream cin.[9] The template argument string specifies that the stream iterator reads elements of this type (string types are covered in Chapter 11). These elements are read with the usual input operator >>. Thus, each time the algorithm wants to process the next element, the istream iterator transforms that desire into a call of

```
    cin >> string
```

The input operator for strings usually reads one word separated by whitespaces (see page 492), so the algorithm reads word-by-word.

2. The expression

```
    istream_iterator<string>()
```

calls the default constructor of istream iterators that creates an *end-of-stream iterator*. It represents a stream from which you can no longer read.

As usual, the copy() algorithm operates as long as the (incremented) first argument differs from the second argument. The end-of-stream iterator is used as the *end of the range*, so the algorithm reads all strings from cin until it can no longer read any more (due to end-of-stream or an error). To summarize, the source of the algorithm is "all words read from cin." These words are copied by inserting them into coll with the help of a back inserter.

The sort() algorithm sorts all elements:

```
sort (coll.begin(), coll.end());
```

Lastly, the statement

```
unique_copy (coll.begin(), coll.end(),
             ostream_iterator<string>(cout,"\n"));
```

copies all elements from the collection into the destination cout. During the process, the unique_copy() algorithm eliminates adjacent duplicate values. The expression

```
ostream_iterator<string>(cout,"\n")
```

---

[9] In older systems you must use ptrdiff_t as the second template parameter to create an istream iterator (see Section 7.4.3, page 280).

creates an output stream iterator that writes `strings` to `cout` by calling operator `<<` for each element. The second argument behind `cout` serves as a separator between the elements. It is optional. In this example, it is a newline, so every element is written on a separate line.

All components of the program are templates, so you can change the program easily to sort other value types, such as integers or more complex objects. Section 7.4.3, page 277, explains more and gives more examples about iostream iterators.

In this example, one declaration and three statements were used to sort all words from standard input. However, you could do the same by using only one declaration and one statement. See page 228 for an example.

5.5.3 Reverse Iterators

The third kind of predefined iterator adapters are reverse iterators. Reverse iterators operate in reverse. They switch the call of an increment operator internally into a call of the decrement operator, and vice versa. All containers can create reverse iterators via their member functions `rbegin()` and `rend()`. Consider the following example:

```
// stl/riter1.cpp

#include <iostream>
#include <vector>
#include <algorithm>
#include <iterator>
using namespace std;

int main()
{
    vector<int> coll;

    // insert elements from 1 to 9
    for (int i=1; i<=9; ++i) {
        coll.push_back(i);
    }

    // print all element in reverse order
    copy (coll.rbegin(), coll.rend(),        // source
          ostream_iterator<int>(cout," "));   // destination
    cout << endl;
}
```

The expression

```
coll.rbegin()
```

returns a reverse iterator for `coll`. This iterator may be used as the beginning of a reverse iteration over the elements of the collection. Its position is the last element of the collection. Thus, the expression

```
*coll.rbegin()
```

returns the value of the last element.

Accordingly, the expression

```
coll.rend()
```

returns a reverse iterator for `coll` that may be used as the end of a reverse iteration. As usual for ranges, its position is past the end of the range, but from the opposite direction; that is, it is the position before the first element in the collection.

The expression

```
*coll.rend()
```

is as undefined as is

```
*coll.end()
```

You should never use operator `*` (or operator `->`) for a position that does not represent a valid element.

The advantage of using reverse iterators is that all algorithms are able to operate in the opposite direction without special code. A step to the next element with operator `++` is redefined into a step backward with operator `--`. For example, in this case, `copy()` iterates over the elements of `coll` from the last to the first element. So, the output of the program is as follows:

```
9 8 7 6 5 4 3 2 1
```

You can also switch "normal" iterators into reverse iterators, and vice versa. However, in doing so the element of an iterator changes. This and other details about reverse iterators are covered in Section 7.4.1, page 264.

5.6   Manipulating Algorithms

Several algorithms modify destination ranges. In particular, they may remove elements. If this happens, special aspects apply. These aspects are explained in this section. They are surprising and show the price of the STL concept that separates containers and algorithms with great flexibility.

5.6.1   "Removing" Elements

The remove() algorithm removes elements from a range. However, if you use it for all elements of a container it operates in a surprising way. Consider the following example:

```
// stl/remove1.cpp

#include <iostream>
#include <list>
#include <algorithm>
#include <iterator>
using namespace std;

int main()
{
    list<int> coll;

    // insert elements from 6 to 1 and 1 to 6
    for (int i=1; i<=6; ++i) {
        coll.push_front(i);
        coll.push_back(i);
    }

    // print all elements of the collection
    cout << "pre:  ";
    copy (coll.begin(), coll.end(),             // source
          ostream_iterator<int>(cout," "));     // destination
    cout << endl;

    // remove all elements with value 3
    remove (coll.begin(), coll.end(),           // range
            3);                                 // value

    // print all elements of the collection
    cout << "post: ";
```

```
    copy (coll.begin(), coll.end(),              // source
          ostream_iterator<int>(cout," "));      // destination
    cout << endl;
}
```

Someone reading this program without deeper knowledge would expect that all elements with value 3 are removed from the collection. However, the output of the program is as follows:

```
pre:  6 5 4 3 2 1 1 2 3 4 5 6
post: 6 5 4 2 1 1 2 4 5 6 5 6
```

Thus, `remove()` did not change the number of elements in the collection for which it was called. The `end()` member function returns the old end, whereas `size()` returns the old number of elements. However, something has changed: The elements changed their order as if the elements were removed. Each element with value 3 was overwritten by the following elements (Figure 5.7). At the end of the collection, the old elements that were not overwritten by the algorithm remain unchanged. Logically, these elements no longer belong to the collection.

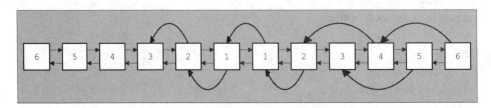

Figure 5.7. How `remove()` *Operates*

However, the algorithm does return the new end. By using it, you can access the resulting range, reduce the size of the collection, or process the number of removed elements. Consider the following modified version of the example:

```
// stl/remove2.cpp

#include <iostream>
#include <list>
#include <algorithm>
#include <iterator>
using namespace std;

int main()
{
    list<int> coll;

    // insert elements from 6 to 1 and 1 to 6
```

```
for (int i=1; i<=6; ++i) {
    coll.push_front(i);
    coll.push_back(i);
}

// print all elements of the collection
copy (coll.begin(), coll.end(),
      ostream_iterator<int>(cout," "));
cout << endl;

// remove all elements with value 3
// - retain new end
list<int>::iterator end = remove (coll.begin(), coll.end(),
                                  3);

// print resulting elements of the collection
copy (coll.begin(), end,
      ostream_iterator<int>(cout," "));
cout << endl;

// print number of resulting elements
cout << "number of removed elements: "
     << distance(end,coll.end()) << endl;

// remove "removed" elements
coll.erase (end, coll.end());

// print all elements of the modified collection
copy (coll.begin(), coll.end(),
      ostream_iterator<int>(cout," "));
cout << endl;
}
```

In this version, the return value of `remove()` is assigned to the iterator end:

```
list<int>::iterator end = remove (coll.begin(), coll.end(),
                                  3);
```

This is the new logical end of the modified collection after the elements are "removed." You can use this return value as the new end for further operations:

```
copy (coll.begin(), end,
      ostream_iterator<int>(cout," "));
```

Another possibility is to process the number of "removed" elements by processing the distance between the "logical" and the real end of the collection:

```
cout << "number of removed elements: "
     << distance(end,coll.end()) << endl;
```

Here, a special auxiliary function for iterators, `distance()`, is used. It returns the distance between two iterators. If the iterators were random access iterators you could process the difference directly with operator `-`. However, the container is a list, so it provides only bidirectional iterators. See Section 7.3.2, page 261, for details about `distance()`.[10]

If you really want to remove the "removed" elements, you must call an appropriate member function of the container. To do this, containers provide the `erase()` member function. `erase()` removes all elements of the range that is specified by its arguments:

```
coll.erase (end, coll.end());
```

Here is the output of the whole program:

```
6 5 4 3 2 1 1 2 3 4 5 6
6 5 4 2 1 1 2 4 5 6
number of removed elements: 2
6 5 4 2 1 1 2 4 5 6
```

If you really want to remove elements in one statement, you can call the following statement:

```
coll.erase (remove(coll.begin(),coll.end(),
                    3),
            coll.end());
```

Why don't algorithms call `erase()` by themselves? Well, this question highlights the price of the flexibility of the STL. The STL separates data structures and algorithms by using iterators as the interface. However, iterators are an abstraction to represent a position in a container. In general, iterators do *not* know their containers. Thus, the algorithms, which use the iterators to access the elements of the container, can't call any member function for it.

This design has important consequences because it allows algorithms to operate on ranges that are different from "all elements of a container." For example, the range might be a subset of all elements of a collection. And, it might even be a container that provides no `erase()` member function (ordinary arrays are an example of such a container). So, to make algorithms as flexible as possible, there are good reasons not to require that iterators know their container.

Note that it is often not necessary to remove the "removed" elements. Often, it is no problem to use the returned new logical end instead of the real end of the container. In particular, you can call all algorithms with the new logical end.

---

[10] The definition of `distance()` has changed, so in older STL versions you must include the file `distance.hpp`, which is mentioned on page 263.

5.6.2 Manipulating Algorithms and Associative Containers

Manipulation algorithms (those that remove elements as well as those that reorder or modify elements) have another problem when you try to use them with associative containers: Associative containers can't be used as a destination. The reason for this is simple: If modifying algorithms would work for associative containers, they could change the value or position of elements so that they are not sorted anymore. This would break the general rule that elements in associative containers are always sorted automatically according to their sorting criterion. So, not to compromise the sorting, every iterator for an associative container is declared as an iterator for a constant value (or key). Thus, manipulating elements of or in associative containers results in a failure at compile time.[11]

Note that this problem prevents you from calling removing algorithms for associative containers because these algorithms manipulate elements implicitly. The values of "removed" elements are overwritten by the following elements that are not removed.

Now the question arises, How does one remove elements in associative containers? Well, the answer is simple: Call their member functions! Every associative container provides member functions to remove elements. For example, you can call the member function `erase()` to remove elements:

```
// stl/remove3.cpp

#include <iostream>
#include <set>
#include <algorithm>
#include <iterator>
using namespace std;

int main()
{
    set<int> coll;

    // insert elements from 1 to 9
    for (int i=1; i<=9; ++i) {
        coll.insert(i);
    }

    // print all elements of the collection
    copy (coll.begin(), coll.end(),
          ostream_iterator<int>(cout," "));
```

---

[11] Unfortunately, some systems provide really bad error handling. You see that something went wrong but have problems finding out why. Some compilers don't even print the source code that caused the trouble. This will change in the future, I hope.

```
        cout << endl;

        /* Remove all elements with value 3
         * - algorithm remove() does not work
         * - instead member function erase() works
         */
        int num = coll.erase(3);

        // print number of removed elements
        cout << "number of removed elements: " << num << endl;

        // print all elements of the modified collection
        copy (coll.begin(), coll.end(),
              ostream_iterator<int>(cout," "));
        cout << endl;
    }
```

Note that containers provide different `erase()` member functions. Only the form that gets the value of the element(s) to remove as a single argument returns the number of removed elements (see page 242). Of course, when duplicates are not allowed, the return value can only be 0 or 1 (as is the case for `sets` and `maps`).

The output of the program is as follows:

```
1 2 3 4 5 6 7 8 9
number of removed elements: 1
1 2 4 5 6 7 8 9
```

5.6.3   Algorithms versus Member Functions

Even if you are able to use an algorithm, it might be a bad idea to do so. A container might have member functions that provide much better performance.

Calling `remove()` for elements of a list is a good example of this. If you call `remove()` for elements of a list, the algorithm doesn't know that it is operating on a list. Thus, it does what it does for any container: It reorders the elements by changing their values. If, for example, it removes the first element, all the following elements are assigned to their previous elements. This behavior contradicts the main advantage of lists — the ability to insert, move, and remove elements by modifying the links instead of the values.

To avoid bad performance, lists provide special member functions for all manipulating algorithms. You should always use them. Furthermore, these member functions really remove "removed" elements, as this example shows:

```
// stl/remove4.cpp

#include <iostream>
#include <list>
#include <algorithm>
using namespace std;

int main()
{
    list<int> coll;

    // insert elements from 6 to 1 and 1 to 6
    for (int i=1; i<=6; ++i) {
        coll.push_front(i);
        coll.push_back(i);
    }

    // remove all elements with value 3
    // - poor performance
    coll.erase (remove(coll.begin(),coll.end(),
                       3),
                coll.end());

    // remove all elements with value 4
    // - good performance
    coll.remove (4);
}
```

You should always prefer a member function over an algorithm if good performance is the goal. The problem is, you have to know that a member function exists that has significantly better performance for a certain container. No warning or error message appears if you use the remove() algorithm for a list. However, if you prefer a member function in these cases you have to change the code when you switch to another container type. In the reference sections of algorithms (Chapter 9) I mention when a member function exists that provides better performance than an algorithm.

5.7 User-Defined Generic Functions

The STL is an extensible framework. This means you can write your own functions and algorithms to process elements of collections. Of course, these operations may also be generic. However, to declare a valid iterator in these operations, you must use the type of the container, which is different for each container type. To facilitate the writing of generic functions, each container type provides some internal type definitions. Consider the following example:

```
// stl/print.hpp

#include <iostream>


/* PRINT_ELEMENTS()
 * - prints optional C-string optcstr followed by
 * - all elements of the collection coll
 * - separated by spaces
 */
template <class T>
inline void PRINT_ELEMENTS (const T& coll, const char* optcstr="")
{
    typename T::const_iterator pos;

    std::cout << optcstr;
    for (pos=coll.begin(); pos!=coll.end(); ++pos) {
        std::cout << *pos << ' ';
    }
    std::cout << std::endl;
}
```

This example defines a generic function that prints an optional string followed by all elements of the passed container. In the declaration

```
typename T::const_iterator pos;
```

pos is declared as having the iterator type of the passed container type. `typename` is necessary to specify that `const_iterator` is a type and not a value of type T (see the introduction of `typename` on page 11).

In addition to `iterator` and `const_iterator`, containers provide other types to facilitate the writing of generic functions. For example, they provide the type of the elements to enable the handling of temporary copies of elements. See Section 7.5.1, page 285, for details.

The optional second argument of `PRINT_ELEMENTS` is a string that is used as a prefix before all elements are written. Thus, by using `PRINT_ELEMENTS()` you could comment or introduce the output like this:

```
PRINT_ELEMENTS (coll, "all elements: ");
```

I introduced this function here because I use it often in the rest of the book to print all elements of containers by using a simple call.

5.8   Functions as Algorithm Arguments

To increase their flexibility and power, several algorithms allow the passing of user-defined auxiliary functions. These functions are called internally by the algorithms.

5.8.1   Examples of Using Functions as Algorithm Arguments

The simplest example is the for_each() algorithm. It calls a user-defined function for each element of the specified range. Consider the following example:

```cpp
// stl/foreach1.cpp

#include <iostream>
#include <vector>
#include <algorithm>
using namespace std;

// function that prints the passed argument
void print (int elem)
{
    cout << elem << ' ';
}

int main()
{
    vector<int> coll;

    // insert elements from 1 to 9
    for (int i=1; i<=9; ++i) {
        coll.push_back(i);
    }

    // print all elements
    for_each (coll.begin(), coll.end(),     // range
              print);                        // operation
    cout << endl;
}
```

The for_each() algorithm calls the passed print() function for every element in the range [coll.begin(),coll.end()). Thus, the output of the program is as follows:

1 2 3 4 5 6 7 8 9

Algorithms use auxiliary functions in several variants — some optional, some mandatory. In particular, you can use them to specify a search criterion, a sorting criterion, or to define a manipulation while transferring elements from one collection to another.

Here is another example program:

```cpp
// stl/transform1.cpp

#include <iostream>
#include <vector>
#include <set>
#include <algorithm>
#include "print.hpp"

int square (int value)
{
    return value*value;
}

int main()
{
    std::set<int>    coll1;
    std::vector<int> coll2;

    // insert elements from 1 to 9 into coll1
    for (int i=1; i<=9; ++i) {
        coll1.insert(i);
    }
    PRINT_ELEMENTS(coll1,"initialized: ");

    // transform each element from coll1 to coll2
    // - square transformed values
    std::transform (coll1.begin(),coll1.end(),    // source
                    std::back_inserter(coll2),    // destination
                    square);                      // operation

    PRINT_ELEMENTS(coll2,"squared:     ");
}
```

In this example, `square()` is used to square each element of `coll1` while it is transformed to `coll2` (Figure 5.8). The program has the following output:

```
initialized: 1 2 3 4 5 6 7 8 9
squared:     1 4 9 16 25 36 49 64 81
```

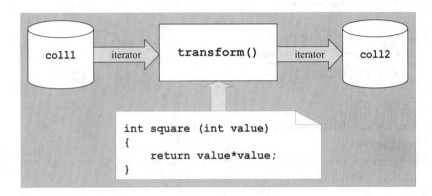

Figure 5.8. How `transform()` *Operates*

5.8.2 Predicates

A special kind of auxiliary function for algorithms is a *predicate*. Predicates are functions that return a Boolean value. They are often used to specify a sorting or a search criterion. Depending on their purpose, predicates are unary or binary. Note that not every unary or binary function that returns a Boolean value is a valid predicate. The STL requires that predicates always yield the same result for the same value. This rules out functions that modify their internal state when they are called. See Section 8.1.4, page 302, for details.

Unary Predicates

Unary predicates check a specific property of a single argument. A typical example is a function that is used as a search criterion to find the first prime number:

```cpp
// stl/prime1.cpp

#include <iostream>
#include <list>
#include <algorithm>
#include <cstdlib>        // for abs()
using namespace std;
```

```cpp
// predicate, which returns whether an integer is a prime number
bool isPrime (int number)
{
    // ignore negative sign
    number = abs(number);

    // 0 and 1 are no prime numbers
    if (number == 0 || number == 1) {
        return false;
    }

    // find divisor that divides without a remainder
    int divisor;
    for (divisor = number/2; number%divisor != 0; --divisor) {
        ;
    }

    // if no divisor greater than 1 is found, it is a prime number
    return divisor == 1;
}

int main()
{
    list<int> coll;

    // insert elements from 24 to 30
    for (int i=24; i<=30; ++i) {
        coll.push_back(i);
    }

    // search for prime number
    list<int>::iterator pos;
    pos = find_if (coll.begin(), coll.end(),     // range
                   isPrime);                     // predicate
    if (pos != coll.end()) {
        // found
        cout << *pos << " is first prime number found" << endl;
    }
    else {
```

```
                // not found
                cout << "no prime number found" << endl;
        }
}
```

In this example, the `find_if()` algorithm is used to search for the first element of the given range for which the passed unary predicate yields `true`. Here, the predicate is the `isPrime()` function. This function checks whether a number is a prime number. By using it, the algorithm returns the first prime number in the given range. If the algorithm does not find any element that matches the predicate, it returns the end of the range (its second argument). This is checked after the call. The collection in this example has a prime number between 24 and 30. So the output of the program is as follows:

```
29 is first prime number found
```

Binary Predicates

Binary predicates typically compare a specific property of two arguments. For example, to sort elements according to your own criterion you could provide it as a simple predicate function. This might be necessary because the elements do not provide operator < or because you wish to use a different criterion.

The following example sorts elements of a set by the first name and last name of a person:

```
// stl/sort1.cpp

#include <iostream>
#include <string>
#include <deque>
#include <algorithm>
using namespace std;

class Person {
  public:
    string firstname() const;
    string lastname() const;
    ...
};

/* binary function predicate:
 * - returns whether a person is less than another person
 */
```

```
bool personSortCriterion (const Person& p1, const Person& p2)
{
    /* a person is less than another person
     * - if the last name is less
     * - if the last name is equal and the first name is less
     */
    return p1.lastname()<p2.lastname() ||
            (p1.lastname()==p2.lastname() &&
             p1.firstname()<p2.firstname());
}

int main()
{
    deque<Person> coll;
    ...

    sort(coll.begin(),coll.end(),        // range
         personSortCriterion);           // sort criterion
    ...
}
```

Note that you can also implement a sorting criterion as a function object. This kind of implementation has the advantage that the criterion is a type, which you could use, for example, to declare sets that use this criterion for sorting its elements. See Section 8.1.1, page 294, for such an implementation of this sorting criterion.

5.9   Function Objects

Functional arguments for algorithms don't have to be functions. They can be objects that behave like functions. Such an object is called a *function object*, or *functor*. Sometimes you can use a function object when an ordinary function won't work. The STL often uses function objects and provides several function objects that are very helpful.

5.9.1   What Are Function Objects?

Function objects are another example of the power of generic programming and the concept of pure abstraction. You could say that anything that *behaves* like a function *is* a function. So, if you define an object that behaves as a function, it can be used as a function.

So, what is the behavior of a function? The answer is: A functional behavior is something that you can call by using parentheses and passing arguments. For example:

```
function(arg1,arg2);      // a function call
```

So, if you want objects to behave this way you have to make it possible to "call" them by using parentheses and passing arguments. Yes, that's possible (there are rarely things that are not possible in C++). All you have to do is define operator () with the appropriate parameter types:

```
class X {
  public:
    // define "function call" operator
    return-value operator() (arguments) const;
    ...
};
```

Now you can use objects of this class to behave as a function that you can call:

```
X fo;
...
fo(arg1,arg2);            // call operator () for function object fo
```

The call is equivalent to:

```
fo.operator()(arg1,arg2); // call operator () for function object fo
```

The following is a complete example. This is the function object version of a previous example (see page 119) that did the same with an ordinary function:

```
// stl/foreach2.cpp

#include <iostream>
#include <vector>
#include <algorithm>
using namespace std;

// simple function object that prints the passed argument
class PrintInt {
  public:
    void operator() (int elem) const {
        cout << elem << ' ';
    }
};

int main()
{
    vector<int> coll;
```

```
// insert elements from 1 to 9
for (int i=1; i<=9; ++i) {
    coll.push_back(i);
}

// print all elements
for_each (coll.begin(), coll.end(),     // range
          PrintInt());                  // operation
cout << endl;
}
```

The class `PrintInt` defines objects for which you can call operator () with an `int` argument. The expression

```
PrintInt()
```

in the statement

```
for_each (coll.begin(), coll.end(),
          PrintInt());
```

creates a temporary object of this class, which is passed to the `for_each()` algorithm as an argument. The `for_each()` algorithm is written like this:

```
namespace std {
    template <class Iterator, class Operation>
    Operation for_each (Iterator act, Iterator end, Operation op)
    {
        while (act != end) {    // as long as not reached the end
            op(*act);           // - call op() for actual element
            ++act;              // - move iterator to the next element
        }
        return op;
    }
}
```

`for_each()` uses the temporary function object `op` to call `op(*act)` for each element `act`. If the third parameter is an ordinary function, it simply calls it with `*act` as an argument. If the third parameter is a function object, it calls operator () for the function object `op` with `*act` as an argument. Thus, in this example program `for_each()` calls:

```
PrintInt::operator()(*act)
```

You may be wondering what all this is good for. You might even think that function objects look strange, nasty, or nonsensical. It is true that they do complicate code. However, function objects are more than functions, and they have some advantages:

1. **Function objects are "smart functions."**

   Objects that behave like pointers are smart pointers. This is similarly true for objects that behave like functions: They can be "smart functions" because they may have abilities beyond operator (). Function objects may have other member functions and attributes. This means that function objects have a state. In fact, the same function, represented by a function object, may have different states at the same time. This is not possible for ordinary functions. Another advantage of function objects is that you can initialize them at runtime before you use/call them.

2. **Each function object has its own type.**

   Ordinary functions have different types only when their signatures differ. However, function objects can have different types even when their signatures are the same. In fact, each functional behavior defined by a function object has its own type. This is a significant improvement for generic programming using templates because you can pass functional behavior as a template parameter. It enables containers of different types to use the same kind of function object as a sorting criterion. This ensures that you don't assign, combine, or compare collections that have different sorting criteria. You can even design hierarchies of function objects so that you can, for example, have different, special kinds of one general criterion.

3. **Function objects are usually faster than ordinary functions.**

   The concept of templates usually allows better optimization because more details are defined at compile time. Thus, passing function objects instead of ordinary functions often results in better performance.

In the rest of this subsection I present some examples that demonstrate how function objects can be "smarter" than ordinary functions. Chapter 8, which deals only with function objects, provides more examples and details. In particular, it shows how to benefit from the ability to pass functional behavior as a template parameter.

Suppose you want to add a certain value to all elements of a collection. If you know the value you want to add at compile time, you could use an ordinary function:

```
void add10 (int& elem)
{
    elem += 10;
}


void f1()
{
    vector<int> coll;
    ...

    for_each (coll.begin(), coll.end(),     // range
              add10);                        // operation
}
```

If you need different values that are known at compile time, you could use a template instead:

```
template <int theValue>
void add (int& elem)
{
    elem += theValue;
}


void f1()
{
    vector<int> coll;
    ...


    for_each (coll.begin(), coll.end(),    // range
              add<10>);                     // operation
}
```

If you process the value to add at runtime, things get complicated. You must pass the value to the function before the function is called. This normally results in some global variable that is used both by the function that calls the algorithm and by the function that is called by the algorithm to add that value. This is messy style.

If you need such a function twice, with two different values to add, and both values are processed at runtime, you can't achieve this with one ordinary function. You must either pass a tag or you must write two different functions. Did you ever copy the definition of a function because it had a static variable to keep its state and you needed the same function with another state at the same time? This is exactly the same type of problem.

With function objects, you can write a "smarter" function that behaves in the desired way. Because the object may have a state, it can be initialized by the correct value. Here is a complete example[12]:

```
// stl/add1.cpp

#include <iostream>
#include <list>
#include <algorithm>
#include "print.hpp"
using namespace std;

// function object that adds the value with which it is initialized
class AddValue {
```

---

[12] The auxiliary function PRINT_ELEMENTS() was introduced on page 118.

```
    private:
      int theValue;      // the value to add
    public:
      // constructor initializes the value to add
      AddValue(int v) : theValue(v) {
      }

      // the "function call" for the element adds the value
      void operator() (int& elem) const {
          elem += theValue;
      }
};

int main()
{
    list<int> coll;

    // insert elements from 1 to 9
    for (int i=1; i<=9; ++i) {
        coll.push_back(i);
    }

    PRINT_ELEMENTS(coll,"initialized:                        ");

    // add value 10 to each element
    for_each (coll.begin(), coll.end(),     // range
            AddValue(10));                  // operation

    PRINT_ELEMENTS(coll,"after adding 10:                    ");

    // add value of first element to each element
    for_each (coll.begin(), coll.end(),     // range
            AddValue(*coll.begin()));       // operation

    PRINT_ELEMENTS(coll,"after adding first element: ");
}
```

After the initialization, the collection contains the values 1 to 9:

```
    initialized:              1 2 3 4 5 6 7 8 9
```

lections are the same, so each element gets multiplied by itself, and the result overwrites the old value.[15]

By using special *function adapters* you can combine predefined function objects with other values or use special cases. Here is a complete example:

```
// stl/fo1.cpp

#include <iostream>
#include <set>
#include <deque>
#include <algorithm>
#include "print.hpp"
using namespace std;

int main()
{
    set<int,greater<int> > coll1;
    deque<int> coll2;

    // insert elements from 1 to 9
    for (int i=1; i<=9; ++i) {
        coll1.insert(i);
    }

    PRINT_ELEMENTS(coll1,"initialized: ");

    // transform all elements into coll2 by multiplying 10
    transform (coll1.begin(),coll1.end(),        // source
               back_inserter(coll2),             // destination
               bind2nd(multiplies<int>(),10));   // operation

    PRINT_ELEMENTS(coll2,"transformed: ");

    // replace value equal to 70 with 42
    replace_if (coll2.begin(),coll2.end(),       // range
                bind2nd(equal_to<int>(),70),     // replace criterion
                42);                             // new value
```

---

[15] In earlier versions of the STL, the function object for multiplication had the name `times`. This was changed due to a name clash with a function of operating system standards (X/Open, POSIX) and because `multiplies` was clearer.

```
    PRINT_ELEMENTS(coll2,"replaced:      ");

    // remove all elements with values less than 50
    coll2.erase(remove_if(coll2.begin(),coll2.end(), // range
                      bind2nd(less<int>(),50)),    // remove criterion
             coll2.end());

    PRINT_ELEMENTS(coll2,"removed:      ");
}
```

With the statement
```
transform (coll1.begin(),coll1.end(),          // source
           back_inserter(coll2),               // destination
           bind2nd(multiplies<int>(),10));     // operation
```
all elements of `coll1` are transformed into `coll2` (inserting) while multiplying each element by 10. Here, the function adapter `bind2nd` causes `multiplies<int>` to be called for each element of the source collection as the first argument and the value 10 as the second.

The way `bind2nd` operates is as follows: `transform()` is expecting as its fourth argument an operation that takes one argument; namely, the actual element. However, we would like to multiply that argument by ten. So, we have to combine an operation that takes two arguments and the value that always should be used as a second argument to get an operation for one argument. `bind2nd` does that job. It stores the operation and the second argument as internal values. When the algorithm calls `bind2nd` with the actual element as the argument, `bind2nd` calls its operation with the element from the algorithm as the first argument and the internal value as the second argument, and returns the result of the operation.

Similarly, in
```
replace_if (coll2.begin(),coll2.end(),          // range
            bind2nd(equal_to<int>(),70),        // replace criterion
            42);
```
the expression
```
bind2nd(equal_to<int>(),70)
```
is used as a criterion to specify the elements that are replaced by 42. `bind2nd` calls the binary predicate `equal_to` with value 70 as the second argument, thus defining a unary predicate for the elements of the processed collection.

The last statement is similar because the expression
```
bind2nd(less<int>(),50)
```
is used to specify the element that should be removed from the collection. It specifies that all elements that are less than value 50 be removed. The output of the program is as follows:

```
initialized:  9 8 7 6 5 4 3 2 1
transformed:  90 80 70 60 50 40 30 20 10
replaced:     90 80 42 60 50 40 30 20 10
removed:      90 80 60 50
```

This kind of programming results in *functional composition*. What is interesting is that all these function objects are usually declared inline. Thus, you use a function-like notation or abstraction, but you get good performance.

There are other kinds of function objects. For example, some function objects provide the ability to call a member function for each element of a collection:

```
for_each (coll.begin(), coll.end(),    // range
          mem_fun_ref(&Person::save)); // operation
```

The function object `mem_fun_ref` calls a specified member function for the element for which it is called. Thus, for each element of the collection `coll`, the member function `save()` of class `Person` is called. Of course, this works only if the elements have type `Person` or a type derived from `Person`.

Section 8.2, page 305, lists and discusses in more detail all predefined function objects, function adapters, and aspects of functional composition. It also explains how you can write your own function objects.

5.10   Container Elements

Elements of containers must meet certain requirements because containers handle them in a special way. In this section I describe these requirements. I also discuss the consequences of the fact that containers make copies of their elements internally.

5.10.1   Requirements for Container Elements

Containers, iterators, and algorithms of the STL are templates. Thus, they can process any type, whether predefined or user defined. However, because of the operations that are called, some requirements apply. The elements of STL containers must meet the following three fundamental requirements:

1. An element must be *copyable* by a copy constructor. The generated copy should be equivalent to the source. This means that any test for equality returns that both are equal and that both source and copy behave the same.

   All containers create internal copies of their elements and return temporary copies of them, so the copy constructor is called very often. Thus, the copy constructor should perform well (this is not a requirement, but a hint to get better performance). If copying objects takes too much time you can avoid copying objects by using the containers with reference semantics. See Section 6.8, page 222, for details.

2. An element must be *assignable* by the assignment operator. Containers and algorithms use assignment operators to overwrite old elements with new elements.

3. An element must be *destroyable* by a destructor. Containers destroy their internal copies of elements when these elements are removed from the container. Thus, the destructor must not be private. Also, as usual in C++, a destructor must not throw; otherwise, all bets are off.

These three operations are generated implicitly for any class. Thus, a class meets the requirements automatically, provided no special versions of these operations are defined and no special members disable the sanity of those operations.

Elements might also have to meet the following requirements[16]:

- For some member functions of sequence containers, the *default constructor* must be available. For example, it is possible to create a nonempty container or increase the number of elements with no hint of the values those new elements should have. These elements are created without any arguments by calling the default constructor of their type.

- For several operations, the *test of equality* with operator == must be defined. It is especially needed when elements are searched.

- For associative containers the operations of the *sorting criterion* must be provided by the elements. By default, this is the operator <, which is called by the less<> function object.

5.10.2 Value Semantics or Reference Semantics

Usually, all containers create internal copies of their elements and return copies of those elements (only for direct access of existing element reference semantics is provided). This means that container elements are equal but not identical to the objects you put into the container. If you modify objects as elements of the container, you modify a copy, not the original object.

Copying values means that the STL containers provide *value semantics*. They contain the values of the objects you insert rather than the objects themselves. In practice, however, you also need *reference semantics*. This means that the containers contain references to the objects that are their elements.

The approach of the STL, only to support value semantics, has strengths and weaknesses. Its strengths are:

- Copying elements is simple.

- References are error prone. You must ensure that references don't refer to objects that no longer exist. You also have to manage circular references, which might occur.

Its weaknesses are:

- Copying elements might result in bad performance or may not even be possible.

- Managing the same object in several containers at the same time is not possible.

---

[16] In some older C++ systems, you may have to implement these additional requirements even if they are not used. For example, some implementations of vector always require the default constructor for elements. Other implementations always require the existence of the comparison operator. However, according to the standard, such a requirement is wrong, and these limitations will likely be eliminated.

In practice you need both approaches; you need copies that are independent of the original data (value semantics) and copies that still refer to the original data and get modified accordingly (reference semantics). Unfortunately, there is no support for reference semantics in the C++ standard library. However, you can implement reference semantics in terms of value semantics.

The obvious approach to implementing reference semantics is to use pointers as elements.[17] However, ordinary pointers have the usual problems. For example, objects to which they refer may no longer exist, and comparisons may not work as desired because pointers instead of the objects are compared. Thus, you should be very careful when you use ordinary pointers as container elements.

A better approach is to use a kind of *smart pointer* — objects that have a pointer-like interface but that do some additional checking or processing internally. The important question here is, how smart do they have to be? The C++ standard library does provide a smart pointer class that might look like it would be useful here: `auto_ptr` (see Section 4.2, page 38). However, you can't use `auto_ptrs` because they don't meet a fundamental requirement for container elements. That is, after a copy or an assignment of an `auto_ptr` is made, source and destination are not equivalent. In fact, the source `auto_ptr` gets modified because its value gets transferred and not copied (see page 43 and page 47). In practice, this means that sorting or even printing the elements of a container might destroy them. So, *do not* use `auto_ptrs` as container elements (if you have a standard-conforming C++ system, you will get an error at compile time if you try to use an `auto_ptr` as a container element). See page 43 for details.

To get reference semantics for STL containers you must write your own smart pointer class. But be aware: Even if you use a smart pointer with reference counting (a smart pointer that destroys its value automatically when the last reference to it gets destroyed), it is troublesome. For example, if you have direct access to the elements, you can modify their values while they are in the container. Thus, you could break the order of elements in an associative container. You don't want to do this.

Section 6.8, page 222, offers more details about containers with reference semantics. In particular, it shows a possible way to implement reference semantics for STL containers by using smart pointers with reference counting.

5.11   Errors and Exceptions Inside the STL

Errors happen. They might be logical errors caused by the program (the programmer) or runtime errors caused by the context or the environment of a program (such as low memory). Both kinds of errors may be handled by exceptions (see page 15 for a short introduction to exceptions). This section discusses how errors and exceptions are handled in the STL.

---

[17] C programmers might recognize the use of pointers to get reference semantics. In C, function arguments are able to get passed only by value, so you need pointers to enable a call-by-reference.

5.11.1   Error Handling

The design goal of the STL was the best performance rather than the highest security. Error checking wastes time, so almost none is done. This is fine if you can program without making any errors, but it can be a catastrophe if you can't. Before the STL was adopted into the C++ standard library, discussions were held regarding whether to introduce more error checking. The majority decided not to, for two reasons:

1. Error checking reduces performance, and speed is still a general goal of programs. As mentioned, good performance was one of the design goals of the STL.

2. If you prefer safety over speed, you can still get it, either by adding wrappers or by using special versions of the STL. But you can't program to avoid error checking to get better performance when error checking is built into all basic operations. For example, when every subscript operation checks whether a range is valid, you can't write your own subscripts without checking. However, it is possible the other way around.

As a consequence, error checking is possible but not required inside the STL.

The C++ standard library states that any use of the STL that violates preconditions results in undefined behavior. Thus, if indexes, iterators, or ranges are not valid, the result is undefined. If you do not use a safe version of the STL, undefined memory access typically results, which causes some nasty side effects or even a crash. In this sense, the STL is as error prone as pointers are in C. Finding such errors could be very hard, especially without a safe version of the STL.

In particular, the use of the STL requires that the following be met:

- Iterators must be valid. For example, they must be initialized before they are used. Note that iterators may become invalid as a side effect of other operations. In particular, they become invalid for vectors and deques if elements are inserted or deleted, or reallocation takes place.

- Iterators that refer to the past-the-end position have no element to which to refer. Thus, calling operator * or operator -> is not allowed. This is especially true for the return values of the end() and rend() container member functions.

- Ranges must be valid:
  - Both iterators that specify a range must refer to the same container.
  - The second iterator must be reachable from the first iterator.

- If more than one source range is used, the second and later ranges must have at least as many elements as the first one.

- Destination ranges must have enough elements that can be overwritten; otherwise, insert iterators must be used.

The following example shows some possible errors:

```
// stl/iterbug1.cpp

#include <iostream>
#include <vector>
#include <algorithm>
using namespace std;
```

```
int main()
{
    vector<int> coll1;      // empty collection
    vector<int> coll2;      // empty collection

    /* RUNTIME ERROR:
     * - beginning is behind the end of the range
     */
    vector<int>::iterator pos = coll1.begin();
    reverse (++pos, coll1.end());

    // insert elements from 1 to 9 into coll2
    for (int i=1; i<=9; ++i) {
        coll2.push_back (i);
    }

    /* RUNTIME ERROR:
     * - overwriting nonexisting elements
     */
    copy (coll2.begin(), coll2.end(),    // source
          coll1.begin());                // destination

    /* RUNTIME ERROR:
     * - collections mistaken
     * - begin() and end() mistaken
     */
    copy (coll1.begin(), coll2.end(),    // source
          coll1.end());                  // destination
}
```

Note that these errors occur at runtime, not at compile time, and thus they cause undefined behavior.

There are many ways to make mistakes when using the STL, and the STL is not required to protect you from yourself. Thus, it is a good idea to use a "safe" STL, at least during software development. A first version of a safe STL was introduced by Cay Horstmann.[18] Unfortunately, most library vendors provide the STL based on the original source code, which doesn't include error handling. But things get better. An exemplary version of the STL is the "STLport," which is available for free for almost any platform at http://www.stlport.org/.

---

[18] You can find the safe STL by Cay Horstmann at http://www.horstmann.com/safestl.html.

5.11.2 Exception Handling

The STL almost never checks for logical errors. Therefore, almost no exceptions are generated by the STL itself due to a logical problem. In fact, there is only one function call for which the standard requires that it might cause an exception directly: the `at()` member function for vectors and deques. (It is the checked version of the subscript operator.) Other than that, the standard requires that only the usual standard exceptions may occur, such as `bad_alloc` for lack of memory or exceptions of user-defined operations.

When are exceptions generated and what happens to STL components when they are? For a long time during the standardization process there was no defined behavior regarding this. In fact, every exception resulted in undefined behavior. Even the destruction of an STL container after an exception was thrown during one of its operations resulted in undefined behavior, such as a crash. Thus, the STL was useless when you needed guaranteed, defined behavior because it was not even possible to unwind the stack.

How to handle exceptions was one of the last topics addressed during the standardization process. Finding a good solution was not easy, and it took a long time for the following reasons:

1. It was very difficult to determine the degree of safety the C++ standard library should provide. You might argue that it is always best to provide as much safety as possible. For example, you could say that the insertion of a new element at any position in a vector ought to either succeed or have no effect. Ordinarily an exception might occur while copying later elements into the next position to make room for the new element, from which a full recovery is impossible. To achieve the stated goal, the insert operation would need to be implemented to copy *every* element of the vector into new storage, which would have a serious impact on performance. If good performance is a design goal (as is the case for the STL), you can't provide perfect exception handling in all cases. You have to find a compromise that meets both needs.

2. There was a concern that the presence of code to handle exceptions could adversely affect performance. This would contradict the design goal of achieving the best possible performance. However, compiler writers state that, in principle, exception handling can be implemented without any significant performance overhead (and many such implementations exist). There is no doubt that it is better to have guaranteed, defined behavior for exceptions without a significant performance penalty instead of the risk that exceptions might crash your system.

As a result of these discussions, the C++ standard library now gives the following *basic guarantee* for exception safety[19]: The C++ standard library will not leak resources or violate container invariants in the face of exceptions.

Unfortunately, for many purposes this is not enough. Often you need a stronger guarantee that specifies that an operation has no effect if an exception is thrown. Such operations can be considered to be *atomic* with respect to exceptions. Or, to use terms from database programming, you could say that these operations support *commit-or-rollback* behavior or are *transaction safe*.

Regarding this stronger guarantee, the C++ standard library now guarantees the following:

---

[19] Many thanks to Dave Abrahams and Greg Colvin for their work on exception safety in the C++ standard library and for the feedback they gave me regarding this topic.

- For all *node-based containers* (lists, sets, multisets, maps and multimaps), any failure to construct a node simply leaves the container as it was. Furthermore, removing a node can't fail (provided destructors don't throw). However, for multiple-element insert operations of associative containers, the need to keep elements sorted makes full recovery from throws impractical. Thus, all single-element insert operations of associative containers support commit-or-rollback behavior. That is, they either succeed or have no effect. In addition, it is guaranteed that all erase operations for both single- and multiple-elements always succeed.

  For lists, even multiple-element insert operations are transaction-safe. In fact, all list operations, except `remove()`, `remove_if()`, `merge()`, `sort()`, and `unique()`, either succeed or have no effect. For some of them the C++ standard library provides conditional guarantees (see page 172). Thus, if you need a transaction-safe container, you should use a list.

- All *array-based containers* (vectors and deques) do not fully recover when an element gets inserted. To do this, they would have to copy all subsequent elements before any insert operation, and handling full recovery for all copy operations would take quite a lot of time. However, push and pop operations that operate at the end do not require that existing elements have to get copied. So if they throw, it is guaranteed that they have no effect. Furthermore, if elements have a type with copy operations (copy constructor and assignment operator) that do not throw, then every container operation for these elements either succeeds or has no effect.

See Section 6.10.10, page 248, for a detailed overview of all container operations that give stronger guarantees in face of exceptions.

Note that all these guarantees are based on the requirement that destructors never throw (which should always be the case in C++). The C++ standard library makes this promise, and so must the application programmer.

If you need a container that has a full commit-or-rollback ability, you should use either a list (without calling the `sort()` and `unique()` member functions) or an associative container (without calling their multiple-element insert operations). This avoids having to make copies before a modifying operation to ensure that no data gets lost. Note that making copies of a container could be very expensive.

If you can't use a node-based container and need the full commit-or-rollback ability, you have to provide wrappers for each critical operation. For example, the following function would almost safely insert a value in any container at a certain position:

```
template <class T, class Cont, class Iter>
void insert (Cont& coll, const Iter& pos, const T& value)
{
    Cont tmp(coll);            // copy container and all elements
    coll.insert(pos,value);    // modify the copy
    coll.swap(tmp);            // use copy (in case no exception was thrown)
}
```

Note that I wrote "almost," because this function still is not perfect. This is because the `swap()` operation throws when, for associative containers, copying the comparison criterion throws. You see, handling exceptions perfectly is not easy.

5.12   Extending the STL

The STL is designed as a framework that may be extended in almost any direction. You can supply your own containers, iterators, algorithms, or function objects, provided they meet certain requirements. In fact, there are some useful extensions that are missing in the C++ standard library. This happened because at some point the committee had to stop introducing new features and concentrate on perfecting the existing parts; otherwise, the job would never have been completed.

The most important component that is missing in the STL is an additional kind of container that is implemented as a hash table. The proposal of having hash tables be part of the C++ standard library simply came too late. However, newer versions of the standard will likely contain some form of hash tables. Most implementations of the C++ library already provide hash containers, but unfortunately they're all different. See Section 6.7.3, page 221, for more details.

Other useful extensions are some additional function objects (see Section 8.3, page 313), iterators (see Section 7.5.2, page 288), containers (see Section 6.7, page 217), and algorithms (see Section 7.5.1, page 285).

Chapter 6

STL Containers

This chapter discusses STL containers in detail. It continues the discussion that was begun in Chapter 5. The chapter starts with a general overview of the general abilities and operations of all container classes, with each container class explained in detail. The explanation includes a description of their internal data structures, their operations, and their performance. It also shows how to use the different operations and gives examples if the usage is not trivial. Each section about the containers ends with examples of the typical use of the container. The chapter then discusses the interesting question of when to use which container. By comparing the general abilities, advantages, and disadvantages of all container types, it shows you how to find the best container to meet your needs. Lastly, the chapter covers all members of all container classes in detail. This part is intended as a kind of a reference manual. You can find the minor details of the container interface and the exact signature of the container operations. When useful, cross-references to similar or supplementary algorithms are included.

The C++ standard library provides some special container classes, the so-called *container adapters* (stack, queue, priority queue), *bitsets*, and *valarrays*. All of these have special interfaces that don't meet the general requirements of STL containers, so they are covered in separate sections.[1] Container adapters and bitsets are covered in Chapter 10. Valarrays are described in Section 12.2, page 547.

---

[1] Historically, container adapters are part of the STL. However, from a conceptional perspective, they are not part of the STL framework; they "only" use the STL.

6.1   Common Container Abilities and Operations

6.1.1   Common Container Abilities

This section covers the common abilities of STL container classes. Most of them are requirements that, in general, every STL container should meet. The three core abilities are as follows:

1. All containers provide value rather than reference semantics. Containers copy elements internally when they are inserted rather than managing references to them. Thus, each element of an STL container must be able to be copied. If objects you want to store don't have a public copy constructor, or copying is not useful (for example, because it takes time or elements must be part of multiple containers), the container elements must be pointers or pointer objects that refer to these objects. Section 5.10.2, page 135, covers this problem in detail.

2. In general, all elements have an order. Thus, you can iterate one or many times over all elements in the same order. Each container type provides operations that return iterators to iterate over the elements. This is the key interface of the STL algorithms.

3. In general, operations are not safe. The caller must ensure that the parameters of the operations meet the requirements. Violating these requirements (such as using an invalid index) results in undefined behavior. Usually the STL does *not* throw exceptions by itself. If user-defined operations called by the STL containers do throw, the behavior is different. See Section 5.11.2, page 139, for details.

6.1.2   Common Container Operations

The operations common to all containers meet the core abilities that were mentioned in the previous subsection. Table 6.1 lists these operations. The following subsections explore some of these common operations.

Initialization

Every container class provides a default constructor, a copy constructor, and a destructor. You can also initialize a container with elements of a given range. This constructor is provided to initialize the container with elements of another container, with an array, or from standard input. These constructors are member templates (see page 11), so not only the container but also the type of the elements may differ, provided there is an automatic conversion from the source element type to the destination element type.[2] The following examples expand on this:

---

[2] If a system does not provide member templates, it will typically allow only the same types. In this case, you can use the copy() algorithm instead. See page 188 for an example.

Operation	Effect
ContType c	Creates an empty container without any element
ContType c1(c2)	Copies a container of the same type
ContType c(beg,end)	Creates a container and initializes it with copies of all elements of [beg,end)
c.~*ContType*()	Deletes all elements and frees the memory
c.size()	Returns the actual number of elements
c.empty()	Returns whether the container is empty (equivalent to size()==0, but might be faster)
c.max_size()	Returns the maximum number of elements possible
c1 == c2	Returns whether c1 is equal to c2
c1 != c2	Returns whether c1 is not equal to c2 (equivalent to !(c1==c2))
c1 < c2	Returns whether c1 is less than c2
c1 > c2	Returns whether c1 is greater than c2 (equivalent to c2<c1)
c1 <= c2	Returns whether c1 is less than or equal to c2 (equivalent to !(c2<c1))
c1 >= c2	Returns whether c1 is greater than or equal to c2 (equivalent to !(c1<c2))
c1 = c2	Assigns all elements of c2 to c1
c1.swap(c2)	Swaps the data of c1 and c2
swap(c1,c2)	Same (as global function)
c.begin()	Returns an iterator for the first element
c.end()	Returns an iterator for the position after the last element
c.rbegin()	Returns a reverse iterator for the first element of a reverse iteration
c.rend()	Returns a reverse iterator for the position after the last element of a reverse iteration
c.insert(pos,elem)	Inserts a copy of elem (return value and the meaning of pos differ)
c.erase(beg,end)	Removes all elements of the range [beg,end) (some containers return next element not removed)
c.clear()	Removes all elements (makes the container empty)
c.get_allocator()	Returns the memory model of the container

Table 6.1. Common Operations of Container Classes

- Initialize with the elements of another container:

```
std::list<int> l;          // l is a linked list of ints

...
// copy all elements of the list as floats into a vector
std::vector<float> c(l.begin(),l.end());
```

- Initialize with the elements of an array:

```
int array[] = { 2, 3, 17, 33, 45, 77 };
...
```

   // copy all elements of the array into a set
```
std::set<int> c(array,array+sizeof(array)/sizeof(array[0]));
```
- Initialize by using standard input:

   // read all integer elements of the deque from standard input
```
std::deque<int> c((std::istream_iterator<int>(std::cin)),
                  (std::istream_iterator<int>()));
```
Don't forget the extra parentheses around the initializer arguments here. Otherwise, this expression does something very different and you probably will get some strange warnings or errors in following statements. Consider writing the statement without extra parentheses:

```
std::deque<int> c(std::istream_iterator<int>(std::cin),
                  std::istream_iterator<int>());
```
In this case, c declares a *function* with a return type that is deque<int>. Its first parameter is of type istream_iterator<int> with the name cin, and its second unnamed parameter is of type "function taking no arguments returning istream_iterator<int>." This construct is valid syntactically as either a declaration or an expression. So, according to language rules, it is treated as a declaration. The extra parentheses force the initializer not to match the syntax of a declaration.[3]

In principle, these techniques are also provided to assign or to insert elements from another range. However, for those operations the exact interfaces either differ due to additional arguments or are not provided for all container classes.

Size Operations

For all container classes, three size operations are provided:

1. **size()**

   Returns the actual number of elements of the container.

2. **empty()**

   Is a shortcut for checking whether the number of elements is zero (size()==0). However, empty() might be implemented more efficiently, so you should use it if possible.

3. **max_size()**

   Returns the maximum number of elements a container might contain. This value is implementation defined. For example, a vector typically contains all elements in a single block of memory, so there might be relevant restrictions on PCs. Otherwise, max_size() is usually the maximum value of the type of the index.

---

[3] Thanks to John H. Spicer from EDG for this explanation.

Comparisons

The usual comparison operators ==, !=, <, <=, >, and >= are defined according to the following three rules:

1. Both containers must have the same type.
2. Two containers are equal if their elements are equal and have the same order. To check equality of elements, use operator ==.
3. To check whether a container is less than another container, a lexicographical comparison is done (see page 360).

To compare containers with different types, you must use the comparing algorithms of Section 9.5.4, page 356.

Assignments and `swap()`

If you assign containers, you copy all elements of the source container and remove all old elements in the destination container. Thus, assignment of containers is relatively expensive.

If the containers have the same type and the source is no longer used, there is an easy optimization: Use `swap()`. `swap()` offers much better efficiency because it swaps only the internal data of the containers. In fact, it swaps only some internal pointers that refer to the data (elements, allocator, sorting criterion, if any). So, `swap()` is guaranteed to have only constant complexity, instead of the linear complexity of an assignment.

6.2   Vectors

A vector models a dynamic array. Thus, it is an abstraction that manages its elements with a dynamic array (Figure 6.1). However, note that the standard does not specify that the implementation uses a dynamic array. Rather, it follows from the constraints and specification of the complexity of its operation.

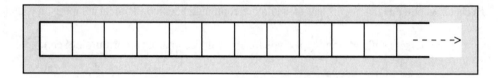

Figure 6.1. Structure of a Vector

To use a vector, you must include the header file `<vector>`[4]:

```
#include <vector>
```

There, the type is defined as a class template inside namespace `std`:

```
namespace std {
    template <class T,
              class Allocator = allocator<T> >
    class vector;
}
```

The elements of a vector may have any type T that is assignable and copyable. The optional second template parameter defines the memory model (see Chapter 15). The default memory model is the model `allocator`, which is provided by the C++ standard library.[5]

6.2.1   Abilities of Vectors

Vectors copy their elements into their internal dynamic array. The elements always have a certain order. Thus, vectors are a kind of *ordered collection*. Vectors provide *random access*. Thus, you can access every element directly in constant time, provided you know its position. The iterators are random access iterators, so you can use any algorithm of the STL.

Vectors provide good performance if you append or delete elements at the end. If you insert or delete in the middle or at the beginning, performance gets worse. This is because every element behind has to be moved to another position. In fact, the assignment operator would be called for every following element.

---

[4] In the original STL, the header file for vectors was `<vector.h>`.

[5] In systems without support for default template parameters, the second argument is typically missing.

Size and Capacity

Part of the way in which vectors give good performance is by allocating more memory than they need to contain all their elements. To use vectors effectively and correctly you should understand how size and capacity cooperate in a vector.

Vectors provide the usual size operations `size()`, `empty()`, and `max_size()` (see Section 6.1.2, page 144). An additional "size" operation is the `capacity()` function. `capacity()` returns the number of elements a vector could contain in its actual memory. If you exceed the `capacity()`, the vector has to reallocate its internal memory.

The capacity of a vector is important for two reasons:

1. Reallocation invalidates all references, pointers, and iterators for elements of the vector.
2. Reallocation takes time.

Thus, if a program manages pointers, references, or iterators into a vector, or if speed is a goal, it is important to take the capacity into account.

To avoid reallocation, you can use `reserve()` to ensure a certain capacity before you really need it. In this way, you can ensure that references remain valid as long as the capacity is not exceeded:

```
std::vector<int> v;      // create an empty vector
v.reserve(80);           // reserve memory for 80 elements
```

Another way to avoid reallocation is to initialize a vector with enough elements by passing additional arguments to the constructor. For example, if you pass a numeric value as parameter, it is taken as the starting size of the vector:

```
std::vector<T> v(5);     // creates a vector and initializes it with five values
                         // (calls five times the default constructor of type T)
```

Of course, the type of the elements must provide a default constructor for this ability. But note that for complex types, even if a default constructor is provided, the initialization takes time. If the only reason for initialization is to reserve memory, you should use `reserve()`.

The concept of capacity for vectors is similar to that for strings (see Section 11.2.5, page 485), with one big difference: Unlike strings, it is not possible to call `reserve()` for vectors to shrink the capacity. Calling `reserve()` with an argument that is less than the current capacity is a no-op. Furthermore, how to reach an optimal performance regarding speed and memory usage is implementation defined. Thus, implementations might increase capacity in larger steps. In fact, to avoid internal fragmentation, many implementations allocate a whole block of memory (such as 2K) the first time you insert anything if you don't call `reserve()` first yourself. This can waste lots of memory if you have many vectors with only a few small elements.

Because the capacity of vectors never shrinks, it is guaranteed that references, pointers, and iterators remain valid even when elements are deleted, provided they refer to a position before the manipulated elements. However, insertions may invalidate references, pointers, and iterators.

There is a way to shrink the capacity indirectly: Swapping the contents with another vector swaps the capacity. The following function shrinks the capacity while preserving the elements:

```
template <class T>
void shrinkCapacity(std::vector<T>& v)
{
```

```
        std::vector<T> tmp(v);      // copy elements into a new vector
        v.swap(tmp);                // swap internal vector data
    }
```

You can even shrink the capacity without calling this function by calling the following statement[6]:

// shrink capacity of vector v for type T
```
    std::vector<T>(v).swap(v);
```

However, note that after `swap()`, all references, pointers, and iterators swap their containers. They still refer to the elements to which they referred on entry. Thus, `shrinkCapacity()` invalidates all references, pointers, and iterators.

6.2.2   Vector Operations

Create, Copy, and Destroy Operations

Table 6.2 lists the constructors and destructors for vectors. You can create vectors with and without elements for initialization. If you pass only the size, the elements are created with their default constructor. Note that an explicit call of the default constructor also initializes fundamental types such as `int` with zero (this language feature is covered on page 14). See Section 6.1.2, page 144, for some remarks about possible initialization sources.

Operation	Effect
`vector<Elem> c`	Creates an empty vector without any elements
`vector<Elem> c1(c2)`	Creates a copy of another vector of the same type (all elements are copied)
`vector<Elem> c(n)`	Creates a vector with n elements that are created by the default constructor
`vector<Elem> c(n,elem)`	Creates a vector initialized with n copies of element `elem`
`vector<Elem> c(beg,end)`	Creates a vector initialized with the elements of the range [beg,end)
`c.~vector<Elem>()`	Destroys all elements and frees the memory

Table 6.2. Constructors and Destructor of Vectors

---

[6] You (or your compiler) might consider this statement as being incorrect because it calls a nonconstant member function for a temporary value. However, standard C++ allows you to call a nonconstant member function for temporary values.

Nonmodifying Operations

Table 6.3 lists all nonmodifying operations of vectors.[7] See additional remarks in Section 6.1.2, page 144, and Section 6.2.1, page 149.

Operation	Effect
c.size()	Returns the current number of elements
c.empty()	Returns whether the container is empty (equivalent to size()==0, but might be faster)
c.max_size()	Returns the maximum number of elements possible
c.capacity()	Returns the maximum possible number of elements without reallocation
c.reserve()	Enlarges capacity, if not enough yet[7]
c1 == c2	Returns whether c1 is equal to c2
c1 != c2	Returns whether c1 is not equal to c2 (equivalent to !(c1==c2))
c1 < c2	Returns whether c1 is less than c2
c1 > c2	Returns whether c1 is greater than c2 (equivalent to c2<c1)
c1 <= c2	Returns whether c1 is less than or equal to c2 (equivalent to !(c2<c1))
c1 >= c2	Returns whether c1 is greater than or equal to c2 (equivalent to !(c1<c2))

Table 6.3. Nonmodifying Operations of Vectors

Assignments

Operation	Effect
c1 = c2	Assigns all elements of c2 to c1
c.assign(n,elem)	Assigns n copies of element elem
c.assign(beg,end)	Assigns the elements of the range [beg,end)
c1.swap(c2)	Swaps the data of c1 and c2
swap(c1,c2)	Same (as global function)

Table 6.4. Assignment Operations of Vectors

Table 6.4 lists the ways to assign new elements while removing all ordinary elements. The set of assign() functions matches the set of constructors. You can use different sources for assignments (containers, arrays, standard input) similar to those described for constructors on page 144. All assignment operations call the default constructor, copy constructor, assignment operator, and/or destructor of the element type, depending on how the number of elements changes. For example:

```
std::list<Elem> l;
std::vector<Elem> coll;
```

---

[7] reserve() manipulates the vector because it invalidates references, pointers, and iterators to elements. However, it is mentioned here because it does not manipulate the logical contents of the container.

...
// make `coll` *be a copy of the contents of* `l`
```
coll.assign(l.begin(),l.end());
```

Element Access

Table 6.5 shows all vector operations for direct element access. As usual in C and C++, the first element has index 0 and the last element has index `size()-1`. Thus, the *n*th element has index *n-1*. For nonconstant vectors, these operations return a reference to the element. Thus you could modify an element by using one of these operations (provided it is not forbidden for other reasons).

Operation	Effect
`c.at(idx)`	Returns the element with index `idx` (throws range error exception if `idx` is out of range)
`c[idx]`	Returns the element with index `idx` (*no* range checking)
`c.front()`	Returns the first element (*no* check whether a first element exists)
`c.back()`	Returns the last element (*no* check whether a last element exists)

Table 6.5. Direct Element Access of Vectors

The most important issue for the caller is whether these operations perform range checking. Only `at()` performs range checking. If the index is out of range, it throws an `out_of_range` exception (see Section 3.3, page 25). All other functions do *not* check. A range error results in undefined behavior. Calling operator `[]`, `front()`, and `back()` for an empty container always results in undefined behavior:

```
std::vector<Elem> coll;        // empty!

coll[5] = elem;                // RUNTIME ERROR ⇒ undefined behavior
std::cout << coll.front();     // RUNTIME ERROR ⇒ undefined behavior
```

So, you must ensure that the index for operator `[]` is valid and the container is not empty when either `front()` or `back()` is called:

```
std::vector<Elem> coll;        // empty!

if (coll.size() > 5) {
    coll[5] = elem;            // OK
}
if (!coll.empty()) {
    cout << coll.front();      // OK
}
coll.at(5) = elem;             // throws out_of_range exception
```

Iterator Functions

Vectors provide the usual operators to get iterators (Table 6.6). Vector iterators are random access iterators (see Section 7.2, page 251, for a discussion of iterator categories). Thus, in principle you could use all algorithms of the STL.

Operation	Effect
c.begin()	Returns a random access iterator for the first element
c.end()	Returns a random access iterator for the position after the last element
c.rbegin()	Returns a reverse iterator for the first element of a reverse iteration
c.rend()	Returns a reverse iterator for the position after the last element of a reverse iteration

Table 6.6. Iterator Operations of Vectors

The exact type of these iterators is implementation defined. However, for vectors the iterators returned by begin() and end() are often ordinary pointers. An ordinary pointer is a random access iterator, and because the internal structure of a vector is usually an array, it has the correct behavior. However, you can't count on it. For example, if a safe version of the STL that checks range errors and other potential problems is used, the iterator type is usually an auxiliary class. See Section 7.2.6, page 258, for a look at the nasty difference between iterators implemented as pointers and iterators implemented as classes.

Iterators remain valid until an element with a smaller index gets inserted or removed, or reallocation occurs and capacity changes (see Section 6.2.1, page 149).

Inserting and Removing Elements

Table 6.7 shows the operations provided for vectors to insert or to remove elements. As usual by using the STL, you must ensure that the arguments are valid. Iterators must refer to valid positions, the beginning of a range must have a position that is not behind the end, and you must not try to remove an element from an empty container.

Regarding performance, you should consider that inserting and removing happens faster when

- Elements are inserted or removed at the end
- The capacity is large enough on entry
- Multiple elements are inserted by a single call rather than by multiple calls

Inserting or removing elements invalidates references, pointers, and iterators that refer to the following elements. If an insertion causes reallocation, it invalidates all references, iterators, and pointers.

Operation	Effect
`c.insert(pos,elem)`	Inserts at iterator position `pos` a copy of `elem` and returns the position of the new element
`c.insert(pos,n,elem)`	Inserts at iterator position pos n copies of `elem` (returns nothing)
`c.insert(pos,beg,end)`	Inserts at iterator position pos a copy of all elements of the range [beg,end) (returns nothing)
`c.push_back(elem)`	Appends a copy of `elem` at the end
`c.pop_back()`	Removes the last element (does not return it)
`c.erase(pos)`	Removes the element at iterator position pos and returns the position of the next element
`c.erase(beg,end)`	Removes all elements of the range [beg,end) and returns the position of the next element
`c.resize(num)`	Changes the number of elements to num (if `size()` grows, new elements are created by their default constructor)
`c.resize(num,elem)`	Changes the number of elements to num (if `size()` grows, new elements are copies of `elem`)
`c.clear()`	Removes all elements (makes the container empty)

Table 6.7. Insert and Remove Operations of Vectors

Vectors provide no operation to remove elements directly that have a certain value. You must use an algorithm to do this. For example, the following statement removes all elements that have the value `val`:

```
std::vector<Elem> coll;
...
// remove all elements with value val
coll.erase(remove(coll.begin(),coll.end(),
                   val),
           coll.end());
```

This statement is explained in Section 5.6.1, page 111.

To remove only the first element that has a certain value, you must use the following statements:

```
std::vector<Elem> coll;
...
// remove first element with value val
std::vector<Elem>::iterator pos;
pos = find(coll.begin(),coll.end(),
           val);
if (pos != coll.end()) {
    coll.erase(pos);
}
```

6.2.3 Using Vectors as Ordinary Arrays

The C++ standard library does not state clearly whether the elements of a vector are required to be in contiguous memory. However, it is the intention that this is guaranteed and it will be fixed due to a defect report. Thus, you can expect that for any valid index i in vector v, the following yields true:

```
&v[i] == &v[0] + i
```

This guarantee has some important consequences. It simply means that you can use a vector in all cases in which you could use a dynamic array. For example, you can use a vector to hold data of ordinary C-strings of type char* or const char*:

```
std::vector<char> v;              // create vector as dynamic array of chars

v.resize(41);                     // make room for 41 characters (including '\0')
strcpy(&v[0],"hello, world");     // copy a C-string into the vector
printf("%s\n", &v[0]);            // print contents of the vector as C-string
```

Of course, you have to be careful when you use a vector in this way (like you always have to be careful when using dynamic arrays). For example, you have to ensure that the size of the vector is big enough to copy some data into it and that you have an '\0' element at the end if you use the contents as a C-string. However, this example shows that whenever you need an array of type T for any reason (such as for an existing C library) you can use a vector<T> and pass the address of the first element.

Note that you must not pass an iterator as the address of the first element. Iterators of vectors have an implementation-specific type, which may be totally different from an ordinary pointer:

```
printf("%s\n", v.begin());        // ERROR (might work, but not portable)
printf("%s\n", &v[0]);            // OK
```

6.2.4 Exception Handling

Vectors provide only minimal support for logical error checking. The only member function for which the standard requires that it may throw an exception is at(), which is the safe version of the subscript operator (see page 152). In addition, the standard requires that only the usual standard exceptions may occur, such as bad_alloc for a lack of memory or exceptions of user-defined operations.

If functions called by a vector (functions for the element type or functions that are user supplied) throw exceptions, the C++ standard library guarantees the following:

1. If an element gets inserted with push_back() and an exception occurs, this function has no effect.

2. insert() either succeeds or has no effect if the copy operations (copy constructor and assignment operator) of the elements do not throw.

3. pop_back() does not throw any exceptions.

4. `erase()` and `clear()` do not throw if the copy operations (copy constructor and assignment operator) of the elements do not throw.

5. `swap()` does not throw.

6. If elements are used that never throw exceptions on copy operations (copy constructor and assignment operator), every operation is either successful or has no effect. Such elements might be "plain old data" (POD). POD describes types that use no special C++ feature. For example, every ordinary C structure is POD.

All these guarantees are based on the requirements that destructors don't throw. See Section 5.11.2, page 139, for a general discussion of exception handling in the STL and Section 6.10.10, page 248, for a list of all container operations that give special guarantees in face of exceptions.

6.2.5 Examples of Using Vectors

The following example shows a simple usage of vectors:

```
// cont/vector1.cpp

#include <iostream>
#include <vector>
#include <string>
#include <algorithm>
#include <iterator>
using namespace std;

int main()
{
    // create empty vector for strings
    vector<string> sentence;

    // reserve memory for five elements to avoid reallocation
    sentence.reserve(5);

    // append some elements
    sentence.push_back("Hello,");
    sentence.push_back("how");
    sentence.push_back("are");
    sentence.push_back("you");
    sentence.push_back("?");

    // print elements separated with spaces
    copy (sentence.begin(), sentence.end(),
          ostream_iterator<string>(cout," "));
```

```
    cout << endl;

    // print "technical data"
    cout << " max_size(): " << sentence.max_size() << endl;
    cout << " size():      " << sentence.size()     << endl;
    cout << " capacity():  " << sentence.capacity() << endl;

    // swap second and fourth element
    swap (sentence[1], sentence[3]);

    // insert element "always" before element "?"
    sentence.insert (find(sentence.begin(),sentence.end(),"?"),
                     "always");

    // assign "!" to the last element
    sentence.back() = "!";

    // print elements separated with spaces
    copy (sentence.begin(), sentence.end(),
          ostream_iterator<string>(cout," "));
    cout << endl;

    // print "technical data" again
    cout << " max_size(): " << sentence.max_size() << endl;
    cout << " size():      " << sentence.size()     << endl;
    cout << " capacity():  " << sentence.capacity() << endl;
}
```

The output of the program might look like this:

```
Hello, how are you ?
  max_size(): 268435455
  size():     5
  capacity(): 5
Hello, you are how always !
  max_size(): 268435455
  size():     6
  capacity(): 10
```

Note my use of the word "might." The values of max_size() and capacity() are implementation defined. Here, for example, you can see that the implementation doubles the capacity if the capacity no longer fits.

6.2.6 Class `vector<bool>`

For Boolean elements of a vector, the C++ standard library provides a specialization of `vector`. The goal is to have a version that is optimized to use less size than a usual implementation of `vector` for type `bool`. Such a usual implementation would reserve at least 1 byte for each element. The `vector<bool>` specialization usually uses internally only 1 bit for an element, so it is typically eight times smaller. Note that such an optimization also has a snag: In C++, the smallest addressable value must have a size of at least 1 byte. Thus, such a specialization of a vector needs special handling for references and iterators.

As a result, a `vector<bool>` does not meet all requirements of other vectors (for example, a `vector<bool>::reference` is not a true lvalue and `vector<bool>::iterator` is not a random access iterator). Therefore, template code might work for vectors of any type except `bool`. In addition, `vector<bool>` might perform slower than normal implementations because element operations have to be transformed into bit operations. However, how `vector<bool>` is implemented is implementation specific. Thus, the performance (speed and memory) might differ.

Note that class `vector<bool>` is more than a specialization of `vector<>` for `bool`. It also provides some special bit operations. You can handle bits or flags in a more convenient way.

`vector<bool>` has a dynamic size, so you can consider it a bitfield with dynamic size. Thus, you can add and remove bits. If you need a bitfield with static size, you should use `bitset` rather than a `vector<bool>`. Class `bitset` is covered in Section 10.4, page 460.

Operation	Effect
`c.flip()`	Negates all Boolean elements (complement of all bits)
`c[idx].flip()`	Negates the Boolean element with index `idx` (complement of a single bit)
`c[idx] = val`	Assigns *val* to the Boolean element with index `idx` (assignment to a single bit)
`c[idx1] = c[idx2]`	Assigns the value of the element with index `idx2` to the element with index `idx1`

Table 6.8. Special Operations of `vector<bool>`

The additional operations of `vector<bool>` are shown in Table 6.8. The operation `flip()`, which processes the complement, can be called for all bits and a single bit of the vector. Note that you can call `flip()` for a single Boolean element. This is surprising, because you might expect that the subscript operator returns `bool` and that calling `flip()` for such a fundamental type is not possible. Here the class `vector<bool>` uses a common trick, called a *proxy*[8]: For `vector<bool>`, the return type of the subscript operator (and other operators that return an element) is an auxiliary class. If

---

[8] A proxy allows you to keep control where usually no control is provided. This is often used to get more security. In this case, it maintains control to allow certain operations, although the return value in principle behaves as `bool`.

you need the return value to be `bool`, an automatic type conversion is used. For other operations, the member functions are provided. The relevant part of the declaration of `vector<bool>` looks like this:

```
namespace std {
    class vector<bool> {
      public:
        // auxiliary type for subscript operator
        class reference {
            ...
          public:
            // automatic type conversion to bool
            operator bool() const;

            // assignments
            reference& operator= (const bool);
            reference& operator= (const reference&);

            // bit complement
            void flip();
        };
        ...

        // operations for element access
        // - return type is reference instead of bool
        reference operator[](size_type n);
        reference at(size_type n);
        reference front();
        reference back();
        ...
    };
}
```

As you can see, all member functions for element access return type `reference`. Thus, you could also use the following statement:

```
c.front().flip();        // negate first Boolean element
c[5] = c.back();         // assign last element to element with index 5
```

As usual, to avoid undefined behavior, the caller must ensure that the first, sixth, and last element exist.

The internal type `reference` is only used for nonconstant containers of type `vector<bool>`. The constant member functions for element access return ordinary values of type `bool`.

6.3 Deques

A deque (pronounced "deck") is very similar to a vector. It manages its elements with a dynamic array, provides random access, and has almost the same interface as a vector. The difference is that with a deque the dynamic array is open at both ends. Thus, a deque is fast for insertions and deletions at both the end and the beginning (Figure 6.2).

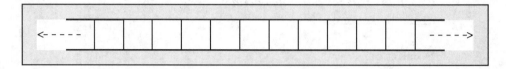

Figure 6.2. Logical Structure of a Deque

To provide this ability, the deque is implemented typically as a bunch of individual blocks, with the first block growing in one direction and the last block growing in the opposite direction (Figure 6.3).

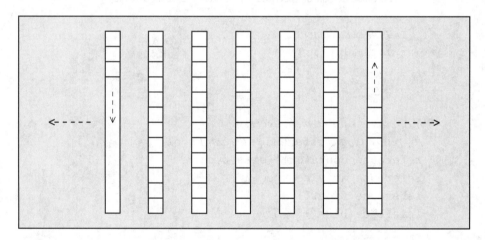

Figure 6.3. Internal Structure of a Deque

To use a deque, you must include the header file <deque>[9]:

```
#include <deque>
```

There, the type is defined as a class template inside namespace std:

```
namespace std {
    template <class T,
```

---

[9] In the original STL, the header file for deques was <deque.h>.

```
              class Allocator = allocator<T> >
    class deque;
}
```

As with vectors, the type of the elements is passed as a first template parameter and may be of any type that is assignable and copyable. The optional second template argument is the memory model, with `allocator` as the default (see Chapter 15).[10]

6.3.1 Abilities of Deques

Deques have the following differences compared with the abilities of vectors:

- Inserting and removing elements is fast both at the beginning and at the end (for vectors it is only fast at the end). These operations are done in amortized constant time.
- The internal structure has one more indirection to access the elements, so element access and iterator movement of deques are usually a bit slower.
- Iterators must be smart pointers of a special type rather than ordinary pointers because they must jump between different blocks.
- In systems that have size limitations for blocks of memory (for example, some PC systems), a deque might contain more elements because it uses more than one block of memory. Thus, `max_size()` might be larger for deques.
- Deques provide no support to control the capacity and the moment of reallocation. In particular, any insertion or deletion of elements other than at the beginning or end invalidates all pointers, references, and iterators that refer to elements of the deque. However, reallocation may perform better than for vectors, because according to their typical internal structure, deques don't have to copy all elements on reallocation.
- Blocks of memory might get freed when they are no longer used, so the memory size of a deque might shrink (however, whether and how this happens is implementation specific).

The following features of vectors also apply to deques:

- Inserting and deleting elements in the middle is relatively slow because all elements up to either of both ends may be moved to make room or to fill a gap.
- Iterators are random access iterators.

In summary, you should prefer a deque if the following is true:

- You insert and remove elements at both ends (this is the classic case for a queue).
- You don't refer to elements of the container.
- It is important that the container frees memory when it is no longer used (however, the standard does not guarantee that this happens).

The interface of vectors and deques is almost the same, so trying both is very easy when no special feature of a vector or a deque is necessary.

---

[10] In systems without support for default template parameters, the second argument is typically missing.

6.3.2   Deque Operations

Table 6.9 through Table 6.11 list all operations provided for deques.

Operation	Effect
deque<Elem> c	Creates an empty deque without any elements
deque<Elem> c1(c2)	Creates a copy of another deque of the same type (all elements are copied)
deque<Elem> c(n)	Creates a deque with n elements that are created by the default constructor
deque<Elem> c(n,elem)	Creates a deque initialized with n copies of element elem
deque<Elem> c(beg,end)	Creates a deque initialized with the elements of the range [beg,end)
c.~deque<Elem>()	Destroys all elements and frees the memory

Table 6.9. Constructors and Destructor of Deques

Operation	Effect
c.size()	Returns the actual number of elements
c.empty()	Returns whether the container is empty (equivalent to size()==0, but might be faster)
c.max_size()	Returns the maximum number of elements possible
c1 == c2	Returns whether c1 is equal to c2
c1 != c2	Returns whether c1 is not equal to c2 (equivalent to !(c1==c2))
c1 < c2	Returns whether c1 is less than c2
c1 > c2	Returns whether c1 is greater than c2 (equivalent to c2<c1)
c1 <= c2	Returns whether c1 is less than or equal to c2 (equivalent to !(c2<c1))
c1 >= c2	Returns whether c1 is greater than or equal to c2 (equivalent to !(c1<c2))
c.at(idx)	Returns the element with index idx (throws range error exception if idx is out of range)
c[idx]	Returns the element with index idx (*no* range checking)
c.front()	Returns the first element (*no* check whether a first element exists)
c.back()	Returns the last element (*no* check whether a last element exists)
c.begin()	Returns a random access iterator for the first element
c.end()	Returns a random access iterator for the position after the last element
c.rbegin()	Returns a reverse iterator for the first element of a reverse iteration
c.rend()	Returns a reverse iterator for the position after the last element of a reverse iteration

Table 6.10. Nonmodifying Operations of Deques

Operation	Effect
`c1 = c2`	Assigns all elements of c2 to c1
`c.assign(n,elem)`	Assigns n copies of element `elem`
`c.assign(beg,end)`	Assigns the elements of the range [beg,end)
`c1.swap(c2)`	Swaps the data of c1 and c2
`swap(c1,c2)`	Same (as global function)
`c.insert(pos,elem)`	Inserts at iterator position pos a copy of `elem` and returns the position of the new element
`c.insert(pos,n,elem)`	Inserts at iterator position pos n copies of `elem` (returns nothing)
`c.insert(pos,beg,end)`	Inserts at iterator position pos a copy of all elements of the range [beg,end) (returns nothing)
`c.push_back(elem)`	Appends a copy of `elem` at the end
`c.pop_back()`	Removes the last element (does not return it)
`c.push_front(elem)`	Inserts a copy of `elem` at the beginning
`c.pop_front()`	Removes the first element (does not return it)
`c.erase(pos)`	Removes the element at iterator position pos and returns the position of the next element
`c.erase(beg,end)`	Removes all elements of the range [beg,end) and returns the position of the next element
`c.resize(num)`	Changes the number of elements to num (if `size()` grows, new elements are created by their default constructor)
`c.resize(num,elem)`	Changes the number of elements to num (if `size()` grows, new elements are copies of `elem`)
`c.clear()`	Removes all elements (makes the container empty)

Table 6.11. Modifying Operations of Deques

Deque operations differ from vector operations only as follows:

1. Deques do not provide the functions for capacity (`capacity()` and `reserve()`).
2. Deques do provide direct functions to insert and to delete the first element (`push_front()` and `pop_front()`).

Because the other operations are the same, they are not reexplained here. See Section 6.2.2, page 150, for a description of them.

Note that you still must consider the following:

1. No member functions for element access (except `at()`) check whether an index or an iterator is valid.
2. An insertion or deletion of elements might cause a reallocation. Thus, any insertion or deletion invalidates all pointers, references, and iterators that refer to other elements of the deque. The exception is when elements are inserted at the front or the back. In this case, references and pointers to elements stay valid (but iterators don't).

6.3.3   Exception Handling

In principle, deques provide the same support for exception handing as do vectors (see page 155). The additional operations `push_front()` and `pop_front()` behave according to `push_back()` and `pop_back()` respectively. Thus, the C++ standard library provides the following behavior:

- If an element gets inserted with `push_back()` or `push_front()` and an exception occurs, these functions have no effect.
- Neither `pop_back()` nor `pop_front()` throw any exceptions.

See Section 5.11.2, page 139, for a general discussion of exception handling in the STL and Section 6.10.10, page 248, for a list of all container operations that give special guarantees in face of exceptions.

6.3.4   Examples of Using Deques

The following program is a simple example that shows the abilities of deques:

```
// cont/deque1.cpp

#include <iostream>
#include <deque>
#include <string>
#include <algorithm>
#include <iterator>
using namespace std;

int main()
{
    // create empty deque of strings
    deque<string> coll;

    // insert several elements
    coll.assign (3, string("string"));
    coll.push_back ("last string");
    coll.push_front ("first string");

    // print elements separated by newlines
    copy (coll.begin(), coll.end(),
          ostream_iterator<string>(cout,"\n"));
    cout << endl;
```

```
// remove first and last element
coll.pop_front();
coll.pop_back();

// insert ''another'' into every element but the first
for (unsigned i=1; i<coll.size(); ++i) {
    coll[i] = "another " + coll[i];
}

// change size to four elements
coll.resize (4, "resized string");

// print elements separated by newlines
copy (coll.begin(), coll.end(),
      ostream_iterator<string>(cout,"\n"));
}
```

The program has the following output:

```
first string
string
string
string
last string

string
another string
another string
resized string
```

6.4   Lists

A list manages its elements as a doubly linked list (Figure 6.4). As usual, the C++ standard library does not specify the kind of the implementation, but it follows from the list's name, constraints, and specifications.

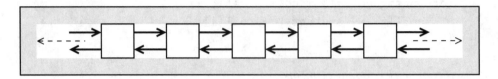

Figure 6.4. Structure of a List

To use a list you must include the header file `<list>`[11]:

```
#include <list>
```

There, the type is defined as a class template inside namespace `std`:

```
namespace std {
    template <class T,
              class Allocator = allocator<T> >
    class list;
}
```

The elements of a list may have any type T that is assignable and copyable. The optional second template parameter defines the memory model (see Chapter 15). The default memory model is the model `allocator`, which is provided by the C++ standard library.[12]

6.4.1   Abilities of Lists

The internal structure of a list is totally different from a vector or a deque. Thus, a list differs in several major ways compared with vectors and deques:

- A list does not provide random access. For example, to access the fifth element, you must navigate the first four elements following the chain of links. Thus, accessing an arbitrary element using a list is slow.
- Inserting and removing elements is fast at each position, and not only at one or both ends. You can always insert and delete an element in constant time because no other elements have to be moved. Internally, only some pointer values are manipulated.

---

[11] In the original STL, the header file for lists was `<list.h>`.

[12] In systems without support for default template parameters, the second argument is typically missing.

- Inserting and deleting elements does not invalidate pointers, references, and iterators to other elements.
- A list supports exception handling in such a way that almost every operation succeeds or is a no-op. Thus, you can't get into an intermediate state in which only half of the operation is complete.

The member functions provided for lists reflect these differences compared with vectors and deques as follows:

- Lists provide neither a subscript operator nor `at()` because no random access is provided.
- Lists don't provide operations for capacity or reallocation because neither is needed. Each element has its own memory that stays valid until the element is deleted.
- Lists provide many special member functions for moving elements. These member functions are faster versions of general algorithms that have the same names. They are faster because they only redirect pointers rather than copy and move the values.

6.4.2 List Operations

Create, Copy, and Destroy Operations

The ability to create, copy, and destroy lists is the same as it is for every sequence container. See Table 6.12 for the list operations that do this. See also Section 6.1.2, page 144, for some remarks about possible initialization sources.

Operation	Effect
`list<Elem> c`	Creates an empty list without any elements
`list<Elem> c1(c2)`	Creates a copy of another list of the same type (all elements are copied)
`list<Elem> c(n)`	Creates a list with n elements that are created by the default constructor
`list<Elem> c(n,elem)`	Creates a list initialized with n copies of element `elem`
`list<Elem> c(beg,end)`	Creates a list initialized with the elements of the range [beg,end)
`c.~list<Elem>()`	Destroys all elements and frees the memory

Table 6.12. Constructors and Destructor of Lists

Nonmodifying Operations

Lists provide the usual operations for size and comparisons. See Table 6.13 for a list and Section 6.1.2, page 144, for details.

Operation	Effect
`c.size()`	Returns the actual number of elements
`c.empty()`	Returns whether the container is empty (equivalent to `size()==0`, but might be faster)
`c.max_size()`	Returns the maximum number of elements possible
`c1 == c2`	Returns whether c1 is equal to c2
`c1 != c2`	Returns whether c1 is not equal to c2 (equivalent to `!(c1==c2)`)
`c1 < c2`	Returns whether c1 is less than c2
`c1 > c2`	Returns whether c1 is greater than c2 (equivalent to `c2<c1`)
`c1 <= c2`	Returns whether c1 is less than or equal to c2 (equivalent to `!(c2<c1)`)
`c1 >= c2`	Returns whether c1 is greater than or equal to c2 (equivalent to `!(c1<c2)`)

Table 6.13. Nonmodifying Operations of Lists

Assignments

Lists also provide the usual assignment operations for sequence containers (Table 6.14).

Operation	Effect
`c1 = c2`	Assigns all elements of c2 to c1
`c.assign(n,elem)`	Assigns n copies of element `elem`
`c.assign(beg,end)`	Assigns the elements of the range [beg,end)
`c1.swap(c2)`	Swaps the data of c1 and c2
`swap(c1,c2)`	Same (as global function)

Table 6.14. Assignment Operations of Lists

As usual, the insert operations match the constructors to provide different sources for initialization (see Section 6.1.2, page 144, for details).

Element Access

Because a list does not have random access, it provides only `front()` and `back()` for accessing elements directly (Table 6.15).

Operation	Effect
`c.front()`	Returns the first element (*no* check whether a first element exists)
`c.back()`	Returns the last element (*no* check whether a last element exists)

Table 6.15. Direct Element Access of Lists

As usual, these operations do *not* check whether the container is empty. If the container is empty, calling them results in undefined behavior. Thus, the caller must ensure that the container contains at least one element. For example:

```
std::list<Elem> coll;              // empty!

std::cout << coll.front();         // RUNTIME ERROR ⇒ undefined behavior

if (!coll.empty()) {
    std::cout << coll.back();      // OK
}
```

Iterator Functions

To access all elements of a list, you must use iterators. Lists provide the usual iterator functions (Table 6.16). However, because a list has no random access, these iterators are only bidirectional. Thus, you can't call algorithms that require random access iterators. All algorithms that manipulate the order of elements a lot (especially sorting algorithms) fall under this category. However, for sorting the elements, lists provide the special member function `sort()` (see page 245).

Operation	Effect
`c.begin()`	Returns a bidirectional iterator for the first element
`c.end()`	Returns a bidirectional iterator for the position after the last element
`c.rbegin()`	Returns a reverse iterator for the first element of a reverse iteration
`c.rend()`	Returns a reverse iterator for the position after the last element of a reverse iteration

Table 6.16. Iterator Operations of Lists

Inserting and Removing Elements

Table 6.17 shows the operations provided for lists to insert and to remove elements. Lists provide all functions of deques, supplemented by special implementations of the `remove()` and `remove_if()` algorithms.

As usual by using the STL, you must ensure that the arguments are valid. Iterators must refer to valid positions, the beginning of a range must have a position that is not behind the end, and you must not try to remove an element from an empty container.

Inserting and removing happens faster if, when working with multiple elements, you use a single call for all elements rather than multiple calls.

For removing elements, lists provide special implementations of the `remove()` algorithms (see Section 9.7.1, page 378). These member functions are faster than the `remove()` algorithms because they manipulate only internal pointers rather than the elements. So, in contrast to vectors or deques, you should call `remove()` as a member function and not as an algorithm (as mentioned on

Operation	Effect
c.insert(pos,elem)	Inserts at iterator position pos a copy of elem and returns the position of the new element
c.insert(pos,n,elem)	Inserts at iterator position pos n copies of elem (returns nothing)
c.insert(pos,beg,end)	Inserts at iterator position pos a copy of all elements of the range [beg,end) (returns nothing)
c.push_back(elem)	Appends a copy of elem at the end
c.pop_back()	Removes the last element (does not return it)
c.push_front(elem)	Inserts a copy of elem at the beginning
c.pop_front()	Removes the first element (does not return it)
c.remove(val)	Removes all elements with value val
c.remove_if(op)	Removes all elements for which op(*elem*) yields true
c.erase(pos)	Removes the element at iterator position pos and returns the position of the next element
c.erase(beg,end)	Removes all elements of the range [beg,end) and returns the position of the next element
c.resize(num)	Changes the number of elements to num (if size() grows, new elements are created by their default constructor)
c.resize(num,elem)	Changes the number of elements to num (if size() grows, new elements are copies of elem)
c.clear()	Removes all elements (makes the container empty)

Table 6.17. Insert and Remove Operations of Lists

page 154). To remove all elements that have a certain value, you can do the following (see Section 5.6.3, page 116, for further details):

```
std::list<Elem> coll;
...
// remove all elements with value val
coll.remove(val);
```

However, to remove only the first occurrence of a value, you must use an algorithm such as that mentioned on page 154 for vectors.

You can use remove_if() to define the criterion for the removal of the elements by a function or a function object.[13] remove_if() removes each element for which calling the passed operation yields true. An example of the use of remove_if() is a statement to remove all elements that have an even value:

```
list.remove_if (not1(bind2nd(modulus<int>(),2)));
```

If you don't understand this statement, don't panic. Turn to page 306 for details. See page 378 for additional examples of remove() and remove_if().

---

[13] The remove_if() member function is usually not provided in systems that do not support member templates.

Splice Functions

Linked lists have the advantage that you can remove and insert elements at any position in constant time. If you move elements from one container to another, this advantage doubles in that you only need to redirect some internal pointers (Figure 6.5).

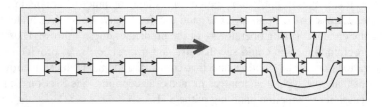

Figure 6.5. Splice Operations to Change the Order of List Elements

To support this ability, lists provide not only `remove()` but also additional modifying member functions to change the order of and relink elements and ranges. You can call these operations to move elements inside a single list or between two lists, provided the lists have the same type. Table 6.18 lists these functions. They are covered in detail in Section 6.10.8, page 244, with examples in Section 6.4.4, page 172.

Operation	Effect
`c.unique()`	Removes duplicates of consecutive elements with the same value
`c.unique(op)`	Removes duplicates of consecutive elements, for which `op()` yields true
`c1.splice(pos,c2)`	Moves all elements of c2 to c1 in front of the iterator position pos
`c1.splice(pos,c2,c2pos)`	Moves the element at c2pos in c2 in front of pos of list c1 (c1 and c2 may be identical)
`c1.splice(pos,c2,` `c2beg,c2end)`	Moves all elements of the range [c2beg,c2end) in c2 in front of pos of list c1 (c1 and c2 may be identical)
`c.sort()`	Sorts all elements with operator <
`c.sort(op)`	Sorts all elements with `op()`
`c1.merge(c2)`	Assuming both containers contain the elements sorted, moves all elements of c2 into c1 so that all elements are merged and still sorted
`c1.merge(c2,op)`	Assuming both containers contain the elements sorted due to the sorting criterion `op()`, moves all elements of c2 into c1 so that all elements are merged and still sorted according to `op()`
`c.reverse()`	Reverses the order of all elements

Table 6.18. Special Modifying Operations for Lists

6.4.3   Exception Handling

Lists have the best support of exception safety of the standard containers in the STL. Almost all list operations will either succeed or have no effect. The only operations that don't give this guarantee in face of exceptions are assignment operations and the member function `sort()` (they give the usual "basic guarantee" that they will not leak resources or violate container invariants in the face of exceptions). `merge()`, `remove()`, `remove_if()`, and `unique()` give guarantees under the condition that comparing the elements (using operator `==` or the predicate) doesn't throw. Thus, to use a term from database programming, you could say that lists are *transaction safe*, provided you don't call assignment operations or `sort()` and ensure that comparing elements doesn't throw. Table 6.19 lists all operations that give special guarantees in face of exceptions. See Section 5.11.2, page 139, for a general discussion of exception handling in the STL.

Operation	Guarantee
`push_back()`	Either succeeds or has no effect
`push_front()`	Either succeeds or has no effect
`insert()`	Either succeeds or has no effect
`pop_back()`	Doesn't throw
`pop_front()`	Doesn't throw
`erase()`	Doesn't throw
`clear()`	Doesn't throw
`resize()`	Either succeeds or has no effect
`remove()`	Doesn't throw if comparing the elements doesn't throw
`remove_if()`	Doesn't throw if the predicate doesn't throw
`unique()`	Doesn't throw if comparing the elements doesn't throw
`splice()`	Doesn't throw
`merge()`	Either succeeds or has no effect if comparing the elements doesn't throw
`reverse()`	Doesn't throw
`swap()`	Doesn't throw

Table 6.19. List Operations with Special Guarantees in Face of Exceptions

6.4.4   Examples of Using Lists

The following example in particular shows the use of the special member functions for lists:

```
// cont/list1.cpp

#include <iostream>
#include <list>
#include <algorithm>
```

```cpp
#include <iterator>
using namespace std;

void printLists (const list<int>& l1, const list<int>& l2)
{
    cout << "list1: ";
    copy (l1.begin(), l1.end(), ostream_iterator<int>(cout," "));
    cout << endl << "list2: ";
    copy (l2.begin(), l2.end(), ostream_iterator<int>(cout," "));
    cout << endl << endl;
}

int main()
{
    // create two empty lists
    list<int> list1, list2;

    // fill both lists with elements
    for (int i=0; i<6; ++i) {
        list1.push_back(i);
        list2.push_front(i);
    }
    printLists(list1, list2);

    // insert all elements of list1 before the first element with value 3 of list2
    // - find() returns an iterator to the first element with value 3
    list2.splice(find(list2.begin(),list2.end(),   // destination position
                      3),
                 list1);                            // source list
    printLists(list1, list2);

    // move first element to the end
    list2.splice(list2.end(),        // destination position
                 list2,              // source list
                 list2.begin());     // source position
    printLists(list1, list2);

    // sort second list, assign to list1 and remove duplicates
    list2.sort();
```

The sorting criterion must define "strict weak ordering." Strict weak ordering is defined by the following three properties:

1. It has to be **antisymmetric**.
    This means for operator <: If x < y is true, then y < x is false.
    This means for a predicate op(): If op(x,y) is true, then op(y,x) is false.

2. It has to be **transitive**.
    This means for operator <: If x < y is true and y < z is true, then x < z is true.
    This means for a predicate op(): If op(x,y) is true and op(y,z) is true, then op(x,z) is true.

3. It has to be **irreflexive**.
    This means for operator <: x < x is always false.
    This means for a predicate op(): op(x,x) is always false.

4. It has to have **transitivity of equivalence**, which means roughly: If a is equivalent to b and b is equivalent to c, then a is equivalent to c.
    This means for operator <: If !(a<b) && !(b<a) is true and !(b<c) && !(c<b) is true then !(a<c) && !(c<a) is true.
    This means for a predicate op(): If op(a,b), op(b,a), op(b,c), and op(c,b) all yield false, then op(a,c) and op(c,a) yield false.

Based on these properties the sorting criterion is also used to check equality. That is, two elements are equal if neither is less than the other (or if both op(x,y) and op(y,x) are false).

6.5.1   Abilities of Sets and Multisets

Like all standardized associative container classes, sets and multisets are usually implemented as balanced binary trees (Figure 6.7). The standard does not specify this, but it follows from the complexity of set and multiset operations.[17]

The major advantage of automatic sorting is that a binary tree performs well when elements with a certain value are searched. In fact, search functions have logarithmic complexity. For example, to search for an element in a set or multiset of 1,000 elements, a tree search (which is performed by the member function) needs, on average, one fiftieth of the comparisons of a linear search (which is performed by the algorithm). See Section 2.3, page 21, for more details about complexity.

However, automatic sorting also imposes an important constraint on sets and multisets: You may *not* change the value of an element directly because this might compromise the correct order. Therefore, to modify the value of an element, you must remove the element that has the old value and insert a new element that has the new value. The interface reflects this behavior:

*   Sets and multisets don't provide operations for direct element access.

*   Indirect access via iterators has the constraint that, from the iterator's point of view, the element value is constant.

---

[17] In fact, sets and multisets are typically implemented as "red-black trees." Red-black trees are good for both changing the number of elements and searching for elements. They guarantee at most two internal relinks on insertions and that the longest path is at most twice as long as the shortest path to a leaf.

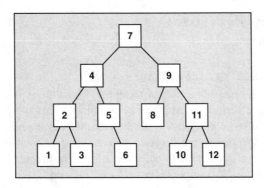

Figure 6.7. Internal Structure of Sets and Multisets

6.5.2 Set and Multiset Operations

Create, Copy, and Destroy Operations

Table 6.20 lists the constructors and destructors of sets and multisets.

Operation	Effect
set c	Creates an empty set/multiset without any elements
set c(op)	Creates an empty set/multiset that uses op as the sorting criterion
set c1(c2)	Creates a copy of another set/multiset of the same type (all elements are copied)
set c(beg,end)	Creates a set/multiset initialized by the elements of the range [beg,end)
set c(beg,end,op)	Creates a set/multiset with the sorting criterion op initialized by the elements of the range [beg,end)
c.~*set*()	Destroys all elements and frees the memory

Here, *set* may be one of the following:

set	Effect
set<Elem>	A set that sorts with less<> (operator <)
set<Elem,Op>	A set that sorts with Op
multiset<Elem>	A multiset that sorts with less<> (operator <)
multiset<Elem,Op>	A multiset that sorts with Op

Table 6.20. Constructors and Destructors of Sets and Multisets

You can define the sorting criterion in two ways:

1. **As a template parameter.**

   For example[18]:

   ```
   std::set<int,std::greater<int> > coll;
   ```

   In this case, the sorting criterion is part of the type. Thus, the type system ensures that only containers with the same sorting criterion can be combined. This is the usual way to specify the sorting criterion. To be more precise, the second parameter is the *type* of the sorting criterion. The concrete sorting criterion is the function object that gets created with the container. To do this, the constructor of the container calls the default constructor of the type of the sorting criterion. See page 294 for an example that uses a user-defined sorting criterion.

2. **As a constructor parameter.**

   In this case, you might have a type for several sorting criteria, and the initial value or state of the sorting criteria might differ. This is useful when processing the sorting criterion at runtime and when sorting criteria are needed that are different but of the same data type. See page 191 for a complete example.

If no special sorting criterion is passed, the default sorting criterion, function object `less<>`, is used, which sorts the elements by using operator `<`.[19]

Note that the sorting criterion is also used to check for equality of the elements. Thus, when the default sorting criterion is used, the check for equality of two elements looks like this:

```
if (! (elem1<elem2 || elem2<elem1))
```

This has three advantages:

1. You need to pass only one argument as the sorting criterion.
2. You don't have to provide operator `==` for the element type.
3. You can have contrary definitions for equality (it doesn't matter if operator `==` behaves differently than in the expression). However, this might be a source of confusion.

However, checking for equality in this way takes a bit more time. This is because two comparisons might be necessary to evaluate the previous expression. Note that if the result of the first comparison yields `true`, the second comparison is not evaluated.

By now the type name of the container might be a bit complicated and boring, so it is probably a good idea to use a type definition. This definition could be used as a shortcut wherever the container type is needed (this also applies to iterator definitions):

```
typedef std::set<int,std::greater<int> >  IntSet;
...
```

---

[18] Note that you have to put a space between the two ">" characters. ">>" would be parsed as shift operator, which would result in a syntax error.

[19] In systems without support for default template parameters, you typically must always pass the sorting criterion as follows:

```
set<int,less<int> > coll;
```

```
IntSet coll;
IntSet::iterator pos;
```

The constructor for the beginning and the end of a range could be used to initialize the container with elements from containers that have other types, from arrays, or from the standard input. See Section 6.1.2, page 144, for details.

Nonmodifying Operations

Sets and multisets provide the usual nonmodifying operations to query the size and to make comparisons (Table 6.21).

Operation	Effect
`c.size()`	Returns the actual number of elements
`c.empty()`	Returns whether the container is empty (equivalent to `size()==0`, but might be faster)
`c.max_size()`	Returns the maximum number of elements possible
`c1 == c2`	Returns whether c1 is equal to c2
`c1 != c2`	Returns whether c1 is not equal to c2 (equivalent to `!(c1==c2)`)
`c1 < c2`	Returns whether c1 is less than c2
`c1 > c2`	Returns whether c1 is greater than c2 (equivalent to `c2<c1`)
`c1 <= c2`	Returns whether c1 is less than or equal to c2 (equivalent to `!(c2<c1)`)
`c1 >= c2`	Returns whether c1 is greater than or equal to c2 (equivalent to `!(c1<c2)`)

Table 6.21. Nonmodifying Operations of Sets and Multisets

Comparisons are provided only for containers of the same type. Thus, the elements *and* the sorting criterion must have the same types; otherwise, a type error occurs at compile time. For example:

```
std::set<float> c1;           // sorting criterion: std::less<>
std::set<float,std::greater<float> > c2;
...
if (c1 == c2) {               // ERROR: different types
    ...
}
```

The check whether a container is less than another container is done by a lexicographical comparison (see page 360). To compare containers of different types (different sorting criteria), you must use the comparing algorithms in Section 9.5.4, page 356.

Special Search Operations

Sets and multisets are optimized for fast searching of elements, so they provide special search functions (Table 6.22). These functions are special versions of general algorithms that have the same name. You should always prefer the optimized versions for sets and multisets to achieve logarithmic complexity instead of the linear complexity of the general algorithms. For example, a search of a collection of 1,000 elements requires on average only 10 comparisons instead of 500 (see Section 2.3, page 21).

Operation	Effect
count(elem)	Returns the number of elements with value elem
find(elem)	Returns the position of the first element with value elem or end()
lower_bound(elem)	Returns the first position, where elem would get inserted (the first element >= elem)
upper_bound(elem)	Returns the last position, where elem would get inserted (the first element > elem)
equal_range(elem)	Returns the first and last position, where elem would get inserted (the range of elements == elem)

Table 6.22. Special Search Operations of Sets and Multisets

The find() member function searches the first element that has the value that was passed as the argument and returns its iterator position. If no such element is found, find() returns end() of the container.

lower_bound() and upper_bound() return the first and last position respectively, at which an element with the passed value would be inserted. In other words, lower_bound() returns the position of the first element that has the same or a greater value than the argument, whereas upper_bound() returns the position of the first element with a greater value. equal_range() returns both return values of lower_bound() and upper_bound() as a pair (type pair is introduced in Section 4.1, page 33). Thus, it returns the range of elements that have the same value as the argument. If lower_bound() or the first value of equal_range() is equal to upper_bound() or the second value of equal_range(), then no elements with the same value exist in the set or multiset. Naturally, in a set the range of elements that have the same values could contain at most one element.

The following example shows how to use lower_bound(), upper_bound(), and equal_range():

```
// cont/set2.cpp

#include <iostream>
#include <set>
using namespace std;
```

```
int main ()
{
    set<int> c;

    c.insert(1);
    c.insert(2);
    c.insert(4);
    c.insert(5);
    c.insert(6);

    cout << "lower_bound(3): " << *c.lower_bound(3) << endl;
    cout << "upper_bound(3): " << *c.upper_bound(3) << endl;
    cout << "equal_range(3): " << *c.equal_range(3).first << " "
                               << *c.equal_range(3).second << endl;
    cout << endl;
    cout << "lower_bound(5): " << *c.lower_bound(5) << endl;
    cout << "upper_bound(5): " << *c.upper_bound(5) << endl;
    cout << "equal_range(5): " << *c.equal_range(5).first << " "
                               << *c.equal_range(5).second << endl;
}
```

The output of the program is as follows:

```
lower_bound(3): 4
upper_bound(3): 4
equal_range(3): 4 4

lower_bound(5): 5
upper_bound(5): 6
equal_range(5): 5 6
```

If you use a multiset instead of a set, the program has the same output.

Assignments

Sets and multisets provide only the fundamental assignment operations that all containers provide (Table 6.23). See page 147 for more details.

For these operations both containers must have the same type. In particular, the type of the comparison criteria must be the same, although the comparison criteria themselves may be different. See page 191 for an example of different sorting criteria that have the same type. If the criteria are different, they will also get assigned or swapped.

Operation	Effect
c1 = c2	Assigns all elements of c2 to c1
c1.swap(c2)	Swaps the data of c1 and c2
swap(c1,c2)	Same (as global function)

Table 6.23. Assignment Operations of Sets and Multisets

Iterator Functions

Sets and multisets do not provide direct element access, so you have to use iterators. Sets and multisets provide the usual member functions for iterators (Table 6.24).

Operation	Effect
c.begin()	Returns a bidirectional iterator for the first element (elements are considered const)
c.end()	Returns a bidirectional iterator for the position after the last element (elements are considered const)
c.rbegin()	Returns a reverse iterator for the first element of a reverse iteration
c.rend()	Returns a reverse iterator for the position after the last element of a reverse iteration

Table 6.24. Iterator Operations of Sets and Multisets

As with all associative container classes, the iterators are bidirectional iterators (see Section 7.2.4, page 255). Thus, you can't use them in algorithms that are provided only for random access iterators (such as algorithms for sorting or random shuffling).

More important is the constraint that, from an iterator's point of view, all elements are considered constant. This is necessary to ensure that you can't compromise the order of the elements by changing their values. However, as a result you can't call any modifying algorithm on the elements of a set or multiset. For example, you can't call the remove() algorithm to remove elements because it "removes" by overwriting "removed" elements the with following arguments (see Section 5.6.2, page 115, for a detailed discussion of this problem). To remove elements in sets and multisets, you can use only member functions provided by the container.

Inserting and Removing Elements

Table 6.25 shows the operations provided for sets and multisets to insert and remove elements.

As usual by using the STL, you must ensure that the arguments are valid. Iterators must refer to valid positions, the beginning of a range must have a position that is not behind the end, and you must not try to remove an element from an empty container.

Inserting and removing happens faster if, when working with multiple elements, you use a single call for all elements rather than multiple calls.

Operation	Effect
c.insert(elem)	Inserts a copy of elem and returns the position of the new element and, for sets, whether it succeeded
c.insert(pos,elem)	Inserts a copy of elem and returns the position of the new element (pos is used as a hint pointing to where the insert should start the search)
c.insert(beg,end)	Inserts a copy of all elements of the range [beg,end) (returns nothing)
c.erase(elem)	Removes all elements with value elem and returns the number of removed elements
c.erase(pos)	Removes the element at iterator position pos (returns nothing)
c.erase(beg,end)	Removes all elements of the range [beg,end) (returns nothing)
c.clear()	Removes all elements (makes the container empty)

Table 6.25. Insert and Remove Operations of Sets and Multisets

Note that the return types of the insert functions differ as follows:

- **Sets** provide the following interface:

```
pair<iterator,bool> insert(const value_type& elem);
iterator            insert(iterator pos_hint,
                           const value_type& elem);
```

- **Multisets** provide the following interface:

```
iterator            insert(const value_type& elem);
iterator            insert(iterator pos_hint,
                           const value_type& elem);
```

The difference in return types results because multisets allow duplicates, whereas sets do not. Thus, the insertion of an element might fail for a set if it already contains an element with the same value. Therefore, the return type of a set returns two values by using a pair structure (pair is discussed in Section 4.1, page 33):

1. The member second of the pair structure returns whether the insertion was successful.
2. The member first of the pair structure returns the position of the newly inserted element or the position of the still existing element.

In all other cases, the functions return the position of the new element (or of the existing element if the set contains an element with the same value already).

The following example shows how to use this interface to insert a new element into a set. It tries to insert the element with value 3.3 into the set c:

```
std::set<double> c;
...
if (c.insert(3.3).second) {
    std::cout << "3.3 inserted" << std::endl;
```

```
}
else {
    std::cout << "3.3 already exists" << std::endl;
}
```

If you also want to process the new or old positions, the code gets more complicated:

```
// define variable for return value of insert()
std::pair<std::set<float>::iterator,bool> status;

// insert value and assign return value
status = c.insert(value);

// process return value
if (status.second) {
    std::cout << value << " inserted as element "
}
else {
    std::cout << value << " already exists as element "
}
std::cout << std::distance(c.begin(),status.first) + 1
          << std::endl;
```

The output of two calls of this sequence might be as follows:

```
8.9 inserted as element 4
7.7 already exists as element 3
```

Note that the return types of the insert functions with an additional position parameter don't differ. These functions return a single iterator for both sets and multisets. However, these functions have the same effect as the functions without the position parameter. They differ only in their performance. You can pass an iterator position, but this position is processed as a hint to optimize performance. In fact, if the element gets inserted right after the position that is passed as the first argument, the time complexity changes from logarithmic to amortized constant (complexity is discussed in Section 2.3, page 21). The fact that the return type for the insert functions with the additional position hint doesn't have the same difference as the insert functions without the position hint ensures that you have one insert function that has the same interface for all container types. In fact, this interface is used by general inserters. See Section 7.4.2, especially page 275, for details about inserters.

To remove an element that has a certain value, you simply call `erase()`:

```
std::set<Elem> coll;

...

// remove all elements with passed value
coll.erase(value);
```

Unlike with lists, the `erase()` member function does not have the name `remove()` (see page 170 for a discussion of `remove()`). It behaves differently because it returns the number of removed elements. When called for sets, it returns only 0 or 1.

If a multiset contains duplicates, you can't use `erase()` to remove only the first element of these duplicates. Instead, you can code as follows:

```
std::multiset<Elem> coll;

...

// remove first element with passed value
std::multiset<Elem>::iterator pos;
pos = coll.find (elem);
if (pos != coll.end()) {
    coll.erase(pos);
}
```

You should use the member function `find()` instead of the `find()` algorithm here because it is faster (see the example on page 154).

Note that there is another inconsistency in return types here. That is, the return types of the `erase()` functions differ between sequence and associative containers as follows:

1. **Sequence containers** provide the following `erase()` member functions:

```
iterator erase(iterator pos);
iterator erase(iterator beg, iterator end);
```

2. **Associative containers** provide the following `erase()` member functions:

```
void      erase(iterator pos);
void      erase(iterator beg, iterator end);
```

The reason for this difference is performance. It might cost time to find and return the successor in an associative container because the container is implemented as a binary tree. However, as a result, to write generic code for all containers you must ignore the return value.

6.5.3 Exception Handling

Sets and multisets are node-based containers, so any failure to construct a node simply leaves the container as it was. Furthermore, because destructors in general don't throw, removing a node can't fail.

However, for multiple-element insert operations, the need to keep elements sorted makes full recovery from throws impractical. Thus, all single-element insert operations support commit-or-rollback behavior. That is, they either succeed or they have no effect. In addition, it is guaranteed that all multiple-element delete operations always succeed. If copying/assigning the comparison criterion may throw, `swap()` may throw.

See Section 5.11.2, page 139, for a general discussion of exception handling in the STL and Section 6.10.10, page 248, for a list of all container operations that give special guarantees in face of exceptions.

6.5.4   Examples of Using Sets and Multisets

The following program demonstrates some abilities of sets[20]:

```
// cont/set1.cpp

#include <iostream>
#include <set>
#include <algorithm>
#include <iterator>
using namespace std;

int main()
{
    /* type of the collection:
     * - no duplicates
     * - elements are integral values
     * - descending order
     */
    typedef set<int,greater<int> > IntSet;

    IntSet coll1;              // empty set container

    // insert elements in random order
    coll1.insert(4);
    coll1.insert(3);
    coll1.insert(5);
    coll1.insert(1);
    coll1.insert(6);
    coll1.insert(2);
    coll1.insert(5);

    // iterate over all elements and print them
    IntSet::iterator pos;
    for (pos = coll1.begin(); pos != coll1.end(); ++pos) {
        cout << *pos << ' ';
    }
```

---

[20] The definition of distance() has changed, so in older STL versions you must include the file distance.hpp, which is mentioned on page 263.

```
    cout << endl;

    // insert 4 again and process return value
    pair<IntSet::iterator,bool> status = coll1.insert(4);
    if (status.second) {
        cout << "4 inserted as element "
             << distance(coll1.begin(),status.first) + 1
             << endl;
    }
    else {
        cout << "4 already exists" << endl;
    }

    // assign elements to another set with ascending order
    set<int> coll2(coll1.begin(),
                   coll1.end());

    // print all elements of the copy
    copy (coll2.begin(), coll2.end(),
          ostream_iterator<int>(cout," "));
    cout << endl;

    // remove all elements up to element with value 3
    coll2.erase (coll2.begin(), coll2.find(3));

    // remove all elements with value 5
    int num;
    num = coll2.erase (5);
    cout << num << " element(s) removed" << endl;

    // print all elements
    copy (coll2.begin(), coll2.end(),
          ostream_iterator<int>(cout," "));
    cout << endl;
}
```

At first, the type definition

```
typedef set<int,greater<int> > IntSet;
```

defines a short type name for a set of `ints` with descending order. After an empty set is created, several elements are inserted by using `insert()`:

```
IntSet coll1;

coll1.insert(4);
...
```

Note that the element with value 5 is inserted twice. However, the second insertion is ignored because sets do not allow duplicates.

After printing all elements, the program tries again to insert the element 4. This time it processes the return values of `insert()` as discussed on page 183.

The statement

```
set<int> coll2(coll1.begin(),coll1.end());
```

creates a new set of `ints` with ascending order and initializes it with the elements of the old set.[21]

Both containers have different sorting criteria, so their types differ and you can't assign or compare them directly. However, you can use algorithms, which in general are able to handle different container types as long as the element types are equal or convertible.

The statement

```
coll2.erase (coll2.begin(), coll2.find(3));
```

removes all elements up to the element with value 3. Note that the element with value 3 is the end of the range, so that it is not removed.

Lastly, all elements with value 5 are removed:

```
int num;
num = coll2.erase (5);
cout << num << " element(s) removed" << endl;
```

The output of the whole program is as follows:

```
6 5 4 3 2 1
4 already exists
1 2 3 4 5 6
1 element(s) removed
3 4 6
```

---

[21] This statement requires several new language features; namely, member templates and default template arguments. If your system does not provide them, you must program as follows:

```
set<int,less<int> > coll2;
copy (coll1.begin(), coll1.end(),
        inserter(coll2,coll2.begin()));
```

For multisets, the same program looks a bit differently and produces different results:

```
// cont/mset1.cpp

#include <iostream>
#include <set>
#include <algorithm>
#include <iterator>
using namespace std;

int main()
{
    /* type of the collection:
     * - duplicates allowed
     * - elements are integral values
     * - descending order
     */
    typedef multiset<int,greater<int> > IntSet;

    IntSet coll1;          // empty multiset container

    // insert elements in random order
    coll1.insert(4);
    coll1.insert(3);
    coll1.insert(5);
    coll1.insert(1);
    coll1.insert(6);
    coll1.insert(2);
    coll1.insert(5);

    // iterate over all elements and print them
    IntSet::iterator pos;
    for (pos = coll1.begin(); pos != coll1.end(); ++pos) {
        cout << *pos << ' ';
    }
    cout << endl;

    // insert 4 again and process return value
    IntSet::iterator ipos = coll1.insert(4);
    cout << "4 inserted as element "
         << distance(coll1.begin(),ipos) + 1 << endl;
```

```
// assign elements to another multiset with ascending order
multiset<int> coll2(coll1.begin(),
                    coll1.end());

// print all elements of the copy
copy (coll2.begin(), coll2.end(),
      ostream_iterator<int>(cout," "));
cout << endl;

// remove all elements up to element with value 3
coll2.erase (coll2.begin(), coll2.find(3));

// remove all elements with value 5
int num;
num = coll2.erase (5);
cout << num << " element(s) removed" << endl;

// print all elements
copy (coll2.begin(), coll2.end(),
      ostream_iterator<int>(cout," "));
cout << endl;
}
```

In all cases type `set` was changed to `multiset`. In addition, the processing of the return value of `insert()` looks different:

```
IntSet::iterator ipos = coll1.insert(4);
cout << "4 inserted as element "
     << distance(coll1.begin(),ipos) + 1
     << endl;
```

Because multisets may contain duplicates, the insertion can fail only if an exception gets thrown. Thus, the return type is only the iterator position of the new element.

The output of the program changed as follows:

```
6 5 5 4 3 2 1
4 inserted as element 5
1 2 3 4 4 5 5 6
2 element(s) removed
3 4 4 6
```

6.5.5   Example of Specifying the Sorting Criterion at Runtime

Normally you define the sorting criterion as part of the type, either by passing it as a second template argument or by using the default sorting criterion less<>. However, sometimes you must process the sorting criterion at runtime, or you may need different sorting criteria with the same data type. In this case, you need a special type for the sorting criterion — one that lets you pass your sorting details at runtime. The following example program demonstrates how to do this:

```cpp
// cont/setcmp.cpp

#include <iostream>
#include <set>
#include "print.hpp"
using namespace std;

// type for sorting criterion
template <class T>
class RuntimeCmp {
  public:
    enum cmp_mode {normal, reverse};
  private:
    cmp_mode mode;
  public:
    // constructor for sorting criterion
    // - default criterion uses value normal
    RuntimeCmp (cmp_mode m=normal) : mode(m) {
    }
    // comparison of elements
    bool operator() (const T& t1, const T& t2) const {
        return mode == normal ? t1 < t2 : t2 < t1;
    }
    // comparison of sorting criteria
    bool operator== (const RuntimeCmp& rc) {
        return mode == rc.mode;
    }
};

// type of a set that uses this sorting criterion
typedef set<int,RuntimeCmp<int> > IntSet;

// forward declaration
```

```
void fill (IntSet& set);

int main()
{
    // create, fill, and print set with normal element order
    // - uses default sorting criterion
    IntSet coll1;
    fill(coll1);
    PRINT_ELEMENTS (coll1, "coll1: ");

    // create sorting criterion with reverse element order
    RuntimeCmp<int> reverse_order(RuntimeCmp<int>::reverse);

    // create, fill, and print set with reverse element order
    IntSet coll2(reverse_order);
    fill(coll2);
    PRINT_ELEMENTS (coll2, "coll2: ");

    // assign elements AND sorting criterion
    coll1 = coll2;
    coll1.insert(3);
    PRINT_ELEMENTS (coll1, "coll1: ");

    // just to make sure...
    if (coll1.value_comp() == coll2.value_comp()) {
        cout << "coll1 and coll2 have same sorting criterion"
            << endl;
    }
    else {
        cout << "coll1 and coll2 have different sorting criterion"
            << endl;
    }
}

void fill (IntSet& set)
{
    // fill insert elements in random order
    set.insert(4);
    set.insert(7);
```

```
        set.insert(5);
        set.insert(1);
        set.insert(6);
        set.insert(2);
        set.insert(5);
    }
```

In this program, `RuntimeCmp<>` is a simple template that provides the general ability to specify, at runtime, the sorting criterion for any type. Its default constructor sorts in ascending order using the default value `normal`. It also is possible to pass `RuntimeCmp<>::reverse` to sort in descending order.

The output of the program is as follows:

```
coll1: 1 2 4 5 6 7
coll2: 7 6 5 4 2 1
coll1: 7 6 5 4 3 2 1
coll1 and coll2 have same sorting criterion
```

Note that `coll1` and `coll2` have the same type, which is used in `fill()`, for example. Note also that the assignment operator assigns the elements *and* the sorting criterion (otherwise an assignment would be an easy way to compromise the sorting criterion).

6.6   Maps and Multimaps

Map and multimap containers are containers that manage key/value pairs as elements. They sort their elements automatically according to a certain sorting criterion that is used for the actual key. The difference between the two is that multimaps allow duplicates, whereas maps do not (Figure 6.8).

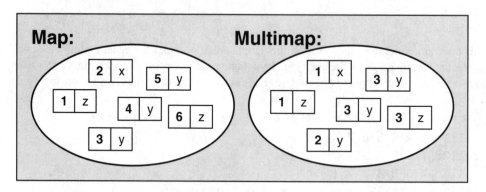

Figure 6.8. Maps and Multimaps

To use a map or multimap, you must include the header file `<map>`[22]:

```
#include <map>
```

There, the types are defined as class templates inside namespace `std`:

```
namespace std {
    template <class Key, class T,
             class Compare = less<Key>,
             class Allocator = allocator<pair<const Key,T> > >
    class map;

    template <class Key, class T,
             class Compare = less<Key>,
             class Allocator = allocator<pair<const Key,T> > >
    class multimap;
}
```

The first template argument is the type of the element's key, and the second template argument is the type of the element's value. The elements of a map or multimap may have any types `Key` and `T` that meet the following two requirements:

---

[22] In the original STL, the header file for maps was `<map.h>`, and for multimaps it was `<multimap.h>`.

1. The key/value pair must be assignable and copyable.

2. The key must be comparable with the sorting criterion.

The optional third template argument defines the sorting criterion. Like sets, this sorting criterion must define a "strict weak ordering" (see page 176). The elements are sorted according to their keys, thus the value doesn't matter for the order of the elements. The sorting criterion is also used to check equality; that is, two elements are equal if neither key is less than the other. If a special sorting criterion is not passed, the default criterion `less` is used. The function object `less` sorts the elements by comparing them with operator < (see page 305 for details about `less`).[23]

The optional fourth template parameter defines the memory model (see Chapter 15). The default memory model is the model `allocator`, which is provided by the C++ standard library.[24]

6.6.1 Abilities of Maps and Multimaps

Like all standardized associative container classes, maps and multimaps are usually implemented as balanced binary trees (Figure 6.9). The standard does not specify this but it follows from the complexity of the map and multimap operations. In fact, sets, multisets, maps, and multimaps typically use the same internal data type. So, you could consider sets and multisets as special maps and multimaps, respectively, for which the value and the key of the elements are the same objects. Thus, maps and multimaps have all the abilities and operations of sets and multisets. Some minor differences exist, however. First, their elements are key/value pairs. In addition, maps can be used as associative arrays.

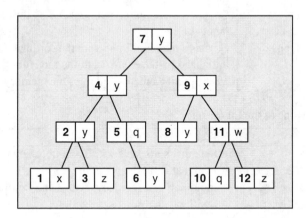

Figure 6.9. Internal Structure of Maps and Multimaps

---

[23] In systems without support for default template parameters, the third argument typically is mandatory.

[24] In systems without support for default template parameters, the fourth argument typically is missing.

Maps and multimaps sort their elements automatically according to the element's keys. Thus they have good performance when searching for elements that have a certain key. Searching for elements that have a certain value promotes bad performance. Automatic sorting imposes an important constraint on maps and multimaps: You may *not* change the key of an element directly because this might compromise the correct order. To modify the key of an element, you must remove the element that has the old key and insert a new element that has the new key and the old value (see page 201 for details). As a consequence, from the iterator's point of view, the element's key is constant. However, a direct modification of the value of the element is still possible (provided the type of the value is not constant).

6.6.2   Map and Multimap Operations

Create, Copy, and Destroy Operations

Table 6.26 lists the constructors and destructors of maps and multimaps.

Operation	Effect
map c	Creates an empty map/multimap without any elements
map c(op)	Creates an empty map/multimap that uses op as the sorting criterion
map c1(c2)	Creates a copy of another map/multimap of the same type (all elements are copied)
map c(beg,end)	Creates a map/multimap initialized by the elements of the range [beg,end)
map c(beg,end,op)	Creates a map/multimap with the sorting criterion op initialized by the elements of the range [beg,end)
c.~*map*()	Destroys all elements and frees the memory

Here, *map* may be one of the following:

map	Effect
map<Key,Elem>	A map that sorts keys with less<> (operator <)
map<Key,Elem,Op>	A map that sorts keys with Op
multimap<Key,Elem>	A multimap that sorts keys with less<> (operator <)
multimap<Key,Elem,Op>	A multimap that sorts keys with Op

Table 6.26. Constructors and Destructors of Maps and Multimaps

You can define the sorting criterion in two ways:

1. **As a template parameter.**
   For example[25]:

   ```
   std::map<float,std::string,std::greater<float> > coll;
   ```

   In this case, the sorting criterion is part of the type. Thus, the type system ensures that only containers with the same sorting criterion can be combined. This is the usual way to specify the sorting criterion. To be more precise, the third parameter is the *type* of the sorting criterion. The concrete sorting criterion is the function object that gets created with the container. To do this, the constructor of the container calls the default constructor of the type of the sorting criterion. See page 294 for an example that uses a user-defined sorting criterion.

2. **As a constructor parameter.**
   In this case you might have a type for several sorting criteria, and the initial value or state of the sorting criteria might differ. This is useful when processing the sorting criterion at runtime, or when sorting criteria are needed that are different but of the same data type. A typical example is specifying the sorting criterion for string keys at runtime. See page 213 for a complete example.

If no special sorting criterion is passed, the default sorting criterion, function object less<>, is used, which sorts the elements by using operator <.[26]

You should make a type definition to avoid the boring repetition of the type whenever it is used:

```
typedef std::map<std::string,float,std::greater<std::string> >
        StringFloatMap;

...

StringFloatMap coll;
```

The constructor for the beginning and the end of a range could be used to initialize the container with elements from containers that have other types, from arrays, or from the standard input. See Section 6.1.2, page 144, for details. However, the elements are key/value pairs, so you must ensure that the elements from the source range have or are convertible into type pair<*key*,*value*>.

Nonmodifying and Special Search Operations

Maps and multimaps provide the usual nonmodifying operations — those that query size aspects and make comparisons (Table 6.27).

---

[25] Note that you have to put a space between the two ">" characters. ">>" would be parsed as shift operator, which would result in a syntax error.

[26] In systems without support for default template parameters, you typically must always pass the sorting criterion as follows:

```
map<float,string,less<float> > coll;
```

Operation	Effect
`c.size()`	Returns the actual number of elements
`c.empty()`	Returns whether the container is empty (equivalent to `size()==0`, but might be faster)
`c.max_size()`	Returns the maximum number of elements possible
`c1 == c2`	Returns whether c1 is equal to c2
`c1 != c2`	Returns whether c1 is not equal to c2 (equivalent to `!(c1==c2)`)
`c1 < c2`	Returns whether c1 is less than c2
`c1 > c2`	Returns whether c1 is greater than c2 (equivalent to `c2<c1`)
`c1 <= c2`	Returns whether c1 is less than or equal to c2 (equivalent to `!(c2<c1)`)
`c1 >= c2`	Returns whether c1 is greater than or equal to c2 (equivalent to `!(c1<c2)`)

Table 6.27. Nonmodifying Operations of Maps and Multimaps

Comparisons are provided only for containers of the same type. Thus, the key, the value, and the sorting criterion must be of the same type. Otherwise, a type error occurs at compile time. For example:

```cpp
std::map<float,std::string> c1;          // sorting criterion: less<>
std::map<float,std::string,std::greater<float> > c2;

...
if (c1 == c2) {                          // ERROR: different types
    ...
}
```

To check whether a container is less than another container is done by a lexicographical comparison (see page 360). To compare containers of different types (different sorting criterion), you must use the comparing algorithms of Section 9.5.4, page 356.

Special Search Operations

Like sets and multisets, maps and multimaps provide special search member functions that perform better because of their internal tree structure (Table 6.28).

The `find()` member function searches for the first element that has the appropriate key and returns its iterator position. If no such element is found, `find()` returns `end()` of the container. You can't use the `find()` member function to search for an element that has a certain value. Instead, you have to use a general algorithm such as the `find_if()` algorithm, or program an explicit loop. Here is an example of a simple loop that does something with each element that has a certain value:

```cpp
std::multimap<std::string,float> coll;
...
// do something with all elements having a certain value
std::multimap<std::string,float>::iterator pos;
for (pos = coll.begin(); pos != coll.end(); ++pos) {
```

Operation	Effect
count(key)	Returns the number of elements with key key
find(key)	Returns the position of the first element with key key or end()
lower_bound(key)	Returns the first position where an element with key key would get inserted (the first element with key >= key)
upper_bound(key)	Returns the last position where an element with key key would get inserted (the first element with key > key)
equal_range(key)	Returns the first and last positions where elements with key key would get inserted (the range of elements with key == key)

Table 6.28. Special Search Operations of Maps and Multimaps

```
if (pos->second == value) {
    do_something();
}
}
```

Be careful when you want to use such a loop to remove elements. It might happen that you saw off the branch on which you are sitting. See page 204 for details about this issue.

Using the find_if() algorithm to search for an element that has a certain value is even more complicated than writing a loop because you have to provide a function object that compares the value of an element with a certain value. See page 211 for an example.

The lower_bound(), upper_bound(), and equal_range() functions behave as they do for sets (see page 180), except that the elements are key/value pairs.

Assignments

Maps and multimaps provide only the fundamental assignment operations that all containers provide (Table 6.29). See page 147 for more details.

Operation	Effect
c1 = c2	Assigns all elements of c2 to c1
c1.swap(c2)	Swaps the data of c1 and c2
swap(c1,c2)	Same (as global function)

Table 6.29. Assignment Operations of Maps and Multimaps

For these operations both containers must have the same type. In particular, the type of the comparison criteria must be the same, although the comparison criteria themselves may be different. See page 213 for an example of different sorting criteria that have the same type. If the criteria are different, they also get assigned or swapped.

Iterator Functions and Element Access

Maps and multimaps do not provide direct element access, so the usual way to access elements is via iterators. An exception to that rule is that maps provide the subscript operator to access elements directly. This is covered in Section 6.6.3, page 205. Table 6.30 lists the usual member functions for iterators that maps and multimaps provide.

Operation	Effect
`c.begin()`	Returns a bidirectional iterator for the first element (keys are considered `const`)
`c.end()`	Returns a bidirectional iterator for the position after the last element (keys are considered `const`)
`c.rbegin()`	Returns a reverse iterator for the first element of a reverse iteration
`c.rend()`	Returns a reverse iterator for the position after the last element of a reverse iteration

Table 6.30. Iterator Operations of Maps and Multimaps

As for all associative container classes, the iterators are bidirectional (see Section 7.2.4, page 255). Thus, you can't use them in algorithms that are provided only for random access iterators (such as algorithms for sorting or random shuffling).

More important is the constraint that the key of all elements inside a map and a multimap is considered to be constant. Thus, the type of the elements is `pair<const Key, T>`. This is also necessary to ensure that you can't compromise the order of the elements by changing their keys. However, you can't call any modifying algorithm if the destination is a map or multimap. For example, you can't call the `remove()` algorithm to remove elements because it "removes" only by overwriting "removed" elements with the following arguments (see Section 5.6.2, page 115, for a detailed discussion of this problem). To remove elements in maps and multimaps, you can use only member functions provided by the container.

The following is an example of the use of iterators:

```
std::map<std::string,float> coll;
...
std::map<std::string,float>::iterator pos;
for (pos = coll.begin(); pos != coll.end(); ++pos) {
    std::cout << "key: "   << pos->first  << "\t"
              << "value: " << pos->second << std::endl;
}
```

Here, the iterator `pos` iterates through the sequence of `string`/`float` pairs. The expression

```
pos->first
```

yields the key of the actual element, whereas the expression

```
pos->second
```

yields the value of the actual element.[27]

Trying to change the value of the key results in an error:

```
pos->first = "hello";      // ERROR at compile time
```

However, changing the value of the element is no problem (as long as the type of the value is not constant):

```
pos->second = 13.5;        // OK
```

To change the key of an element, you have only one choice: You must replace the old element with a new element that has the same value. Here is a generic function that does this:

```
// cont/newkey.hpp

namespace MyLib {
    template <class Cont>
    inline
    bool replace_key (Cont& c,
                      const typename Cont::key_type& old_key,
                      const typename Cont::key_type& new_key)
    {
        typename Cont::iterator pos;
        pos = c.find(old_key);
        if (pos != c.end()) {
            // insert new element with value of old element
            c.insert(typename Cont::value_type(new_key,
                                               pos->second));
            // remove old element
            c.erase(pos);
            return true;
        }
        else {
            // key not found
            return false;
        }
    }
}
```

The `insert()` and `erase()` member functions are discussed in the next subsection.

---

[27] `pos->first` is a shortcut for `(*pos).first`. Some old libraries might only provide the latter.

To use this generic function you simply must pass the container the old key and the new key. For example:

```
std::map<std::string,float> coll;
...
MyLib::replace_key(coll,"old key","new key");
```

It works the same way for multimaps.

Note that maps provide a more convenient way to modify the key of an element. Instead of calling `replace_key()`, you can simply write the following:

```
// insert new element with value of old element
coll["new_key"] = coll["old_key"];
// remove old element
coll.erase("old_key");
```

See Section 6.6.3, page 205, for details about the use of the subscript operator with maps.

Inserting and Removing Elements

Table 6.31 shows the operations provided for maps and multimaps to insert and remove elements.

Operation	Effect
c.insert(elem)	Inserts a copy of elem and returns the position of the new element and, for maps, whether it succeeded
c.insert(pos,elem)	Inserts a copy of elem and returns the position of the new element (pos is used as a hint pointing to where the insert should start the search)
c.insert(beg,end)	Inserts a copy of all elements of the range [beg,end) (returns nothing)
c.erase(key)	Removes all elements with key value key and returns the number of removed elements
c.erase(pos)	Removes the element at iterator position pos (returns nothing)
c.erase(beg,end)	Removes all elements of the range [beg,end) (returns nothing)
c.clear()	Removes all elements (makes the container empty)

Table 6.31. Insert and Remove Operations of Maps and Multimaps

The remarks on page 182 regarding sets and multisets apply here. In particular, the return types of these operations have the same differences as they do for sets and multisets. However, note that the elements here are key/value pairs. So, the use is getting a bit more complicated.

To insert a key/value pair, you must keep in mind that inside maps and multimaps the key is considered to be constant. You either must provide the correct type or you need to provide implicit or explicit type conversions. There are three different ways to pass a value into a map:

1. **Use `value_type`**

   To avoid implicit type conversion, you could pass the correct type explicitly by using `value_type`, which is provided as a type definition by the container type. For example:

   ```
   std::map<std::string,float> coll;
   ...
   coll.insert(std::map<std::string,float>::value_type("otto",
                                                        22.3));
   ```

2. **Use `pair<>`**

   Another way is to use pair<> directly. For example:

   ```
   std::map<std::string,float> coll;
   ...
   // use implicit conversion:
   coll.insert(std::pair<std::string,float>("otto",22.3));
   // use no implicit conversion:
   coll.insert(std::pair<const std::string,float>("otto",22.3));
   ```

   In the first `insert()` statement the type is not quite right, so it is converted into the real element type. For this to happen, the `insert()` member function is defined as a member template.[28]

3. **Use `make_pair()`**

   Probably the most convenient way is to use the `make_pair()` function (see page 36). This function produces a pair object that contains the two values passed as arguments:

   ```
   std::map<std::string,float> coll;
   ...
   coll.insert(std::make_pair("otto",22.3));
   ```

   Again, the necessary type conversions are performed by the `insert()` member template.

Here is a simple example of the insertion of an element into a map that also checks whether the insertion was successful:

```
std::map<std::string,float> coll;
...
if (coll.insert(std::make_pair("otto",22.3)).second) {
    std::cout << "OK, could insert otto/22.3" << std::endl;
}
else {
    std::cout << "Oops, could not insert otto/22.3 "
              << "(key otto already exists)" << std::endl;
}
```

---

[28] If your system does not provide member templates, you must pass an element with the correct type. This usually requires that you make the type conversions explicit.

See page 182 for a discussion regarding the return values of the `insert()` functions and more examples that also apply to maps. Note, again, that maps provide a more convenient way to insert (and set) elements with the subscript operator. This is discussed in Section 6.6.3, page 205.

To remove an element that has a certain value, you simply call `erase()`:

```
std::map<std::string,float> coll;

...
// remove all elements with the passed key
coll.erase(key);
```

This version of `erase()` returns the number of removed elements. When called for maps, the return value of `erase()` can only be 0 or 1.

If a multimap contains duplicates, you can't use `erase()` to remove only the first element of these duplicates. Instead, you could code as follows:

```
typedef std::multimap<std::string,float> StringFloatMMap;
StringFloatMMap coll;

...
// remove first element with passed key
StringFloatMMap::iterator pos;
pos = coll.find(key);
if (pos != coll.end()) {
    coll.erase(pos);
}
```

You should use the member function `find()` instead of the `find()` algorithm here because it is faster (see an example with the `find()` algorithm on page 154). However, you can't use the `find()` member functions to remove elements that have a certain value (instead of a certain key). See page 198 for a detailed discussion of this topic.

When removing elements, be careful not to saw off the branch on which you are sitting. There is a big danger that you will remove an element to which your iterator is referring. For example:

```
typedef std::map<std::string,float> StringFloatMap;
StringFloatMap coll;
StringFloatMap::iterator pos;

...
for (pos = coll.begin(); pos != coll.end(); ++pos) {
    if (pos->second == value) {
        coll.erase(pos);                         // RUNTIME ERROR !!!
    }
}
```

Calling `erase()` for the element to which you are referring with pos invalidates pos as an iterator of `coll`. Thus, if you use pos after removing its element without any reinitialization, then all bets are off. In fact, calling ++pos results in undefined behavior.

A solution would be easy if `erase()` always returned the value of the following element:

```
typedef std::map<std::string,float> StringFloatMap;
StringFloatMap coll;
StringFloatMap::iterator pos;
...
for (pos = coll.begin(); pos != coll.end(); ) {
    if (pos->second == value) {
        pos = coll.erase(pos);   // would be fine, but COMPILE TIME ERROR
    }
    else {
        ++pos;
    }
}
```

It was a design decision not to provide this trait, because if not needed, it costs unnecessary time. I don't agree with this decision however, because code is getting more error prone and complicated (and may cost even more in terms of time).

Here is an example of the correct way to remove elements to which an iterator refers:

```
typedef std::map<std::string,float> StringFloatMap;
StringFloatMap coll;
StringFloatMap::iterator pos;
...
// remove all elements having a certain value
for (pos = coll.begin(); pos != coll.end(); ) {
    if (pos->second == value) {
        coll.erase(pos++);
    }
    else {
        ++pos;
    }
}
```

Note that `pos++` increments `pos` so that it refers to the next element but yields a copy of its original value. Thus, `pos` doesn't refer to the element that is removed when `erase()` is called.

6.6.3 Using Maps as Associative Arrays

Associative containers don't typically provide abilities for direct element access. Instead, you must use iterators. For maps, however, there is an exception to this rule. Nonconstant maps provide a subscript operator for direct element access (Table 6.32). However, the index of the subscript operator is not the integral position of the element. Instead, it is the key that is used to identify the element. This means that the index may have any type rather than only an integral type. Such an interface is the interface of a so-called *associative array*.

Operation	Effect
m[key]	Returns a reference to the value of the element with key key
	Inserts an element with key if it does not yet exist

Table 6.32. Direct Element Access of Maps with Operator [ ]

The type of the index is not the only difference from ordinary arrays. In addition, you can't have a wrong index. If you use a key as the index, for which no element yet exists, a new element gets inserted into the map automatically. The value of the new element is initialized by the default constructor of its type. Thus, to use this feature you can't use a value type that has no default constructor. Note that the fundamental data types provide a default constructor that initializes their values to zero (see page 14).

This behavior of an associative array has both advantages and disadvantages:

- The advantage is that you can insert new elements into a map with a more convenient interface. For example:

```
std::map<std::string,float> coll;      // empty collection

/* insert "otto"/7.7 as key/value pair
 * - first it inserts "otto"/float()
 * - then it assigns 7.7
 */
coll["otto"] = 7.7;
```

The statement

```
coll["otto"] = 7.7;
```

is processed here as follows:

1. Process coll["otto"] expression:
   - If an element with key "otto" exists, the expression returns the value of the element by reference.
   - If, as in this example, no element with key "otto" exists, the expression inserts a new element automatically with "otto" as key and the value of the default constructor of the value type as the element value. It then returns a reference to that new value of the new element.

2. Assign value 7.7:
   - The second part of the statement assigns 7.7 to the value of the new or existing element.

The map then contains an element with key "otto" and value 7.7.

- The disadvantage is that you might insert new elements by accident or mistake. For example, the following statement does something you probably hadn't intended or expected:

```
std::cout << coll["ottto"];
```

It inserts a new element with key `"ottto"` and prints its value, which is 0 by default. However, it should have generated an error message telling you that you wrote `"otto"` incorrectly.

Note, too, that this way of inserting elements is slower than the usual way for maps, which is described on page 202. This is because the new value is first initialized by the default value of its type, which is then overwritten by the correct value.

6.6.4   Exception Handling

Maps and multimaps provide the same behavior as sets and multisets with respect to exception safety. This behavior is mentioned on page 185.

6.6.5   Examples of Using Maps and Multimaps

Using a Map as an Associative Array

The following example shows the use of a map as an associative array. The map is used as a stock chart. The elements of the map are pairs in which the key is the name of the stock and the value is its price:

```
// cont/map1.cpp

#include <iostream>
#include <map>
#include <string>
using namespace std;

int main()
{
    /* create map / associative array
     * - keys are strings
     * - values are floats
     */
    typedef map<string,float> StringFloatMap;

    StringFloatMap stocks;          // create empty container

    // insert some elements
    stocks["BASF"] = 369.50;
```

```cpp
    stocks["VW"] = 413.50;
    stocks["Daimler"] = 819.00;
    stocks["BMW"] = 834.00;
    stocks["Siemens"] = 842.20;

    // print all elements
    StringFloatMap::iterator pos;
    for (pos = stocks.begin(); pos != stocks.end(); ++pos) {
        cout << "stock: " << pos->first << "\t"
             << "price: " << pos->second << endl;
    }
    cout << endl;

    // boom (all prices doubled)
    for (pos = stocks.begin(); pos != stocks.end(); ++pos) {
        pos->second *= 2;
    }

    // print all elements
    for (pos = stocks.begin(); pos != stocks.end(); ++pos) {
        cout << "stock: " << pos->first << "\t"
             << "price: " << pos->second << endl;
    }
    cout << endl;

    /* rename key from "VW" to "Volkswagen"
     * - only provided by exchanging element
     */
    stocks["Volkswagen"] = stocks["VW"];
    stocks.erase("VW");

    // print all elements
    for (pos = stocks.begin(); pos != stocks.end(); ++pos) {
        cout << "stock: " << pos->first << "\t"
             << "price: " << pos->second << endl;
    }
}
```

The program has the following output:

```
stock: BASF       price: 369.5
stock: BMW        price: 834
stock: Daimler    price: 819
stock: Siemens    price: 842.2
stock: VW         price: 413.5

stock: BASF       price: 739
stock: BMW        price: 1668
stock: Daimler    price: 1638
stock: Siemens    price: 1684.4
stock: VW         price: 827

stock: BASF       price: 739
stock: BMW        price: 1668
stock: Daimler    price: 1638
stock: Siemens    price: 1684.4
stock: Volkswagen        price: 827
```

Using a Multimap as a Dictionary

The following example shows how to use a multimap as a dictionary:

```cpp
// cont/mmap1.cpp

#include <iostream>
#include <map>
#include <string>
#include <iomanip>
using namespace std;

int main()
{
    // define multimap type as string/string dictionary
    typedef multimap<string,string> StrStrMMap;

    // create empty dictionary
    StrStrMMap dict;

    // insert some elements in random order
    dict.insert(make_pair("day","Tag"));
```

```cpp
dict.insert(make_pair("strange","fremd"));
dict.insert(make_pair("car","Auto"));
dict.insert(make_pair("smart","elegant"));
dict.insert(make_pair("trait","Merkmal"));
dict.insert(make_pair("strange","seltsam"));
dict.insert(make_pair("smart","raffiniert"));
dict.insert(make_pair("smart","klug"));
dict.insert(make_pair("clever","raffiniert"));

// print all elements
StrStrMMap::iterator pos;
cout.setf (ios::left, ios::adjustfield);
cout << ' ' << setw(10) << "english "
    << "german " << endl;
cout << setfill('-') << setw(20) << ""
    << setfill(' ') << endl;
for (pos = dict.begin(); pos != dict.end(); ++pos) {
    cout << ' ' << setw(10) << pos->first.c_str()
        << pos->second << endl;
}
cout << endl;

// print all values for key "smart"
string word("smart");
cout << word << ": " << endl;
for (pos = dict.lower_bound(word);
    pos != dict.upper_bound(word); ++pos) {
        cout << "    " << pos->second << endl;
}

// print all keys for value "raffiniert"
word = ("raffiniert");
cout << word << ": " << endl;
for (pos = dict.begin(); pos != dict.end(); ++pos) {
    if (pos->second == word) {
        cout << "    " << pos->first << endl;
    }
}
}
```

The program has the following output:

```
english     german
--------------------

car         Auto
clever      raffiniert
day         Tag
smart       elegant
smart       raffiniert
smart       klug
strange     fremd
strange     seltsam
trait       Merkmal

smart:
    elegant
    raffiniert
    klug
raffiniert:
    clever
    smart
```

Find Elements with Certain Values

The following example shows how to use the global find_if() algorithm to find an element with a certain value:

```cpp
// cont/mapfind.cpp

#include <iostream>
#include <algorithm>
#include <map>
using namespace std;

/* function object to check the value of a map element
 */
template <class K, class V>
class value_equals {
  private:
    V value;
  public:
    // constructor (initialize value to compare with)
```

```
        value_equals (const V& v)
          : value(v) {
        }
        // comparison
        bool operator() (pair<const K, V> elem) {
            return elem.second == value;
        }
};

int main()
{
    typedef map<float,float> FloatFloatMap;
    FloatFloatMap coll;
    FloatFloatMap::iterator pos;

    // fill container
    coll[1]=7;
    coll[2]=4;
    coll[3]=2;
    coll[4]=3;
    coll[5]=6;
    coll[6]=1;
    coll[7]=3;

    // search an element with key 3.0
    pos = coll.find(3.0);                       // logarithmic complexity
    if (pos != coll.end()) {
        cout << pos->first << ": "
             << pos->second << endl;
    }

    // search an element with value 3.0
    pos = find_if(coll.begin(),coll.end(),      // linear complexity
                 value_equals<float,float>(3.0));
    if (pos != coll.end()) {
        cout << pos->first << ": "
             << pos->second << endl;
    }
}
```

The output of the program is as follows:

```
3: 2
4: 3
```

6.6.6 Example with Maps, Strings, and Sorting Criterion at Runtime

Here is another example. It is for advanced programmers rather than STL beginners. You can take it as an example of both the power and the snags of the STL. In particular, this example demonstrates the following techniques:

- How to use maps
- How to write and use function objects
- How to define a sorting criterion at runtime
- How to compare strings in a case-insensitive way

```cpp
// cont/mapcmp.cpp

#include <iostream>
#include <iomanip>
#include <map>
#include <string>
#include <algorithm>
using namespace std;

/* function object to compare strings
 * - allows you to set the comparison criterion at runtime
 * - allows you to compare case insensitive
 */
class RuntimeStringCmp {
  public:
    // constants for the comparison criterion
    enum cmp_mode {normal, nocase};
  private:
    // actual comparison mode
    const cmp_mode mode;

    // auxiliary function to compare case insensitive
    static bool nocase_compare (char c1, char c2)
    {
```

The program has the following output:

```
Bestatter        undertaker
Deutschland      Germany
Haken            snag
Hund             dog
Unternehmen      enterprise
arbeiten         work
deutsch          German
gehen            walk
unternehmen      undertake

arbeiten         work
Bestatter        undertaker
deutsch          German
Deutschland      Germany
gehen            walk
Haken            snag
Hund             dog
Unternehmen      undertake
```

The first block of the output prints the contents of the first container that compares with operator <. The output starts with all uppercase keys followed by all lowercase keys.

The second block prints all case-insensitive items, so the order changed. But note, the second block has one item less. This is because the uppercase word "Unternehmen" is, from a case-insensitive point of view, equal to the lowercase word "unternehmen,"[29] and we use a map that does not allow duplicates according to its comparison criterion. Unfortunately the result is a mess because the German key that is the translation for "enterprise" got the value "undertake." So probably a multimap should be used here. This makes sense because a multimap is the typical container for dictionaries.

---

[29] In German all nouns are written with an initial capital letter whereas all verbs are written in lowercase letters.

6.7   Other STL Containers

The STL is a framework. In addition to the standard container classes it allows you to use other data structures as containers. You can use strings or ordinary arrays as STL containers, or you can write and use special containers that meet special needs. Doing this has the advantage that you can benefit from algorithms, such as sorting or merging, for your own type. Such a framework is a good example of the *Open Closed Principle*[30]: *open* for extension; *closed* for modification.

There are three different approaches to making containers "STL-able":

1. **The invasive approach**[31]
   You simply provide the interface that an STL container requires. In particular, you need the usual member functions of containers such as `begin()` and `end()`. This approach is invasive because it requires that a container be written in a certain way.

2. **The noninvasive approach**[31]
   You write or provide special iterators that are used as an interface between the algorithms and special containers. This approach is noninvasive. All it requires is the ability to step through all of the elements of a container, an ability that any container provides in some way.

3. **The wrapper approach**
   Combining the two previous approaches, you write a wrapper class that encapsulates any data structure with an STL container-like interface.

This subsection first discusses strings as a standard container, which is an example of the invasive approach. It then covers an important standard container that uses the noninvasive approach: ordinary arrays. However, you can also use the wrapper approach to access data of an ordinary array. Finally, this section subdiscusses some aspects of an important container that is not part of the standard: a hash table.

Whoever wants to write an STL container might also support the ability to get parameterized for different allocators. The C++ standard library provides some special functions and classes for programming with allocators and uninitialized memory. See Section 15.2, page 728 for details.

6.7.1   Strings as STL Containers

The string classes of the C++ standard library are an example of the invasive approach of writing STL containers (string classes are introduced and discussed in Chapter 11). Strings can be considered containers of characters. The characters inside the string build a sequence over which you can iterate to process the individual characters. Thus, the standard string classes provide the container interface of the STL. They provide the `begin()` and `end()` member functions, which return random access iterators to iterate over a string. They also provide some operations for iterators and iterator adapters. For example, `push_back()` is provided to enable the use of back inserters.

---

[30] I first heard of the Open Closed Principle from Robert C. Martin, who himself heard it from Bertrand Meyer.

[31] Instead of *invasive* and *noninvasive* sometimes the terms *intrusive* and *nonintrusive* are used.

Note that string processing from the STL's point of view is a bit unusual. This is because normally you process strings as a whole object (you pass, copy, or assign strings). However, when individual character processing is of interest, the ability to use STL algorithms might be helpful. For example, you could read the characters with istream iterators or you could transform string characters, such as make them uppercase or lowercase. In addition, by using STL algorithms you can use a special comparison criterion for strings. The standard string interface does not provide that ability.

Section 11.2.13, page 497, which is part of the string chapter, discusses the STL aspects of strings in more detail and gives examples.

6.7.2   Ordinary Arrays as STL Containers

You can use ordinary arrays as STL containers. However, ordinary arrays are not classes, so they don't provide member functions such as begin() and end(), and you can't define member functions for them. Here, either the noninvasive approach or the wrapper approach must be used.

Using Ordinary Arrays Directly

Using the noninvasive approach is simple. You only need objects that are able to iterate over the elements of an array by using the STL iterator interface. Actually, such iterators already exist: ordinary pointers. It was a design decision of the STL to use the pointer interface for iterators so that you could use ordinary pointers as iterators. This again shows the generic concept of pure abstraction: Anything that *behaves* like an iterator *is* an iterator. In fact, pointers are random access iterators (see Section 7.2.5, page 255). The following example demonstrates how to use ordinary arrays as STL containers:

```
// cont/array1.cpp

#include <iostream>
#include <algorithm>
#include <functional>
#include <iterator>
using namespace std;

int main()
{
    int coll[] = { 5, 6, 2, 4, 1, 3 };

    // square all elements
    transform (coll, coll+6,        // first source
               coll,                // second source
               coll,                // destination
               multiplies<int>());  // operation
```

```
// sort beginning with the second element
sort (coll+1, coll+6);

// print all elements
copy (coll, coll+6,
      ostream_iterator<int>(cout," "));
cout << endl;
}
```

You must be careful to pass the correct end of the array, as it is done here by using coll+6. And, as usual, you have to make sure that the end of the range is the position after the last element.

The output of the program is as follows:

```
25 1 4 9 16 36
```

Additional examples are on page 382 and page 421.

An Array Wrapper

In his book *The C++ Programming Language*, 3rd edition, Bjarne Stroustrup introduces a useful wrapper class for ordinary arrays. It is safer and has no worse performance than an ordinary array. It also is a good example of a user-defined STL container. This container uses the wrapper approach because it offers the usual container interface as a wrapper around the array.

The class carray (the name is short for "C array" or for "constant size array") is defined as follows[32]:

```
// cont/carray.hpp

#include <cstddef>

template<class T, std::size_t thesize>
class carray {
  private:
    T v[thesize];      // fixed-size array of elements of type T

  public:
    // type definitions
    typedef T       value_type;
    typedef T*      iterator;
```

---

[32] The original array wrapper class by Bjarne Stroustrup is called c_array and is defined in Section 17.5.4 of his book. I have modified it slightly for this book.

```
    typedef const T*   const_iterator;
    typedef T&         reference;
    typedef const T&   const_reference;
    typedef size_t     size_type;
    typedef ptrdiff_t difference_type;

    // iterator support
    iterator begin() { return v; }
    const_iterator begin() const { return v; }
    iterator end() { return v+thesize; }
    const_iterator end() const { return v+thesize; }

    // direct element access
    reference operator[](size_t i) { return v[i]; }
    const_reference operator[](size_t i) const { return v[i]; }

    // size is constant
    size_type size() const { return thesize; }
    size_type max_size() const { return thesize; }

    // conversion to ordinary array
    T* as_array() { return v; }
};
```

Here is an example of the usage of the `carray` class:

```
// cont/carray1.cpp

#include <algorithm>
#include <functional>
#include "carray.hpp"
#include "print.hpp"
using namespace std;

int main()
{
    carray<int,10> a;

    for (unsigned i=0; i<a.size(); ++i) {
        a[i] = i+1;
```

```
        }
        PRINT_ELEMENTS(a);

        reverse(a.begin(),a.end());
        PRINT_ELEMENTS(a);

        transform(a.begin(),a.end(),      // source
                  a.begin(),              // destination
                  negate<int>());         // operation
        PRINT_ELEMENTS(a);
}
```

As you can see, you can use the general container interface operations (`begin()`, `end()`, and operator `[ ]`) to manipulate the container directly. Therefore, you can also use different operations that call `begin()` and `end()`, such as algorithms and the auxiliary function `PRINT_ELEMENTS()`, which is introduced on page 118.

The output of the program is as follows:

```
1 2 3 4 5 6 7 8 9 10
10 9 8 7 6 5 4 3 2 1
-10 -9 -8 -7 -6 -5 -4 -3 -2 -1
```

6.7.3 Hash Tables

One important data structure for collections is not part of the C++ standard library: the hash table. There were suggestions to incorporate hash tables into the standard; however, they were not part of the original STL and the committee decided that the proposal for their inclusion came too late. (At some point you have to stop introducing features and focus on the details. Otherwise, you never finish the work.)

Nevertheless, inside the C++ community several implementations of hash tables are available. Libraries typically provide four kinds of hash tables: `hash_set`, `hash_multiset`, `hash_map`, and `hash_multimap`. According to the other associative containers, the `multi` versions allow duplicates and maps contain key/value pairs. Bjarne Stroustrup discusses `hash_map` as an example of a supplemented STL container in detail in Section 17.6 of his book *The C++ Programming Language*, 3rd edition. For a concrete implementation of hash containers, see, for example, the "STLport" (`http://www.stlport.org/`). Note that different implementations may differ in details because hash containers are not yet standardized.

6.8   Implementing Reference Semantics

In general, STL container classes provide value semantics and not reference semantics. Thus, they create internal copies of the elements they contain and return copies of those elements. Section 5.10.2, page 135, discusses the pros and cons of this approach and touches on its consequences. To summarize, if you want reference semantics in STL containers (whether because copying elements is expensive or because identical elements will be shared by different collections), you should use a smart pointer class that avoids possible errors. Here is one possible solution to the problem. It uses an auxiliary smart pointer class that enables reference counting for the objects to which the pointers refer[33]:

```
// cont/countptr.hpp

#ifndef COUNTED_PTR_HPP
#define COUNTED_PTR_HPP

/* class for counted reference semantics
 * - deletes the object to which it refers when the last CountedPtr
 *   that refers to it is destroyed
 */
template <class T>
class CountedPtr {
  private:
    T* ptr;           // pointer to the value
    long* count;      // shared number of owners

  public:
    // initialize pointer with existing pointer
    // - requires that the pointer p is a return value of new
    explicit CountedPtr (T* p=0)
      : ptr(p), count(new long(1)) {
    }

    // copy pointer (one more owner)
    CountedPtr (const CountedPtr<T>& p) throw()
      : ptr(p.ptr), count(p.count) {
        ++*count;
    }
```

---

[33] Many thanks to Greg Colvin and Beman Dawes for feedback on implementing this class.

```
// destructor (delete value if this was the last owner)
~CountedPtr () throw() {
    dispose();
}

// assignment (unshare old and share new value)
CountedPtr<T>& operator= (const CountedPtr<T>& p) throw() {
    if (this != &p) {
        dispose();
        ptr = p.ptr;
        count = p.count;
        ++*count;
    }
    return *this;
}

// access the value to which the pointer refers
T& operator*() const throw() {
    return *ptr;
}
T* operator->() const throw() {
    return ptr;
}

private:
void dispose() {
    if (--*count == 0) {
        delete count;
        delete ptr;
    }
}
};

#endif /*COUNTED_PTR_HPP*/
```

This class resembles the standard `auto_ptr` class (see Section 4.2, page 38). It expects that the values with which the smart pointers are initialized are return values of operator `new`. However, unlike `auto_ptr`, it allows you to copy these smart pointers while retaining the validity of the

original and the copy. Only if the last smart pointer to the object gets destroyed does the value to
which it refers get `deleted`.

You could improve the class to allow automatic type conversions or the ability to transfer the
ownership away from the smart pointers to the caller.

The following program demonstrates how to use this class:

```
// cont/refsem1.cpp

#include <iostream>
#include <list>
#include <deque>
#include <algorithm>
#include "countptr.hpp"
using namespace std;

void printCountedPtr (CountedPtr<int> elem)
{
    cout << *elem << ' ';
}

int main()
{
    // array of integers (to share in different containers)
    static int values[] = { 3, 5, 9, 1, 6, 4 };

    // two different collections
    typedef CountedPtr<int> IntPtr;
    deque<IntPtr> coll1;
    list<IntPtr> coll2;

    /* insert shared objects into the collections
     * - same order in coll1
     * - reverse order in coll2
     */
    for (int i=0; i<sizeof(values)/sizeof(values[0]); ++i) {
        IntPtr ptr(new int(values[i]));
        coll1.push_back(ptr);
        coll2.push_front(ptr);
    }
```

```
// print contents of both collections
for_each (coll1.begin(), coll1.end(),
          printCountedPtr);
cout << endl;
for_each (coll2.begin(), coll2.end(),
          printCountedPtr);
cout << endl << endl;

/* modify values at different places
 * - square third value in coll1
 * - negate first value in coll1
 * - set first value in coll2 to 0
 */
*coll1[2] *= *coll1[2];
(**coll1.begin()) *= -1;
(**coll2.begin()) = 0;

// print contents of both collections again
for_each (coll1.begin(), coll1.end(),
          printCountedPtr);
cout << endl;
for_each (coll2.begin(), coll2.end(),
          printCountedPtr);
cout << endl;
}
```

The program has the following output:

```
3 5 9 1 6 4
4 6 1 9 5 3

-3 5 81 1 6 0
0 6 1 81 5 -3
```

Note that if you call an auxiliary function that saves one element of the collections (an `IntPtr`) somewhere else, the value to which it refers stays valid even if the collections get destroyed or all of their elements are removed.

See the Boost repository for C++ libraries at `http://www.boost.org/` for a collection of different smart pointer classes as an extension of the C++ standard library. (Class `CountedPtr<>` will probably be called `shared_ptr<>`.)

6.9   When to Use which Container

The C++ standard library provides different container types with different abilities. The question now is: When do you use which container type? Table 6.33 provides an overview. However, it contains general statements that might not fit in reality. For example, if you manage only a few elements you can ignore the complexity because short element processing with linear complexity is better than long element processing with logarithmic complexity.

As a supplement to the table, the following rules of thumb might help:

- By default, you should use a vector. It has the simplest internal data structure and provides random access. Thus, data access is convenient and flexible, and data processing is often fast enough.

- If you insert and/or remove elements often at the beginning and the end of a sequence, you should use a deque. You should also use a deque if it is important that the amount of internal memory used by the container shrinks when elements are removed. Also, because a vector usually uses one block of memory for its elements, a deque might be able to contain more elements because it uses several blocks.

- If you insert, remove, and move elements often in the middle of a container, consider using a list. Lists provide special member functions to move elements from one container to another in constant time. Note, however, that because a list provides no random access, you might suffer significant performance penalties on access to elements inside the list if you only have the beginning of the list.

  Like all node-based containers, a list doesn't invalidate iterators that refer to elements, as long as those elements are part of the container. Vectors invalidate all of their iterators, pointers, and references whenever they exceed their capacity, and part of their iterators, pointers, and references on insertions and deletions. Deques invalidate iterators, pointers, and references when they change their size, respectively.

- If you need a container that handles exceptions in a way that each operation either succeeds or has no effect, you should use either a list (without calling assignment operations and `sort()` and, if comparing the elements may throw, without calling `merge()`, `remove()`, `remove_if()`, and `unique()`; see page 172) or an associative container (without calling the multiple-element insert operations and, if copying/assigning the comparison criterion may throw, without calling `swap()`). See Section 5.11.2, page 139, for a general discussion of exception handling in the STL and Section 6.10.10, page 248, for a table of all container operations with special guarantees in face of exceptions.

- If you often need to search for elements according to a certain criterion, use a set or a multiset that sorts elements according to this sorting criterion. Keep in mind that the logarithmic complexity involved in sorting 1,000 elements is in principle ten times better than that with linear complexity. In this case, the typical advantages of binary trees apply.

  A hash table commonly provides five to ten times faster lookup than a binary tree. So if a hash container is available, you might consider using it even though hash tables are not standardized. However, hash containers have no ordering, so if you need to rely on element order they're no

	Vector	Deque	List	Set	Multiset	Map	Multimap
Typical internal data structure	Dynamic array	Array of arrays	Doubly linked list	Binary tree	Binary tree	Binary tree	Binary tree
Elements	Value	Value	Value	Value	Value	Key/value pair	Key/value pair
Duplicates allowed	Yes	Yes	Yes	No	Yes	Not for the key	Yes
Random access available	Yes	Yes	No	No	No	With key	No
Iterator category	Random access	Random access	Bidirectional	Bidirectional (element constant)	Bidirectional (element constant)	Bidirectional (key constant)	Bidirectional (key constant)
Search/find elements	Slow	Slow	Very slow	Fast	Fast	Fast for key	Fast for key
Inserting/removing of elements is fast	At the end	At the beginning and the end	Anywhere	—	—	—	—
Inserting/removing invalidates iterators, references, pointers	On reallocation	Always	Never	Never	Never	Never	Never
Frees memory for removed elements	Never	Sometimes	Always	Always	Always	Always	Always
Allows memory reservation	Yes	No	—	—	—	—	—
Transaction safe (success or no effect)	Push/pop at the end	Push/pop at the beginning and the end	All except sort () and assignments	All except multiple-element insertions	All except multiple-element insertions	All except multiple-element insertions	All except multiple-element insertions

Table 6.33. Overview of Container Abilities

good. Because they are not part of the C++ standard library, you should have the source code to
stay portable.

- To process key/value pairs, use a map or a multimap (or the hash version, if available).
- If you need an associative array, use a map.
- If you need a dictionary, use a multimap.

A problem that is not easy to solve is how to sort objects according to two different sorting criteria.
For example, you might have to keep elements in an order provided by the user while providing
search capabilities according to another criterion. And as in databases, you need fast access regarding two or more different criteria. In this case, you could probably use two sets or two maps that
share the same objects with different sorting criteria. However, having objects in two collections is
a special issue, which is covered in Section 6.8, page 222.

The automatic sorting of associative containers does not mean that these containers perform
better when sorting is needed. This is because an associative container sorts each time a new element
gets inserted. An often faster way is to use a sequence container and to sort all elements after they
are all inserted by using one of the several sort algorithms (see Section 9.2.2, page 328).

The following are two simple programs that sort all strings read from the standard input and print
them without duplicates by using two different containers:

1. Using a **set**:

```
// cont/sortset.cpp

#include <iostream>
#include <string>
#include <algorithm>
#include <iterator>
#include <set>
using namespace std;

int main()
{
    /* create a string set
     * - initialized by all words from standard input
     */
    set<string> coll((istream_iterator<string>(cin)),
                      istream_iterator<string>());

    // print all elements
    copy (coll.begin(), coll.end(),
          ostream_iterator<string>(cout, "\n"));
}
```

2. Using a **vector**:

```cpp
// cont/sortvec.cpp

#include <iostream>
#include <string>
#include <algorithm>
#include <iterator>
#include <vector>
using namespace std;

int main()
{
    /* create a string vector
     * - initialized by all words from standard input
     */
    vector<string> coll((istream_iterator<string>(cin)),
                        istream_iterator<string>());

    // sort elements
    sort (coll.begin(), coll.end());

    // print all elements ignoring subsequent duplicates
    unique_copy (coll.begin(), coll.end(),
                ostream_iterator<string>(cout, "\n"));
}
```

When I tried both programs with about 150,000 strings on my system, the vector version was approximately 10% faster. Inserting a call of `reserve()` made the vector version 5% faster. Allowing duplicates (using a `multiset` instead of a `set` and calling `copy()` instead of `unique_copy()` respectively) changed things dramatically: The vector version was more than 40% faster! These measurements are not representative; however, they do show that it is often worth trying different ways of processing elements.

In practice, predicting which container type is the best is often difficult. The big advantage of the STL is that you can try different versions without much effort. The major work — implementing the different data structures and algorithms — is done. You have only to combine them in a way that is best for you.

6.10   Container Types and Members in Detail

This section discusses the different STL containers and presents all of the operations that STL containers provide. The types and members are grouped by functionality. For each type and operation this section describes the signature, the behavior, and the container types that provide it. Possible containers are vector, deques, lists, sets, multisets, maps, multimaps, and strings. In the following subsections, *container* means the container type that provides the member.

6.10.1   Type Definitions

container::**value_type**
- The type of elements.
- For sets and multisets, it is constant.
- For maps and multimaps, it is pair <const *key-type*, *mapped-type*>
- Provided by vectors, deques, lists, sets, multisets, maps, multimaps, and strings.

container::**reference**
- The type of element references.
- Typically: *container*::value_type&.
- For vector<bool>, it is an auxiliary class (see page 158).
- Provided by vectors, deques, lists, sets, multisets, maps, multimaps, and strings.

container::**const_reference**
- The type of constant element references.
- Typically: const *container*::value_type&.
- For vector<bool>, it is bool.
- Provided by vectors, deques, lists, sets, multisets, maps, multimaps, and strings.

container::**iterator**
- The type of iterators.
- Provided by vectors, deques, lists, sets, multisets, maps, multimaps, and strings.

container::**const_iterator**
- The type of constant iterators.
- Provided by vectors, deques, lists, sets, multisets, maps, multimaps, and strings.

container::**reverse_iterator**
- The type of reverse iterators.
- Provided by vectors, deques, lists, sets, multisets, maps, and multimaps.

container::**const_reverse_iterator**
- The type of constant reverse iterators.
- Provided by vectors, deques, lists, sets, multisets, maps, multimaps, and strings.

container::**size_type**
- The unsigned integral type for size values.
- Provided by vectors, deques, lists, sets, multisets, maps, multimaps, and strings.

container::**difference_type**
- The signed integral type for difference values.
- Provided by vectors, deques, lists, sets, multisets, maps, multimaps, and strings.

container::**key_type**
- The type of the key of the elements for associative containers.
- For sets and multisets, it is equivalent to `value_type`.
- Provided by sets, multisets, maps, and multimaps.

container::**mapped_type**
- The type of the value of the elements of associative containers.
- Provided by maps and multimaps.

container::**key_compare**
- The type of the comparison criterion of associative containers.
- Provided by sets, multisets, maps, and multimaps.

container::**value_compare**
- The type of the comparison criterion for the whole element type.
- For sets and multisets, it is equivalent to `key_compare`.
- For maps and multimaps, it is an auxiliary class for a comparison criterion that compares only the key part of two elements.
- Provided by sets, multisets, maps, and multimaps.

container::**allocator_type**
- The type of the allocator.
- Provided by vectors, deques, lists, sets, multisets, maps, multimaps, and strings.

6.10.2 Create, Copy, and Destroy Operations

Containers provide the following constructors and destructors. Also, most constructors allow you to pass an allocator as an additional argument (see Section 6.10.9, page 246).

container::*container* ()
- The default constructor.
- Creates a new empty container.
- Provided by vectors, deques, lists, sets, multisets, maps, multimaps, and strings.

explicit *container*::*container* (**const CompFunc&** *op*)

- Creates a new empty container with *op* used as the sorting criterion (see page 191 and page 213 for examples).
- The sorting criterion must define a "strict weak ordering" (see page 176).
- Provided by sets, multisets, maps, and multimaps.

explicit *container*::*container* (**const** *container&* *c*)

- The copy constructor.
- Creates a new container as a copy of the existing container *c*.
- Calls the copy constructor for every element in *c*.
- Provided by vectors, deques, lists, sets, multisets, maps, multimaps, and strings.

explicit *container*::*container* (**size_type** *num*)

- Creates a container with *num* elements.
- The elements are created with their default constructor.
- Provided by vectors, deques, and lists.

container::*container* (**size_type** *num*, **const T&** *value*)

- Creates a container with *num* elements.
- The elements are created as copies of *value*.
- T is the type of the container elements.
- For strings, *value* is not passed by reference.
- Provided by vectors, deques, lists, and strings.

container::*container* (**InputIterator** *beg*, **InputIterator** *end*)

- Creates a container that is initialized by all elements of the range [*beg,end*).
- This function is a member template (see page 11). Thus, the elements of the source range may have any type that is convertible to the element type of the container.
- Provided by vectors, deques, lists, sets, multisets, maps, multimaps, and strings.

container::*container* (**InputIterator** *beg*, **InputIterator** *end*,
                   const CompFunc& *op*)

- Creates a container that has the sorting criterion *op* and is initialized by all elements of the range [*beg,end*).
- This function is a member template (see page 11). Thus, the elements of the source range may have any type that is convertible to the element type of the container.
- The sorting criterion must define a "strict weak ordering" (see page 176).
- Provided by sets, multisets, maps, and multimaps.

container::˜*container* ()

- The destructor.
- Removes all elements and frees the memory.
- Calls the destructor for every element.
- Provided by vectors, deques, lists, sets, multisets, maps, multimaps, and strings.

6.10.3 Nonmodifying Operations

Size Operations

size_type *container*::**size** () const

- Returns the actual number of elements.
- To check whether the container is empty (contains no elements), you should use empty() because it may be faster.
- Provided by vectors, deques, lists, sets, multisets, maps, multimaps, and strings.

bool *container*::**empty** () const

- Returns whether the container is empty (contains no elements).
- It is equivalent to *container*::size()==0, but it may be faster (especially for lists).
- Provided by vectors, deques, lists, sets, multisets, maps, multimaps, and strings.

size_type *container*::**max_size** () const

- Returns the maximum number of elements a container may contain.
- This is a technical value that may depend on the memory model of the container. In particular, because vectors usually use one memory segment, this value may be less than for other containers.
- Provided by vectors, deques, lists, sets, multisets, maps, multimaps, and strings.

Capacity Operations

size_type *container*::**capacity** () const

- Returns the number of elements the container may contain without reallocation.
- Provided by vectors and strings.

void *container*::**reserve** (size_type *num*)

- Reserves internal memory for at least *num* elements.
- If *num* is less than the actual capacity, this call has no effect on vectors and is a nonbinding shrink request for strings.

- To shrink the capacity of vectors, see the example on page 149.
- Each reallocation invalidates all references, pointers, and iterators, and takes some time. Thus `reserve()` can increase speed and keep references, pointers, and iterators valid (see page 149 for details).
- Provided by vectors and strings.

Comparison Operations

`bool` **comparison** `(const` *container*`& c1, const` *container*`& c2)`

- Returns the result of the comparison of two containers of same type.
- **comparison** might be any of the following:
  ```
  operator ==
  operator !=
  operator <
  operator >
  operator <=
  operator >=
  ```
- Two containers are equal if they have the same number of elements and contain the same elements in the same order (all comparisons of two corresponding elements have to yield `true`).
- To check whether a container is less than another container, the containers are compared lexicographically. See the description of the `lexicographical_compare()` algorithm on page 360 for a description of lexicographical comparison.
- Provided by vectors, deques, lists, sets, multisets, maps, multimaps, and strings.

Special Nonmodifying Operations for Associative Containers

The member functions mentioned here are special implementations of corresponding STL algorithms that are discussed in Section 9.5, page 338, and Section 9.9, page 397. They provide better performance because they rely on the fact that the elements of associative containers are sorted. In fact, they provide logarithmic complexity instead of linear complexity. For example, to search for one of 1,000 elements, no more than ten comparisons on average are needed (see Section 2.3, page 21).

`size_type` *container*`::`**count** `(const T&` *value*`) const`

- Returns the number of elements that are equal to *value*.
- This is the special version of the `count()` algorithm discussed on page 338.
- T is the type of the sorted value:
  - For sets and multisets, it is the type of the elements.
  - For maps and multimaps, it is the type of the keys.
- Complexity: logarithmic.
- Provided by sets, multisets, maps, and multimaps.

`iterator` *container*::**find** (`const T&` *value*)

`const_iterator` *container*::**find** (`const T&` *value*) `const`

- Both return the position of the first element that has a value equal to *value*.
- They return `end()` if no element is found.
- These are the special versions of the `find()` algorithm discussed on page 341.
- T is the type of the sorted value:
  - For sets and multisets, it is the type of the elements.
  - For maps and multimaps, it is the type of the keys.
- Complexity: logarithmic.
- Provided by sets, multisets, maps, and multimaps.

`iterator` *container*::**lower_bound** (`const T&` *value*)

`const_iterator` *container*::**lower_bound** (`const T&` *value*) `const`

- Both return the first position where a copy of *value* would get inserted according to the sorting criterion.
- The return value is the position of the first element that has a value equal to or greater than *value* (which might be `end()`).
- They return `end()` if no such element is found.
- These are the special versions of the `lower_bound()` algorithm discussed on page 413.
- T is the type of the sorted value:
  - For sets and multisets, it is the type of the elements.
  - For maps and multimaps, it is the type of the keys.
- Complexity: logarithmic.
- Provided by sets, multisets, maps, and multimaps.

`iterator` *container*::**upper_bound** (`const T&` *value*)

`const_iterator` *container*::**upper_bound** (`const T&` *value*) `const`

- Both return the last position where a copy of *value* would get inserted according to the sorting criterion.
- The return value is the position of the first element that has a value greater than *value* (which might be `end()`).
- They return `end()` if no such element is found.
- These are the special versions of the `upper_bound()` algorithm discussed on page 413.
- T is the type of the sorted value:
  - For sets and multisets, it is the type of the elements.
  - For maps and multimaps, it is the type of the keys.
- Complexity: logarithmic.
- Provided by sets, multisets, maps, and multimaps.

`pair<iterator,iterator>` *container*::**equal_range** (const T& *value*)
`pair<const_iterator,const_iterator>`
                            container::**equal_range** (const T& *value*) const

- Both return a pair with the first and last positions where a copy of *value* would get inserted according to the sorting criterion.
- The return value is the range of elements equal to *value*.
- They are equivalent to:
    `make_pair(lower_bound(`*value*`),upper_bound(`*value*`))`
- These are the special versions of the `equal_range()` algorithm discussed on page 415.
- T is the type of the sorted value:
    - For sets and multisets, it is the type of the elements.
    - For maps and multimaps, it is the type of the keys.
- Complexity: logarithmic.
- Provided by sets, multisets, maps, and multimaps.

`key_compare` *container*::**key_comp** ()

- Returns the comparison criterion.
- Provided by sets, multisets, maps, and multimaps.

`value_compare` *container*::**value_comp** ()

- Returns the object that is used as the comparison criterion.
- For sets and multisets, it is equivalent to `key_comp()`.
- For maps and multimaps, it is an auxiliary class for a comparison criterion that compares only the key part of two elements.
- Provided by sets, multisets, maps, and multimaps.

6.10.4   Assignments

container& *container*::**operator =** (const *container*& *c*)

- Assigns all elements of *c*; that is, it replaces all existing elements with copies of the elements of *c*.
- The operator may call the assignment operator for elements that have been overwritten, the copy constructor for appended elements, and the destructor of the element type for removed elements.
- Provided by vectors, deques, lists, sets, multisets, maps, multimaps, and strings.

`void` *container*::**assign** (size_type *num*, const T& value)

- Assigns *num* occurrences of *value*; that is, it replaces all existing elements by *num* copies of *value*.

- T has to be the element type.
- Provided by vectors, deques, lists, and strings.

void *container*::**assign** (InputIterator *beg*, InputIterator *end*)

- Assigns all elements of the range [*beg,end*); that is, it replaces all existing elements with copies of the elements of [*beg,end*).
- This function is a member template (see page 11). Thus, the elements of the source range may have any type that is convertible to the element type of the container.
- Provided by vectors, deques, lists, and strings.

void *container*::**swap** (*container*& *c*)

- Swaps the contents with *c*.
- Both containers swap
  - their elements and
  - their sorting criterion if any.
- This function has a constant complexity. You should always prefer it over an assignment when you no longer need the assigned object (see Section 6.1.2, page 147).
- For associative containers, the function may only throw if copying or assigning the comparison criterion may throw. For all other containers, the function does not throw.
- Provided by vectors, deques, lists, sets, multisets, maps, multimaps, and strings.

void **swap** (*container*& *c1*, *container*& *c2*)

- It is equivalent to *c1*.swap(*c2*) (see the previous description).
- For associative containers, the function may only throw if copying or assigning the comparison criterion may throw. For all other containers, the function does not throw.
- Provided by vectors, deques, lists, sets, multisets, maps, multimaps, and strings.

6.10.5 Direct Element Access

reference *container*::**at** (size_type *idx*)

const_reference *container*::**at** (size_type *idx*) const

- Both return the element with the index *idx* (the first element has index 0).
- Passing an invalid index (less than 0 or equal to size() or greater than size()) throws an out_of_range exception.
- Note that the returned reference may get invalidated due to later modifications or reallocations.
- If you are sure that the index is valid, you can use operator [ ], which is faster.
- Provided by vectors, deques, and strings.

```
reference container::operator [ ] (size_type idx)
```
```
const_reference container::operator [ ] (size_type idx) const
```

- Both return the element with the index *idx* (the first element has index 0).
- Passing an invalid index (less than 0 or equal to `size()` or greater than `size()`) results in undefined behavior. Thus, the caller must ensure that the index is valid; otherwise, `at()` should be used.
- The reference returned for the nonconstant string may get invalidated due to string modifications or reallocations (see page 487 for details).
- Provided by vectors, deques, and strings.

```
T& map::operator [ ] (const key_type& key)
```

- Operator [ ] for associative arrays.
- Returns the corresponding value to *key* in a map.
- Note: If no element with a key equal to *key* exists, this operation *creates* a new element automatically with a value that is initialized by the default constructor of the value type. Thus, you can't have an invalid index (only wrong behavior). For example:
    ```
    map<int,string> coll;
    coll[77] = "hello";   // insert key 77 with value "hello"
    cout << coll[42];     // Oops, inserts key 42 with value "" and prints the value
    ```
  See Section 6.6.3, page 205, for details.
- T is the type of the element value.
- It is equivalent to:
    ```
    (*((insert(make_pair(key,T()))).first)).second
    ```
- Provided by maps.

```
reference container::front ()
```
```
const_reference container::front () const
```

- Both return the first element (the element with index 0).
- The caller must ensure that the container contains an element (`size()>0`); otherwise, the behavior is undefined.
- Provided by vectors, deques, and lists.

```
reference container::back ()
```
```
const_reference container::back () const
```

- Both return the last element (the element with index `size()-1`).
- The caller must ensure that the container contains an element (`size()>0`); otherwise, the behavior is undefined.
- Provided by vectors, deques, and lists.

6.10.6   Operations to Generate Iterators

The following member functions return iterators to iterate over the elements of the containers. Table 6.34 lists the iterator category (see Section 7.2, page 251) according to the different container types.

Container	Iterator Category
Vector	Random access
Deque	Random access
List	Bidirectional
Set	Bidirectional, element is constant
Multiset	Bidirectional, element is constant
Map	Bidirectional, key is constant
Multimap	Bidirectional, key is constant
String	Random access

Table 6.34. Iterator Categories According to Container Types

`iterator` *container*::**begin** `()`

`const_iterator` *container*::**begin** `() const`

- Both return an iterator for the beginning of the container (the position of the first element).
- If the container is empty, the calls are equivalent to *container*::`end()`.
- Provided by vectors, deques, lists, sets, multisets, maps, multimaps, and strings.

`iterator` *container*::**end** `()`

`const_iterator` *container*::**end** `() const`

- Both return an iterator for the end of the container (the position after the last element).
- If the container is empty, the calls are equivalent to *container*::`begin()`.
- Provided by vectors, deques, lists, sets, multisets, maps, multimaps, and strings.

`reverse_iterator` *container*::**rbegin** `()`

`const_reverse_iterator` *container*::**rbegin** `() const`

- Both return a reverse iterator for the beginning of a reverse iteration over the elements of the container (the position of the last element).
- If the container is empty, the calls are equivalent to *container*::`rend()`.
- For details about reverse iterators, see Section 7.4.1, page 264.
- Provided by vectors, deques, lists, sets, multisets, maps, multimaps, and strings.

```
reverse_iterator container::rend ()
const_reverse_iterator container::rend () const
```

- Both return a reverse iterator for the end of a reverse iteration over the elements of the container (the position before the first element).
- If the container is empty, the calls are equivalent to *container*::rbegin().
- For details about reverse iterators, see Section 7.4.1, page 264.
- Provided by vectors, deques, lists, sets, multisets, maps, multimaps, and strings.

6.10.7   Inserting and Removing Elements

```
iterator container::insert (const T& value)
pair<iterator,bool> container::insert (const T& value)
```

- Both insert a copy of *value* into an associative container.
- Containers that allow duplicates (multisets and multimaps) have the first signature. They return the position of the new element.
- Containers that do not allow duplicates (sets and maps) have the second signature. If they can't insert the value because an element with an equal value or key exists, they return the position of the existing element and false. If they can insert the value, they return the position of the new element and true.
- T is the type of the container elements. Thus, for maps and multimaps it is a key/value pair.
- The functions either succeed or have no effect.
- Provided by sets, multisets, maps, and multimaps.

```
iterator container::insert (iterator pos, const T& value)
```

- Inserts a copy of *value* at the position of iterator *pos*.
- Returns the position of the new element.
- For associative containers (sets, multisets, maps, and multimaps), the position is only used as hint, pointing to where the insert should start to search. If *value* is inserted right behind *pos* the function has amortized constant complexity; otherwise, it has logarithmic complexity.
- If the container is a set or a map that already contains an element equal to (the key of) *value*, then the call has no effect and the return value is the position of the existing element.
- For vectors and deques, this operation might invalidate iterators and references to other elements.
- T is the type of the container elements. Thus, for maps and multimaps it is a key/value pair.
- For strings, *value* is not passed by reference.
- For vectors and deques, if the copy operations (copy constructor and assignment operator) of the elements don't throw, the function either succeeds or has no effect. For all other standard containers, the function either succeeds or has no effect.
- Provided by vectors, deques, lists, sets, multisets, maps, multimaps, and strings.

void *container*::**insert** (iterator *pos*, size_type *num*, const T& *value*)

- Inserts *num* copies of *value* at the position of iterator *pos*.
- For vectors and deques, this operation might invalidate iterators and references to other elements.
- T is the type of the container elements. Thus, for maps and multimaps it is a key/value pair.
- For strings, *value* is not passed by reference.
- For vectors and deques, if the copy operations (copy constructor and assignment operator) of the elements don't throw, the function either succeeds or has no effect. For lists, the function either succeeds or has no effect.
- Provided by vectors, deques, lists, and strings.

void *container*::**insert** (InputIterator *beg*, InputIterator *end*)

- Inserts copies of all elements of the range [*beg*,*end*) into the associative container.
- This function is a member template (see page 11). Thus, the elements of the source range may have any type that is convertible to the element type of the container.
- Provided by sets, multisets, maps, and multimaps.

void *container*::**insert** (iterator *pos*, InputIterator *beg*, InputIterator *end*)

- Inserts copies of all elements of the range [*beg*,*end*) at the position of iterator *pos*.
- This function is a member template (see page 11). Thus, the elements of the source range may have any type that is convertible to the element type of the container.
- For vectors and deques, this operation might invalidate iterators and references to other elements.
- For lists, the function either succeeds or has no effect.
- Provided by vectors, deques, lists, and strings.

void *container*::**push_front** (const T& *value*)

- Inserts a copy of *value* as the new first element.
- T is the type of the container elements.
- It is equivalent to insert(begin(),*value*).
- For deques, this operation invalidates iterators to other elements. References to other elements stay valid.
- This function either succeeds or has no effect.
- Provided by deques and lists.

void *container*::**push_back** (const T& *value*)

- Appends a copy of *value* as the new last element.
- T is the type of the container elements.
- It is equivalent to insert(end(),*value*).
- For vectors, this operation invalidates iterators and references to other elements when reallocation takes place.

- For deques, this operation invalidates iterators to other elements. References to other elements stay valid.
- This function either succeeds or has no effect.
- Provided by vectors, deques, lists, and strings.

void *list*::**remove** (const T& *value*)

void *list*::**remove_if** (UnaryPredicate *op*)

- `remove()` removes all elements with value `value`.
- `remove_if()` removes all elements for which the unary predicate
    op(*elem*)
  yields `true`.
- Note that *op* should not change its state during a function call. See Section 8.1.4, page 302, for details.
- Both call the destructors of the removed elements.
- The order of the remaining arguments remains stable.
- This is the special version of the `remove()` algorithm, which is discussed on page 378, for lists.
- T is the type of the container elements.
- For further details and examples, see page 170.
- The functions may only throw if the comparison of the elements may throw.
- Provided by lists.

size_type *container*::**erase** (const T& *value*)

- Removes all elements equal to *value* from an associative container.
- Returns the number of removed elements.
- Calls the destructors of the removed elements.
- T is the type of the sorted value:
    - For sets and multisets, it is the type of the elements.
    - For maps and multimaps, it is the type of the keys.
- The function does not throw.
- Provided by sets, multisets, maps, and multimaps.

void *container*::**erase** (iterator *pos*)

iterator *container*::**erase** (iterator *pos*)

- Both remove the element at the position of iterator *pos*.
- Sequence containers (vectors, deques, lists, and strings) have the second signature. They return the position of the following element (or `end()`).
- Associative containers (sets, multisets, maps, and multimaps) have the first signature. They return nothing.
- Both call the destructors of the removed elements.

- Note that the caller must ensure that the iterator *pos* is valid. For example:

  `coll.erase(coll.end());` *// ERROR* ⇒ *undefined behavior*

- For vectors and deques, this operation might invalidate iterators and references to other elements.
- For vectors and deques, the function may only throw if the copy constructor or assignment operator of the elements may throw. For all other containers, the function does not throw.
- Provided by vectors, deques, lists, sets, multisets, maps, multimaps, and strings.

`void` *container*::**erase** `(iterator` *beg*`, iterator` *end*`)`

`iterator` *container*::**erase** `(iterator` *beg*`, iterator` *end*`)`

- Both remove the elements of the range [*beg*,*end*).
- Sequence containers (vectors, deques, lists, and strings) have the second signature. They return the position of the element that was behind the last removed element on entry (or `end()`).
- Associative containers (sets, multisets, maps, and multimaps) have the first signature. They return nothing.
- As always for ranges, all elements including *beg* but excluding *end* are removed.
- Both call the destructors of the removed elements.
- Note that the caller must ensure that *beg* and *end* define a valid range that is part of the container.
- For vectors and deques, this operation might invalidate iterators and references to other elements.
- For vectors and deques, the function may only throw if the copy constructor or the assignment operator of the elements may throw. For all other containers, the function does not throw.
- Provided by vectors, deques, lists, sets, multisets, maps, multimaps, and strings.

`void` *container*::**pop_front** `()`

- Removes the first element of the container.
- It is equivalent to *container*.`erase(`*container*.`begin())`.
- Note: If the container is empty, the behavior is undefined. Thus, the caller must ensure that the container contains at least one element (`size()>0`).
- The function does not throw.
- Provided by deques and lists.

`void` *container*::**pop_back** `()`

- Removes the last element of the container.
- It is equivalent to *container*.`erase(--`*container*.`end())`, provided this expression is valid, which might not be the case for vectors (see page 258).
- Note: If the container is empty, the behavior is undefined. Thus, the caller must ensure that the container contains at least one element (`size()>0`).
- The function does not throw.
- Provided by vectors, deques, and lists.

void *container*::**resize** (size_type *num*)

void *container*::**resize** (size_type *num*, T *value*)

- Both change the number of elements to *num*.
- If size() is *num* on entry, they have no effect.
- If *num* is greater than size() on entry, additional elements are created and appended to the end of the container. The first form creates the new elements by calling their default constructor; the second form creates the new elements as copies of *value*.
- If *num* is less than size() on entry, elements are removed at the end to get the new size. In this case, they call the destructor of the removed elements.
- For vectors and deques, these functions might invalidate iterators and references to other elements.
- For vectors and deques, these functions either succeed or have no effect, provided the copy constructor or the assignment operator of the elements don't throw. For lists, the functions either succeed or have no effect.
- Provided by vectors, deques, lists, and strings.

void *container*::**clear** ()

- Removes all elements (makes the container empty).
- Calls the destructors of the removed elements.
- Invalidates all iterators and references to the container.
- For vectors and deques, the function may only throw if the copy constructor or the assignment operator of the elements may throw. For all other containers, the function does not throw.
- Provided by vectors, deques, lists, sets, multisets, maps, multimaps, and strings.

6.10.8   Special Member Functions for Lists

void *list*::**unique** ()

void *list*::**unique** (BinaryPredicate *op*)

- Both remove subsequent duplicates of list elements so that each element contains a different value than the following element.
- The first form removes all elements for which the previous values are equal.
- The second form removes all elements that follow an element *e* and for which the binary predicate

    op(*elem*,*e*)

yields true.[34] In other words, the predicate is not used to compare an element with its predecessor; the element is compared with the previous element that was not removed.

---

[34] The second version of unique() is available only in systems that support member templates (see page 11).

- Note that *op* should not change its state during a function call. See Section 8.1.4, page 302, for details.
- Both call the destructors of the removed elements.
- These are the special versions of the `unique()` algorithms, which are discussed on page 381, for lists.
- The functions do not throw if the comparisons of the elements do not throw.

void *list*::**splice** (iterator *pos*, *list&* *source*)

- Moves all elements of *source* into `*this` and inserts them at the position of iterator *pos*.
- *source* is empty after the call.
- If *source* and `*this` are identical, the behavior is undefined. Thus, the caller must ensure that *source* is a different list. To move elements inside the same list you must use the following form of `splice()`.
- The caller must ensure that *pos* is a valid position of `*this`; otherwise, the behavior is undefined.
- This function does not throw.

void *list*::**splice** (iterator *pos*, *list&* *source*, iterator *sourcePos*)

- Moves the element at the position *sourcePos* of the list *source* into `*this` and inserts it at the position of iterator *pos*.
- *source* and `*this` may be identical. In this case, the element is moved inside the list.
- If *source* is a different list, it contains one element less after the operation.
- The caller must ensure that *pos* is a valid position of `*this`, *sourcePos* is a valid iterator of *source*, and *sourcePos* is not *source*.`end()`; otherwise, the behavior is undefined.
- This function does not throw.

void *list*::**splice** (iterator *pos*, *list&* *source*,
                  iterator *sourceBeg*, iterator *sourceEnd*)

- Moves the elements of the range [*sourceBeg*,*sourceEnd*) of the list *source* to `*this` and inserts it at the position of iterator *pos*.
- *source* and `*this` may be identical. In this case, *pos* must not be part of the moved range, and the elements are moved inside the list.
- If *source* is a different list, it contains less elements after the operation.
- The caller must ensure that *pos* is a valid position of `*this`, and that *sourceBeg* and *sourceEnd* define a valid range that is part of *source*; otherwise, the behavior is undefined.
- This function does not throw.

void *list*::**sort** ()

void *list*::**sort** (CompFunc *op*)

- Both sort the elements in the list.
- The first form sorts all elements in the list with operator <.

- The second form sorts all elements in the list by calling *op* to compare two elements[35]:
  op(*elem1*,*elem2*)
- The order of elements that have an equal value remains stable (unless an exception is thrown).
- These are the special versions of the `sort()` and `stable_sort()` algorithms, which are discussed on page 397.

void *list*::**merge** (*list& source*)

void *list*::**merge** (*list& source*, CompFunc *op*)

- Both merge all elements of the list *source* into `*this`.
- *source* is empty after the call.
- If `*this` and *source* are sorted on entry according to the sorting criterion < or *op*, the resulting list is also sorted. Strictly speaking, the standard requires that both lists be sorted on entry. In practice, however, merging is also possible for unsorted lists. However, you should check this before you rely on it.
- The first form uses operator < as the sorting criterion.
- The second form uses *op* as the optional sorting criterion and is used to compare two elements[36]:
  op(*elem*,*sourceElem*)
- This is the special version of the `merge()` algorithm, which is discussed on page 416.
- If the comparisons of the elements do not throw, the functions either succeed or have no effect.

void *list*::**reverse** ()

- Reverses the order of the elements in a list.
- This is the special version of the `reverse()` algorithm, which is discussed on page 386.
- This function does not throw.

6.10.9   Allocator Support

All STL containers can be used with a special memory model that is defined by an allocator object (see Chapter 15 for details). This subsection describes the members for allocator support.

Standard containers require that all instances of an allocator type are interchangeable. Thus, storage allocated from one container can be deallocated via another that has the same type. Therefore, it is no problem when elements (and their storage) are moved between containers of the same type.

---

[35] The second form of `sort()` is available only in systems that support member templates (see page 11).

[36] The second form of `merge()` is available only in systems that support member templates (see page 11).

Fundamental Allocator Members

container::**allocator_type**
- The type of the allocator.
- Provided by vectors, deques, lists, sets, multisets, maps, multimaps, and strings.

`allocator_type` *container*::**get_allocator** `() const`
- Returns the memory model of the container.
- Provided by vectors, deques, lists, sets, multisets, maps, multimaps, and strings.

Constructors with Optional Allocator Parameters

`explicit` *container*::*container* `(const Allocator&` *alloc*`)`
- Creates a new empty container that uses the memory model *alloc*.
- Provided by vectors, deques, lists, sets, multisets, maps, multimaps, and strings.

container::*container* `(const CompFunc&` *op*`, const Allocator&` *alloc*`)`
- Creates a new empty container with *op* used as the sorting criterion that uses the memory model *alloc*.
- The sorting criterion must define a "strict weak ordering" (see page 176).
- Provided by sets, multisets, maps, and multimaps.

container::*container* `(size_type` *num*`, const T&` *value*`, const Allocator&` *alloc*`)`
- Creates a container with *num* elements that uses the memory model *alloc*.
- The elements are created as copies of *value*.
- T is the type of the container elements. Note that for strings, *value* is passed by value.
- Provided by vectors, deques, lists, and strings.

container::*container* `(InputIterator` *beg*`, InputIterator` *end*`,`
`                 const Allocator&` *alloc*`)`
- Creates a container that is initialized by all elements of the range [*beg,end*) and uses the memory model *alloc*.
- This function is a member template (see page 11). Thus, the elements of the source range may have any type that is convertible to the element type of the container.
- Provided by vectors, deques, lists, sets, multisets, maps, multimaps, and strings.

container::*container* `(InputIterator` *beg*`, InputIterator` *end*`,`
`                 const CompFunc&` *op*`, const Allocator&` *alloc*`)`
- Creates a container that has the sorting criterion *op*, is initialized by all elements of the range [*beg,end*), and uses the memory model *alloc*.

- This function is a member template (see page 11). Thus, the elements of the source range may have any type that is convertible to the element type of the container.
- The sorting criterion must define a "strict weak ordering" (see page 176).
- Provided by sets, multisets, maps, and multimaps.

6.10.10   Overview of Exception Handling in STL Containers

As mentioned in Section 5.11.2, page 139, containers provide different guarantees in the face of exceptions. In general, the C++ standard library will not leak resources or violate container invariants in the face of exceptions. However, some operations give stronger guarantees (provided the arguments meet some requirements): They may guarantee commit-or-rollback behavior, or they may even guarantee that they will never throw at all. Table 6.35 lists all operations that give these stronger guarantees.[37]

For vectors, deques, and lists, you also have guarantees for `resize()`. It is defined as having the effect of either calling `erase()` or calling `insert()` or doing nothing:

```
void container::resize (size_type num, T value = T())
{
    if (num > size()) {
        insert (end(), num-size(), value);
    }
    else if (num < size()) {
        erase (begin()+num, end());
    }
}
```

Thus, its guarantees are a combination of the guarantees of `erase()` and `insert()` (see page 244).

---

[37] Many thanks to Greg Colvin and Dave Abrahams for providing this table.

Operation	Page	Guarantee
`vector::push_back()`	241	Either succeeds or has no effect
`vector::insert()`	240	Either succeeds or has no effect if copying/assigning elements doesn't throw
`vector::pop_back()`	243	Doesn't throw
`vector::erase()`	242	Doesn't throw if copying/assigning elements doesn't throw
`vector::clear()`	244	Doesn't throw if copying/assigning elements doesn't throw
`vector::swap()`	237	Doesn't throw
`deque::push_back()`	241	Either succeeds or has no effect
`deque::push_front()`	241	Either succeeds or has no effect
`deque::insert()`	240	Either succeeds or has no effect if copying/assigning elements doesn't throw
`deque::pop_back()`	243	Doesn't throw
`deque::pop_front()`	243	Doesn't throw
`deque::erase()`	242	Doesn't throw if copying/assigning elements doesn't throw
`deque::clear()`	244	Doesn't throw if copying/assigning elements doesn't throw
`deque::swap()`	237	Doesn't throw
`list::push_back()`	241	Either succeeds or has no effect
`list::push_front()`	241	Either succeeds or has no effect
`list::insert()`	240	Either succeeds or has no effect
`list::pop_back()`	243	Doesn't throw
`list::pop_front()`	243	Doesn't throw
`list::erase()`	242	Doesn't throw
`list::clear()`	244	Doesn't throw
`list::remove()`	242	Doesn't throw if comparing the elements doesn't throw
`list::remove_if()`	242	Doesn't throw if the predicate doesn't throw
`list::unique()`	244	Doesn't throw if comparing the elements doesn't throw
`list::splice()`	245	Doesn't throw
`list::merge()`	246	Either succeeds or has no effect if comparing the elements doesn't throw
`list::reverse()`	246	Doesn't throw
`list::swap()`	237	Doesn't throw
`[multi]set::insert()`	240	For single elements either succeeds or has no effect
`[multi]set::erase()`	242	Doesn't throw
`[multi]set::clear()`	244	Doesn't throw
`[multi]set::swap()`	237	Doesn't throw if copying/assigning the comparison criterion doesn't throw
`[multi]map::insert()`	240	For single elements either succeeds or has no effect
`[multi]map::erase()`	242	Doesn't throw
`[multi]map::clear()`	244	Doesn't throw
`[multi]map::swap()`	237	Doesn't throw if copying/assigning the comparison criterion doesn't throw

Table 6.35. Container Operations with Special Guarantees in Face of Exceptions

Chapter 7
STL Iterators

7.1 Header Files for Iterators

All containers define their own iterator types, so you don't need a special header file for using iterators of containers. However, there are several definitions for special iterators, such as reverse iterators. These are introduced by the `<iterator>` header file,[1] although you don't need to include this file in your program often. It is needed by containers to define their reverse iterator types and thus it is included by them.

7.2 Iterator Categories

Iterators are objects that can iterate over elements of a sequence. They do this via a common interface that is adapted from ordinary pointers (see the introduction in Section 5.3, page 83). Iterators follow the concept of pure abstraction: Anything that *behaves* like an iterator *is* an iterator. However, iterators have different abilities. These abilities are important because some algorithms require special iterator abilities. For example, sorting algorithms require iterators that can perform random access because otherwise the runtime would be poor. For this reason, iterators have different categories (Figure 7.1). The abilities of these categories are listed in Table 7.1, and discussed in the following subsections.

---

[1] In the original STL, the header file for iterators was called `<iterator.h>`.

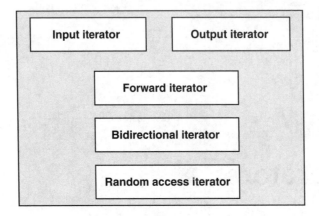

Figure 7.1. Iterator Categories

Iterator Category	Ability	Providers
Input iterator	Reads forward	istream
Output iterator	Writes forward	ostream, inserter
Forward iterator	Reads and writes forward	
Bidirectional iterator	Reads and writes forward and backward	list, set, multiset, map, multimap
Random access iterator	Reads and writes with random access	vector, deque, string, array

Table 7.1. Abilities of Iterator Categories

7.2.1 Input Iterators

Input iterators can only step forward element-by-element with read access. Thus, they return values elementwise. Table 7.2 lists the operations of input iterators.

Note that input iterators can read elements only once. Thus, if you copy an input iterator and let the original and the copy read forward, they might iterate over different values.

Almost all iterators have the abilities of input iterators. However, usually they can have more. A typical example of a pure input iterator is an iterator that reads from the standard input (typically the keyboard). The same value can't be read twice. After a word is read from an input stream (out of the input buffer), the next read access returns another word.

Two input iterators are equal if they occupy the same position. However, as stated previously, this does not mean that they return the same value on element access.

Expression	Effect
iter	Provides read access to the actual element
iter ->*member*	Provides read access to a member (if any) of the actual element
++*iter*	Steps forward (returns new position)
iter++	Steps forward (returns old position)
iter1 == *iter2*	Returns whether two iterators are equal
iter1 != *iter2*	Returns whether two iterators are not equal
TYPE(*iter*)	Copies iterator (copy constructor)

Table 7.2. Operations of Input Iterators

You should always prefer the preincrement operator over the postincrement operator because it might perform better. This is because the preincrement operator does not have to return an old value that must be stored in a temporary object. So, for any iterator pos (and any abstract data type), you should prefer

    ++pos   *// OK and fast*

rather than

    pos++   *// OK, but not so fast*

The same applies to decrement operators, as long as they are defined (they aren't for input iterators).

7.2.2 Output Iterators

Output iterators are the counterparts of input iterators. They can only step forward with write access. Thus, you can assign new values only element-by-element. You can't use an output iterator to iterate twice over the same range. The goal is to write a value into a "black hole" (whatever that means). So, if you write something for the second time at the same position into the same black hole, it is not guaranteed that you will overwrite a previous value. Table 7.3 lists the valid operations for output iterators. The only valid use of operator * is on the left side of an assignment statement.

Expression	Effect
iter = *value*	Writes *value* to where the iterator refers
++*iter*	Steps forward (returns new position)
iter++	Steps forward (returns old position)
TYPE(*iter*)	Copies iterator (copy constructor)

Table 7.3. Operations of Output Iterators

Note that no comparison operations are required for output iterators. You can't check whether an output iterator is valid or whether a "writing" was successful. The only thing you can do is to write, and write, and write values.

Usually iterators can read and write values. So, as for input iterators, almost all iterators also have the abilities of output iterators. A typical example of a pure output iterator is an iterator that writes to the standard output (for example, to the screen or a printer). If you use two output iterators to write to the screen, the second word follows the first rather than overwriting it. Another typical example of output iterators are inserters. Inserters are iterators that insert values into containers. If you assign a value, you insert it. If you then write a second value, you don't overwrite the first value; you just also insert it. Inserters are discussed in Section 7.4.2, page 271.

7.2.3   Forward Iterators

Forward iterators are combinations of input and output iterators. They have all the abilities of input iterators and most of those of output iterators. Table 7.4 summarizes the operations of forward iterators.

Expression	Effect
*iter	Provides access to the actual element
iter->member	Provides access to a member of the actual element
++iter	Steps forward (returns new position)
iter++	Steps forward (returns old position)
iter1 == iter2	Returns whether two iterators are equal
iter1 != iter2	Returns whether two iterators are not equal
TYPE()	Creates iterator (default constructor)
TYPE(iter)	Copies iterator (copy constructor)
iter1 = iter2	Assigns an iterator

Table 7.4. Operations of Forward Iterators

Unlike input iterators and output iterators, forward iterators can refer to the same element in the same collection and process the same element more than once.

You might wonder why a forward iterator does not have all of the abilities of an output iterator. One restriction applies that prohibits valid code for output iterators from being valid for forward iterators:

- For **output iterators**, writing data without checking for the end of a sequence is correct. In fact, you can't compare an output iterator with an end iterator because output iterators do not have to provide a comparison operation. Thus, the following loop is correct for output iterator pos:

```
// OK for output iterators
// ERROR for forward iterators
while (true) {
    *pos = foo();
    ++pos;
}
```

- For **forward iterators**, you must *ensure* that it is correct to dereference (access the data) before you do this. Thus, the previous loop is not correct for forward iterators. This is because it would result in dereferencing the `end()` of a collection, which results in undefined behavior. For forward iterators, the loop must be changed in the following manner:

```
// OK for forward iterators
// IMPOSSIBLE for output iterators
while (pos != coll.end()) {
    *pos = foo();
    ++pos;
}
```

This loop does not compile for output iterators because operator `!=` is not defined for them.

7.2.4 Bidirectional Iterators

Bidirectional iterators are forward iterators that provide the additional ability to iterate backward over the elements. Thus, they provide the decrement operator to step backward (Table 7.5).

Expression	Effect
--iter	Steps backward (returns new position)
iter--	Steps backward (returns old position)

Table 7.5. Additional Operations of Bidirectional Iterators

7.2.5 Random Access Iterators

Random access iterators are bidirectional iterators that can perform random access. Thus, they provide operators for "iterator arithmetic" (in accordance with the "pointer arithmetic" of ordinary pointers). That is, they can add and subtract offsets, process differences, and compare iterators with relational operators such as < and >. Table 7.6 lists the additional operations of random access iterators.

Random access iterators are provided by the following objects and types:

- Containers with random access (`vector`, `deque`)
- Strings (`string`, `wstring`)
- Ordinary arrays (pointers)

Expression	Effect
iter[*n*]	Provides access to the element that has index *n*
iter+=n	Steps *n* elements forward (or backward, if *n* is negative)
iter-=n	Steps *n* elements backward (or forward, if *n* is negative)
iter+n	Returns the iterator of the *n*th next element
n+iter	Returns the iterator of the *n*th next element
iter-n	Returns the iterator of the *n*th previous element
iter1-iter2	Returns the distance between *iter1* and *iter2*
iter1<iter2	Returns whether *iter1* is before *iter2*
iter1>iter2	Returns whether *iter1* is after *iter2*
iter1<=iter2	Returns whether *iter1* is not after *iter2*
iter1>=iter2	Returns whether *iter1* is not before *iter2*

Table 7.6. Additional Operations of Random Access Iterators

The following program demonstrates the special abilities of random access iterators:

```
// iter/itercat.cpp

#include <vector>
#include <iostream>
using namespace std;

int main()
{
    vector<int> coll;

    // insert elements from -3 to 9
    for (int i=-3; i<=9; ++i) {
        coll.push_back (i);
    }

    /* print number of elements by processing the distance between beginning and end
     * - NOTE: uses operator - for iterators
     */
    cout << "number/distance: " << coll.end()-coll.begin() << endl;

    /* print all elements
     * - NOTE: uses operator < instead of operator !=
     */
    vector<int>::iterator pos;
```

```
     for (pos=coll.begin(); pos<coll.end(); ++pos) {
         cout << *pos << ' ';
     }
     cout << endl;

     /* print all elements
      * - NOTE: uses operator [] instead of operator *
      */
     for (int i=0; i<coll.size(); ++i) {
         cout << coll.begin()[i] << ' ';
     }
     cout << endl;

     /* print every second element
      * - NOTE: uses operator +=
      */
     for (pos = coll.begin(); pos < coll.end()-1; pos += 2) {
         cout << *pos << ' ';
     }
     cout << endl;
}
```

The output of the program is as follows:

```
number/distance: 13
-3 -2 -1 0 1 2 3 4 5 6 7 8 9
-3 -2 -1 0 1 2 3 4 5 6 7 8 9
-3 -1 1 3 5 7
```

This example won't work with lists, sets, and maps because all operations that are marked with *NOTE:* are provided only for random access iterators. In particular, keep in mind that you can use operator < as an end criterion in loops for random access iterators only.

Note that in the last loop the expression

```
pos < coll.end()-1
```

requires that coll contains at least one element. If the collection was empty, coll.end()-1 would be the position before coll.begin(). The comparison might still work; but, strictly speaking, moving an iterator to before the beginning results in undefined behavior. Similarly, the expression pos += 2 might result in undefined behavior if it moves the iterator beyond the end() of the collection. Therefore, changing the final loop to the following is very dangerous because it results in undefined behavior if the collection contains an odd number of elements (Figure 7.2):

```
for (pos = coll.begin(); pos < coll.end(); pos += 2) {
    cout << *pos << ' ';
}
```

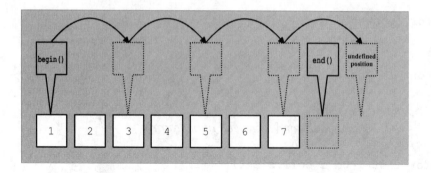

Figure 7.2. Incrementing Iterators by More than One Element

7.2.6   The Increment and Decrement Problem of Vector Iterators

The use of the increment and decrement operators of iterators includes a strange problem. In general, you can increment and decrement temporary iterators. However, for vectors and strings, you typically can't. Consider the following vector example:

```
std::vector<int> coll;
...
// sort, starting with the second element
// - NONPORTABLE version
if (coll.size() > 1) {
    sort(++coll.begin(), coll.end());
}
```

Typically, the compilation of `sort()` fails. However, if you use, for example, a deque rather than a vector, it will compile. It might compile even with vectors, depending on the implementation of class `vector`.

The reason for this strange problem lies in the fact that vector iterators are typically implemented as ordinary pointers. And for all fundamental data types, such as pointers, you are not allowed to modify temporary values. For structures and classes, however, it is allowed. Thus, if the iterator is implemented as an ordinary pointer, the compilation fails; if implemented as a class, it succeeds. It always works with deques, lists, sets, and maps because you can't implement iterators as ordinary pointers for them. But for vectors, whether it works depends on the implementation. Usually, ordinary pointers are used. But if, for example, you use a "safe version" of the STL, the iterators are implemented as classes. To make your code portable you should not code as the previous example, using vectors. Instead, you should use an auxiliary object:

```
std::vector<int> coll;
```

...

// sort, starting with the second element

// - PORTABLE version

```
if (coll.size() > 1) {
    std::vector<int>::iterator beg = coll.begin();
    sort(++beg, coll.end());
}
```

The problem is not as bad as it sounds. You can't get unexpected behavior because it is detected at compile time. But it is tricky enough to spend time solving it. This problem also applies to strings. String iterators are usually also implemented as ordinary character pointers, although this is not required.

7.3 Auxiliary Iterator Functions

The C++ standard library provides three auxiliary functions for iterators: `advance()`, `distance()`, and `iter_swap()`. The first two give all iterators some abilities usually only provided for random access iterators: to step more than one element forward (or backward) and to process the difference between iterators. The third auxiliary function allows you to swap the values of two iterators.

7.3.1 Stepping Iterators Using `advance()`

The function `advance()` increments the position of an iterator passed as the argument. Thus, it lets the iterator step forward (or backward) more than one element:

```
#include <iterator>
```

void **advance** (InputIterator& *pos*, Dist *n*)

- Lets the input iterator *pos* step *n* elements forward (or backward).
- For bidirectional and random access iterators *n* may be negative to step backward.
- `Dist` is a template type. Normally, it must be an integral type because operations such as <, ++, --, and comparisons with 0 are called.
- Note that `advance()` does *not* check whether it crosses the `end()` of a sequence (it can't check because iterators in general do not know the containers on which they operate). Thus, calling this function might result in undefined behavior because calling operator ++ for the end of a sequence is not defined.

Due to the use of iterator traits (introduced in Section 7.5, page 283), the function always uses the best implementation, depending on the iterator category. For random access iterators, it simply calls *pos*+=*n*. Thus, for such iterators `advance()` has constant complexity. For all other iterators, it calls

++*pos* *n* times (or --*pos*, if *n* is negative). Thus, for all other iterator categories advance() has linear complexity.

To be able to change container and iterator types, you should use advance() rather than operator +=. However, in doing so be aware that you risk unintended worse performance. This is because you don't recognize that the performance is worsening when you use other containers that don't provide random access iterators (bad runtime is the reason why operator += is provided only for random access iterators). Note also that advance() does not return anything. Operator += returns the new position, so it might be part of a larger expression. Here is an example of the use of advance():

```
// iter/advance1.cpp

#include <iostream>
#include <list>
#include <algorithm>
using namespace std;

int main()
{
    list<int> coll;

    // insert elements from 1 to 9
    for (int i=1; i<=9; ++i) {
        coll.push_back(i);
    }

    list<int>::iterator pos = coll.begin();

    // print actual element
    cout << *pos << endl;

    // step three elements forward
    advance (pos, 3);

    // print actual element
    cout << *pos << endl;

    // step one element backward
    advance (pos, -1);

    // print actual element
    cout << *pos << endl;
}
```

In this program, `advance()` lets the iterator `pos` step three elements forward and one element backward. Thus, the output is as follows:

```
1
4
3
```

Another way to use `advance()` is to ignore some input for iterators that read from an input stream. See the example on page 282.

7.3.2 Processing Iterator Distance Using `distance()`

The `distance()` function is provided to process the difference between two iterators:

```
#include <iterator>
```
Dist **distance** (InputIterator *pos1*, InputIterator *pos2*)

- Returns the distance between the input iterators *pos1* and *pos2*.
- Both iterators have to refer to elements of the same container.
- If the iterators are not random access iterators, *pos2* must be reachable from *pos1*; that is, it must have the same position or a later position.
- The return type, *Dist*, is the difference type according to the iterator type:

    ```
    iterator_traits<InputIterator>::difference_type
    ```

    See Section 7.5, page 283, for details.

By using iterator tags, this function uses the best implementation according to the iterator category. For random access iterators, it simply returns *pos2-pos1*. Thus, for such iterators `distance()` has constant complexity. For all other iterator categories, *pos1* is incremented until it reaches *pos2* and the number of incrementations is returned. Thus, for all other iterator categories `distance()` has linear complexity. Therefore, `distance()` has bad performance for other than random access iterators. You should consider avoiding it.

The implementation of `distance()` is described in Section 7.5.1, page 287. The following example demonstrates its use:

```
// iter/distance.cpp

#include <iostream>
#include <list>
#include <algorithm>
using namespace std;

int main()
{
    list<int> coll;
```

```
// insert elements from -3 to 9
for (int i=-3; i<=9; ++i) {
    coll.push_back(i);
}

// search element with value 5
list<int>::iterator pos;
pos = find (coll.begin(), coll.end(),      // range
                5);                         // value

if (pos != coll.end()) {
    // process and print difference from the beginning
    cout << "difference between beginning and 5: "
         << distance(coll.begin(),pos) << endl;
}
else {
    cout << "5 not found" << endl;
}
}
```

`find()` assigns the position of the element with value 5 to pos. `distance()` uses this position to process the difference between this position and the beginning. The output of the program is as follows:

```
difference between beginning and 5: 8
```

To be able to change iterator and container types, you should use `distance()` instead of operator -. However, if you use `distance()` you don't recognize that the performance is getting worse when you switch from random access iterators to other iterators.

To process the difference between two iterators that are not random access iterators, you must be careful. The first iterator must refer to an element that is not after the element of the second iterator. Otherwise, the behavior is undefined. If you don't know which iterator position comes first, you have to process the distance between both iterators to the beginning of the container and process the difference of these distances. However, you must then know to which container the iterators refer. If you don't, you have no chance of processing the difference of the two iterators without running into undefined behavior. See the remarks about subranges on page 99 for additional aspects of this problem.

In older versions of the STL, the signature of `distance()` was different. Instead of the difference being returned, it was added to a third argument. This version was very inconvenient because you could not use the difference directly in an expression. If you are using an old version, you should define this simple workaround:

```
// iter/distance.hpp

template <class Iterator>
inline long distance (Iterator pos1, Iterator pos2)
{
    long d = 0;
    distance (pos1, pos2, d);
    return d;
}
```

Here, the return type does not depend on the iterator; it is hard coded as `long`. Type `long` normally should be big enough to fit all possible values, however this is not guaranteed.

7.3.3   Swapping Iterator Values Using `iter_swap()`

The following simple auxiliary function is provided to swap the values to which two iterators refer:

```
#include <algorithm>
void iter_swap (ForwardIterator1 pos1, ForwardIterator2 pos2)
```

- Swaps the values to which iterators *pos1* and *pos2* refer.
- The iterators don't need to have the same type. However, the values must be assignable.

Here is a simple example (function `PRINT_ELEMENTS()` is introduced in Section 5.7, page 118):

```
// iter/swap1.cpp

#include <iostream>
#include <list>
#include <algorithm>
#include "print.hpp"
using namespace std;

int main()
{
    list<int> coll;

    // insert elements from 1 to 9
    for (int i=1; i<=9; ++i) {
        coll.push_back(i);
    }
```

```
    PRINT_ELEMENTS(coll);

    // swap first and second value
    iter_swap (coll.begin(), ++coll.begin());

    PRINT_ELEMENTS(coll);

    // swap first and last value
    iter_swap (coll.begin(), --coll.end());

    PRINT_ELEMENTS(coll);
}
```

The output of the program is as follows:

```
1 2 3 4 5 6 7 8 9
2 1 3 4 5 6 7 8 9
9 1 3 4 5 6 7 8 2
```

Note that this program normally does not work if you use a vector as a container. This is because `++coll.begin()` and `--coll.end()` yield temporary pointers (see Section 7.2.6, page 258, for details regarding this problem).

7.4 Iterator Adapters

This section covers iterator adapters. These special iterators allow algorithms to operate in reverse, in insert mode, and with streams.

7.4.1 Reverse Iterators

Reverse iterators are adapters that redefine increment and decrement operators so that they behave in reverse. Thus, if you use these iterators instead of ordinary iterators, algorithms process elements in reverse order. All standard container classes provide the ability to use reverse iterators to iterate over their elements. Consider the following example:

```
// iter/reviter1.cpp

#include <iostream>
#include <list>
#include <algorithm>
using namespace std;
```

```
void print (int elem)
{
    cout << elem << ' ';
}

int main()
{
    list<int> coll;

    // insert elements from 1 to 9
    for (int i=1; i<=9; ++i) {
        coll.push_back(i);
    }

    // print all elements in normal order
    for_each (coll.begin(), coll.end(),      // range
              print);                         // operation
    cout << endl;

    // print all elements in reverse order
    for_each (coll.rbegin(), coll.rend(),     // range
              print);                         // operations
    cout << endl;
}
```

The `rbegin()` and `rend()` member functions return a reverse iterator. According to `begin()` and `end()`, these iterators define the elements to process as a half-open range. However, they operate in a reverse direction:

- **rbegin()** returns the position of the first element of a reverse iteration. Thus, it returns the position of the last element.
- **rend()** returns the position after the last element of a reverse iteration. Thus, it returns the position *before* the first element.

Iterators and Reverse Iterators

You can convert normal iterators to reverse iterators. Naturally, the iterators must be bidirectional iterators, but note that the logical position of an iterator is moved during the conversion. Consider the following program:

```
// iter/reviter2.cpp

#include <iostream>
#include <vector>
#include <algorithm>
using namespace std;

int main()
{
    vector<int> coll;

    // insert elements from 1 to 9
    for (int i=1; i<=9; ++i) {
        coll.push_back(i);
    }

    // find position of element with value 5
    vector<int>::iterator pos;
    pos = find (coll.begin(), coll.end(),
                5);

    // print value to which iterator pos refers
    cout << "pos:  " << *pos << endl;

    // convert iterator to reverse iterator rpos
    vector<int>::reverse_iterator rpos(pos);

    // print value to which reverse iterator rpos refers
    cout << "rpos: " << *rpos << endl;
}
```

This program has the following output:

```
pos:  5
rpos: 4
```

Thus, if you print the value of an iterator and convert the iterator into a reverse iterator, the value has changed. This is not a bug; it's a feature! This behavior is a consequence of the fact that ranges are half-open. To specify all elements of a container, you must use the position after the last argument. However, for a reverse iterator this is the position before the first element. Unfortunately, such a position may not exist. Containers are not required to guarantee that the position before their first element is valid. Consider that ordinary strings and arrays might also be containers, and the language does not guarantee that arrays don't start at address zero.

As a result, the designers of reverse iterators use a trick: They "physically" reverse the "half-open principle." Physically, in a range defined by reverse iterators, the beginning is *not* included, whereas the end *is*. However, logically, they behave as usual. Thus, there is a distinction between the physical position that defines to which element the iterator refers and the logical position that defines to which value the iterator refers (Figure 7.3). The question is, what happens on a conversion from an iterator to a reverse iterator? Does the iterator keep its logical position (the value) or its physical position (the element)? As the previous example shows, the latter is the case. Thus the value is moved to the previous element (Figure 7.4).

Figure 7.3. Position and Value of Reverse Iterators

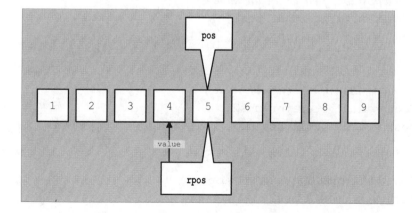

Figure 7.4. Conversion Between Iterator pos *and Reverse Iterator* rpos

You can't understand this decision? Well, it has its advantages: You have nothing to do when you convert a range that is specified by two iterators rather than a single iterator. All elements stay valid. Consider the following example:

```
// iter/reviter3.cpp
#include <iostream>
#include <deque>
#include <algorithm>
using namespace std;

void print (int elem)
{
    cout << elem << ' ';
}

int main()
{
    deque<int> coll;

    // insert elements from 1 to 9
    for (int i=1; i<=9; ++i) {
        coll.push_back(i);
    }

    // find position of element with value 2
    deque<int>::iterator pos1;
    pos1 = find (coll.begin(), coll.end(),    // range
                 2);                          // value

    // find position of element with value 7
    deque<int>::iterator pos2;
    pos2 = find (coll.begin(), coll.end(),    // range
                 7);                          // value

    // print all elements in range [pos1,pos2)
    for_each (pos1, pos2,        // range
              print);            // operation
    cout << endl;

    // convert iterators to reverse iterators
    deque<int>::reverse_iterator rpos1(pos1);
    deque<int>::reverse_iterator rpos2(pos2);
```

```
        // print all elements in range [pos1,pos2) in reverse order
        for_each (rpos2, rpos1,    // range
                    print);        // operation
        cout << endl;
    }
```

The iterators pos1 and pos2 specify the half-open range, including the element with value 2 but excluding the element with value 7. When the iterators describing that range are converted to reverse iterators, the range stays valid and can be processed in reverse order. Thus, the output of the program is as follows:

```
 2 3 4 5 6
 6 5 4 3 2
```

Thus, rbegin() is simply:

```
    container::reverse_iterator(end())
```

and rend() is simply:

```
    container::reverse_iterator(begin())
```

Of course, constant iterators are converted into type const_reverse_iterator.

Converting Reverse Iterators Back Using base()

You can convert reverse iterators back to normal iterators. To do this, reverse iterators provide the base() member function:

```
namespace std {
    template <class Iterator>
    class reverse_iterator ... {
        ...
        Iterator base() const;
        ...
    };
}
```

Here is an example of the use of base():

```
// iter/reviter4.cpp

#include <iostream>
#include <list>
#include <algorithm>
using namespace std;
```

```
int main()
{
    list<int> coll;

    // insert elements from 1 to 9
    for (int i=1; i<=9; ++i) {
        coll.push_back(i);
    }

    // find position of element with value 5
    list<int>::iterator pos;
    pos = find (coll.begin(), coll.end(),     // range
                5);                           // value

    // print value of the element
    cout << "pos:    " << *pos << endl;

    // convert iterator to reverse iterator
    list<int>::reverse_iterator rpos(pos);

    // print value of the element to which the reverse iterator refers
    cout << "rpos:   " << *rpos << endl;

    // convert reverse iterator back to normal iterator
    list<int>::iterator rrpos;
    rrpos = rpos.base();

    // print value of the element to which the normal iterator refers
    cout << "rrpos: " << *rrpos << endl;
}
```

The program has the following output:

```
pos:    5
rpos:   4
rrpos: 5
```

Thus, the conversion with base()

```
*rpos.base()
```

is equivalent to the conversion in a reverse iterator. That is, the physical position (the element of the iterator) is retained, but the logical position (the value of the element) is moved. You can find another example of the use of `base()` on page 353.

7.4.2 Insert Iterators

Insert iterators, also called *inserters*, are iterator adapters that transform an assignment of a new value into an insertion of that new value. By using insert iterators, algorithms can insert rather than overwrite. All insert iterators are in the output iterator category. Thus, they provide only the ability to assign new values (see Section 7.2.2, page 253).

Functionality of Insert Iterators

Usually an algorithm assigns values to a destination iterator. For example, consider the `copy()` algorithm (described on page 363):

```
namespace std {
    template <class InputIterator, class OutputIterator>
    OutputIterator copy (InputIterator from_pos,    // beginning of source
                         InputIterator from_end,    // end of source
                         OutputIterator to_pos)     // beginning of dest.
    {
        while (from_pos != from_end) {
            *to_pos = *from_pos;        // copy values
            ++from_pos;                 // increment iterators
            ++to_pos;
        }
        return to_pos;
    }
}
```

The loop runs until the actual position of the source iterator has reached the end. Inside the loop, the source iterator, `from_pos`, is assigned to the destination iterator, `to_pos`, and both iterators get incremented. The interesting part is the assignment of the new value:

   `*to_pos = ` *value*

An insert iterator transforms such an assignment into an insertion. However, there actually are two operations involved: First, operator `*` returns the actual element of the iterator, and second, operator `=` assigns the new value. Implementations of insert iterators usually use the following two-step trick:

1. Operator `*` is implemented as a no-op that simply returns `*this`. Thus, for insert iterators, `*pos` is equivalent to `pos`.

2. The assignment operator is implemented so that it gets transferred into an insertion. In fact, the insert iterator calls the `push_back()`, `push_front()`, or `insert()` member function of the container.

Thus, for insert iterators, you could write pos=*value* instead of *pos=*value* to insert a new value. However, I'm talking about implementation details of input iterators. The correct expression to assign a new value is *pos=*value*.

Similarly, the increment operator is implemented as a no-op that simply returns `*this`. Thus, you can't modify the position of an insert iterator. Table 7.7 lists all operations of insert iterators.

Expression	Effect
*iter	No-op (returns *iter*)
iter = value	Inserts *value*
++iter	No-op (returns *iter*)
iter++	No-op (returns *iter*)

Table 7.7. Operations of Insert Iterators

Kinds of Insert Iterators

The C++ standard library provides three kinds of insert iterators: back inserters, front inserters, and general inserters. They differ in their handling of the position at which to insert a value. In fact, each uses a different member function, which it calls for the container to which it belongs. Thus, an insert iterator must be always initialized with its container.

Each kind of insert iterator has a convenience function for its creation and initialization. Table 7.8 lists the different kinds of insert iterators and their abilities.

Name	Class	Called Function	Creation
Back inserter	`back_insert_iterator`	`push_back(`*value*`)`	`back_inserter(`*cont*`)`
Front inserter	`front_insert_iterator`	`push_front(`*value*`)`	`front_inserter(`*cont*`)`
General inserter	`insert_iterator`	`insert(`*pos*`,`*value*`)`	`inserter(`*cont*`,`*pos*`)`

Table 7.8. Kinds of Insert Iterators

Of course, the container must provide the member function that the insert iterator calls; otherwise, that kind of insert iterator can't be used. For this reason, back inserters are available only for vectors, deques, lists, and strings; front inserters are available only for deques and lists. The following subsections describe the insert iterators in detail.

Back Inserters

A *back inserter* (or *back insert iterator*) appends a value at the end of a container by calling the `push_back()` member function (see page 241 for details about `push_back()`). `push_back()` is available only for vectors, deques, lists, and strings, so these are the only containers in the C++ standard library for which back inserters are usable.

A back inserter must be initialized with its container at creation time. The `back_inserter()` function provides a convenient way of doing this. The following example demonstrates the use of back inserters:

```cpp
// iter/backins.cpp

#include <iostream>
#include <vector>
#include <algorithm>
#include "print.hpp"
using namespace std;

int main()
{
    vector<int> coll;

    // create back inserter for coll
    // - inconvenient way
    back_insert_iterator<vector<int> > iter(coll);

    // insert elements with the usual iterator interface
    *iter = 1;
    iter++;
    *iter = 2;
    iter++;
    *iter = 3;
    PRINT_ELEMENTS(coll);

    // create back inserter and insert elements
    // - convenient way
    back_inserter(coll) = 44;
    back_inserter(coll) = 55;
    PRINT_ELEMENTS(coll);

    // use back inserter to append all elements again
    // - reserve enough memory to avoid reallocation
    coll.reserve(2*coll.size());
    copy (coll.begin(), coll.end(),      // source
          back_inserter(coll));          // destination
```

```
            PRINT_ELEMENTS(coll);
}
```

The output of the program is as follows:

```
1 2 3
1 2 3 44 55
1 2 3 44 55 1 2 3 44 55
```

Note that you must not forget to reserve enough space before calling `copy()`. This is because the back inserter inserts elements, which might invalidate all other iterators referring to the same vector. Thus, the algorithm invalidates the passed source iterators while running, if not enough space is reserved.

Strings also provide an STL container interface, including `push_back()`. Therefore, you could use back inserters to append characters in a string. See page 502 for an example.

Front Inserters

A *front inserter* (or *front insert iterator*) inserts a value at the beginning of a container by calling the `push_front()` member function (see page 241 for details about `push_front()`). `push_front()` is available only for deques and lists, so these are the only containers in the C++ standard library for which front inserters are usable.

A front inserter must be initialized with its container at creation time. The `front_inserter()` function provides a convenient way of doing this. The following example demonstrates the use of front inserters:

```
// iter/frontins.cpp

#include <iostream>
#include <list>
#include <algorithm>
#include "print.hpp"
using namespace std;

int main()
{
    list<int> coll;

    // create front inserter for coll
    // - inconvenient way
    front_insert_iterator<list<int> > iter(coll);

    // insert elements with the usual iterator interface
    *iter = 1;
    iter++;
    *iter = 2;
```

```
        iter++;
        *iter = 3;

        PRINT_ELEMENTS(coll);

        // create front inserter and insert elements
        // - convenient way
        front_inserter(coll) = 44;
        front_inserter(coll) = 55;

        PRINT_ELEMENTS(coll);

        // use front inserter to insert all elements again
        copy (coll.begin(), coll.end(),    // source
              front_inserter(coll));       // destination

        PRINT_ELEMENTS(coll);
    }
```

The output of the program is as follows:

```
3 2 1
55 44 3 2 1
1 2 3 44 55 55 44 3 2 1
```

Note that the front inserter inserts multiple elements in reverse order. This happens because it always inserts the next element in front of the previous one.

General Inserters

A *general inserter* (or *general insert iterator*)[2] is initialized with two values: the container and the position that is used for the insertions. Using both, it calls the `insert()` member function with the specified position as argument. The `inserter()` function provides a convenient way of creating and initializing a general inserter.

A general inserter is available for all standard containers because all containers provide the needed `insert()` member function. However, for associative containers (set and maps) the position is used only as a hint because the value of the element defines the correct position. See the description of `insert()` on page 240 for details.

---

[2] A general inserter is often simply called *insert iterator* or *inserter*. This means that the words *insert iterator* and *inserter* have different meanings: They are a general term for all kinds of insert iterators. They are also used as names for a special insert iterator that inserts at a specified position rather than in the front or in the back. To avoid this ambiguity, I use the term *general inserter* in this book.

After an insertion, the general inserter gets the position of the new inserted element. In particular, the following statements are called:

> *pos* = *container*.insert(*pos*,*value*);
> ++*pos*;

The assignment of the return value of insert() ensures that the iterator's position is always valid. Without the assignment of the new position for deques, vectors, and strings, the general inserter would invalidate itself. This is because each insertion does, or at least might, invalidate all iterators that refer to the container.

The following example demonstrates the use of general inserters:

```
// iter/inserter.cpp

#include <iostream>
#include <set>
#include <list>
#include <algorithm>
#include "print.hpp"
using namespace std;

int main()
{
    set<int> coll;

    // create insert iterator for coll
    // - inconvenient way
    insert_iterator<set<int> > iter(coll,coll.begin());

    // insert elements with the usual iterator interface
    *iter = 1;
    iter++;
    *iter = 2;
    iter++;
    *iter = 3;

    PRINT_ELEMENTS(coll,"set:   ");

    // create inserter and insert elements
    // - convenient way
    inserter(coll,coll.end()) = 44;
    inserter(coll,coll.end()) = 55;
```

```
        PRINT_ELEMENTS(coll,"set:   ");

        // use inserter to insert all elements into a list
        list<int> coll2;
        copy (coll.begin(), coll.end(),          // source
              inserter(coll2,coll2.begin()));     // destination

        PRINT_ELEMENTS(coll2,"list: ");

        // use inserter to reinsert all elements into the list before the second element
        copy (coll.begin(), coll.end(),          // source
              inserter(coll2,++coll2.begin()));   // destination

        PRINT_ELEMENTS(coll2,"list: ");
    }
```

The output of the program is as follows:

```
    set:  1 2 3
    set:  1 2 3 44 55
    list: 1 2 3 44 55
    list: 1 1 2 3 44 55 2 3 44 55
```

The calls of copy() demonstrate that the general inserter maintains the order of the elements. The second call of copy() uses a certain position inside the range that is passed as argument.

A User-Defined Inserter for Associative Containers

As mentioned previously, for associative containers the position argument of general inserters is only used as a hint. This hint might help to improve speed, however it also might cause bad performance. For example, if the inserted elements are in reverse order, the hint may slow down programs a bit. This is because the search for the correct insertion point always starts at a wrong position. Thus, a bad hint might even be worse than no hint. This is a good example of the need for a supplementation of the C++ standard library. See Section 7.5.2, page 288, for such an extension.

7.4.3   Stream Iterators

A *stream iterator* is an iterator adapter that allows you to use a stream as source or destination of algorithms. In particular, an istream iterator can be used to read elements from an input stream and an ostream iterator can be used to write values to an output stream.

A special form of a stream iterator is a *stream buffer iterator*, which can be used to read from or write to a stream buffer directly. Stream buffer iterators are discussed in Section 13.13.2, page 665.

Ostream Iterators

Ostream iterators write assigned values to an output stream. By using ostream iterators, algorithms can write directly to streams. The implementation of an ostream iterator uses the same concept as the implementation of insert iterators (see page 271). The only difference is that they transform the assignment of a new value into an output operation by using operator <<. Thus, algorithms can write directly to streams using the usual iterator interface. Table 7.9 lists the operations of ostream iterators.

Expression	Effect
`ostream_iterator<T>`(*ostream*)	Creates an ostream iterator for *ostream*
`ostream_iterator<T>`(*ostream*,*delim*)	Creates an ostream iterator for *ostream* with the string *delim* as the delimiter between the values (note that *delim* has type `const char*`)
*iter	No-op (returns *iter*)
iter = value	Writes *value* to *ostream*: *ostream<<value* (followed by *delim* if set)
++iter	No-op (returns *iter*)
iter++	No-op (returns *iter*)

Table 7.9. Operations of ostream Iterators

At creation time of the ostream iterator you must pass the output stream on which the values are written. An optional string can be passed, which is written as a separator between single values. Without the delimiter, the elements directly follow each other.

Ostream iterators are defined for a certain element type T:

```
namespace std {
    template <class T,
              class charT = char,
              class traits = char_traits<charT> >
    class ostream_iterator;
}
```

The optional second and third template arguments specify the type of stream that is used (see Section 13.2.1, page 590, for their meaning).[3]

---

[3] In older systems, the optional template arguments for the stream type are missing.

The following example demonstrates the use of ostream iterators:

```cpp
// iter/ostriter.cpp

#include <iostream>
#include <vector>
#include <algorithm>
#include <iterator>
using namespace std;

int main()
{
    // create ostream iterator for stream cout
    // - values are separated by a newline character
    ostream_iterator<int> intWriter(cout,"\n");

    // write elements with the usual iterator interface
    *intWriter = 42;
    intWriter++;
    *intWriter = 77;
    intWriter++;
    *intWriter = -5;

    // create collection with elements from 1 to 9
    vector<int> coll;
    for (int i=1; i<=9; ++i) {
        coll.push_back(i);
    }

    // write all elements without any delimiter
    copy (coll.begin(), coll.end(),
          ostream_iterator<int>(cout));
    cout << endl;

    // write all elements with " < " as delimiter
    copy (coll.begin(), coll.end(),
          ostream_iterator<int>(cout," < "));
    cout << endl;
}
```

The output of the program is as follows:

```
42
77
-5
123456789
1 < 2 < 3 < 4 < 5 < 6 < 7 < 8 < 9 <
```

Note that the delimiter has type `const char*`. Thus, if you pass an object of type `string` you must call its member function `c_str()` (see Section 11.3.6, page 513) to get the correct type. For example:

```
string delim;
...
ostream_iterator<int>(cout,delim.c_str());
```

Istream Iterators

Istream iterators are the counterparts of ostream iterators. An istream iterator reads elements from an input stream. By using istream iterators, algorithms can read from streams directly. However, istream iterators are a bit more complicated than ostream iterators (as usual, reading is more complicated than writing).

At creation time the istream iterator is initialized by the input stream from which it reads. Then, by using the usual interface of input iterators (see Section 7.2.1, page 252), it reads element-by-element using operator >>. However, reading might fail (due to end-of-file or an error), and source ranges of algorithms need an "end position." To handle both problems, you can use an *end-of-stream iterator*. An end-of-stream iterator is created with the default constructor for istream iterators. If a read fails, every istream iterator becomes an end-of-stream iterator. Thus, after any read access, you should compare an istream iterator with an end-of-stream iterator to check whether the iterator has a valid value. Table 7.10 lists all operations of istream iterators.

Note that the constructor of an istream iterator opens the stream and usually reads the first element. It has to read the first value because otherwise it could not return the first element when operator * is called after the initialization. However, implementations may defer the first read until the first call of operator *. So, you should not define an istream iterator before you really need it.

Istream iterators are defined for a certain element type T:

```
namespace std {
    template <class T,
              class charT = char,
              class traits = char_traits<charT>,
              class Distance = ptrdiff_t>
    class istream_iterator;
}
```

Expression	Effect
`istream_iterator<T>()`	Creates an end-of-stream iterator
`istream_iterator<T>(`*istream*`)`	Creates an istream iterator for *istream* (and might read the first value)
*iter	Returns the actual value, read before (reads first value if not done by the constructor)
iter->member	Returns a member (if any) of the actual value, read before
++*iter*	Reads next value and returns its position
iter++	Reads next value but returns an iterator for the previous value
iter1== *iter2*	Tests *iter1* and *iter2* for equality
iter1!= *iter2*	Tests *iter1* and *iter2* for inequality

Table 7.10. Operations of istream Iterators

The optional second and third template arguments specify the type of stream that is used (see Section 13.2.1, page 590, for their meaning). The optional fourth template argument specifies the difference type for the iterators.[4]

Two istream iterators are equal if

- both are end-of-stream iterators and thus can no longer read, or
- both can read and use the same stream.

The following example demonstrates the operations provided for istream iterators:

```
// iter/istriter.cpp

#include <iostream>
#include <iterator>
using namespace std;

int main()
{
    // create istream iterator that reads integers from cin
    istream_iterator<int> intReader(cin);

    // create end-of-stream iterator
    istream_iterator<int> intReaderEOF;

    /* while able to read tokens with istream iterator
```

---

[4] In older systems without default template parameters, the optional fourth template argument is required as the second argument, and the arguments for the stream type are missing.

```
     * - write them twice
     */
    while (intReader != intReaderEOF) {
        cout << "once:        " << *intReader << endl;
        cout << "once again: " << *intReader << endl;
        ++intReader;
    }
}
```

If you start the program with the following input:

```
1 2 3 f 4
```

the output of the program is as follows:

```
once:        1
once again: 1
once:        2
once again: 2
once:        3
once again: 3
```

As you can see, the input of character f ends the program. Due to a format error, the stream is no longer in a good state. Therefore, the istream iterator intReader is equal to the end-of-stream iterator intReaderEOF. So, the condition of the loop yields false,

Another Example of Stream Iterators

Here is an example that uses both kinds of stream iterators as well as the advance() iterator function:

```
// iter/advance2.cpp

#include <iostream>
#include <string>
#include <algorithm>
#include <iterator>
using namespace std;

int main()
{
    istream_iterator<string> cinPos(cin);
    ostream_iterator<string> coutPos(cout," ");
```

```
/* while input is not at the end of the file
 * - write every third string
 */
while (cinPos != istream_iterator<string>()) {
    // ignore the following two strings
    advance (cinPos, 2);

    // read and write the third string
    if (cinPos != istream_iterator<string>()) {
        *coutPos++ = *cinPos++;
    }
}
cout << endl;
}
```

The advance() iterator function is provided to advance the iterator to another position (see Section 7.3.1, page 259). Used with istream iterators, it skips input tokens. For example, if you have the following input[5]:

```
No one objects if you are doing
a good programming job for
someone whom you respect.
```

the output is as follows:

```
objects are good for you
```

Don't forget to check whether the istream iterator is still valid after calling advance() and before accessing its value with *cinPos. Calling operator * for an end-of-stream iterator results in undefined behavior.

See pages 107, 366, and 385 for other examples that demonstrate how algorithms use stream iterators to read from and write to streams.

7.5 Iterator Traits

Iterators have different categories (see Section 7.2, page 251) that represent special iterator abilities. It might be useful or even necessary to be able to overload behavior for different iterator categories. By using iterator tags and iterator traits (both provided in <iterator>) such an overloading can be performed.

For each iterator category, the C++ standard library provides an *iterator tag* that can be used as a "label" for iterators:

---

[5] Thanks to Andrew Koenig for the nice input of this example.

```
namespace std {
    struct output_iterator_tag {
    };
    struct input_iterator_tag {
    };
    struct forward_iterator_tag
      : public input_iterator_tag {
    };
    struct bidirectional_iterator_tag
      : public forward_iterator_tag {
    };
    struct random_access_iterator_tag
      : public bidirectional_iterator_tag {
    };
}
```

Note that inheritance is used. So, for example, any forward iterator *is a* kind of input iterator. However, note that the tag for forward iterators is only derived from the tag for input iterators, not from the tag for output iterators. Thus, any forward iterator *is not a* kind of output iterator. In fact, forward iterators have requirements that keep them from being output iterators. See page 254 for more details.

If you write generic code, you might not only be interested in the iterator category. For example, you may need the type of the elements to which the iterator refers. Therefore, the C++ standard library provides a special template structure to define the *iterator traits*. This structure contains all relevant information regarding an iterator. It is used as a common interface for all the type definitions an iterator should have (the category, the type of the elements, and so on):

```
namespace std {
    template <class T>
    struct iterator_traits {
        typedef typename T::value_type         value_type;
        typedef typename T::difference_type    difference_type;
        typedef typename T::iterator_category  iterator_category;
        typedef typename T::pointer            pointer;
        typedef typename T::reference          reference;
    };
}
```

In this template, T stands for the type of the iterator. Thus, you can write code that uses for any iterator its category, the type of its elements, and so on. For example, the following expression yields the value type of iterator type T:

```
typename std::iterator_traits<T>::value_type
```

This structure has two advantages:

1. It ensures that an iterator provides all type definitions.
2. It can be (partially) specialized for (sets of) special iterators.

The latter is done for ordinary pointers that also can be used as iterators:

```
namespace std {
    template <class T>
    struct iterator_traits<T*> {
        typedef T                           value_type;
        typedef ptrdiff_t                   difference_type;
        typedef random_access_iterator_tag iterator_category;
        typedef T*                          pointer;
        typedef T&                          reference;
    };
}
```

Thus, for any type "pointer to T," it is defined that it has the random access iterator category. A corresponding partial specialization exists for constant pointers (const T*).

7.5.1 Writing Generic Functions for Iterators

Using iterator traits, you can write generic functions that derive type definitions or use different implementation code depending on the iterator category.

Using Iterator Types

A simple example of the use of iterator traits is an algorithm that needs a temporary variable for the elements. Such a temporary value is declared simply like this

```
typename std::iterator_traits<T>::value_type tmp;
```

whereby T is the type of the iterator.

Another example is an algorithm that shifts elements cyclically:

```
template <class ForwardIterator>
void shift_left (ForwardIterator beg, ForwardIterator end)
{
    // temporary variable for first element
    typedef typename
      std::iterator_traits<ForwardIterator>::value_type value_type;

    if (beg != end) {
        // save value of first element
```

```
value_type tmp(*beg);

// shift following values
    ...
    }
}
```

Using Iterator Categories

To use different implementations for different iterator categories you must follow these two steps:

1. Let your template function call another function with the iterator category as an additional argument. For example:

```
template <class Iterator>
inline void foo (Iterator beg, Iterator end)
{
    foo (beg, end,
        std::iterator_traits<Iterator>::iterator_category());
}
```

2. Implement that other function for any iterator category that provides a special implementation that is not derived from another iterator category. For example:

```
// foo() for bidirectional iterators
template <class BiIterator>
void foo (BiIterator beg, BiIterator end,
        std::bidirectional_iterator_tag)
{
    ...
}
```

```
// foo() for random access iterators
template <class RaIterator>
void foo (RaIterator beg, RaIterator end,
        std::random_access_iterator_tag)
{
    ...
}
```

The version for random access iterators could, for example, use random access operations, whereas the version for bidirectional iterators would not. Due to the hierarchy of iterator tags (see page 283) you could provide one implementation for more than one iterator category.

Implementation of `distance()`

An example of following the steps in the previous subsection is the implementation of the auxiliary `distance()` iterator function. This function returns the distance between two iterator positions and their elements (see Section 7.3.2, page 261). The implementation for random access iterators only uses the operator `-`. For all other iterator categories, the number of increments to reach the end of the range is returned.

```
// general distance()
template <class Iterator>
typename std::iterator_traits<Iterator>::difference_type
distance (Iterator pos1, Iterator pos2)
{
    return distance (pos1, pos2,
                     std::iterator_traits<Iterator>
                         ::iterator_category());
}


// distance() for random access iterators
template <class RaIterator>
typename std::iterator_traits<RaIterator>::difference_type
distance (RaIterator pos1, RaIterator pos2,
          std::random_access_iterator_tag)
{
    return pos2 - pos1;
}


// distance() for input, forward, and bidirectional iterators
template <class InIterator>
typename std::iterator_traits<InIterator>::difference_type
distance (InIterator pos1, InIterator pos2,
          std::input_iterator_tag)
{
    typename std::iterator_traits<InIterator>::difference_type d;
    for (d=0; pos1 != pos2; ++pos1, ++d) {
        ;
    }
    return d;
}
```

The difference type of the iterator is used as the return type. Note that the second version uses the tag for input iterators, so this implementation is also used by forward and bidirectional iterators because their tags are derived from `input_iterator_tag`.

7.5.2   User-Defined Iterators

Let's write an iterator. As mentioned in the previous section, you need iterator traits provided for the user-defined iterator. You can provide them in one of two ways:

1. Provide the necessary five type definitions for the general `iterator_traits` structure (see page 284).
2. Provide a (partial) specialization of the `iterator_traits` structure.

For the first way, the C++ standard library provides a special base class, `iterator<>`, that does the type definitions. You need only to pass the types[6]:

```
class MyIterator
  : public std::iterator <std::bidirectional_iterator_tag,
                          type, std::ptrdiff_t, type*, type&> {
    ...
};
```

The first template parameter defines the iterator category, the second defines the element type *type*, the third defines the difference type, the fourth defines the pointer type, and the fifth defines the reference type. The last three arguments are optional and have the default values `ptrdiff_t`, *type**, and *type&*. Often it is enough to use the following definition:

```
class MyIterator
  : public std::iterator <std::bidirectional_iterator_tag, type> {
    ...
};
```

The following example demonstrates how to write a user-defined iterator. It is an insert iterator for associative containers. Unlike insert iterators of the C++ standard library (see Section 7.4.2, page 271), no insert position is used.

Here is the implementation of the iterator class:

```
// iter/assoiter.hpp

#include <iterator>

/* template class for insert iterator for associative containers
 */
```

---

[6] In older STL versions, the auxiliary types `input_iterator`, `output_iterator`, `forward_iterator`, `bidirectional_iterator`, and `random_access_iterator` were provided instead of `iterator`.

```
template <class Container>
class asso_insert_iterator
  : public std::iterator <std::output_iterator_tag,
                          void, void, void, void>
{
  protected:
    Container& container;      // container in which elements are inserted

  public:
    // constructor
    explicit asso_insert_iterator (Container& c) : container(c) {
    }

    // assignment operator
    // - inserts a value into the container
    asso_insert_iterator<Container>&
    operator= (const typename Container::value_type& value) {
        container.insert(value);
        return *this;
    }

    // dereferencing is a no-op that returns the iterator itself
    asso_insert_iterator<Container>& operator* () {
        return *this;
    }

    // increment operation is a no-op that returns the iterator itself
    asso_insert_iterator<Container>& operator++ () {
        return *this;
    }
    asso_insert_iterator<Container>& operator++ (int) {
        return *this;
    }
};

/* convenience function to create the inserter
 */
template <class Container>
inline asso_insert_iterator<Container> asso_inserter (Container& c)
```

```
{
    return asso_insert_iterator<Container>(c);
}
```

The `asso_insert_iterator` class is derived from the `iterator` class. The first template argument `output_iterator_tag` is passed to `iterator` to specify the iterator category. Output iterators can only be used to write something. Thus, as for all output iterators, element and difference types are `void`.[7]

At creation time the iterator stores its container in its `container` member. Any value that gets assigned is inserted into the container by `insert()`. Operators `*` and `++` are no-ops that simply return the iterator itself. Thus, the iterator maintains control. If the usual iterator interface is used

```
*pos = value
```

the `*pos` expression returns `*this` to which the new value is assigned. That assignment is transfered into a call of `insert(value)` for the container.

After the definition of the inserter class, the usual convenient function `asso_inserter` is defined as convenience function to create and initialize an inserter. The following program uses such an inserter to insert some elements into a set:

```
// iter/assoiter.cpp

#include <iostream>
#include <set>
#include <algorithm>
using namespace std;

#include "print.hpp"

#include "assoiter.hpp"

int main()
{
    set<int> coll;

    // create inserter for coll
    // - inconvenient way
    asso_insert_iterator<set<int> > iter(coll);
```

---

[7] For older STL versions, the `asso_insert_iterator` class must be derived from class `output_iterator` without any template parameter.

```
// insert elements with the usual iterator interface
*iter = 1;
iter++;
*iter = 2;
iter++;
*iter = 3;

PRINT_ELEMENTS(coll);

// create inserter for coll and insert elements
// - convenient way
asso_inserter(coll) = 44;
asso_inserter(coll) = 55;

PRINT_ELEMENTS(coll);

// use inserter with an algorithm
int vals[] = { 33, 67, -4, 13, 5, 2 };
copy (vals, vals+(sizeof(vals)/sizeof(vals[0])),   // source
      asso_inserter(coll));                        // destination

PRINT_ELEMENTS(coll);
}
```

The output of the program is as follows:

```
1 2 3
1 2 3 44 55
-4 1 2 3 5 13 33 44 55 67
```

Chapter 8
STL Function Objects

This chapter discusses in detail *function objects*, or *functors* for short, which were introduced in Section 5.9, page 124. It covers the full set of predefined function objects and function adapters, and the concept of functional composition, and provides examples of self-written function objects.

8.1 The Concept of Function Objects

A function object (or *functor*), is an object that has operator () defined so that in the following example

> *FunctionObjectType* fo;
>
> ...
>
> fo(...);

the expression fo() is a call of operator () for the function object fo instead of a call of the function fo().

At first, you could consider a function object as an ordinary function that is written in a more complicated way: Instead of writing all the function statements inside the function body,

```
void fo() {
    statements
}
```

you write them inside the body of operator () of the function object class:

```
class FunctionObjectType {
  public:
    void operator() () {
        statements
    }
};
```

This kind of definition is more complicated; however, it has three important advantages:

1. A function object might be smarter because it may have a state. In fact, you can have two instances of the same function, represented by a function object, which may have different states at the same time. This is not possible for ordinary functions.

2. Each function object has its own type. Thus, you can pass the type of a function object to a template to specify a certain behavior, and you have the advantage that container types with different function objects differ.

3. A function object is usually faster than a function pointer.

See page 126 for more details about these advantages and page 127 for an example that shows how function objects can be smarter than ordinary functions.

In the next two subsections I present two other examples that go into more detail about function objects. The first example demonstrates how to benefit from the fact that each function object usually has its own type. The second example demonstrates how to benefit from the state of function objects, and leads to an interesting property of the `for_each()` algorithm, which is covered in another subsection.

8.1.1   Function Objects as Sorting Criteria

Programmers often need a sorted collection of elements that have a special class (for example, a collection of `persons`). However, you either don't want to use or you can't use the usual operator < to sort the objects. Instead, you sort the objects according to a special sorting criterion based on some member function. In this regard, a function object can help. Consider the following example:

```
// fo/sort1.cpp

#include <iostream>
#include <string>
#include <set>
#include <algorithm>
using namespace std;

class Person {
  public:
    string firstname() const;
    string lastname() const;
    ...
};

/* class for function predicate
 * - operator () returns whether a person is less than another person
 */
```

```
class PersonSortCriterion {
  public:
    bool operator() (const Person& p1, const Person& p2) const {
        /* a person is less than another person
         * - if the last name is less
         * - if the last name is equal and the first name is less
         */
        return p1.lastname()<p2.lastname() ||
                (p1.lastname()==p2.lastname() &&
                 p1.firstname()<p2.firstname());
    }
};

int main()
{
    // declare set type with special sorting criterion
    typedef set<Person,PersonSortCriterion> PersonSet;

    // create such a collection
    PersonSet coll;
    ...

    // do something with the elements
    PersonSet::iterator pos;
    for (pos = coll.begin(); pos != coll.end(); ++pos) {
        ...
    }
    ...
}
```

The set `coll` uses the special sorting criterion `PersonSortCriterion`, which is defined as a function object class. `PersonSortCriterion` defines operator () in such a way that it compares two Persons according to their last name and (if they are equal) to their first name. The constructor of `coll` creates an instance of class `PersonSortCriterion` automatically so that the elements are sorted according to this sorting criterion.

Note that the sorting criterion `PersonSortCriterion` is a *type*. Thus, you can use it as a template argument for the set. This would not be possible, if you implement the sorting criterion as a plain function (as was done on page 123).

All sets with this sorting criterion have their own type (which is called `PersonSet` in this example). You can't combine or assign a set that has a "normal" or another user-defined sorting criterion. Thus, you can't compromise the automatic sorting of the set by any operation; however, you can design function objects that represent different sorting criteria with the same type (see the next subsection). See page 178 for more details about sets and their sorting criteria.

8.1.2   Function Objects with Internal State

The following example shows how function objects can be used to behave as a function that may have more than one state at the same time:

```
// fo/general.cpp

#include <iostream>
#include <list>
#include <algorithm>
#include "print.hpp"
using namespace std;

class IntSequence {
  private:
    int value;
  public:
    // constructor
    IntSequence (int initialValue)
     : value(initialValue) {
    }

    // "function call"
    int operator() () {
        return value++;
    }
};

int main()
{
    list<int> coll;

    // insert values from 1 to 9
    generate_n (back_inserter(coll),      // start
```

```
                    9,                          // number of elements
                    IntSequence(1));            // generates values

    PRINT_ELEMENTS(coll);

    // replace second to last element but one with values starting at 42
    generate (++coll.begin(),                   // start
                --coll.end(),                   // end
                IntSequence(42));               // generates values

    PRINT_ELEMENTS(coll);
}
```

In this example, a function object is used that generates a sequence of integral values. Each time operator () is called, it returns its actual value and increments it. You can pass the start value as a constructor argument.

Two such function objects are then used by the `generate()` and `generate_n()` algorithms. These algorithms use generated values to write them into a collection: The expression

```
    IntSequence(1)
```

in the statement

```
    generate_n (back_inserter(coll),
                9,
                IntSequence(1));
```

creates such a function object initialized with 1. The `generate_n()` algorithm uses it nine times to write an element, so it generates values 1 to 9. Similarly, the expression

```
    IntSequence(42)
```

generates a sequence beginning with value 42. The `generate()` algorithm replaces the elements beginning with ++coll.begin() up to --coll.end().[1] The output of the program is as follows:

```
    1 2 3 4 5 6 7 8 9
    1 42 43 44 45 46 47 48 9
```

Using other versions of operator (), you can produce more complicated sequences easily.

---

[1] The expressions
```
    ++coll.begin()
```
and
```
    --coll.end()
```
might not work with vectors. This nasty problem is discussed in Section 7.2.6, page 258.

Function objects are passed by value rather than by reference. Thus, the algorithm does not change the state of the function object. For example, the following code generates the sequence starting with value 1 twice:

```
IntSequence seq(1);       // integral sequence starting with value 1
```

```
// insert sequence beginning with 1
generate_n (back_inserter(coll), 9, seq);
```

```
// insert sequence beginning with 1 again
generate_n (back_inserter(coll), 9, seq);
```

Passing function objects by value instead of by reference has the advantage that you can pass constant and temporary expressions. Otherwise, passing `IntSequence(1)` would not be possible.

The disadvantage of passing the function object by value is that you can't benefit from modifications of the state of the function objects. Algorithms can modify the state of the function objects, but you can't access and process their final states because they make internal copies of the function objects. However, access to the final state might be necessary, so the question is how to get a "result" from an algorithm.

There are two ways to get a "result" or "feedback" from using function objects with algorithms:

1. You can pass the function objects by reference.
2. You can use the return value of the `for_each()` algorithm.

The latter is discussed in the next subsection.

To pass a function object by reference you simply have to qualify the call of the algorithm so that the function object type is a reference.[2] For example:

```
// fo/genera2.cpp

#include <iostream>
#include <list>
#include <algorithm>
#include "print.hpp"
using namespace std;

class IntSequence {
  private:
    int value;
  public:
    // constructor
```

---

[2] Thanks to Philip Köster for pointing this out.

```
    IntSequence (int initialValue)
     : value(initialValue) {
    }

    // "function call"
    int operator() () {
        return value++;
    }
};

int main()
{
    list<int> coll;
    IntSequence seq(1);        // integral sequence starting with 1

    // insert values from 1 to 4
    // - pass function object by reference
    //   so that it will continue with 5
    generate_n<back_insert_iterator<list<int> >,
                int, IntSequence&>(back_inserter(coll),     // start
                                        4,        // number of elements
                                        seq);     // generates values
    PRINT_ELEMENTS(coll);

    // insert values from 42 to 45
    generate_n (back_inserter(coll),           // start
                4,                             // number of elements
                IntSequence(42));              // generates values
    PRINT_ELEMENTS(coll);

    // continue with first sequence
    // - pass function object by value
    //   so that it will continue with 5 again
    generate_n (back_inserter(coll),           // start
                4,                             // number of elements
                seq);                          // generates values
    PRINT_ELEMENTS(coll);

    // continue with first sequence again
```

```
        generate_n (back_inserter(coll),        // start
                    4,                           // number of elements
                    seq);                        // generates values
        PRINT_ELEMENTS(coll);
    }
```

The program has the following output:

```
1 2 3 4
1 2 3 4 42 43 44 45
1 2 3 4 42 43 44 45 5 6 7 8
1 2 3 4 42 43 44 45 5 6 7 8 5 6 7 8
```

In the first call of generate_n() the function object seq is passed by reference. To do this, the template arguments are qualified explicitly:

```
    generate_n<back_insert_iterator<list<int> >,
               int, IntSequence&>(back_inserter(coll),    // start
                                  4,           // number of elements
                                  seq);        // generates values
```

As a result, the internal value of seq is modified after the call and the second use of seq by the third call of generate_n() continues the sequence of the first call. However, this call passes seq by value:

```
    generate_n (back_inserter(coll),        // start
                4,                          // number of elements
                seq);                       // generates values
```

Thus, the call does not change the state of seq. As a result, the last call of generate_n() continues the sequence with value 5 again.

8.1.3   The Return Value of for_each()

The effort involved with a reference-counted implementation of a function object to access its final state is not necessary if you use the for_each() algorithm. for_each() has the unique ability to return its function object (no other algorithm can do this). Thus you can query the state of your function object by checking the return value of for_each().

The following program is a nice example of the use of the return value of for_each(). It shows how to process the mean value of a sequence:

```
// fo/foreach3.cpp

#include <iostream>
#include <vector>
#include <algorithm>
```

```cpp
using namespace std;

// function object to process the mean value
class MeanValue {
  private:
    long num;        // number of elements
    long sum;        // sum of all element values
  public:
    // constructor
    MeanValue () : num(0), sum(0) {
    }

    // "function call"
    // - process one more element of the sequence
    void operator() (int elem) {
        num++;               // increment count
        sum += elem;         // add value
    }

    // return mean value
    double value () {
        return static_cast<double>(sum) / static_cast<double>(num);
    }
};

int main()
{
    vector<int> coll;

    // insert elments from 1 to 8
    for (int i=1; i<=8; ++i) {
        coll.push_back(i);
    }

    // process and print mean value
    MeanValue mv = for_each (coll.begin(), coll.end(),   // range
                            MeanValue());                // operation
    cout << "mean value: " << mv.value() << endl;
}
```

The expression

```
MeanValue()
```

creates a function object that counts the number of elements and processes the sum of all element values. By passing it to `for_each()`, it is called for each element of the container `coll`:

```
MeanValue mv = for_each (coll.begin(), coll.end(),
                         MeanValue());
```

The function object is returned and assigned to `mv`, so you can query its state after the statement by calling: `mv.value()`. Therefore, the program has the following output:

```
mean value: 4.5
```

You could even make the class `MeanValue` a bit smarter by defining an automatic type conversion to `double`. Then you could use the mean value that is processed by `for_each()` directly. See page 336 for such an example.

8.1.4 Predicates versus Function Objects

Predicates are functions or function objects that return a Boolean value (a value that is convertible to `bool`). However, not every function that returns a Boolean value is a valid predicate for the STL. This may lead to surprising behavior. Consider the following example:

```
// fo/removeif.cpp

#include <iostream>
#include <list>
#include <algorithm>
#include "print.hpp"
using namespace std;

class Nth {       // function object that returns true for the nth call
  private:
    int nth;        // call for which to return true
    int count;      // call counter
  public:
    Nth (int n) : nth(n), count(0) {
    }
    bool operator() (int) {
        return ++count == nth;
    }
};
```

```
int main()
{
    list<int> coll;

    // insert elements from 1 to 9
    for (int i=1; i<=9; ++i) {
        coll.push_back(i);
    }
    PRINT_ELEMENTS(coll,"coll:          ");

    // remove third element
    list<int>::iterator pos;
    pos = remove_if(coll.begin(),coll.end(),   // range
                    Nth(3));                    // remove criterion
    coll.erase(pos,coll.end());

    PRINT_ELEMENTS(coll,"nth removed: ");
}
```

This program defines a function object Nth that yields true for the *n*th call. However, when passing it to remove_if() (an algorithm that removes all elements for which a unary predicate yields true, see page 378), the result is a big surprise:

```
coll:          1 2 3 4 5 6 7 8 9
nth removed: 1 2 4 5 7 8 9
```

Two elements, namely the third and sixth elements are removed. This happens because the usual implementation of the algorithm copies the predicate internally during the algorithm:

```
template <class ForwIter, class Predicate>
ForwIter std::remove_if(ForwIter beg, ForwIter end,
                        Predicate op)
{
    beg = find_if(beg, end, op);
    if (beg == end) {
        return beg;
    }
    else {
        ForwIter next = beg;
        return remove_copy_if(++next, end, beg, op);
    }
}
```

The algorithm uses `find_if()` to find the first element that should be removed. However, it then uses a copy of the passed predicate op to process the remaining elements if any. Here, `Nth` in its original state is used again and it also removes the third element of the remaining elements, which is in fact the sixth element.

This behavior is not a bug. The standard does not specify how often a predicate might be copied internally by an algorithm. Thus, to get the guaranteed behavior of the C++ standard library you should not pass a function object for which the behavior depends on how often it is copied or called. Thus, if you call a unary predicate for two arguments and both arguments are equal, then the predicate should always yield the same result. That is, a predicate should not change its state due to a call, and a copy of a predicate should have the same state as the original. To ensure that you can't change the state of a predicate due to a function call, you should declare operator () as constant member function.

It is possible to avoid this surprising behavior and to guarantee that this algorithm works as expected even for a function object such as `Nth`, without any performance penalties. You could implement `remove_if()` in such a way that the call of `find_if()` is replaced by its contents:

```
template <class ForwIter, class Predicate>
ForwIter std::remove_if(ForwIter beg, ForwIter end,
                        Predicate op)
{
    while (beg != end && !op(*beg)) {
        ++beg;
    }
    if (beg == end) {
        return beg;
    }
    else {
        ForwIter next = beg;
        return remove_copy_if(++next, end, beg, op);
    }
}
```

So, it might be a good idea to change the implementation of `remove_if()` (or submit a change request to the implementor of the library). To my knowledge, in current implementations this problem only arises with the `remove_if()` algorithm. If you use `remove_copy_if()`, all works as expected.[3] However, to be portable, you should never rely on this implementation detail. You should always declare the function call operator of predicates as being a constant member function.

---

[3] Whether the C++ standard library should guarantee the expected behavior in cases such as those presented in this example is currently under discussion.

8.2   Predefined Function Objects

As mentioned in Section 5.9.2, page 131, the C++ standard library provides many predefined function objects. Table 8.1 lists all predefined function objects.[4]

Expression	Effect
negate<*type*>()	*– param*
plus<*type*>()	*param1 + param2*
minus<*type*>()	*param1 – param2*
multiplies<*type*>()[4]	*param1 * param2*
divides<*type*>()	*param1 / param2*
modulus<*type*>()	*param1 % param2*
equal_to<*type*>()	*param1 == param2*
not_equal_to<*type*>()	*param1 != param2*
less<*type*>()	*param1 < param2*
greater<*type*>()	*param1 > param2*
less_equal<*type*>()	*param1 <= param2*
greater_equal<*type*>()	*param1 >= param2*
logical_not<*type*>()	*! param*
logical_and<*type*>()	*param1 && param2*
logical_or<*type*>()	*param1 || param2*

Table 8.1. Predefined Function Objects

less<> is the default criterion whenever objects are sorted or compared, so it is used often. Default sorting operations always produce an ascending order (*element < nextElement*).

To use these function objects, you must include the header file <functional>[5]:

```
#include <functional>
```

To compare internationalized strings, the C++ standard library provides another function object that can be used as a sorting criterion for strings. See page 703 for details.

---

[4] In earlier versions of the STL, the function object for multiplication had the name times. This was changed due to a name clash with a function of the operating system standards (X/Open, POSIX) and because multiplies was clearer.

[5] In the original STL, the header file for function objects was called <function.h>.

8.2.1   Function Adapters

A function adapter is a function object that enables the combining of function objects with each other, with certain values, or with special functions. Function adapters are also declared in `<functional>`. For example, in the following statement:

```
find_if (coll.begin(),coll.end(),      // range
         bind2nd(greater<int>(),42))    // criterion
```

the expression

```
bind2nd(greater<int>(),42)
```

produces a combined function object that checks whether an `int` value is greater than 42. In fact, `bind2nd` transforms a binary function object, such as `greater<>`, into a unary function object. It always uses its second parameter as the second argument of the binary function object that is passed as the first parameter. Thus, in this example it always calls `greater<>` with 42 as the second argument. Section 5.9.2, page 132, offers some other examples of the use of function adapters.

Table 8.2 lists the predefined function adapter classes provided by the C++ standard library.

Expression	Effect
bind1st(*op*,*value*)	*op*(*value*,*param*)
bind2nd(*op*,*value*)	*op*(*param*,*value*)
not1(*op*)	!*op*(*param*)
not2(*op*)	!*op*(*param1*,*param2*)

Table 8.2. Predefined Function Adapters

Function adapters are function objects themselves, so you can combine function adapters and function objects to form more powerful (and more complicated) expressions. For example, the following statement returns the first even element of a collection:

```
pos = find_if (coll.begin(), coll.end(),        // range
               not1(bind2nd(modulus<int>(),2)));  // criterion
```

In this statement, the expression

```
bind2nd(modulus<int>(),2)
```

returns 1 for all odd values. So this expression as a criterion finds the first element that has an odd value because 1 is equivalent to `true`. `not1()` negates the result, so the whole statement searches for the first element that has an even value.

By using function adapters you can combine different function objects to form very powerful expressions. This kind of programming is called *functional composition*. However, the C++ standard library lacks some function adapters that are necessary and useful for functional composition. For example, some function adapters are missing that allow you to combine two predicates with "and" or "or" (such as, "greater than 4 *and* less than 7"). If you extend the standard function adapters by some composing function adapters you get a lot more power. See Section 8.3, page 313, for a description of such extensions.

8.2.2 Function Adapters for Member Functions

The C++ standard library provides some additional function adapters that enable you to call a member function for each element of a collection (Table 8.3).

Expression	Effect
mem_fun_ref(*op*)	Calls *op*() as a member function for an object
mem_fun(*op*)	Calls *op*() as a member function for a pointer to an object

Table 8.3. Function Adapters for Member Functions

For example, in the following code mem_fun_ref is used to call a member function for objects of a vector:

```cpp
// fo/memfun1a.cpp

class Person {
  private:
    std::string name;
  public:
    ...
    void print () const {
        std::cout << name << std::endl;
    }
    void printWithPrefix (std::string prefix) const {
        std::cout << prefix << name << std::endl;
    }
};

void foo (const std::vector<Person>& coll)
{
    using std::for_each;
    using std::bind2nd;
    using std::mem_fun_ref;

    // call member function print() for each element
    for_each (coll.begin(), coll.end(),
              mem_fun_ref(&Person::print));
```

      // call member function `printWithPrefix()` *for each element*
      // - `"person: "` *is passed as an argument to the member function*

```
      for_each (coll.begin(), coll.end(),
                bind2nd(mem_fun_ref(&Person::printWithPrefix),
                        "person: "));
  }
```

In `foo()`, two different member functions of class `Person` are called for each element in the vector
`coll`: (1) `Person::print()`, which has no parameter, and (2) `Person::printWithPrefix()`,
which has an additional parameter. To call the `Person::print()` member function, the function
object

```
    mem_fun_ref(&Person::print)
```

is passed to the `for_each()` algorithm:

```
    for_each (coll.begin(), coll.end(),
              mem_fun_ref(&Person::print));
```

The `mem_fun_ref` adapter transforms the function call for the element into a call of the passed
member function.

    The adapter is necessary because you can't pass a member function directly to an algorithm.
Doing so would cause a compile-time error:

```
    for_each (coll.begin(), coll.end(),
              &Person::print);    // ERROR: can't call operator ()
              //          for a member function pointer
```

The problem is that `for_each()` would call operator () for the pointer passed as the third argument
instead of calling the member function to which it points. The `mem_fun_ref` adapter solves this
problem by transforming the call of operator ().

    By using `bind2nd` it is also possible to pass one argument to the called member function, as the
second call of `for_each()` shows[6]:

```
    for_each (coll.begin(), coll.end(),
              bind2nd(mem_fun_ref(&Person::printWithPrefix),
                      "person: "));
```

You might wonder why the adapter is called `mem_fun_ref` instead of simply `mem_fun`. The reason
is historical: Another version of member function adapters was introduced first and got the name
`mem_fun`. Those `mem_fun` adapters are for sequences that contain *pointers* to elements. Probably
`mem_fun_ptr` would have been a less confusing name for them. So, if you have a sequence of
pointers to objects, you can also call member functions for them. For example:

---

[6] In older versions of the STL and the C++ standard library, the member function adapters for one argument
were called `mem_fun1` and `mem_fun1_ref` instead of `mem_fun` and `mem_fun_ref`.

```
// fo/memfun1b.cpp
void ptrfoo (const std::vector<Person*>& coll)
                                    // ^^^ pointer !
{
    using std::for_each;
    using std::bind2nd;
    using std::mem_fun;

    // call member function print() for each referred object
    for_each (coll.begin(), coll.end(),
              mem_fun(&Person::print));

    // call member function printWithPrefix() for each referred object
    // - "person: " is passed as an argument to the member function
    for_each (coll.begin(), coll.end(),
              bind2nd(mem_fun(&Person::printWithPrefix),
                      "person: "));
}
```

Both `mem_fun_ref` and `mem_fun` can call member functions with zero or one argument. However, you can't call member functions with two or more arguments in this way. This is because for the implementation of these adapters you need auxiliary function objects that are provided for each kind of member function. For example, the auxiliary classes for `mem_fun` and `mem_fun_ref` are `mem_fun_t`, `mem_fun_ref_t`, `const_mem_fun_t`, `const_mem_fun_ref_t`, `mem_fun1_t`, `mem_fun1_ref_t`, `const_mem_fun1_t`, and `const_mem_fun1_ref_t`.

Note that the member functions called by `mem_fun_ref` and `mem_fun` must be *constant* member functions. Unfortunately, the C++ standard library does not provide function adapters for nonconstant member functions (I discovered this while writing this book). It seems to have been simply an oversight because nobody knew that this was not possible, and it is possible to solve this problem without much effort. Hopefully, implementations (and the standard) will fix this problem in the future.

8.2.3 Function Adapters for Ordinary Functions

Another function adapter enables ordinary functions to be used from other function adapters: `ptr_fun` (Table 8.4).

For example, suppose you have a global function such as the following that checks something for each parameter:

```
bool check(int elem);
```

Expression	Effect
ptr_fun(*op*)	**op*(*param*)
	*op(*param1*, *param2*)

Table 8.4. Function Adapters for Ordinary Functions

If you want to find the first element for which the check does not succeed you could call the following statement:

```
pos = find_if (coll.begin(), coll.end(),        // range
               not1(ptr_fun(check)));           // search criterion
```

You could not use not1(check) because not1() uses special type members that function objects provide. See Section 8.2.4 for more details.

The second form is used when you have a global function for two parameters and, for example, you want to use it as a unary function:

```
// find first string that is not empty
pos = find_if (coll.begin(), coll.end(),        // range
               bind2nd(ptr_fun(strcmp),""));     // search criterion
```

Here, the strcmp() C function is used to compare each element with the empty C-string. strcmp() returns 0, which is equivalent to false, when both strings match. So, this call of find_if() returns the position of the first element that is not the empty string. See another example of the use of ptr_fun on page 319.

8.2.4   User-Defined Function Objects for Function Adapters

You can write your own function objects, but to use them in combination with function adapters they must meet certain requirements: They must provide type members for the type of their arguments and the result. The C++ standard library provides structures to make this more convenient:

```
template <class Arg, class Result>
struct unary_function {
    typedef Arg    argument_type;
    typedef Result result_type;
};

template <class Arg1, class Arg2, class Result>
struct binary_function {
    typedef Arg1   first_argument_type;
    typedef Arg2   second_argument_type;
    typedef Result result_type;
};
```

Thus, by deriving your function object from one of these types you meet the requirements easily so that your function object becomes "adapter-able."

The following example shows a complete definition for a function object that processes the first argument raised to the power of the second argument:

```
// fo/fopow.hpp

#include <functional>
#include <cmath>

template <class T1, class T2>
struct fopow : public std::binary_function<T1, T2, T1>
{
    T1 operator() (T1 base, T2 exp) const {
        return std::pow(base,exp);
    }
};
```

Here, the first argument and the return value have the same type, T1, and the exponent may have a different type T2. These types are passed to binary_function to make the required type definitions. However, instead of passing them to binary_function you could make the type definition directly. As usual in the STL, the concept of function adapters is pure abstraction: Anything that *behaves* like a function object for function adapters *is* a function object for function adapters.

The following program shows how to use the user-defined function object fopow. In particular, it uses fopow with the bind1st and bind2nd function adapters:

```
// fo/fopow1.cpp

#include <iostream>
#include <vector>
#include <algorithm>
#include <iterator>
using namespace std;

// include self-defined fopow<>
#include "fopow.hpp"

int main()
{
    vector<int> coll;

    // insert elements from 1 to 9
```

```
for (int i=1;  i<=9;  ++i) {
    coll.push_back(i);
}
```

```
// print 3 raised to the power of all elements
transform (coll.begin(), coll.end(),           // source
           ostream_iterator<float>(cout," "),  // destination
           bind1st(fopow<float,int>(),3));     // operation
cout << endl;
```

```
// print all elements raised to the power of 3
transform (coll.begin(), coll.end(),           // source
           ostream_iterator<float>(cout," "),  // destination
           bind2nd(fopow<float,int>(),3));     // operation
cout << endl;
```
```
}
```

The program has the following output:

```
3 9 27 81 243 729 2187 6561 19683
1 8 27 64 125 216 343 512 729
```

Note that `fopow` is realized for types `float` and `int`. If you use `int` for both base and exponent, you'd call `pow()` with two arguments of type `int`, but this isn't portable because according to the standard `pow()` is overloaded for more than one but not all fundamental types:

```
transform (coll.begin(), coll.end(),
           ostream_iterator<int>(cout," "),
           bind1st(fopow<int,int>(),3));        // ERROR: ambiguous
```

See page 581 for details about this problem.

8.3   Supplementary Composing Function Objects

The ability to compose function objects is important for building software components from other components. It enables you to construct very complicated function objects from simple ones. So in general it should be possible to define almost every functional behavior as a combination of function objects. However, the C++ standard library does not provide enough adapters to support this. For example, it is not possible to combine the result of two unary operations to formulate a criterion such as "this *and* that."

In principle, the following compose adapters are useful:

- **f(g(***elem***))**
  This is the general form of a unary compose function. It allows nested calls of unary predicates such that the result of calling predicate g() for *elem* is used as input for predicate f(). The whole expression operates as a unary predicate.

- **f(g(***elem1***,***elem2***))**
  This is a form in which two elements, *elem1* and *elem2*, are passed as arguments to a binary predicate g(). Again the result is used as input for the unary predicate f(). The whole expression operates as a binary predicate.

- **f(g(***elem***),h(***elem***))**
  This is a form in which *elem* is passed as an argument to two different unary predicates g() and h(), and the result of both is processed by the binary predicate f(). In a way, this form "injects" a single argument into a composed function. The whole expression operates as a unary predicate.

- **f(g(***elem1***),h(***elem2***))**
  This is a form in which two elements, *elem1* and *elem2*, are passed as an argument to two different unary predicates g() and h(), and the result of both is processed by the binary predicate f(). In a way, this form "distributes" a composed function over two arguments. The whole expression operates as a binary predicate.

Unfortunately, these compose adapters were not standardized, so we don't have standard names for them. SGI's implementation of the STL has names for two of them, however the community is currently looking for general names for all these adapters. See Table 8.5 for the names I chose to use in this book.

Functionality	This Book	SGI STL
f(g(*elem*))	compose_f_gx	compose1
f(g(*elem1*,*elem2*))	compose_f_gxy	
f(g(*elem*),h(*elem*))	compose_f_gx_hx	compose2
f(g(*elem1*),h(*elem2*))	compose_f_gx_hy	

Table 8.5. Possible Names of Compose Function Object Adapters

Look at the Boost repository for C++ libraries at `http://www.boost.org/` for the names that should be used in the future and for a complete implementation of all of them. In the next few subsections I discuss three of them — those that I need most often.

8.3.1   Unary Compose Function Object Adapters

This subsection describes the most fundamental compose function object adapters. They are also part of SGI's STL implementation.

Nested Computations by Using `compose_f_gx`

The simplest and most fundamental compose function adapter uses the result of a unary operation as input to another unary operation. Thus, it is simply a nested call of two unary function objects. You need this function adapter to formulate something like "add 10 and multiply by 4."

I use the name `compose_f_gx` for this function object adapter. SGI's implementation of the STL uses the name `compose1`. You can implement `compose_f_gx` as follows:

```
// fo/compose11.hpp

#include <functional>

/* class for the compose_f_gx adapter
 */
template <class OP1, class OP2>
class compose_f_gx_t
  : public std::unary_function<typename OP2::argument_type,
                               typename OP1::result_type>
{
  private:
    OP1 op1;      // process: op1(op2(x))
    OP2 op2;
  public:
    // constructor
    compose_f_gx_t(const OP1& o1, const OP2& o2)
     : op1(o1), op2(o2) {
    }

    // function call
    typename OP1::result_type
    operator()(const typename OP2::argument_type& x) const {
        return op1(op2(x));
    }
};
```

```
/* convenience functions for the compose_f_gx adapter
 */
template <class OP1, class OP2>
inline compose_f_gx_t<OP1,OP2>
compose_f_gx (const OP1& o1, const OP2& o2) {
    return compose_f_gx_t<OP1,OP2>(o1,o2);
}
```

Here is a complete example that demonstrates the use of `compose_f_gx`:

```
// fo/compose1.cpp

#include <iostream>
#include <vector>
#include <algorithm>
#include <functional>
#include <iterator>
#include "print.hpp"
#include "compose11.hpp"
using namespace std;

int main()
{
    vector<int> coll;

    // insert elements from 1 to 9
    for (int i=1; i<=9; ++i) {
        coll.push_back(i);
    }
    PRINT_ELEMENTS(coll);

    // for each element add 10 and multiply by 5
    transform (coll.begin(),coll.end(),
               ostream_iterator<int>(cout," "),
               compose_f_gx(bind2nd(multiplies<int>(),5),
                            bind2nd(plus<int>(),10)));
    cout << endl;
}
```

Note that the second operation passed to `compose_f_gx` is performed first. Thus,

```
compose_f_gx(bind2nd(multiplies<int>(),5),
             bind2nd(plus<int>(),10))
```

yields a unary function object that first adds ten and then multiplies the result by five. The program has the following output:

```
1 2 3 4 5 6 7 8 9
55 60 65 70 75 80 85 90 95
```

Combining Two Criteria by Using `compose_f_gx_hx`

Probably the most important supplementary function adapter is one that allows you to combine two criteria logically to formulate a single criterion. You need this function adapter to formulate something like "greater than 4 *and* less than 7."

I use the name `compose_f_gx_hx` for this function object adapter. In SGI's implementation of the STL it is called compose2. You can implement `compose_f_gx_hx` as follows:

```
// fo/compose21.hpp

#include <functional>


/* class for the compose_f_gx_hx adapter
 */
template <class OP1, class OP2, class OP3>
class compose_f_gx_hx_t
  : public std::unary_function<typename OP2::argument_type,
                               typename OP1::result_type>
{
  private:
    OP1 op1;      // process: op1(op2(x),op3(x))
    OP2 op2;
    OP3 op3;
  public:
    // constructor
    compose_f_gx_hx_t (const OP1& o1, const OP2& o2, const OP3& o3)
      : op1(o1), op2(o2), op3(o3) {
    }

    // function call
    typename OP1::result_type
    operator()(const typename OP2::argument_type& x) const {
        return op1(op2(x),op3(x));
    }
};
```

```
/* convenience functions for the compose_f_gx_hx adapter
 */
template <class OP1, class OP2, class OP3>
inline compose_f_gx_hx_t<OP1,OP2,OP3>
compose_f_gx_hx (const OP1& o1, const OP2& o2, const OP3& o3) {
    return compose_f_gx_hx_t<OP1,OP2,OP3>(o1,o2,o3);
}
```

`compose_f_gx_hx` uses the first operation to combine the results of two unary operations for the same object. Thus, the expression

```
compose_f_gx_hx(op1,op2,op3)
```

results in the unary predicate that calls for each value x:

```
op1(op2(x),op3(x))
```

Here is a complete example that demonstrates the use of `compose_f_gx_hx`:

```
// fo/compose2.cpp

#include <iostream>
#include <vector>
#include <algorithm>
#include <functional>
#include "print.hpp"
#include "compose21.hpp"
using namespace std;

int main()
{
    vector<int> coll;

    // insert elements from 1 to 9
    for (int i=1; i<=9; ++i) {
        coll.push_back(i);
    }
    PRINT_ELEMENTS(coll);

    // remove all elements that are greater than four and less than seven
    // - retain new end
    vector<int>::iterator pos;
    pos = remove_if (coll.begin(),coll.end(),
```

```
compose_f_gx_hx(logical_and<bool>(),
                bind2nd(greater<int>(),4),
                bind2nd(less<int>(),7)));
```

```
    // remove "removed" elements in coll
    coll.erase(pos,coll.end());

    PRINT_ELEMENTS(coll);
}
```

The expression

```
compose_f_gx_hx(logical_and<bool>(),
                bind2nd(greater<int>(),4),
                bind2nd(less<int>(),7))
```

yields a unary predicate that returns whether a value is greater than four and less than seven. The program has the following output:

```
1 2 3 4 5 6 7 8 9
1 2 3 4 7 8 9
```

8.3.2   Binary Compose Function Object Adapters

One of the binary compose function object adapters processes the result of two unary operations that use different elements as parameters. I use the name `compose_f_gx_hy` for this function object adapter. Here is a possible implementation:

```
// fo/compose22.hpp

#include <functional>

/* class for the compose_f_gx_hy adapter
 */
template <class OP1, class OP2, class OP3>
class compose_f_gx_hy_t
  : public std::binary_function<typename OP2::argument_type,
                                typename OP3::argument_type,
                                typename OP1::result_type>
{
  private:
    OP1 op1;    // process: op1(op2(x),op3(y))
```

```
        OP2 op2;
        OP3 op3;
    public:
        // constructor
        compose_f_gx_hy_t (const OP1& o1, const OP2& o2, const OP3& o3)
         : op1(o1), op2(o2), op3(o3) {
        }

        // function call
        typename OP1::result_type
        operator()(const typename OP2::argument_type& x,
                   const typename OP3::argument_type& y) const {
            return op1(op2(x),op3(y));
        }
};

/* convenience function for the compose_f_gx_hy adapter
 */
template <class OP1, class OP2, class OP3>
inline compose_f_gx_hy_t<OP1,OP2,OP3>
compose_f_gx_hy (const OP1& o1, const OP2& o2, const OP3& o3) {
    return compose_f_gx_hy_t<OP1,OP2,OP3>(o1,o2,o3);
}
```

The following example shows the use of `compose_f_gx_hy`. It searches for a substring in a string in a case-insensitive way:

```
// fo/compose3.cpp

#include <iostream>
#include <algorithm>
#include <functional>
#include <string>
#include <cctype>
#include "compose22.hpp"
using namespace std;

int main()
{
    string s("Internationalization");
```

```
    string sub("Nation");

    // search substring case insensitive
    string::iterator pos;
    pos = search (s.begin(),s.end(),              // string to search in
                  sub.begin(),sub.end(),          // substring to search
                  compose_f_gx_hy(equal_to<int>(), // compar. criterion
                                  ptr_fun(::toupper),
                                  ptr_fun(::toupper)));

    if (pos != s.end()) {
        cout << "\"" << sub << "\" is part of \"" << s << "\""
             << endl;
    }
}
```

The program has the following output:

```
    "Nation" is part of "Internationalization"
```

On page 499 you will find an example program that searches a substring in a case-insensitive way without using compose_f_gx_hy.

Chapter 9
STL Algorithms

This chapter describes all of the algorithms of the C++ standard library. It begins with an overview of all algorithms and some general remarks about the algorithms. It then presents the exact signature of each algorithm and one or more examples of its use.

9.1 Algorithm Header Files

To use the algorithms of the C++ standard library you must include the header file `<algorithm>`[1]:

```
#include <algorithm>
```

This header file also includes some auxiliary functions. `min()`, `max()`, and `swap()` were presented in Section 4.4.1, page 66, and Section 4.4.2, page 67. The `iter_swap()` iterator function was discussed in Section 7.3.3, page 263.

Some of the STL algorithms are provided for numeric processing. Thus, they are defined in `<numeric>`[1]:

```
#include <numeric>
```

In general, Chapter 12 discusses the numeric components of the C++ standard library. However, I decided to discuss the numeric algorithms here because, in my opinion, the fact that they are STL algorithms is more important than the fact that they are used for numeric processing.

When you use algorithms, you often also need function objects and function adapters. These were described in Chapter 8 and are defined in `<functional>`[2]:

```
#include <functional>
```

---

[1] In the original STL the header file for all algorithms was `<algo.h>`.

[2] In the original STL the header file for function objects and function adapters was `<function.h>`.

9.2   Algorithm Overview

This section presents an overview of all of the C++ standard library algorithms. From it you can get an idea of their abilities and be better able to find the best algorithm to solve a certain problem.

9.2.1   A Brief Introduction

Algorithms were introduced in Chapter 5 along with the STL. In particular, Section 5.4, page 94, and Section 5.6, page 111, discuss the role of algorithms and some important constraints regarding their use. All STL algorithms process one or more iterator ranges. The first range is usually specified by its beginning and its end. For additional ranges, in most cases you need to pass only the beginning because the end follows from the number of elements of the first range. The caller must ensure that the ranges are valid. That is, the beginning must refer to a previous or the same element of the same container as the end. Additional ranges must have enough elements.

Algorithms work in overwrite mode rather than in insert mode. Thus, the caller must ensure that destination ranges have enough elements. You can use special insert iterators (see Section 7.4.2, page 271) to switch from overwrite to insert mode.

To increase their flexibility and power, several algorithms allow the user to pass user-defined operations, which they call internally. These operations might be ordinary functions or function objects. If these functions return a Boolean value they are called *predicates*. You can use predicates for the following tasks:

- You can pass a function or function object that specifies a unary predicate as the search criterion for a search algorithm. The unary predicate is used to check whether an element fits the criterion. For example, you could search the first element that is less than 50.

- You can pass a function or function object that specifies a binary predicate as the sorting criterion for a sort algorithm. The binary predicate is used to compare two elements. For example, you could pass a criterion that lets objects that represent a person sort according to their last name (see page 294 for an example).

- You can pass a unary predicate as the criterion that specifies for which elements an operation should apply. For example, you could specify that only elements with an odd value should be removed.

- You can specify the numeric operation of numeric algorithms. For example, you could use `accumulate()`, which normally processes the sum of elements, to process the product of all elements.

Note that predicates should not modify their state due to a function call (see Section 8.1.4, page 302).

See Section 5.8, page 119, Section 5.9, page 124, and Chapter 8 for examples and details about functions and function objects that are used as algorithm parameters.

9.2.2 Classification of Algorithms

Different algorithms meet different needs. Thus, they can be classified by their main purposes. For example, some algorithms operate as read only, some modify elements, and some change the order of elements. This subsection gives you a brief idea of the functionality of each algorithm and in which aspect it differs from similar algorithms.

The name of an algorithm gives you a first impression of its purpose. The designers of the STL introduced two special suffixes:

1. **The `_if` suffix**

   The `_if` suffix is used when you can call two forms of an algorithm that have the same number of parameters either by passing a value or by passing a function or function object. In this case, the version without the suffix is used for values, and the version with the `_if` suffix is used for functions and function objects. For example, `find()` searches for an element that has a certain value, whereas `find_if()` searches for an element that meets the criterion passed as a function or function object.

   However, not all algorithms that have a parameter for functions and function objects have the `_if` suffix. When the function or function object version of an algorithm has an additional argument, it has the same name. For example, `min_element()` called with two arguments returns the minimum element in the range according to a comparison with operator <. If you pass a third element, it is used as comparison criterion.

2. **The `_copy` suffix**

   The `_copy` suffix is used as an indication that elements are not only manipulated but also copied into a destination range. For example, `reverse()` reverses the order of elements inside a range, whereas `reverse_copy()` copies the elements into another range in reverse order.

The following subsections and sections describe the algorithms according to the following classification:

- Nonmodifying algorithms
- Modifying algorithms
- Removing algorithms
- Mutating algorithms
- Sorting algorithms
- Sorted range algorithms
- Numeric algorithms

If algorithms belong to more than one category I describe them in the category that I consider to be the most important.

Nonmodifying Algorithms

Nonmodifying algorithms neither change the order nor the value of the elements they process. They operate with input and forward iterators; therefore, you can call them for all standard containers. Table 9.1 lists the nonmodifying algorithms of the C++ standard library. See page 330 for nonmodifying algorithms that are provided especially for sorted input ranges.

Name	Effect	Page
`for_each()`	Performs an operation for each element	334
`count()`	Returns the number of elements	338
`count_if()`	Returns the number of elements that match a criterion	338
`min_element()`	Returns the element with the smallest value	340
`max_element()`	Returns the element with the largest value	340
`find()`	Searches for the first element with the passed value	341
`find_if()`	Searches for the first element that matches a criterion	341
`search_n()`	Searches for the first n consecutive elements with certain properties	344
`search()`	Searches for the first occurrence of a subrange	347
`find_end()`	Searches for the last occurrence of a subrange	350
`find_first_of()`	Searches the first of several possible elements	352
`adjacent_find()`	Searches for two adjacent elements that are equal (by some criterion)	354
`equal()`	Returns whether two ranges are equal	356
`mismatch()`	Returns the first elements of two sequences that differ	358
`lexicographical_compare()`	Returns whether a range is lexicographically less than another range	360

Table 9.1. Nonmodifying Algorithms

One of the most important algorithms is `for_each()`. `for_each()` calls an operation provided by the caller for each element. That operation is usually used to process each element of the range individually. For example, you can pass `for_each()` a function that prints each element. However, `for_each()` can also call a modifying operation for the elements. So `for_each()` can be used as both a nonmodifying and a modifying algorithm. However, you should avoid using `for_each()` when possible, and use other algorithms to meet your needs because the other algorithms are implemented specifically for that purpose.

Several of the nonmodifying algorithms perform searching. Unfortunately, the naming scheme of searching algorithms is a mess. In addition, the naming schemes of searching algorithms and searching string functions differ (Table 9.2). As is often the case, there are historical reasons for this. First, the STL and string classes were designed independently. Second, the `find_end()`, `find_first_of()`, and `search_n()` algorithms were not part of the original STL. So, for example, by accident the name `find_end()` instead of `search_end()` was chosen (it is easy to forget aspects of the whole picture, such as consistency, when you are caught up in the details). Also by accident, a form of `search_n()` breaks the general concept of the original STL. See page 346 for a description of this problem.

Search for	String Function	STL Algorithm
First occurrence of one element	`find()`	`find()`
Last occurrence of one element	`rfind()`	`find()` with reverse iterators
First occurrence of a subrange	`find()`	`search()`
Last occurrence of a subrange	`rfind()`	`find_end()`
First occurrence of several elements	`find_first_of()`	`find_first_of()`
Last occurrence of several elements	`find_last_of()`	`find_first_of()` with reverse iterators
First occurrence of *n* consecutive elements		`search_n()`

Table 9.2. Comparison of Searching String Operations and Algorithms

Modifying Algorithms

Modifying algorithms change the value of elements. They might modify the elements of a range directly or modify them while they are being copied into another range. If elements are copied into a destination range, the source range is not changed. Table 9.3 lists the modifying algorithms of the C++ standard library.

The fundamental modifying algorithms are `for_each()` (again) and `transform()`. You can use both to modify elements of a sequence. However, their behavior differs as follows:

- **`for_each()`** accepts an operation that modifies its argument. Thus, the argument has to be passed by reference. For example:

```
void square (int& elem)        // call-by-reference
{
    elem = elem * elem;        // assign processed value directly
}
...
for_each(coll.begin(),coll.end(),        // range
        square);                         // operation
```

- **`transform()`** uses an operation that returns the modified argument. The trick is that it can be used to assign the result to the original element. For example:

```
int square (int elem)        // call-by-value
{
    return elem * elem;        // return processed value
}
...
transform (coll.begin(), coll.end(),     // source range
          coll.begin(),                  // destination range
          square);                       // operation
```

Name	Effect	Page
`for_each()`	Performs an operation for each element	334
`copy()`	Copies a range starting with the first element	363
`copy_backward()`	Copies a range starting with the last element	363
`transform()`	Modifies (and copies) elements; combines elements of two ranges	367 368
`merge()`	Merges two ranges	416
`swap_ranges()`	Swaps elements of two ranges	370
`fill()`	Replaces each element with a given value	372
`fill_n()`	Replaces *n* elements with a given value	372
`generate()`	Replaces each element with the result of an operation	373
`generate_n()`	Replaces *n* elements with the result of an operation	373
`replace()`	Replaces elements that have a special value with another value	375
`replace_if()`	Replaces elements that match a criterion with another value	375
`replace_copy()`	Replaces elements that have a special value while copying the whole range	376
`replace_copy_if()`	Replaces elements that match a criterion while copying the whole range	376

Table 9.3. Modifying Algorithms

The approach of `transform()` is a bit slower because it returns and assigns the result instead of modifying the element directly. However, it is more flexible because it can also be used to modify elements while they are being copied into a different destination sequence. `transform()` also has another version, one that can process and combine elements of two source ranges.

Strictly speaking, `merge()` does not necessarily have to be part of the list of modifying algorithms. This is because it requires that its input ranges must be sorted. So it should be part of the algorithms for sorted ranges (see page 330). However, in practice, `merge()` also merges the elements of unsorted ranges. Of course, then the result is unsorted. Nevertheless, to be safe you should call `merge()` only for sorted ranges.

Note that elements of associative containers are constant to ensure that you can't compromise the sorted order of the elements due to an element modification. Therefore, you can't use associative containers as a destination for modifying algorithms.

In addition to these modifying algorithms, the C++ standard library provides modifying algorithms for sorted ranges. See page 330 for details.

Removing Algorithms

Removing algorithms are a special form of modifying algorithms. They can remove the elements either in a single range or while they are being copied into another range. As with modifying algorithms, you can't use an associative container as a destination because the elements of the associative container are considered to be constant. Table 9.4 lists the removing algorithms of the C++ standard library.

Name	Effect	Page
remove()	Removes elements with a given value	378
remove_if()	Removes elements that match a given criterion	378
remove_copy()	Copies elements that do not match a given value	380
remove_copy_if()	Copies elements that do not match a given criterion	380
unique()	Removes adjacent duplicates (elements that are equal to their predecessor)	381
unique_copy()	Copies elements while removing adjacent duplicates	384

Table 9.4. Removing Algorithms

Note that removing algorithms remove elements logically only by overwriting them with the following elements that were not removed. Thus, they do not change the number of elements in the ranges on which they operate. Instead, they return the position of the new "end" of the range. It's up to the caller to use that new end, such as to remove the elements physically. See Section 5.6.1, page 111, for a detailed discussion of this behavior.

Mutating Algorithms

Mutating algorithms are algorithms that change the order of elements (and not their values) by assigning and swapping their values. Table 9.5 lists the mutating algorithms of the C++ standard library. As with modifying algorithms, you can't use an associative container as a destination because the elements of the associative container are considered to be constant.

Name	Effect	Page
reverse()	Reverses the order of the elements	386
reverse_copy()	Copies the elements while reversing their order	386
rotate()	Rotates the order of the elements	388
rotate_copy()	Copies the elements while rotating their order	389
next_permutation()	Permutates the order of the elements	391
prev_permutation()	Permutates the order of the elements	391
random_shuffle()	Brings the elements into a random order	393
partition()	Changes the order of the elements so that elements that match a criterion are at the front	395
stable_partition()	Same as partition() but preserves the relative order of matching and nonmatching elements	395

Table 9.5. Mutating Algorithms

Sorting Algorithms

Sorting algorithms are a special kind of mutating algorithm because they also change the order of the elements. However, sorting is more complicated and therefore usually takes more time than simple mutating operations. In fact, these algorithms usually have worse than linear complexity[3] and require random access iterators (for the destination). Table 9.6 lists the sorting algorithms.

Name	Effect	Page
`sort()`	Sorts all elements	397
`stable_sort()`	Sorts while preserving order of equal elements	397
`partial_sort()`	Sorts until the first *n* elements are correct	400
`partial_sort_copy()`	Copies elements in sorted order	402
`nth_element()`	Sorts according to the *n*th position	404
`partition()`	Changes the order of the elements so that elements that match a criterion are at the front	395
`stable_partition()`	Same as `partition()` but preserves the relative order of matching and nonmatching elements	395
`make_heap()`	Converts a range into a heap	406
`push_heap()`	Adds an element to a heap	406
`pop_heap()`	Removes an element from a heap	407
`sort_heap()`	Sorts the heap (it is no longer a heap after the call)	407

Table 9.6. Sorting Algorithms

Time often is critical for sorting algorithms. Therefore, the C++ standard library provides more than one sorting algorithm. The algorithms use different ways of sorting, and some algorithms don't sort all elements. For example, `nth_element()` stops when the *n*th element of the sequence is correct according to the sorting criterion. For the other elements it guarantees only that the previous elements have a lesser or equal value and that the following elements have a greater or equal value. To sort all elements of a sequence, you should consider the following algorithms:

- **`sort()`** is based historically on *quicksort*. Thus, it guarantees a good runtime ($n * log(n)$ complexity) on average but may have a very bad runtime (quadratic complexity) in the worst case:

  ```
  /* sort all elements
   * - best n*log(n) complexity on average
   * - n*n complexity in worst case
   */
  sort (coll.begin(), coll.end());
  ```

---

[3] See Section 2.3, page 21, for an introduction to and a discussion of complexity.

So if avoiding the worst-case behavior is important, you should use another algorithm, such as `partial_sort()` or `stable_sort()`, which are discussed next.

- **`partial_sort()`** is based historically on *heapsort*. Thus, it guarantees $n*log(n)$ complexity in any case. However, in most circumstances, heapsort is slower than quicksort by a factor of two to five. So, provided `sort()` is implemented as quicksort and `partial_sort()` is implemented as heapsort, `partial_sort()` has the better complexity, but `sort()` has the better runtime in most cases. The advantage of `partial_sort()` is that it guarantees $n * log(n)$ complexity in any case, so it never becomes quadratic complexity.

  `partial_sort()` also has the special ability to stop sorting when only the first n elements need to be sorted. To sort all the elements you have to pass the end of the sequence as second and last argument:

  ```
  /* sort all elements
   * - always n*log(n) complexity
   * - but usually twice as long as sort()
   */
  partial_sort (coll.begin(), coll.end(), coll.end());
  ```

- **`stable_sort()`** is based historically on *mergesort*. It sorts all the elements:

  ```
  /* sort all elements
   * - n*log(n) or n*log(n)*log(n) complexity
   */
  stable_sort (coll.begin(), coll.end());
  ```

  However, it needs enough additional memory to have $n * log(n)$ complexity. Otherwise, it has $n * log(n) * log(n)$ complexity. The advantage of `stable_sort()` is that it preserves the order of equal elements.

Now you have a brief idea of which sorting algorithm might best meet your needs. But the story doesn't end here. The standard guarantees complexity, but not how it is implemented. This is an advantage in that an implementation could benefit from algorithm innovations and use a better way of sorting without breaking the standard. For example, the `sort()` algorithm in the SGI implementation of the STL is implemented by using *introsort*. Introsort is a new algorithm that, by default, operates like quicksort, but switches to heapsort when it is going to have quadratic complexity. The disadvantage of the fact that the standard does not guarantee exact complexity is that an implementation could use a standard-conforming but very bad algorithm. For example, using heapsort to implement `sort()` would be standard conforming. Of course, you simply could test which algorithm fits best, but be aware that measurements might not be portable.

There are even more algorithms to sort elements. For example, the heap algorithms are provided to call the functions that implement a heap directly (a heap is a binary tree, which is used internally by heapsort). The heap algorithms are provided and used as the base for efficient implementations of priority queues (see Section 10.3, page 453). You can use them to sort all elements of a collection by calling them as follows:

```
/* sort all elements
 * - n+n*log(n) complexity
```

```
*/
make_heap (coll.begin(), coll.end());
sort_heap (coll.begin(), coll.end());
```

See Section 9.9.4, page 406, for details about heaps and heap algorithms.

The nth_element() algorithms are provided if you need only the *n*th sorted element or the set of the *n* highest or *n* lowest elements (not sorted). Thus, nth_element() is a way to split elements into two subsets according to a sorting criterion. However, you could also use partition() or stable_partition() to do this. The difference is as follows:

- For **nth_element()** you pass the number of elements you want to have in the first part (and therefore also in the second part). For example:

    // move the four lowest elements to the front
    ```
    nth_element (coll.begin(),        // beginning of range
                 coll.begin()+3,      // position between first and second part
                 coll.end());         // end of range
    ```

    However, after the call you don't know the exact criterion that is the difference between the first and the second parts. Both parts may, in fact, have elements with the same value as the *n*th element.

- For **partition()** you pass the exact sorting criterion that serves as the difference between the first and the second parts:

    // move all elements less than seven to the front
    ```
    vector<int>::iterator pos;
    pos = partition (coll1.begin(), coll1.end(),      // range
                     bind2nd(less<int>(),7));         // criterion
    ```

    Here, after the call, you don't know how many elements are owned by the first and the second parts. The return value pos refers to the first element of the second part that contains all elements that don't match the criterion, if any.

- **stable_partition()** behaves similarly to partition(), with an additional ability. It guarantees that the order of the elements in both parts remains stable according to their relative positions to the other elements in the same part.

You can always pass the sorting criterion to all sorting algorithms as an optional argument. The default sorting argument is the function object less<>, so that elements are sorted in ascending order of their values.

As with modifying algorithms, you can't use an associative container as a destination because the elements of the associative containers are considered to be constant.

Lists do not provide random access iterators, so you can't call sorting algorithms for them either. However, lists provide a member function sort() to sort their elements; see page 245.

Sorted Range Algorithms

Sorted range algorithms require that the ranges on which they operate are sorted according to their sorting criterion. Table 9.7 lists all algorithms of the C++ standard library that are especially written for sorted ranges. Like associative containers, these algorithms have the advantage of a better complexity.

Name	Effect	Page
binary_search()	Returns whether the range contains an element	410
includes()	Returns whether each element of a range is also an element of another range	411
lower_bound()	Finds the first element greater than or equal to a given value	413
upper_bound()	Finds the first element greater than a given value	413
equal_range()	Returns the range of elements equal to a given value	415
merge()	Merges the elements of two ranges	416
set_union()	Processes the sorted union of two ranges	418
set_intersection()	Processes the sorted intersection of two ranges	419
set_difference()	Processes a sorted range that contains all elements of a range that are not part of another	420
set_symmetric_difference()	Processes a sorted range that contains all elements that are in exactly one of two ranges	421
inplace_merge()	Merges two consecutive sorted ranges	423

Table 9.7. Algorithms for Sorted Ranges

The first five sorted range algorithms in Table 9.7 are nonmodifying because they search only according to their purpose. The other algorithms combine two sorted input ranges and write the result to a destination range. In general, the result of these algorithms is also sorted.

Numeric Algorithms

These algorithms combine numeric elements in different ways. Table 9.8 lists the numeric algorithms of the C++ standard library. If you understand the names, you get an idea of the purpose of the algorithms. However, these algorithms are more flexible and more powerful than they may seem at first. For example, by default, accumulate() processes the sum of all elements. When you use strings as elements, you concatenate them using this algorithm. When you switch from operator + to operator *, you get the product of all elements. As another example, you should know that adjacent_difference() and partial_sum() transfer a range of absolute values into a range of relative values and vice versa.

accumulate() and inner_product() process and return a single value without modifying the ranges. The other algorithms write the results to a destination range that has the same number of elements as the source range.

Name	Effect	Page
`accumulate()`	Combines all element values (processes sum, product, and so forth)	425
`inner_product()`	Combines all elements of two ranges	427
`adjacent_difference()`	Combines each element with its predecessor	431
`partial_sum()`	Combines each element with all of its predecessors	429

Table 9.8. Numeric Algorithms

9.3 Auxiliary Functions

The rest of this chapter discusses the algorithms in detail. It includes at least one example of each algorithm. To simplify the examples, I use some auxiliary functions so that you can concentrate on the essence of the examples:

```
// algo/algostuff.hpp

#ifndef ALGOSTUFF_HPP
#define ALGOSTUFF_HPP

#include <iostream>
#include <vector>
#include <deque>
#include <list>
#include <set>
#include <map>
#include <string>
#include <algorithm>
#include <iterator>
#include <functional>
#include <numeric>

/* PRINT_ELEMENTS()
 * - prints optional C-string optcstr followed by
 * - all elements of the collection coll
 * - separated by spaces
 */
template <class T>
inline void PRINT_ELEMENTS (const T& coll, const char* optcstr="")
{
    typename T::const_iterator pos;
```

```
      std::cout << optcstr;
      for (pos=coll.begin(); pos!=coll.end(); ++pos) {
          std::cout << *pos << ' ';
      }
      std::cout << std::endl;
  }


  /* INSERT_ELEMENTS (collection, first, last)
   * - fill values from first to last into the collection
   * - NOTE: NO half-open range
   */
  template <class T>
  inline void INSERT_ELEMENTS (T& coll, int first, int last)
  {
      for (int i=first; i<=last; ++i) {
          coll.insert(coll.end(),i);
      }
  }


  #endif /*ALGOSTUFF_HPP*/
```

First, `algostuff.hpp` includes all header files that may be necessary to implement the examples, thus the program doesn't have to do it. Second, it defines two auxiliary functions:

1. `PRINT_ELEMENTS()` prints all elements of the container that is passed as the first argument separated by spaces. You can pass a second argument optionally for a string that is used as a prefix in front of the elements (see page 118).
2. `INSERT_ELEMENTS()` inserts elements into the container that is passed as the first argument. These elements get the values from the value passed as the second argument up to the value passed as the third argument. Both argument values are included (so this is not a half-open range).

9.4   The `for_each()` Algorithm

The `for_each()` algorithm is very flexible because it allows you to access, process, and modify each element in many different ways.

UnaryProc
for_each   (InputIterator *beg*, InputIterator *end*, UnaryProc *op*)

- Calls

    op(*elem*)

    for each element in the range [*beg*,*end*).
- Returns a copy of the (internally modified) *op*.
- *op* might modify the elements. However, see page 325 for a comparison with the `transform()` algorithm, which is able to do the same thing in a slightly different way.
- Any return value of *op* is ignored.
- See page 126 for the implementation of the `for_each()` algorithm.
- Complexity: linear (*numberOfElements* calls of *op*()).

The following example of `for_each()` calls the `print()` function, which is passed as the operation for each element. Thus, the call prints each element:

```cpp
// algo/foreach1.cpp

#include "algostuff.hpp"
using namespace std;

// function called for each element
void print (int elem)
{
    cout << elem << ' ';
}

int main()
{
    vector<int> coll;

    INSERT_ELEMENTS(coll,1,9);

    // call print() for each element
    for_each (coll.begin(), coll.end(),   // range
              print);                      // operation
    cout << endl;
}
```

The program has the following output:

```
1 2 3 4 5 6 7 8 9
```

To call a member function of the elements you can use the mem_fun adapters. See Section 8.2.2, page 307, for details and an example.

The following example demonstrates how to modify each element using a function object:

```cpp
// algo/foreach2.cpp

#include "algostuff.hpp"
using namespace std;

// function object that adds the value with which it is initialized
template <class T>
class AddValue {
  private:
    T theValue;      // value to add
  public:
    // constructor initializes the value to add
    AddValue (const T& v) : theValue(v) {
    }

    // the function call for the element adds the value
    void operator() (T& elem) const {
        elem += theValue;
    }
};

int main()
{
    vector<int> coll;

    INSERT_ELEMENTS(coll,1,9);

    // add ten to each element
    for_each (coll.begin(), coll.end(),        // range
              AddValue<int>(10));              // operation
    PRINT_ELEMENTS(coll);

    // add value of first element to each element
    for_each (coll.begin(), coll.end(),        // range
```

```
            AddValue<int>(*coll.begin())); // operation
    PRINT_ELEMENTS(coll);
}
```

The `AddValue<>` class defines function objects that add a value to each element that is passed to the constructor. Using the function object has the advantage that you can process the added value at runtime. The program has the following output:

```
11 12 13 14 15 16 17 18 19
22 23 24 25 26 27 28 29 30
```

See page 128 for more details regarding this example. Note also that you can do the same by using the `transform()` algorithm (see page 367) in the following way:

```
transform (coll.begin(), coll.end(),          // source range
           coll.begin(),                      // destination range
           bind2nd(plus<int>(),10));          // operation
...
transform (coll.begin(), coll.end(),          // source range
           coll.begin(),                      // destination range
           bind2nd(plus<int>(),*coll.begin())); // operation
```

See page 325 for a general comparison between `for_each()` and `transform()`.

A third example demonstrates how to use the return value of the `for_each()` algorithm. Because `for_each()` has the special property that it returns its operation, you can process and return a result inside the operation:

```
// algo/foreach3.cpp

#include "algostuff.hpp"
using namespace std;

// function object to process the mean value
class MeanValue {
  private:
    long num;      // number of elements
    long sum;      // sum of all element values
  public:
    // constructor
    MeanValue () : num(0), sum(0) {
    }

    // function call
    // - process one more element of the sequence
```

```
        void operator() (int elem) {
            num++;              // increment count
            sum += elem;        // add value
        }

        // return mean value (implicit type conversion)
        operator double() {
            return static_cast<double>(sum) / static_cast<double>(num);
        }
    };

    int main()
    {
        vector<int> coll;

        INSERT_ELEMENTS(coll,1,8);

        // process and print mean value
        double mv = for_each (coll.begin(), coll.end(),   // range
                              MeanValue());                // operation
        cout << "mean value: " << mv << endl;
    }
```

The program has the following output:

```
    mean value: 4.5
```

This example, in a slightly different form, is discussed in detail on page 300.

9.5   Nonmodifying Algorithms

The algorithms presented in this section enable you to access elements without modifying their values or changing their order.

9.5.1   Counting Elements

difference_type
count (InputIterator *beg*, InputIterator *end*, const T& *value*)

difference_type
count_if (InputIterator *beg*, InputIterator *end*, UnaryPredicate *op*)

- The first form counts the elements in the range [*beg*,*end*) that are equal to value *value*.
- The second form counts the elements in the range [*beg*,*end*) for which the unary predicate
    op(*elem*)
  yields true.
- The type of the return value, *difference_type*, is the difference type of the iterator:
    typename iterator_traits<InputIterator>::difference_type
  (Section 7.5, page 283, introduces iterator traits.)[4]
- Note that *op* should not change its state during a function call. See Section 8.1.4, page 302, for details.
- *op* should not modify the passed arguments.
- Associative containers (sets, multisets, maps, and multimaps) provide a similar member function, count(), to count the number of elements that have a certain value as key (see page 234).
- Complexity: linear (*numberOfElements* comparisons or calls of *op*() respectively).

The following example counts elements according to different criteria:

```
// algo/count1.cpp

#include "algostuff.hpp"
using namespace std;

bool isEven (int elem)
{
    return elem % 2 == 0;
}
```

---

[4] In the original STL the count() and count_if() had a fourth input/output parameter that was used as a counter and the return type was void.

```
int main()
{
    vector<int> coll;
    int num;
    INSERT_ELEMENTS(coll,1,9);
    PRINT_ELEMENTS(coll,"coll: ");

    // count and print elements with value 4
    num = count (coll.begin(), coll.end(),      // range
                 4);                            // value
    cout << "number of elements equal to 4:      " << num << endl;

    // count elements with even value
    num = count_if (coll.begin(), coll.end(),   // range
                    isEven);                    // criterion
    cout << "number of elements with even value: " << num << endl;

    // count elements that are greater than value 4
    num = count_if (coll.begin(), coll.end(),   // range
                    bind2nd(greater<int>(),4)); // criterion
    cout << "number of elements greater than 4:  " << num << endl;
}
```

The program has the following output:

```
coll: 1 2 3 4 5 6 7 8 9
number of elements equal to 4:      1
number of elements with even value: 4
number of elements greater than 4:  5
```

Instead of using the self-written isEven() function, you could use the following expression:

```
not1(bind2nd(modulus<int>(),2))
```

See page 306 for more details regarding this expression.

9.5.2 Minimum and Maximum

```
ForwardIterator
```
min_element (ForwardIterator *beg*, ForwardIterator *end*)

```
ForwardIterator
```
min_element (ForwardIterator *beg*, ForwardIterator *end*, CompFunc *op*)

```
ForwardIterator
max_element (ForwardIterator beg, ForwardIterator end)
```

```
ForwardIterator
max_element (ForwardIterator beg, ForwardIterator end, CompFunc op)
```

- All algorithms return the position of the minimum or maximum element in the range [*beg,end*).
- The versions without *op* compare the elements with operator <.
- *op* is used to compare two elements:
    op(elem1,elem2)
  It should return true when the first element is less than the second element.
- If more than one minimum or maximum element exists, they return the first found.
- *op* should not modify the passed arguments.
- Complexity: linear (*numberOfElements*-1 comparisons or calls of *op()* respectively).

The following program prints the minimum and the maximum of the elements in coll and, by using absLess(), prints the minimum and the maximum of the absolute values:

```
// algo/minmax1.cpp

#include <cstdlib>
#include "algostuff.hpp"
using namespace std;

bool absLess (int elem1, int elem2)
{
    return abs(elem1) < abs(elem2);
}

int main()
{
    deque<int> coll;

    INSERT_ELEMENTS(coll,2,8);
    INSERT_ELEMENTS(coll,-3,5);

    PRINT_ELEMENTS(coll);

    // process and print minimum and maximum
    cout << "minimum: "
         << *min_element(coll.begin(),coll.end())
         << endl;
    cout << "maximum: "
```

```
          << *max_element(coll.begin(),coll.end())
          << endl;

    // process and print minimum and maximum of absolute values
    cout << "minimum of absolute values: "
         << *min_element(coll.begin(),coll.end(),
                          absLess)
         << endl;
    cout << "maximum of absolute values: "
         << *max_element(coll.begin(),coll.end(),
                          absLess)
         << endl;
}
```

The program has the following output:

```
2 3 4 5 6 7 8 -3 -2 -1 0 1 2 3 4 5
minimum: -3
maximum: 8
minimum of absolute values: 0
maximum of absolute values: 8
```

Note that the algorithms return the *position* of the maximum or minimum element respectively. Thus, you must use the unary operator ∗ to print their values.

9.5.3 Searching Elements

Search First Matching Element

```
InputIterator
find (InputIterator beg, InputIterator end, const T& value)
```

```
InputIterator
find_if (InputIterator beg, InputIterator end, UnaryPredicate op)
```

- The first form returns the position of the first element in the range [*beg,end*) that has a value equal to *value*.
- The second form returns the position of the first element in the range [*beg,end*) for which the unary predicate
    op(*elem*)
  yields true.
- Both forms return *end* if no matching elements are found.

- Note that *op* should not change its state during a function call. See Section 8.1.4, page 302, for details.
- *op* should not modify the passed arguments.
- If the range is sorted, you should use the `lower_bound()`, `upper_bound()`, `equal_range()`, or `binary_search()` algorithms (see Section 9.10, page 409).
- Associative containers (sets, multisets, maps, and multimaps) provide an equivalent member function, `find()`, that has logarithmic instead of linear complexity (see page 235).
- Complexity: linear (at most, *numberOfElements* comparisons or calls of *op()* respectively).

The following example demonstrates how to use `find()` to find a subrange starting with the first element with value 4 and ending after the second 4, if any:

```
// algo/find1.cpp

#include "algostuff.hpp"
using namespace std;

int main()
{
    list<int> coll;

    INSERT_ELEMENTS(coll,1,9);
    INSERT_ELEMENTS(coll,1,9);

    PRINT_ELEMENTS(coll,"coll: ");

    // find first element with value 4
    list<int>::iterator pos1;
    pos1 = find (coll.begin(), coll.end(),    // range
                 4);                          // value

    /* find second element with value 4
     * - note: continue the search behind the first 4 (if any)
     */
    list<int>::iterator pos2;
    if (pos1 != coll.end()) {
        pos2 = find (++pos1, coll.end(),      // range
                     4);                      // value
    }

    /* print all elements from first to second 4 (both included)
```

```
 *  - note: now we need the position of the first 4 again (if any)
 *  - note: we have to pass the position behind the second 4 (if any)
 */
if (pos1!=coll.end() && pos2!=coll.end()) {
    copy (--pos1, ++pos2,
            ostream_iterator<int>(cout," "));
    cout << endl;
}
}
```

To find the second 4 you must increment the position of the first 4. However, incrementing the
end() of a collection results in undefined behavior. Thus, if you are not sure, you should check the
return value of find() before you increment it. The program has the following output:

```
coll: 1 2 3 4 5 6 7 8 9 1 2 3 4 5 6 7 8 9
4 5 6 7 8 9 1 2 3 4
```

You can call find() twice for the same range but with two different values. However, you have to
be careful to use the results as the beginning and the end of a subrange of elements; otherwise, the
subrange might not be valid. See page 97 for a discussion of possible problems and for an example.

The following example demonstrates how to use find_if() to find elements according to very
different search criteria:

```
// algo/find2.cpp

#include "algostuff.hpp"
using namespace std;

int main()
{
    vector<int> coll;
    vector<int>::iterator pos;

    INSERT_ELEMENTS(coll,1,9);

    PRINT_ELEMENTS(coll,"coll: ");

    // find first element greater than 3
    pos = find_if (coll.begin(), coll.end(),      // range
                    bind2nd(greater<int>(),3));   // criterion

    // print its position
```

```
cout << "the "
     << distance(coll.begin(),pos) + 1
     << ". element is the first greater than 3" << endl;

// find first element divisible by 3
pos = find_if (coll.begin(), coll.end(),
               not1(bind2nd(modulus<int>(),3)));

// print its position
cout << "the "
     << distance(coll.begin(),pos) + 1
     << ". element is the first divisible by 3" << endl;
}
```

The first call of find_if() uses a simple function object combined with the bind2nd adapter to search for the first element that is greater than 3. The second call uses a more complicated combination to find the first element that is divisible by 3 without remainder.

The program has the following output:

```
coll: 1 2 3 4 5 6 7 8 9
the 4. element is the first greater than 3
the 3. element is the first divisible by 3
```

See page 121 for an example that lets find_if() find the first prime number.

Search First *n* Matching Consecutive Elements

```
ForwardIterator
search_n (ForwardIterator beg, ForwardIterator end,
          Size count, const T& value)
```

```
ForwardIterator
search_n (ForwardIterator beg, ForwardIterator end,
          Size count, const T& value, BinaryPredicate op)
```

- The first form returns the position of the first of *count* consecutive elements in the range [*beg*,*end*) that all have a value equal to *value*.
- The second form returns the position of the first of *count* consecutive elements in the range [*beg*,*end*) for which the binary predicate
    op(*elem*,*value*)
  yields true.
- Both forms return *end* if no matching elements are found.

- Note that *op* should not change its state during a function call. See Section 8.1.4, page 302, for details.
- *op* should not modify the passed arguments.
- These algorithms were not part of the original STL and were not introduced very carefully. The fact that the second form uses a binary predicate instead of a unary predicate breaks the consistency of the original STL. See the remarks on page 346.
- Complexity: linear (at most, *numberOfElements*count* comparisons or calls of *op*() respectively).

The following example searches for four consecutive elements that have a value equal to or greater than 3:

```cpp
// algo/searchn1.cpp

#include "algostuff.hpp"
using namespace std;

int main()
{
    deque<int> coll;

    INSERT_ELEMENTS(coll,1,9);
    PRINT_ELEMENTS(coll);

    // find four consecutive elements with value 3
    deque<int>::iterator pos;
    pos = search_n (coll.begin(), coll.end(),    // range
                    4,                           // count
                    3);                          // value

    // print result
    if (pos != coll.end()) {
        cout << "four consecutive elements with value 3 "
             << "start with " << distance(coll.begin(),pos) +1
             << ". element" << endl;
    }
    else {
        cout << "no four consecutive elements with value 3 found"
             << endl;
    }
```

```
// find four consecutive elements with value greater than 3
pos = search_n (coll.begin(), coll.end(),      // range
                4,                              // count
                3,                              // value
                greater<int>());                // criterion

// print result
if (pos != coll.end()) {
    cout << "four consecutive elements with value > 3 "
         << "start with " << distance(coll.begin(),pos) +1
         << ". element" << endl;
}
else {
    cout << "no four consecutive elements with value > 3 found"
         << endl;
}
}
```

The program has the following output:

```
1 2 3 4 5 6 7 8 9
no four consecutive elements with value 3 found
four consecutive elements with value > 3 start with 4. element
```

There is a nasty problem with the second form of search_n(). Consider the second call of search_n():

```
pos = search_n (coll.begin(), coll.end(),      // range
                4,                              // count
                3,                              // value
                greater<int>());                // criterion
```

This kind of searching for elements that matches a special criterion does not conform with the rest of the STL. Following the usual concepts of the STL, the call should be as follows:

```
pos = search_n_if (coll.begin(), coll.end(),   // range
                4,                              // count
                bind2nd(greater<int>(),3));     // criterion
```

Unfortunately, nobody noticed this inconsistency when these new algorithms were introduced to the standard (they were not part of the original STL). You might argue that the version with four arguments is more convenient. However, it requires a binary predicate even if you only need a unary predicate. For example, to use a self-written unary predicate function, normally you would write:

```
bool isPrime (int elem);
...
pos = search_n_if (coll.begin(), coll.end(),    // range
                   4,                           // count
                   isPrime);                    // criterion
```

However, with the actual definition you must use a binary predicate. So, either you change the signature of your function or you write a simple wrapper:

```
bool binaryIsPrime (int elem1, int) {
    return isPrime(elem1);
}
...
pos = search_n (coll.begin(), coll.end(),    // range
                4,                           // count
                0,                           // required dummy value
                binaryIsPrime);              // binary criterion
```

Search First Subrange

```
ForwardIterator1
search (ForwardIterator1 beg, ForwardIterator1 end,
        ForwardIterator2 searchBeg, ForwardIterator2 searchEnd)

ForwardIterator1
search (ForwardIterator1 beg, ForwardIterator1 end,
        ForwardIterator2 searchBeg, ForwardIterator2 searchEnd,
        BinaryPredicate op)
```

- Both forms return the position of the first element of the first subrange matching the range [*searchBeg,searchEnd*) in the range [*beg,end*).
- In the first form the elements of the subrange have to be equal to the elements of the whole range.
- In the second form for every comparison between elements, the call of the binary predicate
    op(*elem*,*searchElem*)
  has to yield true.
- Both forms return *end* if no matching elements are found.
- Note that *op* should not change its state during a function call. See Section 8.1.4, page 302, for details.
- *op* should not modify the passed arguments.
- See page 97 for a discussion of how to find a subrange for which you know only the first and the last elements.

- Complexity: linear (at most, *numberOfElements∗numberOfSearchElements* comparisons or calls of *op()* respectively).

The following example demonstrates how to find a sequence as the first subrange of another sequence (compare with the example of find_end() on page 351):

```
// algo/search1.cpp

#include "algostuff.hpp"
using namespace std;

int main()
{
    deque<int> coll;
    list<int> subcoll;

    INSERT_ELEMENTS(coll,1,7);
    INSERT_ELEMENTS(coll,1,7);

    INSERT_ELEMENTS(subcoll,3,6);

    PRINT_ELEMENTS(coll,   "coll:    ");
    PRINT_ELEMENTS(subcoll,"subcoll: ");

    // search first occurrence of subcoll in coll
    deque<int>::iterator pos;
    pos = search (coll.begin(), coll.end(),          // range
                  subcoll.begin(), subcoll.end());   // subrange

    // loop while subcoll found as subrange of coll
    while (pos != coll.end()) {
        // print position of first element
        cout << "subcoll found starting with element "
             << distance(coll.begin(),pos) + 1
             << endl;

        // search next occurrence of subcoll
        ++pos;
        pos = search (pos, coll.end(),               // range
                      subcoll.begin(), subcoll.end());   // subrange
    }
}
```

The program has the following output:

```
coll:    1 2 3 4 5 6 7 1 2 3 4 5 6 7
subcoll: 3 4 5 6
subcoll found starting with element 3
subcoll found starting with element 10
```

The next example demonstrates how to use the second form of the `search()` algorithm to find a subsequence that matches a more complicated criterion. Here, the subsequence *even, odd, and even value* is searched:

```cpp
// algo/search2.cpp

#include "algostuff.hpp"
using namespace std;

// checks whether an element is even or odd
bool checkEven (int elem, bool even)
{
    if (even) {
        return elem % 2 == 0;
    }
    else {
        return elem % 2 == 1;
    }
}

int main()
{
    vector<int> coll;

    INSERT_ELEMENTS(coll,1,9);
    PRINT_ELEMENTS(coll,"coll: ");

    /* arguments for checkEven()
     * - check for: ''even odd even''
     */
    bool checkEvenArgs[3] = { true, false, true };

    // search first subrange in coll
    vector<int>::iterator pos;
    pos = search (coll.begin(), coll.end(),          // range
```

```
                         checkEvenArgs, checkEvenArgs+3, // subrange values
                         checkEven);                     // subrange criterion

    // loop while subrange found
    while (pos != coll.end()) {
        // print position of first element
        cout << "subrange found starting with element "
             << distance(coll.begin(),pos) + 1
             << endl;

        // search next subrange in coll
        pos = search (++pos, coll.end(),                  // range
                      checkEvenArgs, checkEvenArgs+3,     // subr. values
                      checkEven);                         // subr. criterion
    }
}
```

The program has the following output:

```
coll: 1 2 3 4 5 6 7 8 9
subrange found starting with element 2
subrange found starting with element 4
subrange found starting with element 6
```

Search Last Subrange

```
ForwardIterator
find_end (ForwardIterator beg, ForwardIterator end,
          ForwardIterator searchBeg, ForwardIterator searchEnd)
```

```
ForwardIterator
find_end (ForwardIterator beg, ForwardIterator end,
          ForwardIterator searchBeg, ForwardIterator searchEnd,
          BinaryPredicate op)
```

- Both forms return the position of the first element of the last subrange matching the range [searchBeg,searchEnd) in the range [beg,end).
- In the first form the elements of the subrange have to be equal to the elements of the whole range.
- In the second form, for every comparison between elements, the call of the binary predicate
      op(elem,searchElem)
  has to yield true.

- Both forms return *end* if no matching elements are found.
- Note that *op* should not change its state during a function call. See Section 8.1.4, page 302, for details.
- *op* should not modify the passed arguments.
- See page 97 for a discussion of how to find a subrange for which you only know the first and the last elements.
- These algorithms were not part of the original STL. Unfortunately they were called `find_end()` instead of `search_end()`, which would be more consistent, because the algorithm used to search the first subrange is called `search()`.
- Complexity: linear (at most, *numberOfElements*numberOfSearchElements* comparisons or calls of *op*() respectively).

The following example demonstrates how to find a sequence as the last subrange of another sequence (compare with the example of `search()` on page 348):

```
// algo/findend1.cpp

#include "algostuff.hpp"
using namespace std;

int main()
{
    deque<int> coll;
    list<int> subcoll;

    INSERT_ELEMENTS(coll,1,7);
    INSERT_ELEMENTS(coll,1,7);

    INSERT_ELEMENTS(subcoll,3,6);

    PRINT_ELEMENTS(coll,    "coll:    ");
    PRINT_ELEMENTS(subcoll,"subcoll: ");

    // search last occurrence of subcoll in coll
    deque<int>::iterator pos;
    pos = find_end (coll.begin(), coll.end(),          // range
                    subcoll.begin(), subcoll.end());   // subrange

    // loop while subcoll found as subrange of coll
    deque<int>::iterator end(coll.end());
    while (pos != end) {
```

```
                    // print position of first element
                    cout << "subcoll found starting with element "
                         << distance(coll.begin(),pos) + 1
                         << endl;

                    // search next occurrence of subcoll
                    end = pos;
                    pos = find_end (coll.begin(), end,              // range
                                    subcoll.begin(), subcoll.end()); // subrange
            }
    }
```

The program has the following output:

```
coll:     1 2 3 4 5 6 7 1 2 3 4 5 6 7
subcoll: 3 4 5 6
subcoll found starting with element 10
subcoll found starting with element 3
```

For the second form of this algorithm, see the second example of search() on page 349. You can use find_end() in a similar manner.

Search First of Several Possible Elements

```
ForwardIterator
```
find_first_of (ForwardIterator1 *beg*, ForwardIterator1 *end*,
         ForwardIterator2 *searchBeg*, ForwardIterator2 *searchEnd*)

```
ForwardIterator
```
find_first_of (ForwardIterator1 *beg*, ForwardIterator1 *end*,
         ForwardIterator2 *searchBeg*, ForwardIterator2 *searchEnd*,
         BinaryPredicate *op*)

- The first form returns the position of the first element in the range [*beg,end*) that is also in the range [*searchBeg,searchEnd*).
- The second form returns the position of the first element in the range [*beg,end*) for which any call with all elements of [*searchBeg,searchEnd*)
    op(*elem*,*searchElem*)
  yields true.
- Both forms return *end* if no matching elements are found.
- Note that *op* should not change its state during a function call. See Section 8.1.4, page 302, for details.

- *op* should not modify the passed arguments.
- By using reverse iterators, you can find the last of several possible values.
- These algorithms were not part of the original STL.
- Complexity: linear (at most, *numberOfElements*numberOfSearchElements* comparisons or calls of *op*() respectively).

The following example demonstrates the use of find_first_of():

```
// algo/findof1.cpp

#include "algostuff.hpp"
using namespace std;

int main()
{
    vector<int> coll;
    list<int> searchcoll;

    INSERT_ELEMENTS(coll,1,11);
    INSERT_ELEMENTS(searchcoll,3,5);

    PRINT_ELEMENTS(coll,      "coll:        ");
    PRINT_ELEMENTS(searchcoll,"searchcoll: ");

    // search first occurrence of an element of searchcoll in coll
    vector<int>::iterator pos;
    pos = find_first_of (coll.begin(), coll.end(),      // range
                         searchcoll.begin(),     // beginning of search set
                         searchcoll.end());      // end of search set
    cout << "first element of searchcoll in coll is element "
         << distance(coll.begin(),pos) + 1
         << endl;

    // search last occurrence of an element of searchcoll in coll
    vector<int>::reverse_iterator rpos;
    rpos = find_first_of (coll.rbegin(), coll.rend(),  // range
                          searchcoll.begin(),   // beginning of search set
                          searchcoll.end());    // end of search set
    cout << "last element of searchcoll in coll is element "
         << distance(coll.begin(),rpos.base())
         << endl;
}
```

The second call uses reverse iterators to find the last element that has a value equal to one element in searchcoll. To print the position of the element, base() is called to transform the reverse iterator into an iterator. Thus, you can process the distance from the beginning. Normally you would have to add 1 to the result of distance() because the first element has distance 0 but actually is element 1. However, because base() moves the position of the value to which it refers, you have the same effect (see Section 7.4.1, page 269, for the description of base()).

The program has the following output:

```
coll:        1 2 3 4 5 6 7 8 9 10 11
searchcoll: 3 4 5
first element of searchcoll in coll is element 3
last element of searchcoll in coll is element 5
```

Search Two Adjacent, Equal Elements

```
ForwardIterator
```
adjacent_find (ForwardIterator *beg*, ForwardIterator *end*)

```
ForwardIterator
```
adjacent_find (ForwardIterator *beg*, ForwardIterator *end*,
                  BinaryPredicate *op*)

- The first form returns the first element in the range [*beg*,*end*) that has a value equal to the value of the following element.
- The second form returns the first element in the range [*beg*,*end*) for which the binary predicate
    op(*elem*,*nextElem*)
  yields true.
- Both forms return *end* if no matching elements are found.
- Note that *op* should not change its state during a function call. See Section 8.1.4, page 302, for details.
- *op* should not modify the passed arguments.
- Complexity: linear (at most, *numberOfElements* comparisons or calls of *op*() respectively).

The following program demonstrates both forms of adjacent_find():

```
// algo/adjfind1.cpp

#include "algostuff.hpp"
using namespace std;

// return whether the second object has double the value of the first
bool doubled (int elem1, int elem2)
{
```

```cpp
        return elem1 * 2 == elem2;
}

int main()
{
    vector<int> coll;

    coll.push_back(1);
    coll.push_back(3);
    coll.push_back(2);
    coll.push_back(4);
    coll.push_back(5);
    coll.push_back(5);
    coll.push_back(0);

    PRINT_ELEMENTS(coll,"coll: ");

    // search first two elements with equal value
    vector<int>::iterator pos;
    pos = adjacent_find (coll.begin(), coll.end());

    if (pos != coll.end()) {
        cout << "first two elements with equal value have position "
             << distance(coll.begin(),pos) + 1
             << endl;
    }

    // search first two elements for which the second has double the value of the first
    pos = adjacent_find (coll.begin(), coll.end(),   // range
                         doubled);                   // criterion

    if (pos != coll.end()) {
        cout << "first two elements with second value twice the "
             << "first have pos. "
             << distance(coll.begin(),pos) + 1
             << endl;
    }
}
```

The first call of `adjacent_find()` searches for equal values. The second form uses `doubled()` to find the first element for which the successor has the double value. The program has the following output:

```
coll: 1 3 2 4 5 5 0
first two elements with equal value have position 5
first two elements with second value twice the first have pos. 3
```

9.5.4 Comparing Ranges

Testing Equality

```
bool
equal (InputIterator1 beg, InputIterator1 end,
       InputIterator2 cmpBeg)

bool
equal (InputIterator1 beg, InputIterator1 end,
       InputIterator2 cmpBeg,
       BinaryPredicate op)
```

- The first form returns whether the elements in the range [*beg,end*) are equal to the elements in the range starting with *cmpBeg*.

- The second form returns whether each call of the binary predicate
  op(elem,cmpElem)
  with the corresponding elements in the range [*beg,end*) and in the range starting with *cmpBeg* yields `true`.

- Note that *op* should not change its state during a function call. See Section 8.1.4, page 302, for details.

- *op* should not modify the passed arguments.

- The caller must ensure that the range starting with *cmpBeg* contains enough elements.

- To determine the differences when the sequences are not equal, you should use the `mismatch()` algorithm (see page 358).

- Complexity: linear (at most, *numberOfElements* comparisons or calls of *op()* respectively).

The following example demonstrates both forms of `equal()`. The first call checks whether the elements have values with equal elements. The second call uses an auxiliary predicate function to check whether the elements of both collections have corresponding even and odd elements:

```
// algo/equal1.cpp

#include "algostuff.hpp"
using namespace std;
```

```cpp
bool bothEvenOrOdd (int elem1, int elem2)
{
    return elem1 % 2 == elem2 % 2;
}

int main()
{
    vector<int> coll1;
    list<int> coll2;

    INSERT_ELEMENTS(coll1,1,7);
    INSERT_ELEMENTS(coll2,3,9);

    PRINT_ELEMENTS(coll1,"coll1: ");
    PRINT_ELEMENTS(coll2,"coll2: ");

    // check whether both collections are equal
    if (equal (coll1.begin(), coll1.end(),   // first range
               coll2.begin())) {             // second range
        cout << "coll1 == coll2" << endl;
    }
    else {
        cout << "coll1 != coll2" << endl;
    }

    // check for corresponding even and odd elements
    if (equal (coll1.begin(), coll1.end(),   // first range
               coll2.begin(),                // second range
               bothEvenOrOdd)) {             // comparison criterion
        cout << "even and odd elements correspond" << endl;
    }
    else {
        cout << "even and odd elements do not correspond" << endl;
    }
}
```

The program has the following output:

```
coll1: 1 2 3 4 5 6 7
coll2: 3 4 5 6 7 8 9
coll1 != coll2
even and odd elements correspond
```

Search the First Difference

```
pair<InputIterator1,InputIterator2>
```
mismatch (InputIterator1 *beg*, InputIterator1 *end*,
            InputIterator2 *cmpBeg*)

```
pair<InputIterator1,InputIterator2>
```
mismatch (InputIterator1 *beg*, InputIterator1 *end*,
            InputIterator2 *cmpBeg*,
            BinaryPredicate *op*)

- The first form returns the first two corresponding elements of range [*beg,end*) and the range starting with *cmpBeg* that differ.
- The second form returns the first two corresponding elements of range [*beg,end*) and the range starting with *cmpBeg* for which the binary predicate
    op(*elem*,*cmpElem*)
  yields `false`.
- If no difference is found, a pair of *end* and the corresponding element of the second range is returned. Note that this does not mean that both sequences are equal, because the second sequence might contain more elements.
- Note that *op* should not change its state during a function call. See Section 8.1.4, page 302, for details.
- *op* should not modify the passed arguments.
- The caller must ensure that the range starting with *cmpBeg* contains enough elements.
- To check whether two ranges are equal, you should use the `equal()` algorithm (see page 356).
- Complexity: linear (at most, *numberOfElements* comparisons or calls of *op*() respectively).

The following example demonstrates both forms of `mismatch()`:

```
// algo/misma1.cpp

#include "algostuff.hpp"
using namespace std;

int main()
{
    vector<int> coll1;
    list<int> coll2;

    INSERT_ELEMENTS(coll1,1,6);

    for (int i=1; i<=16; i*=2) {
        coll2.push_back(i);
```

```
    }
    coll2.push_back(3);

    PRINT_ELEMENTS(coll1,"coll1: ");
    PRINT_ELEMENTS(coll2,"coll2: ");

    // find first mismatch
    pair<vector<int>::iterator,list<int>::iterator> values;
    values = mismatch (coll1.begin(), coll1.end(),   // first range
                       coll2.begin());               // second range
    if (values.first == coll1.end()) {
        cout << "no mismatch" << endl;
    }
    else {
        cout << "first mismatch: "
             << *values.first  << " and "
             << *values.second << endl;
    }


    /* find first position where the element of coll1 is not
     * less than the corresponding element of coll2
     */
    values = mismatch (coll1.begin(), coll1.end(),   // first range
                       coll2.begin(),                // second range
                       less_equal<int>());           // criterion
    if (values.first == coll1.end()) {
        cout << "always less-or-equal" << endl;
    }
    else {
        cout << "not less-or-equal: "
             << *values.first << " and "
             << *values.second << endl;
    }
}
```

The first call of `mismatch()` searches for the first corresponding elements that are not equal. If such elements exist, their values are written to standard output. The second call searches for the first pair of elements in which the element of the first collection is greater than the corresponding element of the second collection, and returns these elements. The program has the following output:

```
coll1: 1 2 3 4 5 6
coll2: 1 2 4 8 16 3
first mismatch: 3 and 4
not less-or-equal: 6 and 3
```

Testing for "Less Than"

```
bool
```
lexicographical_compare (InputIterator1 *beg1*, InputIterator1 *end1*,
                        InputIterator2 *beg2*, InputIterator2 *end2*)

```
bool
```
lexicographical_compare (InputIterator1 *beg1*, InputIterator1 *end1*,
                        InputIterator2 *beg2*, InputIterator2 *end2*,
                        CompFunc *op*)

- Both forms return whether the elements in the range [*beg1*,*end1*) are "lexicographically less than" the elements in the range [*beg2*,*end2*).
- The first form compares the elements by using operator <.
- The second form compares the elements by using the binary predicate
    op(*elem1*,*elem2*)
  It should return `true` when *elem1* is less than *elem2*.
- *Lexicographical comparison* means that sequences are compared element-by-element until any of the following occurs:
  - When two elements are not equal, the result of their comparison is the result of the whole comparison.
  - When one sequence has no more elements, then the sequence that has no more elements is less than the other. Thus, the comparison yields `true` if the first sequence is the one that has no more elements.
  - When both sequences have no more elements, then both sequences are equal, and the result of the comparison is `false`.
- Note that *op* should not change its state during a function call. See Section 8.1.4, page 302, for details.
- *op* should not modify the passed arguments.
- Complexity: linear (at most, min(*numberOfElements1*,*numberOfElements2*) comparisons or calls of *op*() respectively).

The following example demonstrates the use of a lexicographical sorting of collections:

```
// algo/lexico1.cpp

#include "algostuff.hpp"
using namespace std;
```

```
void printCollection (const list<int>& l)
{
    PRINT_ELEMENTS(l);
}

bool lessForCollection (const list<int>& l1, const list<int>& l2)
{
    return lexicographical_compare
                (l1.begin(), l1.end(),    // first range
                 l2.begin(), l2.end());   // second range
}

int main()
{
    list<int> c1, c2, c3, c4;

    // fill all collections with the same starting values
    INSERT_ELEMENTS(c1,1,5);
    c4 = c3 = c2 = c1;

    // and now some differences
    c1.push_back(7);
    c3.push_back(2);
    c3.push_back(0);
    c4.push_back(2);

    // create collection of collections
    vector<list<int> > cc;

    cc.push_back(c1);
    cc.push_back(c2);
    cc.push_back(c3);
    cc.push_back(c4);
    cc.push_back(c3);
    cc.push_back(c1);
    cc.push_back(c4);
    cc.push_back(c2);

    // print all collections
```

```
    for_each (cc.begin(), cc.end(),
              printCollection);
    cout << endl;

    // sort collection lexicographically
    sort (cc.begin(), cc.end(),      // range
          lessForCollection);        // sorting criterion

    // print all collections again
    for_each (cc.begin(), cc.end(),
              printCollection);
}
```

The vector cc is initialized with several collections (all lists). The call of sort() uses the binary predicate lessForCollection() to compare two collections (see page 397 for a description of sort()). In lessForCollection(), the lexicographical_compare() algorithm is used to compare the collections lexicographically. The program has the following output:

```
1 2 3 4 5 7
1 2 3 4 5
1 2 3 4 5 2 0
1 2 3 4 5 2
1 2 3 4 5 2 0
1 2 3 4 5 7
1 2 3 4 5 2
1 2 3 4 5

1 2 3 4 5
1 2 3 4 5
1 2 3 4 5 2
1 2 3 4 5 2
1 2 3 4 5 2 0
1 2 3 4 5 2 0
1 2 3 4 5 7
1 2 3 4 5 7
```

9.6   Modifying Algorithms

This section describes algorithms that modify the elements of a range. There are two ways to modify elements:

1. Modify them directly while iterating through a sequence.
2. Modify them while copying them from a source range to a destination range.

Several modifying algorithms provide both ways of modifying the elements of a range. In this case, the name of the latter uses the `_copy` suffix.

You can't use an associative container as a destination range because the elements in an associative container are constant. If you could, it would be possible to compromise the automatic sorting.

All algorithms that have a separate destination range return the position after the last copied element of that range.

9.6.1   Copying Elements

```
OutputIterator
```
copy (InputIterator *sourceBeg*, InputIterator *sourceEnd*,
       OutputIterator *destBeg*)

```
BidirectionalIterator1
```
copy_backward (BidirectionalIterator1 *sourceBeg*,
                  BidirectionalIterator1 *sourceEnd*,
                  BidirectionalIterator2 *destEnd*)

- Both algorithms copy all elements of the source range [*sourceBeg*,*sourceEnd*) into the destination range starting with *destBeg* or ending with *destEnd* respectively.
- They return the position after the last copied element in the destination range (the first element that is not overwritten).
- *destBeg* or *destEnd* should not be part of [*sourceBeg*,*sourceEnd*).
- `copy()` iterates forward through the sequence, whereas `copy_backward()` iterates backward. This difference matters only if the source and destination ranges overlap.
    - To copy a range to the front, use `copy()`. Thus, for `copy()`, *destBeg* should have a position in front of *sourceBeg*.
    - To copy a range to the back, use `copy_backward()`. Thus, for `copy_backward()`, *destEnd* should have a position after *sourceEnd*.
  So whenever the third argument is an element of the source range specified by the first two arguments, use the other algorithm. Note that switching to the other algorithm means that you switch from passing the beginning of the destination range to passing the end. See page 365 for an example that demonstrates the differences.
- There is no `copy_if()` algorithm provided. To copy only those elements that meet a certain criterion, use `remove_copy_if()` (see page 380).

- Use `reverse_copy()` to reverse the order of the elements during the copy (see page 386). `reverse_copy()` may be slightly more efficient than using `copy()` with reverse iterators.
- The caller must ensure that the destination range is big enough or that insert iterators are used.
- See page 271 for the implementation of the `copy()` algorithm.
- To assign all elements of a container, use the assignment operator (if the containers have the same type; see page 236) or the `assign()` member function (if the containers have different types; see page 237) of the containers.
- To remove elements while they are being copied, use `remove_copy()` and `remove_copy_if()` (see page 380).
- To modify elements while they are being copied, use `transform()` (see page 367) or `replace_copy()` (see page 376).
- Complexity: linear (*numberOfElements* assignments).

The following example shows some simple calls of `copy()`:

```cpp
// algo/copy1.cpp

#include "algostuff.hpp"
using namespace std;

int main()
{
    vector<int> coll1;
    list<int> coll2;

    INSERT_ELEMENTS(coll1,1,9);

    /* copy elements of coll1 into coll2
     * - use back inserter to insert instead of overwrite
     */
    copy (coll1.begin(), coll1.end(),        // source range
          back_inserter(coll2));             // destination range

    /* print elements of coll2
     * - copy elements to cout using an ostream iterator
     */
    copy (coll2.begin(), coll2.end(),        // source range
          ostream_iterator<int>(cout," "));  // destination range
    cout << endl;

    /* copy elements of coll1 into coll2 in reverse order
```

```
    * - now overwriting
    */
    copy (coll1.rbegin(), coll1.rend(),        // source range
          coll2.begin());                      // destination range

    // print elements of coll2 again
    copy (coll2.begin(), coll2.end(),          // source range
          ostream_iterator<int>(cout," "));    // destination range
    cout << endl;
}
```

In this example, back inserters (see Section 7.4.2, page 272) are used to insert the elements in the destination range. Without using inserters, copy() would overwrite the empty collection coll2, which results in undefined behavior. Similarly, the example uses ostream iterators (see Section 7.4.3, page 278) to use standard output as the destination.

The program has the following output:

```
1 2 3 4 5 6 7 8 9
9 8 7 6 5 4 3 2 1
```

The following example demonstrates the difference between copy() and copy_backward():

```
// algo/copy2.cpp

#include "algostuff.hpp"
using namespace std;

int main()
{
    /* initialize source collection with "..........abcdef.........."
     */
    vector<char> source(10,'.');
    for (int c='a'; c<='f'; c++) {
        source.push_back(c);
    }
    source.insert(source.end(),10,'.');
    PRINT_ELEMENTS(source,"source: ");

    // copy all letters three elements in front of the 'a'
    vector<char> c1(source.begin(),source.end());
    copy (c1.begin()+10, c1.begin()+16,   // source range
          c1.begin()+7);                  // destination range
```

```
    PRINT_ELEMENTS(c1,"c1:       ");

    // copy all letters three elements behind the 'f'
    vector<char> c2(source.begin(),source.end());
    copy_backward (c2.begin()+10, c2.begin()+16,    // source range
                   c2.begin()+19);                  // destination range
    PRINT_ELEMENTS(c2,"c2:       ");
}
```

Note that in both calls of copy() and copy_backward(), the third argument is not part of the source range. The program has the following output:

```
source: . . . . . . . . . . a b c d e f . . . . . . . . .
c1:       . . . . . . . a b c d e f d e f . . . . . . . . .
c2:       . . . . . . . . . a b c a b c d e f . . . . . . .
```

A third example demonstrates how to use copy() as a data filter between standard input and standard output. The program reads strings and prints them, each on one line:

```
// algo/copy3.cpp

#include <iostream>
#include <algorithm>
#include <iterator>
#include <string>
using namespace std;

int main()
{
    copy (istream_iterator<string>(cin),           // beginning of source
          istream_iterator<string>(),              // end of source
          ostream_iterator<string>(cout,"\n"));    // destination
}
```

9.6.2   Transforming and Combining Elements

The transform() algorithms provide two abilities:

1. The first form has four arguments. It transforms elements from a source to a destination range. Thus, it copies and modifies elements in one step.

2. The second form has five arguments. It combines elements from two source sequences and writes the result to a destination range.

Transforming Elements

OutputIterator
transform (InputIterator *sourceBeg*, InputIterator *sourceEnd*,
          OutputIterator *destBeg*,
          UnaryFunc *op*)

- Calls
    op(*elem*)
  for each element in the source range [*sourceBeg*,*sourceEnd*) and writes each result of *op* to the destination range starting with *destBeg*:

- Returns the position after the last transformed element in the destination range (the first element that is not overwritten with a result).
- The caller must ensure that the destination range is big enough or that insert iterators are used.
- *sourceBeg* and *destBeg* may be identical. Thus, as with for_each() you can use this algorithm to modify elements inside a sequence. See the comparison with the for_each() algorithm on page 325 for this kind of usage.
- To replace elements matching a criterion with a particular value, use the replace() algorithms (see page 375).
- Complexity: linear (*numberOfElements* calls of *op*()).

The following program demonstrates how to use this kind of transform():

```
// algo/transf1.cpp

#include "algostuff.hpp"
using namespace std;

int main()
{
    vector<int> coll1;
    list<int> coll2;

    INSERT_ELEMENTS(coll1,1,9);
    PRINT_ELEMENTS(coll1,"coll1:    ");

    // negate all elements in coll1
    transform (coll1.begin(), coll1.end(),      // source range
               coll1.begin(),                   // destination range
               negate<int>());                  // operation
```

```
      PRINT_ELEMENTS(coll1,"negated: ");

      // transform elements of coll1 into coll2 with ten times their value
      transform (coll1.begin(), coll1.end(),        // source range
                 back_inserter(coll2),              // destination range
                 bind2nd(multiplies<int>(),10));    // operation
      PRINT_ELEMENTS(coll2,"coll2:    ");

      // print coll2 negatively and in reverse order
      transform (coll2.rbegin(), coll2.rend(),      // source range
                 ostream_iterator<int>(cout," "),   // destination range
                 negate<int>());                    // operation
      cout << endl;
}
```

The program has the following output:

```
    coll1:    1 2 3 4 5 6 7 8 9
    negated: -1 -2 -3 -4 -5 -6 -7 -8 -9
    coll2:    -10 -20 -30 -40 -50 -60 -70 -80 -90
    90 80 70 60 50 40 30 20 10
```

See the example on page 315 of how to combine two different operations while processing the elements.

Combining Elements of Two Sequences

```
OutputIterator
transform (InputIterator1 source1Beg, InputIterator1 source1End,
           InputIterator2 source2Beg,
           OutputIterator destBeg,
           BinaryFunc op)
```

- Calls

    op (source1Elem , source2Elem)

    for all corresponding elements from the first source range [*source1Beg,source1End*) and the second source range starting with *source2Beg*, and writes each result to the the destination range starting with *destBeg*:

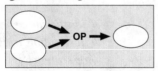

- Returns the position after the last transformed element in the destination range (the first element that is not overwritten with a result).
- The caller must ensure that the second source range is big enough (has at least as many elements as the source range).
- The caller must ensure that the destination range is big enough or that insert iterators are used.
- *source1Beg*, *source2Beg*, and *destBeg* may be identical. Thus, you can process the results of elements that are combined with themselves and you can overwrite the elements of a source with the results.
- Complexity: linear (*numberOfElements* calls of *op*()).

The following program demonstrates how to use this form of `transform()`:

```
// algo/transf2.cpp

#include "algostuff.hpp"
using namespace std;

int main()
{
    vector<int> coll1;
    list<int> coll2;

    INSERT_ELEMENTS(coll1,1,9);
    PRINT_ELEMENTS(coll1,"coll1:    ");

    // square each element
    transform (coll1.begin(), coll1.end(),       // first source range
               coll1.begin(),                    // second source range
               coll1.begin(),                    // destination range
               multiplies<int>());               // operation
    PRINT_ELEMENTS(coll1,"squared: ");

    /* add each element traversed forward with each element traversed backward
     * and insert result into coll2
     */
    transform (coll1.begin(), coll1.end(),       // first source range
               coll1.rbegin(),                   // second source range
               back_inserter(coll2),             // destination range
               plus<int>());                     // operation
    PRINT_ELEMENTS(coll2,"coll2:    ");
```

```
        // print differences of two corresponding elements
        cout << "diff:      ";
        transform (coll1.begin(), coll1.end(),      // first source range
                   coll2.begin(),                   // second source range
                   ostream_iterator<int>(cout, " "), // destination range
                   minus<int>());                   // operation
        cout << endl;
}
```

The program has the following output:

```
        coll1:    1 2 3 4 5 6 7 8 9
        squared: 1 4 9 16 25 36 49 64 81
        coll2:    82 68 58 52 50 52 58 68 82
        diff:     -81 -64 -49 -36 -25 -16 -9 -4 -1
```

9.6.3   Swapping Elements

```
ForwardIterator2
swap_ranges (ForwardIterator1 beg1, ForwardIterator1 end1,
             ForwardIterator2 beg2)
```

- Swaps the elements in the range [*beg1,end1*) with the corresponding elements starting with *beg2*.
- Returns the position after the last swapped element in the second range.
- The caller must ensure that the second range is big enough.
- Both ranges shall not overlap.
- To swap all elements of a container of the same type, use its `swap()` member function because the member function usually has constant complexity (see page 237).
- Complexity: linear (*numberOfElements* swap operations).

The following example demonstrates how to use `swap_ranges()`:

```
    // algo/swap1.cpp

    #include "algostuff.hpp"
    using namespace std;

    int main()
    {
        vector<int> coll1;
        deque<int> coll2;
```

```
INSERT_ELEMENTS(coll1,1,9);
INSERT_ELEMENTS(coll2,11,23);

PRINT_ELEMENTS(coll1,"coll1: ");
PRINT_ELEMENTS(coll2,"coll2: ");

// swap elements of coll1 with corresponding elements of coll2
deque<int>::iterator pos;
pos = swap_ranges (coll1.begin(), coll1.end(),    // first range
                   coll2.begin());                // second range

PRINT_ELEMENTS(coll1,"\ncoll1: ");
PRINT_ELEMENTS(coll2,"coll2: ");
if (pos != coll2.end()) {
    cout << "first element not modified: "
         << *pos << endl;
}

// mirror first three with last three elements in coll2
swap_ranges (coll2.begin(), coll2.begin()+3,      // first range
             coll2.rbegin());                     // second range

PRINT_ELEMENTS(coll2,"\ncoll2: ");
}
```

The first call of `swap_ranges()` swaps the elements of `coll1` with the corresponding elements of `coll2`. The remaining elements of `coll2` are not modified. The `swap_ranges()` algorithm returns the position of the first element not modified. The second call swaps the first and the last three elements of `coll2`. One of the iterators is a reverse iterator, so the elements are mirrored (swapped from outside to inside). The program has the following output:

```
coll1: 1 2 3 4 5 6 7 8 9
coll2: 11 12 13 14 15 16 17 18 19 20 21 22 23

coll1: 11 12 13 14 15 16 17 18 19
coll2: 1 2 3 4 5 6 7 8 9 20 21 22 23
first element not modified: 20

coll2: 23 22 21 4 5 6 7 8 9 20 3 2 1
```

9.6.4   Assigning New Values

Assigning the Same Value

```
void
fill (ForwardIterator beg, ForwardIterator end,
    const T& newValue)
```

```
void
fill_n (OutputIterator beg, Size num,
        const T& newValue)
```

- `fill()` assigns *newValue* to each element in the range [*beg,end*).
- `fill_n()` assigns *newValue* to the first *num* elements in the range starting with *beg*.
- The caller must ensure that the destination range is big enough or that insert iterators are used.
- Complexity: linear (*numberOfElements* or *num* assignments respectively).

The following program demonstrates the use of `fill()` and `fill_n()`:

```
// algo/fill1.cpp

#include "algostuff.hpp"
using namespace std;

int main()
{
    // print ten times 7.7
    fill_n(ostream_iterator<float>(cout, " "),   // beginning of destination
           10,                                    // count
           7.7);                                  // new value
    cout << endl;

    list<string> coll;

    // insert "hello" nine times
    fill_n(back_inserter(coll),        // beginning of destination
           9,                          // count
           "hello");                   // new value
    PRINT_ELEMENTS(coll,"coll: ");

    // overwrite all elements with "again"
    fill(coll.begin(), coll.end(),     // destination
```

```
            "again");                       // new value
        PRINT_ELEMENTS(coll,"coll: ");


        // replace all but two elements with "hi"
        fill_n(coll.begin(),                // beginning of destination
               coll.size()-2,               // count
               "hi");                       // new value
        PRINT_ELEMENTS(coll,"coll: ");


        // replace the second and up to the last element but one with "hmmm"
        list<string>::iterator pos1, pos2;
        pos1 = coll.begin();
        pos2 = coll.end();
        fill (++pos1, --pos2,               // destination
              "hmmm");                      // new value
        PRINT_ELEMENTS(coll,"coll: ");
    }
```

The first call shows how to use `fill_n()` to print a certain number of values. The other calls of `fill()` and `fill_n()` insert and replace values in a list of strings. The program has the following output:

```
7.7 7.7 7.7 7.7 7.7 7.7 7.7 7.7 7.7 7.7
coll: hello hello hello hello hello hello hello hello hello
coll: again again again again again again again again again
coll: hi hi hi hi hi hi hi again again
coll: hi hmmm hmmm hmmm hmmm hmmm hmmm hmmm again
```

Assigning Generated Values

```
void
generate (ForwardIterator beg, ForwardIterator end,
          Func op)

void
generate_n (OutputIterator beg, Size num,
            Func op)
```

- `generate()` assigns the values that are generated by a call of
    `op()`
  to each element in the range *[beg,end]*.

- `generate_n()` assigns the values that are generated by a call of
  op()
  to the first *num* elements in the range starting with *beg*.
- The caller must ensure that the destination range is big enough or that insert iterators are used.
- Complexity: linear (*numberOfElements* or *num* calls of *op()* and assignments).

The following program demonstrates how to use `generate()` and `generate_n()` to insert or assign some random numbers:

```
// algo/generate.cpp

#include <cstdlib>
#include "algostuff.hpp"
using namespace std;

int main()
{
    list<int> coll;

    // insert five random numbers
    generate_n (back_inserter(coll),        // beginning of destination range
                5,                           // count
                rand);                       // new value generator
    PRINT_ELEMENTS(coll);

    // overwrite with five new random numbers
    generate (coll.begin(), coll.end(),      // destination range
              rand);                         // new value generator
    PRINT_ELEMENTS(coll);
}
```

The `rand()` function is described in Section 12.3, page 581. The program might have the following output:

```
41 18467 6334 26500 19169
15724 11478 29358 26962 24464
```

The output is platform dependent because the random number sequence that `rand()` generates is not standardized.

See Section 8.1.2, page 296, for an example that demonstrates how to use `generate()` with function objects so that it generates a sequence of numbers.

9.6.5   Replacing Elements

Replacing Values Inside a Sequence

```
void
replace (ForwardIterator beg, ForwardIterator end,
         const T& oldValue, const T& newValue)

void
replace_if (ForwardIterator beg, ForwardIterator end,
            UnaryPredicate op, const T& newValue)
```

- `replace()` replaces each element in the range [*beg,end*) that is equal to *oldValue* with *newValue*.
- `replace_if()` replaces each element in the range [*beg,end*) for which the unary predicate
    op(*elem*)
  yields `true` with *newValue*.
- Note that *op* should not change its state during a function call. See Section 8.1.4, page 302, for details.
- Complexity: linear (*numberOfElements* comparisons or calls of *op*() respectively).

The following program demonstrates some examples of the use of `replace()` and `replace_if()`:

```cpp
// algo/replace1.cpp

#include "algostuff.hpp"
using namespace std;

int main()
{
    list<int> coll;

    INSERT_ELEMENTS(coll,2,7);
    INSERT_ELEMENTS(coll,4,9);
    PRINT_ELEMENTS(coll,"coll: ");

    // replace all elements with value 6 with 42
    replace (coll.begin(), coll.end(),    // range
             6,                            // old value
             42);                          // new value
    PRINT_ELEMENTS(coll,"coll: ");

    // replace all elements with value less than 5 with 0
```

```
            replace_if (coll.begin(), coll.end(),   // range
                        bind2nd(less<int>(),5),      // criterion for replacement
                        0);                          // new value
        PRINT_ELEMENTS(coll,"coll: ");
    }
```

The program has the following output:

```
    coll: 2 3 4 5 6 7 4 5 6 7 8 9
    coll: 2 3 4 5 42 7 4 5 42 7 8 9
    coll: 0 0 0 5 42 7 0 5 42 7 8 9
```

Copying and Replacing Elements

```
OutputIterator
```
replace_copy (InputIterator *sourceBeg*, InputIterator *sourceEnd*,
              OutputIterator *destBeg*,
              const T& *oldValue*, const T& *newValue*)

```
OutputIterator
```
replace_copy_if (InputIterator *sourceBeg*, InputIterator *sourceEnd*,
                OutputIterator *destBeg*,
                UnaryPredicate *op*, const T& *newValue*)

- replace_copy() is a combination of copy() and replace(). It replaces each element in the source range [*beg,end*) that is equal to *oldValue* with *newValue* while the elements are copied into the destination range starting with *destBeg*.
- replace_copy_if() is a combination of copy() and replace_if(). It replaces each element in the source range [*beg,end*) for which the unary predicate
    op(*elem*)
  yields true with *newValue* while the elements are copied into the destination range starting with *destBeg*.
- Both algorithms return the position after the last copied element in the destination range (the first element that is not overwritten).
- Note that *op* should not change its state during a function call. See Section 8.1.4, page 302, for details.
- The caller must ensure that the destination range is big enough or that insert iterators are used.
- Complexity: linear (*numberOfElements* comparisons or calls of *op*() and assignments respectively).

The following program demonstrates how to use replace_copy() and replace_copy_if():

```cpp
// algo/replace2.cpp

#include "algostuff.hpp"
using namespace std;

int main()
{
    list<int> coll;

    INSERT_ELEMENTS(coll,2,6);
    INSERT_ELEMENTS(coll,4,9);
    PRINT_ELEMENTS(coll);

    // print all elements with value 5 replaced with 55
    replace_copy(coll.begin(), coll.end(),          // source
                 ostream_iterator<int>(cout," "),   // destination
                 5,                                  // old value
                 55);                                // new value
    cout << endl;

    // print all elements with a value less than 5 replaced with 42
    replace_copy_if(coll.begin(), coll.end(),          // source
                    ostream_iterator<int>(cout," "),   // destination
                    bind2nd(less<int>(),5),            // replacement criterion
                    42);                               // new value
    cout << endl;

    // print each element while each odd element is replaced with 0
    replace_copy_if(coll.begin(), coll.end(),          // source
                    ostream_iterator<int>(cout," "),   // destination
                    bind2nd(modulus<int>(),2),         // replacement criterion
                    0);                                // new value
    cout << endl;
}
```

The program has the following output:

```
2 3 4 5 6 4 5 6 7 8 9
2 3 4 55 6 4 55 6 7 8 9
42 42 42 5 6 42 5 6 7 8 9
2 0 4 0 6 4 0 6 0 8 0
```

9.7   Removing Algorithms

The following algorithms remove elements from a range according to their value or to a criterion. These algorithms, however, *cannot* change the number of elements. They only move logically by overwriting "removed" elements with the following elements that were not removed. They return the new logical end of the range (the position after the last element not removed). See Section 5.6.1, page 111, for details.

9.7.1   Removing Certain Values

Removing Elements in a Sequence

```
ForwardIterator
remove (ForwardIterator beg, ForwardIterator end,
        const T& value)
```

```
ForwardIterator
remove_if (ForwardIterator beg, ForwardIterator end,
           UnaryPredicate op)
```

- `remove()` removes each element in the range [*beg*,*end*) that is equal to *value*.
- `remove_if()` removes each element in the range [*beg*,*end*) for which the unary predicate
    op(*elem*)
  yields `true`.
- Both algorithms return the logical new end of the modified sequence (the position after the last element not removed).
- The algorithms overwrite "removed" elements by the following elements that were not removed.
- The order of elements that were not removed remains stable.
- It is up to the caller, after calling this algorithm, to use the returned new logical end instead of the original end *end* (see Section 5.6.1, page 111, for more details).
- Note that *op* should not change its state during a function call. See Section 8.1.4, page 302, for details.
- Note that `remove_if()` usually copies the unary predicate inside the algorithm and uses it twice. This may lead to problems if the predicate changes its state due to the function call. See Section 8.1.4, page 302, for details.
- Due to modifications, you can't use these algorithms for an associative container (see Section 5.6.2, page 115). However, associative containers provide a similar member function, `erase()` (see page 242).
- Lists provide an equivalent member function, `remove()`, which offers better performance because it relinks pointers instead of assigning element values (see page 242).
- Complexity: linear (*numberOfElements* comparisons or calls of *op*() respectively).

The following program demonstrates how to use `remove()` and `remove_if()`:

```
// algo/remove1.cpp

#include "algostuff.hpp"
using namespace std;

int main()
{
    vector<int> coll;

    INSERT_ELEMENTS(coll,2,6);
    INSERT_ELEMENTS(coll,4,9);
    INSERT_ELEMENTS(coll,1,7);
    PRINT_ELEMENTS(coll,"coll:                    ");

    // remove all elements with value 5
    vector<int>::iterator pos;
    pos = remove(coll.begin(), coll.end(),   // range
                 5);                          // value to remove

    PRINT_ELEMENTS(coll,"size not changed:    ");

    // erase the "removed" elements in the container
    coll.erase(pos, coll.end());
    PRINT_ELEMENTS(coll,"size changed:        ");

    // remove all elements less than 4
    coll.erase(remove_if(coll.begin(), coll.end(),   // range
                         bind2nd(less<int>(),4)),    // remove criterion
               coll.end());
    PRINT_ELEMENTS(coll,"<4 removed:          ");
}
```

The program has the following output:

```
coll:                 2 3 4 5 6 4 5 6 7 8 9 1 2 3 4 5 6 7
size not changed:     2 3 4 6 4 6 7 8 9 1 2 3 4 6 7 5 6 7
size changed:         2 3 4 6 4 6 7 8 9 1 2 3 4 6 7
<4 removed:           4 6 4 6 7 8 9 4 6 7
```

Removing Elements While Copying

```
OutputIterator
```
remove_copy (InputIterator *sourceBeg*, InputIterator *sourceEnd*,
           OutputIterator *destBeg*,
           const T& *value*)

```
OutputIterator
```
remove_copy_if (InputIterator *sourceBeg*, InputIterator *sourceEnd*,
              OutputIterator *destBeg*,
              UnaryPredicate *op*)

- `remove_copy()` is a combination of `copy()` and `remove()`. It copies each element in the source range [*beg,end*) that is not equal to *value* into the destination range starting with *destBeg*.
- `remove_copy_if()` is a combination of `copy()` and `remove_if()`. It copies each element in the source range [*beg,end*) for which the unary predicate
    op(*elem*)
  yields `false` into the destination range starting with *destBeg*.
- Both algorithms return the position after the last copied element in the destination range (the first element that is not overwritten).
- Note that *op* should not change its state during a function call. See Section 8.1.4, page 302, for details.
- The caller must ensure that the destination range is big enough or that insert iterators are used.
- Complexity: linear (*numberOfElements* comparisons or calls of *op*() and assignments respectively).

The following program demonstrates how to use `remove_copy()` and `remove_copy_if()`:

```
// algo/remove2.cpp

#include "algostuff.hpp"
using namespace std;

int main()
{
    list<int> coll1;

    INSERT_ELEMENTS(coll1,1,6);
    INSERT_ELEMENTS(coll1,1,9);
    PRINT_ELEMENTS(coll1);

    // print elements without those having the value 3
```

```
        remove_copy(coll1.begin(), coll1.end(),        // source
                    ostream_iterator<int>(cout," "),    // destination
                    3);                                 // removed value
        cout << endl;

        // print elements without those having a value greater than 4
        remove_copy_if(coll1.begin(), coll1.end(),      // source
                    ostream_iterator<int>(cout," "),    // destination
                    bind2nd(greater<int>(),4));         // removed elements
        cout << endl;

        // copy all elements greater than 3 into a multiset
        multiset<int> coll2;
        remove_copy_if(coll1.begin(), coll1.end(),      // source
                    inserter(coll2,coll2.end()),        // destination
                    bind2nd(less<int>(),4));            // elements not copied
        PRINT_ELEMENTS(coll2);
}
```

The program has the following output:

```
1 2 3 4 5 6 1 2 3 4 5 6 7 8 9
1 2 4 5 6 1 2 4 5 6 7 8 9
1 2 3 4 1 2 3 4
4 4 5 5 6 6 7 8 9
```

9.7.2   Removing Duplicates

Removing Consecutive Duplicates

```
ForwardIterator
unique (ForwardIterator beg, ForwardIterator end)

ForwardIterator
unique (ForwardIterator beg, ForwardIterator end,
        BinaryPredicate op)
```

- Both forms collapse consecutive equal elements by removing the following duplicates.
- The first form removes from the range [beg,end) all elements that are equal to the previous elements. Thus, only when the elements in the sequence are sorted (or at least when all elements of the same value are adjacent), does it remove all duplicates.

- The second form removes all elements that follow an element *e* and for which the binary predicate
    op(elem,e)
  yields `true`. In other words, the predicate is not used to compare an element with its predecessor;
  the element is compared with the previous element that was not removed (see the following
  examples).
- Both forms return the logical new end of the modified sequence (the position after the last element
  not removed).
- The algorithms overwrite "removed" elements by the following elements that were not removed.
- The order of elements that were not removed remains stable.
- It is up to the caller, after calling this algorithm, to use the returned new logical end instead of
  the original end *end* (see Section 5.6.1, page 111, for more details).
- Note that *op* should not change its state during a function call. See Section 8.1.4, page 302, for
  details.
- Due to modifications you can't use these algorithms for an associative container (see Section 5.6.2,
  page 115).
- Lists provide an equivalent member function, `unique()`, which offers better performance because it relinks pointers instead of assigning element values (see page 244).
- Complexity: linear (*numberOfElements* comparisons or calls of *op()* respectively).

The following program demonstrates how to use `unique()`:

```
// algo/unique1.cpp

#include "algostuff.hpp"
using namespace std;

int main()
{
    // source data
    int source[] = { 1, 4, 4, 6, 1, 2, 2, 3, 1, 6, 6, 6, 5, 7,
                     5, 4, 4 };
    int sourceNum = sizeof(source)/sizeof(source[0]);

    list<int> coll;

    // initialize coll with elements from source
    copy (source, source+sourceNum,             // source
          back_inserter(coll));                  // destination
    PRINT_ELEMENTS(coll);

    // remove consecutive duplicates
    list<int>::iterator pos;
```

```
    pos = unique (coll.begin(), coll.end());

    /* print elements not removed
     * - use new logical end
     */
    copy (coll.begin(), pos,                    // source
          ostream_iterator<int>(cout," "));     // destination
    cout << "\n\n";

    // reinitialize coll with elements from source
    copy (source, source+sourceNum,             // source
          coll.begin());                        // destination
    PRINT_ELEMENTS(coll);

    // remove elements if there was a previous greater element
    coll.erase (unique (coll.begin(), coll.end(),
                        greater<int>()),
                coll.end());
    PRINT_ELEMENTS(coll);
}
```

The program has the following output:

```
1 4 4 6 1 2 2 3 1 6 6 6 5 7 5 4 4
1 4 6 1 2 3 1 6 5 7 5 4

1 4 4 6 1 2 2 3 1 6 6 6 5 7 5 4 4
1 4 4 6 6 6 6 7
```

The first call of unique() removes consecutive duplicates. The second call shows the behavior of the second form. It removes all the consecutive following elements of an element for which the comparison with greater yields true. For example, the first 6 is greater than the following 1, 2, 2, 3, and 1, so all these elements are removed. In other words, the predicate is not used to compare an element with its predecessor; the element is compared with the previous element that was not removed (see the following description of unique_copy() for another example).

Removing Duplicates While Copying

```
OutputIterator
unique_copy (InputIterator sourceBeg, InputIterator sourceEnd,
            OutputIterator destBeg)

OutputIterator
unique_copy (InputIterator sourceBeg, InputIterator sourceEnd,
            OutputIterator destBeg,
            BinaryPredicate op)
```

- Both forms are a combination of copy() and unique().
- They copy all elements of the source range [*sourceBeg,sourceEnd*) into the destination range starting with *destBeg* except for consecutive duplicates.
- Both forms return the position after the last copied element in the destination range (the first element that is not overwritten).
- The caller must ensure that the destination range is big enough or that insert iterators are used.
- Complexity: linear (*numberOfElements* comparisons or calls of *op*() and assignments respectively).

The following program demonstrates how to use unique_copy():

```
// algo/unique2.cpp

#include "algostuff.hpp"
using namespace std;

bool differenceOne (int elem1, int elem2)
{
    return elem1 + 1 == elem2 || elem1 - 1 == elem2;
}

int main()
{
    // source data
    int source[] = { 1, 4, 4, 6, 1, 2, 2, 3, 1, 6, 6, 6, 5, 7,
                     5, 4, 4 };
    int sourceNum = sizeof(source)/sizeof(source[0]);

    // initialize coll with elements from source
    list<int> coll;
    copy(source, source+sourceNum,          // source
         back_inserter(coll));              // destination
```

```
        PRINT_ELEMENTS(coll);

        // print elements with consecutive duplicates removed
        unique_copy(coll.begin(), coll.end(),              // source
                    ostream_iterator<int>(cout," "));      // destination
        cout << endl;

        // print elements without consecutive entries that differ by one
        unique_copy(coll.begin(), coll.end(),              // source
                    ostream_iterator<int>(cout," "),       // destination
                    differenceOne);                        // duplicates criterion
        cout << endl;
    }
```

The program has the following output:

```
1 4 4 6 1 2 2 3 1 6 6 6 5 7 5 4 4
1 4 6 1 2 3 1 6 5 7 5 4
1 4 4 6 1 3 1 6 6 6 4 4
```

Note that the second call of `unique_copy()` does not remove the elements that differ from their predecessor by one. Instead it removes all elements that differ from their previous element *that is not removed* by one. For example, after the three occurrences of 6, the following 5, 7, and 5 differ by one compared with 6, so they are removed. However, the following two occurrences of 4 remain in the sequence because compared with 6 the difference is not one.

Another example compresses sequences of spaces:

```
// algo/unique3.cpp

#include <iostream>
#include <algorithm>
#include <iterator>
using namespace std;

bool bothSpaces (char elem1, char elem2)
{
    return elem1 == ' ' && elem2 == ' ';
}

int main()
{
    // don't skip leading whitespaces by default
    cin.unsetf(ios::skipws);
```

```
/* copy standard input to standard output
 * - while compressing spaces
 */
unique_copy(istream_iterator<char>(cin),    // beginning of source: cin
            istream_iterator<char>(),        // end of source: end-of-file
            ostream_iterator<char>(cout),    // destination: cout
            bothSpaces);                     // duplicate criterion
}
```

With the input of

```
Hello, here are   sometimes more  and sometimes fewer    spaces.
```
this example produces the following output:

```
Hello, here are sometimes more and sometimes fewer spaces.
```

9.8   Mutating Algorithms

Mutating algorithms change the order of elements (but not their values). Because elements of associative containers have a fixed order, you can't use them as a destination for mutating algorithms.

9.8.1   Reversing the Order of Elements

```
void
reverse (BidirectionalIterator beg, BidirectionalIterator end)
```

```
OutputIterator
reverse_copy (BidirectionalIterator sourceBeg, BidirectionalIterator sourceEnd,
              OutputIterator destBeg)
```

- reverse() reverses the order of the elements inside the range [beg,end).
- reverse_copy() reverses the order of the elements while copying them from the source range [sourceBeg,sourceEnd) to the destination range starting with destBeg.
- reverse_copy() returns the position after the last copied element in the destination range (the first element that is not overwritten).
- The caller must ensure that the destination range is big enough or that insert iterators are used.
- Lists provide an equivalent member function, reverse(), which offers better performance because it relinks pointers instead of assigning element values (see page 246).
- Complexity: linear (numberOfElements/2 swaps or numberOfElements assignments respectively).

The following program demonstrates how to use reverse() and reverse_copy():

```cpp
// algo/reverse1.cpp

#include "algostuff.hpp"
using namespace std;

int main()
{
    vector<int> coll;

    INSERT_ELEMENTS(coll,1,9);
    PRINT_ELEMENTS(coll,"coll: ");

    // reverse order of elements
    reverse (coll.begin(), coll.end());
    PRINT_ELEMENTS(coll,"coll: ");

    // reverse order from second to last element but one
    reverse (coll.begin()+1, coll.end()-1);
    PRINT_ELEMENTS(coll,"coll: ");

    // print all of them in reverse order
    reverse_copy (coll.begin(), coll.end(),          // source
                  ostream_iterator<int>(cout," "));  // destination
    cout << endl;
}
```

The program has the following output:

```
coll: 1 2 3 4 5 6 7 8 9
coll: 9 8 7 6 5 4 3 2 1
coll: 9 2 3 4 5 6 7 8 1
1 8 7 6 5 4 3 2 9
```

9.8.2   Rotating Elements

Rotating Elements Inside a Sequence

void
rotate (ForwardIterator *beg*, ForwardIterator *newBeg*, ForwardIterator *end*)

- Rotates elements in the range [*beg,end*) so that *newBeg* is the new first element after the call.
- The caller must ensure that *newBeg* is a valid position in the range [*beg,end*); otherwise, the call results in undefined behavior.
- Complexity: linear (at most, *numberOfElements* swaps).

The following program demonstrates how to use rotate():

```
// algo/rotate1.cpp

#include "algostuff.hpp"
using namespace std;

int main()
{
    vector<int> coll;

    INSERT_ELEMENTS(coll,1,9);
    PRINT_ELEMENTS(coll,"coll:       ");

    // rotate one element to the left
    rotate (coll.begin(),        // beginning of range
            coll.begin() + 1,    // new first element
            coll.end());         // end of range
    PRINT_ELEMENTS(coll,"one left:  ");

    // rotate two elements to the right
    rotate (coll.begin(),        // beginning of range
            coll.end() - 2,      // new first element
            coll.end());         // end of range
    PRINT_ELEMENTS(coll,"two right: ");

    // rotate so that element with value 4 is the beginning
    rotate (coll.begin(),                         // beginning of range
            find(coll.begin(),coll.end(),4),      // new first element
            coll.end());                          // end of range
```

```
        PRINT_ELEMENTS(coll,"4 first:    ");
}
```

As the example shows, you can rotate to the left with a positive offset for the beginning and rotate to
the right with a negative offset to the end. However, adding the offset to the iterator is possible only
when you have random access iterators, as you have for vectors. Without such iterators, you must
use advance() (see the example of rotate_copy() on page 389).

The program has the following output:

```
coll:       1 2 3 4 5 6 7 8 9
one left:   2 3 4 5 6 7 8 9 1
two right:  9 1 2 3 4 5 6 7 8
4 first:    4 5 6 7 8 9 1 2 3
```

Rotating Elements While Copying

```
OutputIterator
```
rotate_copy (ForwardIterator *sourceBeg*, ForwardIterator *newBeg*,
                ForwardIterator *sourceEnd*,
                OutputIterator *destBeg*)

- Is a combination of copy() and rotate().
- Copies the elements of the source range [*sourceBeg*,*sourceEnd*) into the destination range start-
  ing with *destBeg* in rotated order so that *newBeg* is the new first element.
- Returns the position after the last copied element in the destination range.
- The caller must ensure that *newBeg* is an element in the range [*beg*,*end*); otherwise, the call
  results in undefined behavior.
- The caller must ensure that the destination range is big enough or that insert iterators are used.
- The source and destination ranges should not overlap.
- Complexity: linear (*numberOfElements* assignments).

The following program demonstrates how to use rotate_copy():

```
// algo/rotate2.cpp

#include "algostuff.hpp"
using namespace std;

int main()
{
    set<int> coll;

    INSERT_ELEMENTS(coll,1,9);
```

```
PRINT_ELEMENTS(coll);

// print elements rotated one element to the left
set<int>::iterator pos = coll.begin();
advance(pos,1);
rotate_copy(coll.begin(),              // beginning of source
            pos,                       // new first element
            coll.end(),                // end of source
            ostream_iterator<int>(cout," ")); // destination
cout << endl;

// print elements rotated two elements to the right
pos = coll.end();
advance(pos,-2);
rotate_copy(coll.begin(),              // beginning of source
            pos,                       // new first element
            coll.end(),                // end of source
            ostream_iterator<int>(cout," ")); // destination
cout << endl;

// print elements rotated so that element with value 4 is the beginning
rotate_copy(coll.begin(),              // beginning of source
            coll.find(4),              // new first element
            coll.end(),                // end of source
            ostream_iterator<int>(cout," ")); // destination
cout << endl;
}
```

Unlike the previous example of `rotate()` (see page 388), here a set is used instead of a vector. This has two consequences:

1. You must use `advance()` (see Section 7.3.1, page 259) to change the value of the iterator because bidirectional iterators do not provide operator +.

2. You should use the `find()` member function instead of the `find()` algorithm because the former has better performance.

The program has the following output:

```
1 2 3 4 5 6 7 8 9
2 3 4 5 6 7 8 9 1
8 9 1 2 3 4 5 6 7
4 5 6 7 8 9 1 2 3
```

9.8.3 Permuting Elements

```
bool
next_permutation (BidirectionalIterator beg, BidirectionalIterator end)

bool
next_permutation (BidirectionalIterator beg, BidirectionalIterator end,
                  CompFunc op)

bool
prev_permutation (BidirectionalIterator beg, BidirectionalIterator end)

bool
prev_permutation (BidirectionalIterator beg, BidirectionalIterator end,
                  CompFunc op)
```

- `next_permutation()` changes the order of the elements in [*beg,end*) according to the next permutation.

- `prev_permutation()` changes the order of the elements in [*beg,end*) according to the previous permutation.

- The first forms compare the elements by using operator <.

- The second forms compare the elements by using the binary predicate
    op(elem1,elem2)
  It should return `true` when *elem1* is less than *elem2*.

- Both algorithms return `false` if the elements have the "normal" (lexicographical) order; that is, ascending order for `next_permutation()` and descending order for `prev_permutation()`. So, to run through all permutations you have to sort all elements (ascending or descending), and start a loop that calls `next_permutation()` or `prev_permutation()` as long as these algorithms return true.[5]
  Lexicographical sorting is explained on page 360.

- Complexity: linear (at most, *numberOfElements*/2 swaps).

The following example demonstrates how `next_permutation()` and `prev_permutation()` run through all permutations of the elements:

```
// algo/perm1.cpp

#include "algostuff.hpp"
using namespace std;

int main()
{
    vector<int> coll;
    INSERT_ELEMENTS(coll,1,3);
    PRINT_ELEMENTS(coll,"on entry:   ");
```

---

[5] `next_permutation()` and `prev_permutation()` could also be used to sort elements in a range. You just call them for a range as long as they return `true`. However, doing so would produce really bad performance.

```
/* permute elements until they are sorted
 * - runs through all permutations because the elements are sorted now
 */
while (next_permutation(coll.begin(),coll.end())) {
    PRINT_ELEMENTS(coll," ");
}
PRINT_ELEMENTS(coll,"afterward: ");

/* permute until descending sorted
 * - this is the next permutation after ascending sorting
 * - so the loop ends immediately
 */
while (prev_permutation(coll.begin(),coll.end())) {
    PRINT_ELEMENTS(coll," ");
}
PRINT_ELEMENTS(coll,"now:        ");

/* permute elements until they are sorted in descending order
 * - runs through all permutations because the elements are sorted
 *   in descending order now
 */
while (prev_permutation(coll.begin(),coll.end())) {
    PRINT_ELEMENTS(coll," ");
}
PRINT_ELEMENTS(coll,"afterward: ");
}
```

The program has the following output:

```
on entry:  1 2 3
  1 3 2
  2 1 3
  2 3 1
  3 1 2
  3 2 1
afterward: 1 2 3
now:        3 2 1
  3 1 2
  2 3 1
  2 1 3
```

```
1 3 2
1 2 3
afterward: 3 2 1
```

9.8.4   Shuffling Elements

void
random_shuffle (RandomAccessIterator *beg*, RandomAccessIterator *end*)

void
random_shuffle (RandomAccessIterator *beg*, RandomAccessIterator *end*,
                    RandomFunc& *op*)

- The first form shuffles the order of the elements in the range [*beg*,*end*) using a uniform distribution random number generator.
- The second form shuffles the order of the elements in the range [*beg*,*end*) using *op*. *op* is called with an integral value of difference_type of the iterator:

  op (*max*)

  It should return a random number greater than or equal to zero and less than *max*. Thus, it should not return *max* itself.
- Note that *op* is a nonconstant reference, so you can't pass a temporary value or an ordinary function.
- Complexity: linear (*numberOfElements*-1 swaps).

You might wonder why random_shuffle() uses its optional operation as a nonconstant reference. It does so because random number generators typically have a local state. Old global C functions such as rand() store their local state in a static variable. However, this has some disadvantages: For example, the random number generator is inherently thread unsafe, and you can't have two independent streams of random numbers. Therefore, function objects provide a better solution by encapsulating their local state as one or more member variables. Thus, the random number generator can't be constant because it has to change its local state while generating a new random number. However, to have the random number generator nonconstant, you could still pass it by value instead of passing it by nonconstant reference. In this case each call would copy the random number generator and its state so that you get the same random sequence each time you pass the generator to the algorithm. Thus the generator is passed as a nonconstant reference.[6]

If you need the same random number sequence twice, you can simply copy it. However, if the generator is implemented in a way that uses a global state, you would still get different sequences.

The following example demonstrates how to shuffle elements by calling random_shuffle():

```
// algo/random1.cpp

#include <cstdlib>
#include "algostuff.hpp"
```

---

[6] Thanks to Matt Austern for this explanation.

```
using namespace std;

class MyRandom {
  public:
    ptrdiff_t operator() (ptrdiff_t max) {
        double tmp;
        tmp = static_cast<double>(rand())
                / static_cast<double>(RAND_MAX);
        return static_cast<ptrdiff_t>(tmp * max);
    }
};

int main()
{
    vector<int> coll;

    INSERT_ELEMENTS(coll,1,9);
    PRINT_ELEMENTS(coll,"coll:       ");

    // shuffle all elements randomly
    random_shuffle (coll.begin(), coll.end());

    PRINT_ELEMENTS(coll,"shuffled: ");

    // sort them again
    sort (coll.begin(), coll.end());
    PRINT_ELEMENTS(coll,"sorted:    ");

    /* shuffle elements with self-written random number generator
     * - to pass an lvalue we have to use a temporary object
     */
    MyRandom rd;
    random_shuffle (coll.begin(), coll.end(),    // range
                    rd);                          // random number generator

    PRINT_ELEMENTS(coll,"shuffled: ");
}
```

The second call of `random()` uses the self-written random number generator `rd()`. It is an object of the auxiliary function object class `MyRandom`, which uses an algorithm for random numbers that often is better than the usual direct call of `rand()`.[7]

A possible (but not portable) output of the program is as follows:

```
coll:     1 2 3 4 5 6 7 8 9
shuffled: 2 6 9 5 4 3 1 7 8
sorted:   1 2 3 4 5 6 7 8 9
shuffled: 2 6 9 3 1 8 7 4 5
```

9.8.5 Moving Elements to the Front

```
BidirectionalIterator
```
partition (`BidirectionalIterator` *beg*, `BidirectionalIterator` *end*,
          `UnaryPredicate` *op*)

```
BidirectionalIterator
```
stable_partition (`BidirectionalIterator` *beg*, `BidirectionalIterator` *end*,
                   `UnaryPredicate` *op*)

- Both algorithms move all elements in the range [*beg*,*end*) to the front for which the unary predicate
    op(*elem*)
  yields `true`.
- Both algorithms return the first position for which `op()` yields `false`.
- The difference between `partition()` and `stable_partition()` is that `stable_partition()` preserves the relative order of elements that match the criterion and those that do not.
- You could use this algorithm to split elements into two parts according to a sorting criterion. The `nth_element()` algorithm has a similar ability. See page 330 for a discussion of the differences between these algorithms and `nth_element()`.
- Note that *op* should not change its state during a function call. See Section 8.1.4, page 302, for details.
- Complexity:
    - For `partition()`: linear (*numberOfElements* calls of *op*() and, at most, *numberOfElements*/2 swaps).
    - For `stable_partition()`: linear if there is enough extra memory (*numberOfElements* calls of *op*() and swaps), or n-log-n otherwise (*numberOfElements**`log`(*numberOfElements*) calls of *op*()).

The following program demonstrates the use of and the difference between `partition()` and `stable_partition()`:

---

[7] The way `MyRandom` generates random numbers is introduced and described in Bjarne Stroustrup's *The C++ Programming Language*, 3rd edition.

```cpp
// algo/part1.cpp

#include "algostuff.hpp"
using namespace std;

int main()
{
    vector<int> coll1;
    vector<int> coll2;

    INSERT_ELEMENTS(coll1,1,9);
    INSERT_ELEMENTS(coll2,1,9);
    PRINT_ELEMENTS(coll1,"coll1: ");
    PRINT_ELEMENTS(coll2,"coll2: ");
    cout << endl;

    // move all even elements to the front
    vector<int>::iterator pos1, pos2;
    pos1 = partition(coll1.begin(), coll1.end(),        // range
                   not1(bind2nd(modulus<int>(),2)));    // criterion
    pos2 = stable_partition(coll2.begin(), coll2.end(), // range
                   not1(bind2nd(modulus<int>(),2)));    // crit.

    // print collections and first odd element
    PRINT_ELEMENTS(coll1,"coll1: ");
    cout << "first odd element: " << *pos1 << endl;
    PRINT_ELEMENTS(coll2,"coll2: ");
    cout << "first odd element: " << *pos2 << endl;
}
```

The program has the following output:

```
coll1: 1 2 3 4 5 6 7 8 9
coll2: 1 2 3 4 5 6 7 8 9

coll1: 8 2 6 4 5 3 7 1 9
first odd element: 5
coll2: 2 4 6 8 1 3 5 7 9
first odd element: 1
```

As this example shows, stable_partition(), unlike partition(), preserves the relative order of the even and the odd elements.

9.9   Sorting Algorithms

The STL provides several algorithms to sort elements of a range. In addition to full sorting, it provides different variants of partial sorting. If their result is enough, you should prefer them because they usually have better performance.

You might also use associative containers to have elements sorted automatically. However, note that sorting all elements once is usually faster than keeping them sorted always (see page 228 for details).

9.9.1   Sorting All Elements

```
void
sort (RandomAccessIterator beg, RandomAccessIterator end)
```

```
void
sort (RandomAccessIterator beg, RandomAccessIterator end, BinaryPredicate op)
```

```
void
stable_sort (RandomAccessIterator beg, RandomAccessIterator end)
```

```
void
stable_sort (RandomAccessIterator beg, RandomAccessIterator end,
             BinaryPredicate op)
```

- The first forms of sort() and stable_sort() sort all elements in the range [*beg,end*) with operator <.
- The second forms of sort() and stable_sort() sort all elements by using the binary predicate *op(elem1,elem2)* as the sorting criterion.
- Note that *op* should not change its state during a function call. See Section 8.1.4, page 302, for details.
- The difference between sort() and stable_sort() is that stable_sort() guarantees that the order of equal elements remains stable.
- You can't call these algorithms for lists because lists do not provide random access iterators. However, lists provide a special member function to sort elements: sort() (see page 245).
- sort() guarantees a good performance (n-log-n) on average. However, if avoiding worst-case performance is important, you should use partial_sort() or stable_sort(). See the discussion about sorting algorithms on page 328.
- Complexity:
  - For sort(): n-log-n on average (approximately *numberOfElements*∗log(*numberOfElements*) comparisons on average).

- For `stable_sort()`: n-log-n if there is enough extra memory (*numberOfElements* * log(*numberOfElements*) comparisons), or n-log-n*log-n otherwise (*numberOfElements* * log(*numberOfElements*)^2 comparisons).

The following example demonstrates the use of `sort()`:

```
// algo/sort1.cpp

#include "algostuff.hpp"
using namespace std;

int main()
{
    deque<int> coll;

    INSERT_ELEMENTS(coll,1,9);
    INSERT_ELEMENTS(coll,1,9);

    PRINT_ELEMENTS(coll,"on entry: ");

    // sort elements
    sort (coll.begin(), coll.end());

    PRINT_ELEMENTS(coll,"sorted:    ");

    // sorted reverse
    sort (coll.begin(), coll.end(),      // range
          greater<int>());               // sorting criterion

    PRINT_ELEMENTS(coll,"sorted >: ");
}
```

The program has the following output:

```
on entry: 1 2 3 4 5 6 7 8 9 1 2 3 4 5 6 7 8 9
sorted:    1 1 2 2 3 3 4 4 5 5 6 6 7 7 8 8 9 9
sorted >: 9 9 8 8 7 7 6 6 5 5 4 4 3 3 2 2 1 1
```

See page 123 for an example that demonstrates how to sort according to a member of a class.

The following program demonstrates how `sort()` and `stable_sort()` differ. The program uses both algorithms to sort strings only according to their number of characters by using the sorting criterion `lessLength()`:

```cpp
// algo/sort2.cpp

#include "algostuff.hpp"
using namespace std;

bool lessLength (const string& s1, const string& s2)
{
    return s1.length() < s2.length();
}

int main()
{
    vector<string> coll1;
    vector<string> coll2;

    // fill both collections with the same elements
    coll1.push_back ("1xxx");
    coll1.push_back ("2x");
    coll1.push_back ("3x");
    coll1.push_back ("4x");
    coll1.push_back ("5xx");
    coll1.push_back ("6xxxx");
    coll1.push_back ("7xx");
    coll1.push_back ("8xxx");
    coll1.push_back ("9xx");
    coll1.push_back ("10xxx");
    coll1.push_back ("11");
    coll1.push_back ("12");
    coll1.push_back ("13");
    coll1.push_back ("14xx");
    coll1.push_back ("15");
    coll1.push_back ("16");
    coll1.push_back ("17");
    coll2 = coll1;

    PRINT_ELEMENTS(coll1,"on entry:\n ");

    // sort (according to the length of the strings)
    sort (coll1.begin(), coll1.end(),            // range
```

```
                       lessLength);                              // criterion
            stable_sort (coll2.begin(), coll2.end(),            // range
                       lessLength);                              // criterion

            PRINT_ELEMENTS(coll1,"\nwith sort():\n ");
            PRINT_ELEMENTS(coll2,"\nwith stable_sort():\n ");
    }
```

The program has the following output:

```
on entry:
 1xxx 2x 3x 4x 5xx 6xxxx 7xx 8xxx 9xx 10xxx 11 12 13 14xx 15 16 17

with sort():
 17 2x 3x 4x 16 15 13 12 11 9xx 7xx 5xx 8xxx 14xx 1xxx 10xxx 6xxxx

with stable_sort():
 2x 3x 4x 11 12 13 15 16 17 5xx 7xx 9xx 1xxx 8xxx 14xx 6xxxx 10xxx
```

Only `stable_sort()` preserves the relative order of the elements (the leading numbers tag the order of the elements on entry).

9.9.2   Partial Sorting

```
void
partial_sort (RandomAccessIterator beg, RandomAccessIterator sortEnd,
              RandomAccessIterator end)

void
partial_sort (RandomAccessIterator beg, RandomAccessIterator sortEnd,
              RandomAccessIterator end, BinaryPredicate op)
```

- The first form sorts the elements in the range [*beg*,*end*) with operator < so that range [*beg*,*sortEnd*) contains the elements in sorted order.
- The second form sorts the elements by using the binary predicate
    op(*elem1*,*elem2*)
  as the sorting criterion so that range [*beg*,*sortEnd*) contains the elements in sorted order.
- Note that *op* should not change its state during a function call. See Section 8.1.4, page 302, for details.
- Unlike `sort()`, `partial_sort()` does not sort all elements, but stops the sorting once the first elements up to *sortEnd* are sorted correctly. Thus, if after sorting the sequence you need only the first three elements, this algorithm saves time because it does not sort the remaining elements unnecessarily.

- If *sortEnd* is equal to *end*, `partial_sort()` sorts the full sequence. It has worse performance than `sort()` on average but better performance in the worst case. See the discussion about sorting algorithms on page 328.
- Complexity: between linear and n-log-n (approximately *numberOfElements*∗log(*numberOf-SortedElements*) comparisons).

The following program demonstrates how to use `partial_sort()`:

```
// algo/psort1.cpp

#include "algostuff.hpp"
using namespace std;

int main()
{
    deque<int> coll;

    INSERT_ELEMENTS(coll,3,7);
    INSERT_ELEMENTS(coll,2,6);
    INSERT_ELEMENTS(coll,1,5);
    PRINT_ELEMENTS(coll);

    // sort until the first five elements are sorted
    partial_sort (coll.begin(),          // beginning of the range
                  coll.begin()+5,        // end of sorted range
                  coll.end());           // end of full range
    PRINT_ELEMENTS(coll);

    // sort inversely until the first five elements are sorted
    partial_sort (coll.begin(),          // beginning of the range
                  coll.begin()+5,        // end of sorted range
                  coll.end(),            // end of full range
                  greater<int>());       // sorting criterion
    PRINT_ELEMENTS(coll);

    // sort all elements
    partial_sort (coll.begin(),          // beginning of the range
                  coll.end(),            // end of sorted range
                  coll.end());           // end of full range
    PRINT_ELEMENTS(coll);
}
```

The program has the following output:

```
3 4 5 6 7 2 3 4 5 6 1 2 3 4 5
1 2 2 3 3 7 6 5 5 6 4 4 3 4 5
7 6 6 5 5 1 2 2 3 3 4 4 3 4 5
1 2 2 3 3 3 4 4 4 5 5 5 6 6 7
```

RandomAccessIterator
partial_sort_copy (InputIterator *sourceBeg*, InputIterator *sourceEnd*,
                        RandomAccessIterator *destBeg*, RandomAccessIterator *destEnd*)

RandomAccessIterator
partial_sort_copy (InputIterator *sourceBeg*, InputIterator *sourceEnd*,
                        RandomAccessIterator *destBeg*, RandomAccessIterator *destEnd*,
                        BinaryPredicate *op*)

- Both forms are a combination of copy() and partial_sort().
- They copy elements from the source range [*sourceBeg*,*sourceEnd*) sorted into the destination range [*destBeg*,*destEnd*).
- The number of elements that are sorted and copied is the minimum number of elements in the source range and in the destination range.
- Both forms return the position after the last copied element in the destination range (the first element that is not overwritten).
- If the destination range [*destBeg*,*destEnd*) has more or an equal number of elements than the source range [*sourceBeg*,*sourceEnd*), all elements are copied and sorted. Thus, the behavior is a combination of copy() and sort().
- Complexity: between linear and n-log-n (approximately *numberOfElements**log(*numberOf-SortedElements*) comparisons).

The following program demonstrates some examples of partial_sort_copy():

```
// algo/psort2.cpp

#include "algostuff.hpp"
using namespace std;

int main()
{
    deque<int> coll1;
    vector<int> coll6(6);       // initialize with 6 elements
    vector<int> coll30(30);     // initialize with 30 elements

    INSERT_ELEMENTS(coll1,3,7);
    INSERT_ELEMENTS(coll1,2,6);
```

```
    INSERT_ELEMENTS(coll1,1,5);
    PRINT_ELEMENTS(coll1);

    // copy elements of coll1 sorted into coll6
    vector<int>::iterator pos6;
    pos6 = partial_sort_copy (coll1.begin(), coll1.end(),
                              coll6.begin(), coll6.end());

    // print all copied elements
    copy (coll6.begin(), pos6,
          ostream_iterator<int>(cout," "));
    cout << endl;

    // copy elements of coll1 sorted into coll30
    vector<int>::iterator pos30;
    pos30 = partial_sort_copy (coll1.begin(), coll1.end(),
                               coll30.begin(), coll30.end(),
                               greater<int>());

    // print all copied elements
    copy (coll30.begin(), pos30,
          ostream_iterator<int>(cout," "));
    cout << endl;
}
```

The program has the following output:

```
3 4 5 6 7 2 3 4 5 6 1 2 3 4 5
1 2 2 3 3 3
7 6 6 5 5 5 4 4 4 3 3 3 2 2 1
```

The destination of the first call of `partial_sort_copy()` has only six elements, so the algorithm copies only six elements and returns the end of `coll6`. The second call of `partial_sort_copy()` copies all elements of `coll1` into `coll30`, which has enough room for them, and thus all elements are copied and sorted.

9.9.3   Sorting According to the *n*th Element

```
void
nth_element (RandomAccessIterator beg, RandomAccessIterator nth,
             RandomAccessIterator end)
```

```
void
nth_element (RandomAccessIterator beg, RandomAccessIterator nth,
             RandomAccessIterator end, BinaryPredicate op)
```

- Both forms sort the elements in the range [*beg,end*) so that the correct element is at the *n*th position and all elements in front are less than or equal to this element, and all elements that follow are greater than or equal to it. Thus, you get two subsequences separated by the element at position *n*, whereby each element of the first subsequence is less than or equal to each element of the second subsequence. This is helpful if you need only the set of the *n* highest or lowest elements without having all the elements sorted.

- The first form uses operator < as the sorting criterion.

- The second form uses the binary predicate

     op(*elem1*,*elem2*)

  as the sorting criterion.

- Note that *op* should not change its state during a function call. See Section 8.1.4, page 302, for details.

- The `partition()` algorithm (see page 395) is also provided to split elements of a sequence into two parts according to a sorting criterion. See page 330 for a discussion of how `nth_element()` and `partition()` differ.

- Complexity: linear on average.

The following program demonstrates how to use `nth_element()`:

```
// algo/nth1.cpp

#include "algostuff.hpp"
using namespace std;

int main()
{
    deque<int> coll;

    INSERT_ELEMENTS(coll,3,7);
    INSERT_ELEMENTS(coll,2,6);
    INSERT_ELEMENTS(coll,1,5);
    PRINT_ELEMENTS(coll);
```

```
            // extract the four lowest elements
            nth_element (coll.begin(),        // beginning of range
                         coll.begin()+3,      // element that should be sorted correctly
                         coll.end());         // end of range

            // print them
            cout << "the four lowest elements are:   ";
            copy (coll.begin(), coll.begin()+4,
                  ostream_iterator<int>(cout," "));
            cout << endl;

            // extract the four highest elements
            nth_element (coll.begin(),        // beginning of range
                         coll.end()-4,        // element that should be sorted correctly
                         coll.end());         // end of range

            // print them
            cout << "the four highest elements are: ";
            copy (coll.end()-4, coll.end(),
                  ostream_iterator<int>(cout," "));
            cout << endl;

            // extract the four highest elements (second version)
            nth_element (coll.begin(),        // beginning of range
                         coll.begin()+3,      // element that should be sorted correctly
                         coll.end(),          // end of range
                         greater<int>());     // sorting criterion

            // print them
            cout << "the four highest elements are: ";
            copy (coll.begin(), coll.begin()+4,
                  ostream_iterator<int>(cout," "));
            cout << endl;
        }
```

The program has the following output:

```
    3 4 5 6 7 2 3 4 5 6 1 2 3 4 5
    the four lowest elements are:   2 1 2 3
    the four highest elements are: 5 6 7 6
    the four highest elements are: 6 7 6 5
```

9.9.4 Heap Algorithms

A *heap*, in the context of sorting, is used as a particular way to sort elements. It is used by heapsort. A heap can be considered a binary tree that is implemented as a sequential collection. Heaps have two properties:

1. The first element is always the largest element.
2. You can add or remove an element in logarithmic time.

A heap is the ideal way to implement a priority queue (a queue that sorts its elements automatically). Therefore, the heap algorithms are used by the `priority_queue` container (see Section 10.3, page 453). The STL provides four algorithms to handle a heap:

1. `make_heap()` converts a range of elements into a heap.
2. `push_heap()` adds one element to the heap.
3. `pop_heap()` removes the next element from the heap.
4. `sort_heap()` converts the heap into a sorted collection (after that, it is no longer a heap).

As usual, you can pass a binary predicate as the sorting criterion. The default sorting criterion is operator <.

Heap Algorithms in Detail

```
void
```
make_heap (RandomAccesIterator *beg*, RandomAccesIterator *end*)

```
void
```
make_heap (RandomAccesIterator *beg*, RandomAccesIterator *end*,
              BinaryPredicate *op*)

- Both forms convert the elements in the range [*beg,end*) into a heap.
- *op* is an optional binary predicate that is used as the sorting criterion:
    op(elem1,elem2)
- You need these functions only to start processing a heap for more than one element (one element automatically is a heap).
- Complexity: linear (at most, 3*numberOfElements* comparisons).

```
void
```
push_heap (RandomAccesIterator *beg*, RandomAccesIterator *end*)

```
void
```
push_heap (RandomAccesIterator *beg*, RandomAccesIterator *end*,
              BinaryPredicate *op*)

- Both forms add the last element that is in front of *end* to the existing heap in the range [*beg,end*-1] so that the whole range [*beg,end*) becomes a heap.

- *op* is an optional binary predicate that is used as the sorting criterion:
     op(*elem1*,*elem2*)
- The caller has to ensure that, on entry, the elements in the range [*beg*,*end*-1) are a heap (according to the same sorting criterion) and that the new element immediately follows these elements.
- Complexity: logarithmic (at most, log(*numberOfElements*) comparisons).

```
void
pop_heap (RandomAccesIterator beg, RandomAccesIterator end)

void
pop_heap (RandomAccesIterator beg, RandomAccesIterator end,
          BinaryPredicate op)
```

- Both forms move the highest element of the heap [*beg*,*end*), which is the first element, to the last position and create a new heap from the remaining elements in the range [*beg*,*end*-1).
- *op* is an optional binary predicate that is used as the sorting criterion:
     op(*elem1*,*elem2*)
- The caller has to ensure that, on entry, the elements in the range [*beg*,*end*) are a heap (according to the same sorting criterion).
- Complexity: logarithmic (at most, 2*log(*numberOfElements*) comparisons).

```
void
sort_heap (RandomAccesIterator beg, RandomAccesIterator end)

void
sort_heap (RandomAccesIterator beg, RandomAccesIterator end,
           BinaryPredicate op)
```

- Both forms convert the heap [*beg*,*end*) into a sorted sequence.
- *op* is an optional binary predicate that is used as the sorting criterion:
     op(*elem1*,*elem2*)
- Note that after this call, the range is no longer a heap.
- The caller has to ensure that, on entry, the elements in the range [*beg*,*end*) are a heap (according to the same sorting criterion).
- Complexity: n-log-n (at most, *numberOfElements**log(*numberOfElements*) comparisons).

Example Using Heaps

The following program demonstrates how to use the different heap algorithms:

```
// algo/heap1.cpp

#include "algostuff.hpp"
using namespace std;
```

```
int main()
{
    vector<int> coll;

    INSERT_ELEMENTS(coll,3,7);
    INSERT_ELEMENTS(coll,5,9);
    INSERT_ELEMENTS(coll,1,4);

    PRINT_ELEMENTS (coll, "on entry:             ");

    // convert collection into a heap
    make_heap (coll.begin(), coll.end());

    PRINT_ELEMENTS (coll, "after make_heap(): ");

    // pop next element out of the heap
    pop_heap (coll.begin(), coll.end());
    coll.pop_back();

    PRINT_ELEMENTS (coll, "after pop_heap():   ");

    // push new element into the heap
    coll.push_back (17);
    push_heap (coll.begin(), coll.end());

    PRINT_ELEMENTS (coll, "after push_heap(): ");

    /* convert heap into a sorted collection
     * - NOTE: after the call it is no longer a heap
     */
    sort_heap (coll.begin(), coll.end());

    PRINT_ELEMENTS (coll, "after sort_heap():  ");
}
```

The program has the following output:

```
on entry:            3 4 5 6 7 5 6 7 8 9 1 2 3 4
after make_heap():   9 8 6 7 7 5 5 3 6 4 1 2 3 4
after pop_heap():    8 7 6 7 4 5 5 3 6 4 1 2 3
```

```
after push_heap():  17 7 8 7 4 5 6 3 6 4 1 2 3 5
after sort_heap():  1 2 3 3 4 4 5 5 6 6 7 7 8 17
```

After `make_heap()`, the elements are sorted as a heap:

```
9 8 6 7 7 5 5 3 6 4 1 2 3 4
```

Transform the elements into a binary tree, and you'll see that the value of each node is less than or equal to its parent node (Figure 9.1). Both `push_heap()` and `pop_heap()` change the elements so that the invariant of this binary tree structure (each node not greater than its parent node) remains stable.

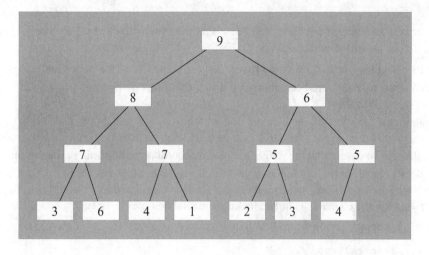

Figure 9.1. Elements of a Heap as a Binary Tree

9.10 Sorted Range Algorithms

Sorted range algorithms require that the source ranges have the elements sorted according to their sorting criterion. They may have significantly better performance than similar algorithms for unsorted ranges (usually logarithmic instead of linear complexity). You can use these algorithms with iterators that are not random access iterators. However, in this case, the algorithms have linear complexity because they have to step through the sequence element-by-element. Nevertheless, the number of comparisons may still have logarithmic complexity.

According to the standard, calling these algorithms for sequences that are not sorted on entry results in undefined behavior. However, for most implementations calling these algorithms also works for unsorted sequences. Nevertheless, to rely on this fact is not portable.

Associative containers provide special member functions for the searching algorithms presented here. When searching for a special value or key, you should use them.

9.10.1   Searching Elements

The following algorithms search certain values in sorted ranges.

Checking Whether One Element Is Present

```
bool
```
binary_search (ForwardIterator *beg*, ForwardIterator *end*, const T& *value*)

```
bool
```
binary_search (ForwardIterator *beg*, ForwardIterator *end*, const T& *value*,
                 BinaryPredicate *op*)

- Both forms return whether the sorted range [*beg*,*end*) contains an element equal to *value*.
- *op* is an optional binary predicate that is used as the sorting criterion:
    op(*elem1*,*elem2*)
- To obtain the position of an element for which you are searching, use lower_bound(),
  upper_bound(), or equal_range() (see page 413 and page 415).
- The caller has to ensure that the ranges are sorted according to the sorting criterion on entry.
- Complexity: logarithmic for random access iterators, linear otherwise (at most, log(*numberOf-Elements*) + 2 comparisons, but for other than random access iterators the number of operations to step through the elements is linear, making the total complexity linear).

The following program demonstrates how to use binary_search():

```cpp
// algo/bsearch1.cpp

#include "algostuff.hpp"
using namespace std;

int main()
{
    list<int> coll;

    INSERT_ELEMENTS(coll,1,9);
    PRINT_ELEMENTS(coll);

    // check existence of element with value 5
    if (binary_search(coll.begin(), coll end(), 5)) {
        cout << "5 is present" << endl;
    }
    else {
        cout << "5 is not present" << endl;
```

```
    }

    // check existence of element with value 42
    if (binary_search(coll.begin(), coll.end(), 42)) {
        cout << "42 is present" << endl;
    }
    else {
        cout << "42 is not present" << endl;
    }
}
```

The program has the following output:

```
1 2 3 4 5 6 7 8 9
5 is present
42 is not present
```

Checking Whether Several Elements Are Present

bool
includes (InputIterator1 *beg*, InputIterator1 *end*,
          InputIterator2 *searchBeg*, InputIterator2 *searchEnd*)

bool
includes (InputIterator1 *beg*, InputIterator1 *end*,
          InputIterator2 *searchBeg*, InputIterator2 *searchEnd*,
          BinaryPredicate *op*)

- Both forms return whether the sorted range [*beg,end*) contains all elements in the sorted range [*searchBeg,searchEnd*). That is, for each element in [*searchBeg,searchEnd*) there must be an equal element in [*beg,end*). If elements in [*searchBeg,searchEnd*) are equal, [*beg,end*) must contain the same number of elements. Thus, [*searchBeg,searchEnd*) must be a subset of [*beg,end*).
- *op* is an optional binary predicate that is used as the sorting criterion:
     op(elem1,elem2)
- The caller has to ensure that both ranges are sorted according to the same sorting criterion on entry.
- Complexity: linear (at most, 2∗(*numberOfElements+searchElements*) − 1 comparisons).

The following program demonstrates the usage of includes():

```
// algo/includes.cpp

#include "algostuff.hpp"
using namespace std;

int main()
{
    list<int> coll;
    vector<int> search;

    INSERT_ELEMENTS(coll,1,9);
    PRINT_ELEMENTS(coll,"coll:    ");

    search.push_back(3);
    search.push_back(4);
    search.push_back(7);
    PRINT_ELEMENTS(search,"search: ");

    // check whether all elements in search are also in coll
    if (includes (coll.begin(), coll.end(),
                    search.begin(), search.end())) {
        cout << "all elements of search are also in coll"
            << endl;
    }
    else {
        cout << "not all elements of search are also in coll"
            << endl;
    }
}
```

The program has the following output:

```
coll:    1 2 3 4 5 6 7 8 9
search: 3 4 7
all elements of search are also in coll
```

Searching First or Last Possible Position

```
ForwardIterator
lower_bound (ForwardIterator beg, ForwardIterator end, const T& value)

ForwardIterator
lower_bound (ForwardIterator beg, ForwardIterator end, const T& value,
             BinaryPredicate op)

ForwardIterator
upper_bound (ForwardIterator beg, ForwardIterator end, const T& value)

ForwardIterator
upper_bound (ForwardIterator beg, ForwardIterator end, const T& value,
             BinaryPredicate op)
```

- `lower_bound()` returns the position of the first element that has a value equal to or greater than *value*. This is the first position where an element with value *value* could get inserted without breaking the actual sorting of the range [*beg,end*].
- `upper_bound()` returns the position of the first element that has a value greater than *value*. This is the last position where an element with value *value* could get inserted without breaking the actual sorting of the range [*beg,end*].
- All algorithms return *end* if there is no such value.
- *op* is an optional binary predicate that is used as the sorting criterion:
    op(elem1 ,elem2)
- The caller has to ensure that the ranges are sorted according to the sorting criterion on entry.
- To obtain the result from both `lower_bound()` and `upper_bound()`, use `equal_range()`, which returns both (see the next algorithm).
- Associative containers (set, multiset, map, and multimap) provide equivalent member functions that provide better performance (see page 235).
- Complexity: logarithmic for random access iterators, linear otherwise (at most, log (*numberOf-Elements*) + 1 comparisons, but for other than random access iterators the number of operations to step through the elements is linear, making the total complexity linear).

The following program demonstrates how to use `lower_bound()` and `upper_bound()`[8]:

```
// algo/bounds1.cpp

#include "algostuff.hpp"
using namespace std;
```

---

[8] Older STL versions might need the file `distance.hpp` from page 263.

```
int main()
{
    list<int> coll;

    INSERT_ELEMENTS(coll,1,9);
    INSERT_ELEMENTS(coll,1,9);
    coll.sort ();
    PRINT_ELEMENTS(coll);

    // print first and last position 5 could get inserted
    list<int>::iterator pos1, pos2;

    pos1 = lower_bound (coll.begin(), coll.end(),
                        5);
    pos2 = upper_bound (coll.begin(), coll.end(),
                        5);

    cout << "5 could get position "
         << distance(coll.begin(),pos1) + 1
         << " up to "
         << distance(coll.begin(),pos2) + 1
         << " without breaking the sorting" << endl;

    // insert 3 at the first possible position without breaking the sorting
    coll.insert (lower_bound(coll.begin(),coll.end(),
                             3),
                 3);

    // insert 7 at the last possible position without breaking the sorting
    coll.insert (upper_bound(coll.begin(),coll.end(),
                             7),
                 7);

    PRINT_ELEMENTS(coll);
}
```

The program has the following output:

```
1 1 2 2 3 3 4 4 5 5 6 6 7 7 8 8 9 9
5 could get position 9 up to 11 without breaking the sorting
1 1 2 2 3 3 3 4 4 5 5 6 6 7 7 7 8 8 9 9
```

Searching First and Last Possible Positions

```
pair<ForwardIterator,ForwardIterator>
```
equal_range (ForwardIterator *beg*, ForwardIterator *end*, const T& *value*)

```
pair<ForwardIterator,ForwardIterator>
```
equal_range (ForwardIterator *beg*, ForwardIterator *end*, const T& *value*,
                BinaryPredicate *op*)

- Both forms return the range of elements that is equal to *value*. This is the first and the last position an element with value *value* could get inserted without breaking the actual sorting of the range [*beg,end*).
- This is equivalent to
    make_pair(lower_bound(...),upper_bound(...))
- *op* is an optional binary predicate that is used as the sorting criterion:
    op (*elem1* , *elem2*)
- The caller has to ensure that the ranges are sorted according to the sorting criterion on entry.
- Associative containers (set, multiset, map, and multimap) provide an equivalent member function that has better performance (see page 236).
- Complexity: logarithmic for random access iterators, linear otherwise (at most, 2*log(*number-OfElements*) + 1 comparisons, but for other than random access iterators the number of operations to step through the elements is linear, making the total complexity linear).

The following program demonstrates how to use equal_range()[9]:

```
// algo/eqrange1.cpp

#include "algostuff.hpp"
using namespace std;

int main()
{
    list<int> coll;

    INSERT_ELEMENTS(coll,1,9);
    INSERT_ELEMENTS(coll,1,9);
    coll.sort ();
    PRINT_ELEMENTS(coll);

    // print first and last position 5 could get inserted
    pair<list<int>::iterator,list<int>::iterator> range;
```

---

[9] Older STL versions might need the file distance.hpp from page 263.

```
        range = equal_range (coll.begin(), coll.end(),
                             5);

        cout << "5 could get position "
             << distance(coll.begin(),range.first) + 1
             << " up to "
             << distance(coll.begin(),range.second) + 1
             << " without breaking the sorting" << endl;
    }
```

The program has the following output:

```
    1 1 2 2 3 3 4 4 5 5 6 6 7 7 8 8 9 9
    5 could get position 9 up to 11 without breaking the sorting
```

9.10.2   Merging Elements

The following algorithms merge elements of two ranges. They process the sum, the union, the intersection, and so on.

Processing the Sum of Two Sorted Sets

```
OutputIterator
```
merge (InputIterator *source1Beg*, InputIterator *source1End*,
       InputIterator *source2Beg*, InputIterator *source2End*,
       OutputIterator *destBeg*)

```
OutputIterator
```
merge (InputIterator *source1Beg*, InputIterator *source1End*,
       InputIterator *source2Beg*, InputIterator *source2End*,
       OutputIterator *destBeg*, BinaryPredicate *op*)

- Both forms merge the elements of the sorted source ranges [*source1Beg,source1End*) and [*source2Beg,source2End*) so that the destination range starting with destBeg contains all elements that are in the first source range plus those that are in the second source range. For example, calling merge() for
    ```
    1 2 2 4 6 7 7 9
    ```
    and
    ```
    2 2 2 3 6 6 8 9
    ```
    results in
    ```
    1 2 2 2 2 2 3 4 6 6 6 7 7 8 9 9
    ```
- All elements in the destination range are in sorted order.

- Both forms return the position after the last copied element in the destination range (the first element that is not overwritten).

- *op* is an optional binary predicate that is used as the sorting criterion:
   op(elem1,elem2)

- The source ranges are not modified.

- According to the standard, the caller has to ensure that both source ranges are sorted on entry. However, in most implementations this algorithm also merges elements of two unsorted source ranges into an unsorted destination range. Nevertheless, for unsorted ranges you should call `copy()` twice, instead of `merge()`, to be portable.

- The caller must ensure that the destination range is big enough or that insert iterators are used.

- The destination range should not overlap the source ranges.

- Lists provide a special member function, `merge()`, to merge the elements of two lists (see page 246).

- To ensure that elements that are in both source ranges end up in the destination range only once, use `set_union()` (see page 418).

- To process only the elements that are in both source ranges, use `set_intersection()` (see page 419).

- Complexity: linear (at most, *numberOfElements1+numberOfElements2*-1 comparisons).

The following example demonstrates how to use `merge()`:

```cpp
// algo/merge1.cpp

#include "algostuff.hpp"
using namespace std;

int main()
{
    list<int> coll1;
    set<int> coll2;

    // fill both collections with some sorted elements
    INSERT_ELEMENTS(coll1,1,6);
    INSERT_ELEMENTS(coll2,3,8);

    PRINT_ELEMENTS(coll1,"coll1:  ");
    PRINT_ELEMENTS(coll2,"coll2:  ");

    // print merged sequence
    cout << "merged: ";
    merge (coll1.begin(), coll1.end(),
           coll2.begin(), coll2.end(),
```

```
            ostream_iterator<int>(cout," "));
    cout << endl;
}
```

The program has the following output:

```
coll1:  1 2 3 4 5 6
coll2:  3 4 5 6 7 8
merged: 1 2 3 3 4 4 5 5 6 6 7 8
```

See page 421 for another example. It demonstrates how the different algorithms that are provided to combine sorted sequences differ.

Processing the Union of Two Sorted Sets

```
OutputIterator
set_union (InputIterator source1Beg, InputIterator source1End,
           InputIterator source2Beg, InputIterator source2End,
           OutputIterator destBeg)
```

```
OutputIterator
set_union (InputIterator source1Beg, InputIterator source1End,
           InputIterator source2Beg, InputIterator source2End,
           OutputIterator destBeg, BinaryPredicate op)
```

- Both forms merge the elements of the sorted source ranges [*source1Beg,source1End*) and [*source2Beg,source2End*) so that the destination range starting with destBeg contains all elements that are either in the first source range, in the second source range, or in both. For example, calling set_union() for

    ```
    1 2 2 4 6 7 7 9
    ```
    and
    ```
    2 2 2 3 6 6 8 9
    ```
    results in
    ```
    1 2 2 2 3 4 6 6 7 7 8 9
    ```

- All elements in the destination range are in sorted order.

- Elements that are in both ranges are in the union range only once. However, duplicates are possible if elements occur more than once in one of the source ranges. The number of occurrences of equal elements in the destination range is the maximum of the number of their occurrences in both source ranges.

- Both forms return the position after the last copied element in the destination range (the first element that is not overwritten).

- *op* is an optional binary predicate that is used as the sorting criterion:

    op(elem1,elem2)

- The source ranges are not modified.
- The caller has to ensure that the ranges are sorted according to the sorting criterion on entry.
- The caller must ensure that the destination range is big enough or that insert iterators are used.
- The destination range should not overlap the source ranges.
- To obtain all elements of both source ranges without removing elements that are in both, use `merge()` (see page 416).
- Complexity: linear (at most, 2*(*numberOfElements1*+*numberOfElements2*) – 1 comparisons).

See page 421 for an example of the use of `set_union()`. This example also demonstrates how it differs from other algorithms that combine elements of two sorted sequences.

Processing the Intersection of Two Sorted Sets

```
OutputIterator
```
set_intersection (InputIterator *source1Beg*, InputIterator *source1End*,
InputIterator *source2Beg*, InputIterator *source2End*,
OutputIterator *destBeg*)

```
OutputIterator
```
set_intersection (InputIterator *source1Beg*, InputIterator *source1End*,
InputIterator *source2Beg*, InputIterator *source2End*,
OutputIterator *destBeg*, BinaryPredicate *op*)

- Both forms merge the elements of the sorted source ranges [*source1Beg*,*source1End*) and [*source2Beg*,*source2End*) so that the destination range starting with `destBeg` contains all elements that are in both source ranges. For example, calling `set_intersection()` for
    1 2 2 4 6 7 7 9
  and
    2 2 2 3 6 6 8 9
  results in
    2 2 6 9
- All elements in the destination range are in sorted order.
- Duplicates are possible if elements occur more than once in both source ranges. The number of occurrences of equal elements in the destination range is the minimum number of their occurrences in both source ranges.
- Both forms return the position after the last merged element in the destination range.
- *op* is an optional binary predicate that is used as the sorting criterion:
    op(*elem1*,*elem2*)
- The source ranges are not modified.
- The caller has to ensure that the ranges are sorted according to the sorting criterion on entry.
- The caller must ensure that the destination range is big enough or that insert iterators are used.
- The destination range should not overlap the source ranges.

- Complexity: linear (at most, 2∗(*numberOfElements1*+*numberOfElements2*) − 1 comparisons).

See page 421 for an example of the use of `set_intersection()`. This example also demonstrates how it differs from other algorithms that combine elements of two sorted sequences.

Processing the Difference of Two Sorted Sets

```
OutputIterator
set_difference (InputIterator source1Beg, InputIterator source1End,
                InputIterator source2Beg, InputIterator source2End,
                OutputIterator destBeg)
```

```
OutputIterator
set_difference (InputIterator source1Beg, InputIterator source1End,
                InputIterator source2Beg, InputIterator source2End,
                OutputIterator destBeg, BinaryPredicate op)
```

- Both forms merge the elements of the sorted source ranges [*source1Beg,source1End*) and [*source2Beg,source2End*) so that the destination range starting with `destBeg` contains all elements that are in the first source range but not in the second source range. For example, calling `set_difference()` for
  ```
  1 2 2 4 6 7 7 9
  ```
  and
  ```
  2 2 2 3 6 6 8 9
  ```
  results in
  ```
  1 4 7 7
  ```
- All elements in the destination range are in sorted order.
- Duplicates are possible if elements occur more than once in the first source range. The number of occurrences of equal elements in the destination range is the difference between the number of their occurrences in the first source range less the number of occurrences in the second source range. If there are more occurrences in the second source range, the number of occurrences in the destination range is zero.
- Both forms return the position after the last merged element in the destination range.
- *op* is an optional binary predicate that is used as the sorting criterion:
    op(*elem1*,*elem2*)
- The source ranges are not modified.
- The caller has to ensure that the ranges are sorted according to the sorting criterion on entry.
- The caller must ensure that the destination range is big enough or that insert iterators are used.
- The destination range should not overlap the source ranges.
- Complexity: linear (at most, 2∗(*numberOfElements1*+*numberOfElements2*) − 1 comparisons).

See page 421 for an example of the use of `set_difference()`. This example also demonstrates how it differs from other algorithms that combine elements of two sorted sequences.

```
OutputIterator
```
set_symmetric_difference (InputIterator *source1Beg*, InputIterator *source1End*,
                            InputIterator *source2Beg*, InputIterator *source2End*,
                            OutputIterator *destBeg*)

```
OutputIterator
```
set_symmetric_difference (InputIterator *source1Beg*, InputIterator *source1End*,
                            InputIterator *source2Beg*, InputIterator *source2End*,
                            OutputIterator *destBeg*, BinaryPredicate *op*)

- Both forms merge the elements of the sorted source ranges [*source1Beg*,*source1End*) and [*source2Beg*,*source2End*) so that the destination range starting with destBeg contains all elements that are either in the first source range or in the second source range, but not in both. For example, calling set_symmetric_difference() for

      1 2 2 4 6 7 7 9

  and

      2 2 2 3 6 6 8 9

  results in

      1 2 3 4 6 7 7 8

- All elements in the destination range are in sorted order
- Duplicates are possible if elements occur more than once in one of the source ranges. The number of occurrences of equal elements in the destination range is the difference between the number of their occurrences in the source ranges.
- Both forms return the position after the last merged element in the destination range.
- *op* is an optional binary predicate that is used as the sorting criterion:
    op(elem1,elem2)
- The source ranges are not modified.
- The caller has to ensure that the ranges are sorted according to the sorting criterion on entry.
- The caller must ensure that the destination range is big enough or that insert iterators are used.
- The destination range should not overlap the source ranges.
- Complexity: linear (at most, 2*(*numberOfElements1+numberOfElements2*) − 1 comparisons).

See the following subsection for an example of the use of set_symmetric_difference(). This example also demonstrates how it differs from other algorithms that combine elements of two sorted sequences.

Example of All Merging Algorithms

The following example compares the different algorithms that combine elements of two sorted source ranges, demonstrating how they work and differ:

```
// algo/setalgos.cpp

#include "algostuff.hpp"
using namespace std;
```

```cpp
int main()
{
    int c1[] = { 1, 2, 2, 4, 6, 7, 7, 9 };
    int num1 = sizeof(c1) / sizeof(int);

    int c2[] = { 2, 2, 2, 3, 6, 6, 8, 9 };
    int num2 = sizeof(c2) / sizeof(int);

    // print source ranges
    cout << "c1:                          " ;
    copy (c1, c1+num1,
          ostream_iterator<int>(cout," "));
    cout << endl;
    cout << "c2:                          " ;
    copy (c2, c2+num2,
          ostream_iterator<int>(cout," "));
    cout << '\n' << endl;

    // sum the ranges by using merge()
    cout << "merge():                    ";
    merge (c1, c1+num1,
           c2, c2+num2,
           ostream_iterator<int>(cout," "));
    cout << endl;

    // unite the ranges by using set_union()
    cout << "set_union():                ";
    set_union (c1, c1+num1,
               c2, c2+num2,
               ostream_iterator<int>(cout," "));
    cout << endl;

    // intersect the ranges by using set_intersection()
    cout << "set_intersection():         ";
    set_intersection (c1, c1+num1,
                      c2, c2+num2,
                      ostream_iterator<int>(cout," "));
    cout << endl;
```

```
        // determine elements of first range without elements of second range
        // by using set_difference()
        cout << "set_difference():              ";
        set_difference (c1, c1+num1,
                        c2, c2+num2,
                        ostream_iterator<int>(cout," "));
        cout << endl;

        // determine difference the ranges with set_symmetric_difference()
        cout << "set_symmetric_difference(): ";
        set_symmetric_difference (c1, c1+num1,
                                  c2, c2+num2,
                                  ostream_iterator<int>(cout," "));
        cout << endl;
}
```

The program has the following output:

```
    c1:                         1 2 2 4 6 7 7 9
    c2:                         2 2 2 3 6 6 8 9

    merge():                     1 2 2 2 2 2 3 4 6 6 6 7 7 8 9 9
    set_union():                 1 2 2 2 3 4 6 6 7 7 8 9
    set_intersection():          2 2 6 9
    set_difference():            1 4 7 7
    set_symmetric_difference(): 1 2 3 4 6 7 7 8
```

Merging Consecutive Sorted Ranges

```
void
```
inplace_merge (BidirectionalIterator *beg1*, BidirectionalIterator *end1beg2*,
          BidirectionalIterator *end2*)

```
void
```
inplace_merge (BidirectionalIterator *beg1*, BidirectionalIterator *end1beg2*,
          BidirectionalIterator *end2*, BinaryPredicate *op*)

- Both forms merge the consecutive sorted source ranges [*beg1*,*end1beg2*) and [*end1beg2*,*end2*) so that the range [*beg1*,*end2*) contains the elements as a sorted summary range.
- Complexity: linear (*numberOfElements*-1 comparisons) if enough memory available, or n-log-n otherwise (*numberOfElements**log(*numberOfElements*) comparisons).

The following program demonstrates the use of `inplace_merge()`:

```
// algo/imerge1.cpp

#include "algostuff.hpp"
using namespace std;

int main()
{
    list<int> coll;

    // insert two sorted sequences
    INSERT_ELEMENTS(coll,1,7);
    INSERT_ELEMENTS(coll,1,8);
    PRINT_ELEMENTS(coll);

    // find beginning of second part (element after 7)
    list<int>::iterator pos;
    pos = find (coll.begin(), coll.end(),    // range
                7);                          // value
    ++pos;

    // merge into one sorted range
    inplace_merge (coll.begin(), pos, coll.end());

    PRINT_ELEMENTS(coll);
}
```

The program has the following output:

```
1 2 3 4 5 6 7 1 2 3 4 5 6 7 8
1 1 2 2 3 3 4 4 5 5 6 6 7 7 8
```

9.11   Numeric Algorithms

This section presents the STL algorithms that are provided for numeric processing. However, you can process other than numeric values. For example, you can use `accumulate()` to process the sum of several strings. To use the numeric algorithms you have to include the header file `<numeric>`[10]:

```
#include <numeric>
```

9.11.1   Processing Results

Computing the Result of One Sequence

T
accumulate (InputIterator *beg*, InputIterator *end*,
            T *initValue*)

T
accumulate (InputIterator *beg*, InputIterator *end*,
            T *initValue*, BinaryFunc *op*)

- The first form computes and returns the sum of *initValue* and all elements in the range [*beg,end*). In particular, it calls
    initValue = *initValue* + *elem*
  for each element.
- The second form computes and returns the result of calling *op* for *initValue* and all elements in the range [*beg,end*). In particular, it calls
    initValue = *op*(*initValue*,*elem*)
  for each element.
- Thus, for the values
    a1 a2 a3 a4 ...
  they compute and return either
    initValue + a1 + a2 + a3 + ...
  or
    initValue *op* a1 *op* a2 *op* a3 *op* ...
  respectively.
- If the range is empty (*beg==end*), both forms return *initValue*.
- *op* must not modify the passed arguments.
- Complexity: linear (*numberOfElements* calls of operator + or *op*() respectively).

The following program demonstrates how to use `accumulate()` to process the sum and the product of all elements of a range:

---

[10] In the original STL the numeric algorithms were defined in `<algo.h>`.

```
// algo/accu1.cpp
#include "algostuff.hpp"
using namespace std;

int main()
{
    vector<int> coll;

    INSERT_ELEMENTS(coll,1,9);
    PRINT_ELEMENTS(coll);

    // process sum of elements
    cout << "sum: "
         << accumulate (coll.begin(), coll.end(),    // range
                        0)                            // initial value
         << endl;

    // process sum of elements less 100
    cout << "sum: "
         << accumulate (coll.begin(), coll.end(),    // range
                        -100)                         // initial value
         << endl;

    // process product of elements
    cout << "product: "
         << accumulate (coll.begin(), coll.end(),    // range
                        1,                            // initial value
                        multiplies<int>())            // operation
         << endl;

    // process product of elements (use 0 as initial value)
    cout << "product: "
         << accumulate (coll.begin(), coll.end(),    // range
                        0,                            // initial value
                        multiplies<int>())            // operation
         << endl;
}
```

The program has the following output:

```
1 2 3 4 5 6 7 8 9
sum: 45
sum: -55
product: 362880
product: 0
```

The last output is 0 because any value multiplied by zero is zero.

Computing the Inner Product of Two Sequences

T
inner_product (InputIterator1 *beg1*, InputIterator1 *end1*,
InputIterator2 *beg2*, T *initValue*)

T
inner_product (InputIterator1 *beg1*, InputIterator1 *end1*,
InputIterator2 *beg2*, T *initValue*,
BinaryFunc *op1*, BinaryFunc *op2*)

- The first form computes and returns the inner product of *initValue* and all elements in the range [*beg,end*) combined with the elements in the range starting with *beg2*. In particular, it calls
    initValue = *initValue* + *elem1* * *elem2*
  for all corresponding elements.
- The second form computes and returns the result of calling *op* for *initValue* and all elements in the range [*beg,end*) combined with the elements in the range starting with *beg2*. In particular, it calls
    initValue = *op1*(*initValue*,*op2*(*elem1*,*elem2*))
  for all corresponding elements.
- Thus, for the values
    a1 a2 a3 ...
    b1 b2 b3 ...
  they compute and return either
    initValue + (a1 * b1) + (a2 * b2) + (a3 * b3) + ...
  or
    initValue *op1* (a1 *op2* b1) *op1* (a2 *op2* b2) *op1* (a3 *op2* b3) *op1* ...
  respectively.
- If the first range is empty (*beg1==end1*), both forms return *initValue*.
- The caller has to ensure that the range starting with *beg2* contains enough elements.
- *op1* and *op2* must not modify their arguments.
- Complexity: linear (*numberOfElements* calls of operators + and * or *numberOfElements* calls of *op1* () and *op2* () respectively).

The following program demonstrates how to use `inner_product()`. It processes the sum of products and the product of the sums for two sequences:

```
// algo/inner1.cpp

#include "algostuff.hpp"
using namespace std;

int main()
{
    list<int> coll;

    INSERT_ELEMENTS(coll,1,6);
    PRINT_ELEMENTS(coll);

    /* process sum of all products
     * (0 + 1*1 + 2*2 + 3*3 + 4*4 + 5*5 + 6*6)
     */
    cout << "inner product: "
         << inner_product (coll.begin(), coll.end(),   // first range
                           coll.begin(),               // second range
                           0)                          // initial value
         << endl;

    /* process sum of 1*6 ... 6*1
     * (0 + 1*6 + 2*5 + 3*4 + 4*3 + 5*2 + 6*1)
     */
    cout << "inner reverse product: "
         << inner_product (coll.begin(), coll.end(),   // first range
                           coll.rbegin(),              // second range
                           0)                          // initial value
         << endl;

    /* process product of all sums
     * (1 * 1+1 * 2+2 * 3+3 * 4+4 * 5+5 * 6+6)
     */
    cout << "product of sums: "
         << inner_product (coll.begin(), coll.end(),   // first range
                           coll.begin(),               // second range
                           1,                          // initial value
```

```
                                    multiplies<int>(),      // outer operation
                                    plus<int>())            // inner operation
            << endl;
    }
```

The program has the following output:

```
1 2 3 4 5 6
inner product: 91
inner reverse product: 56
product of sums: 46080
```

9.11.2 Converting Relative and Absolute Values

The following two algorithms provide the ability to convert a sequence of relative values into a sequence of absolute values, and vice versa.

Converting Relative Values into Absolute Values

OutputIterator
partial_sum (InputIterator *sourceBeg*, InputIterator *sourceEnd*,
            OutputIterator *destBeg*)

OutputIterator
partial_sum (InputIterator *sourceBeg*, InputIterator *sourceEnd*,
            OutputIterator *destBeg*, BinaryFunc *op*)

- The first form computes the partial sum for each element in the source range [*sourceBeg*, *sourceEnd*) and writes each result to the destination range starting with *destBeg*.
- The second form calls *op* for each element in the source range [*sourceBeg*,*sourceEnd*) combined with all previous values and writes each result to the destination range starting with *destBeg*.
- Thus, for the values
    ```
    a1 a2 a3 ...
    ```
  they compute either
    ```
    a1,  a1 + a2,  a1 + a2 + a3,  ...
    ```
  or
    ```
    a1,  a1 op a2,  a1 op a2 op a3,  ...
    ```
  respectively.
- Both forms return the position after the last written value in the destination range (the first element that is not overwritten).

- The first form is equivalent to the conversion of a sequence of relative values into a sequence of absolute values. In this regard, `partial_sum()` is the complement of `adjacent_difference()`.
- The source and destination range may be identical.
- The caller must ensure that the destination range is big enough or that insert iterators are used.
- *op* should not modify the passed arguments.
- Complexity: linear (*numberOfElements* calls of operator + or *op*() respectively).

The following program demonstrates some examples of using `partial_sum()`:

```
// algo/partsum1.cpp

#include "algostuff.hpp"
using namespace std;

int main()
{
    vector<int> coll;

    INSERT_ELEMENTS(coll,1,6);
    PRINT_ELEMENTS(coll);

    // print all partial sums
    partial_sum (coll.begin(), coll.end(),                 // source range
                 ostream_iterator<int>(cout," "));         // destination
    cout << endl;

    // print all partial products
    partial_sum (coll.begin(), coll.end(),                 // source range
                 ostream_iterator<int>(cout," "),          // destination
                 multiplies<int>());                       // operation
    cout << endl;
}
```

The program has the following output:

```
1 2 3 4 5 6
1 3 6 10 15 21
1 2 6 24 120 720
```

See also the example of converting relative values into absolute values, and vice versa, on page 432.

Converting Absolute Values into Relative Values

```
OutputIterator
```
adjacent_difference (InputIterator *sourceBeg*, InputIterator *sourceEnd*,
                    OutputIterator *destBeg*)

```
OutputIterator
```
adjacent_difference (InputIterator *sourceBeg*, InputIterator *sourceEnd*,
                    OutputIterator *destBeg*, BinaryFunc *op*)

- The first form computes the difference of each element in the range [*sourceBeg*,*sourceEnd*) with its predecessor and writes the result to the destination range starting with *destBeg*.
- The second form calls *op* for each element in the range [*sourceBeg*,*sourceEnd*) with its predecessor and writes the result to the destination range starting with *destBeg*.
- The first element only is copied.
- Thus, for the values

      a1 a2 a3 a4 ...

  they compute and write either the values

      a1,   a2 - a1,   a3 - a2,   a4 - a3,   ...

  or the values

      a1,   a2 *op* a1,   a3 *op* a2,   a4 *op* a3,   ...

  respectively.
- Both forms return the position after the last written value in the destination range (the first element that is not overwritten).
- The first form is equivalent to the conversion of a sequence of absolute values into a sequence of relative values. In this regard, adjacent_difference() is the complement of partial_sum().
- The source and destination range may be identical.
- The caller must ensure that the destination range is big enough or that insert iterators are used.
- *op* should not modify the passed arguments.
- Complexity: linear (*numberOfElements*-1 calls of operator - or *op*() respectively).

The following program demonstrates some examples of using adjacent_difference():

```cpp
// algo/adjdiff1.cpp

#include "algostuff.hpp"
using namespace std;

int main()
{
    deque<int> coll;

    INSERT_ELEMENTS(coll,1,6);
```

```
    PRINT_ELEMENTS(coll);

    // print all differences between elements
    adjacent_difference (coll.begin(), coll.end(),          // source
                         ostream_iterator<int>(cout," "));  // dest.
    cout << endl;

    // print all sums with the predecessors
    adjacent_difference (coll.begin(), coll.end(),          // source
                         ostream_iterator<int>(cout," "),   // dest.
                         plus<int>());                      // operation
    cout << endl;

    // print all products between elements
    adjacent_difference (coll.begin(), coll.end(),          // source
                         ostream_iterator<int>(cout," "),   // dest.
                         multiplies<int>());                // operation
    cout << endl;
}
```

The program has the following output:

```
1 2 3 4 5 6
1 1 1 1 1 1
1 3 5 7 9 11
1 2 6 12 20 30
```

See also the example of converting relative values into absolute values, and vice versa, in the next subsection.

Example of Converting Relative Values into Absolute Values

The following example demonstrates how to use `partial_sum()` and `adjacent_difference()` to convert a sequence of relative values into a sequence of absolute values, and vice versa:

```
// algo/relabs.cpp

#include "algostuff.hpp"
using namespace std;

int main()
{
```

```
      vector<int> coll;

      coll.push_back(17);
      coll.push_back(-3);
      coll.push_back(22);
      coll.push_back(13);
      coll.push_back(13);
      coll.push_back(-9);
      PRINT_ELEMENTS(coll,"coll:      ");

      // convert into relative values
      adjacent_difference (coll.begin(), coll.end(),     // source
                            coll.begin());               // destination
      PRINT_ELEMENTS(coll,"relative: ");

      // convert into absolute values
      partial_sum (coll.begin(), coll.end(),             // source
                   coll.begin());                        // destination
      PRINT_ELEMENTS(coll,"absolute: ");
  }
```

The program has the following output:

```
  coll:     17 -3 22 13 13 -9
  relative: 17 -20 25 -9 0 -22
  absolute: 17 -3 22 13 13 -9
```

Chapter 10

Special Containers

The C++ standard library provides not only the containers for the STL framework, but also some containers that fit some special needs and provide simple, almost self-explanatory interfaces. You can group these containers into

- The so-called *container adapters*

  These containers adapt standard STL containers to fit special needs. There are three standard container adapters:

  1. Stacks
  2. Queues
  3. Priority queues

  Priority queues are queues in which the elements are sorted automatically according to a sorting criterion. Thus, the "next" element of a priority queue is the element with the "highest" value.

- A special container, called a *bitset*

  A bitset is a bitfield with an arbitrary but fixed number of bits. You can consider it a container for bits or Boolean values. Note that the C++ standard library also provides a special container with a variable size for Boolean values: `vector<bool>`. It is described in Section 6.2.6, page 158.

10.1   Stacks

The class `stack<>` implements a stack (also known as LIFO). With `push()`, you can insert any number of elements into the stack (Figure 10.1). With `pop()`, you can remove the elements in the opposite order in which they were inserted ("last in, first out").

To use a stack, you have to include the header file `<stack>`[1]:

```
#include <stack>
```

---

[1] In the original STL the header file for stacks was `<stack.h>`.

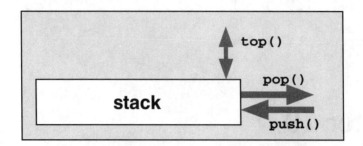

Figure 10.1. Interface of a Stack

In <stack>, the class stack is defined as follows:

```
namespace std {
    template <class T,
              class Container = deque<T> >
    class stack;
}
```

The first template parameter is the type of the elements. The optional second template parameter defines the container that is used internally by the stack for its elements. The default container is a deque. It was chosen because, unlike vectors, deques free their memory when elements are removed and don't have to copy all elements on reallocation (see Section 6.9, page 226, for a discussion of when to use which container).

For example, the following declaration defines a stack of integers[2]:

```
std::stack<int> st;        // integer stack
```

The stack implementation simply maps the operations into appropriate calls of the container that is used internally (Figure 10.2). You can use any sequence container class that provides the member functions back(), push_back(), and pop_back(). For example, you could also use a vector or a list as the container for the elements:

```
std::stack<int,std::vector<int> > st;        // integer stack that uses a vector
```

10.1.1   The Core Interface

The core interface of stacks is provided by the member functions push(), top(), and pop():

- **push()** inserts an element into the stack.
- **top()** returns the next element in the stack.
- **pop()** removes an element from the stack.

---

[2] In previous versions of the STL you could pass the container as the only template parameter. Thus, a stack of integers had to be declared as follows:

```
stack<deque<int> > st;
```

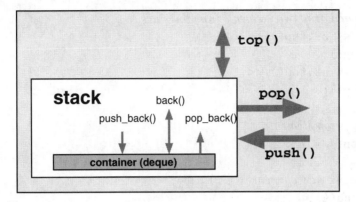

Figure 10.2. Internal Interface of a Stack

Note that pop() removes the next element but does not return it, whereas top() returns the next element without removing it. Thus, you must always call both functions to process and remove the next element from the stack. This interface is somewhat inconvenient, but it performs better if you only want to remove the next element without processing it. Note that the behavior of top() and pop() is undefined if the stack contains no elements. To check whether the stack contains elements, the member functions size() and empty() are provided.

If you don't like the standard interface of stack<>, you can easily write a more convenient interface. See Section 10.1.4, page 441, for an example.

10.1.2 Example of Using Stacks

The following program demonstrates the use of class stack<>:

```
// cont/stack1.cpp

#include <iostream>
#include <stack>
using namespace std;

int main()
{
    stack<int> st;

    // push three elements into the stack
    st.push(1);
    st.push(2);
    st.push(3);
```

```cpp
// pop and print two elements from the stack
cout << st.top() << ' ';
st.pop();
cout << st.top() << ' ';
st.pop();

// modify top element
st.top() = 77;

// push two new elements
st.push(4);
st.push(5);

// pop one element without processing it
st.pop();

// pop and print remaining elements
while (!st.empty()) {
    cout << st.top() << ' ';
    st.pop();
}
cout << endl;
}
```

The output of the program is as follows:

```
3 2 4 77
```

10.1.3   Class **stack<>** in Detail

The stack<> interface is so small, you can understand it easily by reading its typical implementation:

```cpp
namespace std {
    template <class T, class Container = deque<T> >
    class stack {
      public:
        typedef typename Container::value_type value_type;
        typedef typename Container::size_type size_type;
        typedef          Container            container_type;
```

```
    protected:
      Container c;      // container
    public:
      explicit stack(const Container& = Container());

      bool        empty() const              { return c.empty(); }
      size_type   size()   const             { return c.size(); }
      void        push(const value_type& x)  { c.push_back(x); }
      void        pop()                      { c.pop_back(); }
      value_type& top()                      { return c.back(); }
      const value_type& top() const          { return c.back(); }
  };

  template <class T, class Container>
    bool operator==(const stack<T, Container>&,
                    const stack<T, Container>&);
  template <class T, class Container>
    bool operator< (const stack<T, Container>&,
                    const stack<T, Container>&);
  ... // (other comparison operators)
}
```

The following subsections describe the members and operations in detail.

Type Definitions

stack::**value_type**
- The type of the elements.
- It is equivalent to *container*::value_type.

stack::**size_type**
- The unsigned integral type for size values.
- It is equivalent to *container*::size_type.

stack::**container_type**
- The type of the container.

Operations

stack::**stack** ()

- The default constructor.
- Creates an empty stack.

explicit *stack*::**stack** (const Container& *cont*)

- Creates a stack that is initialized by the elements of *cont*.
- All elements of *cont* are copied.

size_type *stack*::**size** () const

- Returns the current number of elements.
- To check whether the stack is empty (contains no elements), use empty() because it might be faster.

bool *stack*::**empty** () const

- Returns whether the stack is empty (contains no elements).
- It is equivalent to *stack*::size()==0, but it might be faster.

void *stack*::**push** (const *value_type*& *elem*)

- Inserts a copy of *elem* as the new first element in the stack.

value_type& *stack*::**top** ()

const *value_type*& *stack*::**top** () const

- Both forms return the next element of the stack. The next element is the element that was inserted last (after all other elements in the stack).
- The caller has to ensure that the stack contains an element (size()>0); otherwise, the behavior is undefined.
- The first form for nonconstant stacks returns a reference. Thus, you could modify the next element while it is in the stack. It is up to you to decide whether this is good style.

void *stack*::**pop** ()

- Removes the next element from the stack. The next element is the element that was inserted last (after all other elements in the stack).
- This function has no return value. To process this next element, you must call top() first.
- The caller must ensure that the stack contains an element (size()>0); otherwise, the behavior is undefined.

bool *comparison* (const *stack*& *stack1*, const *stack*& *stack2*)

- Returns the result of the comparison of two stacks of the same type.

- *comparison* might be any of the following:
  ```
  operator ==
  operator !=
  operator <
  operator >
  operator <=
  operator >=
  ```
- Two stacks are equal if they have the same number of elements and contain the same elements in the same order (all comparisons of two corresponding elements must yield `true`).
- To check whether a stack is less than another stack, the stacks are compared lexicographically. See the description of the `lexicographical_compare()` algorithm on page 360.

10.1.4 A User-Defined Stack Class

The standard class `stack<>` prefers speed over convenience and safety. This is not what I usually prefer. I have written my own stack class. It has the following two advantages:

1. `pop()` returns the next element.
2. `pop()` and `top()` throw exceptions when the stack is empty.

In addition, I have skipped the members that are not necessary for the ordinary stack user, such as the comparison operations. My stack class is defined as follows:

```
// cont/Stack.hpp

/* ************************************************************
 *  Stack.hpp
 *  - safer and more convenient stack class
 * ************************************************************/
#ifndef STACK_HPP
#define STACK_HPP

#include <deque>
#include <exception>

template <class T>
class Stack {
  protected:
    std::deque<T> c;          // container for the elements

  public:
    /* exception class for pop() and top() with empty stack
```

```
      */
    class ReadEmptyStack : public std::exception {
      public:
        virtual const char* what() const throw() {
            return "read empty stack";
        }
    };

    // number of elements
    typename std::deque<T>::size_type size() const {
        return c.size();
    }

    // is stack empty?
    bool empty() const {
        return c.empty();
    }

    // push element into the stack
    void push (const T& elem) {
        c.push_back(elem);
    }

    // pop element out of the stack and return its value
    T pop () {
        if (c.empty()) {
            throw ReadEmptyStack();
        }
        T elem(c.back());
        c.pop_back();
        return elem;
    }

    // return value of next element
    T& top () {
        if (c.empty()) {
            throw ReadEmptyStack();
        }
        return c.back();
```

```
    }
};

#endif /* STACK_HPP */
```

With this stack class, the previous stack example could be written as follows:

```
// cont/stack2.cpp

#include <iostream>
#include "Stack.hpp"          // use special stack class
using namespace std;

int main()
{
    try {
        Stack<int> st;

        // push three elements into the stack
        st.push(1);
        st.push(2);
        st.push(3);

        // pop and print two elements from the stack
        cout << st.pop() << ' ';
        cout << st.pop() << ' ';

        // modify top element
        st.top() = 77;

        // push two new elements
        st.push(4);
        st.push(5);

        // pop one element without processing it
        st.pop();

        /* pop and print three elements
         * - ERROR: one element too many
         */
```

```
        cout << st.pop() << ' ';
        cout << st.pop() << endl;
        cout << st.pop() << endl;
    }
    catch (const exception& e) {
        cerr << "EXCEPTION: " << e.what() << endl;
    }
}
```

The additional final call of pop() forces an error. Unlike the standard stack class, this one throws
an exception rather than resulting in undefined behavior. The output of the program is as follows:

```
3 2 4 77
EXCEPTION: read empty stack
```

10.2   Queues

The class queue<> implements a queue (also known as FIFO). With push(), you can insert any
number of elements (Figure 10.3). With pop(), you can remove the elements in the same order in
which they were inserted ("first in, first out"). Thus, a queue serves as a classic data buffer.

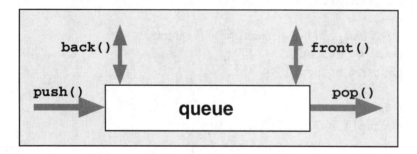

Figure 10.3. Interface of a Queue

To use a queue, you must include the header file <queue>[3]:

```
#include <queue>
```

In <queue>, the class queue is defined as follows:

```
namespace std {
    template <class T,
```

---

[3] In the original STL the header file for queues was <stack.h>.

```
                    class Container = deque<T> >
        class queue;
   }
```

The first template parameter is the type of the elements. The optional second template parameter defines the container that is used internally by the queue for its elements. The default container is a deque.

For example, the following declaration defines a queue of strings[4]:

```
std::queue<std::string> buffer;      // string queue
```

The queue implementation simply maps the operations into appropriate calls of the container that is used internally (Figure 10.4). You can use any sequence container class that provides the member functions `front()`, `back()`, `push_back()`, and `pop_front()`. For example, you could also use a list as the container for the elements:

```
std::queue<std::string,std::list<std::string> > buffer;
```

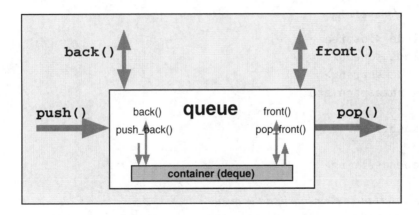

Figure 10.4. Internal Interface of a Queue

10.2.1   The Core Interface

The core interface of queues is provided by the member functions `push()`, `front()`, `back()` and `pop()`:

- **push()** inserts an element into the queue.
- **front()** returns the next element in the queue (the element that was inserted first).

---

[4] In previous versions of the STL you could pass the container as the only template parameter. Thus, a queue of strings had to be declared as follows:

```
queue<deque<string> > buffer;
```

- **back()** returns the last element in the queue (the element that was inserted last).
- **pop()** removes an element from the queue.

Note that pop() removes the next element but does not return it, whereas front() and back() return the element without removing it. Thus, you must always call front() and pop() to process and remove the next element from the queue. This interface is somewhat inconvenient, but it performs better if you only want to remove the next element without processing it. Note that the behavior of front(), back(), and pop() is undefined if the queue contains no elements. To check whether the queue contains elements, the member functions size() and empty() are provided.

If you don't like the standard interface of queue<>, you can easily write a more convenient interface. See Section 10.2.4, page 450, for an example.

10.2.2 Example of Using Queues

The following program demonstrates the use of class queue<>:

```
// cont/queue1.cpp

#include <iostream>
#include <queue>
#include <string>
using namespace std;

int main()
{
    queue<string> q;

    // insert three elements into the queue
    q.push("These ");
    q.push("are ");
    q.push("more than ");

    // read and print two elements from the queue
    cout << q.front();
    q.pop();
    cout << q.front();
    q.pop();

    // insert two new elements
    q.push("four ");
    q.push("words!");
```

```
    // skip one element
    q.pop();

    // read and print two elements
    cout << q.front();
    q.pop();
    cout << q.front() << endl;
    q.pop();

    // print number of elements in the queue
    cout << "number of elements in the queue: " << q.size()
         << endl;
}
```

The output of the program is as follows:

```
These are four words!
number of elements in the queue: 0
```

10.2.3 Class queue<> in Detail

Similar to stack<>, the typical queue<> implementation is rather self-explanatory:

```
namespace std {
    template <class T, class Container = deque<T> >
    class queue {
      public:
        typedef typename Container::value_type value_type;
        typedef typename Container::size_type  size_type;
        typedef          Container             container_type;
      protected:
        Container c;      // container
      public:
        explicit queue(const Container& = Container());

        bool      empty() const                 { return c.empty(); }
        size_type size()  const                 { return c.size(); }
        void      push(const value_type& x)     { c.push_back(x); }
        void      pop()                         { c.pop_front(); }
        value_type&       front()               { return c.front(); }
```

```
              const value_type& front() const      { return c.front(); }
              value_type&        back()             { return c.back(); }
              const value_type& back() const        { return c.back(); }
       };

       template <class T, class Container>
         bool operator==(const queue<T, Container>&,
                         const queue<T, Container>&);
       template <class T, class Container>
         bool operator< (const queue<T, Container>&,
                         const queue<T, Container>&);
       ... // (other comparison operators)
  }
```

The following subsections describe the members and operations in detail.

Type Definitions

queue::**value_type**
- The type of the elements.
- It is equivalent to *container*::value_type.

queue::**size_type**
- The unsigned integral type for size values.
- It is equivalent to *container*::size_type.

queue::**container_type**
- The type of the container.

Operations

queue::**queue** ()
- The default constructor.
- Creates an empty queue.

explicit *queue*::**queue** (const Container& *cont*)
- Creates a queue that is initialized by the elements of *cont*.
- All elements of *cont* are copied.

size_type *queue*::**size** () const
- Returns the current number of elements.

- To check whether the queue is empty (contains no elements), use `empty()` because it might be faster.

`bool` *queue*`::`**empty** `()` `const`

- Returns whether the queue is empty (contains no elements).
- It is equivalent to *queue*`::size()==0`, but it might be faster.

`void` *queue*`::`**push** `(const` *value_type*`&` *elem*`)`

- Insert a copy of *elem* as the new last element in the queue.

value_type`&` *queue*`::`**front** `()`
`const` *value_type*`&` *queue*`::`**front** `()` `const`

- Both forms return next element of the queue. The next element is the element that was inserted first (before all other elements in the queue).
- The caller has to ensure that the queue contains an element (`size()>0`); otherwise, the behavior is undefined.
- The first form for nonconstant queues returns a reference. Thus, you could modify the next element while it is in the queue. It is up to you to decide whether this is good style.

value_type`&` *queue*`::`**back** `()`
`const` *value_type*`&` *queue*`::`**back** `()` `const`

- Both forms return the last element of the queue. The last element is the element that was inserted last (after all other elements in the queue).
- The caller must ensure that the queue contains an element (`size()>0`); otherwise, the behavior is undefined.
- The first form for nonconstant queues returns a reference. Thus, you could modify the last element while it is in the queue. It is up to you to decide whether this is good style.

`void` *queue*`::`**pop** `()`

- Removes the next element from the queue. The next element is the element that was inserted first (before all other elements in the queue).
- Note that this function has no return value. To process the next element, you must call `front()` first.
- The caller must ensure that the queue contains an element (`size()>0`); otherwise, the behavior is undefined.

`bool` *comparison* `(const` *queue*`&` *queue1*`, const` *queue*`&` *queue2*`)`

- Returns the result of the comparison of two queues of the same type.

- *comparison* might be any of the following:
  ```
  operator ==
  operator !=
  operator <
  operator >
  operator <=
  operator >=
  ```
- Two queues are equal if they have the same number of elements and contain the same elements in the same order (all comparisons of two corresponding elements must yield `true`).
- To check whether a queue is less than another queue, the queues are compared lexicographically. See the description of the `lexicographical_compare()` algorithm on page 360.

10.2.4   A User-Defined Queue Class

The standard class `queue<>` prefers speed over convenience and safety. This is not what I usually prefer. I have written my own queue class. It has the following two advantages:

1. `pop()` returns the next element.
2. `pop()` and `front()` throw exceptions when the queue is empty.

In addition, I have skipped the members that are not necessary for the ordinary queue user, such as the comparison operations and the `back()` member function. My queue class is defined as follows:

```cpp
// cont/Queue.hpp

/* **********************************************************
 * Queue.hpp
 *  - safer and more convenient queue class
 * *********************************************************/
#ifndef QUEUE_HPP
#define QUEUE_HPP

#include <deque>
#include <exception>

template <class T>
class Queue {
  protected:
    std::deque<T> c;          // container for the elements

  public:
    /* exception class for pop() and top() with empty queue
```

```
      */
    class ReadEmptyQueue : public std::exception {
      public:
        virtual const char* what() const throw() {
            return "read empty queue";
        }
    };
```

```
    // number of elements
    typename std::deque<T>::size_type size() const {
        return c.size();
    }
```

```
    // is queue empty?
    bool empty() const {
        return c.empty();
    }
```

```
    // insert element into the queue
    void push (const T& elem) {
        c.push_back(elem);
    }
```

```
    // read element from the queue and return its value
    T pop () {
        if (c.empty()) {
            throw ReadEmptyQueue();
        }
        T elem(c.front());
        c.pop_front();
        return elem;
    }
```

```
    // return value of next element
    T& front () {
        if (c.empty()) {
            throw ReadEmptyQueue();
        }
        return c.front();
```

```
        }
    };

    #endif /* QUEUE_HPP */
```

With this queue class, the previous queue example could be written as follows:

```
// cont/queue2.cpp

#include <iostream>
#include <string>
#include "Queue.hpp"          // use special queue class
using namespace std;

int main()
{
    try {
        Queue<string> q;

        // insert three elements into the queue
        q.push("These ");
        q.push("are ");
        q.push("more than ");

        // read and print two elements from the queue
        cout << q.pop();
        cout << q.pop();

        // push two new elements
        q.push("four ");
        q.push("words!");

        // skip one element
        q.pop();

        // read and print two elements from the queue
        cout << q.pop();
        cout << q.pop() << endl;

        // print number of remaining elements
```

```
            cout << "number of elements in the queue: " << q.size()
                 << endl;

            // read and print one element
            cout << q.pop() << endl;
        }
        catch (const exception& e) {
            cerr << "EXCEPTION: " << e.what() << endl;
        }
    }
```

The additional final call of pop() forces an error. Unlike the standard queue class, this one throws an exception rather than resulting in undefined behavior. The output of the program is as follows:

```
These are four words!
number of elements in the queue: 0
EXCEPTION: read empty queue
```

10.3   Priority Queues

The class priority_queue<> implements a queue from which elements are read according to their priority. The interface is similar to queues. That is, push() inserts an element into the queue, whereas top() and pop() access and remove the next element (Figure 10.5). However, the next element is not the first inserted element. Rather, it is the element that has the highest priority. Thus, elements are partially sorted according to their value. As usual, you can provide the sorting criterion as a template parameter. By default, the elements are sorted by using operator < in descending order. Thus, the next element is always the "highest" element. If more than one "highest" element exists, which element comes next is undefined.

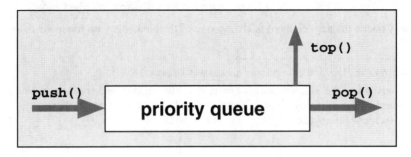

Figure 10.5. Interface of a Priority Queue

Priority queues are defined in the same header file as ordinary queues, `<queue>`[5]:

```
#include <queue>
```

In `<queue>`, the class `priority_queue` is defined as follows:

```
namespace std {
    template <class T,
              class Container = vector<T>,
              class Compare = less<typename Container::value_type> >
    class priority_queue;
}
```

The first template parameter is the type of the elements. The optional second template parameter defines the container that is used internally by the priority queue for its elements. The default container is a vector. The optional third template parameter defines the sorting criterion that is used to find the next element with the highest priority. By default, it compares the elements by using operator <.

For example, the following declaration defines a priority queue of `floats`[6]:

```
std::priority_queue<float> pbuffer;       // priority queue for floats
```

The priority queue implementation simply maps the operations into appropriate calls of the container that is used internally. You can use any sequence container class that provides random access iterators and the member functions `front()`, `push_back()`, and `pop_back()`. Random access is necessary for sorting the elements, which is performed by the heap algorithms of the STL (the heap algorithms are described in Section 9.9.4, page 406). For example, you could also use a deque as the container for the elements:

```
std::priority_queue<float,std::deque<float> > pbuffer;
```

To define your own sorting criterion you must pass a function or function object as a binary predicate that is used by the sorting algorithms to compare two elements (for more about sorting criteria, see Section 6.5.2, page 178, and Section 8.1.1, page 294). For example, the following declaration defines a priority queue with reverse sorting:

```
std::priority_queue<float,std::vector<float>,
                    std::greater<float> > pbuffer;
```

In this priority queue the next element is always one of the elements with the lowest value.

---

[5] In the original STL the header file for priority queues was `<stack.h>`.

[6] In previous versions of the STL you always had to pass the container and sorting criterion as mandatory template arguments. Thus, a priority queue of floating values had to be declared as follows:

```
priority_queue<vector<float>,less<float> > buffer;
```

10.3.1   The Core Interface

The core interface of priority queues is provided by the member functions push(), top(), and
pop():
- **push()** inserts an element into the priority queue.
- **top()** returns the next element in the priority queue.
- **pop()** removes an element from the priority queue.

As for the other container adapters, pop() removes the next element but does not return it, whereas
top() returns the next element without removing it. Thus, you must always call both functions to
process and remove the next element from the priority queue. And, as usual, the behavior of top()
and pop() is undefined if the priority queue contains no elements. If in doubt, you must use the
member functions size() and empty().

10.3.2   Example of Using Priority Queues

The following program demonstrates the use of class priority_queue<>:

```
// cont/pqueue1.cpp

#include <iostream>
#include <queue>
using namespace std;

int main()
{
    priority_queue<float> q;

    // insert three elements into the priority queue
    q.push(66.6);
    q.push(22.2);
    q.push(44.4);

    // read and print two elements
    cout << q.top() << ' ';
    q.pop();
    cout << q.top() << endl;
    q.pop();

    // insert three more elements
    q.push(11.1);
```

```
    q.push(55.5);
    q.push(33.3);

    // skip one element
    q.pop();

    // pop and print remaining elements
    while (!q.empty()) {
        cout << q.top() << ' ';
        q.pop();
    }
    cout << endl;
}
```

The output of the program is as follows:

```
66.6 44.4
33.3 22.2 11.1
```

As you can see, after 66.6, 22.2, and 44.4 are inserted, the program prints 66.6 and 44.4 as the highest elements. After three other elements are inserted, the priority queue contains the elements 22.2, 11.1, 55.5, and 33.3 (in the order of insertion). The next element is skipped simply via a call of pop(), so the final loop prints 33.3, 22.2, and 11.1 in that order.

10.3.3   Class `priority_queue<>` in Detail

Most of the priority_queue<> operations are as self-explanatory as stack<> and queue<>:

```
namespace std {
    template <class T, class Container = vector<T>,
              class Compare = less<typename Container::value_type> >
    class priority_queue {
      public:
        typedef typename Container::value_type value_type;
        typedef typename Container::size_type  size_type;
        typedef          Container             container_type;
      protected:
        Compare comp;      // sorting criterion
        Container c;       // container
      public:
        // constructors
```

```
        explicit priority_queue(const Compare& cmp = Compare(),
                                 const Container& cont = Container())
         : comp(cmp), c(cont) {
            make_heap(c.begin(),c.end(),comp);
        }

        template <class InputIterator>
        priority_queue(InputIterator first, InputIterator last,
                       const Compare& cmp = Compare(),
                       const Container& cont = Container())
         : comp(cmp), c(cont) {
            c.insert(c.end(),first,last);
            make_heap(c.begin(),c.end(),comp);
        }

        void push(const value_type& x) {
            c.push_back(x);
            push_heap(c.begin(),c.end(),comp);
        }
        void pop() {
            pop_heap(c.begin(),c.end(),comp);
            c.pop_back();
        }

        bool               empty() const { return c.empty(); }
        size_type          size() const  { return c.size(); }
        const value_type&  top() const   { return c.front(); }
    };
}
```

As you can see, the priority queue uses the STL's heap algorithms. These algorithms are described in Section 9.9.4, page 406. Note that, unlike other container adapters, no comparison operators are defined.

The following subsections describe the members and operations in detail.

Type Definitions

priority_queue::**value_type**
- The type of the elements.
- It is equivalent to *container*::value_type.

priority_queue::**size_type**
- The unsigned integral type for size values.
- It is equivalent to *container*::size_type.

priority_queue::**container_type**
- The type of the container.

Constructors

priority_queue::**priority_queue** ()
- The default constructor.
- Creates an empty priority queue.

explicit *priority_queue*::**priority_queue** (const CompFunc& *op*)
- Creates an empty priority queue with *op* used as the sorting criterion.
- See page 191 and page 213 for examples that demonstrate how to pass a sorting criterion as a constructor argument.

priority_queue::**priority_queue** (const CompFunc& *op* const Container& *cont*)
- Creates a priority queue that is initialized by the elements of *cont* and that uses *op* as the sorting criterion.
- All elements of *cont* are copied.

priority_queue::**priority_queue** (InputIterator *beg*, InputIterator *end*)
- Creates a priority queue that is initialized by all elements of the range [*beg*,*end*).
- This function is a member template (see page 11), so the elements of the source range might have any type that is convertible into the element type of the container.

priority_queue::**priority_queue** (InputIterator *beg*, InputIterator *end*,
                                      const CompFunc& *op*)
- Creates a priority queue that is initialized by all elements of the range [*beg*,*end*) and that uses *op* as the sorting criterion.
- This function is a member template (see page 11), so the elements of the source range might have any type that is convertible into the element type of the container.
- See page 191 and page 213 for examples that demonstrate how to pass a sorting criterion as a constructor argument.

priority_queue::**priority_queue** (InputIterator *beg*, InputIterator *end*,
const CompFunc& *op*, const Container& *cont*)

- Creates a priority queue that is initialized by all elements of the container *cont* plus all elements of the range [*beg*,*end*) and that uses *op* as the sorting criterion.
- This function is a member template (see page 11). So, the elements of the source range might have any type that is convertible into the element type of the container.

Other Operations

size_type *priority_queue*::**size** () const

- Returns the current number of elements.
- To check whether the priority queue is empty (contains no elements), use empty() because it might be faster.

bool *priority_queue*::**empty** () const

- Returns whether the priority queue is empty (contains no elements).
- It is equivalent to *priority_queue*::size()==0, but it might be faster.

void *priority_queue*::**push** (const *value_type*& *elem*)

- Inserts a copy of *elem* into the priority queue.

const *value_type*& *priority_queue*::**top** () const

- Returns the next element of the priority queue. The next element is the element that, of all elements in the priority queue, has the maximum value. If more than one element has the maximum value, which element it returns is undefined.
- The caller must ensure that the queue contains an element (size()>0); otherwise, the behavior is undefined.

void *priority_queue*::**pop** ()

- Removes the next element from the queue. The next element is the element that, of all elements in the priority queue, has the maximum value. If more than one element has the maximum value, which element it removes is undefined.
- Note that this function has no return value. To process the next element, you must call top() first.
- The caller must ensure that the queue contains an element (size()>0); otherwise, the behavior is undefined.

10.4   Bitsets

Bitsets model fixed-sized arrays of bits or Boolean values. They are useful to manage sets of flags, where variables may represent any combination of flags. C and old C++ programs usually use type `long` for arrays of bits and manipulate the bits with the bit operators, such as &, |, and ˜. The class `bitset` has the advantage that bitsets may contain any number of bits, and additional operations are provided. For example, you can assign single bits, and read and write bitsets as a sequence of zeros and ones.

Note that you can't change the number of bits in a bitset. The number of bits is the template parameter. If you need a container for a variable number of bits or Boolean values, you can use the class `vector<bool>` (described in Section 6.2.6, page 158).

The class `bitset` is defined in the header file `<bitset>`:

```
#include <bitset>
```

In `<bitset>`, the class `bitset` is defined as a template class with the number of bits as the template parameter:

```
namespace std {
    template <size_t Bits>
    class bitset;
}
```

In this case the template parameter is not a type but an unsigned integral value (see page 10 for details about this language feature).

Templates with different template arguments are different types. You can compare and combine bitsets only with the same number of bits.

10.4.1   Examples of Using Bitsets

Using Bitsets as Set of Flags

The first example of using bitsets demonstrates how to use bitsets to manage a set of flags. Each flag has a value that is defined by an enumeration type. The value of the enumeration type is used as the position of the bit in the bitset. In particular, the bits represent colors. Thus, each enumeration value defines one color. By using a bitset, you can manage variables that might contain any combination of colors:

```
// cont/bitset1.cpp

#include <bitset>
#include <iostream>
using namespace std;
```

```
int main()
{
    /* enumeration type for the bits
     * - each bit represents a color
     */
    enum Color { red, yellow, green, blue, white, black, ...,
                 numColors };

    // create bitset for all bits/colors
    bitset<numColors> usedColors;

    // set bits for two colors
    usedColors.set(red);
    usedColors.set(blue);

    // print some bitset data
    cout << "bitfield of used colors:   " << usedColors
         << endl;
    cout << "number   of used colors:   " << usedColors.count()
         << endl;
    cout << "bitfield of unused colors: " << ~usedColors
         << endl;

    // if any color is used
    if (usedColors.any()) {
        // loop over all colors
        for (int c = 0; c < numColors; ++c) {
            // if the actual color is used
            if (usedColors[(Color)c]) {
                ...
            }
        }
    }
}
```

Using Bitsets for I/O with Binary Representation

A useful feature of bitsets is the ability to convert integral values into a sequence of bits and vice versa. This is done simply by creating a temporary bitset:

```
// cont/bitset2.cpp

#include <bitset>
#include <iostream>
#include <string>
#include <limits>
using namespace std;

int main()
{
    /* print some numbers in binary representation
     */
    cout << "267 as binary short:    "
         << bitset<numeric_limits<unsigned short>::digits>(267)
         << endl;

    cout << "267 as binary long:     "
         << bitset<numeric_limits<unsigned long>::digits>(267)
         << endl;

    cout << "10,000,000 with 24 bits: "
         << bitset<24>(1e7) << endl;

    /* transform binary representation into integral number
     */
    cout << "\"1000101011\" as number:   "
         << bitset<100>(string("1000101011")).to_ulong() << endl;
}
```

Depending on the number of bits for `short` and `long`, the program might produce the following output:

```
267 as binary short:    0000000100001011
267 as binary long:     00000000000000000000000100001011
10,000,000 with 24 bits: 100110001001011010000000
"1000101011" as number:  555
```

In this example,

```
bitset<numeric_limits<unsigned short>::digits>(267)
```

converts 267 into a bitset with the number of bits of type `unsigned short` (see Section 4.3, page 60, for a discussion of numeric limits). The output operator for `bitset` prints the bits as a sequence of characters 0 and 1.

Similarly,

```
bitset<100>(string("1000101011"))
```

converts a sequence of binary characters into a bitset, for which `to_ulong()` yields the integral value. Note that the number of bits in the bitset should be smaller than `sizeof(unsigned long)`. This is because you get an exception when the value of the bitset can't be represented as `unsigned long`.[7]

10.4.2 Class **bitset** in Detail

The `bitset` class provides the following operations.

Create, Copy, and Destroy Operations

For bitsets, some special constructors are defined. However, there is no special copy constructor, assignment operator, and destructor defined. Thus, bitsets are assigned and copied with the default operations that copy bitwise.

bitset<*bits*>::**bitset** ()

- The default constructor.
- Creates a bitset with all bits initialized with zero.
- For example:
    ```
    bitset<50> flags;        // flags: 0000...000000
                             // thus, 50 unset bits
    ```

bitset<*bits*>::**bitset** (`unsigned long` *value*)

- Creates a bitset that is initialized according to the bits of the integral value *value*.
- If the number of bits of *value* is too small, the leading bit positions are initialized to zero.
- For example:
    ```
    bitset<50> flags(7);     // flags: 0000...000111
    ```

---

[7] Note that you have to convert the initial value to type `string` explicitly. This is probably a mistake in the standard because it was possible to use

```
bitset<100>("1000101011")
```

in earlier versions of the standard. By accident this implicit type conversion was ruled out when this constructor was templified for different string types. There is a proposed resolution to fix this problem.

explicit **bitset**<*bits*>::**bitset** (const *string& str*)

bitset<*bits*>::**bitset** (const *string& str*, *string*::size_type *str_idx*)

bitset<*bits*>::**bitset** (const *string& str*, *string*::size_type *str_idx*,
                        string::size_type *str_num*)

- All forms create a bitset that is initialized by the string *str* or a substring of *str*.
- The string or substring may contain only the characters '0' and '1'.
- *str_idx* is the index of the first character of *str* that is used for initialization.
- If *str_num* is missing, all characters from *str_idx* to the end of *str* are used.
- If the string or substring has fewer characters than necessary, the leading bit positions are initialized to zero.
- If the string or substring has more characters than necessary, the remaining characters are ignored.
- Throw out_of_range if *str_idx* > *str*.size().
- Throw invalid_argument if one of the characters is neither '0' nor '1'.
- Note that this constructor is a member template (see page 11). For this reason no implicit type conversion from const char* to string for the first parameter is provided.[8]
- For example:

      bitset<50> flags(string("1010101"));   // flags: 0000...0001010101
      bitset<50> flags(string("1111000"),2,3); // flags: 0000...0000000110

Nonmanipulating Operations

size_t **bitset**<*bits*>::**size** () const

- Returns the number of bits (thus, *bits*).

size_t **bitset**<*bits*>::**count** () const

- Returns the number of set bits (bits with value 1).

bool **bitset**<*bits*>::**any** () const

- Returns whether any bit is set.

bool **bitset**<*bits*>::**none** () const

- Returns whether no bit is set.

---

[8] This is probably a mistake in the standard because it was possible to use

   bitset<50> flags("1010101")

in earlier versions of the standard. By accident this implicit type conversion was ruled out when this constructor was templified for different string types. There is a proposed resolution to fix this problem.

```
bool bitset<bits>::test (size_t idx) const
```

- Returns whether the bit at position *idx* is set.
- Throws out_of_range if *idx* >= size().

```
bool bitset<bits>::operator == (const bitset<bits>& bits) const
```

- Returns whether all bits of *this and *bits* have the same value.

```
bool bitset<bits>::operator != (const bitset<bits>& bits) const
```

- Returns whether any bits of *this and *bits* have a different value.

Manipulating Operations

```
bitset<bits>& bitset<bits>::set ()
```

- Sets all bits to true.
- Returns the modified bitset.

```
bitset<bits>& bitset<bits>::set (size_t idx)
```

- Sets the bit at position *idx* to true.
- Returns the modified bitset.
- Throws out_of_range if *idx* >= size().

```
bitset<bits>& bitset<bits>::set (size_t idx, int value)
```

- Sets the bit at position *idx* according to *value*.
- Returns the modified bitset.
- *value* is processed as a Boolean value. If *value* is equal to 0, the bit is set to false. Any other value sets the bit to true.
- Throws out_of_range if *idx* >= size().

```
bitset<bits>& bitset<bits>::reset ()
```

- Resets all bits to false (assigns 0 to all bits).
- Returns the modified bitset.

```
bitset<bits>& bitset<bits>::reset (size_t idx)
```

- Resets the bit at position *idx* to false.
- Returns the modified bitset.
- Throws out_of_range if *idx* >= size().

```
bitset<bits>& bitset<bits>::flip ()
```

- Toggles all bits (sets unset bits and vice versa).
- Returns the modified bitset.

`bitset<`*bits*`>& `**`bitset<`***bits***`>::`**flip** `(size_t` *idx*`)`

- Toggles the bit at position *idx*.
- Returns the modified bitset.
- Throws `out_of_range` if *idx* `>= size()`.

`bitset<`*bits*`>& `**`bitset<`***bits***`>::`**operator ˆ=** `(const bitset<`*bits*`>& `*bits*`)`

- The bitwise exclusive-or operator.
- Toggles the value of all bits that are set in *bits* and leaves all other bits unchanged.
- Returns the modified bitset.

`bitset<`*bits*`>& `**`bitset<`***bits***`>::`**operator |=** `(const bitset<`*bits*`>& `*bits*`)`

- The bitwise or operator.
- Sets all bits that are set in *bits* and leaves all other bits unchanged.
- Returns the modified bitset.

`bitset<`*bits*`>& `**`bitset<`***bits***`>::`**operator &=** `(const bitset<`*bits*`>& `*bits*`)`

- The bitwise and operator.
- Resets all bits that are not set in *bits* and leaves all other bits unchanged.
- Returns the modified bitset.

`bitset<`*bits*`>& `**`bitset<`***bits***`>::`**operator <<=** `(size_t` *num*`)`

- Shifts all bits by *num* positions to the left.
- Returns the modified bitset.
- The first *num* bits are set to `false`.

`bitset<`*bits*`>& `**`bitset<`***bits***`>::`**operator >>=** `(size_t` *num*`)`

- Shifts all bits by *num* positions to the right.
- Returns the modified bitset.
- The last *num* bits are set to `false`.

Access with Operator [ ]

`bitset<`*bits*`>::reference `**`bitset<`***bits***`>::`**operator [ ]** `(size_t` *idx*`)`
`bool `**`bitset<`***bits***`>::`**operator [ ]** `(size_t` *idx*`) const`

- Both forms return the bit at position *idx*
- The first form for nonconstant bitsets uses a proxy type to enable the use of the return value as a modifiable value (lvalue). See the next paragraphs for details.
- The caller must ensure that *idx* is a valid index; otherwise, the behavior is undefined.

Operator [ ] returns a special temporary object of type `bitset<>::reference` when it is called for nonconstant bitsets. That object is used as a proxy[9] that allows certain modifications with the bit that is accessed by operator [ ]. In particular, for `reference`s the following five operations are provided:

1. `reference&` **operator=** `(bool)`
   Sets the bit according to the passed value.
2. `reference&` **operator=** `(const reference&)`
   Sets the bit according to another reference.
3. `reference&` **flip** `()`
   Toggles the value of the bit.
4. **operator bool** `() const`
   Converts the value into a Boolean value (automatically).
5. `bool` **operator~** `() const`
   Returns the complement (toggled value) of the bit.

For example, you can write the following statements:

```
bitset<50> flags;
...
flags[42] = true;             // set bit 42
flags[13] = flags[42];        // assign value of bit 42 to bit 13
flags[42].flip();             // toggle value of bit 42
if (flags[13]) {              // if bit 13 is set,
    flags[10] = ~flags[42];   // then assign complement of bit 42 to bit 10
}
```

Creating New Modified Bitsets

`bitset<`*bits*`>` **bitset<***bits***>::operator ~** `() const`

- Returns a new bitset that has all bits toggled with respect to `*this`.

`bitset<`*bits*`>` **bitset<***bits***>::operator <<** `(size_t `*num*`) const`

- Returns a new bitset that has all bits shifted to the left by *num* position.

`bitset<`*bits*`>` **bitset<***bits***>::operator >>** `(size_t `*num*`) const`

- Returns a new bitset that has all bits shifted to the right by *num* position.

---

[9] A proxy allows you to keep control where usually no control is provided. This is often used to get more security. In this case, it maintains control to allow certain operations, although the return value in principle behaves as `bool`.

bitset<*bits*> **operator &** (const bitset<*bits*>& *bits1*,
                                            const bitset<*bits*>& *bits2*)

- Returns the bitwise computing of operator and of *bits1* and *bits2*.
- Returns a new bitset that has only those bits set in *bits1* and in *bits2*.

bitset<*bits*> **operator |** (const bitset<*bits*>& *bits1*,
                                            const bitset<*bits*>& *bits2*)

- Returns the bitwise computing of operator or of *bits1* and *bits2*.
- Returns a new bitset that has only those bits set in *bits1* or in *bits2*.

bitset<*bits*> **operator ^** (const bitset<*bits*>& *bits1*,
                                            const bitset<*bits*>& *bits2*)

- Returns the bitwise computing of operator exclusive-or of *bits1* and *bits2*.
- Returns a new bitset that has only those bits set in *bits1* and not set in *bits2* or vice versa.

Operations for Type Conversions

unsigned long **bitset**<*bits*>::**to_ulong** () const

- Returns the integral value that the bits of the bitset represent.
- Throws overflow_error if the integral value can't be represented by type unsigned long.

string **bitset**<*bits*>::**to_string** () const

- Returns a string that contains the value of the bitset as a binary representation written with characters '0' for unset bits and '1' for set bits.
- The order of the characters is equivalent to the order of the bits with descending index.
- This function is a template function that is parameterized only by the return type. According to the language rules, you must write the following:

  ```
  bitset<50> b;
  ...
  b.template to_string<char,char_traits<char>,allocator<char> >()
  ```

Input/Output Operations

istream& **operator >>** (*istream&* *strm*, bitset<*bits*>& *bits*)

- Reads into *bits* a bitset as a character sequence of characters '0' and '1'.
- Reads until any one of the following happens:
  - At most, *bits* characters are read.
  - End-of-file occurs in *strm*.
  - The next character is neither '0' nor '1'.

- Returns *strm*.
- If the number of bits read is less than the number of bits in the bitset, the bitset is filled with leading zeros.
- If this operator can't read any character, it sets `ios::failbit` in *strm*, which might throw the corresponding exception (see Section 13.4.4, page 602).

ostream& **operator <<** *(ostream&* *strm,* `const bitset<`*bits*`>&` *bits)*

- Writes *bits* converted into a string that contains the binary representation (thus, as a sequence of '0' and '1').
- Uses `to_string()` (see page 468) to create the output characters.
- Returns *strm*.
- See page 462 for an example.

Chapter 11
Strings

This chapter presents the string types of the C++ standard library. It describes the basic template class `basic_string<>` and its standard specializations `string` and `wstring`.

Strings can be a source of confusion. This is because it is not clear what is meant by the term *string*. Does it mean an ordinary character array of type `char*` (with or without the `const` qualifier), or an instance of class `string`, or is it a general name for objects that are kind of strings? In this chapter I use the term *string* for objects of one of the string types in the C++ standard library (whether it is `string` or `wstring`). For "ordinary strings" of type `char*` or `const char*`, I use the term *C-string*.

Note that the type of string literals (such as `"hello"`) was changed into `const char*`. However, to provide backward compatibility there is an implicit but deprecated conversion to `char*` for them.

11.1 Motivation

The string classes of the C++ standard library enable you to use strings as normal types that cause no problems for the user. Thus, you can copy, assign, and compare strings as fundamental types without worrying or bothering about whether there is enough memory or for how long the internal memory is valid. You simply use operators, such as assignment by using =, comparison by using ==, and concatenation by using +. In short, the string types of the C++ standard library are designed in such a way that they behave as if they were a kind of fundamental data type that does not cause any trouble (at least in principle). Modern data processing is mostly string processing, so this is an important step for programmers coming from C, Fortran, or similar languages in which strings are a source of trouble.

The following sections offer two examples that demonstrate the abilities and uses of the string classes. They aren't very useful because they are written only for demonstration purposes.

11.1.1   A First Example: Extracting a Temporary File Name

The first example program uses command-line arguments to generate temporary file names. For example, if you start the program as

```
string1 prog.dat mydir hello. oops.tmp end.dat
```

the output is

```
prog.dat => prog.tmp
mydir => mydir.tmp
hello. => hello.tmp
oops.tmp => oops.xxx
end.dat => end.tmp
```

Usually, the generated file name has the extension `.tmp`, whereas the temporary file name for a name with the extension `.tmp` is `.xxx`.

The program is written in the following way:

```cpp
// string/string1.cpp

#include <iostream>
#include <string>
using namespace std;

int main (int argc, char* argv[])
{
    string filename, basename, extname, tmpname;
    const string suffix("tmp");

    /* for each command-line argument
     * (which is an ordinary C-string)
     */
    for (int i=1; i<argc; ++i) {
        // process argument as file name
        filename = argv[i];

        // search period in file name
        string::size_type idx = filename.find('.');
        if (idx == string::npos) {
            // file name does not contain any period
            tmpname = filename + '.' + suffix;
        }
        else {
```

```
                    /* split file name into base name and extension
                      * - base name contains all characters before the period
                      * - extension contains all characters after the period
                      */
                    basename = filename.substr(0, idx);
                    extname = filename.substr(idx+1);
                    if (extname.empty()) {
                         // contains period but no extension: append tmp
                         tmpname = filename;
                         tmpname += suffix;
                    }
                    else if (extname == suffix) {
                         // replace extension tmp with xxx
                         tmpname = filename;
                         tmpname.replace (idx+1, extname.size(), "xxx");
                    }
                    else {
                         // replace any extension with tmp
                         tmpname = filename;
                         tmpname.replace (idx+1, string::npos, suffix);
                    }
               }

               // print file name and temporary name
               cout << filename << " => " << tmpname << endl;
          }
     }
```

At first,

```
    #include <string>
```

includes the header file for the C++ standard string classes. As usual, these classes are declared in namespace std.

The declaration

```
    string filename, basename, extname, tmpname;
```

creates four string variables. No argument is passed, so for their initialization the default constructor for string is called. The default constructor initializes them as empty strings.

The declaration

```
    const string suffix("tmp");
```

creates a constant string `suffix` that is used in the program as the normal suffix for temporary file names. The string is initialized by an ordinary C-string, so it has the value `tmp`. Note that C-strings can be combined with objects of class `string` in almost any situation in which two `strings` can be combined. In particular, in the entire program every occurrence of `suffix` could be replaced with `"tmp"` so that a C-string is used directly.

In each iteration of the `for` loop, the statement

```
filename = argv[i];
```

assigns a new value to the string variable `filename`. In this case, the new value is an ordinary C-string. However, it could also be another object of class `string` or a single character that has type `char`.

The statement

```
string::size_type idx = filename.find('.');
```

searches for the first occurrence of a period inside the string `filename`. The `find()` function is one of several functions that search for something inside strings. You could also search backward, for substrings, only in a part of a string, or for more than one character simultaneously. All these find functions return an index of the first matching position. Yes, the return value is an integer and not an iterator. The usual interface for strings is not based on the concept of the STL. However, some iterator support for strings is provided (see Section 11.2.13, page 497). The return type of all find functions is `string::size_type`, an unsigned integral type that is defined inside the string class.[1] As usual, the index of the first character is the value 0. The index of the last character is the value "numberOfCharacters-1." Note that "numberOfCharacters" is *not* a valid index. Unlike C-strings, objects of class `string` have *no* special character `'\0'` at the end of the string.

If the search fails, a special value is needed to return the failure. That value is `npos`, which is also defined by the string class. Thus, the line

```
if (idx == string::npos)
```

checks whether the search for the period failed.

The type and value of `npos` are a big pitfall for the use of strings. Be very careful that you always use `string::size_type` and *not* `int` or `unsigned` for the return type when you want to check the return value of a find function. Otherwise, the comparison with `string::npos` might not work. See Section 11.2.12, page 495, for details.

If the search for the period fails in this example, the file name has no extension. In this case, the temporary file name is the concatenation of the original file name, the period character, and the previously defined extension for temporary files:

```
tmpname = filename + '.' + suffix;
```

Thus, you can simply use operator + to concatenate two strings. It is also possible to concatenate strings with ordinary C-strings and single characters.

---

[1] In particular, the `size_type` of a string depends on the memory model of the string class. See Section 11.3.12, page 526, for details.

If the period is found, the `else` part is used. Here, the index of the period is used to split the file name into a base part and the extension. This is done by the `substr()` member function:

```
basename = filename.substr(0, idx);
extname = filename.substr(idx+1);
```

The first parameter of the `substr()` function is the starting index. The optional second argument is the number of characters (not the end index). If the second argument is not used, all remaining characters of the string are returned as a substring.

At all places where an index and a length are used as arguments, strings behave according to the following two rules:

1. An argument specifying the **index** must have a valid value. That value must be less than the number of characters of the string (as usual, the index of the first character is 0). In addition, the index of the position after the last character could be used to specify the end.

   In most cases, any use of an index greater than the actual number of characters throws `out_of_range`. However, all functions that search for a character or a position (all find functions) allow any index. If the index exceeds the number of characters these functions simply return `string::npos` ("not found").

2. An argument specifying the **number of characters** could have any value. If the size is greater than the remaining number of characters, all remaining characters are used. In particular, `string::npos` always works as a synonym for "all remaining characters."

Thus, the following expression throws an exception if the period is not found:

```
filename.substr(filename.find('.'))
```

But, the following expression does not throw an exception:

```
filename.substr(0, filename.find('.'))
```

If the period is not found, it results in the whole file name.

Even if the period is found, the extension that is returned by `substr()` might be empty because there are no more characters after the period. This is checked by

```
if (extname.empty())
```

If this condition yields `true`, the generated temporary file name becomes the ordinary file name that has the normal extension appended:

```
tmpname = filename;
tmpname += suffix;
```

Here, operator `+=` is used to append the extension.

The file name might already have the extension for temporary files. To check this, operator `==` is used to compare two strings:

```
if (extname == suffix)
```

If this comparison yields `true` the normal extension for temporary files is replaced by the extension `xxx`:

```
tmpname = filename;
tmpname.replace (idx+1, extname.size(), "xxx");
```

Here,

```
extname.size()
```

returns the number of characters of the string `extname`. Instead of `size()` you could use `length()`, which does exactly the same thing. So, both `size()` and `length()` return the number of characters. In particular, `size()` has nothing to do with the memory that the string uses.[2]

Next, after all special conditions are considered, normal processing takes place. The program replaces the whole extension by the ordinary extension for temporary file names:

```
tmpname = filename;
tmpname.replace (idx+1, string::npos, suffix);
```

Here, `string::npos` is used as a synonym for "all remaining characters." Thus, all remaining characters after the period are replaced with `suffix`. This replacement would also work if the file name contained a period but no extension. It would just replace "nothing" with `suffix`.

The statement that writes the original file name and the generated temporary file name shows that you can print the strings by using the usual output operators of streams (surprise, surprise):

```
cout << filename << " => " << tmpname << endl;
```

11.1.2 A Second Example: Extracting Words and Printing Them Backward

The second example extracts single words from standard input and prints the characters of each word in reverse order. The words are separated by the usual whitespaces (newline, space, and tab), and by commas, periods, or semicolons.

```
// string/string2.cpp

#include <iostream>
#include <string>
using namespace std;

int main (int argc, char** argv)
{
    const string delims(" \t,.;");
    string line;
```

---

[2] In this case, two member functions do the same with respect to the two different design approaches that are merged here. `length()` returns the length of the string as `strlen()` does for ordinary C-strings, whereas `size()` is the common member function for the number of elements according to the concept of the STL.

```
    // for every line read successfully
    while (getline(cin,line)) {
        string::size_type begIdx, endIdx;

        // search beginning of the first word
        begIdx = line.find_first_not_of(delims);

        // while beginning of a word found
        while (begIdx != string::npos) {
            // search end of the actual word
            endIdx = line.find_first_of (delims, begIdx);
            if (endIdx == string::npos) {
                // end of word is end of line
                endIdx = line.length();
            }

            // print characters in reverse order
            for (int i=endIdx-1; i>=static_cast<int>(begIdx); --i) {
                cout << line[i];
            }
            cout << ' ';

            // search beginning of the next word
            begIdx = line.find_first_not_of (delims, endIdx);
        }
        cout << endl;
    }
}
```

In this program, all characters used as word separators are defined in a special string constant:

```
const string delims(" \t,.;");
```

The newline is also used as a delimiter. However, no special processing is necessary for it because the program reads line-by-line.

The outer loop runs as far as a line can be read into the string line:

```
string line;
while (getline(cin,line)) {
    ...
}
```

The function `getline()` is a special function to read input from streams into a string. It reads every character up to the next end-of-line, which by default is the newline character. The line delimiter itself is extracted but not appended. By passing your special line delimiter as an optional third character argument you can use `getline()` to read token-by-token, where the tokens are separated by that special delimiter.

Inside the outer loop, the individual words are searched and printed. The first statement

```
begIdx = line.find_first_not_of(delims);
```

searches for the beginning of the first word. The `find_first_not_of()` function returns the first index of a character that is not part of the passed string argument. Thus, this function returns the first character that is not one of the separators in `delims`. As usual for find functions, if no matching index is found, `string::npos` is returned.

The inner loop iterates as long as the beginning of a word can be found:

```
while (begIdx != string::npos) {
    ...
}
```

The first statement of the inner loop searches for the end of the current word:

```
endIdx = line.find_first_of (delims, begIdx);
```

The `find_first_of()` function searches for the first occurrence of one of the characters passed as the first argument. In this case, an optional second argument is used that specifies where to start the search in the string. Thus, the first delimiter after the beginning of the word is searched.

If no such character is found, the end-of-line is used:

```
if (endIdx == string::npos) {
    endIdx = line.length();
}
```

Here, `length()` is used, which does the same thing as `size()`: It returns the number of characters.

In the next statement, all characters of the word are printed in reverse order:

```
for (int i=endIdx-1; i>=static_cast<int>(begIdx); --i) {
    cout << line[i];
}
```

Accessing a single character of the string is done with operator `[ ]`. Note that this operator does *not* check whether the index of the string is valid. Thus, you have to ensure that the index is valid (as was done here). A safer way to access a character is to use the `at()` member function. However, such a check costs runtime, so the check is not provided for the usual accessing of characters of a string.

Another nasty problem results from using the index of the string. That is, if you omit the cast of `begIdx` to `int`, this program might run in an endless loop or might crash. Similar to the first example program, the problem is that `string::size_type` is an unsigned integral type. Without the cast, the signed value `i` is converted automatically into an unsigned value because it is compared with a unsigned type. In this case, the expression

```
    i>=begIdx
```

always yields `true` if the current word starts at the beginning of the line. This is because `begIdx` is then zero and any unsigned value is greater than or equal to zero. So, an endless loop results that might get stopped by a crash due to an illegal memory access.

For this reason, I really don't like the concept of `string::size_type` and `string::npos`. See Section 11.2.12, page 496, for a workaround that is safer (but not perfect).

The last statement of the inner loop reinitializes `begIdx` to the beginning of the next word, if any:

```
begIdx = line.find_first_not_of (delims, endIdx);
```

Unlike with the first call of `find_first_not_of()` in the example, here the end of the previous word is passed as the starting index for the search. If the previous word was the rest of the line, `endIdx` is the index of the end of the line. This simply means that the search starts from the end of the string, which returns `string::npos`.

Let's try this "useful and important" program. Here is some possible input:

```
pots & pans
I saw a reed
```

The output for this input is as follows:

```
stop & snap
I was a deer
```

I'd appreciate other examples of input for the next edition of this book.

11.2   Description of the String Classes

11.2.1   String Types

Header File

All types and functions for strings are defined in the header file `<string>`:

```
#include <string>
```

As usual, it defines all identifiers in namespace `std`.

Template Class `basic_string<>`

Inside `<string>`, the type `basic_string<>` is defined as a basic template class for all string types:

```
namespace std {
    template<class charT,
             class traits = char_traits<charT>,
```

```
            class Allocator = allocator<charT> >
    class basic_string;
}
```

It is parameterized by the character type, the traits of the character type, and the memory model:

- The first parameter is the data type of a single character.
- The optional second parameter is a traits class, which provides all core operations for the characters of the string class. Such a traits class specifies how to copy or to compare characters (see Section 14.1.2, page 687, for details). If it is not specified, the default traits class according to the current character type is used. See Section 11.2.14, page 503, for a user-defined traits class that lets strings behave in a case-insensitive manner.
- The third optional argument defines the memory model that is used by the string class. As usual, the default value is the default memory model `allocator` (see Section 3.4, page 31, and Chapter 15 for details).[3]

Types `string` and `wstring`

Two specializations of class `basic_string<>` are provided by the C++ standard library:

1. `string` is the predefined specialization of that template for characters of type `char`:
   ```
   namespace std {
       typedef basic_string<char> string;
   }
   ```
2. `wstring` is the predefined specialization of that template for characters of type `wchar_t`:
   ```
   namespace std {
       typedef basic_string<wchar_t> wstring;
   }
   ```
   Thus, you can use strings that use wider character sets, such as Unicode or some Asian character sets (see Chapter 14 for details about internationalization).

In the following sections no distinction is made between these different kinds of strings. The usage and the problems are the same because all string classes have the same interface. So, "string" means any string type, such as `string` and `wstring`. The examples in this book usually use type `string` because the European and Anglo-American environment is the common environment for software development.

---

[3] In systems that do not support default template parameters, the third argument is usually missing.

11.2.2   Operation Overview

Table 11.1 lists all operations that are provided for strings.

Operation	Effect
constructors	Create or copy a string
destructor	Destroys a string
=, assign()	Assign a new value
swap()	Swaps values between two strings
+=, append(), push_back()	Append characters
insert()	Inserts characters
erase()	Deletes characters
clear()	Removes all characters (makes it empty)
resize()	Changes the number of characters (deletes or appends characters at the end)
replace()	Replaces characters
+	Concatenates strings
==, !=, <, <=, >, >=, compare()	Compare strings
size(), length()	Return the number of characters
max_size()	Returns the maximum possible number of characters
empty()	Returns whether the string is empty
capacity()	Returns the number of characters that can be held without reallocation
reserve()	Reserves memory for a certain number of characters
[], at()	Access a character
>>, getline()	Read the value from a stream
<<	Writes the value to a stream
copy()	Copies or writes the contents to a character array
c_str()	Returns the value as C-string
data()	Returns the value as character array
substr()	Returns a certain substring
find functions	Search for a certain substring or character
begin(), end()	Provide normal iterator support
rbegin(), rend()	Provide reverse iterator support
get_allocator()	Returns the allocator

Table 11.1. String Operations

String Operation Arguments

Many operations are provided to manipulate strings. In particular, the operations that manipulate the value of a string have several overloaded versions that specify the new value with one, two, or three arguments. All these operations use the argument scheme of Table 11.2.

Arguments	Interpretation
const *string&* *str*	The whole string *str*
const *string&* *str*, size_type *idx*, size_type *num*	At most, the first *num* characters of *str* starting with index *idx*
const *char** *cstr*	The whole C-string *cstr*
const *char** *chars*, size_type *len*	*len* characters of the character array *chars*
char *c*	The character *c*
size_type *num*, *char* *c*	*num* occurrences of the character *c*
iterator *beg*, iterator *end*	All characters in the range [*beg*,*end*)

Table 11.2. Scheme of String Operation Arguments

Note that only the single-argument version char* handles the character '\0' as a special character that terminates the string. In all other cases '\0' is *not* a special character:

```
std::string s1("nico");      // initializes s1 with: 'n' 'i' 'c' 'o'
std::string s2("nico",5);    // initializes s2 with: 'n' 'i' 'c' 'o' '\0'
std::string s3(5,'\0');      // initializes s3 with: '\0' '\0' '\0' '\0' '\0'

s1.length()                  // yields 4
s2.length()                  // yields 5
s3.length()                  // yields 5
```

Thus, in general a string might contain any character. In particular, a string might contain the contents of a binary file.

See Table 11.3 for an overview of which operation uses which kind of arguments. All operators can only handle objects as single values. Therefore, to assign, compare, or append a part of a string or C-string, you must use the function that has the corresponding name.

Operations that Are Not Provided

The string classes of the C++ standard library do not solve every possible string problem. In fact, they do not provide direct solutions for

- Regular expressions
- Text processing (capitalization, case-insensitive comparisons)

Text processing, however, is not a big problem. See Section 11.2.13, page 497, for some examples.

	Full String	Part of String	C-string (*char∗*)	*char* Array	Single *char*	*num* chars	Iterator Range
constructors	Yes	Yes	Yes	Yes	—	Yes	Yes
=	Yes	—	Yes	—	Yes	—	—
`assign()`	Yes	Yes	Yes	Yes	—	Yes	Yes
+=	Yes	—	Yes	—	Yes	—	—
`append()`	Yes	Yes	Yes	Yes	—	Yes	Yes
`push_back()`	—	—	—	—	Yes	—	—
`insert()`, index version	Yes	Yes	Yes	Yes	—	Yes	—
`insert()`, iterator version	—	—	—	—	Yes	Yes	Yes
`replace()`, index version	Yes	Yes	Yes	Yes	Yes	Yes	—
`replace()`, iterator vers.	Yes	—	Yes	Yes	—	Yes	Yes
find functions	Yes	—	Yes	Yes	Yes	—	—
+	Yes	—	Yes	—	Yes	—	—
==, !=, <, <=, >, >=	Yes	—	Yes	—	—	—	—
`compare()`	Yes	Yes	Yes	Yes	—	—	—

Table 11.3. Available Operations that Have String Parameters

11.2.3 Constructors and Destructors

Table 11.4 lists all constructors and destructors for strings. These are described in this section. The initialization by a range that is specified by iterators is described in Section 11.2.13, page 497.

Expression	Effect
`string s`	Creates the empty string `s`
`string s(str)`	Creates a string as a copy of the existing string `str`
`string s(str,stridx)`	Creates a string `s` that is initialized by the characters of string `str` starting with index `stridx`
`string s(str,stridx,strlen)`	Creates a string `s` that is initialized by, at most, `strlen` characters of string `str` starting with index `stridx`
`string s(cstr)`	Creates a string `s` that is initialized by the C-string `cstr`
`string s(chars,chars_len)`	Creates a string `s` that is initialized by `chars_len` characters of the character array `chars`
`string s(num,c)`	Creates a string that has `num` occurrences of character `c`
`string s(beg,end)`	Creates a string that is initialized by all characters of the range [beg,end)
`s.~string()`	Destroys all characters and frees the memory

Table 11.4. Constructors and Destructor of Strings

You can't initialize a string with a single character. Instead, you must use its address or an additional number of occurrences:

```
std::string s('x');    // ERROR
std::string s(1,'x');  // OK, creates a string that has one character 'x'
```

This means that there is an automatic type conversion from type `const char*` but not from type `char` to type `string`.

11.2.4   Strings and C-Strings

In standard C++ the type of string literals was changed from `char*` to `const char*`. However, to provide backward compatibility there is an implicit but deprecated conversion to `char*` for them. However, because string literals don't have type `string`, there is a strong relationship between "new" string class objects and ordinary C-strings: You can use ordinary C-strings in almost every situation where strings are combined with other string-like objects (comparing, appending, inserting, etc.). In particular, there is an automatic type conversion from `const char*` into strings. However, there is *no* automatic type conversion from a string object to a C-string. This is for safety reasons to prevent unintended type conversions that result in strange behavior (type `char*` often has strange behavior) and ambiguities (for example, in an expression that combines a `string` and a C-string it would be possible to convert `string` into `char*` and vice versa). Instead, there are several ways to create or write/copy in a C-string. In particular, `c_str()` is provided to generate the value of a string as a C-string (as a character array that has '\0' as its last character). By using `copy()`, you can copy or write the value to an existing C-string or character array.

Note that strings do *not* provide a special meaning for the character '\0', which is used as special character in an ordinary C-string to mark the end of the string. The character '\0' may be part of a string just like every other character.

Note also that you must not use a null pointer (`NULL`) instead of a `char*` parameter. Doing so results in strange behavior. This is because `NULL` has an integral type and is interpreted as the number zero or the character with value 0 if the operation is overloaded for a single integral type.

There are three possible ways to convert the contents of the string into a raw array of characters or C-string:

1. **data()**
   Returns the contents of the string as an array of characters. Note that the return type is *not* a valid C-string because no '\0' character gets appended.

2. **c_str()**
   Returns the contents of the string as a C-string. Thus, the '\0' character is appended.

3. **copy()**
   Copies the contents of the string into a character array provided by the caller. An '\0' character is not appended.

Note that `data()` and `c_str()` return an array that is owned by the string. Thus, the caller must not modify or free the memory. For example:

```
std::string s("12345");

atoi(s.c_str())          // convert string into integer
f(s.data(),s.length())   // call function for a character array
                         // and the number of characters

char buffer[100];
s.copy(buffer,100);      // copy at most 100 characters of s into buffer
s.copy(buffer,100,2);    // copy at most 100 characters of s into buffer
                         // starting with the third character of s
```

You usually should use strings in the whole program and convert them into C-strings or character arrays only just immediately before you need the contents as type `char*`. Note that the return value of `c_str()` and `data()` is valid only until the next call of a nonconstant member function for the same string:

```
std::string s;
...
foo(s.c_str());          // s.c_str() is valid during the whole statement

const char* p;
p = s.c_str();           // p refers to the contents of s as a C-string
foo(p);                  // OK (p is still valid)
s += "ext";              // invalidates p
foo(p);                  // ERROR: argument p is not valid
```

11.2.5 Size and Capacity

To use strings effectively and correctly you need to understand how the size and capacity of strings cooperate. For strings, three "sizes" exist:

1. **`size()`** and **`length()`**

   Return the current number of characters of the string. Both functions are equivalent.[4]

   The **`empty()`** member function is a shortcut for checking whether the numbers of characters is zero. Thus, it checks whether the string is empty. You should use it instead of `length()` or `size()` because it might be faster.

---

[4] In this case, two member functions do the same thing because `length()` returns the length of the string, as `strlen()` does for ordinary C-strings, whereas `size()` is the common member function for the number of elements according to the concept of the STL.

2. **`max_size()`**

   Returns the maximum number of characters that a string may contain. A string typically contains all characters in a single block of memory, so there might be relevant restrictions on PCs. Otherwise, this value usually is the maximum value of the type of the index less one. It is "less one" for two reasons: (a) The maximum value itself is `npos` and (b) an implementation might append `'\0'` internally at the end of the internal buffer so that it simply returns that buffer when the string is used as a C-string (for example, by `c_str()`). Whenever an operation results in a string that has a length greater than `max_size()`, the class throws `length_error`.

3. **`capacity()`**

   Returns the number of characters that a string could contain without having to reallocate its internal memory.

Having sufficient capacity is important for two reasons:

1. Reallocation invalidates all references, pointers, and iterators that refer to characters of the string.

2. Reallocation takes time.

Thus, the capacity must be taken into account if a program uses pointers, references, or iterators that refer to a string or to characters of a string, or if speed is a goal.

The member function `reserve()` is provided to avoid reallocations. `reserve()` lets you reserve a certain capacity before you really need it to ensure that references are valid as long as the capacity is not exceeded:

```
std::string s;        // create empty string
s.reserve(80);        // reserve memory for 80 characters
```

The concept of capacity for strings is, in principle, the same as for vector containers (see Section 6.2.1, page 149); however, there is one big difference: Unlike vectors, you can call `reserve()` for strings to shrink the capacity. Calling `reserve()` with an argument that is less than the current capacity is, in effect, a nonbinding shrink request. If the argument is less than the current number of characters, it is a nonbinding shrink-to-fit request. Thus, although you might *want* to shrink the capacity, it is not guaranteed to happen. The default value of `reserve()` for string is 0. So, a call of `reserve()` without any argument is always a nonbinding shrink-to-fit request:

```
s.reserve();        // "would like to shrink capacity to fit the current size"
```

The call to shrink capacity is nonbinding because how to reach an optimal performance is implementation-defined. Implementations of the string class might have different design approaches with respect to speed and memory usage. Therefore, implementations might increase capacity in larger steps and might never shrink the capacity.

The standard, however, specifies that capacity may shrink only because of a call of `reserve()`. Thus, it is guaranteed that references, pointers, and iterators remain valid even when characters are deleted or changed, provided they refer to characters that have a position that is before the manipulated characters.

11.2.6 Element Access

A string allows you to have read or write access to the characters it contains. You can access a single character via either of two methods: the subscript operator [ ] and the `at()` member function. Both return the character at the position of the passed index. As usual, the first character has index 0 and the last character has index `length()-1`. However, note the following differences:

- Operator [ ] does *not* check whether the index passed as an argument is valid; `at()` does. If `at()` is called with an invalid index, it throws an `out_of_range` exception. If operator [ ] is called with an invalid index, the behavior is undefined. The effect might be an illegal memory access that might then cause some nasty side effects or a crash (you're lucky if the result is a crash, because then you know that you did something wrong).

- For the *constant* version of operator [ ], the position after the last character is valid. In this case, the current number of characters is a valid index. The operator returns the value that is generated by the default constructor of the character type. Thus, for objects of type `string` it returns the char `'\0'`.

    In all other cases (for the nonconstant version of operator [ ] and for the `at()` member function), the current number of characters is an invalid index. Using it might cause an exception or result in undefined behavior.

For example:

```
const std::string cs("nico");   // cs contains: 'n' 'i' 'c' 'o'
std::string s("abcde");         // s contains: 'a' 'b' 'c' 'd' 'e'

s[2]                            // yields 'c'
s.at(2)                         // yields 'c'

s[100]                          // ERROR: undefined behavior
s.at(100)                       // throws out_of_range

s[s.length()]                   // ERROR: undefined behavior
cs[cs.length()]                 // yields '\0'
s.at(s.length())                // throws out_of_range
cs.at(cs.length())              // throws out_of_range
```

To enable you to modify a character of a string, the nonconstant versions of [ ] and `at()` return a character reference. Note that this reference becomes invalid on reallocation:

```
std::string s("abcde");    // s contains: 'a' 'b' 'c' 'd' 'e'

char& r = s[2];            // reference to third character
char* p = &s[3];           // pointer to fourth character

r = 'X';                   // OK, s contains: 'a' 'b' 'X' 'd' 'e'
```

```
*p = 'Y';                    // OK, s contains: 'a' 'b' 'X' 'Y' 'e'

s = "new long value";        // reallocation invalidates r and p

r = 'X';                     // ERROR: undefined behavior
*p = 'Y';                    // ERROR: undefined behavior
```

Here, to avoid runtime errors, you would have had to `reserve()` enough capacity before r and p were initialized.

References and pointers that refer to characters of a string may be invalidated by the following operations:

- If the value is swapped with `swap()`
- If a new value is read by `operator>>()` or `getline()`
- If the contents are exported by `data()` or `c_str()`
- If any nonconstant member function is called, except operator `[]`, `at()`, `begin()`, `rbegin()`, `end()`, or `rend()`
- If any of these functions is followed by operator `[]`, `at()`, `begin()`, `rbegin()`, `end()`, or `rend()`

The same applies to iterators (see Section 11.2.13, page 497).

11.2.7 Comparisons

The usual comparison operators are provided for strings. The operands may be strings or C-strings:

```
std::string s1, s2;
...
```

```
s1 == s2        // returns true if s1 and s2 contain the same characters
s1 < "hello"    // return whether s1 is less than the C-string "hello"
```

If strings are compared by <, <=, >, or >=, their characters are compared lexicographically according to the current character traits. For example, all of the following comparisons yield `true`:

```
std::string("aaaa") < std::string("bbbb")
std::string("aaaa") < std::string("abba")
std::string("aaaa") < std::string("aaaaaa")
```

By using the `compare()` member functions you can compare substrings. The `compare()` member functions can process more than one argument for each string so that you can specify a substring by its index and by its length. Note that `compare()` returns an integral value rather than a Boolean value. This return value has the following meaning: 0 means equal, a value less than zero means less than, and a value greater than zero means greater than. For example:

```
std::string s("abcd");
```

```
s.compare("abcd")          // returns 0
s.compare("dcba")          // returns a value < 0 (s is less)
s.compare("ab")            // returns a value > 0 (s is greater)

s.compare(s)               // returns 0 (s is equal to s)
s.compare(0,2,s,2,2)       // returns a value < 0 ("ab" is less than "cd")
s.compare(1,2,"bcx",2)     // returns 0 ("bc" is equal to "bc")
```

To use a different comparison criterion you can define your own comparison criterion and use STL comparison algorithms (see Section 11.2.13, page 499, for an example), or you can use special character traits that make comparisons on a case-insensitive basis. However, because a string type that has a special traits class is a different data type, you cannot combine or process these strings with objects of type `string`. See Section 11.2.14, page 503, for an example.

In programs for the international market it might be necessary to compare strings according to a specific locale. Class `locale` provides the parenthesis operator as convenient way to do this (see page 703). It uses the string collation facet, which is provided to compare strings for sorting according to some locale conventions. See Section 14.4.5, page 724, for details.

11.2.8 Modifiers

You can modify strings by using different member functions and operators.

Assignments

To modify a string you can use operator = to assign a new value. The new value may be a string, a C-string, or a single character. In addition, you can use the `assign()` member functions to assign strings when more than one argument is needed to describe the new value. For example:

```
const std::string aString("othello");
std::string s;
```

```
s = aString;               // assign "othello"
s = "two\nlines";          // assign a C-string
s = ' ';                   // assign a single character

s.assign(aString);         // assign "othello" (equivalent to operator =)
s.assign(aString,1,3);     // assign "the"
s.assign(aString,2,std::string::npos);     // assign "hello"

s.assign("two\nlines");    // assign a C-string (equivalent to operator =)
```

```
s.assign("nico",5);        // assign the character array: 'n' 'i' 'c' 'o' '\0'
s.assign(5,'x');           // assign five characters: 'x' 'x' 'x' 'x' 'x'
```

You also can assign a range of characters that is defined by two iterators. See Section 11.2.13, page 497, for details.

Swapping Values

As with many nontrivial types, the string type provides a specialization of the swap() function, which swaps the contents of two strings (the global swap() function was introduced in Section 4.4.2, page 67). The specialization of swap() for strings guarantees constant complexity. So you should use it to swap the value of strings and to assign strings if you don't need the assigned string after the assignment.

Making Strings Empty

To remove all characters in a string, you have several possibilities. For example:

```
std::string s;
```

```
s = "";            // assign the empty string
s.clear();         // clear contents
s.erase();         // erase all characters
```

Inserting and Removing Characters

There are a lot of member functions to insert, remove, replace, and erase characters of a string. To append characters, you can use operator +=, append(), and push_back(). For example:

```
const std::string aString("othello");
std::string s;
```

```
s += aString;              // append "othello"
s += "two\nlines";         // append C-string
s += '\n';                 // append single character

s.append(aString);         // append "othello" (equivalent to operator +=)
s.append(aString,1,3);     // append "the"
s.append(aString,2,std::string::npos);     // append "hello"

s.append("two\nlines");    // append C-string (equivalent to operator +=)
s.append("nico",5);        // append character array: 'n' 'i' 'c' 'o' '\0'
s.append(5,'x');           // append five characters: 'x' 'x' 'x' 'x' 'x'

s.push_back('\n');         // append single character (equivalent to operator +=)
```

Operator += appends single-argument values. append() lets you specify the appended value by using multiple arguments. One additional version of append() lets you append a range of characters specified by two iterators (see Section 11.2.13, page 497). The push_back() member function is provided for back inserters so that STL algorithms are able to append characters to a string (see Section 7.4.2, page 272, for details about back inserters and Section 11.2.13, page 502, for an example of their use with strings).

Similar to append(), several insert() member functions enable you to insert characters. They require the index of the character, behind which the new characters are inserted:

```
const std::string aString("age");
std::string s("p");

s.insert(1,aString);     // s: page
s.insert(1,"ersifl");    // s: persiflage
```

Note that no insert() member function is provided to pass the index and a single character. Thus you must pass a string or an additional number:

```
s.insert(0,' ');     // ERROR
s.insert(0," ");     // OK
```

You might also try

```
s.insert(0,1,' ');   // ERROR: ambiguous
```

However, this results in a nasty ambiguity because insert() is overloaded for the following signatures:

```
insert (size_type idx, size_type num, charT c);   // position is index
insert (iterator  pos, size_type num, charT c);   // position is iterator
```

For type string, size_type is usually defined as unsigned and iterator is often defined as char*. In this case, the first argument 0 has two equivalent conversions. So, to get the correct behavior you have to write:

```
s.insert((std::string::size_type)0,1,' ');  // OK
```

The second interpretation of the ambiguity described here is an example of the use of iterators to insert characters. If you wish to specify the insert position as an iterator, you can do it in three ways: insert a single character, insert a certain number of the same character, and insert a range of characters specified by two iterators (see Section 11.2.13, page 497).

Similar to append() and insert(), several erase() functions remove characters, and several replace() functions replace characters. For example:

```
std::string s = "i18n";                     // s: i18n
s.replace(1,2,"nternationalizatio");        // s: internationalization
s.erase(13);                                // s: international
s.erase(7,5);                               // s: internal
s.replace(0,2,"ex");                        // s: external
```

`resize()` lets you change the number of characters. If the new size that is passed as an argument is less than the current number of characters, characters are removed from the end. If the new size is greater than the current number of characters, characters are appended at the end. You can pass the character that is appended if the size of the string grows. If you don't, the default constructor for the character type is used (which is the `'\0'` character for type `char`).

11.2.9   Substrings and String Concatenation

You can extract a substring from any string by using the `substr()` member function. For example:

```
std::string s("interchangeability");
```

```
s.substr()              // returns a copy of s
s.substr(11)            // returns string("ability")
s.substr(5,6)           // returns string("change")
s.substr(s.find('c'))   // returns string("changeability")
```

You can concatenate two strings or C-strings, or one of those with single characters by using operator +. For example, the statements

```
std::string s1("enter");
std::string s2("nation");
std::string i18n;

i18n = 'i' + s1.substr(1) + s2 + "aliz" + s2.substr(1);
std::cout << "i18n means: " + i18n << std::endl;
```

have the following output:

```
i18n means: internationalization
```

11.2.10   Input/Output Operators

The usual I/O operators are defined for strings:

- **Operator >>** reads a string from an input stream.
- **Operator <<** writes a string to an output stream.

These operators behave as they do for ordinary C-strings. In particular, operator >> operates as follows:

1. It skips leading whitespaces if the `skipws` flag (see Section 13.7.7, page 625) is set.
2. It reads all characters until any of the following happens:
   - The next character is a whitespace
   - The stream is no longer in a good state (for example due to end-of-file)

- The current `width()` of the stream (see Section 13.7.3, page 618) is greater than zero and `width()` characters are read
- `max_size()` characters are read

3. It sets `width()` of the stream to 0.

Thus, in general, the input operator reads the next word while skipping leading whitespaces. A whitespace is any character for which `isspace(c,`*strm*`.getloc())` is `true` (`isspace()` is explained in Section 14.4.4, page 718).

The output operator also takes the `width()` of the stream in consideration. That is, if `width()` is greater than 0, operator `<<` writes at least `width()` characters.

The string classes also provide a special function in namespace `std` for reading line-by-line: `std::getline()`. This reads all characters (including leading whitespaces) until the line delimiter or end-of-file is reached. The line delimiter is extracted but not appended. By default, the line delimiter is the newline character, but you can pass your own "line" delimiter as an optional argument[5]. This way, you can read token-by-token separated by any arbitrary character:

```
std::string s;

while (getline(std::cin,s)) {        // for each line read from cin
    ...
}

while (getline(std::cin,s,':')) {  // for each token separated by ':'
    ...
}
```

Note that if you read token-by-token, the newline character is not a special character. In this case, the tokens might contain a newline character.

11.2.11 Searching and Finding

Strings provide a lot of functions to search and find characters or substrings.[6] You can search

- A single character, a character sequence (substring), or one of a certain set of characters
- Forward and backward
- Starting from any position at the beginning or inside the string

---

[5] You don't have to qualify `getline()` with `std::` because "Koenig lookup" will always consider the namespace where the class of an argument was defined when calling a function (see page 17).

[6] Don't be confused because I write about searching "and" finding. They are (almost) synonymous. The search functions use "find" in their name. However, unfortunately they don't guarantee to find anything. In fact, they "search" for something or "try to find" something. So I use the term *search* for the behavior of these functions and *find* with respect to their name.

In addition, all search algorithms of the STL can be called when iterators are used.

All search functions have the word *find* inside their name. They try to find a character position given a *value* that is passed as an argument. How the search proceeds depends on the exact name of the find function. Table 11.5 lists all of the search functions for strings.

String Function	Effect
`find()`	Finds the first occurrence of *value*
`rfind()`	Finds the last occurrence of *value* (reverse find)
`find_first_of()`	Finds the first character that is part of *value*
`find_last_of()`	Finds the last character that is part of *value*
`find_first_not_of()`	Finds the first character that is not part of *value*
`find_last_not_of()`	Finds the last character that is not part of *value*

Table 11.5. Search Functions for Strings

All search functions return the index of the first character of the character sequence that matches the search. If the search fails, they return `npos`. The search functions use the following argument scheme:

- The first argument is always the value that is searched for.
- The second optional value indicates an index at which to start the search in the string.
- The optional third argument is the number of characters of the value to search.

Unfortunately, this argument scheme differs from that of the other string functions. With the other string functions, the starting index is the first argument, and the value and its length are adjacent arguments. In particular, each search function is overloaded with the following set of arguments:

- **const** *string&* *value*
  The function searches against the characters of the string *value*.
- **const** *string&* *value*, *size_type idx*
  The function searches against the characters of *value*, starting with index *idx* in *this.
- **const** *char** *value*
  The function searches against the characters of the C-string *value*.
- **const** *char** *value*, *size_type idx*
  The function searches against the characters of the C-string *value*, starting with index *idx* in *this.
- **const** *char** *value*, *size_type idx*, *size_type value_len*
  The function searches against the *value_len* characters of the character array *value*, starting with index *idx* in *this. Thus, the null character ('\0') has *no* special meaning here inside *value*.
- **const** *char value*
  The function searches against the character *value*.
- **const** *char value*, *size_type idx*
  The function searches against the characters *value*, starting with index *idx* in *this.

For example:

```
std::string s("Hi Bill, I'm ill, so please pay the bill");
```

```
s.find("il")                   // returns 4 (first substring "il")
s.find("il",10)                // returns 13 (first substring "il" starting from s[10])
s.rfind("il")                  // returns 37 (last substring "il")
s.find_first_of("il")          // returns 1 (first char 'i' or 'l')
s.find_last_of("il")           // returns 39 (last char 'i' or 'l')
s.find_first_not_of("il")      // returns 0 (first char neither 'i' nor 'l')
s.find_last_not_of("il")       // returns 36 (last char neither 'i' nor 'l')
s.find("hi")                   // returns npos
```

You could also use STL algorithms to find characters or substrings in strings. They allow you to use your own comparison criterion (see Section 11.2.13, page 499, for an example). However, note that the naming scheme of the STL search algorithms differs from the naming scheme for string search functions (see Section 9.2.2, page 324, for details).

11.2.12   The Value npos

If a search function fails, it returns *string*::npos. Consider the following example:

```
std::string s;
std::string::size_type idx;         // be careful: don't use any other type!
...

idx = s.find("substring");
if (idx == std::string::npos) {
    ...
}
```

The condition of the if statement yields true if and only if "substring" is not part of string s.

Be very careful when using the string value npos and its type. When you want to check the return value always use string::size_type and *not* int or unsigned for the type of the return value; otherwise, the comparison of the return value with string::npos might not work.

This behavior is the result of the design decision that npos is defined as -1:

```
namespace std {
    template<class charT,
             class traits = char_traits<charT>,
             class Allocator = allocator<charT> >
    class basic_string {
      public:
```

```
        typedef typename Allocator::size_type size_type;
        ...
        static const size_type npos = -1;
        ...
    };
}
```

Unfortunately, `size_type` (which is defined by the allocator of the string) must be an unsigned integral type. The default allocator, `allocator`, uses type `size_t` as `size_type` (see Section 15.3, page 732). Because `-1` is converted into an unsigned integral type, `npos` is the maximum unsigned value of its type. However, the exact value depends on the exact definition of type `size_type`. Unfortunately, these maximum values differ. In fact, `(unsigned long)-1` *differs* from `(unsigned short)-1` (provided the size of the types differ). Thus, the comparison

```
    idx == std::string::npos
```

might yield `false`, if `idx` has the value −1 and `idx` and `string::npos` have different types:

```
    std::string s;
    ...
    int idx = s.find("not found");       // assume it returns npos
    if (idx == std::string::npos) {      // ERROR: comparison might not work
        ...
    }
```

One way to avoid this error is to check whether the search fails directly:

```
    if (s.find("hi") == std::string::npos) {
        ...
    }
```

However, often you need the index of the matching character position. Thus, another simple solution is to define your own signed value for `npos`:

```
    const int NPOS = -1;
```

Now the comparison looks a bit different (and even more convenient):

```
    if (idx == NPOS) {       // works almost always
        ...
    }
```

Unfortunately, this solution is not perfect because the comparison fails if either `idx` has type `unsigned short` or the index is greater than the maximum value of `int` (because of these problems the standard did not define it that way). However, because both might happen very rarely, the solution works in most situations. To write portable code, however, you should always use *string*`::size_type` for any index of your string type. For a perfect solution you'd need some overloaded functions that consider the exact type of `string::size_type`. I hope the standard will provide a better solution in the future.

11.2.13   Iterator Support for Strings

A string is an ordered collection of characters. As a consequence, the C++ standard library provides an interface for strings that lets you use strings as STL containers.[7]

In particular, you can call the usual member functions to get iterators that iterate over the characters of a string. If you are not familiar with iterators, consider them as something that can refer to a single character inside a string, just as ordinary pointers do for C-strings. By using these objects, you can iterate over all characters of a string by calling several algorithms that either are provided by the C++ standard library or that are user defined. For example, you can sort the characters of a string, reverse the order, or find the character that has the maximum value.

String iterators are random access iterators. This means that they provide random access and that you can use all algorithms (see Section 5.3.2, page 93, and Section 7.2, page 251, for a discussion about iterator categories). As usual, the types of string iterators (`iterator`, `const_iterator`, and so on) are defined by the string class itself. The exact type is implementation defined, but usually string iterators are defined simply as ordinary pointers. See Section 7.2.6, page 258, for a discussion of a nasty difference between iterators that are implemented as pointers and iterators that are implemented as classes.

Iterators are invalidated when reallocation occurs or when certain changes are made to the values to which they refer. See Section 11.2.6, page 487, for details.

Iterator Functions for Strings

Table 11.6 shows all of the member functions that strings provide for iterators. As usual, the range specified by `beg` and `end` is a half-open range that includes `beg` but excludes `end` (often written as [beg,end), see Section 5.3, page 83).

To support the use of back inserters for string, the `push_back()` function is defined. See Section 7.4.2, page 272, for details about back inserters and page 502 for an example of their use with strings.

Example of Using String Iterators

A very useful thing that you can do with string iterators is to make all characters of a string lowercase or uppercase via a single statement. For example:

```
// string/iter1.cpp

#include <string>
#include <iostream>
#include <algorithm>
#include <cctype>
using namespace std;
```

---

[7] The STL is introduced in Chapter 5.

Expression	Effect
`s.begin()`	Returns a random access iterator for the first character
`s.end()`	Returns a random access iterator for the position after the last character
`s.rbegin()`	Returns a reverse iterator for the first character of a reverse iteration (thus, for the last character)
`s.rend()`	Returns a reverse iterator for the position after the last character of a reverse iteration (thus, the position before the first character)
`string s(beg,end)`	Creates a string that is initialized by all characters of the range [beg,end)
`s.append(beg,end)`	Appends all characters of the range [beg,end)
`s.assign(beg,end)`	Assigns all characters of the range [beg,end)
`s.insert(pos,c)`	Inserts the character c at iterator position pos and returns the iterator position of the new character
`s.insert(pos,num,c)`	Inserts num occurrences of the character c at iterator position pos and returns the iterator position of the first new character
`s.insert(pos,beg,end)`	Inserts all characters of the range [beg,end) at iterator position pos
`s.erase(pos)`	Deletes the character to which iterator pos refers and returns the position of the next character
`s.erase(beg,end)`	Deletes all characters of the range [beg,end) and returns the next position of the next character
`s.replace(beg,end,str)`	Replaces all characters of the range [beg,end) with the characters of string str
`s.replace(beg,end,cstr)`	Replaces all characters of the range [beg,end) with the characters of the C-string cstr
`s.replace(beg,end,cstr,len)`	Replaces all characters of the range [beg,end) with len characters of the character array cstr
`s.replace(beg,end,num,c)`	Replaces all characters of the range [beg,end) with num occurrences of the character c
`s.replace(beg,end, newBeg,newEnd)`	Replaces all characters of the range [beg,end) with all characters of the range [newBeg,newEnd)

Table 11.6. Iterator Operations of Strings

```
int main()
{
    // create a string
    string s("The zip code of Hondelage in Germany is 38108");
    cout << "original: " << s << endl;

    // lowercase all characters
    transform (s.begin(), s.end(),    // source
               s.begin(),             // destination
               tolower);              // operation
    cout << "lowered:  " << s << endl;

    // uppercase all characters
    transform (s.begin(), s.end(),    // source
               s.begin(),             // destination
               toupper);              // operation
    cout << "uppered:  " << s << endl;
}
```

The output of the program is as follows:

```
original: The zip code of Hondelage in Germany is 38108
lowered:  the zip code of hondelage in germany is 38108
uppered:  THE ZIP CODE OF HONDELAGE IN GERMANY IS 38108
```

Note that `tolower()` and `toupper()` are old C functions that use the global locale. If you have a different locale or more than one locale in your program, you should use the new form of `tolower()` and `toupper()`. See Section 14.4.4, page 718, for details.

The following example demonstrates how the STL enables you to use your own search and sort criteria. It compares and searches strings in a case-insensitive way:

```
// string/iter2.cpp

#include <string>
#include <iostream>
#include <algorithm>
using namespace std;

bool nocase_compare (char c1, char c2)
{
    return toupper(c1) == toupper(c2);
}
```

```
int main()
{
    string s1("This is a string");
    string s2("STRING");

    // compare case insensitive
    if (s1.size() == s2.size() &&            // ensure same sizes
        equal (s1.begin(),s1.end(),          // first source string
               s2.begin(),                   // second source string
               nocase_compare)) {            // comparison criterion
        cout << "the strings are equal" << endl;
    }
    else {
        cout << "the strings are not equal" << endl;
    }

    // search case insensitive
    string::iterator pos;
    pos = search (s1.begin(),s1.end(),       // source string in which to search
                  s2.begin(),s2.end(),       // substring to search
                  nocase_compare);           // comparison criterion
    if (pos == s1.end()) {
        cout << "s2 is not a substring of s1" << endl;
    }
    else {
        cout << '"' << s2 << "\" is a substring of \""
             << s1 << "\" (at index " << pos - s1.begin() << ")"
             << endl;
    }
}
```

Note that the caller of equal() has to ensure that the second range has at least as many elements/characters as the first range. Thus, comparing the string size is necessary; otherwise, the behavior will be undefined.

In the last output statement you can process the difference of two string iterators to get the index of the character position:

```
pos - s1.begin()
```

This is because string iterators are random access iterators. Similar to transferring an index into the iterator position, you can simply add the value of the index.

In this example the user-defined auxiliary function `nocase_compare()` is provided to compare two strings in a case-insensitive way. Instead, you can also use a combination of some function adapters and replace the expression `nocase_compare` with the following expression:

```
compose_f_gx_hy(equal_to<int>(),
                ptr_fun(toupper),
                ptr_fun(toupper))
```

See page 309 and page 318 for further details.

If you use strings in sets or maps, you might need a special sorting criterion to let the collections sort the string in a case-insensitive way. See page 213 for an example that demonstrates how to do this.

The following program demonstrates other examples of strings using iterator functions:

```cpp
// string/iter3.cpp

#include <string>
#include <iostream>
#include <algorithm>
using namespace std;

int main()
{
    // create constant string
    const string hello("Hello, how are you?");

    // initialize string s with all characters of string hello
    string s(hello.begin(),hello.end());

    // iterate through all of the characters
    string::iterator pos;
    for (pos = s.begin(); pos != s.end(); ++pos) {
        cout << *pos;
    }
    cout << endl;

    // reverse the order of all characters inside the string
    reverse (s.begin(), s.end());
    cout << "reverse:       " << s << endl;

    // sort all characters inside the string
    sort (s.begin(), s.end());
    cout << "ordered:       " << s << endl;
```

```
        /* remove adjacent duplicates
         * - unique() reorders and returns new end
         * - erase() shrinks accordingly
         */
        s.erase (unique(s.begin(),
                        s.end()),
                 s.end());
        cout << "no duplicates: " << s << endl;
    }
```

The program has the following output:

```
Hello, how are you?
reverse:         ?uoy era woh ,olleH
ordered:            ,?Haeehlloooruwy
no duplicates:   ,?Haehloruwy
```

The following example uses back inserters to read the standard input into a string:

```
// string/unique.cpp

#include <iostream>
#include <string>
#include <algorithm>
#include <iterator>
#include <locale>
using namespace std;

class bothWhiteSpaces {
  private:
    const locale& loc;      // locale
  public:
    /* constructor
     * - save the locale object
     */
    bothWhiteSpaces (const locale& l) : loc(l) {
    }
    /* function call
     * - returns whether both characters are whitespaces
     */
    bool operator() (char elem1, char elem2) {
```

```
            return isspace(elem1,loc) && isspace(elem2,loc);
    }
};

int main()
{
    string contents;

    // don't skip leading whitespaces
    cin.unsetf (ios::skipws);

    // read all characters while compressing whitespaces
    unique_copy(istream_iterator<char>(cin),        // beginning of source
                istream_iterator<char>(),           // end of source
                back_inserter(contents),            // destination
                bothWhiteSpaces(cin.getloc()));     // criterion for removing

    // process contents
    // - here: write it to the standard output
    cout << contents;
}
```

By using the `unique_copy()` algorithm (see Section 9.7.2, page 384), all characters are read from the input stream `cin` and inserted into the string `contents`. The `bothWhiteSpaces` function object is used to check whether two consecutive characters are both whitespaces. To do this, it is initialized by the locale of `cin` and calls `isspace()`, which checks whether a character is a whitespace character (see Section 14.4.4, page 718, for a discussion of `isspace()`). `unique_copy()` uses the criterion `bothWhiteSpaces` to remove adjacent duplicate whitespaces. You can find a similar example in the reference section about `unique_copy()` on page 385.

11.2.14   Internationalization

As mentioned in the introduction of the string class (see Section 11.2.1, page 479), the template string class `basic_string<>` is parameterized by the character type, the traits of the character type, and the memory model. Type `string` is the specialization for characters of type `char`, and type `wstring` is the specialization for characters of type `wchar_t`.

The character traits are provided to specify the details of how to deal with aspects depending on the representation of a character type. An additional class is necessary because you can't change the interface of built-in types (such as `char` and `wchar_t`), and the same character type may have different traits. The details about the traits classes are described in Section 14.1.2, page 687.

The following code defines a special traits class for strings so that they operate in a case-insensitive way:

```cpp
// string/icstring.hpp

#ifndef ICSTRING_HPP
#define ICSTRING_HPP

#include <string>
#include <iostream>
#include <cctype>

/* replace functions of the standard char_traits<char>
 * so that strings behave in a case-insensitive way
 */
struct ignorecase_traits : public std::char_traits<char> {
    // return whether c1 and c2 are equal
    static bool eq(const char& c1, const char& c2) {
        return std::toupper(c1)==std::toupper(c2);
    }
    // return whether c1 is less than c2
    static bool lt(const char& c1, const char& c2) {
        return std::toupper(c1)<std::toupper(c2);
    }
    // compare up to n characters of s1 and s2
    static int compare(const char* s1, const char* s2,
                       std::size_t n) {
        for (std::size_t i=0; i<n; ++i) {
            if (!eq(s1[i],s2[i])) {
                return lt(s1[i],s2[i])?-1:1;
            }
        }
        return 0;
    }
    // search c in s
    static const char* find(const char* s, std::size_t n,
                            const char& c) {
        for (std::size_t i=0; i<n; ++i) {
            if (eq(s[i],c)) {
                return &(s[i]);
            }
        }
        return 0;
    }
};
```

```
// define a special type for such strings
typedef std::basic_string<char,ignorecase_traits> icstring;

/* define an output operator
 * because the traits type is different than that for std::ostream
 */
inline
std::ostream& operator << (std::ostream& strm, const icstring& s)
{
    // simply convert the icstring into a normal string
    return strm << std::string(s.data(),s.length());
}


#endif     // ICSTRING_HPP
```

The definition of the output operator is necessary because the standard only defines I/O operators for streams that use the same character and traits type. But here, the traits type differs, so we have to define our own output operator. For input operators the same problem occurs.

The following program demonstrates how to use these special kinds of strings:

```
// string/icstring1.cpp

#include "icstring.hpp"

int main()
{
    using std::cout;
    using std::endl;

    icstring s1("hallo");
    icstring s2("otto");
    icstring s3("hALLo");

    cout << std::boolalpha;
    cout << s1 << " == " << s2 << " : " << (s1==s2) << endl;
    cout << s1 << " == " << s3 << " : " << (s1==s3) << endl;

    icstring::size_type idx = s1.find("All");
    if (idx != icstring::npos) {
        cout << "index of \"All\" in \"" << s1 << "\": "
             << idx << endl;
    }
```

```
    else {
        cout << "\"All\" not found in \"" << s1 << endl;
    }
}
```

The program has the following output:

```
hallo == otto : false
hallo == hALLo : true
index of "All" in "hallo": 1
```

See Chapter 14 for more details about internationalization.

11.2.15   Performance

The standard does *not* specify *how* the string class is to be implemented. It only specifies the interface. There may be important differences in speed and memory usage depending on the concept and priorities of the implementation.

If you prefer better speed, make sure that your string class uses a concept such as *reference counting*. Reference counting makes copies and assignments faster because the implementation only copies and assigns references instead of the contents of a string (see Section 6.8, page 222, for a smart pointer class that enables reference counting for any type). By using reference counting you might not even need to pass strings by constant reference; however, to maintain flexibility and portability, you always should.

11.2.16   Strings and Vectors

Strings and vectors behave similarly. This is not a surprise because both are containers that are typically implemented as dynamic arrays. Thus, you could consider a string as a special kind of a vector that has characters as elements. In fact, you can use a string as an STL container. This is covered by Section 11.2.13, page 497. However, considering a string as a special kind of vector is dangerous because there are many fundamental differences between the two. Chief of these are their two primary goals:

- The primary goal of vectors is to handle and to manipulate the elements of the container, not the container as a whole. Thus, vector implementations are optimized to operate on elements inside the container.

- The primary goal of strings is to handle and to manipulate the container (the string) as a whole. Thus, strings are optimized to reduce the costs of assigning and passing the whole container.

These different goals typically result in completely different implementations. For example, strings are often implemented by using reference counting; vectors never are. Nevertheless, you can also use vectors as ordinary C-strings. See Section 6.2.3, page 155, for details.

11.3   String Class in Detail

In this section *string* means the actual string class. It might be `string`, `wstring`, or any other specialization of class `basic_string<>`. Type *char* means the actual character type, which is `char` for `string` and `wchar_t` for `wstring`. Other types and values that are in italic type have definitions that depend on individual definitions of the character type or traits class. The details about traits classes are provided in Section 14.1.2, page 687.

11.3.1   Type Definitions and Static Values

string`::`**traits_type**
- The type of the character traits.
- The second template parameter of class `basic_string`.
- For type `string`, it is equivalent to `char_traits<char>`.

string`::`**value_type**
- The type of the characters.
- It is equivalent to `traits_type::char_type`.
- For type `string`, it is equivalent to `char`.

string`::`**size_type**
- The unsigned integral type for size values and indices.
- It is equivalent to `allocator_type::size_type`.
- For type `string`, it is equivalent to `size_t`.

string`::`**difference_type**
- The signed integral type for difference values.
- It is equivalent to `allocator_type::difference_type`.
- For type `string`, it is equivalent to `ptrdiff_t`.

string`::`**reference**
- The type of character references.
- It is equivalent to `allocator_type::reference`.
- For type `string`, it is equivalent to `char&`.

string`::`**const_reference**
- The type of constant character references.
- It is equivalent to `allocator_type::const_reference`.
- For type `string`, it is equivalent to `const char&`.

string : : **pointer**
- The type of character pointers.
- It is equivalent to `allocator_type::pointer`.
- For type `string`, it is equivalent to `char*`.

string : : **const_pointer**
- The type of constant character pointers.
- It is equivalent to `allocator_type::const_pointer`.
- For type `string`, it is equivalent to `const char*`.

string : : **iterator**
- The type of iterators.
- The exact type is implementation defined.
- For type `string`, it is typically `char*`.

string : : **const_iterator**
- The type of constant iterators.
- The exact type is implementation defined.
- For type `string`, it is typically `const char*`.

string : : **reverse_iterator**
- The type of reverse iterators.
- It is equivalent to `reverse_iterator<iterator>`.

string : : **const_reverse_iterator**
- The type of constant reverse iterators.
- It is equivalent to `reverse_iterator<const_iterator>`.

`static const` *size_type* *string* : : **npos**
- A special value that indicates one of the following:
  - "not found"
  - "all remaining characters"
- It is an unsigned integral value that is initialized by `-1`.
- Be careful when you use `npos`. See Section 11.2.12, page 495, for details.

11.3.2   Create, Copy, and Destroy Operations

string : : **string** ( )
- The default constructor.
- Creates an empty string.

string::**string** (const *string&* *str*)

- The copy constructor.
- Creates a new string as a copy of *str*.

string::**string** (const *string&* *str*, size_type *str_idx*)

string::**string** (const *string&* *str*, size_type *str_idx*, size_type *str_num*)

- Create a new string that is initialized by, at most, the first *str_num* characters of *str* starting with index *str_idx*.
- If *str_num* is missing, all characters from *str_idx* to the end of *str* are used.
- Throws out_of_range if *str_idx* > *str*.size().

string::**string** (const *char** *cstr*)

- Creates a string that is initialized by the C-string *cstr*.
- The string is initialized by all characters of *cstr* up to but not including '\0'.
- Note that *cstr* must not be a null pointer (NULL).
- Throws length_error if the resulting size exceeds the maximum number of characters.

string::**string** (const *char** *chars*, size_type *chars_len*)

- Creates a string that is initialized by *chars_len* characters of the character array *chars*.
- Note that *chars* must have at least *chars_len* characters. The characters may have arbitrary values. Thus, '\0' has no special meaning.
- Throws length_error if *chars_len* is equal to *string*::npos.
- Throws length_error if the resulting size exceeds the maximum number of characters.

string::**string** (size_type *num*, *char* *c*)

- Creates a string that is initialized by *num* occurrences of character *c*.
- Throws length_error if *num* is equal to *string*::npos.
- Throws length_error if the resulting size exceeds the maximum number of characters.

string::**string** (InputIterator *beg*, InputIterator *end*)

- Creates a string that is initialized by all characters of the range [*beg*,*end*).
- Throws length_error if the resulting size exceeds the maximum number of characters.

string::~**string** ()

- The destructor.
- Destroys all characters and frees the memory.

Most constructors allow you to pass an allocator as an additional argument (see Section 11.3.12, page 526).

11.3.3   Operations for Size and Capacity

Size Operations

size_type *string*::**size** () const

size_type *string*::**length** () const

- Both functions return the current number of characters.
- They are equivalent.
- To check whether the string is empty, you should use `empty()` because it might be faster.

bool *string*::**empty** () const

- Returns whether the string is empty (contains no characters).
- It is equivalent to *string*::`size()==0`, but it might be faster.

size_type *string*::**max_size** () const

- Returns the maximum number of characters a string could contain.
- Whenever an operation results in a string that has a length greater than `max_size()`, the class throws `length_error`.

Capacity Operations

size_type *string*::**capacity** () const

- Returns the number of characters the string could contain without reallocation.

void *string*::**reserve** ()

void *string*::**reserve** (size_type *num*)

- The second form reserves internal memory for at least *num* characters.
- If *num* is less than the current capacity, the call is taken as a nonbinding request to shrink the capacity.
- If *num* is less than the current number of characters, the call is taken as a nonbinding request to shrink the capacity to fit the current number of characters.
- If no argument is passed, the call is always a nonbinding shrink-to-fit request.
- The capacity is never reduced below the current number of characters.
- Each reallocation invalidates all references, pointers, and iterators and takes some time, so a preemptive call to `reserve()` is useful to increase speed and to keep references, pointers, and iterators valid (see Section 11.2.5, page 486, for details).

11.3.4 Comparisons

bool **comparison** (const *string*& *str1*, const *string*& *str2*)
bool **comparison** (const *string*& *str*, const *char** *cstr*)
bool **comparison** (const *char** *cstr*, const *string*& *str*)

- The first form returns the result of the comparison of two strings.
- The second and third form return the result of the comparison of a string with a C-string.
- *comparison* might be any of the following:
  operator ==
  operator !=
  operator <
  operator >
  operator <=
  operator >=
- The values are compared lexicographically (see page 488).

int *string*::**compare** (const *string*& *str*) const

- Compares the string *this with the string *str*.
- Returns
  - 0 if both strings are equal
  - A value < 0 if *this is lexicographically less than *str*
  - A value > 0 if *this is lexicographically greater than *str*
- For the comparison, traits::compare() is used (see Section 14.1.2, page 689).
- See Section 11.2.7, page 488, for details.

int *string*::**compare** (size_type *idx*, size_type *len*, const *string*& *str*) const

- Compares, at most, *len* characters of string *this, starting with index *idx* with the string *str*.
- Throws out_of_range if *idx* > size().
- The comparison is performed as just described for compare(*str*).

int *string*::**compare** (size_type *idx*, size_type *len*,
                   const *string*& *str*, size_type *str_idx*,
                   size_type *str_len*) const

- Compares, at most, *len* characters of string *this, starting with index *idx* with, at most, *str_len* characters of string *str* starting with index *str_idx*.
- Throws out_of_range if *idx* > size().
- Throws out_of_range if *str_idx* > *str*.size().
- The comparison is performed as just described for compare(*str*).

int *string*::**compare** (const *char* cstr*) const

- Compares the characters of string *this with the characters of the C-string *cstr*.
- The comparison is performed as just described for compare(*str*).

int *string*::**compare** (size_type *idx*, size_type *len*, const *char* cstr*) const

- Compares, at most, *len* characters of string *this, starting with index *idx* with all characters of the C-string *cstr*.[8]
- The comparison is performed as just described for compare(*str*).
- Note that *cstr* must not be a null pointer (NULL).

int *string*::**compare** (size_type *idx*, size_type *len*,
                         const *char* chars*, size_type *chars_len*) const

- Compares, at most, *len* characters of string *this, starting with index *idx* with *chars_len* characters of the character array *chars*.
- The comparison is performed as just described for compare(*str*).
- Note that *chars* must have at least *chars_len* characters. The characters may have arbitrary values. Thus, '\0' has no special meaning.
- Throws length_error if *chars_len* is equal to *string*::npos.

11.3.5   Character Access

char& *string*::**operator [ ]** (size_type *idx*)

const *char&* *string*::**operator [ ]** (size_type *idx*) const

- Both forms return the character with the index *idx* (the first character has index 0).
- For constant strings, length() is a valid index and the operator returns the value generated by the default constructor of the character type (for string: '\0').
- For nonconstant strings, using length() as index value is invalid.
- Passing an invalid index results in undefined behavior.
- The reference returned for the nonconstant string may become invalidated due to string modifications or reallocations (see Section 11.2.6, page 487, for details).
- If the caller can't ensure that the index is valid, at() should be used.

---

[8] The standard specifies the behavior of this form of compare() differently: It states that *cstr* is not considered a C-string but a character array, and passes npos as its length (in fact, it calls the following form of compare() by using npos as an additional parameter). This is a bug in the standard (it would always throw a length_error exception).

char& ***string***::**at** (size_type *idx*)

const *char&* ***string***::**at** (size_type *idx*) const

- Both forms return the character that has the index *idx* (the first character has index 0).
- For all strings, an index with length() as value is invalid.
- Passing an invalid index (less than 0 or greater than or equal to size()) throws an out_of_range exception.
- The reference returned for the nonconstant string may become invalidated due to string modifications or reallocations (see Section 11.2.6, page 487, for details).
- If the caller ensures that the index is valid, she can use operator [ ], which is faster.

11.3.6   Generating C-Strings and Character Arrays

const *char** ***string***::**c_str** () const

- Returns the contents of the string as a C-string (an array of characters that has the null character '\0' appended).
- The return value is owned by the string. Thus, the caller must neither modify nor free or delete the return value.
- The return value is valid only as long as the string exists, and as long as only constant functions are called for it.

const *char** ***string***::**data** () const

- Returns the contents of the string as a character array.
- The return value contains all characters of the string without any modification or extension. In particular, no null character is appended. Thus, the return value is, in general, *not* a valid C-string.
- The return value is owned by the string. Thus, the caller must neither modify nor free or delete the return value.
- The return value is valid only as long as the string exists, and as long as only constant functions are called for it.

size_type ***string***::**copy** (*char** *buf*, size_type *buf_size*) const

size_type ***string***::**copy** (*char** *buf*, size_type *buf_size*, size_type *idx*) const

- Both forms copy, at most, *buf_size* characters of the string (beginning with index *idx*) into the character array *buf*.
- They return the number of characters copied.
- No null character is appended. Thus, the contents of *buf* might *not* be a valid C-string after the call.
- The caller must ensure that *buf* has enough memory; otherwise, the call results in undefined behavior.
- Throws out_of_range if *idx* > size().

11.3.7 Modifying Operations

Assignments

string& ***string***::**operator =** (const *string&* *str*)

string& ***string***::**assign** (const *string&* *str*)

- Both operations assign the value of string *str*.
- They return *this.

string& ***string***::**assign** (const *string&* *str*, size_type *str_idx*, size_type *str_num*)

- Assigns at most *str_num* characters of *str* starting with index *str_idx*.
- Returns *this.
- Throws out_of_range if *str_idx* > *str*.size().

string& ***string***::**operator =** (const *char** *cstr*)

string& ***string***::**assign** (const *char** *cstr*)

- Both operations assign the characters of the C-string *cstr*.
- They assign all characters of *cstr* up to but not including '\0'.
- Both operations return *this.
- Note that *cstr* must not be a null pointer (NULL).
- Both operations throw length_error if the resulting size exceeds the maximum number of characters.

string& ***string***::**assign** (const *char** *chars*, size_type *chars_len*)

- Assigns *chars_len* characters of the character array *chars*.
- Returns *this.
- Note that *chars* must have at least *chars_len* characters. The characters may have arbitrary values. Thus, '\0' has no special meaning.
- Throws length_error if the resulting size exceeds the maximum number of characters.

string& ***string***::**operator =** (*char* *c*)

- Assigns character *c* as the new value.
- Returns *this.
- After this call, *this contains only this single character.

string& ***string***::**assign** (size_type *num*, *char* *c*)

- Assigns *num* occurrences of character *c*.
- Returns *this.
- Throws length_error if *num* is equal to *string*::npos.
- Throws length_error if the resulting size exceeds the maximum number of characters.

void *string*::**swap** (*string& str*)

void **swap** (*string& str1*, *string& str2*)

- Both forms swap the value of two strings:
  - The member function swaps the contents of *this and *str*.
  - The global function swaps the contents of *str1* and *str2*.
- You should prefer these functions over assignment if possible because they are faster. In fact, they are guaranteed to have constant complexity. See Section 11.2.8, page 490, for details.

Appending Characters

string& string::**operator +=** (const *string& str*)

string& string::**append** (const *string& str*)

- Both operations append the characters of *str*.
- They return *this.
- Both operations throw `length_error` if the resulting size exceeds the maximum number of characters.

string& string::**append** (const *string& str*, `size_type` *str_idx*, `size_type` *str_num*)

- Appends, at most, *str_num* characters of *str*, starting with index *str_idx*.
- Returns *this.
- Throws `out_of_range` if *str_idx* > *str*.`size()`.
- Throws `length_error` if the resulting size exceeds the maximum number of characters.

string& string::**operator +=** (const *char* cstr*)

string& string::**append** (const *char* cstr*)

- Both operations append the characters of the C-string *cstr*.
- They return *this.
- Note that *cstr* must not be a null pointer (NULL).
- Both operations throw `length_error` if the resulting size exceeds the maximum number of characters.

string& string::**append** (const *char* chars*, `size_type` *chars_len*)

- Appends *chars_len* characters of the character array *chars*.
- Returns *this.
- Note that *chars* must have at least *chars_len* characters. The characters may have arbitrary values. Thus, '\0' has no special meaning.
- Throws `length_error` if the resulting size exceeds the maximum number of characters.

string& **string**::**append** (size_type *num*, *char c*)

- Appends *num* occurrences of character *c*.
- Returns *this.
- Throws length_error if the resulting size exceeds the maximum number of characters.

string& **string**::**operator +=** (*char c*)
void **string**::**push_back** (*char c*)

- Both operations append character *c*.
- Operator += returns *this.
- Both operations throw length_error if the resulting size exceeds the maximum number of characters.

string& **string**::**append** (InputIterator *beg*, InputIterator *end*)

- Appends all characters of the range [*beg,end*).
- Returns *this.
- Throws length_error if the resulting size exceeds the maximum number of characters.

Inserting Characters

string& **string**::**insert** (size_type *idx*, const *string& str*)

- Inserts the characters of *str* so that the new characters start with index *idx*.
- Returns *this.
- Throws out_of_range if *idx* > size().
- Throws length_error if the resulting size exceeds the maximum number of characters.

string& **string**::**insert** (size_type *idx*, const *string& str*,
                                  size_type *str_idx*, size_type *str_num*)

- Inserts, at most, *str_num* characters of *str*, starting with index *str_idx*, so that the new characters start with index *idx*.
- Returns *this.
- Throws out_of_range if *idx* > size().
- Throws out_of_range if *str_idx* > *str*.size().
- Throws length_error if the resulting size exceeds the maximum number of characters.

string& **string**::**insert** (size_type *idx*, const *char* cstr*)

- Inserts the characters of the C-string *cstr* so that the new characters start with index *idx*.
- Returns *this.
- Note that *cstr* must not be a null pointer (NULL).

- Throws `out_of_range` if *idx* > `size()`.
- Throws `length_error` if the resulting size exceeds the maximum number of characters.

string& ***string***::**insert** (`size_type` *idx*, `const` *char** *chars*, `size_type` *chars_len*)

- Inserts *chars_len* characters of the character array *chars* so that the new characters start with index *idx*.
- Returns *`this`.
- Note that *chars* must have at least *chars_len* characters. The characters may have arbitrary values. Thus, `'\0'` has no special meaning.
- Throws `out_of_range` if *idx* > `size()`.
- Throws `length_error` if the resulting size exceeds the maximum number of characters.

string& ***string***::**insert** (`size_type` *idx*, `size_type` *num*, *char* *c*)

`void` ***string***::**insert** (`iterator` *pos*, `size_type` *num*, *char* *c*)

- Both forms insert *num* occurrences of character *c* at the position specified by *idx* or *pos* respectively.
- The first form inserts the new characters so that they start with index *idx*.
- The second form inserts the new characters before the character to which iterator *pos* refers.
- Note that the overloading of these two functions results in a possible ambiguity. If you pass 0 as first argument, it can be interpreted as an index (which is typically a conversion to `unsigned`) or as an iterator (which is often a conversion to `char*`). So in this case you should pass an index as the exact type. For example:

```
std::string s;
...
s.insert(0,1,' ');                        // ERROR: ambiguous
s.insert((std::string::size_type)0,1,' '); // OK
```

- The first form returns *`this`.
- Both forms throw `out_of_range` if *idx* > `size()`.
- Both forms throw `length_error` if the resulting size exceeds the maximum number of characters.

`iterator` ***string***::**insert** (`iterator` *pos*, *char* *c*)

- Inserts a copy of character *c* before the character to which iterator *pos* refers.
- Returns the position of the character inserted.
- Throws `length_error` if the resulting size exceeds the maximum number of characters.

`void` ***string***::**insert** (`iterator` *pos*, `InputIterator` *beg*, `InputIterator` *end*)

- Inserts all characters of the range [*beg,end*) before the character to which iterator *pos* refers.
- Throws `length_error` if the resulting size exceeds the maximum number of characters.

Erasing Characters

void *string*::**clear** ()

string& *string*::**erase** ()

- Both functions delete all characters of the string. Thus, the string is empty after the call.
- erase() returns *this.

string& *string*::**erase** (size_type *idx*)

string& *string*::**erase** (size_type *idx*, size_type *len*)

- Both forms erase, at most, *len* characters of *this, starting at index *idx*.
- They return *this.
- If *len* is missing, all remaining characters are removed.
- Both forms throw out_of_range if *idx* > size().

iterator *string*::**erase** (iterator *pos*)

iterator *string*::**erase** (iterator *beg*, iterator *end*)

- Both forms erase the single character at iterator position *pos* or all characters of the range [*beg*,*end*) respectively.
- They return the position of the first character after the last character removed (thus, the second form returns *end*).[9]

Changing the Size

void *string*::**resize** (size_type *num*)

void *string*::**resize** (size_type *num*, *char c*)

- Both forms change the number of characters of *this to *num*. Thus, if *num* is not equal to size(), they append or remove characters at the end according to the new size.
- If the number of characters increases, the new characters are initialized by *c*. If *c* is missing, the characters are initialized by the default constructor of the character type (for string: '\0').
- Both forms throw length_error if *num* is equal to *string*::npos.
- Both forms throw length_error if the resulting size exceeds the maximum number of characters.

---

[9] The standard specifies that the second form of this function returns the position after *end*. This is a bug in the standard.

Replacing Characters

string& *string*::**replace** (size_type *idx*, size_type *len*, const *string&* *str*)

string& *string*::**replace** (iterator *beg*, iterator *end*, const *string&* *str*)

- The first form replaces, at most, *len* characters of *this, starting with index *idx*, with all characters of *str*.
- The second form replaces all characters of the range [*beg*,*end*) with all characters of *str*.
- Both forms return *this.
- Both forms throw out_of_range if *idx* > size().
- Both forms throw length_error if the resulting size exceeds the maximum number of characters.

string& *string*::**replace** (size_type *idx*, size_type *len*,
                         const *string&* *str*, size_type *str_idx*, size_type *str_num*)

- Replaces, at most, *len* characters of *this, starting with index *idx*, with at most *str_num* characters of *str* starting with index *str_idx*.
- Returns *this.
- Throws out_of_range if *idx* > size().
- Throws out_of_range if *str_idx* > *str*.size().
- Throws length_error if the resulting size exceeds the maximum number of characters.

string& *string*::**replace** (size_type *idx*, size_type *len*, const *char** *cstr*)

string& *string*::**replace** (iterator *beg*, iterator *end*, const *char** *cstr*)

- Both forms replace, at most, *len* characters of *this, starting with index *idx*, or all characters of the range [*beg*,*end*), respectively, with all characters of the C-string *cstr*.
- Both forms return *this.
- Note that *cstr* must not be a null pointer (NULL).
- Both forms throw out_of_range if *idx* > size().
- Both forms throw length_error if the resulting size exceeds the maximum number of characters.

string& *string*::**replace** (size_type *idx*, size_type *len*,
                     const *char** *chars*, size_type *chars_len*)

string& *string*::**replace** (iterator *beg*, iterator *end*,
                     const *char** *chars*, size_type *chars_len*)

- Both forms replace, at most, *len* characters of *this, starting with index *idx*, or all characters of the range [*beg*,*end*), respectively, with *chars_len* characters of the character array *chars*.
- They return *this.

- Note that *chars* must have at least *chars_len* characters. The characters may have arbitrary values. Thus, '\0' has no special meaning.
- Both forms throw out_of_range if *idx* > size().
- Both forms throw length_error if the resulting size exceeds the maximum number of characters.

string& *string*::**replace** (size_type *idx*, size_type *len*, size_type *num*, *char c*)

string& *string*::**replace** (iterator *beg*, iterator *end*, size_type *num*, *char c*)

- Both forms replace, at most, *len* characters of *this, starting with index *idx*, or all characters of the range [*beg,end*), respectively, with *num* occurrences of character *c*
- They return *this.
- Both forms throw out_of_range if *idx* > size().
- Both forms throw length_error if the resulting size exceeds the maximum number of characters.

string& *string*::**replace** (iterator *beg*, iterator *end*
                                   InputIterator *newBeg*, InputIterator *newEnd*)

- Replaces all characters of the range [*beg,end*) with all characters of the range [*newBeg,newEnd*).
- Returns *this.
- Throws length_error if the resulting size exceeds the maximum number of characters.

11.3.8   Searching and Finding

Find a Character

size_type *string*::**find** (*char c*) const

size_type *string*::**find** (*char c*, size_type *idx*) const

size_type *string*::**rfind** (*char c*) const

size_type *string*::**rfind** (*char c*, size_type *idx*) const

- These functions search for the first/last character *c* (starting at index *idx*).
- The find() functions search forward and return the first substring.
- The rfind() functions search backward and return the last substring.
- These functions return the index of the character when successful or *string*::npos if they fail.

Find a Substring

size_type *string*::**find** (const *string&* str) const

size_type *string*::**find** (const *string&* str, size_type *idx*) const

size_type *string*::**rfind** (const *string&* str) const

size_type *string*::**rfind** (const *string&* str, size_type *idx*) const

- These functions search for the first/last substring *str* (starting at index *idx*).
- The find() functions search forward and return the first substring.
- The rfind() functions search backward and return the last substring.
- These functions return the index of the first character of the substring when successful or *string*::npos if they fail.

size_type *string*::**find** (const *char** cstr) const

size_type *string*::**find** (const *char** cstr, size_type *idx*) const

size_type *string*::**rfind** (const *char** cstr) const

size_type *string*::**rfind** (const *char** cstr, size_type *idx*) const

- These functions search for the first/last substring that has the characters of the C-string *cstr* (starting at index *idx*).
- The find() functions search forward and return the first substring.
- The rfind() functions search backward and return the last substring.
- These functions return the index of the first character of the substring when successful or *string*::npos if they fail.
- Note that *cstr* must not be a null pointer (NULL).

size_type *string*::**find** (const *char** chars, size_type *idx*,
                    size_type *chars_len*) const

size_type *string*::**rfind** (const *char** chars, size_type *idx*,
                    size_type *chars_len*) const

- These functions search for the first/last substring that has *chars_len* characters of the character array *chars* (starting at index *idx*).
- find() searches forward and returns the first substring.
- rfind() searches backward and returns the last substring.
- These functions return the index of the first character of the substring when successful or *string*::npos if they fail.
- Note that *chars* must have at least *chars_len* characters. The characters may have arbitrary values. Thus, '\0' has no special meaning.

Find First of Different Characters

size_type *string*::**find_first_of** (const *string&* str) const

size_type *string*::**find_first_of** (const *string&* str, size_type *idx*) const

size_type *string*::**find_first_not_of** (const *string&* str) const

size_type *string*::**find_first_not_of** (const *string&* str, size_type *idx*) const

- These functions search for the first character that is or is not also an element of the string *str* (starting at index *idx*).
- These functions return the index of that character or substring when successful or *string*::npos if they fail.

size_type *string*::**find_first_of** (const *char** cstr) const

size_type *string*::**find_first_of** (const *char** cstr, size_type *idx*) const

size_type *string*::**find_first_not_of** (const *char** cstr) const

size_type *string*::**find_first_not_of** (const *char** cstr, size_type *idx*) const

- These functions search for the first character that is or is not also an element of the C-string *cstr* (starting at index *idx*).
- These functions return the index of that character when successful or *string*::npos if they fail.
- Note that *cstr* must not be a null pointer (NULL).

size_type *string*::**find_first_of** (const *char** chars, size_type *idx*,
                                 size_type *chars_len*) const

size_type *string*::**find_first_not_of** (const *char** chars, size_type *idx*,
                                 size_type *chars_len*) const

- These functions search for the first character that is or is not also an element of the *chars_len* characters of the character array *chars* (starting at index *idx*).
- These functions return the index of that character when successful or *string*::npos if they fail.
- Note that *chars* must have at least *chars_len* characters. The characters may have arbitrary values. Thus, '\0' has no special meaning.

size_type *string*::**find_first_of** (*char* c) const

size_type *string*::**find_first_of** (*char* c, size_type *idx*) const

size_type *string*::**find_first_not_of** (*char* c) const

size_type *string*::**find_first_not_of** (*char* c, size_type *idx*) const

- These functions search for the first character that has or does not have the value *c* (starting at index *idx*).
- These functions return the index of that character when successful or *string*::npos if they fail.

Find Last of Different Characters

```
size_type string::find_last_of (const string& str) const
size_type string::find_last_of (const string& str, size_type idx) const
size_type string::find_last_not_of (const string& str) const
size_type string::find_last_not_of (const string& str, size_type idx) const
```

- These functions search for the last character that is or is not also an element of the string *str* (starting at index *idx*).
- These functions return the index of that character or substring when successful or *string*::npos if they fail.

```
size_type string::find_last_of (const char* cstr) const
size_type string::find_last_of (const char* cstr, size_type idx) const
size_type string::find_last_not_of (const char* cstr) const
size_type string::find_last_not_of (const char* cstr, size_type idx) const
```

- These functions search for the last character that is or is not also an element of the C-string *cstr* (starting at index *idx*).
- These functions return the index of that character when successful or *string*::npos if they fail.
- Note that *cstr* must not be a null pointer (NULL).

```
size_type string::find_last_of (const char* chars, size_type idx,
                                size_type chars_len) const
size_type string::find_last_not_of (const char* chars, size_type idx,
                                    size_type chars_len) const
```

- These functions search for the last character that is or is not also an element of the *chars_len* characters of the character array *chars* (starting at index *idx*).
- These functions return the index of that character when successful or *string*::npos if they fail.
- Note that *chars* must have at least *chars_len* characters. The characters may have arbitrary values. Thus, '\0' has no special meaning.

```
size_type string::find_last_of (char c) const
size_type string::find_last_of (char c, size_type idx) const
size_type string::find_last_not_of (char c) const
size_type string::find_last_not_of (char c, size_type idx) const
```

- These functions search for the last character that has or does not have the value *c* (starting at index *idx*).
- These functions return the index of that character when successful or *string*::npos if they fail.

11.3.9   Substrings and String Concatenation

string **string**::**substr** () const

string **string**::**substr** (size_type *idx*) const

string **string**::**substr** (size_type *idx*, size_type *len*) const

- All forms return a substring of, at most, *len* characters of the string *this starting with index *idx*.
- If *len* is missing, all remaining characters are used.
- If *idx* and *len* are missing, a copy of the string is returned.
- All forms throw out_of_range if *idx* > size().

string **operator +** (const *string*& *str1*, const *string*& *str2*)

string **operator +** (const *string*& *str*, const *char** *cstr*)

string **operator +** (const *char** *cstr*, const *string*& *str*)

string **operator +** (const *string*& *str*, *char c*)

string **operator +** (*char c*, const *string*& *str*)

- All forms concatenate all characters of both operands and return the sum string.
- The operands may be any of the following:
  - A string
  - A C-string
  - A single character
- All forms throw length_error if the resulting size exceeds the maximum number of characters.

11.3.10   Input/Output Functions

ostream& **operator <<** (*ostream*& *strm*, const *string*& *str*)

- Writes the characters of *str* to the stream *strm*.
- If *strm*.width() is greater than 0, at least width() characters are written and width() is set to 0.
- *ostream* is the ostream type basic_ostream<*char*> according to the character type (see Section 13.2.1, page 588).

istream& **operator >>** (*istream*& *strm*, *string*& *str*)

- Reads the characters of the next word from *strm* into the string *str*.
- If the skipws flag is set for *strm*, leading whitespaces are ignored.

- Characters are extracted until any of the following happens:
  - *strm*.width() is greater than 0 and width() characters are stored
  - *strm*.good() is false (which might cause an appropriate exception)
  - isspace(*c*,*strm*.getloc()) is true for the next character *c*
  - *str*.max_size() characters are stored
- The internal memory is reallocated accordingly.
- *istream* is the istream type basic_istream<*char*> according to the character type (see Section 13.2.1, page 588).

istream& **getline** (*istream*& *strm*, *string*& *str*)

istream& **getline** (*istream*& *strm*, *string*& *str*, *char delim*)

- Read the characters of the next line from *strm* into the string *str*.
- All characters (including leading whitespaces) are extracted until any of the following happens:
  - *strm*.good() is false (which might cause an appropriate exception)
  - *delim* or *strm*.widen('\n') is extracted
  - *str*.max_size() characters are stored
- The line delimiter is extracted but not appended.
- The internal memory is reallocated accordingly.
- *istream* is the istream type basic_istream<*char*> according to the character type (see Section 13.2.1, page 588).

11.3.11   Generating Iterators

iterator *string*::**begin** ()

const_iterator *string*::**begin** () const

- Both forms return a random access iterator for the beginning of the string (the position of the first character).
- If the string is empty, the call is equivalent to end().

iterator *string*::**end** ()

const_iterator *string*::**end** () const

- Both forms return a random access iterator for the end of the string (the position after the last character).
- Note that the character at the end is not defined. Thus, *∗s*.end() results in undefined behavior.
- If the string is empty, the call is equivalent to begin().

```
reverse_iterator  string::rbegin ()
```
```
const_reverse_iterator  string::rbegin () const
```

- Both forms return a random access iterator for the beginning of a reverse iteration over the string (the position of the last character).
- If the string is empty, the call is equivalent to `rend()`.
- For details about reverse iterators see Section 7.4.1, page 264.

```
reverse_iterator  string::rend ()
```
```
const_reverse_iterator  string::rend () const
```

- Both forms return a random access iterator for the end of the reverse iteration over the string (the position before the first character).
- Note that the character at the reverse end is not defined. Thus, `*s.rend()` results in undefined behavior.
- If the string is empty, the call is equivalent to `rbegin()`.
- For details about reverse iterators see Section 7.4.1, page 264.

11.3.12 Allocator Support

Strings provide the usual members of classes with allocator support.

string::**allocator_type**
- The type of the allocator.
- Third template parameter of class `basic_string<>`.
- For type `string`, it is equivalent to `allocator<char>`.

allocator_type *string*::**get_allocator** () const
- Returns the memory model of the string.

Strings also provide all constructors with optional allocator arguments. The following are all of the string constructors, including their optional allocator arguments, according to the standard:

```
namespace std {
    template<class charT,
             class traits = char_traits<charT>,
             class Allocator = allocator<charT> >
    class basic_string {
      public:
        // default constructor
        explicit basic_string(const Allocator& a = Allocator());

        // copy constructor and substrings
```

```
        basic_string(const basic_string& str,
                     size_type str_idx = 0,
                     size_type str_num = npos);
        basic_string(const basic_string& str,
                     size_type str_idx, size_type str_num,
                     const Allocator&);

        // constructor for C-strings
        basic_string(const charT* cstr,
                     const Allocator& a = Allocator());

        // constructor for character arrays
        basic_string(const charT* chars, size_type chars_len,
                     const Allocator& a = Allocator());

        // constructor for num occurrences of a character
        basic_string(size_type num, charT c,
                     const Allocator& a = Allocator());

        // constructor for a range of characters
        template<class InputIterator>
        basic_string(InputIterator beg, InputIterator end,
                     const Allocator& a = Allocator());
        ...
    };
}
```

These constructors behave as described in Section 11.3.2, page 508, with the additional ability that you can pass your own memory model object. If the string is initialized by another string, the allocator also gets copied.[10] See Chapter 15 for more details about allocators.

---

[10] The original standard states that the default allocator is used when a string gets copied. However, this does not make much sense, so this is the proposed resolution to fix this behavior.

Chapter 12
Numerics

This chapter describes the numeric components of the C++ standard library. In particular, it presents the class for complex numbers, the classes for value arrays, and the global numeric functions, which are inherited from the C library.

Two other numeric components in the C++ standard library are described in other parts of this book:

1. The STL contains some numeric algorithms that are described in Section 9.11, page 425.
2. For all fundamental numeric data types, the implementation-specific aspects of their representation are described by `numeric_limits`, as described in Section 4.3, page 59.

12.1   Complex Numbers

The C++ standard library provides the template class `complex<>` to operate on complex numbers. Just to remind you: Complex numbers are numbers that have two parts — real and imaginary. The imaginary part has the property that its square is a negative number. In other words, the imaginary part of a complex number is the factor i, which is the square root of minus 1.

The class `complex` is declared in the header file `<complex>`:

```
#include <complex>
```

In `<complex>`, the class `complex` is defined as follows:

```
namespace std {
    template <class T>
    class complex;
}
```

The template parameter T is used as the scalar type of both the real and the imaginary parts of the complex number.

In addition, the C++ standard library provides three specializations for `float`, `double`, and `long double`:

```
namespace std {
    template<> class complex<float>;
    template<> class complex<double>;
    template<> class complex<long double>;
}
```

These types are provided to allow certain optimizations and some safer conversions from one complex type to the other.

12.1.1   Examples Using Class Complex

The following program demonstrates some of the abilities of class `complex` to create complex numbers, print different representations of complex numbers, and perform some common operations on complex numbers.

```
// num/complex1.cpp

#include <iostream>
#include <complex>
using namespace std;

int main()
{
    /* complex number with real and imaginary parts
     * - real part: 4.0
     * - imaginary part: 3.0
     */
    complex<double> c1(4.0,3.0);

    /* create complex number from polar coordinates
     * - magnitude: 5.0
     * - phase angle: 0.75
     */
    complex<float> c2(polar(5.0,0.75));

    // print complex numbers with real and imaginary parts
    cout << "c1: " << c1 << endl;
    cout << "c2: " << c2 << endl;
```

```
// print complex numbers as polar coordinates
cout << "c1: magnitude: " << abs(c1)
     << " (squared magnitude: " << norm(c1) << ") "
     <<    " phase angle: " << arg(c1) << endl;
cout << "c2: magnitude: " << abs(c2)
     << " (squared magnitude: " << norm(c2) << ") "
     <<    " phase angle: " << arg(c2) << endl;

// print complex conjugates
cout << "c1 conjugated:  " << conj(c1) << endl;
cout << "c2 conjugated:  " << conj(c2) << endl;

// print result of a computation
cout << "4.4 + c1 * 1.8: " << 4.4 + c1 * 1.8 << endl;

/* print sum of c1 and c2:
 * - note: different types
 */
cout << "c1 + c2:             "
     << c1 + complex<double>(c2.real(),c2.imag()) << endl;

// add square root of c1 to c1 and print the result
cout << "c1 += sqrt(c1): " << (c1 += sqrt(c1)) << endl;
}
```

The program might have the following output (the exact output depends on the implementation specific properties of the type double):

```
c1: (4,3)
c2: (3.65844,3.40819)
c1: magnitude: 5 (squared magnitude: 25)  phase angle: 0.643501
c2: magnitude: 5 (squared magnitude: 25)  phase angle: 0.75
c1 conjugated:  (4,-3)
c2 conjugated:  (3.65844,-3.40819)
4.4 + c1 * 1.8: (11.6,5.4)
c1 + c2:        (7.65844,6.40819)
c1 += sqrt(c1): (6.12132,3.70711)
```

A second example contains a loop that reads two complex numbers and processes the first complex number raised to the power of the second complex number:

```cpp
// num/complex2.cpp

#include <iostream>
#include <complex>
#include <cstdlib>
#include <limits>
using namespace std;

int main()
{
    complex<long double> c1, c2;

    while (cin.peek() != EOF) {

        // read first complex number
        cout << "complex number c1: ";
        cin >> c1;
        if (!cin) {
            cerr << "input error" << endl;
            return EXIT_FAILURE;
        }

        // read second complex number
        cout << "complex number c2: ";
        cin >> c2;
        if (!cin) {
            cerr << "input error" << endl;
            return EXIT_FAILURE;
        }

        if (c1 == c2) {
            cout << "c1 and c2 are equal !" << endl;
        }

        cout << "c1 raised to the c2: " << pow(c1,c2)
             << endl << endl;

        // skip rest of line
        cin.ignore(numeric_limits<int>::max(),'\n');
    }
}
```

Table 12.1 shows some possible input and output of this program.

c1	c2	Output
2	2	c1 raised to c2: (4,0)
(16)	0.5	c1 raised to c2: (4,0)
(8,0)	0.333333333	c1 raised to c2: (2,0)
0.99	(5)	c1 raised to c2: (0.95099,0)
(0,2)	2	c1 raised to c2: (-4,4.89843e-16)
(1.7,0.3)	0	c1 raised to c2: (1,0)
(3,4)	(-4,3)	c1 raised to c2: (4.32424e-05,8.91396e-05)
(1.7,0.3)	(4.3,2.8)	c1 raised to c2: (-4.17622,4.86871)

Table 12.1. Possible I/O of `complex2` *Example*

Note that you can input a complex number by passing only the real part as a single value with or without parentheses or by passing the real and imaginary parts separated by a comma in parentheses.

12.1.2   Operations for Complex Numbers

The template class `complex` provides the operations described in the following subsections.

Create, Copy, and Assign Operations

Table 12.2 lists the constructors and assignment operations for `complex`. The constructors provide the ability to pass the initial values of the real and the imaginary parts. If they are not passed, they are initialized by the default constructor of the value type.

The assignment operators are the only way to modify the value of an existing complex number. The computed assignment operators +=, -=, *=, and /= add, subtract, multiply, and divide the value of the second operand to, from, by, and into the first operand.

The auxiliary `polar()` function provides the ability to create a complex number that is initialized by polar coordinates (magnitude and phase angle in radians):

```
// create a complex number initialized from polar coordinates
std::complex<double> c2(std::polar(4.2,0.75));
```

A problem exists when you have an implicit type conversion during the creation. For example, this notation works:

```
std::complex<float> c2(std::polar(4.2,0.75));     // OK
```

However, the following notation with the equal sign does not:

```
std::complex<float> c2 = std::polar(4.2,0.75);     // ERROR
```

Expression	Effect
complex c	Creates a complex number with 0 as the real part and 0 as the imaginary part ($0 + 0i$)
complex c(1.3)	Creates a complex number with 1.3 as the real part and 0 as the imaginary part ($1.3 + 0i$)
complex c(1.3,4.2)	Creates a complex number with 1.3 as the real part and 4.2 as the imaginary part ($1.3 + 4.2i$)
complex c1(c2)	Creates c1 as a copy of c2
polar(4.2)	Creates a temporary complex number from polar coordinates (4.2 as magnitude rho and 0 as phase angle theta)
polar(4.2,0.75)	Creates a temporary complex number from polar coordinates (4.2 as magnitude rho and 0.75 as phase angle theta)
conj(c)	Creates a temporary complex number that is the conjugated complex number of c (the complex number with the negated imaginary part)
c1 = c2	Assigns the values of c2 to c1
c1 += c2	Adds the value of c2 to c1
c1 -= c2	Subtracts the value of c2 from c1
c1 *= c2	Multiplies the value of c2 by c1
c1 /= c2	Divides the value of c2 into c1

Table 12.2. Constructors and Assignment Operations of Class `complex<>`

This problem is discussed in the next subsection.

The auxiliary `conj()` function provides the ability to create a complex number that is initialized by the conjugated complex value of another complex number (a conjugated complex value is the value with a negated imaginary part):

```
std::complex<double> c1(1.1,5.5);
std::complex<double> c2(conj(c1));    // initialize c2 with
                                      // complex<double>(1.1,-5.5)
```

Implicit Type Conversions

The constructors of the specializations for `float`, `double`, and `long double` are designed in such a way that safe conversions such as `complex<float>` to `complex<double>` are allowed to be implicit, but less safe conversions such as `complex<long double>` to `complex<double>` must be explicit (see page 542 for the declarations in detail):

```
std::complex<float> cf;
std::complex<double> cd;
std::complex<long double> cld;
...
std::complex<double> cd1 = cf;     // OK: safe conversion
std::complex<double> cd2 = cld;    // ERROR: no implicit conversion
std::complex<double> cd3(cld);     // OK: explicit conversion
```

In addition, there are no constructors from any other complex type defined. In particular, you can't convert a `complex` with an integral value type into a complex with value type `float`, `double`, or `long double`. However, you can convert the values by passing the real and imaginary parts as separate arguments:

```
std::complex<double> cd;
std::complex<int> ci;
...
std::complex<double> cd4 = ci;     // ERROR: no implicit conversion
std::complex<double> cd5(ci);      // ERROR: no explicit conversion
std::complex<double> cd6(ci.real(),ci.imag());   // OK
```

Unfortunately, the assignment operators allow less safe conversions. They are provided as template functions for all types. So, you can assign any complex type as long as the value types are convertible[1]:

```
std::complex<double> cd;
std::complex<long double> cld;
std::complex<int> ci;
...
cd = ci;     // OK
cd = cld;    // OK
```

This problem also relates to `polar()` and `conj()`. For example, the following notation works fine:

```
std::complex<float> c2(std::polar(4.2,0.75));     // OK
```

But, the notation with the equal sign does not:

```
std::complex<float> c2 = std::polar(4.2,0.75);    // ERROR
```

The reason for this is that the expression

```
std::polar(4.2,0.75)
```

---

[1] The fact that constructors for the complex specializations allow only safe implicit conversions, whereas the assignment operations allow any implicit conversion, is probably a mistake in the standard.

creates a temporary complex<double> and the implicit conversion from complex<double> to complex<float> is not defined.[2]

Value Access

Table 12.3 shows the different functions provided to access the attributes of complex numbers.

Expression	Effect
c.real()	Returns the value of the real part (as a member function)
real(c)	Returns the value of the real part (as a global function)
c.imag()	Returns the value of the imaginary part (as a member function)
imag(c)	Returns the value of the imaginary part (as a global function)
abs(c)	Returns the absolute value of c ($\sqrt{\text{c.real}()^2 + \text{c.imag}()^2}$)
norm(c)	Returns the squared absolute value of c ($\text{c.real}()^2 + \text{c.imag}()^2$)
arg(c)	Returns the angle of the polar representation of c (φ) (equivalent to atan2(c.imag(),c.real()) as phase angle)

Table 12.3. Operations for Value Access of Class complex<>

Note that real() and imag() provide only read access to the real and the imaginary parts. To change only the real part or only the imaginary part you must assign a new complex number. For example, the following statement sets the imaginary part of c to 3.7:

```
std::complex<double> c;
...
c = std::complex<double>(c.real(),3.7);
```

---

[2] There is a minor difference between

```
    X x;
    Y y(x); // explicit conversion
```
and
```
    X x;
    Y y = x; // implicit conversion
```
The former creates a new object of type Y by using an explicit conversion from type X, whereas the latter creates a new object of type Y by using an implicit conversion.

Comparison Operations

To compare complex numbers, you can only check for equality (Table 12.4). The operators == and
!= are defined as global functions so that one of the operands may be a scalar value. If you use a
scalar value as the operand it is interpreted as the real part, with the imaginary part having the default
value of its type (which is usually 0).

Expression	Effect
c1 == c2	Returns whether c1 is equal to c2 (c1.real()==c2.real() && c1.imag()==c2.imag())
c == 1.7	Returns whether c is equal to 1.7 (c.real()==1.7 && c.imag()==0.0)
1.7 == c	Returns whether c is equal to 1.7 (c.real()==1.7 && c.imag()==0.0)
c1 != c2	Returns whether c1 differs from c2 (c1.real()!=c2.real() || c1.imag()!=c2.imag())
c != 1.7	Returns whether c differs from 1.7 (c.real()!=1.7 || c.imag()!=0.0)
1.7 != c	Returns whether c differs from 1.7 (c.real()!=1.7 || c.imag()!=0.0)

Table 12.4. Comparison Operations of Class complex<>

Other comparison operations, such as operator <, are not defined. Although it is not impossible
to define an ordering for complex values, such orderings are neither very intuitive nor very useful.
Note, for example, that the magnitude of complex numbers by itself is not a good basis to order
complex values because two complex values can be very different and yet have identical magnitude
(1 and −1 are two such numbers). An add hoc criterion can be added to create a valid ordering. For
example, given two complex values c1 and c2, you could deem c1 < c2 when |c1| < |c2| or,
if both magnitudes are equal, when arg(c1) < arg(c2). However, such a criterion invariably has
little or no mathematical meaning.[3]

As a consequence, you can't use complex as the element type of an associative container (provided you use no user-defined sorting criterion). This is because associative containers use the
function object less<>, which calls operator <, to be able to sort the elements (see Section 5.10.1,
page 134).

By implementing a user-defined operator < you could sort complex numbers and use them in
associative containers. Note that you should be very careful not to pollute the standard namespace.
For example:

---

[3] Thanks to David Vandevoorde for pointing this out.

```
template <class T>
bool operator< (const std::complex<T>& c1,
                const std::complex<T>& c2)
{
    return std::abs(c1)<std::abs(c2) ||
           (std::abs(c1)==std::abs(c2) &&
            std::arg(c1)<std::arg(c2));
}
```

Arithmetic Operations

Complex numbers provide the four basic arithmetic operations and the negative and positive signs
(Table 12.5).

Expression	Effect
c1 + c2	Returns the sum of c1 and c2
c + 1.7	Returns the sum of c and 1.7
1.7 + c	Returns the sum of 1.7 and c
c1 - c2	Returns the difference between c1 and c2
c - 1.7	Returns the difference between c and 1.7
1.7 - c	Returns the difference between 1.7 and c
c1 * c2	Returns the product of c1 and c2
c * 1.7	Returns the product of c and 1.7
1.7 * c	Returns the product of 1.7 and c
c1 / c2	Returns the quotient of c1 and c2
c / 1.7	Returns the quotient of c and 1.7
1.7 / c	Returns the quotient of 1.7 and c
- c	Returns the negated value of c
+ c	Returns c
c1 += c2	Equivalent to c1 = c1 + c2
c1 -= c2	Equivalent to c1 = c1 - c2
c1 *= c2	Equivalent to c1 = c1 * c2
c1 /= c2	Equivalent to c1 = c1 / c2

Table 12.5. Arithmetic Operations of Class `complex<>`

Input/Output Operations

Class `complex` provides the common I/O operators `<<` and `>>` (Table 12.6).

Expression	Effect
`strm << c`	Writes the complex number c to the output stream `strm`
`strm >> c`	Reads the complex number c from the input stream `strm`

Table 12.6. I/O Operations of Class `complex<>`

The output operator writes the complex number with respect to the current stream state with the format:

(*realpart*,*imagpart*)

In particular, the output operator is defined as equivalent to the following implementation:

```
template <class T, class charT, class traits>
std::basic_ostream<charT,traits>&
operator<< (std::basic_ostream<charT,traits>& strm,
            const std::complex<T>& c)
{
    // temporary value string to do the output with one argument
    std::basic_ostringstream<charT,traits> s;

    s.flags(strm.flags());          // copy stream flags
    s.imbue(strm.getloc());         // copy stream locale
    s.precision(strm.precision());  // copy stream precision

    // prepare the value string
    s << '(' << c.real() << ',' << c.imag() << ')';

    // write the value string
    strm << s.str();

    return strm;
}
```

The input operator provides the ability to read a complex number with one of the following formats:

(*realpart*,*imagpart*)

(*realpart*)

realpart

If none of the formats fits according to the next characters in the input stream, the `ios::failbit` is set, which might throw a corresponding exception (see Section 13.4.4, page 602).

Unfortunately, you can't specify the separator of complex numbers between the real and the imaginary parts. So if you have a comma as a "decimal point" (as is the case in German), I/O looks really strange. For example, a complex number with `4.6` as the real part and `2.7` as the imaginary part would be written as

    (4,6,2,7)

See page 532 for an example of how to use the I/O operations.

Transcendental Functions

Table 12.7 lists the transcendental functions (trigonometric, exponential, and so on) for `complex`.

Expression	Effect
`pow(c,3)`	Complex power c^3
`pow(c,1.7)`	Complex power $c^{1.7}$
`pow(c1,c2)`	Complex power $c1^{c2}$
`pow(1.7,c)`	Complex power 1.7^c
`exp(c)`	Base e exponential of c (e^c)
`sqrt(c)`	Square root of c ($\sqrt{c}$)
`log(c)`	Complex natural logarithm of c with base e ($\ln c$)
`log10(c)`	Complex common logarithm of c with base 10 ($\lg c$)
`sin(c)`	Sine of c ($\sin c$)
`cos(c)`	Cosine of c ($\cos c$)
`tan(c)`	Tangent of c ($\tan c$)
`sinh(c)`	Hyperbolic sine of c ($\sinh c$)
`cosh(c)`	Hyperbolic cosine of c ($\cosh c$)
`tanh(c)`	Hyperbolic tangent of c ($\tanh c$)

Table 12.7. Transcendental Functions of Class `complex<>`

12.1.3   Class `complex<>` in Detail

This subsection describes all operations of class `complex<>` in detail. In the following definitions, T is the template parameter of class `complex<>`, which is the type of the real and the imaginary parts of the `complex` value.

Type Definitions

complex :: **value_type**

- The type of the real and the imaginary parts.

Create, Copy, and Assign Operations

complex :: **complex** ()

- The default constructor.
- Creates a complex value in which the real and the imaginary parts are initialized by an explicit call of their default constructor. Thus, for fundamental types, the initial value of the real and the imaginary parts is 0 (see page 14 for the default value of fundamental types).

complex :: **complex** (const T& *re*)

- Creates a complex value in which *re* is the value of the real part, and the imaginary part is initialized by an explicit call of its default constructor (0 for fundamental data types).
- This constructor also defines an automatic type conversion from T to `complex`.

complex :: **complex** (const T& *re*, const T& *im*)

- Creates a complex value, with *re* as the real part and *im* as the imaginary part.

complex **polar** (const T& *rho*)
complex **polar** (const T& *rho*, const T& *theta*)

- Both forms create and return the complex number that is initialized by polar coordinates.
- *rho* is the magnitude.
- *theta* is the phase angle in radians (default: 0).

complex **conj** (const *complex*& *cmplx*)

- Creates and returns the complex number that is initialized by the conjugated complex value (the value with the negated imaginary part) of *cmplx*.

complex :: **complex** (const *complex*& *cmplx*)

- The copy constructor.
- Creates a new complex as a copy of *cmplx*.

- Copies the real and imaginary parts.
- In general, this function is provided as both a nontemplate and a template function (see page 11 for an introduction to member templates). Thus, in general, automatic type conversions of the element type are provided.
- However, the specializations for `float`, `double`, and `long double` restrict copy constructors, so the less safe conversions from `double` and `long double` to `float`, as well as from `long double` to `double`, must be explicit and allow *no* other element type conversions:

```
namespace std {
    template<> class complex<float> {
      public:
        explicit complex(const complex<double>&);
        explicit complex(const complex<long double>&);
        // no other kinds of copy constructors

        ...
    };
    template<> class complex<double> {
      public:
        complex(const complex<float>&);
        explicit complex(const complex<long double>&);
        // no other kinds of copy constructors

        ...
    };
    template<> class complex<long double> {
      public:
        complex(const complex<float>&);
        complex(const complex<double>&);
        // no other kinds of copy constructors

        ...
    };
}
```

See page 534 for more information about the implications from this.

complex& ***complex***::**operator =** (const *complex& cmplx*)

- Assigns the value of complex *cmplx*.
- Returns `*this`.
- This function is provided as both a nontemplate and a template function (see page 11 for an introduction to member templates). Thus, automatic type conversions of the element type are provided. (This is also the case for the specializations that are provided by the C++ standard library.)

complex& ***complex***::**operator +=** (const *complex&* *cmplx*)

complex& ***complex***::**operator -=** (const *complex&* *cmplx*)

complex& ***complex***::**operator *=** (const *complex&* *cmplx*)

complex& ***complex***::**operator /=** (const *complex&* *cmplx*)

- These operations add, subtract, multiply, and divide the value of *cmplx* to, from, by, and into `*this` respectively and store the result in `*this`.
- They return `*this`.
- These operations are provided as both a nontemplate and a template function (see page 11 for an introduction to member templates). Thus, automatic type conversions of the element type are provided. (This is also the case for the specializations that are provided by the C++ standard library.)

Note that the assignment operators are the only functions that allow you to modify the value of an existing `complex`.

Element Access

T *complex*::**real** () const

T **real** (const *complex&* *cmplx*)

T *complex*::**imag** () const

T **imag** (const *complex&* *cmplx*)

- These functions return the real or imaginary part respectively.
- Note that the return value is not a reference. Thus, you can't use these functions to modify the real or the imaginary parts. To change only the real part or only the imaginary part you must assign a new complex number (see page 536).

T **abs** (const *complex&* *cmplx*)

- Returns the absolute value (magnitude) of *cmplx*.
- The absolute value is $\sqrt{cmplx.\texttt{real}()^2 + cmplx.\texttt{imag}()^2}$.

T **norm** (const *complex&* *cmplx*)

- Returns the squared absolute value (squared magnitude) of *cmplx*.
- The squared absolute value is $cmplx.\texttt{real}()^2 + cmplx.\texttt{imag}()^2$.

T **arg** (const *complex&* *cmplx*)

- Returns the angle of the polar representation (φ) of *cmplx* in radians.
- It is equivalent to `atan2(`*cmplx*`.imag(),`*cmplx*`.real())` as the phase angle.

Input/Output Operations

ostream& **operator** `<<` (*ostream&* *strm*, `const` *complex&* *cmplx*)

- Writes the value of *cmplx* to the stream *strm* in the format
     (*realpart*,*imagpart*)
- Returns *strm*.
- See page 539 for the exact behavior of this operation.

istream& **operator** `>>` (*istream&* *strm*, *complex&* *cmplx*)

- Reads a new value from *strm* into *cmplx*.
- Valid input formats are
     (*realpart*,*imagpart*)
     (*realpart*)
     realpart
- Returns *strm*.
- See page 539 for the exact behavior of this operation.

Operators

complex **operator** `+` (`const` *complex&* *cmplx*)

- The positive sign.
- Returns *cmplx*.

complex **operator** `-` (`const` *complex&* *cmplx*)

- The negative sign.
- Returns the value of *cmplx* with the negated real and the negated imaginary parts.

complex ***binary-op*** (`const` *complex&* *cmplx1*, `const` *complex&* *cmplx2*)
complex ***binary-op*** (`const` *complex&* *cmplx*, `const` T& *value*)
complex ***binary-op*** (`const` T& *value*, `const` *complex&* *cmplx*)

- All forms return a complex number with the result of ***binary-op***.
- ***binary-op*** may be any of the following:
     ```
     operator +
     operator -
     operator *
     operator /
     ```
- If a scalar value of the element type is passed, it is interpreted as the real part, with the imaginary part having the default value of its type (which is 0 for fundamental types).

bool ***comparison*** (const *complex&* *cmplx1*, const *complex&* *cmplx2*)

bool ***comparison*** (const *complex&* *cmplx*, const T& *value*)

bool ***comparison*** (const T& *value*, const *complex&* *cmplx*)

- Returns the result of the comparison of two complex numbers or the result of the comparison of a complex number with a scalar value.
- ***comparison*** may be any of the following:
  ```
  operator ==
  operator !=
  ```
- If a scalar value of the element type is passed, it is interpreted as the real part, with the imaginary part having the default value of its type (which is 0 for fundamental types).
- Note that no operators <, <=, >, and >= are provided.

Transcendental Functions

complex **pow** (const *complex&* *base*, int *exp*)

complex **pow** (const *complex&* *base*, const T& *exp*)

complex **pow** (const *complex&* *base*, const *complex&* *exp*)

complex **pow** (const T& *base*, const *complex&* *exp*)

- All forms return the complex power of *base* raised to the *exp*th power, defined as exp(*exp**log(*base*)).
- The branch cuts are along the negative real axis.
- The value returned for pow(0,0) is implementation defined.

complex **exp** (const *complex&* *cmplx*)

- Returns the complex base *e* exponential of *cmplx*.

complex **sqrt** (const *complex&* *cmplx*)

- Returns the complex square root of *cmplx* in the range of the right half plane.
- If the argument is a negative real number, the value returned lies on the positive imaginary axis.
- The branch cuts are along the negative real axis.

complex **log** (const *complex&* *cmplx*)

- Returns the complex natural base *e* logarithm of *cmplx*.
- When *cmplx* is a negative real number, imag(log(*cmplx*)) is pi.
- The branch cuts are along the negative real axis.

complex **log10** (const *complex&* *cmplx*)

- Returns the complex base 10 logarithm of *cmplx*.
- It is equivalent to log(*cmplx*)/log(10).
- The branch cuts are along the negative real axis.

complex **sin** (const *complex& cmplx*)

complex **cos** (const *complex& cmplx*)

complex **tan** (const *complex& cmplx*)

complex **sinh** (const *complex& cmplx*)

complex **cosh** (const *complex& cmplx*)

complex **tanh** (const *complex& cmplx*)

- These operations return the corresponding complex trigonometric operation on *cmplx*.

12.2   Valarrays

The C++ standard library provides the class `valarray` for the processing of arrays of numeric values. A valarray is a representation of the mathematical concept of a linear sequence of values. It has one dimension, but you can get the illusion of higher dimensionality by special techniques of computed indices and powerful subsetting capabilities. Therefore, a valarray can be used as a base both for vector and matrix operations as well as for the processing of mathematical systems of polynomial equations with good performance.

The valarray classes enable some tricky optimizations to get good performance for the processing of value arrays. However, it is not clear how important this component of the C++ standard library will be in the future because there are other interesting developments that perform even better. One of the most interesting examples is the Blitz system. If you are interested in numeric processing, you should look at it. For details, see `http://www.oonumerics.org/blitz/`.

The valarray classes were not designed very well. In fact, nobody tried to determine whether the final specification worked. This happened because nobody felt "responsible" for these classes. The people who introduced valarrays to the C++ standard library left the committee a long time before the standard was finished. For example, to use valarrays, you often need some inconvenient and time-consuming type conversions (see page 554).

12.2.1   Getting to Know Valarrays

Valarrays are one-dimensional arrays with elements numbered sequentially from zero. They provide the ability to do some numeric processing for all or a subset of the values in one or more value arrays. For example, you can process the statement

```
z = a*x*x + b*x + c
```

with a, b, c, x, and z being arrays that contain hundreds of numeric values. In doing this, you have the advantage of a simple notation. Also, the processing is done with good performance because the classes provide some optimizations that avoid the creation of temporary objects while processing the whole statement. In addition, special interfaces and auxiliary classes provide the ability to process only a certain subset of value arrays or to do some multidimensional processing. In this way, the valarray concept also helps to implement vector and matrix operations and classes.

The standard guarantees that valarrays are alias free. That is, any value of a nonconstant valarray is accessed through a unique path. Thus, operations on these values can get optimized better because the compiler does not have to take into account that the data could be accessed through another path.

Header File

Valarrays are declared in the header file `<valarray>`:

```
#include <valarray>
```

In particular, in `<valarray>` the following classes are declared:

```
namespace std {
    template<class T> class valarray;          // numeric array of type T

    class slice;                               // slice out of a valarray
    template<class T> class slice_array;

    class gslice;                              // a generalized slice
    template<class T> class gslice_array;

    template<class T> class mask_array;        // a masked valarray

    template<class T> class indirect_array;    // an indirected valarray
}
```

The classes have the following meanings:

- valarray is the core class that manages an array of numeric values.
- slice and gslice are provided to define a BLAS-like[4] slice as a subset of a valarray.
- slice_array, gslice_array, mask_array, and indirect_array are internal auxiliary classes that are used to store temporary values or data. You can't use them in your programming interface directly. They are created indirectly by certain valarray operations.

All classes are templatized for the type of the elements. In principle, the type could be any data type. However, according to the nature of valarrays it should be a numeric data type.

Creating Valarrays

When you create a valarray you usually pass the number of elements as a parameter:

```
std::valarray<int>   va1(10);        // valarray of ten ints with value 0
std::valarray<float> va2(5.7,10);    // valarray of ten floats with value 5.7
                                     // (note the order)
```

If you pass one argument, it is used as the size. The elements are initialized by the default constructor of their type. Elements of fundamental data types are initialized by zero (see Section 2.2.2, page 14, for a description of why fundamental data types may be initialized by a default constructor). If you pass a second value, the first is used as the initial value for the elements, whereas the second specifies the number of elements. Note that the order of passing two arguments to the constructor differs from that of all other classes of the C++ standard library. All STL container classes use the first numeric argument as the number of elements and the second argument as the initial value.

---

[4] The Basic Linear Algebra Subprograms (BLAS) library provides computational kernels for several of the fundamental linear algebra operations, such as matrix multiply, the solution of triangular systems, and simple vector operations.

You can also initialize a valarray with an ordinary array:

```
int array[] = { 3, 6, 18, 3, 22 };
```

```
// initialize valarray by elements of an ordinary array
std::valarray<int> va3(array,sizeof(array)/sizeof(array[0]));
```

```
// initialize by the second to the fourth element
std::valarray<int> va4(array+1,3);
```

The valarray creates copies of the passed values. Thus, you can pass temporary data for initialization.

Valarray Operations

For valarrays, the subscript operator is defined to access the element of a valarray. As usual, the first element has the index 0:

```
va[0] = 3 * va[1] + va[2];
```

In addition, all ordinary numeric operators are defined (addition, subtraction, multiplication, modulo, negation, bit operators, comparison operators, and logical operators, as well as all assignment operators). These operators are called for each element in the valarrays that is processed by the operation. Thus, the result of a valarray operation is a valarray that has the same number of elements as the operands and that contains the result of the elementwise computation. For example, the statement

```
va1 = va2 * va3;
```

is equivalent to

```
va1[0] = va2[0] * va3[0];
va1[1] = va2[1] * va3[1];
va1[2] = va2[2] * va3[2];
...
```

If the number of elements of the combined valarrays differs, the result is undefined.

Of course, the operations are available only if the element's type supports them. And the exact meaning of the operation depends on the meaning of the operation for the elements. Thus, all of these operations simply do the same for each element or pair of elements in the valarrays they process.

For binary operations, one of the operands may be a single value of the element's type. In this case, the single value is combined with each element of the valarray that is used as the other operand. For example, the statement

```
va1 = 4 * va2;
```

is equivalent to

```
va1[0] = 4 * va2[0];
va1[1] = 4 * va2[1];
va1[2] = 4 * va2[2];
...
```

Note that the type of the single value has to match exactly the element type of the valarray. Thus, the previous example works only if the element type is int. The following statement would fail:

```
std::valarray<double> va(20);
...
va = 4 * va;        // ERROR: type mismatch
```

The schema of binary operations also applies to comparison operators. Thus, operator == does *not* return a single Boolean value that shows whether both valarrays are equal. Instead, it returns a new valarray with the same number of elements of type bool, where each value is the result of the individual comparison. For example, in the following code

```
std::valarray<double> va1(10);
std::valarray<double> va2(10);
std::valarray<bool> vab(10);
...
vab = (va1 == va2);
```

the last statement is equivalent to

```
vab[0] = (va1[0] == va2[0]);
vab[1] = (va1[1] == va2[1]);
vab[2] = (va1[2] == va2[2]);
...
vab[9] = (va1[9] == va2[9]);
```

For this reason, you can't sort valarrays by using operator <, and you can't use them as elements in STL containers if the test for equality is performed with operator == (see Section 5.10.1, page 134, for the requirements of elements of STL containers).

The following program demonstrates a simple use of valarrays:

```
// num/val1.cpp

#include <iostream>
#include <valarray>
using namespace std;

// print valarray
template <class T>
void printValarray (const valarray<T>& va)
{
    for (int i=0; i<va.size(); i++) {
        cout << va[i] << ' ';
    }
    cout << endl;
}
```

```
int main()
{
    // define two valarrays with ten elements
    valarray<double> va1(10), va2(10);

    // assign values 0.0, 1.1, up to 9.9 to the first valarray
    for (int i=0; i<10; i++) {
        va1[i] = i * 1.1;
    }

    // assign -1 to all elements of the second valarray
    va2 = -1;

    // print both valarrays
    printValarray(va1);
    printValarray(va2);

    // print minimum, maximum, and sum of the first valarray
    cout << "min(): " << va1.min() << endl;
    cout << "max(): " << va1.max() << endl;
    cout << "sum(): " << va1.sum() << endl;

    // assign values of the first to the second valarray
    va2 = va1;

    // remove all elements of the first valarray
    va1.resize(0);

    // print both valarrays again
    printValarray(va1);
    printValarray(va2);
}
```

The program has the following output:

```
0 1.1 2.2 3.3 4.4 5.5 6.6 7.7 8.8 9.9
-1 -1 -1 -1 -1 -1 -1 -1 -1 -1
min(): 0
max(): 9.9
sum(): 49.5

0 1.1 2.2 3.3 4.4 5.5 6.6 7.7 8.8 9.9
```

Transcendental Functions

The transcendental operations (trigonometric and exponential) are defined as equivalent to the numeric operators. The operations are performed with all elements in the valarrays, and for binary operations, one of the operands may be a single value, which is used as one operand, with all elements of the valarrays as the other operand.

All of these operations are defined as global functions instead of member functions. This is to provide automatic type conversion for subsets of valarrays for both operands (subsets of valarrays are covered in Section 12.2.2, page 553).

Here is a second example of the use of valarrays. It demonstrates the use of transcendental operations:

```
// num/val2.cpp

#include <iostream>
#include <valarray>
using namespace std;

// print valarray
template <class T>
void printValarray (const valarray<T>& va)
{
    for (int i=0; i<va.size(); i++) {
        cout << va[i] << ' ';
    }
    cout << endl;
}

int main()
{
    // create and initialize valarray with nine elements
    valarray<double> va(9);
    for (int i=0; i<va.size(); i++) {
        va[i] = i * 1.1;
    }

    // print valarray
    printValarray(va);

    // double values in the valarray
    va *= 2.0;
```

```
// print valarray again
printValarray(va);

// create second valarray initialized by the values of the first plus 10
valarray<double> vb(va+10.0);

// print second valarray
printValarray(vb);

// create third valarray as a result of processing both existing valarrays
valarray<double> vc(9);
vc = sqrt(va) + vb/2.0 - 1.0;

// print third valarray
printValarray(vc);
}
```

The program has the following output:

```
0 1.1 2.2 3.3 4.4 5.5 6.6 7.7 8.8
0 2.2 4.4 6.6 8.8 11 13.2 15.4 17.6
10 12.2 14.4 16.6 18.8 21 23.2 25.4 27.6
4 6.58324 8.29762 9.86905 11.3665 12.8166 14.2332 15.6243 16.9952
```

12.2.2   Valarray Subsets

The subscript operator [] is overloaded for special auxiliary objects of valarrays. These auxiliary objects define subsets of valarrays in different ways. In doing this, they provide an elegant way to operate on certain subsets of valarrays (with both read and write access).

The subset of a valarray is defined by using a certain subset definition as the index. For example:

```
va[std::slice(2,4,3)]    // four elements with distance 3 starting from index 2
va[va>7]                 // all elements with a value greater than 7
```

If a subset definition such as std::slice(2,4,3) or va>7 is used with a constant valarray, the expression returns a new valarray with the corresponding elements. However, if such a subset definition is used with a nonconstant valarray, the expression returns a temporary object of a special auxiliary valarray class. This temporary object does not contain the subset values, only the definition of the subset. Thus, the evaluation of expressions is deferred until the values are needed to compute a final result.

This mechanism is called *lazy evaluation*. It has the advantage that no temporary values for expressions are computed. This saves time and memory. In addition, the technique provides reference semantics. Thus, the subsets are logical sets of references to the original values. You can use these subsets as the destination (lvalue) of a statement. For example, you could assign one subset of a valarray the result of a multiplication of two other subsets of the same valarray (examples follow shortly).

However, because "temporaries" are avoided, some unexpected conditions might occur when elements in the destination subset are also used in a source subset. Therefore, any operation of valarrays is guaranteed to work only if the elements of the destination subset and the elements of all source subsets are distinct.

With smart definitions of subsets you can give valarrays the semantics of two or more dimensions. Thus, in a way, valarrays may be used as multidimensional arrays.

There are four ways to define subsets of valarrays:

1. Slices
2. General slices
3. Masked subsets
4. Indirect subsets

The following subsections discuss them and give examples.

Valarray Subset Problems

Before I start with the individual subsets, I have to mention a general problem. The handling of valarray subsets is not well designed. You can create subsets easily, but you can't combine them easily with other subsets. Unfortunately, you almost always need an explicit type conversion to `valarray`. This is because the C++ standard library does not specify that valarray subsets provide the same operations as valarrays.

For example, to multiply two subsets and assign the result to a third subset, you can't write the following:

```
// ERROR: conversions missing
va[std::slice(0,4,3)]
    = va[std::slice(1,4,3)] * va[std::slice(2,4,3)];
```

Instead, you have to code by using a new-style cast (see page 19)[5]:

```
va[std::slice(0,4,3)]
    = static_cast<std::valarray<double> >(va[std::slice(1,4,3)]) *
      static_cast<std::valarray<double> >(va[std::slice(2,4,3)]);
```

or by using an old-style cast:

---

[5] Note that you have to put a space between the two ">" characters. ">>" would be parsed as shift operator, which would result in a syntax error.

```
va[std::slice(0,4,3)]
    = std::valarray<double>(va[std::slice(1,4,3)]) *
        std::valarray<double>(va[std::slice(2,4,3)]);
```

This is tedious and error prone. Even worse, without good optimization it may cost performance because each cast creates a temporary object, which could be avoided without the cast.

To make the handling a bit more convenient, you can use the following template function:

```
/* template to convert valarray subset into valarray
 */
template <class T>
inline
std::valarray<typename T::value_type> VA (const T& valarray_subset)
{
    return std::valarray<typename T::value_type>(valarray_subset);
}
```

By using this template, you could write

```
va[std::slice(0,4,3)] = VA(va[std::slice(1,4,3)]) *
                        VA(va[std::slice(2,4,3)]);     // OK
```

However, the performance penalty remains.

If you use a certain element type you could also use a simple type definition:

```
typedef valarray<double> VAD;
```

By using this type definition you could also write

```
va[std::slice(0,4,3)] = VAD(va[std::slice(1,4,3)]) *
                        VAD(va[std::slice(2,4,3)]);    // OK
```

provided the elements of va have type double.

Slices

A slice defines a set of indices that has three properties:

1. The starting index
2. The number of elements (size)
3. The distance between elements (stride)

You can pass these three properties exactly in the same order as parameters to the constructor of class slice. For example, the following expression specifies four elements, starting with index 2 with distance 3:

```
std::slice(2,4,3)
```

In other words, the expression specifies the following set of indices:

```
2   5   8   11
```

The stride may be negative. For example, the expression

```
std::slice(9,5,-2)
```

specifies the following indices:

```
9   7   5   3   1
```

To define the subset of a valarray, you simply use a slice as an argument of the subscript operator. For example, the following expression specifies the subset of the valarray `va` that contains the elements with the indices 2, 5, 8, and 11:

```
va[std::slice(2,4,3)]
```

It's up to the caller to ensure that all these indices are valid.

If the subset qualified by a slice is a subset of a constant valarray, the subset is a new valarray. If the valarray is nonconstant, the subset has reference semantics to the original valarray. The auxiliary class `slice_array` is provided for this:

```
namespace std {
    class slice;

    template <class T>
    class slice_array;

    template <class T>
    class valarray {
      public:
        // slice of a constant valarray returns a new valarray
        valarray<T> operator[] (slice) const;

        // slice of a variable valarray returns a slice_array
        slice_array<T> operator[] (slice);

        ...
    };
}
```

For `slice_arrays`, the following operations are defined:

- Assign a single value to all elements.
- Assign another valarray (or valarray subset).
- Call any computed assignment operation, such as operators `+=` and `*=`.

For any other operation you have to convert the subset to a valarray (see page 554). Note that the class `slice_array<>` is intended purely as an internal helper class for slices, and it should be transparent to the user. Thus, all constructors and the assignment operator of class `slice_array<>` are private.

For example, the statement

```
va[std::slice(2,4,3)] = 2;
```

assigns 2 to the third, sixth, ninth, and twelfth elements of the valarray va. It is equivalent to the following statements:

```
va[2]  = 2;
va[5]  = 2;
va[8]  = 2;
va[11] = 2;
```

As another example, the following statement squares the values of the elements with index 2, 5, 8, and 11:

```
va[std::slice(2,4,3)]
    *= std::valarray<double>(va[std::slice(2,4,3)]);
```

As mentioned on page 554, you can't write

```
va[std::slice(2,4,3)] *= va[std::slice(2,4,3)];          // ERROR
```

But using the VA() template function mentioned on page 555, you can write

```
va[std::slice(2,4,3)] *= VA(va[std::slice(2,4,3)]);      // OK
```

By passing different slices of the same valarray you can combine different subsets and store the result in another subset of the valarray. For example, the statement

```
va[std::slice(0,4,3)] = VA(va[std::slice(1,4,3)]) *
                        VA(va[std::slice(2,4,3)]);
```

is equivalent to the following:

```
va[0] = va[1]  * va[2];
va[3] = va[4]  * va[5];
va[6] = va[7]  * va[8];
va[9] = va[10] * va[11];
```

If you consider your valarray as a two-dimensional matrix, this example is nothing else but vector multiplication (Figure 12.1). However, note that the order of the individual assignments is not defined. Therefore, the behavior is undefined if the destination subset contains elements that are used in the source subsets.

In the same way, more complicated statements are possible. For example:

```
va[std::slice(0,100,3)]
    = std::pow(VA(va[std::slice(1,100,3)]) * 5.0,
               VA(va[std::slice(2,100,3)]));
```

Note again that a single value, such as 5.0 in this example, has to match the element type of the valarray exactly.

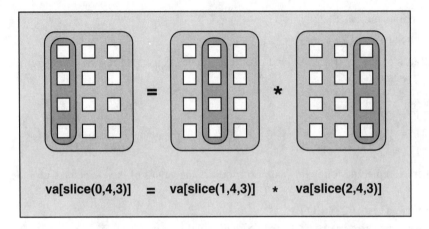

Figure 12.1. Vector Multiplication by Valarray Slices

The following program demonstrates a complete example of using valarray slices:

```
// num/slice1.cpp

#include <iostream>
#include <valarray>
using namespace std;

// print valarray line-by-line
template<class T>
void printValarray (const valarray<T>& va, int num)
{
    for (int i=0; i<va.size()/num; ++i) {
        for (int j=0; j<num; ++j) {
            cout << va[i*num+j] << ' ';
        }
        cout << endl;
    }
    cout << endl;
}

int main()
{
    /* valarray with 12 elements
     * - four rows
```

```
    * - three columns
    */
   valarray<double> va(12);

   // fill valarray with values
   for (int i=0; i<12; i++) {
       va[i] = i;
   }

   printValarray (va, 3);

   // first column = second column raised to the third column
   va[slice(0,4,3)] = pow (valarray<double>(va[slice(1,4,3)]),
                           valarray<double>(va[slice(2,4,3)]));

   printValarray (va, 3);

   // create valarray with three times the third element of va
   valarray<double> vb(va[slice(2,4,0)]);

   // multiply the third column by the elements of vb
   va[slice(2,4,3)] *= vb;

   printValarray (va, 3);

   // print the square root of the elements in the second row
   printValarray (sqrt(valarray<double>(va[slice(3,3,1)])), 3);

   // double the elements in the third row
   va[slice(2,4,3)] = valarray<double>(va[slice(2,4,3)]) * 2.0;

   printValarray (va, 3);
}
```

The program has the following output:

```
0  1  2
3  4  5
6  7  8
9  10  11
```

```
1 1 2
1024 4 5
5.7648e+006 7 8
1e+011 10 11

1 1 4
1024 4 10
5.7648e+006 7 16
1e+011 10 22

32 2 3.16228

1 1 8
1024 4 20
5.7648e+006 7 32
1e+011 10 44
```

General Slices

General slices, or *gslices*, are the general form of slices. Similar to slices, which provide the ability to handle a subset that is one dimension out of two dimensions, gslices allow the handling of subsets of multidimensional arrays. In principle, gslices have the same properties as slices:

- Starting index
- Number of elements (size)
- Distance between elements (stride)

Unlike slices, however, the number and distance of elements in a gslice are arrays of values. The number of elements in such an array is equivalent to the number of dimensions used. For example, if a gslice has the state

```
start:  2
size:   [ 4 ]
stride: [ 3 ]
```

then the gslice is equivalent to a slice because the array handles one dimension. Thus, it defines four elements with distance 3, starting with index 2:

```
2   5   8   11
```

However, if a gslice has the state

```
start:  2
size:   [  2 4 ]
stride: [ 10 3 ]
```

then the gslice handles two dimensions. The smallest index handles the highest dimension. Thus, this gslice specifies starting from index 2, twice with distance 10, four elements with distance 3:

```
 2    5    8   11
12   15   18   21
```

Here is an example of a slice with three dimensions:

```
start:   2
size:    [  3  2 4 ]
stride:  [ 30 10 3 ]
```

It specifies starting from index 2, three times with distance 30, twice with distance 10, four elements with distance 3:

```
 2    5    8   11
12   15   18   21

32   35   38   41
42   45   48   51

62   65   68   71
72   75   78   81
```

The ability to use arrays to define size and stride is the only difference between gslices and slices. Apart from this, gslices behave the same as slices:

1. To define a concrete subset of a valarray, you simply pass a gslice as the argument to the subscript operator of the valarray.

2. If the valarray is constant, the resulting expression is a new valarray.

3. If the valarray is nonconstant, the resulting expression is a `gslice_array` that represents the elements of the valarray with reference semantics:

```
namespace std {
    class gslice;

    template <class T>
    class gslice_array;

    template <class T>
    class valarray {
      public:
        // gslice of a constant valarray returns a new valarray
        valarray<T> operator[] (const gslice&) const;

        // gslice of a variable valarray returns a gslice_array
```

```
        gslice_array<T> operator[] (const gslice&);
        ...

    };
}
```

4. For `gslice_array`, the assignment and computed assignment operators are provided to modify the elements of the subset.

5. By using type conversions you can combine a gslice array with other valarrays and subsets of valarrays (see page 554).

The following program demonstrates the use of valarray gslices:

// num/gslice1.cpp

```
#include <iostream>
#include <valarray>
using namespace std;


// print three-dimensional valarray line-by-line
template<class T>
void printValarray3D (const valarray<T>& va, int dim1, int dim2)
{
    for (int i=0; i<va.size()/(dim1*dim2); ++i) {
        for (int j=0; j<dim2; ++j) {
            for (int k=0; k<dim1; ++k) {
                cout << va[i*dim1*dim2+j*dim1+k] << ' ';
            }
            cout << '\n';
        }
        cout << '\n';
    }
    cout << endl;
}


int main()
{
    /* valarray with 24 elements
     * - two groups
     * - four rows
     * - three columns
     */
```

```
valarray<double> va(24);

// fill valarray with values
for (int i=0; i<24; i++) {
    va[i] = i;
}

// print valarray
printValarray3D (va, 3, 4);

// we need two two-dimensional subsets of three times 3 values
// in two 12-element arrays
size_t lengthvalues[] = {  2, 3 };
size_t stridevalues[] = { 12, 3 };
valarray<size_t> length(lengthvalues,2);
valarray<size_t> stride(stridevalues,2);

// assign the second column of the first three rows
// to the first column of the first three rows
va[gslice(0,length,stride)]
    = valarray<double>(va[gslice(1,length,stride)]);

// add and assign the third of the first three rows
// to the first of the first three rows
va[gslice(0,length,stride)]
    += valarray<double>(va[gslice(2,length,stride)]);

// print valarray
printValarray3D (va, 3, 4);
}
```

The program has the following output:

```
0  1  2
3  4  5
6  7  8
9  10 11

12 13 14
15 16 17
```

```
18 19 20
21 22 23


3  1  2
9  4  5
15 7  8
9  10 11


27 13 14
33 16 17
39 19 20
21 22 23
```

Masked Subsets

Mask arrays provide another way to define a subset of a valarray. You can mask the elements with a Boolean expression. For example, in the expression

```
va[va > 7]
```

the subexpression

```
va > 7
```

returns a valarray with the size of va, where for each element a Boolean value states whether the element is greater than 7. The Boolean valarray is used by the subscript operator to specify all elements for which the Boolean expression yields true. Thus,

```
va[va > 7]
```

specifies the subset of elements in the valarray va that is greater than 7.

Apart from this, mask arrays behave the same as all valarray subsets:

1. To define a concrete subset of a valarray, you simply pass a valarray of Boolean values as the argument to the subscript operator of the valarray.
2. If the valarray is constant, the resulting expression is a new valarray.
3. If the valarray is nonconstant, the resulting expression is a `mask_array` that represents the elements of the valarray with reference semantics:

```
namespace std {
    template <class T>
    class mask_array;
```

```
        template <class T>
        class valarray {
          public:
            // masking a constant valarray returns a new valarray
            valarray<T> operator[] (const valarray<bool>&) const;

            // masking a variable valarray returns a mask_array
            mask_array<T> operator[] (const valarray<bool>&);
            ...
        };
    }
```

4. For `mask_array`, the assignment and computed assignment operators are provided to modify the elements of the subset.

5. By using type conversions you can combine a mask array with other valarrays and subsets of valarrays (see page 554).

The following program demonstrates the use of masked subsets of valarrays:

```
// num/masked1.cpp

#include <iostream>
#include <valarray>
using namespace std;

// print valarray line-by-line
template<class T>
void printValarray (const valarray<T>& va, int num)
{
    for (int i=0; i<va.size()/num; ++i) {
        for (int j=0; j<num; ++j) {
            cout << va[i*num+j] << ' ';
        }
        cout << endl;
    }
    cout << endl;
}

int main()
{
    /* valarray with 12 elements
     * - four rows
```

```
   * - three columns
   */
valarray<double> va(12);

// fill valarray with values
for (int i=0; i<12; i++) {
    va[i] = i;
}

printValarray (va, 3);

// assign 77 to all values that are less than 5
va[va<5.0] = 77.0;

// add 100 to all values that are greater than 5 and less than 9
va[va>5.0 && va<9.0]
    = valarray<double>(va[va>5.0 && va<9.0]) + 100.0;

printValarray (va, 3);
}
```

The program has the following output:

```
0  1  2
3  4  5
6  7  8
9  10  11

77  77  77
77  77  5
106  107  108
9  10  11
```

Note that the type of a numeric value that is compared with the valarray has to match the type of the valarray exactly. So, using an int value to compare it with a valarray of doubles would not compile:

```
valarray<double> va(12);
...
va[va<5] = 77;    // ERROR
```

Indirect Subsets

The fourth and last way to define a subset of a valarray is provided by indirect arrays. Here you simply define the subset of a valarray by passing an array of indices. Note that the indices that specify the subset don't have to be sorted and may occur twice.

Apart from this, indirect arrays behave the same as all valarray subsets:

1. To define a concrete subset of a valarray you simply pass a valarray of elements of type `size_t` as the argument to the subscript operator of the valarray.
2. If the valarray is constant, the resulting expression is a new valarray.
3. If the valarray is nonconstant, the resulting expression is an `indirect_array` that represents the elements of the valarray with reference semantics:

```
namespace std {
    template <class T>
    class indirect_array;

    template <class T>
    class valarray {
      public:
        // indexing a constant valarray returns a new valarray
        valarray<T> operator[] (const valarray<size_t>&) const;

        // indexing a variable valarray returns an indirect_array
        indirect_array<T> operator[] (const valarray<size_t>&);
        ...
    };
}
```

4. For `indirect_array`, the assignment and computed assignment operators are provided to modify the elements of the subset.
5. By using type conversions you can combine an indirect array with other valarrays and subsets of valarrays (see page 554).

The following program demonstrates how to use indirect arrays:

```
// num/indi1.cpp

#include <iostream>
#include <valarray>
using namespace std;

// print valarray as two-dimensional array
template<class T>
void printValarray (const valarray<T>& va, int num)
```

```cpp
{
    for (int i=0; i<va.size()/num; i++) {
        for (int j=0; j<num; j++) {
            cout << va[i*num+j] << ' ';
        }
        cout << endl;
    }
    cout << endl;
}

int main()
{
    // create valarray for 12 elements
    valarray<double> va(12);

    // initialize valarray by values 1.01, 2.02, ... 12.12
    for (int i=0; i<12; i++) {
        va[i] = (i+1) * 1.01;
    }
    printValarray(va,4);

    /* create array of indexes
     * - note: element type has to be size_t
     */
    valarray<size_t> idx(4);
    idx[0] = 8;
    idx[1] = 0;
    idx[2] = 3;
    idx[3] = 7;

    // use array of indexes to print the ninth, first, fourth, and eighth elements
    printValarray(valarray<double>(va[idx]), 4);

    // change the first and fourth elements and print them again indirectly
    va[0] = 11.11;
    va[3] = 44.44;
    printValarray(valarray<double>(va[idx]), 4);

    // now select the second, third, sixth, and ninth elements
```

```
// and assign 99 to them
idx[0] = 1;
idx[1] = 2;
idx[2] = 5;
idx[3] = 8;
va[idx] = 99;

// print the whole valarray again
printValarray (va, 4);
}
```

The valarray `idx` is used to define the subset of the elements in valarray `va`. The program has the following output:

```
1.01 2.02 3.03 4.04
5.05 6.06 7.07 8.08
9.09 10.1 11.11 12.12

9.09 1.01 4.04 8.08

9.09 11.11 44.44 8.08

11.11 99 99 44.44
5.05 99 7.07 8.08
99 10.1 11.11 12.12
```

12.2.3   Class `valarray` in Detail

The class `valarray<>` is the core part of the valarray component. It is defined as a template class parameterized on the type of the elements:

```
namespace std {
    template <class T>
    class valarray;
}
```

The size is not part of the type. Thus, in principle you can process valarrays with different sizes and you can change the size. However, changing the size of a valarray is provided only to make a two-step initialization (creating and setting the size), which you can't avoid to manage arrays of valarrays. Beware that the result of combining valarrays of different size is undefined.

Create, Copy, and Destroy Operations

valarray::**valarray** ()

- The default constructor.
- Creates an empty valarray.
- This constructor is provided only to enable the creation of arrays of valarrays. The next step is to give them the correct size using the `resize()` member function.

`explicit` *valarray*::**valarray** (`size_t` *num*)

- Creates a valarray that contains *num* elements.
- The elements are initialized by their default constructor (which is 0 for fundamental data types).

valarray::**valarray** (`const T&` *value*, `size_t` *num*)

- Creates a valarray that contains *num* elements.
- The elements are initialized by *value*.
- Note that the order of parameters is unusual. All other classes of the C++ standard library provide an interface in which *num* is the first parameter and *value* is the second parameter.

valarray::**valarray** (`const T*` *array*, `size_t` *num*)

- Creates a valarray that contains *num* elements.
- The elements are initialized by the values of the elements in *array*.
- The caller must ensure that *array* contains *num* elements; otherwise, the behavior is undefined.

valarray::**valarray** (`const` *valarray&* *va*)

- The copy constructor.
- Creates a valarray as a copy of *va*.

valarray::~**valarray** ()

- The destructor.
- Destroys all elements and frees the memory.

In addition, you can create valarrays initialized by objects of the internal auxiliary classes `slice_array`, `gslice_array`, `mask_array`, and `indirect_array`. See pages 575, 577, 578, and 579, respectively, for details about these classes.

Assignment Operations

valarray& *valarray*::**operator =** (`const` *valarray&* *va*)

- Assigns the elements of the valarray *va*.

- If *va* has a different size, the behavior is undefined.
- The value of an element on the left side of any valarray assignment operator should not depend on the value of another element on that left side. In other words, if an assignment overwrites values that are used on the right side of the assignment, the result is undefined. This means you should not use an element on the left side anywhere in the expression on the right side. The reason for this is that the order of the evaluation of valarray statements is not defined. See page 557 and page 554 for details.

valarray& *valarray*::**operator =** (const T& *value*)

- Assigns *value* to each element of the valarray.[6]
- The size of the valarray is not changed. Pointers and references to the elements remain valid.

In addition, you can assign values of the internal auxiliary classes `slice_array`, `gslice_array`, `mask_array`, and `indirect_array`. See pages 575, 577, 578, and 579, respectively, for details about these classes.

Member Functions

Class `valarray` provides the following member functions.

`size_t` *valarray*::**size** () const

- Returns the current number of elements.[7]

void *valarray*::**resize** (size_t *num*)
void *valarray*::**resize** (size_t *num*, T *value*)

- Both forms change the size of the valarray to *num*.
- If the size grows, the new elements are initialized by their default constructor or with *value* respectively.
- Both forms invalidate all pointers and references to elements of the valarray.
- These functions are provided only to enable the creation of arrays of valarrays. After creating them with the default constructor you should give them the correct size by calling this function.

T *valarray*::**min** () const
T *valarray*::**max** () const

- The first form returns the minimum value of all elements.
- The second form returns the maximum value of all elements.
- The elements are compared with operator < or >. Thus, these operators must be provided for the element type.
- If the valarray contains no elements, the return value is undefined.

---

[6] In earlier versions single values were assigned by the member function `fill()`.

[7] The member function `size()` was called `length()` in earlier versions.

T *valarray*::**sum** () const

- Returns the sum of all elements.
- The elements are processed by operator +=. Thus, this operator has to be provided for the element type.
- If the valarray contains no elements, the return value is undefined.

valarray *valarray*::**shift** (int *num*) const

- Returns a new valarray in which all elements are shifted by *num* positions.
- The returned valarray has the same number of elements.
- Elements of positions that were shifted are initialized by their default constructor.
- The direction of the shifting depends on the sign of *num*:
  - If *num* is positive, it shifts to the left/front. Thus, elements get a smaller index.
  - If *num* is negative, it shifts to the right/back. Thus, elements get a higher index.

valarray *valarray*::**cshift** (int *num*) const

- Returns a new valarray in which all elements are shifted cyclically by *num* positions.
- The returned valarray has the same number of elements.
- The direction of the shifting depends on the sign of *num*:
  - If *num* is positive, it shifts to the left/front. Thus, elements get a smaller index or are inserted at the back.
  - If *num* is negative, it shifts to the right/back. Thus, elements get a higher index or are inserted at the front.

valarray *valarray*::**apply** (T *op*(T)) const

valarray *valarray*::**apply** (T *op*(const T&)) const

- Both forms return a new valarray with all elements processed by *op*().
- The returned valarray has the same number of elements.
- For each element of *this, it calls
  op(*elem*)
  and initializes the corresponding element in the new returned valarray by its result.

Element Access

T& *valarray*::**operator** [] (size_t *idx*)

T *valarray*::**operator** [] (size_t *idx*) const

- Both forms return the valarray element that has index *idx* (the first element has index 0).
- The nonconstant version returns a reference. So, you can modify the element that is specified and returned by this operator. The reference is guaranteed to be valid as long as the valarray exists, and no function is called that modifies the size of the valarray.

Valarray Operators

Unary valarray operators have the following format:

valarray **valarray**::**unary-op** () const

- A unary operator returns a new valarray that contains all values of `*this` modified by **unary-op**.
- **unary-op** may be any of the following:
    ```
    operator +
    operator -
    operator ~
    operator !
    ```
- The return type for operator ! is `valarray<bool>`.

The binary operators for valarrays (except comparison and assignment operators) have the following format:

valarray **binary-op** (const *valarray&* *va1*, const *valarray&* *va2*)

valarray **binary-op** (const *valarray&* *va*, const T& *value*)

valarray **binary-op** (const T& *value*, const *valarray&* *va*)

- These operators return a new valarray with the same number of elements as `va`, `va1`, or `va2`. The new valarray contains the result of computing **binary-op** for each value pair.
- If only one operand is passed as a single *value*, it is combined with each element of *va*.
- **binary-op** may be any of the following:
    ```
    operator +
    operator -
    operator *
    operator /
    operator %
    operator ^
    operator &
    operator |
    operator <<
    operator >>
    ```
- If *va1* and *va2* have different numbers of elements, the result is undefined.

The logical and comparison operators follow the same schema. However, their return values are a valarray of Boolean values:

`valarray<bool>` **logical-op** (const *valarray&* *va1*, const *valarray&* *va2*)

`valarray<bool>` **logical-op** (const *valarray&* *va*, const T& *value*)

`valarray<bool>` **logical-op** (const T& *value*, const *valarray&* *va*)

- These operators return a new valarray with the same number of elements as `va`, `va1`, or `va2`. The new valarray contains the result of computing *logical-op* for each value pair.
- If only one operand is passed as a single *value*, it is combined with each element of *va*.
- *logical-op* may be any of the following:
  ```
  operator ==
  operator !=
  operator <
  operator <=
  operator >
  operator >=
  operator &&
  operator ||
  ```
- If *va1* and *va2* have different numbers of elements, the result is undefined.

Similarly, computed assignment operators are defined for valarrays:

valarray& **valarray::*assign-op*** (const *valarray&* va)

valarray& **valarray::*assign-op*** (const T& *value*)

- Both forms call for each element in `*this` *assign-op* with the corresponding element of *va* or *value*, respectively, as the second operand.
- They return a reference to the modified valarray.
- *assign-op* may be any of the following:
  ```
  operator +=
  operator -=
  operator *=
  operator /=
  operator %=
  operator ^=
  operator &=
  operator |=
  operator <<=
  operator >>=
  ```
- If `*this` and *va2* have different numbers of elements, the result is undefined.
- References and pointers to modified elements stay valid as long as the valarray exists, and no function is called that modifies the size of the valarray.

Transcendental Functions

valarray **abs** (const *valarray&* va)

valarray **pow** (const *valarray&* va1, const *valarray&* va2)

valarray **pow** (const *valarray&* va, const T& *value*)

valarray **pow** (const T& *value*, const *valarray*& *va*)

valarray **exp** (const *valarray*& *va*)

valarray **sqrt** (const *valarray*& *va*)

valarray **log** (const *valarray*& *va*)

valarray **log10** (const *valarray*& *va*)

valarray **sin** (const *valarray*& *va*)

valarray **cos** (const *valarray*& *va*)

valarray **tan** (const *valarray*& *va*)

valarray **sinh** (const *valarray*& *va*)

valarray **cosh** (const *valarray*& *va*)

valarray **tanh** (const *valarray*& *va*)

valarray **asin** (const *valarray*& *va*)

valarray **acos** (const *valarray*& *va*)

valarray **atan** (const *valarray*& *va*)

valarray **atan2** (const *valarray*& *va1*, const *valarray*& *va2*)

valarray **atan2** (const *valarray*& *va*, const T& *value*)

valarray **atan2** (const T& *value*, const *valarray*& *va*)

- All of these functions return a new valarray with the same number of elements as va, va1, or va2. The new valarray contains the result of the corresponding operation called for each element or pair of elements.
- If *va1* and *va2* have different numbers of elements, the result is undefined.

12.2.4 Valarray Subset Classes in Detail

This subsection describes the subset classes for valarray in detail. However, these classes are very simple and do not provide many operations, thus I provide only their declarations along with a few remarks.

Class `slice` and Class `slice_array`

Objects of class `slice_array` are created by using a `slice` as the index of a nonconstant valarray:

```
namespace std {
    template<class T>
    class valarray {
      public:
        ...
        slice_array<T> operator[](slice);
        ...
```

```
        };
    }
```

The exact definition of the public interface of class `slice` is as follows:

```
namespace std {
    class slice {
      public:
        slice ();              // empty subset
        slice (size_t start, size_t size, size_t stride);

        size_t start()  const;
        size_t size() const;
        size_t stride() const;
    };
}
```

The default constructor creates an empty subset. With the `start()`, `size()`, and `stride()` member functions, you can query the properties of a slice.

The class `slice_array` provides the following operations:

```
namespace std {
    template <class T>
    class slice_array {
      public:
        typedef T value_type;

        void operator= (const T&);
        void operator= (const valarray<T>&) const;
        void operator*= (const valarray<T>&) const;
        void operator/= (const valarray<T>&) const;
        void operator%= (const valarray<T>&) const;
        void operator+= (const valarray<T>&) const;
        void operator-= (const valarray<T>&) const;
        void operator^= (const valarray<T>&) const;
        void operator&= (const valarray<T>&) const;
        void operator|= (const valarray<T>&) const;
        void operator<<=(const valarray<T>&) const;
        void operator>>=(const valarray<T>&) const;
        ~slice_array();
      private:
        slice_array();
```

```
            slice_array(const slice_array&);
            slice_array& operator=(const slice_array&);
            ...
        };
    }
```

Note that class `slice_array<>` is intended purely as an internal helper class for slices and should be transparent to the user. Thus, all constructors and the assignment operator of class `slice_array<>` are private.

Class `gslice` and Class `gslice_array`

Objects of class `gslice_array` are created by using a `gslice` as the index of a nonconstant valarray:

```
    namespace std {
        template<class T>
        class valarray {
          public:
            ...
            gslice_array<T> operator[](const gslice&);
            ...
        };
    }
```

The exact definition of the public interface of `gslice` is as follows:

```
    namespace std {
        class gslice {
          public:
            gslice ();              // empty subset
            gslice (size_t start,
                    const valarray<size_t>& size,
                    const valarray<size_t>& stride);

            size_t start() const;
            valarray<size_t> size() const;
            valarray<size_t> stride() const;
        };
    }
```

The default constructor creates an empty subset. With the `start()`, `size()`, and `stride()` member functions you can query the properties of a gslice.

The class `gslice_array` provides the following operations:

```
namespace std {
    template <class T>
    class gslice_array {
      public:
        typedef T value_type;

        void operator= (const T&);
        void operator= (const valarray<T>&) const;
        void operator*= (const valarray<T>&) const;
        void operator/= (const valarray<T>&) const;
        void operator%= (const valarray<T>&) const;
        void operator+= (const valarray<T>&) const;
        void operator-= (const valarray<T>&) const;
        void operator^= (const valarray<T>&) const;
        void operator&= (const valarray<T>&) const;
        void operator|= (const valarray<T>&) const;
        void operator<<=(const valarray<T>&) const;
        void operator>>=(const valarray<T>&) const;
        ~gslice_array();
      private:
        gslice_array();
        gslice_array(const gslice_array<T>&);
        gslice_array& operator=(const gslice_array<T>&);
        ...
    };
}
```

As with slice_array<>, note that class gslice_array<> is intended purely as an internal helper class for gslices and should be transparent to the user. Thus, all constructors and the assignment operator of class gslice_array<> are private.

Class mask_array

Objects of class mask_array are created by using a valarray<bool> as the index of a nonconstant valarray:

```
namespace std {
    template<class T>
    class valarray {
      public:
        ...
```

```
        mask_array<T> operator[](const valarray<bool>&);
        ...
    };
}
```

The class `mask_array` provides the following operations:

```
namespace std {
    template <class T>
    class mask_array {
      public:
        typedef T value_type;

        void operator= (const T&);
        void operator= (const valarray<T>&) const;
        void operator*= (const valarray<T>&) const;
        void operator/= (const valarray<T>&) const;
        void operator%= (const valarray<T>&) const;
        void operator+= (const valarray<T>&) const;
        void operator-= (const valarray<T>&) const;
        void operator^= (const valarray<T>&) const;
        void operator&= (const valarray<T>&) const;
        void operator|= (const valarray<T>&) const;
        void operator<<=(const valarray<T>&) const;
        void operator>>=(const valarray<T>&) const;
        ~mask_array();
      private:
        mask_array();
        mask_array(const mask_array<T>&);
        mask_array& operator=(const mask_array<T>&);
        ...
    };
}
```

Again, note that class `mask_array<>` is intended purely as an internal helper class and should be transparent to the user. Thus, all constructors and the assignment operator of class `mask_array<>` are private.

Class `indirect_array`

Objects of class `indirect_array` are created by using a `valarray<size_t>` as the index of a nonconstant valarray:

```
namespace std {
    template<class T>
    class valarray {
      public:
        ...
        indirect_array<T> operator[](const valarray<size_t>&);
        ...
    };
}
```

The class `indirect_array` provides the following operations:

```
namespace std {
    template <class T>
    class indirect_array {
      public:
        typedef T value_type;

        void operator= (const T&);
        void operator= (const valarray<T>&) const;
        void operator*= (const valarray<T>&) const;
        void operator/= (const valarray<T>&) const;
        void operator%= (const valarray<T>&) const;
        void operator+= (const valarray<T>&) const;
        void operator-= (const valarray<T>&) const;
        void operator^= (const valarray<T>&) const;
        void operator&= (const valarray<T>&) const;
        void operator|= (const valarray<T>&) const;
        void operator<<=(const valarray<T>&) const;
        void operator>>=(const valarray<T>&) const;
        ~indirect_array();
      private:
        indirect_array();
        indirect_array(const indirect_array<T>&);
        indirect_array& operator=(const indirect_array<T>&);
        ...
    };
}
```

As usual, class `indirect_array<>` is intended purely as an internal helper class and should be transparent to the user. Thus, all constructors and the assignment operator of `indirect_array<>` are private.

12.3   Global Numeric Functions

The header files `<cmath>` and `<cstdlib>` provide the global numeric functions that are inherited from C. Tables 12.8 and 12.9 list these functions.[8]

Function	Effect
`pow()`	Power function
`exp()`	Exponential function
`sqrt()`	Square root
`log()`	Natural logarithm
`log10()`	Base 10 logarithm
`sin()`	Sine
`cos()`	Cosine
`tan()`	Tangent
`sinh()`	Hyperbolic sine
`cosh()`	Hyperbolic cosine
`tanh()`	Hyperbolic tangent
`asin()`	Arc sine
`acos()`	Arc cosine
`atan()`	Arc tangent
`atan2()`	Arc tangent of a quotient
`ceil()`	Floating-point value rounded up to the next integral value
`floor()`	Floating-point value rounded down to the next integral value
`fabs()`	Absolute value of a floating-point value
`fmod()`	Remainder after division for floating-point value (modulo)
`frexp()`	Converts floating-point value to fractional and integral components
`ldexp()`	Multiplies floating-point value by integral power of two
`modf()`	Extracts signed integral and fractional values from floating-point value

Table 12.8. Functions of the Header File `<cmath>`

In contrast to C, C++ overloads some operations for different types, which makes some numeric functions of C obsolete. For example, C provides `abs()`, `labs()`, and `fabs()` to process the absolute value of `int`, `long`, and `double`, respectively. In C++, `abs()` is overloaded for different data types so that you can use it for all data types.

---

[8] For historical reasons, some numeric functions are defined in `<cstdlib>` rather than in `<cmath>`.

Function	Effect
abs()	Absolute value of an int value
labs()	Absolute value of a long
div()	Quotient and remainder of int division
ldiv()	Quotient and remainder of long division
srand()	Random number generator (seed new sequence)
rand()	Random number generator (next number of sequence)

Table 12.9. Numeric Functions of the Header File <cstdlib>

In particular, all numeric functions for floating-point values are overloaded for types float, double, and long double. However, this has an important side effect: When you pass an integral value, the expression is ambiguous:[9]:

```
std::sqrt(7)          // AMBIGUOUS: sqrt(float), sqrt(double), or
                      //            sqrt(long double)?
```

Instead, you have to write

```
std::sqrt(7.0)        // OK
```

or, if you use a variable, you must write

```
int x;
...
std::sqrt(float(x))   // OK
```

Library vendors handle this problem completely differently: some don't provide the overloading, some provide standard conforming behavior (overload for all floating-point types), some overload for all numeric types, and some allow you to switch between different policies by using the preprocessor. Thus, in practice, the ambiguity might or might not occur. To write portable code, you should always write the code in a way that the arguments match exactly.

---

[9] Thanks to David Vandevoorde for pointing this out.

Chapter 13

Input/Output Using Stream Classes

The classes for I/O form an important part of the C++ standard library; a program without I/O is not of much use. Actually, the I/O classes from the C++ standard library are not restricted to files or to screen and keyboard. Instead, they form an extensible framework for the formatting of arbitrary data and access to arbitrary "external representations."

The *IOStream library*, as the classes for I/O are called, is the only part of the C++ standard library that was used widely prior to the standardization of C++. Early distributions of C++ systems came with a set of classes developed at AT&T that established a de facto standard for doing I/O. Although these classes have undergone several changes to fit consistently into the C++ standard library and to suit new needs, the basic principles of the IOStream library remain unchanged.

This chapter first presents a general overview of the most important components and techniques, and then demonstrates in detail how the IOStream library can be used in practice. Its use ranges from simple formatting to the integration of new external representations (a topic that is often addressed improperly).

This chapter does not attempt to discuss all aspects of the IOStream library in detail; to do that would take an entire book by itself. For details not found here, please consult one of the books that focus on the I/O stream library or the reference manual of the C++ standard library.

Many thanks to Dietmar Kühl, who is an expert on I/O and internationalization in the C++ standard library and gave very much feedback and wrote some parts of this chapter.

Recent Changes in the IOStream Library

For those already familiar with the "old-fashioned" IOStream library, this section outlines changes introduced during the standardization process. Although the basics of the I/O stream classes remained unchanged, some important features allowing additional customization were introduced. Here is a brief list of the major changes:

- I/O became internationalized.
- The string stream classes for character arrays of type `char*` were replaced with classes that use the `string` types of the C++ standard library. The former classes are still retained for backward compatibility, but their use is deprecated.[1]
- Exception handling was integrated into state and error handling.
- The IOStream library classes supporting assignment (those ending in `_withassign`) were replaced with a different approach available to all stream classes.
- The classes from the IOStream library were made templates to support different character representations. As a side effect, this renders simple forward declarations of stream classes illegal. A header was introduced to provide the appropriate declarations. So, instead of using

      class ostream;   // wrong

  this new header should be used:

      #include <iosfwd>   // OK

- Like the other parts of the C++ standard library, all symbols of the IOStream library are now declared in the namespace `std`.

13.1 Common Background of I/O Streams

Before going into details about stream classes, I briefly discuss the generally known aspects of streams to provide a common background. This section could be skipped by readers familiar with iostream basics.

13.1.1 Stream Objects

In C++, I/O is performed by using streams. A stream is a "stream of data" in which character sequences "flow." Following the principles of object orientation, a stream is an object with properties that are defined by a class. Output is interpreted as data flowing into a stream; input is interpreted as data flowing out of a stream. Global objects are predefined for the standard I/O channels.

13.1.2 Stream Classes

Just as there are different kinds of I/O (for example, input, output, and file access), there are different classes depending on the type of I/O. The following are the most important stream classes:

- **Class `istream`**
  Defines input streams that can be used to read data.

---

[1] *Deprecated* means that a feature is not recommended because some superior feature exists. Also, deprecated features are likely to disappear from a future version of the standard.

- **Class `ostream`**

  Defines output streams that can be used to write data.

Both classes are instantiations of template classes, namely of the classes `basic_istream<>` and `basic_ostream<>` using `char` as the character type. Actually, the whole IOStream library does not depend on a specific character type. Instead the character type used is a template argument for most of the classes in the IOStream library. This parameterization corresponds to the string classes and is used for internationalization (see also Chapter 14).

This section concentrates on output to and input from "narrow streams"; that is, streams dealing with `char` as the character type. Later in this chapter the discussion is extended to streams that have other character types.

13.1.3 Global Stream Objects

The IOStream library defines several global objects of type `istream` and `ostream`. These objects correspond to the standard I/O channels:

- **cin**

  `cin` (of class `istream`) is the standard input channel that is used for user input. This stream corresponds to C's `stdin`. Normally, this stream is connected to the keyboard by the operating system.

- **cout**

  `cout` (of class `ostream`) is the standard output channel that is used for program output. This stream corresponds to C's `stdout`. Normally, this stream is connected to the monitor by the operating system.

- **cerr**

  `cerr` (of class `ostream`) is the standard error channel that is used for all kinds of error messages. This stream corresponds to C's `stderr`. Normally, this stream is also connected to the monitor by the operating system. By default, `cerr` is not buffered.

- **clog**

  `clog` (of class `ostream`) is the standard logging channel. There is no C equivalent for this stream. By default, this stream is connected to the same destination as `cerr`, with the difference that output to `clog` is buffered.

The separation of "normal" output and error messages makes it possible to treat these two kinds of output differently when executing a program. For example, the normal output of a program can be redirected into a file while the error messages are still appearing on the console. Of course, this requires that the operating system supports redirection of the standard I/O channels (most operating systems do). This separation of standard channels originates from the UNIX concept of I/O redirection.

13.1.4   Stream Operators

The shift operators >> for input and << for output are overloaded for the corresponding stream classes. For this reason, in C++ the "shift operators" became the "I/O operators."[2] Using these operators, it is possible to chain multiple I/O operations.

For example, for each iteration, the following loop reads two integers from the standard input (as long as only integers are entered) and writes them to the standard output:

```
int a, b;
```

```
// as long as input of a and b is successful
while (std::cin >> a >> b) {
    // output a and b
    std::cout << "a: " << a << " b: " << b << std::endl;
}
```

13.1.5   Manipulators

At the end of most output statements, a so-called manipulator is written:

```
std::cout << std::endl
```

Manipulators are special objects that are used to, guess what, manipulate a stream. Often, manipulators only change the way input is interpreted or output is formatted, like the manipulators for the numeric bases dec, hex, and oct. Thus, manipulators for ostreams do not necessarily create output, and manipulators for istreams do not necessary consume input. But there are also manipulators that actually trigger some immediate action. For example, a manipulator can be used to flush the output buffer or to skip whitespace in the input buffer.

The manipulator endl means "end line" and does two things:

1. Outputs a newline (that is, the character '\n')
2. Flushes the output buffer (forces a write of all buffered data for the given stream using the stream method flush())

The most important manipulators defined by the IOStream library are provided in Table 13.1.

Section 13.6, page 612, discusses manipulators in more detail, including those that are defined in the IOStream library, and describes how to define your own manipulators.

---

[2] According to the fact that these operators insert characters into a stream or extract characters from a stream, some people also call the I/O operators *inserters* and *extractors*.

Manipulator	Class	Meaning
endl	ostream	Outputs '\n' and flushes the output buffer
ends	ostream	Outputs '\0'
flush	ostream	Flushes the output buffer
ws	istream	Reads and discards whitespaces

Table 13.1. The IOStream Library's Most Important Manipulators

13.1.6 A Simple Example

The use of the stream classes is demonstrated by the following example. This program reads two floating-point values and outputs their product:

```cpp
// io/io1.cpp

#include <cstdlib>
#include <iostream>
using namespace std;

int main()
{
    double x, y;              // operands

    // print header string
    cout << "Multiplication of two floating point values" << endl;

    // read first operand
    cout << "first operand:   ";
    if (! (cin >> x)) {
        /* input error
         * => error message and exit program with error status
         */
        cerr << "error while reading the first floating value"
             << endl;
        return EXIT_FAILURE;
    }

    // read second operand
    cout << "second operand: ";
    if (! (cin >> y)) {
        /* input error
```

```
    *  => error message and exit program with error status
    */
    cerr << "error while reading the second floating value"
         << endl;
    return EXIT_FAILURE;
}

// print operands and result
cout << x << " times " << y << " equals " << x * y << endl;
}
```

13.2   Fundamental Stream Classes and Objects

13.2.1   Classes and Class Hierarchy

The stream classes of the IOStream library form a hierarchy, as shown in Figure 13.1. For template classes, the upper row shows the name of the template class, and the lower row presents the names of the instantiations for the character types char and wchar_t.

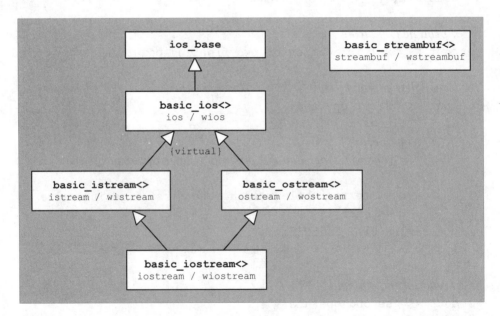

Figure 13.1. Class Hierarchy of the Fundamental Stream Classes

The classes in this class hierarchy play the following roles:

- The base class **ios_base** defines the properties of all stream classes independent of the character type and the corresponding character traits. Most of this class consists of components and functions for state and format flags.

- The class template **basic_ios<>** is derived from ios_base and it defines the common properties of all stream classes that depend on the character types and the corresponding character traits. These properties include the definition of the buffer used by the stream. The buffer is an object of a class derived from the template class basic_streambuf<> with the corresponding template instantiation. It performs the actual reading and/or writing.

- The class templates **basic_istream<>** and **basic_ostream<>** derive virtually from basic_ios<>, and define objects that can be used for reading or writing respectively. Like basic_ios<>, these classes are templates that are parameterized with a character type and its traits. When internationalization does not matter, the corresponding instantiations for the character type char (namely, istream and ostream) are used.

- The class template **basic_iostream<>** derives from both basic_istream<> and basic_ostream<>. This class template defines objects that can be used for both reading and writing.

- The class template **basic_streambuf<>** is the heart of the IOStream library. This class defines the interface to all representations that can be written to or read from by streams. It is used by the other stream classes to perform the actual reading and writing of characters. For access to some external representation, classes are derived from basic_streambuf<>. See the following subsection for details.

Purpose of the Stream Buffer Classes

The IOStream library is designed with a rigid separation of responsibilities. The classes derived from basic_ios "only" handle formatting of the data.[3] The actual reading and writing of characters is performed by the stream buffers maintained by the basic_ios subobjects. The stream buffers supply character buffers for reading and writing. In addition, an abstraction from the external representation (for example files or strings) is formed by the stream buffers.

Thus, stream buffers play an important role when performing I/O with new external representations (such as sockets or graphical user interface components), redirecting streams, or combining streams to form pipelines (for example, to compress output before writing to another stream). Also, the stream buffer synchronizes the I/O when doing simultaneous I/O on the same external representation. The details about these techniques are explained in Section 13.10.2, page 638.

By using stream buffers it is quite easy to define access to a new "external representation" like a new storage device. All that has to be done is to derive a new stream buffer class from basic_streambuf<> (or an appropriate specialization) and define functions for reading and/or writing characters for this new external representation. All options for formatted I/O are avail-

---

[3] Actually, they don't even do the formatting! The actual formatting is delegated to corresponding facets in the locale library. See Section 14.2.2, page 698, and Section 14.4, page 704, for details on facets.

able automatically if a stream object is initialized to use an object of the new stream buffer class. Section 13.13, page 663, explains how to define new stream buffers for access to special storage devices.

Detailed Class Definitions

Like all template classes in the IOStream library, the template class `basic_ios<>` is parameterized with two arguments and defined as

```
namespace std {
    template <class charT,
              class traits = char_traits<charT> >
    class basic_ios;
}
```

The template arguments are the character type used by the stream classes and a class describing the traits of the character type that are used by the stream classes.

Examples of traits defined in the traits class are the value used to represent end-of-file[4] and the instructions for how to copy or move a sequence of characters. Normally, the traits for a character type are coupled with the character type, thereby making it reasonable to define a template class that is specialized for specific character types. Hence, the traits class defaults to `char_traits<charT>` if `charT` is the character type argument. The C++ standard library provides specializations of the class `char_traits` for the character types `char` and `wchar_t`. For more details about character traits, see Section 14.1.2, page 687.

There are two instantiations of the class `basic_ios<>` for the two character types used most often:

```
namespace std {
    typedef basic_ios<char>    ios;
    typedef basic_ios<wchar_t> wios;
}
```

The type `ios` corresponds to the base class of the "old-fashioned" IOStream library from AT&T and can be used for compatibility in older C++ programs.

The stream buffer class used by `basic_ios` is defined similarly:

```
namespace std {
    template <class charT,
              class traits = char_traits<charT> >
    class basic_streambuf;
    typedef basic_streambuf<char>    streambuf;
    typedef basic_streambuf<wchar_t> wstreambuf;
}
```

---

[4] I use the term *end-of-file* for the "end of input data." This is according to the constant EOF in C.

Of course, the class templates `basic_istream<>`, `basic_ostream<>`, and `basic_iostream<>` are also parameterized with the character type and a traits class:

```
namespace std {
    template <class charT,
              class traits = char_traits<charT> >
    class basic_istream;

    template <class charT,
              class traits = char_traits<charT> >
    class basic_ostream;

    template <class charT,
              class traits = char_traits<charT> >
    class basic_iostream;
}
```

As for the other classes, there are also type definitions for the instantiations of the two most important character types:

```
namespace std {
    typedef basic_istream<char>     istream;
    typedef basic_istream<wchar_t>  wistream;

    typedef basic_ostream<char>     ostream;
    typedef basic_ostream<wchar_t>  wostream;

    typedef basic_iostream<char>    iostream;
    typedef basic_iostream<wchar_t> wiostream;
}
```

The types `istream` and `ostream` are the types normally used in the western hemisphere. They are mostly compatible with the "old-fashioned" stream classes of AT&T.

The classes `istream_withassign`, `ostream_withassign`, and `iostream_withassign`, which are present in some older stream libraries (derived from `istream`, `ostream`, and `iostream` respectively) are not supported by the standard. The corresponding functionality is achieved differently (see Section 13.10.3, page 641).

There are additional classes for formatted I/O with files and strings. These classes are discussed in Section 13.9, page 627, and Section 13.11, page 645.

13.2.2   Global Stream Objects

Several global stream objects are defined for the stream classes. These objects are the objects for access to the standard I/O channels that are mentioned previously for streams with `char` as the character type and a set of corresponding objects for the streams using `wchar_t` as the character type (see Table 13.2).

Type	Name	Purpose
istream	**cin**	Reads input from the standard input channel
ostream	**cout**	Writes "normal" output to the standard output channel
ostream	**cerr**	Writes error messages to the standard error channel
ostream	**clog**	Writes log messages to the standard logging channel
wistream	**wcin**	Reads wide-character input from the standard input channel
wostream	**wcout**	Writes "normal" wide-character output to the standard output channel
wostream	**wcerr**	Writes wide-character error messages to the standard error channel
wostream	**wclog**	Writes wide-character log messages to the standard logging channel

Table 13.2. Global Stream Objects

By default, these standard streams are synchronized with the standard streams of C. That is, the C++ standard library ensures that the order of mixed output with C++ streams and C streams is preserved. Before any buffer of standard C++ streams writes data it flushes the buffer of the corresponding C streams and vice versa. Of course, this synchronization takes some time. If it isn't necessary you can turn it off by calling `sync_with_stdio(false)` before any input or output is done (see page 682).

13.2.3   Header Files

The definitions of the stream classes are scattered among several header files:

* **<iosfwd>**
  Contains forward declarations for the stream classes. This header file is necessary because it is no longer permissible to use a simple forward declaration such as `class ostream`.

* **<streambuf>**
  Contains the definitions for the stream buffer base class (`basic_streambuf<>`).

* **<istream>**
  Contains the definitions for the classes that support input only (`basic_istream<>`) and for the classes that support both input and output (`basic_iostream<>`).[5]

* **<ostream>**
  Contains the definitions for the output stream class (`basic_ostream<>`).

* **<iostream>**
  Contains declarations of the global stream objects (such as `cin` and `cout`).

---

[5] At first, `<istream>` might not appear to be a logical choice for declaration of the classes for input *and* output. However, because there may be some initialization overhead at start-up for every translation unit that includes `<iostream>` (see the following paragraph for details), the declarations for input *and* output were put into `<istream>`.

Most of the headers exist for the internal organization of the C++ standard library. For the application programmer it should be sufficient to include `<iosfwd>` for the declaration of the stream classes and `<istream>` or `<ostream>` when actually using the input or output functions respectively. The header `<iostream>` should only be included if the standard stream objects are to be used. For some implementations some code is executed at start-up for each translation unit including this header. The actual code being executed is not that expensive but it requires loading of the corresponding pages of the executable, which might be expensive. In general, only those headers defining necessary "stuff" should be included. In particular, header files should only include `<iosfwd>`, and the corresponding implementation files should then include the header with the complete definition.

For special stream features, such as parameterized manipulators, file streams, or string streams, there are additional headers (`<iomanip>`, `<fstream>`, `<sstream>`, and `<strstream>`). The details regarding these headers are provided in the sections that introduce these special features.

13.3   Standard Stream Operators << and >>

In C and C++, operators `<<` and `>>` are used for shifting bits of an integer to the right or the left respectively. The classes `basic_istream<>` and `basic_ostream<>` overload operators `>>` and `<<` as the standard I/O operators. Thus, in C++ the "shift operators" became the "I/O operators."[6]

13.3.1   Output Operator <<

The class `basic_ostream` (and thus also the classes `ostream` and `wostream`) defines `<<` as an output operator. It overloads this operator for all fundamental types, including `char*`, `void*`, and `bool`.

The output operators for streams are defined to send their second argument to the corresponding stream. Thus, the data is sent in the direction of the arrow:

```
int i = 7;
std::cout << i;            // outputs: 7

float f = 4.5;
std::cout << f;            // outputs: 4.5
```

The `<<` operator can be overloaded such that the second argument is an arbitrary data type. This allows the integration of your own data types into the I/O system. The compiler ensures that the correct function for outputting the second argument is called. Of course, this function should in fact transform the second argument into a sequence of characters sent to the stream.

The C++ standard library also uses this mechanism to provide output operators for strings (see page 524), bitsets (see page 468), and complex numbers (see page 539):

---

[6] Some people also call the I/O operators *inserters* and *extractors*.

```
std::string s("hello");
s += ", world";
std::cout << s;            // outputs: hello, world

std::bitset<10> flags(7);
std::cout << flags;        // outputs: 0000000111

std::complex<float> c(3.1,7.4);
std::cout << c;            // outputs: (3.1,7.4)
```

The details about writing output operators for your own data types are explained in Section 13.12, page 652.

The fact that the output mechanism can be extended to incorporate your own data types is a significant improvement over C's I/O mechanism that uses `printf()`: It is not necessary to specify the type of an object to be printed. Instead, the overloading of different types ensures that the correct function for printing is deduced automatically. The mechanism is not limited to standard types. Thus, the user has only one mechanism that works for all types.

Operator << can also be used to print multiple objects in one statement. By convention, the output operators return their first argument. Thus, the result of an output operator is the output stream. This allows you to chain calls to output operators like this:

```
std::cout << x << " times " << y << " is " << x * y << std::endl;
```

Operator << is evaluated from left to right. Thus,

```
std::cout << x
```

is executed first. Note that the evaluative order of the operator does not imply any specific order in which the arguments are evaluated; only the order in which the operators are executed is defined. This expression returns its first operand — `std::cout`. So,

```
std::cout << " times "
```

is executed next. The object y, the string literal " is ", and the result of x * y are printed accordingly. Note that the multiplication operator has a higher priority than operator <<, so you need no parentheses around x * y. However, there are operators that have lower priority, such as all logical operators. In this example, if x and y are floating-point numbers with the values 2.4 and 5.1, the following is printed:

```
2.4 times 5.1 is 12.24
```

13.3.2   Input Operator >>

The class `basic_istream` (and thus also the classes `istream` and `wistream`) defines >> as an input operator. Similar to `basic_ostream`, this operator is overloaded for all fundamental types including, `char*`, `void*`, and `bool`. The input operators for streams are defined to store the value read in their second argument. As with operator <<, the data is sent in the direction of the arrow:

```
int i;
std::cin >> i;        // reads an int from standard input and stores it in i

float f;
std::cin >> f;        // reads a float from standard input and stores it in f
```

Note that the second argument is modified. To make this possible, the second argument is passed by nonconstant reference.

Like output operator <<, it is also possible to overload the input operator for arbitrary data types and to chain the calls:

```
float f;
std::complex<double> c;

std::cin >> f >> c;
```

To make this possible, leading whitespace is skipped by default. However, this automatic skipping of whitespace can be turned off (see page 625).

13.3.3   Input/Output of Special Types

The standard I/O operators are also defined for types bool, char*, and void*. In addition, you can extend it for your own types.

Type bool

By default, Boolean values are printed and read numerically: false is converted from and to 0, and true is converted from and to 1. When reading, values different from 0 and 1 are considered to be an error. In this case the ios::failbit is set, which might throw a corresponding exception (see page 602).

It is also possible to set up the formatting options of the stream to use character strings for the I/O of Boolean values (see page 617). This touches on the topic of internationalization: Unless a special locale object is used, the strings "true" and "false" are used. In other locale objects, different strings might be used. For example, a German locale object would use the strings "wahr" and "falsch". See Chapter 14, especially page 698, for more details.

Types char and wchar_t

When a char or wchar_t is being read with operator >>, leading whitespace is skipped by default. To read any character (whether or not it is whitespace) you can either clear the flag skipws (see page 625) or use the member function get() (see page 608).

Type `char*`

A C-string (that is, a `char*`) is read word wise. That is, when a C-string is being read, leading whitespace is skipped by default and the string is read until another whitespace character or end-of-file is encountered. Whether leading whitespace is skipped automatically can be controlled with the flag `skipws` (see Section 13.7.7, page 625).

Note that this behavior means that the string you read can become arbitrarily long. It is already a common error in C programs to assume that a string can be a maximum of 80 characters long. There is no such restriction. Thus, you must arrange for a premature termination of the input when the string is too long. To do this, you should *always* set the maximum length of the string to be read. This normally looks something like this:

```
char buffer[81];      // 80 characters and '\0'
std::cin >> std::setw(81) >> buffer;
```

The manipulator `setw()` and the corresponding stream parameter are described in detail in Section 13.7.3, page 618.

The type `string` from the C++ standard library (see Chapter 11) grows as needed to accommodate a lengthy string. It is much easier and safer to use the string class instead of `char*`. In addition, it provides a convenient function for reading line-by-line (see page 493). So, whenever you can avoid the use of C-strings and use strings.

Type `void*`

Operators `<<` and `>>` also provide the possibility of printing a pointer and reading it back in again. An address is printed in an implementation-dependent format if a parameter of type `void*` is passed to the output operator. For example, the following statement prints the contents of a C-string and its address:

```
char* cstring = "hello";

std::cout << "string \"" << cstring << "\" is located at address: "
          << static_cast<void*>(cstring) << std::endl;
```

The result of this statement might appear as follows:

```
string "hello" is located at address: 0x10000018
```

It is even possible to read an address again with the input operator. However, note that addresses are normally transient. The same object can get a different address in a newly started program. A possible application of printing and reading addresses may be programs that exchange addresses for object identification or programs that share memory.

Stream Buffers

You can use operators >> and << to read directly into a stream buffer and to write directly out of a stream buffer respectively. This is probably the fastest way to copy files by using C++ I/O streams. See page 683 for examples.

User-Defined Types

In principle it is very easy to extend this technique to your own types. However, to be able to pay attention to all possible formatting data and error conditions, this takes more effort than you might think. See Section 13.12, page 652, for a detailed discussion about extending the standard I/O mechanism for your own types.

13.4   State of Streams

Streams maintain a state. The state identifies whether I/O was successful and, if not, the reason for the failure.

13.4.1   Constants for the State of Streams

For the general state of streams, several constants of type `iostate` are defined to be used as flags (Table 13.3). The type `iostate` is a member of the class `ios_base`. The exact type of the constants is an implementation detail (in other words, it is not defined whether `iostate` is an enumeration, a type definition for an integral type, or an instantiation of the class `bitset`).

Constant	Meaning
goodbit	Everything is OK; none of the other bits is set
eofbit	End-of-file was encountered
failbit	Error; an I/O operation was not successful
badbit	Fatal error; undefined state

Table 13.3. Constants of Type `iostate`

goodbit is defined to have the value 0. Thus, having goodbit set actually means that all other bits are cleared. The name goodbit may be somewhat confusing because it doesn't mean that one bit is set; it means that all bits are cleared.

The difference between failbit and badbit is basically that badbit indicates a more fatal error:

- **failbit** is set if an operation was not processed correctly but the stream is generally OK. Normally this flag is set as a result of a format error during reading. For example, this flag is set if an integer is to be read but the next character is a letter.

- **badbit** is set if the stream is somehow corrupted or if data is lost. For example, this flag is set when positioning a stream that refers to a file before the beginning of a file.

Note that `eofbit` normally happens with `failbit` because the end-of-file condition is checked and detected when an attempt is made to read beyond end-of-file. After reading the last character, the flag `eofbit` is not yet set. The next attempt to read a character sets `eofbit` *and* `failbit`, because the read fails.

Some former implementations supported the flag `hardfail`. This flag is not supported in the standard.

These constants are not defined globally. Instead, they are defined within the class `ios_base`. Thus, you must always use them with the scope operator or with some object. For example:

```
std::ios_base::eofbit
```

Of course, it is also possible to use a class derived from `ios_base`. These constants were defined in the class `ios` in old implementations. Because `ios` is a type derived from `ios_base` and its use involves less typing, the use often looks like this:

```
std::ios::eofbit
```

These flags are maintained by the class `basic_ios` and are thus present in all objects of type `basic_istream` or `basic_ostream`. However, the stream buffers don't have state flags. One stream buffer can be shared by multiple stream objects, so the flags only represent the state of the stream as found in the last operation. Even this is only the case if `goodbit` was set prior to this operation. Otherwise the flags may have been set by some earlier operation.

13.4.2   Member Functions Accessing the State of Streams

The current state of the flags can be determined by the member functions, as presented in Table 13.4.

Member Function	Meaning
`good()`	Returns `true` if the stream is OK (`goodbit` is "set")
`eof()`	Returns `true` if end-of-file was hit (`eofbit` is set)
`fail()`	Returns `true` if an error has occurred (`failbit` or `badbit` is set)
`bad()`	Returns `true` if a fatal error has occurred (`badbit` is set)
`rdstate()`	Returns the currently set flags
`clear()`	Clears all flags
`clear(`*state*`)`	Clears all and sets *state* flags
`setstate(`*state*`)`	Sets additional *state* flags

Table 13.4. Member Functions for Stream States

The first four member functions in Table 13.4 determine certain states and return a Boolean value. Note that `fail()` returns whether `failbit` or `badbit` is set. Although this is done mainly for historical reasons, it also has the advantage that one test suffices to determine whether an error has occurred.

In addition, the state of the flags can be determined and modified with the more general member functions. When `clear()` is called without parameters, all error flags (including `eofbit`) are cleared (this is the origin of the name *clear*):

```
// clear all error flags (including eofbit):
strm.clear();
```

If a parameter is given to `clear()`, the state of the stream is adjusted to be the state given by the parameter; that is, the flags set in the parameter are set for the stream, while the other flags are cleared. The only exception is that the `badbit` is always set if there is no stream buffer (this is the case if `rdbuf() == 0`; see Section 13.10.2, page 638, for details).

The following example checks whether `failbit` is set and clears it if necessary:

```
// check whether failbit is set
if (strm.rdstate() & std::ios::failbit) {
    std::cout << "failbit was set" << std::endl;


    // clear only failbit
    strm.clear (strm.rdstate() & ~std::ios::failbit);
}
```

This example uses the bit operators `&` and `~`: Operator `~` returns the bitwise complement of its argument. Thus, the expression

```
~ios::failbit
```

returns a temporary value that has all bits except `failbit` set. Operator `&` returns a bitwise "and" of its operands. Only the bits set in both operands remain set. Applying bitwise "and" to all currently set flags (`rdstate()`) and to all bits except `failbit` retains the value of all other bits while `failbit` is cleared.

Streams can be configured to throw exceptions if certain flags are set with `clear()` or `setstate()` (see Section 13.4.4, page 602). Such streams always throw an exception if the corresponding flag is set at the end of the method used to manipulate the flags.

Note that you always have to clear error bits explicitly. In C it was possible to read characters after a format error. For example, if `scanf()` failed to read an integer, you could still read the remaining characters. Thus, the read operation failed, but the input stream was still in a good state. This is different in C++. If `failbit` is set, each following stream operation is a no-op until `failbit` is cleared explicitly.

In general, it has to be mentioned that the set bits reflect only what happened sometime in the past: If a bit is set after some operation this does not necessarily mean that this operation caused the flag to be set. Instead, the flag might have been set before the operation. Thus, `goodbit` should be set (if it is not known to be set) before an operation is executed if the flags are then used to tell you what went wrong. Also, after clearing the flags the operations may yield different results. For example, even if `eofbit` was set by an operation, this does not mean that after clearing `eofbit` (and any other bits set) the operation will set `eofbit` again. This can be the case, for example, if the accessed file grew between the two calls.

13.4.3   Stream State and Boolean Conditions

Two functions are defined for the use of streams in Boolean expressions (Table 13.5).

Member Function	Meaning
`operator void* ()`	Returns whether the stream has not run into an error (corresponds to `!fail()`)
`operator ! ()`	Returns whether the stream has run into an error (corresponds to `fail()`)

Table 13.5. Stream Operators for Boolean Expressions

With `operator void*()`, streams can be tested in control structures in a short and idiomatic way for their current state:

```
// while the standard input stream is OK
while (std::cin) {
    ...
}
```

For the Boolean condition in a control structure, the type does not need a direct conversion to `bool`. Instead, a unique conversion to an integral type (such as `int` or `char`) or to a pointer type is sufficient. The conversion to `void*` is often used to read objects and test for success in the same expression:

```
if (std::cin >> x) {
    // reading x was successful
    ...
}
```

As discussed earlier, the expression

```
std::cin >> x
```

returns `cin`. So after `x` is read, the statement is

```
if (std::cin) {
    ...
}
```

Because `cin` is being used in the context of a condition, its operator `void*` is called, which returns whether the stream has run into an error.

A typical application of this technique is a loop that reads and processes objects:

```
// as long as obj can be read
while (std::cin >> obj) {
    // process obj (in this case, simply output it)
    std::cout << obj << std::endl;
}
```

This is C's classic filter framework for C++ objects. The loop is terminated if the `failbit` or `badbit` is set. This happens when an error occurred or at end-of-file (the attempt to read at end-of-file results in setting `eofbit` *and* `failbit`; see page 598). By default, operator `>>` skips leading whitespaces. This is normally exactly what is desired. However, if `obj` is of type `char`, whitespace is normally considered to be significant. In this case you can use the `put()` and `get()` member functions of streams (see page 611) or, even better, an `istreambuf_iterator` (see page 667) to implement an I/O filter.

With operator `!`, the inverse test can be performed. The operator is defined to return whether a stream has run into an error; that is, it returns `true` if `failbit` or `badbit` is set. It can be used like this:

```
if (! std::cin) {
    // the stream cin is not OK
    ...
}
```

Like the implicit conversion to a Boolean value, this operator is often used to test for success in the same expression in which an object was read:

```
if (! (std::cin >> x)) {
    // the read failed
    ...
}
```

Here, the expression

```
std::cin >> x
```

returns `cin`, to which operator `!` is applied. The expression after `!` must be placed within parentheses. This is due to the operator precedence rules: without the parentheses, operator `!` would be evaluated first. In other words, the expression

```
!std::cin >> x
```

is equivalent to the expression

```
(!std::cin) >> x
```

This is probably not what is intended.

Although these operators are very convenient in Boolean expressions, one oddity has to be noted: Double "negation" does *not* yield the original object:

- `cin` is a stream object of class `istream`.
- `!!cin` is a Boolean value describing the state of `cin`.

As with other features of C++, it can be argued whether the use of the conversions to a Boolean value is good style. The use of member functions such as `fail()` normally yields a more readable program:

```
std::cin >> x;
if (std::cin.fail()) {
    ...
}
```

13.4.4   Stream State and Exceptions

Exception handling was introduced to C++ for the handling of errors and exceptions (see page 15). However, this was done after streams were already in wide use. To stay backward compatible, by default, streams throw no exceptions. However, for the standardized streams, it is possible to define, for every state flag, whether setting that flag will trigger an exception. This definition is done by the exceptions() member function (Table 13.6).

Member Function	Meaning
exceptions(*flags*)	Sets flags that trigger exceptions
exceptions()	Returns the flags that trigger exceptions

Table 13.6. Stream Member Functions for Exceptions

Calling exceptions() without an argument yields the current flags for which exceptions are triggered. No exceptions are thrown if the function returns goodbit. This is the default, to maintain backward compatibility. When exceptions() is called with an argument, exceptions are thrown as soon as the corresponding state flags are set. If a state flag is already set when exceptions() is called with an argument, an exception is thrown if the corresponding flag is set in the argument.

The following example configures the stream so that, for all flags, an exception is thrown:

```
// throw exceptions for all "errors"
strm.exceptions (std::ios::eofbit | std::ios::failbit |
                 std::ios::badbit);
```

If 0 or goodbit is passed as an argument, no exceptions are generated:

```
// do not generate exceptions
strm.exceptions (std::ios::goodbit);
```

Exceptions are thrown when the corresponding state flags are set after calling clear() or setstate(). An exception is even thrown if the flag was already set and not cleared:

```
// this call throws an exception if failbit is set on entry
strm.exceptions (std::ios::failbit);
...
// throw an exception (even if failbit was already set)
strm.setstate (std::ios::failbit);
```

The exceptions thrown are objects of the class std::ios_base::failure, which is derived from class exception (see Section 3.3.1, page 25):

```
namespace std {
    class ios_base::failure : public exception {
      public:
        // constructor
```

```
        explicit failure (const string& msg);
```

// destructor
```
        virtual ~failure();
```

// return information about the exception
```
        virtual const char* what() const;
    };
}
```

Unfortunately, the standard does not require that the exception object includes any information about the erroneous stream or the kind of error. The only portable method that can be used to get information about the error is the error message returned from `what()`. But note, only *calling* `what()` is portable; the string it returns is not. If additional information is necessary, the programmer must arrange to get the required information.

This behavior shows that exception handling is intended to be used more for unexpected situations. It is called *exception handling* rather than *error handling*. Expected errors, such as format errors during input from the user, are considered to be "normal" and are usually better handled using the state flags.

The major area in which stream exceptions are useful is reading preformatted data such as automatically written files. But even then, problems arise if exception handling is used. For example, if it is desired to read data until end-of-file, you can't get exceptions for errors without getting an exception for end-of-file. This is because the detection of end-of-file also sets the `failbit` (meaning that reading an object was not successful). To distinguish end-of-file from an input error you have to check the state of the stream.

The next example demonstrates how this might look. It shows a function that reads floating-point values from a stream until end-of-file is reached. Then it returns the sum of the floating-point values read:

```
// io/sum1a.cpp

#include <istream>

namespace MyLib {
    double readAndProcessSum (std::istream& strm)
    {
        using std::ios;
        double value, sum;
```

// save current state of exception flags
```
        ios::iostate oldExceptions = strm.exceptions();
```

```
/* let failbit and badbit throw exceptions
 * - NOTE: failbit is also set at end-of-file
 */
strm.exceptions (ios::failbit | ios::badbit);

try {
    /* while stream is OK
     * - read value and add it to sum
     */
    sum = 0;
    while (strm >> value) {
        sum += value;
    }
}
catch (...) {
    /* if exception not caused by end-of-file
     * - restore old state of exception flags
     * - rethrow exception
     */
    if (!strm.eof()) {
        strm.exceptions(oldExceptions);    // restore exception flags
        throw;                             // rethrow
    }
}

// restore old state of exception flags
strm.exceptions (oldExceptions);

// return sum
return sum;
    }
}
```

First the function stores the set stream exceptions in `oldExceptions` to restore them later. Then the stream is configured to throw an exception on certain conditions. In a loop, all values are read and added as long as the stream is OK. If end-of-file is reached, the stream is no longer OK, and a corresponding exception is thrown even though no exception is thrown for setting `eofbit`. This happens because end-of-file is detected on an unsuccessful attempt to read more data, which also sets the `failbit`. To avoid the behavior that end-of-file throws an exception, the exception is caught locally to check the state of the stream by using eof(). The exception is propagated only if eof() yields false.

Note that restoring the original exception flags may cause exceptions. exceptions() throws an exception if a corresponding flag is set in the stream already. Thus, if the state did throw exceptions for eofbit, failbit, or badbit on function entry, these exceptions are propagated to the caller.

This function can be called in the simplest case from the following main function:

```cpp
// io/summain.cpp

#include <iostream>
#include <cstdlib>

namespace MyLib {
    double readAndProcessSum (std::istream&);
}

int main()
{
    using namespace std;
    double sum;

    try {
        sum = MyLib::readAndProcessSum(cin);
    }
    catch (const ios::failure& error) {
        cerr << "I/O exception: " << error.what() << endl;
        return EXIT_FAILURE;
    }
    catch (const exception& error) {
        cerr << "standard exception: " << error.what() << endl;
        return EXIT_FAILURE;
    }
    catch (...) {
        cerr << "unknown exception" << endl;
        return EXIT_FAILURE;
    }

    // print sum
    cout << "sum: " << sum << endl;
}
```

The question arises whether this is worth the effort. It is also possible to work with streams not throwing an exception. In this case, an exception is thrown if an error is detected. This has the additional advantage that user-defined error messages and error classes can be used:

```cpp
// io/sum2a.cpp

#include <istream>

namespace MyLib {
    double readAndProcessSum (std::istream& strm)
    {
        double value, sum;

        /* while stream is OK
         * - read value and add it to sum
         */
        sum = 0;
        while (strm >> value) {
            sum += value;
        }

        if (!strm.eof()) {
            throw std::ios::failure
                    ("input error in readAndProcessSum()");
        }

        // return sum
        return sum;
    }
}
```

This looks somewhat simpler, doesn't it? This version of the function needs the header <string> because the constructor of the class failure takes a reference to a constant string as an argument. To construct an object of this type, the definition is needed but the header <istream> is only required to provide a declaration.

13.5 Standard Input/Output Functions

Instead of using the standard operators for streams (operator << and operator >>), you can use several other member functions for reading and writing, which are presented in this section.

The functions in this section read or write "unformatted" data (unlike operators >> or <<, which read or write "formatted" data). When reading, they never skip leading whitespaces (unlike the operators that are, by default, configured to skip leading whitespace). Also, they handle exceptions differently than the formatted I/O functions: If an exception is thrown, either from a called function or as a result of setting a state flag (see Section 13.4.4, page 602), the badbit flag is set. The exception is then rethrown if the exception mask has badbit set. However, the unformatted functions create a sentry object like the formatted functions do (see Section 13.12.4, page 658).

These functions use type streamsize to specify counts, which is defined in <ios>:

```
namespace std {
    typedef ... streamsize;
    ...
}
```

The type streamsize usually is a signed version of size_t. It is signed because it is also used to specify negative values.

13.5.1 Member Functions for Input

In the following definitions, *istream* is a placeholder for the stream class used for reading. It can stand for istream, wistream, or some other instantiation of the template class basic_istream. The type *char* is a placeholder for the corresponding character type, which is char for istream and wchar_t for wistream. Other types or values printed in italics depend on the exact definition of the character type or on the traits class associated with the stream.

The C++ standard library provides several member functions to read character sequences. Table 13.7 compares their abilities.

Member Function	Reads Until	Number of Characters	Appends Termin.	Returns
get(s,num)	Excluding newline or end-of-file	Up to num−1	Yes	istream
get(s,num,t)	Excluding t or end-of-file	Up to num−1	Yes	istream
getline(s,num)	Including newline or end-of-file	Up to num−1	Yes	istream
getline(s,num,t)	Including t or end-of-file	Up to num−1	Yes	istream
read(s,num)	end-of-file	num	No	istream
readsome(s,num)	end-of-file	Up to num	No	count

Table 13.7. Abilities of Stream Operators Reading Character Sequences

int **istream** : :**get** ()

- Reads the next character.
- Returns the read character or *EOF*.
- In general, the return type is `traits::int_type` and *EOF* is the value returned by `traits::eof()`. For `istream`, the return type is `int` and *EOF* is the constant `EOF`. Hence, for `istream` this function corresponds to C's `getchar()` or `getc()`.
- Note that the returned value is not necessarily of the character type but can be of a type with a larger range of values. Otherwise, it would be impossible to distinguish *EOF* from characters with the corresponding value.

istream& **istream** : :**get** (*char& c*)

- Assigns the next character to the passed argument *c*.
- Returns the stream. The stream's state tells whether the read was successful.

istream& **istream** : :**get** (*char* str*, `streamsize` *count*)
istream& **istream** : :**get** (*char* str*, `streamsize` *count, char delim*)

- Both forms read up to *count*-1 characters into the character sequence pointed to by *str*.
- The first form terminates the reading if the next character to be read is the newline character of the corresponding character set. For `istream`, it is the character `'\n'` and for `wistream` it is `wchar_t('\n')` (see page 691). In general, `widen('\n')` is used (see page 626).
- The second form terminates the reading if the next character to be read is *delim*.
- Both forms return the stream. The stream's state tells whether the read was successful.
- The terminating character (*delim*) is not read.
- The read character sequence is terminated by a string termination character.
- The caller must ensure that *str* is large enough for *count* characters.

istream& **istream** : :**getline** (*char* str*, `streamsize` *count*)
istream& **istream** : :**getline** (*char* str*, `streamsize` *count, char delim*)

- Both forms are identical to their previous counterparts of `get()` except the following:
  - They terminate the reading *including* but not before the newline character or *delim* respectively. Thus, the newline character or *delim* is read if it occurs within *count*-1 characters, but it is *not* stored in *str*.
  - If they read lines with more than *count*-1 characters, they set `failbit`

istream& **istream** : :**read** (*char* str*, `streamsize` *count*)

- Reads *count* characters into the string *str*.
- Returns the stream. The stream's state tells whether the read was successful.
- The string in *str* is *not* terminated automatically with the string termination character.
- The caller must ensure that *str* has sufficient space to store *count* characters.
- Encountering end-of-file during reading is considered an error, and `failbit` is set (in addition to `eofbit`).

streamsize *istream*::**readsome** (*char* str*, streamsize *count*)

- Reads up to *count* characters into the string *str*.
- Returns the number of characters read.
- The string in *str* is *not* terminated automatically with the string termination character.
- The caller must ensure that *str* has sufficient space to store *count* characters.
- In contrast to read(), readsome() reads all available characters of the stream buffer (using the in_avail() member function of the buffer). This is useful when it is undesirable to wait for the input because it comes from the keyboard or other processes. Encountering end-of-file is not considered an error and sets neither eofbit nor failbit.

streamsize *istream*::**gcount** () const

- Returns the number of characters read by the last *unformatted* read operation.

istream& *istream*::**ignore** ()

istream& *istream*::**ignore** (streamsize *count*)

istream& *istream*::**ignore** (streamsize *count*, int *delim*)

- All forms extract and discard characters.
- The first form ignores one character.
- The second form ignores up to *count* characters.
- The third form ignores up to *count* characters until *delim* is extracted and discarded.
- If *count* is std::numeric_limits<std::streamsize>::max() (the largest value of type std::streamsize, see Section 4.3, page 59), all characters are discarded until either *delim* or end-of-file is reached.
- All forms return the stream.
- Examples:
  - The following call discards the rest of the line:
        cin.ignore(numeric_limits<std::streamsize>::max(),'\n');
  - The following call discards the complete remainder of cin:
        cin.ignore(numeric_limits<std::streamsize>::max());

int istream::**peek** ()

- Returns the next character to be read from the stream without extracting it. The next read will read this character (unless the read position is modified).
- Returns *EOF*, if no more characters can be read.
- *EOF* is the value returned from traits::eof(). For istream, this is the constant EOF.

istream& *istream*::**unget** ()

istream& *istream*::**putback** (*char c*)

- Both functions put the last character read back into the stream so that it is read again by the next read (unless the read position is modified).

- The difference between `ungetc()` and `putback()` is that for `putback()` a check is made whether the character *c* passed is indeed the last character read.

- If the character cannot be put back or if the wrong character is put back with `putback()`, `badbit` is set, which may throw a corresponding exception (see Section 13.4.4, page 602).

- The maximum number of characters that can be put back with these functions is implementation defined. Only one call of these functions between two reads is guaranteed to work by the standard and thus is portable.

When C-strings are read it is safer to use the functions from this section than to use operator >>. This is because the maximum string size to be read must be passed explicitly as an argument. Although it is possible to limit the number of characters read when using operator >> (see page 618), this is easily forgotten.

It is often better to use the stream buffer directly instead of using istream member functions. Stream buffers provide member functions that read single characters or character sequences efficiently without overhead due to the construction of `sentry` objects (see Section 13.12.4, page 658, for more information on `sentry` objects). Section 13.13, page 663, explains the stream buffer interface in detail. Another alternative is to use the template class `istreambuf_iterator`, which provides an iterator interface to the stream buffer (see Section 13.13.2, page 665).

Two other functions for manipulating the read position are `tellg()` and `seekg()`. These are relevant mainly in conjunction with files, so their descriptions are deferred until Section 13.9.2, page 634.

13.5.2   Member Functions for Output

In the following definitions *ostream* is a placeholder for the stream class used for writing. It can stand for `ostream`, `wostream`, or some other instantiation of the template class `basic_ostream`. The type *char* is a placeholder for the corresponding character type, which is `char` for `ostream` and `wchar_t` for `wostream`. Other types or values printed in italics depend on the exact definition of the character type or on the traits class associated with the stream.

ostream& ostream::**put** (*char c*)

- Writes the argument *c* to the stream.
- Returns the stream. The stream's state tells whether the write was successful.

ostream& ostream::**write** (const *char* str*, streamsize *count*)

- Writes *count* characters of the string *str* to the stream.
- Returns the stream. The stream's state tells whether the write was successful.
- The string termination character does *not* terminate the write and will be written.
- The caller must ensure that *str* really contains at least *count* characters; otherwise, the behavior is undefined.

ostream& ostream::**flush** ()

- Flushes the buffers of the stream (forces a write of all buffered data to the device or I/O channel to which it belongs).

Two other functions modify the write position: `tellp()` and `seekp()`. These functions are relevant mainly in conjunction with files, so their descriptions are deferred until Section 13.9.2, page 634.

Like the input functions, it may also be reasonable to use the stream buffer directly or to use the template class `ostreambuf_iterator` for unformatted writing. There is actually no point in using the unformatted output functions, except that these functions might handle some locks in multithreaded environments using `sentry` objects. See Section 13.14.3, page 683, for details.

13.5.3   Example Uses

The classic filter framework that simply writes all read characters looks like this in C++:

```
// io/charcat1.cpp

#include <iostream>
using namespace std;

int main()
{
    char c;

    // while it is possible to read a character
    while (cin.get(c)) {
        // print it
        cout.put(c);
    }
}
```

With each call of

```
cin.get(c)
```

the next character is simply assigned to c, which is passed by reference. The return value of `get()` is the stream; thus, `while` tests whether `cin` is still in a good state.[7]

To perform better, you can operate directly on stream buffers. See page 667 for a version of this example that uses stream buffer iterators for I/O and page 683 for a version that copies the whole input in one statement.

---

[7] Note that this interface is better than the usual C interface for filters. In C, you have to use `getchar()` or `getc()`, which return both the next character or whether end-of-file was reached. This causes the problem that you have to process the return value as `int` to distinguish any `char` value from the value for end-of-file.

13.6   Manipulators

Manipulators for streams were introduced in Section 13.1.5, page 586. They are objects that modify a stream when applied with the standard I/O operators. This does not necessarily mean that something is read or written. The basic manipulators defined in `<istream>` or `<ostream>` are presented in Table 13.8.

Manipulator	Class	Meaning
flush	basic_ostream	Flushes the output buffer to its device
endl	basic_ostream	Inserts a newline character into the buffer and flushes the output buffer to its device
ends	basic_ostream	Inserts a string termination character into the buffer
ws	basic_istream	Reads and ignores whitespaces

Table 13.8. Manipulators Defined in `<istream>` *or* `<ostream>`

There are additional manipulators, for example, to change I/O formats. These manipulators are introduced in Section 13.7, page 615, about formatting.

13.6.1   How Manipulators Work

Manipulators are implemented using a very simple trick. This trick not only enables the convenient manipulation of streams, it also demonstrates the power provided by function overloading. Manipulators are nothing more than functions that are passed to the I/O operators as arguments. The functions are then called by the operator. For example, the output operator for class `ostream` is basically overloaded like this[7]:

```
ostream& ostream::operator << ( ostream& (*op)(ostream&))
{
    // call the function passed as parameter with this stream as the argument
    return (*op)(*this);
}
```

The argument op is a pointer to a function. More precisely, it is a function that takes *ostream* as an argument and returns *ostream* (it is assumed that the *ostream* given as the argument is returned). If the second operand of operator << is such a function, this function is called with the first operand of operator << as the argument.

This may sound very complicated, but it is actually relatively simple. An example should make it clearer. The manipulator (that is, the function) `endl()` for `ostream` is implemented basically like this:

---

[7] The real implementation looks a little bit more complicated because it has to construct a `sentry` object and because it is actually a function template.

```
std::ostream& std::endl (std::ostream& strm)
{
    // write newline
    strm.put('\n');

    // flush the output buffer
    strm.flush();

    // return strm to allow chaining
    return strm;
}
```

You can use this manipulator in an expression such as the following:

```
std::cout << std::endl
```

Here, operator << is called for stream cout with the endl() function as the second operand. The implementation of operator << transforms this call into a call of the passed function with the stream as the argument:

```
std::endl(std::cout)
```

The same effect as "writing" the manipulator can also be achieved by calling this expression directly. There is actually an advantage in using the function notation: It is not necessary to provide the namespace:

```
endl(std::cout)
```

This is because functions are looked up in the namespaces where their arguments are defined if they are not found otherwise (see page 17).

Because the stream classes are actually template classes parameterized with the character type, the real implementation of endl() looks like this:

```
template<class charT, class traits>
std::basic_ostream<charT,traits>&
std::endl (std::basic_ostream<charT,traits>& strm)
{
    strm.put(strm.widen('\n'));
    strm.flush();
    return strm;
}
```

The member function widen() is used to convert the newline character into the character set currently used by the stream. See Section 13.8, page 625, for more details.

The C++ standard library also contains manipulators with arguments. How these manipulators work exactly is implementation dependent, and there is no standard way to implement user-defined manipulators with arguments.

The standard manipulators with arguments are defined in the header file `<iomanip>`, which must be included to work with the standard manipulators taking arguments:

```
#include <iomanip>
```

The standard manipulators taking arguments are all concerned with details of formatting, so they are described when formatting options are described.

13.6.2   User-Defined Manipulators

You can define your own manipulators. All you need to do is to write a function such as `endl()`. For example, the following function defines a manipulator that ignores all characters until end-of-line:

```cpp
// io/ignore.hpp

#include <istream>
#include <limits>

template <class charT, class traits>
inline
std::basic_istream<charT,traits>&
ignoreLine (std::basic_istream<charT,traits>& strm)
{
    // skip until end-of-line
    strm.ignore(std::numeric_limits<int>::max(),strm.widen('\n'));

    // return stream for concatenation
    return strm;
}
```

The manipulator simply delegates the work to the function `ignore()`, which in this case discards all characters until end-of-line (`ignore()` was introduced on page 609).

The application of the manipulator is very simple:

```cpp
// ignore the rest of the line
std::cin >> ignoreLine;
```

Applying this manipulator multiple times enables you to ignore multiple lines:

```cpp
// ignore two lines
std::cin >> ignoreLine >> ignoreLine;
```

This works because a call to the function `ignore(max,c)` ignores all characters until the c is found in the input stream (or `max` characters are read or the end of the stream was reached). However, this character is discarded, too, before the function returns.

13.7 Formatting

Two concepts influence the definition of I/O formats: Most obviously, there are format flags that define, for example, numeric precision, the fill character, or the numeric base. Apart from this, there exists the possibility of adjusting the formats to meet special national conventions. This section introduces the format flags. Section 13.8, page 625, and Chapter 14 describe the aspects of internationalized formatting.

13.7.1 Format Flags

The class `ios_base` has several members that are used for the definition of various I/O formats. For example, it has members that store the minimum field width, the precision of floating-point numbers, or the fill character. A member of type `ios::fmtflags` stores configuration flags defining, for example, whether positive numbers should be preceded by a positive sign or whether Boolean values should be printed numerically or as words.

Some of the format flags form groups. For example, the flags for octal, decimal, and hexadecimal formats of integer numbers form a group. Special masks are defined to make dealing with such groups easier.

Member Function	Meaning
`setf` (*flags*)	Sets *flags* as additional format flags and returns the previous state of all flags
`setf` (*flags, mask*)	Sets *flags* as the new format flags of the group identified by *mask* and returns the previous state of all flags
`unsetf` (*flags*)	Clears *flags*
`flags()`	Returns all set format flags
`flags` (*flags*)	Sets *flags* as the new format flags and returns the previous state of all flags
`copyfmt` (*stream*)	Copies *all* format definitions from *stream*

Table 13.9. Member Function to Access Format Flags

Several member functions can be used to handle all of the format definitions of a stream. These are presented in Table 13.9. The functions `setf()` and `unsetf()` set or clear, respectively, one or more flags. You can manipulate multiple flags at once by combining them using the "binary or" operator; that is, operator |. The function `setf()` can take a mask as the second argument to clear all flags in a group before setting the flags of the first argument, which are also limited to a group. This does not happen with the version of `setf()` that takes only one argument. For example:

```
// set flags showpos and uppercase
std::cout.setf (std::ios::showpos | std::ios::uppercase);
```

```
// set only the flag hex in the group basefield
std::cout.setf (std::ios::hex, std::ios::basefield);
```

```
// clear the flag uppercase
std::cout.unsetf (std::ios::uppercase);
```

Using `flags()` you can manipulate all format flags at once. Calling `flags()` without an argument returns the current format flags. Calling `flags()` with an argument takes this argument as the new state of all format flags and returns the old state. Thus, `flags()` with an argument clears all flags and sets the flags that were passed. Using `flags()` is useful, for example, for saving the current state of the flags to restore the original state later. The following statements demonstrate an example:

```
using std::ios, std::cout;
```

```
// save current format flags
ios::fmtflags oldFlags = cout.flags();
```

```
// do some changes
cout.setf(ios::showpos | ios::showbase | ios::uppercase);
cout.setf(ios::internal, ios::adjustfield);
cout << std::hex << x << std::endl;
```

```
// restore saved format flags
cout.flags(oldFlags);
```

By using `copyfmt()` you can copy all the format information from one stream to another. See page 653 for an example.

You can also use manipulators to set and clear format flags. These are presented in Table 13.10.

Manipulator	Effect
setiosflags(*flags*)	Sets *flags* as format flags (calls setf(*flags*) for the stream)
resetiosflags(*mask*)	Clears all flags of the group identified by *mask* (calls setf(0,*mask*) for the stream)

Table 13.10. Manipulators to Access Format Flags

The manipulators `setiosflags()` and `resetiosflags()` provide the possibility of setting or clearing, respectively, one or more flags in a write or read statement with operator `<<` or `>>` respectively. To use one of these manipulators, you must include the header file `<iomanip>`. For example:

```
#include <iostream>
#include <iomanip>
...
std::cout << resetiosflags(std::ios::adjustfield) // clear adjustm. flags
          << setiosflags(std::ios::left);         // left-adjust values
```

Some flag manipulations are performed by specialized manipulators. These manipulators are used often because they are more convenient and more readable. They are discussed in the following subsections.

13.7.2   Input/Output Format of Boolean Values

The `boolalpha` flag defines the format used to read or to write Boolean values. It defines whether a numeric or a textual representation is used for Boolean values (Table 13.11).

Flag	Meaning
boolalpha	If set, specifies the use of textual representation; if not set, specifies the use of numeric representation

Table 13.11. Flag for Boolean Representation

If the flag is not set (this is the default), Boolean values are represented using numeric strings. In this case, the value 0 is always used for `false` and the value 1 is always used for `true`. When reading a Boolean value as a numeric string it is considered to be an error (setting `failbit` for the stream) if the value is different from 0 or 1.

If the flag is set, Boolean values are written using a textual representation. When a Boolean value is read, the string has to match the textual representation of either `true` or `false`. The stream's locale object is used to determine the strings used to represent `true` and `false` (see page 626 and page 698). The standard "C" locale object uses the strings "true" and "false" as representations of the Boolean values.

Special manipulators are defined for the convenient manipulation of this flag (Table 13.12).

Manipulator	Meaning
boolalpha	Forces textual representation (sets the flag ios::boolalpha)
noboolalpha	Forces numeric representation (clears the flag ios::boolalpha)

Table 13.12. Manipulators for Boolean Representation

For example, the following statements print b first in numeric and then in textual representation:

```
bool b;
...
std::cout << std::noboolalpha << b << " == "
          << std::boolalpha << b << std::endl;
```

13.7.3   Field Width, Fill Character, and Adjustment

Two member functions are used to define the field width and the fill character: `width()` and `fill()` (Table 13.13).

Member Function	Meaning
`width()`	Returns the current field width
`width(`*val*`)`	Sets the field width to *val* and returns the previous field width
`fill()`	Returns the current fill character
`fill(`*c*`)`	Defines *c* as the fill character and returns the previous fill character

Table 13.13. Member Functions for the Field Width and the Fill Character

Using Field Width, Fill Character, and Adjustment for Output

For the output `width()` defines a minimum field. This definition applies only to the next formatted field written. Calling `width()` without arguments returns the current field width. Calling `width()` with an integral argument changes the width and returns the former value. The default value for the minimum field width is 0, which means that the field may have any length. This is also the value to which the field width is set after a value was written.

Note that the field width is never used to truncate output. Thus, you can't specify a maximum field width. Instead, you have to program it. For example, you could write to a string and output only a certain number of characters.

`fill()` defines the fill character that is used to fill the difference between the formatted representation of a value and the minimum field width. The default fill character is a space.

To adjust values within a field, three flags are defined, as shown in Table 13.14. These flags are defined in the class `ios_base` together with the corresponding mask.

Mask	Flag	Meaning
`adjustfield`	`left`	Left-adjusts the value
	`right`	Right-adjusts the value
	`internal`	Left-adjusts the sign and right-adjusts the value
	None	Right-adjusts the value (the default)

Table 13.14. Masks to Adjust Values within a Field

After any formatted I/O operation is performed, the default field width is restored. The values of the fill character and the adjustment remain unchanged until they are modified explicitly.

Table 13.15 presents the effect of the functions and the flags used for different values. The underscore is used as the fill character.

Adjustment	`width()`	-42	0.12	`"Q"`	`'Q'`
`left`	6	-42___	0.12__	Q_____	Q_____
`right`	6	___-42	__0.12	_____Q	_____Q
`internal`	6	-___42	__0.12	_____Q	_____Q

Table 13.15. Examples of Adjustment

Note that the adjustment for single characters has changed during the standardization. Before standardization, the field width was ignored if single characters were written. It was used for the next formatted output that was not a single character. This bug was fixed. However, for programs that used this bug as a feature, the fix breaks backward compatibility.

Several manipulators are defined to handle the field width, the fill character, and the adjustment (Table 13.16).

Manipulator	Meaning
`setw(`*val*`)`	Sets the field width for input and output to *val* (corresponds to `width()`)
`setfill(`*c*`)`	Defines *c* as the fill character (corresponds to `fill()`)
`left`	Left-adjusts the value
`right`	Right-adjusts the value
`internal`	Left-adjusts the sign and right-adjusts the value

Table 13.16. Manipulators for Adjustment

The manipulators `setw()` and `setfill()` use an argument, so you must include the header file `<iomanip>` to use them. For example, the statements

```
#include <iostream>
#include <iomanip>
...
std::cout << std::setw(8) << std::setfill('_') << -3.14
          << ' ' << 42 << std::endl;
std::cout << std::setw(8) << "sum: "
          << std::setw(8) << 42 << std::endl;
```

produce this output:

```
___-3.14 42
___sum: _____42
```

Using Field Width for Input

You can use the field width also to define the maximum number of characters read when character sequences of type `char*` are read. If the value of `width()` is not 0, then at most `width()-1` characters are read.

Because of the fact that ordinary C-strings can't grow while values are read, `width()` or `setw()` should always be used when reading them with operator `>>`. For example:

```
char buffer[81];


// read, at most, 80 characters:
cin >> setw(sizeof(buffer)) >> buffer;
```

This reads, at most, 80 characters, although `sizeof(buffer)` is 81 because one character is used for the string termination character (which is appended automatically). Note that the following code is a common error:

```
char* s;
cin >> setw(sizeof(s)) >> s;      // RUNTIME ERROR
```

This is because s is only declared as a pointer without any storage for characters, and `sizeof(s)` is the size of the pointer instead of the size of the storage to which it points. This is a typical example of the problems you encounter if you use C-strings. By using strings, you won't run into these problems:

```
string buffer;
cin >> buffer;                        // OK
```

13.7.4   Positive Sign and Uppercase Letters

Two format flags are defined to influence the general appearance of numeric values: `showpos` and `uppercase` (Table 13.17).

Flag	Meaning
showpos	Writes a positive sign on positive numbers
uppercase	Uses uppercase letters

Table 13.17. Flags Affecting Sign and Letters of Numeric Values

`ios::showpos` dictates that a positive sign for positive numeric values be written. If the flag is not set, only negative values are written with a sign. `ios::uppercase` dictates that letters in numeric values be written using uppercase letters. This flag applies to integers using hexadecimal format and to floating-point numbers using scientific notation. By default, letters are written as lowercase and no positive sign is written. For example, the statements

```
std::cout << 12345678.9 << std::endl;

std::cout.setf (std::ios::showpos | std::ios::uppercase);
std::cout << 12345678.9 << std::endl;
```

produce this output:

```
1.23457e+07
+1.23457E+07
```

Both flags can be set or cleared using the manipulators presented in Table 13.18.

Manipulator	Meaning
showpos	Forces to write a positive sign on positive numbers (sets the flag `ios::showpos`)
noshowpos	Forces not to write a positive sign (clears the flag `ios::showpos`)
uppercase	Forces uppercase letters (sets the flag `ios::uppercase`)
nouppercase	Forces lowercase letters (clears the flag `ios::uppercase`)

Table 13.18. Manipulators for Sign and Letters of Numeric Values

13.7.5   Numeric Base

A group of three flags defines which base is used for I/O of integer values. The flags are defined in the class `ios_base` with the corresponding mask (Table 13.19).

Mask	Flag	Meaning
basefield	oct	Writes and reads octal
	dec	Writes and reads decimal (default)
	hex	Writes and reads hexadecimal
	None	Writes decimal and reads according to the leading characters of the integral value

Table 13.19. Flags Defining the Base of Integral Values

A change in base applies to the processing of all integer numbers until the flags are reset. By default, decimal format is used. There is no support for binary notation. However, you can read and write integral values in binary by using class `bitset`. See Section 10.4.1, page 462, for details.

If none of the base flags is set, output uses a decimal base. If more than one flag is set, decimal is used as the base.

The flags for the numeric base also affect input. If one of the flags for the numeric base is set, all numbers are read using this base. If no flag for the base is set when numbers are read the base is determined by the leading characters: A number starting with 0x or 0X is read as a hexadecimal number. A number starting with 0 is read as an octal number. In all other cases, the number is read as a decimal value.

There are basically two ways to switch these flags:

1. Clear one flag and set another:

```
std::cout.unsetf (std::ios::dec);
std::cout.setf (std::ios::hex);
```

2. Set one flag and clear all other flags in the group automatically:

```
std::cout.setf (std::ios::hex, std::ios::basefield);
```

In addition, manipulators are defined that make the handling of these flags significantly simpler (Table 13.20).

Manipulator	Meaning
oct	Writes and reads octal
dec	Writes and reads decimal
hex	Writes and reads hexadecimal

Table 13.20. Manipulators Defining the Base of Integral Values

For example, the following statements write x and y in hexadecimal, and z in decimal:

```
int x, y, z;
...
std::cout << std::hex << x << std::endl;
std::cout << y << ' ' << std::dec << z << std::endl;
```

An additional flag, showbase, lets you write numbers according to the usual C/C++ convention for indicating numeric bases of literal values (Table 13.21).

Flag	Meaning
showbase	If set, indicates the numeric base

Table 13.21. Flags to Indicate the Numeric Base

If ios::showbase is set, octal numbers are preceded by a 0 and hexadecimal numbers are preceded by 0x (or, if ios::uppercase is set, by 0X). For example, the statements

```
std::cout << 127 << ' ' << 255 << std::endl;

std::cout << std::hex << 127 << ' ' << 255 << std::endl;

std::cout.setf(std::ios::showbase);
std::cout << 127 << ' ' << 255 << std::endl;
```

```
std::cout.setf(std::ios::uppercase);
std::cout << 127 << ' ' << 255 << std::endl;
```

produce this output:

```
127 255
7f ff
0x7f 0xff
0X7F 0XFF
```

`ios::showbase` can also be manipulated using the manipulators presented in Table 13.22.

Manipulator	Meaning
showbase	Indicates numeric base (sets the flag `ios::showbase`)
noshowbase	Does not indicate numeric base (clears the flag `ios::showbase`)

Table 13.22. Manipulators to Indicate the Numeric Base

13.7.6   Floating-Point Notation

Several flags and members control the output of floating-point values. The flags, presented in Table 13.23, define whether output is written using decimal or scientific notation. These flags are defined in the class `ios_base` together with the corresponding mask. If `ios::fixed` is set, floating-point values are printed using decimal notation. If `ios::scientific` is set scientific (that is, exponential) notation is used.

Mask	Flag	Meaning
floatfield	fixed	Uses decimal notation
	scientific	Uses scientific notation
	None	Uses the "best" of these two notations (default)

Table 13.23. Flags for the Floating-Point Notation

To define the precision, the member function `precision()` is provided (see Table 13.24).

Member Function	Meaning
precision()	Returns the current precision of floating-point values
precision(*val*)	Sets *val* as the new precision of floating-point values and returns the old

Table 13.24. Member Function for the Precision of Floating-Point Values

If scientific notation is used, `precision()` defines the number of decimal places in the fractional part. In all cases, the remainder is not cut off but rounded. Calling `precision()` without arguments returns the current precision. Calling it with an argument sets the precision to that value and returns the previous precision. The default precision is six decimal places.

By default, neither `ios::fixed` nor `ios::scientific` is set. In this case, the notation used depends on the value written. All meaningful but, at most, `precision()` decimal places are written as follows: A leading zero before the decimal point and/or all trailing zeros, and potentially even the decimal point, are removed. If `precision()` places are sufficient, decimal notation is used; otherwise, scientific notation is used.

Using the flag `showpoint`, you can force the stream to write a decimal point and trailing zeros until `precision()` places are written (Table 13.25).

Flag	Meaning
showpoint	Always writes a decimal point

Table 13.25. Flag to Force Decimal Point

Table 13.26 shows the somewhat complicated dependencies between flags and precision, using two concrete values as an example.

	precision()	421.0	0.0123456789
Normal	2	4.2e+02	0.012
	6	421	0.0123457
With showpoint	2	4.2e+02	0.012
	6	421.000	0.0123457
fixed	2	421.00	0.01
	6	421.000000	0.012346
scientific	2	4.21e+02	1.23e-02
	6	4.210000e+02	1.234568e-02

Table 13.26. Example of Floating-Point Formatting

As for integral values, `ios::showpos` can be used to write a positive sign. `ios::uppercase` can be used to dictate whether the scientific notation should use an uppercase E or a lowercase e.

The flag `ios::showpoint`, the notation, and the precision can be configured using the manipulators presented in Table 13.27.

For example, the statement

```
std::cout << std::scientific << std::showpoint
        << std::setprecision(8)
        << 0.123456789 << std::endl;
```

produces this output:

```
1.23456789e-01
```

Manipulator	Meaning
`showpoint`	Always writes a decimal point (sets the flag `ios::showpoint`)
`noshowpoint`	Does not require a decimal point (clears the flag `showpoint`)
`setprecision(val)`	Sets *val* as the new value for the precision
`fixed`	Uses decimal notation
`scientific`	Uses scientific notation

Table 13.27. Manipulators for Floating-Point Values

`setprecision()` is a manipulator with an argument, so you must include the header file `<iomanip>` to use it.

13.7.7   General Formatting Definitions

Two more format flags complete the list of formatting flags: `skipws` and `unitbuf` (Table 13.28).

Flag	Meaning
`skipws`	Skips leading whitespaces automatically when reading a value with operator `>>`
`unitbuf`	Flushes the output buffer after each write operation

Table 13.28. Other Formatting Flags

`ios::skipws` is set by default, meaning that by default leading whitespaces are skipped by certain read operations. Normally, it is useful to have this flag set. For example, with it set, reading the separating spaces between numbers explicitly is not necessary. However, this implies reading space characters using operator `>>` is not possible because leading whitespaces are always skipped.

`ios::unitbuf` controls the buffering of the output. With `ios::unitbuf` set, output is basically unbuffered. The output buffer is flushed after each write operation. By default, this flag is not set. However, for the streams `cerr` and `wcerr` this flag is set initially.

Both flags can be manipulated using the manipulators presented in Table 13.29.

13.8   Internationalization

You can adapt I/O formats to national conventions. The class `ios_base` defines for this purpose the member functions presented in Table 13.30.

Each stream uses an associated locale object. The initial default locale object is a copy of the global locale object at the construction time of the stream. The locale object defines, for example, details about numeric formatting, such as the character used as the decimal point or the strings used for the textual representation of Boolean values.

Manipulator	Meaning
skipws	Skips leading whitespaces with operator >> (sets the flag ios::skipws)
noskipws	Does not skip leading whitespaces with operator >> (clears the flag ios::skipws)
unitbuf	Flushes the output buffer after each write operation (sets the flag ios::unitbuf)
nounitbuf	Does not flush the output buffer after each write operation (clears the flag ios::unitbuf)

Table 13.29. Manipulators for Other Formatting Flags

Member Function	Meaning
imbue(*loc*)	Sets the locale object
getloc()	Returns the current locale object

Table 13.30. Member Functions for Internationalization

In contrast to the C localization facilities, you can configure each stream individually with a specific locale object. This capability can be used, for example, to read floating-point values according to American format and to write them using German format (in German, a comma is used as the "decimal point"). Section 14.2.1, page 694, presents an example and discusses the details.

Several characters, mainly special characters, are often needed in the character set of the stream. For this reason, some conversion functions are provided by streams (Table 13.31).

Member Function	Meaning
widen(*c*)	Converts the char character *c* to a character of the stream's character set
narrow(*c*,*def*)	Converts character *c* from the stream's character set to a char (if there is no such char, *def* is returned)

Table 13.31. Stream Functions for the Internationalization of Characters

For example, to get the newline character from the character set of the stream strm, you can use a statement like

```
strm.widen('\n')
```

For additional details on locales and on internationalization in general, see Chapter 14.

13.9   File Access

Streams can be used to access files. The C++ standard library provides four class templates for which the following standard specializations are predefined:

1. The template class `basic_ifstream<>` with the specializations `ifstream` and `wifstream` is for read access to files ("input file stream").
2. The template class `basic_ofstream<>` with the specializations `ofstream` and `wofstream` is for write access to files ("output file stream").
3. The template class `basic_fstream<>` with the specializations `fstream` and `wfstream` is for access to files that should be both read and written.
4. The template class `basic_filebuf<>` with the specializations `filebuf` and `wfilebuf` is used by the other file stream classes to perform the actual reading and writing of characters.

The classes are related to the stream base classes, as depicted in Figure 13.2.

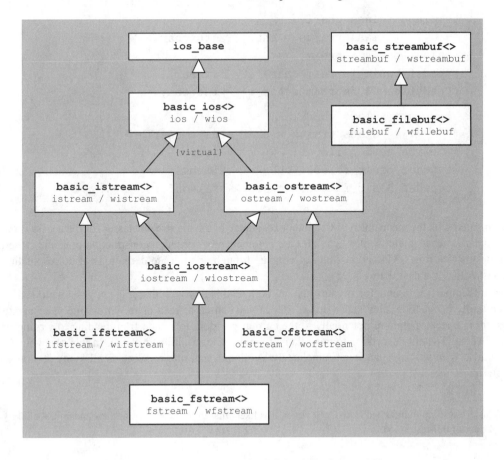

Figure 13.2. Class Hierarchy of the File Stream Classes

These classes are declared in the header file `<fstream>` as follows:

```
namespace std {
    template <class charT,
              class traits = char_traits<charT> >
      class basic_ifstream;
    typedef basic_ifstream<char>    ifstream;
    typedef basic_ifstream<wchar_t> wifstream;

    template <class charT,
              class traits = char_traits<charT> >
      class basic_ofstream;
    typedef basic_ofstream<char>    ofstream;
    typedef basic_ofstream<wchar_t> wofstream;

    template <class charT,
              class traits = char_traits<charT> >
      class basic_fstream;
    typedef basic_fstream<char>     fstream;
    typedef basic_fstream<wchar_t>  wfstream;

    template <class charT,
              class traits = char_traits<charT> >
      class basic_filebuf;
    typedef basic_filebuf<char>     filebuf;
    typedef basic_filebuf<wchar_t>  wfilebuf;
}
```

Compared with the mechanism of C, a major advantage of the file stream classes for file access is the automatic management of files. The files are automatically opened at construction time and closed at destruction time. This is possible, of course, through appropriate definitions of corresponding constructors and destructors.

It is important to note for streams that are both read and written that it is *not* possible to switch arbitrarily between reading and writing![8] Once you started to read or to write a file you have to perform a seek operation, potentially to the current position, to switch from reading to writing or vice versa. The only exception to this rule is if you have read until end-of-file. In this case you can continue with writing characters immediately. Violating this rule can lead to all kinds of strange effects.

---

[8] This is a restriction inherited from C. However, it is likely that implementations of the standard C++ library make use of this restriction.

If a file stream object is constructed with a C-string (type `char*`) as an argument, opening the file for reading and/or writing is attempted automatically. Whether this attempt was successful is reflected in the stream's state. Thus, the state should be examined after construction.

The following program opens the file `charset.out` and writes the current character set (all characters for the values between 32 and 255) into this file:

```cpp
// io/charset.cpp

#include <string>          // for strings
#include <iostream>        // for I/O
#include <fstream>         // for file I/O
#include <iomanip>         // for setw()
#include <cstdlib>         // for exit()
using namespace std;

// forward declarations
void writeCharsetToFile (const string& filename);
void outputFile (const string& filename);

int main ()
{
    writeCharsetToFile("charset.out");
    outputFile("charset.out");
}

void writeCharsetToFile (const string& filename)
{
    // open output file
    ofstream file(filename.c_str());

    // file opened?
    if (! file) {
        // NO, abort program
        cerr << "can't open output file \"" << filename << "\""
             << endl;
        exit(EXIT_FAILURE);
    }

    // write character set
    for (int i=32; i<256; i++) {
```

```
        file << "value: " << setw(3) << i << "   "
             << "char:  " << static_cast<char>(i) << endl;
    }

}    // closes file automatically

void outputFile (const string& filename)
{
    // open input file
    ifstream file(filename.c_str());

    // file opened?
    if (! file) {
        // NO, abort program
        cerr << "can't open input file \"" << filename << "\""
             << endl;
        exit(EXIT_FAILURE);
    }

    // copy file contents to cout
    char c;
    while (file.get(c)) {
        cout.put(c);
    }

}    // closes file automatically
```

In `writeCharsetToFile()`, the constructor of the class `ofstream` takes care of opening the file named by the given file name:

```
std::ofstream file(filename.c_str());
```

The file name is a `string`, so `c_str()` is used to convert it to `const char*` (see page 484 for details about `c_str()`). Unfortunately, there is no constructor for the file stream classes that takes `string` as the argument type. After this, it is determined whether the stream is in a good state:

```
if (! file) {
    ...
}
```

If opening the stream was not successful, this test will fail. After this check, a loop prints the values 32 to 255 together with the corresponding characters.

In the function `outputFile()`, the constructor of the class `ifstream` opens the file. Then the contents of the file are written characterwise.

At the end of both functions the file opened locally is closed automatically when the corresponding stream goes out of scope. The destructors of the classes `ifstream` and `ofstream` take care of closing the file if it is still open at destruction time.

If a file should be used longer than the scope in which it was created, you can allocate the file object on the heap and delete it later when it is no longer needed:

```
std::ofstream* filePtr = new std::ofstream("xyz");
...
delete filePtr;
```

In this case, some smart pointer class, such as `CountedPtr` (see Section 6.8, page 222) or `auto_ptr` (see Section 4.2, page 38), should be used.

Instead of copying the file contents character-by-character, you could also output the whole contents in one statement by passing a pointer to the stream buffer of the file as an argument to operator `<<`:

```
// copy file contents to cout
std::cout << file.rdbuf();
```

See page 683 for details.

13.9.1   File Flags

For precise control over the processing mode of a file, a set of flags is defined in the class `ios_base` (Table 13.32). These flags are of type `openmode`, which is a bit mask type similar to `fmtflags`.

Flag	Meaning
in	Opens for reading (default for `ifstream`)
out	Opens for writing (default for `ofstream`)
app	Always appends at the end when writing
ate	Positions at the end of the file after opening ("at end")
trunc	Removes the former file contents
binary	Does not replace special characters

Table 13.32. Flags for Opening Files

`binary` configures the stream to suppress conversion of special characters or character sequences such as end-of-line or end-of-file. In operating systems, such as MS-DOS or OS/2, a line end in text files is represented by two characters (CR and LF). In normal text mode (`binary` is not set), newline characters are replaced by the two-character sequence, and vice versa, when reading or writing to avoid special processing. In binary mode (`binary` is set), none of these conversions take place.

`binary` should always be used if the contents of a file do not consist of a character sequence but are processed as binary data. An example is the copying of files by reading the file to be copied character-by-character and writing those characters without modifying them. If the file is processed as text, the flag should not be set because special handling of newlines would be required. For example, a newline would still consist of two characters.

Some implementations provide additional flags such as `nocreate` (the file must exist when it is opened) and `noreplace` (the file must not exist). However, these flags are not standard and thus are not portable.

The flags can be combined by using operator `|`. The resulting `openmode` can be passed as an optional second argument to the constructor. For example, the following statement opens a file for appending text at the end:

```
std::ofstream file("xyz.out", std::ios::out|std::ios::app);
```

Table 13.33 correlates the various combinations of flags with the strings used in the interface of C's function for opening files: `fopen()`. The combinations with the `binary` and the `ate` flags set are not listed. A set `binary` corresponds to strings with b appended, and a set `ate` corresponds to a seek to the end of the file immediately after opening. Other combinations not listed in the table, such as `trunc|app`, are not allowed.

`ios_base` Flags	Meaning	C Mode
`in`	Reads (file must exist)	`"r"`
`out`	Empties and writes (creates if necessary)	`"w"`
`out|trunc`	Empties and writes (creates if necessary)	`"w"`
`out|app`	Appends (creates if necessary)	`"a"`
`in|out`	Reads and writes; initial position is the start (file must exist)	`"r+"`
`in|out|trunc`	Empties, reads, and writes (creates if necessary)	`"w+"`

Table 13.33. Meaning of Open Modes in C++

Whether a file is opened for reading and/or for writing is independent of the corresponding stream object's class. The class only determines the default open mode if no second argument is used. This means that files used only by the class `ifstream` or the class `ofstream` can be opened for reading *and* writing. The open mode is passed to the corresponding stream buffer class, which opens the file. However, the operations possible for the object are determined by the stream's class.

The file owned by a file stream can also be opened or closed explicitly. For this, three member functions are defined (Table 13.34).

These functions are useful mainly if a file stream is created without being initialized. The following example demonstrates their use. It opens all files with names that are given as arguments to the program, and writes their contents (this corresponds to the UNIX program `cat`).

Member Function	Meaning
open(*name*)	Opens a file for the stream using the default mode
open(*name*,*flags*)	Opens a file for the stream using *flags* as the mode
close()	Closes the streams file
is_open()	Returns whether the file is opened

Table 13.34. Member Functions to Open and Close Files

```
// io/cat1.cpp
// header files for file I/O
#include <fstream>
#include <iostream>
using namespace std;

/* for all file names passed as command-line arguments
 * - open, print contents, and close file
 */
int main (int argc, char* argv[])
{
    ifstream file;

    // for all command-line arguments
    for (int i=1; i<argc; ++i) {

        // open file
        file.open(argv[i]);

        // write file contents to cout
        char c;
        while (file.get(c)) {
            cout.put(c);
        }

        // clear eofbit and failbit set due to end-of-file
        file.clear();

        // close file
        file.close();
    }
}
```

Note that after the processing of a file, `clear()` must be called to clear the state flags that are set at end-of-file. This is required because the stream object is used for multiple files. `open()` *never* clears any state flags. Thus, if a stream was not in a good state, after closing and reopening it you still have to call `clear()` to get to a good state. This is also the case, if you open a different file.

Instead of processing character-by-character, you could also print the entire contents of the file in one statement by passing a pointer to the stream buffer of the file as an argument to operator <<:

```
// write file contents to cout
std::cout << file.rdbuf();
```

See page 683 for details.

13.9.2   Random Access

Table 13.35 lists the member function defined for positioning within C++ streams.

Class	Member Function	Meaning
`basic_istream<>`	`tellg()`	Returns the read position
	`seekg(`*pos*`)`	Sets the read position as an absolute value
	`seekg(`*offset*`,`*rpos*`)`	Sets the read position as a relative value
`basic_ostream<>`	`tellp()`	Returns the write position
	`seekp(`*pos*`)`	Sets the write position as an absolute value
	`seekp(`*offset*`,`*rpos*`)`	Sets the write position as a relative value

Table 13.35. Member Functions for Stream Positions

These functions distinguish between read and write position (g stands for *get* and p stands for *put*). Read position functions are defined in `basic_istream`, and write position functions are defined in `basic_ostream`. However, not all stream classes support positioning. For example, positioning the streams `cin`, `cout`, and `cerr` is not defined. The positioning of files is defined in the base classes because, usually, references to objects of type `istream` and `ostream` are passed around.

The functions `seekg()` and `seekp()` can be called with absolute or relative positions. To handle absolute positions, you must use `tellg()` and `tellp()`. They return an absolute position as the value of type `pos_type`. This value is *not* an integral value or simply the position of the character as an index. This is because the logical position and the real position can differ. For example, in MS-DOS text files, newline characters are represented by two characters in the file even though it is logically only one character. Things are even worse if the file uses some multibyte representation for the characters.

The exact definition of `pos_type` is a bit complicated: The C++ standard library defines a global template class `fpos<>` for file positions. Class `fpos<>` is used to define types `streampos` for `char` and `wstreampos` for `wchar_t` streams. These types are used to define the `pos_type` of the corresponding character traits (see Section 14.1.2, page 689). And the `pos_type` member of the traits is used to define `pos_type` of the corresponding stream classes. Thus, you could also use `streampos` as the type for the stream positions. However, using `long` or `unsigned long` is wrong because `streampos` is *not* an integral type (anymore).[9] For example:

```
// save current file position
std::ios::pos_type pos = file.tellg();
...
// seek to file position saved in pos
file.seekg(pos);
```

Instead of

```
std::ios::pos_type pos;
```

you could also write:

```
std::streampos pos;
```

For relative values, the offset can be relative to three positions, for which corresponding constants are defined (Table 13.36). The constants are defined in class `ios_base` and are of type `seekdir`.

Constant	Meaning
beg	Position is relative to the beginning ("beginning")
cur	Position is relative to the current position ("current")
end	Position is relative to the end ("end")

Table 13.36. Constants for Relative Positions

The type for the offset is `off_type`, which is an indirect definition of `streamoff`. Similar to `pos_type`, `streamoff` is used to define `off_type` of the traits (see page 689) and the stream classes. However, `streamoff` is a signed integral type, so you can use integral values as stream offsets. For example:

```
// seek to the beginning of the file
file.seekg (0, std::ios::beg);
...
// seek 20 character forward
file.seekg (20, std::ios::cur);
...
// seek 10 characters before the end
file.seekg (-10, std::ios::end);
```

In all cases, care must be taken to position only within a file. If a position ends up before the beginning of a file or beyond the end, the behavior is undefined.

---

[9] Formerly, `streampos` was used for stream positions, and it was simply defined as `unsigned long`.

The following example demonstrates the use of `seekg()`. It uses a function that writes the contents of a file twice:

```cpp
// io/cat2.cpp

// header files for file I/O
#include <iostream>
#include <fstream>

void printFileTwice (const char* filename)
{
    // open file
    std::ifstream file(filename);

    // print contents the first time
    std::cout << file.rdbuf();

    // seek to the beginning
    file.seekg(0);

    // print contents the second time
    std::cout << file.rdbuf();
}

int main (int argc, char* argv[])
{
    // print all files passed as a command-line argument twice
    for (int i=1; i<argc; ++i) {
        printFileTwice(argv[i]);
    }
}
```

Note that `file.rdbuf()` is used to print the contents of `file` (see page 683). Thus, you operate directly on the stream buffer, which can't manipulate the state of the stream. If you print the contents of `file` by using the stream interface functions (such as `getline()`, see Section 13.5.1 on page 607), you'd have to `clear()` the state of `file` before it can be manipulated in any way (including changes of the read position) because these functions set `ios::eofbit` and `ios::failbit` when end-of-file is reached.

Different functions are provided for the manipulation of the read and the write positions; but for the standard streams, the same position is maintained for the read and write positions in the same stream buffer. This is important if multiple streams use the same stream buffer. It is explained in more detail in Section 13.10.2, page 638.

13.9.3 Using File Descriptors

Some implementations provide the possibility of attaching a stream to an already opened I/O channel. To do this, you initialize the file stream with a *file descriptor*.

File descriptors are integers that identify an open I/O channel. In UNIX-like systems, file descriptors are used in the low-level interface to the I/O functions of the operating system. Three file descriptors are predefined:

1. 0 for the standard input channel
2. 1 for the standard output channel
3. 2 for the standard error channel

These channels may be connected to files, the console, other processes, or some other I/O facility.

The C++ standard library unfortunately does not provide this possibility of attaching a stream to an I/O channel using file descriptors. This is because the language is supposed to be independent of any operating system. In practice, though, the possibility probably still exists. The only drawback is that using it is not portable to all systems. What is missing at this point is a corresponding specification in a standard of operating system interfaces such as POSIX or X/OPEN. However, such a standard is not yet planned.

However, it is possible to initialize a stream by a file descriptor. See Section 13.13.3, page 672, for a description and implementation of a possible solution.

13.10 Connecting Input and Output Streams

Often you need to connect two streams. For example, you may want to ensure that text asking for input is written on the screen before the input is read. Another example is reading from and writing to the same stream. This is mainly of interest regarding files. A third example is the need to manipulate the same stream using different formats. This section discusses all of these techniques.

13.10.1 Loose Coupling Using `tie()`

You can tie a stream to an output stream. This means the buffers of both streams are synchronized in a way that the buffer of the output stream is flushed before each input or output of the other stream. That is, for the output stream, the function `flush()` is called. Table 13.37 lists the member functions defined in `basic_ios` for tieing one stream to another.

Calling the function `tie()` without any argument returns a pointer to the output stream that is currently tied to a stream. To tie a new output stream to a stream, a pointer to that output stream must be passed as the argument to `tie()`. The argument is a pointer because you can also pass 0 or NULL as an argument. This argument means "no tie," and unties any tied output stream. 0 is also

Member Function	Meaning
tie()	Returns a pointer to the output stream that is tied to the stream
tie(*ostream* strm*)	Ties the output stream to which the argument refers to the stream and returns a pointer to the previous output stream that was tied to the stream (if any)

Table 13.37. Tieing One Stream to Another

returned by tie() if no output stream is tied. For each stream, you can only have one output stream that is tied to this stream. However, you can tie an output stream to different streams.

By default, the standard input is connected to the standard output using this mechanism:

```
// predefined connections:
std::cin.tie (&std::cout);
std::wcin.tie (&std::wcout);
```

This ensures that a message asking for input is flushed before requesting the input. For example, during the statements

```
std::cout << "Please enter x: ";
std::cin >> x;
```

the function flush() is called implicitly for cout before reading x.

To remove the connection between two streams, you pass 0 or NULL to tie(). For example:

```
// decouple cin from any output stream
std::cin.tie (static_cast<std::ostream*>(0));
```

This might improve the performance of a program because it avoids unnecessary additional flushing of streams (see Section 13.14.2, page 683, for a discussion of stream performance).

You can also tie one output stream to another output stream. For example, the following statement arranges that before something is written to the error stream, the normal output is flushed:

```
// tieing cout to cerr
cerr.tie (&cout);
```

13.10.2   Tight Coupling Using Stream Buffers

Using the function rdbuf(), you can couple streams tightly by using a common stream buffer (Table 13.38). These functions suit several purposes, which are discussed in this and the following subsections.

rdbuf() allows several stream objects to read from the same input channel or to write to the same output channel without garbling the order of the I/O. The use of multiple stream buffers does not work smoothly because the I/O operations are buffered. Thus, when using different streams with different buffers for the same I/O channel means that I/O may pass other I/O. An additional

Member Function	Meaning
rdbuf()	Returns a pointer to the stream buffer
rdbuf(*streambuf**)	Installs the stream buffer pointed to by the argument and returns a pointer to the previously used stream buffer

Table 13.38. Stream Buffer Access

constructor of `basic_istream` and `basic_ostream` is used to initialize the stream with a stream buffer passed as the argument. For example:

```
// io/rdbuf1.cpp

#include <iostream>
#include <fstream>
using namespace std;

int main()
{
    // stream for hexadecimal standard output
    ostream hexout(cout.rdbuf());
    hexout.setf (ios::hex, ios::basefield);
    hexout.setf (ios::showbase);

    // switch between decimal and hexadecimal output
    hexout << "hexout: " << 177 << " ";
    cout   << "cout: "   << 177 << " ";
    hexout << "hexout: " << -49 << " ";
    cout   << "cout: "   << -49 << " ";
    hexout << endl;
}
```

Note that the destructor of the classes `basic_istream` and `basic_ostream` does *not* delete the corresponding stream buffer (it was not opened by these classes anyway). Thus, you can pass a stream device by using a pointer to the stream buffer instead of a stream reference:

```
// io/rdbuf2.cpp

#include <iostream>
#include <fstream>

void hexMultiplicationTable (std::streambuf* buffer, int num)
{
```

```
        std::ostream hexout(buffer);
        hexout << std::hex << std::showbase;

        for (int i=1; i<=num; ++i) {
            for (int j=1; j<=10; ++j) {
                hexout << i*j << ' ';
            }
            hexout << std::endl;
        }

}       // does NOT close buffer

int main()
{
        using namespace std;
        int num = 5;

        cout << "We print " << num
             << " lines hexadecimal" << endl;

        hexMultiplicationTable(cout.rdbuf(),num);

        cout << "That was the output of " << num
             << " hexadecimal lines " << endl;
}
```

The advantage of this approach is that the format does not need to be restored to its original state after it is modified because the format applies to the stream object, not to the stream buffer. Thus, the corresponding output of the program is as follows:

```
We print 5 lines hexadecimal
0x1 0x2 0x3 0x4 0x5 0x6 0x7 0x8 0x9 0xa
0x2 0x4 0x6 0x8 0xa 0xc 0xe 0x10 0x12 0x14
0x3 0x6 0x9 0xc 0xf 0x12 0x15 0x18 0x1b 0x1e
0x4 0x8 0xc 0x10 0x14 0x18 0x1c 0x20 0x24 0x28
0x5 0xa 0xf 0x14 0x19 0x1e 0x23 0x28 0x2d 0x32
That was the output of 5 hexadecimal lines
```

However, this has the disadvantage that construction and destruction of a stream object involves more overhead than just setting and restoring some format flags. Also note that the destruction of a stream object does not flush the buffer. To make sure that an output buffer is flushed, it has to be flushed manually.

The fact that the stream buffer is not destroyed applies only to `basic_istream` and `basic_ostream`. The other stream classes destroy the stream buffers they allocated originally, but they do not destroy stream buffers set with `rdbuf()` (for more details see the next subsection).

13.10.3 Redirecting Standard Streams

In the old implementation of the IOStream library, the global streams `cin`, `cout`, `cerr`, and `clog` were objects of the classes `istream_withassign` and `ostream_withassign`. It was therefore possible to redirect the streams by assigning streams to other streams. This possibility was removed from the C++ standard library. However, the possibility to redirect streams was retained and extended to apply to all streams. A stream can be redirected by setting a stream buffer.

The setting of stream buffers means the redirection of I/O streams controlled by the program without help from the operating system. For example, the following statements set things up such that output written to `cout` is not sent to the standard output channel but rather to the file `cout.txt`:

```
std::ofstream file ("cout.txt");
std::cout.rdbuf (file.rdbuf());
```

The function `copyfmt()` can be used to assign all format information of a given stream to another stream object:

```
std::ofstream file ("cout.txt");
file.copyfmt (std::cout);
std::cout.rdbuf (file.rdbuf());
```

Caution! The object `file` is local and is destroyed at the end of the block. This also destroys the corresponding stream buffer. This differs from the "normal" streams because file streams allocate their stream buffer objects at construction time and destroy them on destruction. Thus, in this example, `cout` can no longer be used for writing. Actually, it cannot even be destroyed safely at program termination. Thus, the old buffer should *always* be saved and restored later! The following example does this in the function `redirect()`:

```
// io/redirect.cpp

#include <iostream>
#include <fstream>
using namespace std;

void redirect(ostream&);

int main()
{
```

```
    cout << "the first row" << endl;

    redirect(cout);

    cout << "the last row" << endl;
}

void redirect (ostream& strm)
{
    ofstream file("redirect.txt");

    // save output buffer of the stream
    streambuf* strm_buffer = strm.rdbuf();

    // redirect ouput into the file
    strm.rdbuf (file.rdbuf());

    file << "one row for the file" << endl;
    strm << "one row for the stream" << endl;

    // restore old output buffer
    strm.rdbuf (strm_buffer);

}       // closes file AND its buffer automatically
```

The output of the program is this

```
the first row
the last row
```

and the contents of the file redirect.txt are

```
one row for the file
one row for the stream
```

As you can see, the output written in redirect() to cout (using the parameter name strm) is sent to the file. The output written after the execution of redirect() in main() is sent to the restored output channel.

13.10.4 Streams for Reading and Writing

A final example of the connection between streams is the use of the same stream for reading and writing. Normally, a file can be opened for reading and writing using the class `fstream`:

```
std::fstream file ("example.txt", std::ios::in | std::ios::out);
```

It is also possible to use two different stream objects, one for reading and one for writing. This can be done, for example, with the following declarations:

```
std::ofstream out ("example.txt", ios::in | ios::out);
std::istream  in (out.rdbuf());
```

The declaration of `out` opens the file. The declaration of `in` uses the stream buffer of `out` to read from it. Note that `out` must be opened for both reading and writing. If it is only opened for writing, reading from the stream will result in undefined behavior. Also note that `in` is not of type `ifstream` but only of type `istream`. The file is already opened and there is a corresponding stream buffer. All that is needed is a second stream object. As in previous examples, the file is closed when the file stream object `out` is destroyed.

It is also possible to create a file stream buffer and install it in both stream objects. The code looks like this:

```
std::filebuf buffer;
std::ostream out (&buffer);
std::istream in (&buffer);
buffer.open("example.txt", std::ios::in | std::ios::out);
```

`filebuf` is the usual specialization of the class `basic_filebuf<>` for the character type `char`. This class defines the stream buffer class used by file streams.

The following program is a complete example. In a loop, four lines are written to a file. After each writing of a line, the whole contents of the file are written to standard output:

```
// io/rw1.cpp

#include <iostream>
#include <fstream>
using namespace std;

int main()
{
    // open file "example.dat" for reading and writing
    filebuf buffer;
    ostream output(&buffer);
    istream input(&buffer);
    buffer.open ("example.dat", ios::in | ios::out | ios::trunc);
```

```
for (int i=1; i<=4; i++) {
    // write one line
    output << i << ". line" << endl;

    // print all file contents
    input.seekg(0);                 // seek to the beginning
    char c;
    while (input.get(c)) {
        cout.put(c);
    }
    cout << endl;
    input.clear();                  // clear eofbit and failbit
}
}
```

The output of the program is as follows:

```
1. line

1. line
2. line

1. line
2. line
3. line

1. line
2. line
3. line
4. line
```

Although two different stream objects are used for reading and writing, the read and write positions are tightly coupled. seekg() and seekp() call the same member function of the stream buffer.[10] Thus, the read position must always be set to the beginning of the file in order for the complete contents of the file to be written. After the whole contents of the file are written, the read/write position is again at the end of the file so that new lines are appended to the file.

---

[10] Actually, this function can distinguish whether the read position, the write position, or both positions are to be modified. Only the standard stream buffers maintain one position for reading and writing.

It is important to perform a seek between read and write operations to the same file unless you have reached the end of the file while reading. Without this seek you are likely to end up with a garbled file or with even more fatal errors.

As mentioned before, instead of processing character-by-character, you could also print the entire contents in one statement by passing a pointer to the stream buffer of the file as an argument to operator << (see page 683 for details):

```
std::cout << input.rdbuf();
```

13.11   Stream Classes for Strings

The mechanisms of stream classes can also be used to read from strings or to write to strings. String streams provide a buffer but don't have an I/O channel. This buffer/string can be manipulated with special functions. A major use of this is the processing of I/O independent of the actual I/O. For example, text for output can be formatted in a string and then sent to an output channel sometime later. Another use is reading input line-by-line and processing each line using string streams.

The original stream classes for strings are replaced by a set of new ones in the C++ standard library. Formerly, the string stream classes used type `char*` to represent a string. Now, type `string` (or in general `basic_string<>`) is used. The old string stream classes are also part of the C++ standard library, but they are deprecated. They are retained for backward compatibility, but they might be removed in future versions of the standard. Thus, they should not be used in new code and should be replaced in legacy code. Still, a brief description of these classes is found at the end of this section.

13.11.1   String Stream Classes

The following stream classes are defined for strings (they correspond to the stream classes for files):
- The class `basic_istringstream` with the specializations `istringstream` and `wistringstream` for reading from strings ("input string stream")
- The class `basic_ostringstream` with the specializations `ostringstream` and `wostringstream` for writing to strings ("output string stream")
- The class `basic_stringstream` with the specializations `stringstream` and `wstringstream` for reading from and writing to strings
- The template class `basic_stringbuf<>` with the specializations `stringbuf` and `wstringbuf` is used by the other string stream classes to perform the actual reading and writing of characters.

These classes have a similar relationship to the stream base classes, as do the file stream classes. The class hierarchy is depicted in Figure 13.3.

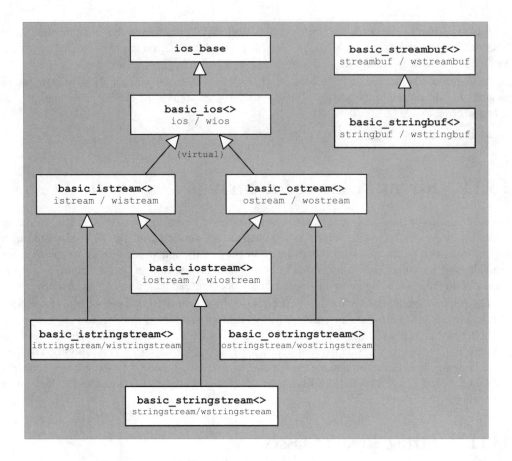

Figure 13.3. Class Hierarchy of the String Stream Classes

The classes are declared in the header file <sstream> like this:

```
namespace std {
    template <class charT,
              class traits = char_traits<charT>,
              class Allocator = allocator<charT> >
      class basic_istringstream;
    typedef basic_istringstream<char>    istringstream;
    typedef basic_istringstream<wchar_t> wistringstream;

    template <class charT,
              class traits = char_traits<charT>,
              class Allocator = allocator<charT> >
```

```
    class basic_ostringstream;
    typedef basic_ostringstream<char>    ostringstream;
    typedef basic_ostringstream<wchar_t> wostringstream;

    template <class charT,
             class traits = char_traits<charT>,
             class Allocator = allocator<charT> >
      class basic_stringstream;
    typedef basic_stringstream<char>    stringstream;
    typedef basic_stringstream<wchar_t> wstringstream;

    template <class charT,
             class traits = char_traits<charT>,
             class Allocator = allocator<charT> >
      class basic_stringbuf;
    typedef basic_stringbuf<char>    stringbuf;
    typedef basic_stringbuf<wchar_t> wstringbuf;
}
```

The major function in the interface of the string stream classes is the member function `str()`. This function is used to manipulate the buffer of the string stream classes (Table 13.39).

Member Function	Meaning
str()	Returns the buffer as a string
str(*string*)	Sets the contents of the buffer to *string*

Table 13.39. Fundamental Operations for String Streams

The following program demonstrates the use of string streams:

```
// io/sstr1.cpp

#include <iostream>
#include <sstream>
#include <bitset>
using namespace std;

int main()
{
    ostringstream os;

    // decimal and hexadecimal value
```

```
os << "dec: " << 15 << hex << " hex: " << 15 << endl;
cout << os.str() << endl;

// append floating value and bitset
bitset<15> b(5789);
os << "float: " << 4.67 << " bitset: " << b << endl;

// overwrite with octal value
os.seekp(0);
os << "oct: " << oct << 15;
cout << os.str() << endl;
}
```

The output of this program is as follows:

```
dec: 15 hex: f

oct: 17 hex: f
float: 4.67 bitset: 001011010011101
```

First a decimal and a hexadecimal value are written to os. Next a floating-point value and a bitset (written in binary) are appended. Using seekp(), the write position is moved to the beginning of the stream. So, the following call of operator << writes at the beginning of the string, thus overwriting the beginning of the existing string stream. However, the characters that are not overwritten remain valid. If you want to remove the current contents from the stream, you can use the function str() to assign new contents to the buffer:

```
strm.str("");
```

The first lines written to os are each terminated with endl. This means that the string ends with a newline. Because the string is printed followed by endl, two adjacent newlines are written. This explains the empty lines in the output.

A typical programming error when dealing with string streams is to forget to extract the string with the function str(), and instead to write to the stream directly. This is, from a compiler's point of view, a possible and reasonable thing to do in that there is a conversion to void*. As a result, the state of the stream is written in the form of an address (see page 596).

A typical use for writing to an output string stream is to define output operators for user-defined types (see Section 13.12.1, page 652).

Input string streams are used mainly for formatted reading from existing strings. For example, it is often easier to read data line-by-line and then analyze each line individually. The following lines read the integer x with the value 3 and the floating-point f with the value 0.7 from the string s:

```
int x;
float f;
std::string s = "3.7";

std::istringstream is(s);
is >> x >> f;
```

A string stream can be created with the flags for the file open modes (see Section 13.9.1, page 631) and/or an existing string. With the flag `ios::app` or `ios::ate`, the characters written to a string stream can be appended to an existing string:

```
std::string s;
...
std::ostringstream os (s, ios::out|ios::app);
os << 77 << std::hex << 77;
```

However, this means that the string returned from `str()` is a copy of the string `s`, with a decimal and a hexadecimal version of 77 appended. The string `s` itself is not modified.

13.11.2 `char*` Stream Classes

The `char*` stream classes are retained only for backward compatibility. Their interface is error prone and they are rarely used correctly. However, they are still in heavy use and thus are described briefly here. Note that the standard version described here has slightly modified the old interface.

In this subsection, the term *character sequence* will be used instead of *string*. This is because the character sequence maintained by the `char*` stream classes is not always terminated with the string termination character (and thus it is not really a string).

The `char*` stream classes are defined only for the character type `char`. They include

- The class `istrstream` for reading from character sequences (input string stream)
- The class `ostrstream` for writing to character sequences (output string stream)
- The class `strstream` for reading from and writing to character sequences
- The class `strstreambuf` used as a stream buffer for `char*` streams

The `char*` stream classes are defined in the header file `<strstream>`.

An `istrstream` can be initialized with a character sequence (of type `char*`) that is either terminated with the string termination character 0 or for which the number of characters is passed as the argument. A typical use is the reading and processing of whole lines:

```
char buffer[1000];      // buffer for at most 999 characters

// read line
std::cin.get(buffer,sizeof(buffer));

// read/process line as stream
```

```
std::istrstream input(buffer);
...
input >> x;
```

A `char*` stream for writing can either maintain a character sequence that grows as needed or it can be initialized with a buffer of fixed size. Using the flag `ios::app` or `ios:ate`, you can append the characters written to a character sequence that is already stored in the buffer.

Care must be taken when using `char*` stream as a string. In contrast to string streams, `char*` streams are not always responsible for the memory used to store the character sequence.

With the member function `str()`, the character sequence is made available to the caller together with the responsibility for the corresponding memory. Unless the stream is initialized with a buffer of fixed size (for which the stream is never responsible), the following three rules have to be obeyed:

1. Because ownership of the memory is transferred to the caller, unless the stream was initialized with a buffer of fixed size, the character sequence has to be released. However, there is no guarantee how the memory was allocated,[11] thus it is not always safe to release it using `delete[]`. Your best bet is to return the memory to the stream by calling the member function `freeze()` with the argument `false` (the following paragraphs present an example).

2. With the call to `str()`, the stream is no longer allowed to modify the character sequence. It calls the member function `freeze()` implicitly, which freezes the character sequence. The reason for this is to avoid complications if the allocated buffer is not sufficiently large and new memory has to be allocated.

3. The member function `str()` does *not* append a string termination character (`'\0'`). This character has to be appended explicitly to the stream to terminate the character sequence. This can be done using the `ends` manipulator. Some implementations append a string termination character automatically, but this behavior is not portable.

The following example demonstrates the use of a `char*` stream:

```
float x;
...
/* create and fill char* stream
/* - don't forget ends or '\0' !!!
 */
std::ostrstream buffer;        // dynamic stream buffer
buffer << "float x: " << x << std::ends;

// pass resulting C-string to foo() and return memory to buffer
char* s = buffer.str();
foo(s);
buffer.freeze(false);
```

---

[11] There is actually a constructor that takes two function pointers as an argument: a function to allocate memory and a function to release memory.

A frozen `char*` stream can be restored to its normal state for additional manipulation. To do so, the member function `freeze()` has to be called with the argument `false`. With this operation, ownership of the character sequence is returned to the stream object. This is the only safe way to release the memory for the character sequence. The next example demonstrates this:

```
float x;
...
std::ostrstream buffer;        // dynamic char* stream

// fill char* stream
buffer << "float x: " << x << std::ends;

/* pass resulting C-string to foo()
 * - freezes the char* stream
 */
foo(buffer.str());

// unfreeze the char* stream
buffer.freeze(false);

// seek writing position to the beginning
buffer.seekp (0, ios::beg);

// refill char* stream
buffer << "once more float x: " << x << std::ends;

/* pass resulting C-string to foo() again
 * - freezes the char* stream
 */
foo(buffer.str());

// return memory to buffer
buffer.freeze(false);
```

The problems related to freezing the stream are removed from the string stream classes. This is mainly because the strings are copied and because the string class takes care of the used memory.

13.12   Input/Output Operators for User-Defined Types

As mentioned earlier in this chapter, a major advantage of streams over the old I/O mechanism of C is the possibility that the stream mechanism can be extended to user-defined types. To do this, you must overload operators << and >>. This is demonstrated using a class for fractions in the following subsection.

13.12.1   Implementing Output Operators

In an expression with the output operator, the left operand is a stream and the right operand is the object to be written:

> *stream* << *object*

According to language rules this can be interpreted in two ways:

1. As *stream*.operator<<(*object*)
2. As operator<<(*stream*,*object*)

The first way is used for built-in types. For user-defined types you have to use the second way because the stream classes are closed for extensions. All you have to do is implement global operator << for your user-defined type. This is rather easy, unless access to private members of the objects is necessary (which I cover later).

For example, to print an object of class `Fraction` with the format *numerator/denominator*, you can write the following function:

```
// io/frac1out.hpp

#include <iostream>

inline
std::ostream& operator << (std::ostream& strm, const Fraction& f)
{
    strm << f.numerator() << '/' << f.denominator();
    return strm;
}
```

The function writes the numerator and the denominator, separated by the character '/', to the stream that is passed as the argument. The stream can be a file stream, a string stream, or some other stream. To support the chaining of write operations or the access to the streams state in the same statement, the stream is returned by the function.

This simple form has two drawbacks:

1. Because `ostream` is used in the signature, the function applies only to streams with the character type `char`. If the function is intended only for use in Western Europe or in North America, this is no problem. On the other hand, a more general version requires only a little extra work, so it should at least be considered.

2. Another problem arises if a field width is set. In this case, the result is probably not what might be expected. The field width applies to the immediately following write; in this case, to the numerator. Thus, the statements

```
Fraction vat(16,100);    // I'm German and we have a uniform VAT of 16%...
std::cout << "VAT: \"" << std::left << std::setw(8)
          << vat << '"' << std::endl;
```

result in this output:

```
VAT: "16      /100"
```

The next version solves both of these problems:

```
// io/frac2out.hpp

#include <iostream>
#include <sstream>

template <class charT, class traits>
inline
std::basic_ostream<charT,traits>&
operator << (std::basic_ostream<charT,traits>& strm,
             const Fraction& f)
{
    /* string stream
     * - with same format
     * - without special field width
     */
    std::basic_ostringstream<charT,traits> s;
    s.copyfmt(strm);
    s.width(0);

    // fill string stream
    s << f.numerator() << '/' << f.denominator();

    // print string stream
    strm << s.str();

    return strm;
}
```

The operator has become a template function that is parameterized to suit all kinds of streams. The problem with the field width is addressed by writing the fraction first to a string stream without setting any specific width. The constructed string is then sent to the stream passed as the argument. This results in the characters representing the fraction being written with only one write operation, to which the field width is applied. Thus, the statements

```
Fraction vat(16,100);        // I'm German ...
std::cout << "VAT: \"" << std::left << std::setw(8)
          << vat << '"' << std::endl;
```

now produce the following output:

```
VAT: "16/100  "
```

13.12.2 Implementing Input Operators

Input operators are implemented according to the same principle as output operators (described in the previous subsection). However, input incurs the likely problem of read failures. Input functions normally need special handling of cases in which reading might fail.

When implementing a read function you can choose between simple or flexible approaches. For example, the following function uses a simple approach. It reads a fraction without checking for error situations:

```
// io/frac1in.hpp

#include <iostream>

inline
std::istream& operator >> (std::istream& strm, Fraction& f)
{
    int n, d;

    strm >> n;        // read value of the numerator
    strm.ignore();    // skip '/'
    strm >> d;        // read value of the denominator

    f = Fraction(n,d);  // assign the whole fraction

    return strm;
}
```

This implementation has the problem that it can be used only for streams with the character type char. In addition, whether the character between the two numbers is indeed the character '/' is not checked.

Another problem arises when undefined values are read. When reading a zero for the denominator, the value of the read fraction is not well-defined. This problem is detected in the constructor of the class Fraction that is invoked by the expression Fraction(n,d). However, handling inside class Fraction means that a format error automatically results in an error handling of the class Fraction. Because it is common practice to record format errors in the stream, it might be better to set ios_base::failbit in this case.

Lastly, the fraction passed by reference might be modified even if the read operation is not successful. This can happen, for example, when the read of the numerator succeeds, but the read of the denominator fails. This behavior contradicts common conventions established by the predefined input operators, and thus is best avoided. A read operation should be successful or have no effect.

The following implementation is improved to avoid these problems. It is also more flexible because it is parameterized to be applicable to all stream types:

```
// io/frac2in.hpp

#include <iostream>

template <class charT, class traits>
inline
std::basic_istream<charT,traits>&
operator >> (std::basic_istream<charT,traits>& strm, Fraction& f)
{
    int n, d;

    // read value of numerator
    strm >> n;

    /* if available
     * - read '/' and value of demonimator
     */
    if (strm.peek() == '/') {
        strm.ignore();
        strm >> d;
    }
    else {
        d = 1;
    }
```

```
/* if denominator is zero
 * - set failbit as I/O format error
 */
if (d == 0) {
    strm.setstate(std::ios::failbit);
    return strm;
}


/* if everything is fine so far
 * change the value of the fraction
 */
if (strm) {
    f = Fraction(n,d);
}


return strm;
}
```

Here the denominator is read only if the first number is followed by the character '/'; otherwise, a denominator of one is assumed and the integer read is interpreted as the whole fraction. Hence, the denominator is optional.

This implementation also tests whether a denominator with value 0 was read. In this case, the `ios_base::failbit` is set, which might trigger a corresponding exception (see Section 13.4.4, page 602). Of course, the behavior can be implemented differently if the denominator is zero. For example, an exception could be thrown directly, or the check could be skipped so that the fraction is initialized with zero, which would throw the appropriate exception by class `Fraction`.

Lastly, the state of the stream is checked and the new value is assigned to the fraction only if no input error occurred. This final check should always be done to make sure that the value of an object is changed only if the read was successful.

Of course, it can be argued whether it is reasonable to read integers as fractions. In addition, there are other subtleties that may be improved. For example, the numerator must be followed by the character '/' without separating whitespaces. But the denominator may be preceded by arbitrary whitespaces because normally these are skipped. This hints at the complexity involved in reading nontrivial data structures.

13.12.3   Input/Output Using Auxiliary Functions

If the implementation of an I/O operator requires access to the private data of an object, the standard operators should delegate the actual work to auxiliary member functions. This technique also allows polymorphic read and write functions. This might look as follows:

```
class Fraction {
  ...
  public:
    virtual void printOn (std::ostream& strm) const;   // output
    virtual void scanFrom (std::istream& strm);         // input
    ...
};

std::ostream& operator << (std::ostream& strm, const Fraction& f)
{
    f.printOn (strm);
    return strm;
}

std::istream& operator >> (std::istream& strm, Fraction& f)
{
    f.scanFrom (strm);
    return strm;
}
```

A typical example is the direct access to the numerator and denominator of a fraction during input:

```
void Fraction::scanFrom (std::istream& strm)
{
    ...
    // assign values directly to the components
    num = n;
    denom = d;
}
```

If a class is not intended to be used as a base class, the I/O operators can be made `friends` of the class. However, note that this approach reduces the possibilities significantly when inheritance is used. Friend functions cannot be virtual; so as a result, the wrong function might be called. For example, if a reference to a base class actually refers to an object of a derived class and is used as an argument for the input operator, the operator for the base class is called. To avoid this problem, derived classes should not implement their own I/O operators. Thus, the implementation sketched previously is more general than the use of friend functions. It should be used as a standard approach, although most examples use friend functions instead.

13.12.4   User-Defined Operators Using Unformatted Functions

The I/O operators implemented in the previous subsections delegate most of the work to some pre-defined operators for formatted I/O. That is, operators << and >> are implemented in terms of the corresponding operators for more basic types.

The I/O operators defined in the C++ standard library are defined differently. The common scheme used for these operators is as follows: First, with some preprocessing the stream is prepared for actual I/O. Then the actual I/O is done, followed by some postprocessing. This scheme should be used for your own I/O operators, too, to provide consistency for I/O operators.

The classes `basic_istream` and `basic_ostream` each define an auxiliary class `sentry`. The constructor of these classes does the preprocessing, and the destructor does the corresponding post-processing. These classes replace the member functions that were used in former implementations of the IOStream library (`ipfx()`, `isfx()`, `opfx()`, and `osfx()`). Using the new classes ensures that the postprocessing is invoked even if the I/O is aborted with an exception.

If an I/O operator uses a function for unformatted I/O or operates directly on the stream buffer, the first thing to be done should be the construction of a corresponding `sentry` object. The remaining processing should then depend on the state of this object, which indicates whether the stream is OK. This state can be checked using the conversion of the `sentry` object to `bool`. Thus, I/O operators generally look like this:

```
sentry se(strm);        // indirect pre- and postprocessing
if (se) {
    ...                 // the actual processing
}
```

The `sentry` object takes the stream `strm`, on which the preprocessing and postprocessing should be done, as the constructor argument.

The additional processing is used to arrange general tasks of the I/O operators. These tasks include synchronizing several streams, checking whether the stream is OK, and skipping whitespaces, as well as possibly implementation-specific tasks. For example, in a multithreaded environment, the additional processing can be used for corresponding locking.

For input streams, the `sentry` object can be constructed with an optional Boolean value that indicates whether skipping of whitespace should be avoided even though the flag `skipws` is set:

```
sentry se(strm,true);  // don't skip whitespaces during the additional processing
```

The following examples demonstrate this for class `Row`, which is used to represent the lines in a text processor or editor:

- The output operator writes a line by using the stream's member function `write()`:

```
std::ostream& operator<< (std::ostream& strm, const Row& row)
{
    // ensure pre- and postprocessing
    std::ostream::sentry se(strm);
```

```
        if (se) {
            // perform the output
            strm.write(row.c_str(),row.len());
        }

        return strm;
    }
```

- The input operator reads a line character-by-character in a loop. The argument `true` is passed to the constructor of the `sentry` object to avoid the skipping of whitespaces:

```
    std::istream& operator>> (std::istream& strm, Row& row)
    {
        /* ensure pre- and postprocessing
         * - true: Yes, don't ignore leading whitespaces
         */
        std::istream::sentry se(strm,true);
        if (se) {
            // perform the input
            char c;
            row.clear();
            while (strm.get(c) && c != '\n') {
                row.append(c);
            }
        }

        return strm;
    }
```

Of course, it is also possible to use this framework even if functions do not use unformatted functions for their implementation but use I/O operators instead. However, using `basic_istream` or `basic_ostream` members for reading or writing characters within code guarded by `sentry` objects is unnecessarily expensive. Whenever possible, the corresponding `basic_streambuf` should be used instead.

13.12.5 User-Defined Format Flags

When user-defined I/O operators are being written, it is often desirable to have formatting flags specific to these operators, probably set by using a corresponding manipulator. For example, it would be nice if the output operator for fractions, shown previously, could be configured to place spaces around the slash that separates numerator and denominator.

The stream objects support this by providing a mechanism to associate data with a stream. This mechanism can be used to associate corresponding data (for example, using a manipulator), and later retrieve the data. The class ios_base defines the two functions iword() and pword(), each taking an int argument as the index, to access a specific long& or void*& respectively. The idea is that iword() and pword() access long or void* objects in an array of arbitrary size stored with a stream object. Formatting flags to be stored for a stream are then placed at the same index for all streams. The static member function xalloc() of the class ios_base is used to obtain an index that is not yet used for this purpose.

Initially, the objects accessed with iword() or pword() are set to 0. This value can be used to represent the default formatting or to indicate that the corresponding data was not yet accessed. Here is an example:

```
// get index for new ostream data
static const int iword_index = std::ios_base::xalloc();

// define manipulator that sets this data
std::ostream& fraction_spaces (std::ostream& strm)
{
    strm.iword(iword_index) = true;
    return strm;
}

std::ostream& operator<< (std::ostream& strm, const Fraction& f)
{
    /* query the ostream data
     * - if true, use spaces between numerator and denominator
     * - if false, use no spaces between numerator and denominator
     */
    if (strm.iword(iword_index)) {
        strm << f.numerator() << " / " << f.denominator();
    }
    else {
        strm << f.numerator() << "/" << f.denominator();
    }
    return strm;
}
```

This example uses a simple approach to the implementation of the output operator because the main feature to be exposed is the use of the function iword(). The format flag is considered to be a Boolean value that defines whether spaces between numerator and denominator should be written.

In the first line, the function `ios_base::xalloc()` is used to obtain an index that can be used to store the format flag. The result of this call is stored in a constant because it is never modified. The function `fraction_spaces()` is a manipulator that sets the `int` value that is stored at the index `iword_index` in the integer array associated with the stream `strm` to `true`. The output operator retrieves that value and writes the fraction according the value stored. If the value is `false`, the default formatting using no spaces is used. Otherwise, spaces are placed around the slash.

When `iword()` and `pword()` are used, references to `int` or `void*` objects are returned. These references stay valid only until the next call of `iword()` or `pword()` for the corresponding stream object or until the stream object is destroyed. Normally, the results from `iword()` and `pword()` should not be saved. It is assumed that the access is fast, although it is not required that the data is really represented by using an array.

The function `copyfmt()` copies all format information (see page 615). This includes the arrays accessed with `iword()` and `pword()`. This may pose a problem for the objects stored with a stream using `pword()`. For example, if a value is the address of an object, the address is copied instead of the object. If you copy only the address, it may happen that if the format of one stream is changed, the format of other streams would be affected. In addition, it may be desirable that an object associated with a stream using `pword()` is destroyed when the stream is destroyed. So, a deep copy rather than a shallow copy may be necessary for such an object.

A callback mechanism is defined by `ios_base` to support behavior, such as making a deep copy if necessary or deleting an object when destroying a stream. The function `register_callback()` can be used to register a function that is called if certain operations are performed on the `ios_base` object. It is declared as follows:

```
namespace std {
  class ios_base {
    public:
      // kinds of callback events
      enum event { erase_event, imbue_event, copyfmt_event };
      // type of callbacks
      typedef void (*event_callback) (event e, ios_base& strm,
                                      int arg);

      // function to register callbacks
      void register_callback (event_callback cb, int arg);
      ...
  };
}
```

`register_callback()` takes a function pointer as the first argument and an `int` argument as the second. The `int` argument is passed as the third argument when a registered function is called. It can, for example, be used to identify an index for `pword()` to signal which member of the array has to be processed. The argument `strm` that is passed to the callback function is the `ios_base` object that caused the call to the callback function. The argument `e` identifies the reason why the callback function was called. The reasons for calling the callback functions are listed in Table 13.40.

Event	Reason
ios_base::imbue_event	A locale is set with imbue()
ios_base::erase_event	The stream is destroyed or copyfmt() is used
ios_base::copy_event	copyfmt() is used

Table 13.40. Reasons for Callback Events

If copyfmt() is used, the callbacks are called twice for the object on which copyfmt() is called. First, before anything is copied, the callbacks are invoked with the argument erase_event to do all the cleanup necessary (for example, deleting objects stored in the pword() array). The callbacks called are those registered for the object. After the format flags are copied, which includes the list of callbacks from the argument stream, the callbacks are called again, this time with the argument copy_event. This pass can, for example, be used to arrange for deep copying of objects stored in the pword() array. Note that the callbacks are also copied and the original list of callbacks is removed. Thus, the callbacks invoked for the second pass are the callbacks just copied.

The callback mechanism is very primitive. It does not allow callback functions to be unregistered, except by using copyfmt() with an argument that has no callbacks registered. Also, registering a callback function twice, even with the same argument, results in calling the callback function twice. It is, however, guaranteed that the callbacks are called in the opposite order of registration. This has the effect that a callback function registered from within some other callback function is not called before the next time the callback functions are invoked.

13.12.6   Conventions for User-Defined Input/Output Operators

Several conventions that should be obeyed by the implementations of your own I/O operators have been presented. They correspond to the behavior that is typical for the predefined I/O operators. To summarize, these conventions are the following:

- The output format should allow an input operator that can read the data without loss of information. Especially for strings, this is close to impossible because a problem with spaces arises. A space character in the string cannot be distinguished from a space character between two strings.
- The current formatting specification of the stream should be taken into account when doing I/O. This applies especially to the width for writing.
- If an error occurs, an appropriate state flag should be set.
- The objects should not be modified in case of an error. If multiple data is read, the data should first be stored in auxiliary objects before the value of the object passed to the read operator is set.
- Output should not be terminated with a newline, mainly because it is otherwise impossible to write other objects on the same line.
- Even values that are too large should be read completely. After the read, a corresponding error flag should be set, and the value returned should be some meaningful value, such as the maximum value.
- If a format error is detected, no character should be read, if possible.

13.13   The Stream Buffer Classes

As mentioned in Section 13.2.1, page 589, the actual reading and writing is not done by the streams directly, but is delegated to stream buffers. This section describes how these classes operate. The discussion not only gives a deeper understanding of what is going on when I/O streams are used, but also provides the basis to define new I/O channels. Before going into the details of stream buffer operation, the public interface is presented for those only interested in using stream buffers.

13.13.1   User's View of Stream Buffers

To the user of a stream buffer the class `basic_streambuf` is not much more than something that characters can be sent to or extracted from. Table 13.41 lists the public function for writing characters.

Member Function	Meaning
`sputc(c)`	Sends the character c to the stream buffer
`sputn(s, n)`	Sends n characters from the sequence s to the stream buffer

Table 13.41. Public Members for Writing Characters

The function `sputc()` returns `traits_type::eof()` in case of an error, where `traits_type` is a type definition in the class `basic_streambuf`. The function `sputn()` writes the number of characters specified by the second argument unless the stream buffer cannot consume them. It does not care about string termination characters. This function returns the number of characters written.

The interface to reading characters from a stream buffer is a little bit more complex (Table 13.42). This is because for input it is necessary to have a look at a character without consuming it. Also, it is desirable that characters can be put back into the stream buffer when parsing. Thus, the stream buffer classes provide corresponding functions.

Member Function	Meaning
`in_avail()`	Returns a lower bound on the characters available
`sgetc()`	Returns the current character without consuming it
`sbumpc()`	Returns the current character and consumes it
`snextc()`	Consumes the current character and returns the next character
`sgetn(b, n)`	Reads n characters and stores them in the buffer b
`sputbackc(c)`	Returns the character c to the stream buffer
`sungetc()`	Steps one step back to the previous character

Table 13.42. Public Members for Reading Characters

The function `in_avail()` can be used to determine how many characters are at least available. This can be used, for example, to make sure that reading does not block when reading from the keyboard. However, there can be more characters available.

Until the stream buffer has reached the end of the stream, there is a current character. The function `sgetc()` is used to get the current character without moving on to the next character. The function `sbumpc()` reads the current character and moves on to next character, making this the new current character. The last function reading a single character, `snextc()` makes the next character the current one and then reads this character. All three functions return `traits_type::eof()` to indicate failure. The function `sgetn()` reads a sequence of characters into a buffer. The maximum number of characters to be read is passed as an argument. The function returns the number of characters read.

The two functions `sputbackc()` and `sungetc()` are used to move one step back, making the previous character the current one. The function `sputbackc()` can be used to replace the previous character by some other character. These two functions should only be used with care. Often it is only possible to put back just one character.

Finally, there are functions to access the imbued locale object, to change the position, and to influence buffering. Table 13.43 lists these functions.

Member Function	Meaning
`pubimbue`(*loc*)	Imbues the stream buffer with the locale *loc*
`getloc()`	Returns the current locale
`pubseekpos`(*pos*)	Repositions the current position to an absolute position
`pubseekpos`(*pos*, *which*)	Same with specifying the I/O direction
`pubseekoff`(*offset*, *rpos*)	Repositions the current position relative to another position
`pubseekoff`(*offset*, *rpos*, *which*)	Same with specifying the I/O direction
`pubsetbuf`(*b*, *n*)	Influences buffering

Table 13.43. Miscellaneous Public Stream Buffer Functions

`pubimbue()` and `getloc()` are used for internationalization (see page 625). `pubimbue()` installs a new locale object in the stream buffer returning the previously installed locale object. `getloc()` returns the currently installed locale object.

The function `pubsetbuf()` is intended to provide some control over the buffering strategy of stream buffers. However, whether it is honored depends on the concrete stream buffer class. For example, it makes no sense to use `pubsetbuf()` for string stream buffers. Even for file stream buffers the use of this function is only portable if it is called before the first I/O operation is performed and if it is called as `pubsetbuf(0,0)` (that is, no buffer is to be used). This function returns 0 on failure and the stream buffer otherwise.

The functions `pubseekoff()` and `pubseekpos()` are used to manipulate the current position used for reading and/or writing. Which position is manipulated depends on the last argument, which is of type `ios_base::openmode` and which defaults to `ios_base::in|ios_base::out` if it is not specified. If `ios_base::in` is set, the read position is modified. Correspondingly, the write position is modified if `ios_base::out` is set. The function `pubseekpos()` moves the stream to an absolute position specified as the first argument whereas the function `pubseekoff()` moves the stream relative to some other position. The offset is specified as the first argument. The position used as starting point is specified as the second argument and can be either `ios_base::cur`, `ios_base::beg`, or `ios_base::end` (see page 635 for details). Both functions return the position to which the stream was positioned or an invalid stream position. The invalid stream position can be detected by comparing the result with the object `pos_type(off_type(-1))` (`pos_type` and `off_type` are types for handling stream positions; see page 634). The current position of a stream can be obtained using `pubseekoff()`:

```
sbuf.pubseekoff(0, std::ios::cur)
```

13.13.2   Stream Buffer Iterators

An alternative way to use a member function for unformatted I/O is to use the stream buffer iterator classes. These classes provide iterators that conform to input iterator or output iterator requirements and read or write individual characters from stream buffers. This fits character-level I/O into the algorithm library of the C++ standard library.

The template classes `istreambuf_iterator` and `ostreambuf_iterator` are used to read or to write individual characters from or to objects of type `basic_streambuf`. The classes are defined in the header `<iterator>` like this:

```
namespace std {
    template <class charT,
              class traits = char_traits<charT> >
    istreambuf_iterator;
    template <class charT,
              class traits = char_traits<charT> >
    ostreambuf_iterator;
}
```

These iterators are special forms of stream iterators, which are described in Section 7.4.3, page 277. The only difference is that their elements are characters.

Output Stream Buffer Iterators

Here is how a string can be written to a stream buffer using an `ostreambuf_iterator`:

```
// create iterator for buffer of output stream cout
std::ostreambuf_iterator<char> bufWriter(std::cout);

std::string hello("hello, world\n");
std::copy(hello.begin(), hello.end(),       // source: string
          bufWriter);                       // destination: output buffer of cout
```

The first line of this example constructs an output iterator of type `ostreambuf_iterator` from the object `cout`. Instead of passing the output stream you could also pass a pointer to the stream buffer directly. The remainder constructs a `string` object and copies the characters in this object to the constructed output iterator.

Table 13.44 lists all operations of output stream buffer iterators. The implementation is similar to ostream iterators (see page 278). In addition, you can initialize the iterator with a buffer and you can call `failed()` to query whether the iterator is able to write. If any prior writing of a character failed, `failed()` yields `true`. In this case, any writing with operator = has no effect.

Expression	Effect
`ostreambuf_iterator<`*char*`>(`*ostream*`)`	Creates an output stream buffer iterator for *ostream*
`ostreambuf_iterator<`*char*`>(`*buffer_ptr*`)`	Creates an output stream buffer iterator for the buffer to which *buffer_ptr* refers
`*`*iter*	No-op (returns *iter*)
iter `=` *c*	Writes character *c* to the buffer by calling `sputc(`*c*`)` for it
`++`*iter*	No-op (returns *iter*)
iter`++`	No-op (returns *iter*)
`failed()`	Returns whether the output stream iterator is not able to write anymore

Table 13.44. Operations of Output Stream Buffer Iterators

Input Stream Buffer Iterators

Table 13.45 lists all operations of input stream buffer iterators. The implementation is similar to istream iterators (see page 280). In addition, you can initialize the iterator with a buffer, and a member function, `equal()`, is provided, which returns whether two input stream buffer iterators are equal. Two input stream buffer iterators are equal when they are both end-of-stream iterators or when neither is an end-of-stream iterator.

What is somewhat obscure is what it means for two objects of type `istreambuf_iterator` to be equivalent: Two `istreambuf_iterator` objects are equivalent if both iterators are end-of-stream iterators or if neither of them is an end-of-stream iterator (whether the output buffer is the same doesn't matter). One possibility to get an end-of-stream iterator is to construct an iterator with the default constructor. In addition, an `istreambuf_iterator` becomes an end-of-stream iterator when an attempt is made to advance the iterator past the end of the stream (in other words, if `sbumpc()` returns `traits_type::eof()`. This behavior has two major implications:

Expression	Effect
`istreambuf_iterator<`*char*`>()`	Creates an end-of-stream iterator
`istreambuf_iterator<`*char*`>(`*istream*`)`	Creates an input stream buffer iterator for *istream* and might read the first character using `sgetc()`
`istreambuf_iterator<`*char*`>(`*buffer_ptr*`)`	Creates an input stream buffer iterator for the buffer to which *buffer_ptr* refers and might read the first character using `sgetc()`
`*`*iter*	Returns the current character, read with `sgetc()` before (reads the first character if not done by the constructor)
`++`*iter*	Reads the next character with `sbumpc()` and returns its position
iter`++`	Reads the next character with `sbumpc()` but returns an iterator for the previous character
iter1`.equal(`*iter2*`)`	Returns whether both iterators are equal
iter1`==` *iter2*	Tests *iter1* and *iter2* for equality
iter1`!=` *iter2*	Tests *iter1* and *iter2* for inequality

Table 13.45. Operations of Input Stream Buffer Iterators

1. A range from the current position in a stream to the end of the stream is defined by the two iterators `istreambuf_iterator<charT,traits>(`*stream*`)` (for the current position) and `istreambuf_iterator<charT,traits>()` (for the end of the stream), where *stream* is of type `basic_istream<charT,traits>` or `basic_streambuf<charT,traits>`.

2. It is not possible to create subranges using `istreambuf_iterators`.

Example Use of Stream Buffer Iterators

The following example is the classic filter framework that simply writes all read characters with stream buffer iterators. It is a modified version of the example on page 611:

```
// io/charcat2.cpp

#include <iostream>
#include <iterator>
using namespace std;

int main()
{
    // input stream buffer iterator for cin
    istreambuf_iterator<char> inpos(cin);
```

```
// end-of-stream iterator
istreambuf_iterator<char> endpos;

// output stream buffer iterator for cout
ostreambuf_iterator<char> outpos(cout);

// while input iterator is valid
while (inpos != endpos) {
    *outpos = *inpos;      // assign its value to the output iterator
    ++inpos;
    ++outpos;
}
}
```

13.13.3   User-Defined Stream Buffers

Stream buffers are buffers for I/O. Their interface is defined by class `basic_streambuf<>`. For the character types `char` and `wchar_t`, the specializations `streambuf` and `wstreambuf`, respectively, are predefined. These classes are used as base classes when implementing the communication over special I/O channels. However, doing this requires an understanding of the stream buffer's operation.

The central interface to the buffers is formed by three pointers for each of the two buffers. The pointers returned from the functions `eback()`, `gptr()`, and `egptr()` form the interface to the read buffer. The pointers returned from the functions `pbase()`, `pptr()`, and `epptr()` form the interface to the write buffer. These pointers are manipulated by the read and write operations, which may result in corresponding reactions in the corresponding read or write channel. The exact operation is examined separately for reading and writing.

User-Defined Output Buffers

A buffer used to write characters is maintained with three pointers that can be accessed by the three functions `pbase()`, `pptr()`, and `epptr()` (Figure 13.4). Here is what these pointers represent:

1. `pbase()` ("put base") is the beginning of the output buffer.
2. `pptr()` ("put pointer") is the current write position.
3. `epptr()` ("end put pointer") is the end of the output buffer. This means that `epptr()` points to one past the last character that can be buffered.

The characters in the range from `pbase()` to `pptr()` (not including the character pointed to by `pptr()`) are already written but not yet transported (flushed) to the corresponding output channel.

A character is written using the member function `sputc()`. This character is copied to the current write position if there is a spare write position. Then the pointer to the current write position is

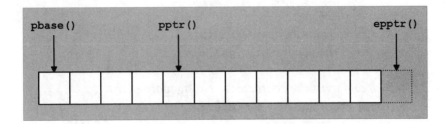

Figure 13.4. The Interface to the Output Buffer

incremented. If the buffer is full (pptr() == epptr()), the contents of the output buffer are sent to the corresponding output channel. This is done by calling the virtual function overflow(). This function is effectively responsible for the actual sending of the characters to some "external representation" (which may actually be internal, as in the case of string streams). The implementation of overflow() in the base class basic_streambuf only returns end-of-file, which indicates that no more characters could be written.

The member function sputn() can be used to write multiple characters at once. This function delegates the work to the virtual function xsputn(), which can be implemented for more efficient writing of multiple characters. The implementation of xsputn() in class basic_streambuf basically calls sputc() for each character. Thus, overriding xsputn() is not necessary. However, often, writing multiple characters can be implemented more efficiently than writing characters one at a time. Thus, this function can be used to optimize the processing of character sequences.

Writing to a stream buffer does not necessarily involve using the buffer. Instead, the characters can be written as soon as they are received. In this case, the value 0 or NULL has to be assigned to the pointers that maintain the write buffer. The default constructor does this automatically.

With this information, the following example of a simple stream buffer can be implemented. This stream buffer does not use a buffer. Thus, the function overflow() is called for each character. Implementing this function is all that is necessary:

```
// io/outbuf1.hpp

#include <streambuf>
#include <locale>
#include <cstdio>

class outbuf : public std::streambuf
{
  protected:
    /* central output function
     * - print characters in uppercase mode
     */
    virtual int_type overflow (int_type c) {
```

```
                    if (c != EOF) {
                        // convert lowercase to uppercase
                        c = std::toupper(c,getloc());

                        // and write the character to the standard output
                        if (putchar(c) == EOF) {
                            return EOF;
                        }
                    }
                    return c;
            }
    };
```

In this case, each character sent to the stream buffer is written using the C function `putchar()`. However, before the character is written it is turned into an uppercase character using `toupper()` (see page 718). The function `getloc()` is used to get the locale object that is associated with the stream buffer (see also page 626).

In this example, the output buffer is implemented specifically for the character type `char` (`streambuf` is the specialization of `basic_streambuf<>` for the character type `char`). If other character types are used, you have to implement this function using character traits, which are introduced in Section 14.1.2, page 687. In this case, the comparison of `c` with end-of-file looks different. `traits::eof()` has to be returned instead of EOF, and if the argument `c` is EOF, the value `traits::not_eof(c)` should be returned (where `traits` is the second template argument to `basic_streambuf`). This might look as follows:

```
// io/outbuf1x.hpp

#include <streambuf>
#include <locale>
#include <cstdio>

template <class charT, class traits = std::char_traits<charT> >
class basic_outbuf : public std::basic_streambuf<charT,traits>
{
  protected:
    /* central output function
     * - print characters in uppercase mode
     */
    virtual typename traits::int_type
            overflow (typename traits::int_type c) {
        if (!traits::eq_int_type(c,traits::eof())) {
```

```
            // convert lowercase to uppercase
            c = std::toupper(c,getloc());

            // and write the character to the standard output
            if (putchar(c) == EOF) {
                return traits::eof();
            }
        }
    }
    return traits::not_eof(c);
    }
};

typedef basic_outbuf<char>    outbuf;
typedef basic_outbuf<wchar_t> woutbuf;
```

Using this stream buffer in the following program:

```
// io/outbuf1.cpp

#include <iostream>
#include "outbuf1.hpp"

int main()
{
    outbuf ob;                  // create special output buffer
    std::ostream out(&ob);      // initialize output stream with that output buffer

    out << "31 hexadecimal: " << std::hex << 31 << std::endl;
}
```

produces the following output:

```
31 HEXADECIMAL: 1F
```

The same approach can be used to write to other arbitrary destinations. For example, the constructor of a stream buffer may take a file descriptor, the name of a socket connection, or two other stream buffers used for simultaneous writing to initialize the object. Writing to the corresponding destination requires only that overflow() be implemented. In addition, the function xsputn() should also be implemented to make writing to the stream buffer more efficient.

For convenient construction of the stream buffer, it is also reasonable to implement a special stream class that mainly passes the constructor argument to the corresponding stream buffer. The next example demonstrates this. It defines a stream buffer class initialized with a file descriptor, to which characters are written with the function write() (a low-level I/O function used on UNIX-like operating systems). In addition, a class derived from `ostream` is defined that maintains such a stream buffer, to which the file descriptor is passed:

```cpp
// io/outbuf2.hpp

#include <iostream>
#include <streambuf>
#include <cstdio>

// for write():
#ifdef _MSC_VER
# include <io.h>
#else
# include <unistd.h>
#endif

class fdoutbuf : public std::streambuf {
  protected:
    int fd;       // file descriptor
  public:
    // constructor
    fdoutbuf (int _fd) : fd(_fd) {
    }
  protected:
    // write one character
    virtual int_type overflow (int_type c) {
        if (c != EOF) {
            char z = c;
            if (write (fd, &z, 1) != 1) {
                return EOF;
            }
        }
        return c;
    }
    // write multiple characters
    virtual std::streamsize xsputn (const char* s,
                                    std::streamsize num) {
        return write(fd,s,num);
    }
};
```

```
class fdostream : public std::ostream {
  protected:
    fdoutbuf buf;
  public:
    fdostream (int fd) : std::ostream(0), buf(fd) {
        rdbuf(&buf);
    }
};
```

This stream buffer also implements the function `xsputn()` to avoid calling `overflow()` for each character if a character sequence is sent to this stream buffer. This function writes the whole character sequence with one call to the file identified by the file descriptor `fd`. The function `xsputn()` returns the number of characters written successfully. Here is a sample application:

```
// io/outbuf2.cpp

#include <iostream>
#include "outbuf2.hpp"

int main()
{
    fdostream out(1);        // stream with buffer writing to file descriptor 1

    out << "31 hexadecimal: " << std::hex << 31 << std::endl;
}
```

This program creates a output stream that is initialized with the file descriptor 1. This file descriptor, by convention, identifies the standard output channel. Thus, in this example the characters are simply printed. If some other file descriptor is available (for example, for a file or a socket), it can also be used as the constructor argument.

To implement a stream buffer that really buffers, the write buffer has to be initialized using the function `setp()`. This is demonstrated by the next example:

```
// io/outbuf3.hpp

#include <cstdio>
#include <streambuf>

// for write():
#ifdef _MSC_VER
# include <io.h>
#else
# include <unistd.h>
#endif
```

```
class outbuf : public std::streambuf {
  protected:
    static const int bufferSize = 10;    // size of data buffer
    char buffer[bufferSize];             // data buffer

  public:
    /* constructor
     * - initialize data buffer
     * - one character less to let the bufferSizeth character
     *   cause a call of overflow()
     */
    outbuf() {
        setp (buffer, buffer+(bufferSize-1));
    }

    /* destructor
     * - flush data buffer
     */
    virtual ~outbuf() {
        sync();
    }

  protected:
    // flush the characters in the buffer
    int flushBuffer () {
        int num = pptr()-pbase();
        if (write (1, buffer, num) != num) {
            return EOF;
        }
        pbump (-num);        // reset put pointer accordingly
        return num;
    }

    /* buffer full
     * - write c and all previous characters
     */
    virtual int_type overflow (int_type c) {
        if (c != EOF) {
            // insert character into the buffer
```

```
            *pptr() = c;
            pbump(1);
        }
        // flush the buffer
        if (flushBuffer() == EOF) {
            // ERROR
            return EOF;
        }
        return c;
    }


    /* synchronize data with file/destination
     * - flush the data in the buffer
     */
    virtual int sync () {
        if (flushBuffer() == EOF) {
            // ERROR
            return -1;
        }
        return 0;
    }
};
```

The constructor initializes the write buffer with `setp()`:

```
setp (buffer, buffer+(size-1));
```

The write buffer is set up such that `overflow()` is already called when there is still room for one character. If `overflow()` is not called with EOF as the argument, the corresponding character can be written to the write position because the pointer to the write position is not increased beyond the end pointer. After the argument to `overflow()` is placed in the write position, the whole buffer can be emptied.

The member function `flushBuffer()` does exactly this. It writes the characters to the standard output channel (file descriptor 1) using the function `write()`. The stream buffer's member function `pbump()` is used to move the write position back to the beginning of the buffer.

The function `overflow()` inserts the character that caused the call of `overflow()` into the buffer if it is not EOF. Then, `pbump()` is used to advance the write position to reflect the new end of the buffered characters. This moves the write position beyond the end position (`epptr()`) temporarily.

This class also features the virtual function `sync()` that is used to synchronize the current state of the stream buffer with the corresponding storage medium. Normally, all that needs to be done is to flush the buffer. For the unbuffered versions of the stream buffer, overriding this function was not necessary because there was no buffer to be flushed.

The virtual destructor ensures that data is written that is still buffered when the stream buffer is destroyed.

These are the functions that are overridden for most stream buffers. If the external representation has some special structure, overriding additional functions may be useful. For example, the functions `seekoff()` and `seekpos()` may be overridden to allow manipulation of the write position.

User-Defined Input Buffers

The input mechanism works basically the same as the output mechanism. However, for input there is also the possibility of undoing the last read. The functions `sungetc()` (called by `unget()` of the input stream) or `sputbackc()` (called by `putback()` of the input stream) can be used to restore the stream buffer to its state before the last read. It is also possible to read the next character without moving the read position beyond this character. Thus, you must override more functions to implement reading from a stream buffer than is necessary to implement writing to a stream buffer.

A stream buffer maintains a read buffer with three pointers that can be accessed through the member function `eback()`, `gptr()`, and `egptr()` (Figure 13.5):

1. `eback()` ("end back") is the beginning of the input buffer, or (this is where the name comes from) the end of the putback area. The character can only be put back up to this position without taking special action.
2. `gptr()` ("get pointer") is the current read position.
3. `egptr()` ("end get pointer") is the end of the input buffer.

The characters between the read position and the end position have been transported from the external representation to the program's memory, but they still await processing by the program.

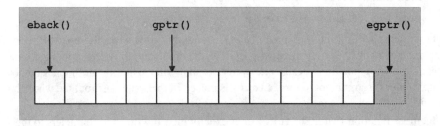

Figure 13.5. The Interface for Reading from Stream Buffers

Single characters can be read using the function `sgetc()` or `sbumpc()`. These two functions differ in that the read pointer is incremented by `sbumpc()`, but not by `sgetc()`. If the buffer is read completely (`gptr()` == `egptr()`), there is no character available and the buffer has to be refilled. This is done by a call of the virtual function `underflow()`. This function is responsible for the reading of data. The function `sbumpc()` calls the virtual function `uflow()` instead, if no characters are available. The default implementation of `uflow()` is to call `underflow()` and then increment the read pointer. The default implementation of `underflow()` in the base class `basic_streambuf` is to return EOF. This means it is impossible to read characters with the default implementation.

The function `sgetn()` is used for reading multiple characters at once. This function delegates the processing to the virtual function `xsgetn()`. The default implementation of `xsgetn()` simply extracts multiple characters by calling `sbumpc()` for each character. Like the function `xsputn()` for writing, `xsgetn()` can be implemented to optimize the reading of multiple characters.

For input it is not sufficient just to override one function as it is the case of output. Either a buffer has to be set up, or at the very least `underflow()` and `uflow()` have to implemented. This is because `underflow()` does not move past the current character, but `underflow()` may be called from `sgetc()`. Moving on to the next character has to be done using buffer manipulation or using a call to `uflow()`. In any case, `underflow()` has to be implemented for any stream buffer capable of reading characters. If both `underflow()` and `uflow()` are implemented, there is no need to set up a buffer.

A read buffer is set up with the member function `setg()`, which takes three arguments in this order:

1. A pointer to the beginning of the buffer (`eback()`)
2. A pointer to the current read position (`gptr()`)
3. A pointer to the end of the buffer (`egptr()`)

Unlike `setp()`, `setg()` takes three arguments. This is necessary to be able to define the room for storing characters that are put back into the stream. Thus, when the pointers to the read buffer are being set up, it is reasonable to have some characters (at least one) that are already read but still stored in the buffer.

As mentioned, characters can be put back into the read buffer using the functions `sputbackc()` and `sungetc()`. `sputbackc()` gets the character to be put back as its argument and ensures that this character was indeed the character read. Both functions decrement the read pointer, if possible. Of course, this only works as long as the read pointer is not at the beginning of the read buffer. If you attempt to put a character back after the beginning of the buffer is reached, the virtual function `pbackfail()` is called. By overriding this function you can implement a mechanism to restore the old read position even in this case. In the base class `basic_streambuf`, no corresponding behavior is defined. Thus, in practice, it is not possible to go back an arbitrary number of characters. For streams that do not use a buffer, the function `pbackfail()` should be implemented because it is generally assumed that at least one character can be put back into the stream.

If a new buffer was just read, another problem arises: Not even one character can be put back if the old data is not saved in the buffer. Thus, the implementation of `underflow()` often moves the last few characters (for example, four characters) of the current buffer to the beginning of the buffer and appends the newly read characters thereafter. This allows some characters to be moved back before `pbackfail()` is called.

The following example demonstrates how such an implementation might look. In the class `inbuf`, an input buffer with ten characters is implemented. This buffer is split into a maximum of four characters for the putback area and six characters for the "normal" input buffer:

```
// io/inbuf1.hpp

#include <cstdio>
#include <cstring>
#include <streambuf>

// for read():
#ifdef _MSC_VER
# include <io.h>
#else
# include <unistd.h>
#endif

class inbuf : public std::streambuf {
  protected:
    /* data buffer:
     * - at most, four characters in putback area plus
     * - at most, six characters in ordinary read buffer
     */
    static const int bufferSize = 10;    // size of the data buffer
    char buffer[bufferSize];             // data buffer
  public:
    /* constructor
     * - initialize empty data buffer
     * - no putback area
     * => force underflow()
     */
    inbuf() {
        setg (buffer+4,         // beginning of putback area
              buffer+4,         // read position
              buffer+4);        // end position
    }
  protected:
    // insert new characters into the buffer
    virtual int_type underflow () {

        // is read position before end of buffer?
        if (gptr() < egptr()) {
            return traits_type::to_int_type(*gptr());
        }
```

```
/* process size of putback area
 * - use number of characters read
 * - but at most four
 */
int numPutback;
numPutback = gptr() - eback();
if (numPutback > 4) {
    numPutback = 4;
}

/* copy up to four characters previously read into
 * the putback buffer (area of first four characters)
 */
std::memmove (buffer+(4-numPutback), gptr()-numPutback,
              numPutback);

// read new characters
int num;
num = read (0, buffer+4, bufferSize-4);
if (num <= 0) {
    // ERROR or EOF
    return EOF;
}

// reset buffer pointers
setg (buffer+(4-numPutback),    // beginning of putback area
      buffer+4,                  // read position
      buffer+4+num);             // end of buffer

// return next character
return traits_type::to_int_type(*gptr());
    }
};
```

The constructor initializes all pointers so that the buffer is completely empty (Figure 13.6). If a character is read from this stream buffer, the function underflow() is called. This function is always used by this stream buffer to read the next characters. It starts by checking for read characters in the input buffer. If characters are present, they are moved to the putback area using the function memcpy(). These are, at most, the last four characters of the input buffer. Then POSIX's low-level

I/O function `read()` is used to read the next character from the standard input channel. After the buffer is adjusted to the new situation, the first character read is returned.

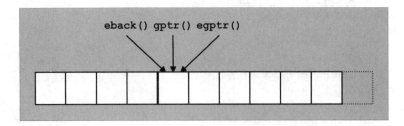

Figure 13.6. Get Buffer After Initialization

For example, if the characters 'H', 'a', 'l', 'l', 'o', and 'w' are read by the first call to `read()`, the state of the input buffer changes, as shown in Figure 13.7. The putback area is empty because the buffer was filled for the first time, and there are no characters yet that can be put back.

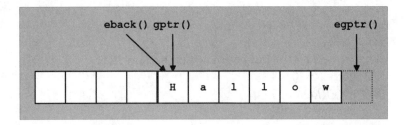

Figure 13.7. Get Buffer After Reading H a l l o w

After these characters are extracted, the last four characters are moved into the putback area and new characters are read. For example, if the characters 'e', 'e', 'n', and '\n' are read by the next call of `read()` the result is as shown in Figure 13.8.

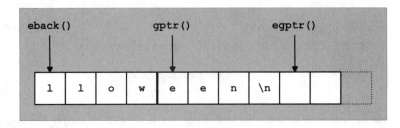

Figure 13.8. Get Buffer After Reading Four More Characters

Here is an example of the use of this stream buffer:

```cpp
// io/inbuf1.cpp

#include <iostream>
#include "inbuf1.hpp"

int main()
{
    inbuf ib;                    // create special stream buffer
    std::istream in(&ib);        // initialize input stream with that buffer

    char c;
    for (int i=1; i<=20; i++) {
        // read next character (out of the buffer)
        in.get(c);

        // print that character (and flush)
        std::cout << c << std::flush;

        // after eight characters, put two characters back into the stream
        if (i == 8) {
            in.unget();
            in.unget();
        }
    }
    std::cout << std::endl;
}
```

The program reads characters in a loop and writes them out. After the eighth character is read, two characters are put back. Thus, the seventh and eighth characters are printed twice.

13.14   Performance Issues

This section specifically addresses issues that focus on performance. In general the stream classes should be pretty efficient, but performance can be improved further in applications in which I/O is performance critical.

One performance issue was mentioned in Section 13.2.3, page 593, already: You should only include those headers that are necessary to compile your code. In particular, you should avoid including <iostream> if the standard stream objects are not used.

13.14.1   Synchronization with C's Standard Streams

By default, the eight C++ standard streams (the four narrow character streams `cin`, `cout`, `cerr`, and `clog`, and their wide-character counterpart) are synchronized with the corresponding files from the C standard library (`stdin`, `stdout`, and `stderr`). By default `clog` and `wclog` use the same stream buffer as `cerr` and `wcerr` respectively. Thus, they are also synchronized with `stderr` by default, although there is no direct counterpart in the C standard library.

Depending on the implementation, this synchronization might imply some often unnecessary overhead. For example, if the standard C++ streams are implemented using the standard C files, this basically inhibits buffering in the corresponding stream buffers. However, the buffer in the stream buffers is necessary for some optimizations especially during formatted reading (see Section 13.14.2, page 682). To allow switching to a better implementation, the static member function `sync_with_stdio()` is defined for the class `ios_base` (Table 13.46).

Static Function	Meaning
`sync_with_stdio()`	Returns whether the standard stream objects are synchronized with standard C streams
`sync_with_stdio(false)`	Disables the synchronization of C++ and C streams provided it is called before any I/O

Table 13.46. Synchronizing Standard C++ and Standard C Streams

`sync_with_stdio()` takes an optional Boolean value as argument that determines whether the synchronization with the standard C streams should be turned on. Thus, to turn the synchronization off you have to pass `false` as the argument:

    std::ios::sync_with_stdio(false);   // disable synchronization

Note that you have to disable the synchronization before any other I/O operation. Calling this function after any I/O has occurred results in implementation-defined behavior.

The function returns the previous value with which the function was called. If not called before, it always returns `true` to reflect the default setup of the standard streams.

13.14.2   Buffering in Stream Buffers

Buffering I/O is important for efficiency. One reason for this is that system calls are, in general, relatively expensive and it pays to avoid them if possible. There is, however, another more subtle reason in C++ for doing buffering in stream buffers, at least for input: The functions for formatted I/O use stream buffer iterators to access the streams, and operating on stream buffer iterators is slower than operating on pointers. The difference is not that big, but it is sufficient to justify improved implementations for frequently used operations like formatted reading of numeric values. However, for such improvements it is essential that stream buffers are buffered.

Thus, all I/O is done using stream buffers, which implement a mechanism for buffering. However, it is not sufficient to rely solely on this buffering because there are three aspects that conflict with effective buffering:

1. It is often simpler to implement stream buffers without buffering. If the corresponding streams are not used frequently or are only used for output (for output the difference between stream buffer iterators and pointers is not as bad as for input; the main problem is comparing stream buffer iterators), buffering is probably not that important. However, for stream buffers that are used extensively, buffering should definitely be implemented.

2. The flag `unitbuf` causes output streams to flush the stream after each output operation. Correspondingly, the manipulators `flush` and `endl` also flush the stream. For the best performance all three should probably be avoided. However, when writing to the console, for example, it is probably still reasonable to flush the stream after writing complete lines. If you are stuck with a program that makes heavy use of `unitbuf`, `flush`, or `endl`, you might consider using a special stream buffer that does not use `sync()` to flush the stream buffer but uses some other function that is called when appropriate.

3. Tieing streams with the `tie()` function (see Section 13.10.1, page 637) also results in additional flushing of streams. Thus, streams should only be tied if it is really necessary.

When implementing new stream buffers, it may be reasonable to implement them without buffering first. Then, if the stream buffer is identified as a bottleneck, it is still possible to implement buffering without affecting anything in the remainder of the application.

13.14.3 Using Stream Buffers Directly

All member functions of the class `basic_istream` and `basic_ostream` that read or write characters operate according to the same schema: First, a corresponding `sentry` object is constructed, then the actual operation is performed. The construction of the `sentry` object results in flushing of potentially tied objects, skipping of whitespace (for input only), and implementation-specific operations like locking in multithreaded environments (see Section 13.12.4, page 658).

For unformatted I/O, most of the operations are normally useless anyway. Only the locking operation might be useful if the streams are used in multithreaded environments (note that the C++ standard does not address multithreading). Thus, when doing unformatted I/O it is normally much better to use stream buffers directly.

To support this behavior, you can use operators `<<` and `>>` with stream buffers as follows:

- By passing a pointer to a stream buffer to operator `<<`, you can output all input of its device. This is probably the fastest way to copy files by using C++ I/O streams. For example:

```
// io/copy1.cpp

#include <iostream>

int main ()
{
```

```
// copy all standard input to standard output
std::cout << std::cin.rdbuf();
}
```

Here, rdbuf() yields the buffer of cin (see page 638). Thus, the program copies all standard input to standard output.

- By passing a pointer to a stream buffer to operator >>, you can read directly into a stream buffer. For example, you could also copy all standard input to standard output in the following way:

```
// io/copy2.cpp

#include <iostream>

int main ()
{
    // copy all standard input to standard output
    std::cin >> std::noskipws >> std::cout.rdbuf();
}
```

Note that you have to clear the flag skipws. Otherwise, leading whitespace of the input is skipped (see page 625).

Even for formatted I/O it may be reasonable to use stream buffers directly. For example, if lots of numeric values are read in a loop, it is sufficient to construct just one sentry object that exists for the whole time the loop is executed. Then, within the loop, whitespace is skipped manually (using the ws manipulator would also construct a sentry object) and then the facet num_get (see Section 14.4.1, page 707) is used for reading the numeric values directly.

Note that a stream buffer has no error state of its own. It also has no knowledge of the input or ouput stream that might connect to it. So, inside of

```
// copy contents of in to out
out << in.rdbuf();
```

there is no way to change the error state of in due to a failure or end-of-file.

Chapter 14

Internationalization

As the global market has increased in importance, so has *internationalization* (or *i18n* for short)[1] become more important for software development. As a consequence, the C++ standard library provides concepts to write code for international programs. These concepts influence mainly the use of I/O and string processing. This chapter describes these concepts. Many thanks to **Dietmar Kühl**, who is an expert on I/O and internationalization in the C++ standard library and wrote major parts of this chapter.

The C++ standard library provides a general approach to support national conventions without being bound to specific conventions. This goes to the extent, for example, that strings are not bound to a specific character type to support 16-bit characters in Asia. For the internationalization of programs, two related aspects are important:

1. Different character sets have different properties. Handling them requires flexible solutions for problems, such as what is considered to be a letter or, worse, what type to use to represent characters. For character sets with more than 256 characters, type `char` is not sufficient as a representation.

2. The user of a program expects to see national or cultural conventions obeyed (for example, the formatting of dates, monetary values, numbers, and Boolean values).

For both aspects, the C++ standard library provides related solutions.

The major approach toward internationalization is to use *locale objects* to represent an extensible collection of aspects to be adapted to specific local conventions. Locales are already used in C to adapt to specific local conventions. In the C++ standard, this mechanism was generalized and made more flexible. Actually, the C++ locale mechanism can be used to address all kinds of customization, depending on the user's environment or preferences. For example, it can be extended to deal with measurement systems, time zones, or paper size.

---

[1] *i18n* is a common abbreviation for *internationalization*. It stands for *the letter i, followed by 18 characters, followed by the letter n.*

Most of the mechanisms of internationalization involve no or only minimal additional work for the programmer. For example, when doing I/O with the C++ stream mechanism, numeric values are formatted according to the rules of some locale. The only work for the programmer is to instruct the I/O stream classes to use the user's preferences.

In addition to such automatic use, the programmer may use locale objects directly for formatting, collation, character classification, and so on. Some internationalized aspects supported by the C++ standard library are not used by the C++ standard library itself, and to use them the programmer has to call those functions manually. For example, there are no stream functions defined in the C++ standard library that do time, date, or monetary formatting. To use these services, it is necessary to call them directly (for example, in user-defined stream operators writing objects of a money class).

Strings and streams use another concept for internationalization: *character traits*. They define fundamental properties and operations that differ for different character sets, such as the value of "end-of-file" as well as functions to compare, assign, and copy strings.

The classes for internationalization were introduced to the standard relatively late. Although the general approach is extremely flexible, it still needs some work to make it really complete. For example, the functions for string collation (that is, comparing strings for sorting according to some locale conventions) use only iterators of type const charT*, where charT is some character type. Although it is very likely that basic_string<charT> uses this type as an iterator type, it is not at all guaranteed. Thus, it is not guaranteed that string iterators can be used as arguments to the functions for string collation. However, it is possible to use the result of basic_string data() member functions with the string collation functions.

14.1   Different Character Encodings

One area internationalization addresses is how to handle different character encodings. This issue arises mainly in Asia, where different encodings are used to represent the same character set. The issue normally comes in conjunction with character encodings that use more than 8 bits. To process such characters, it is necessary to use new concepts and functions for text processing.

14.1.1   Wide-Character and Multibyte Text

Two different approaches are common to address character sets that have more than 256 characters: multibyte representation and wide-character representation:

1. With *multibyte representation*, the number of bytes used for a character is variable. A 1-byte character, such as an ISO Latin-1 character, can be followed by a 3-byte character, such as a Japanese ideogram.

2. With *wide-character representation*, the number of bytes used to represent a character is always the same, independent of the character being represented. Typical representations use 2 or 4 bytes. Conceptually, this does not differ from representations that use just 1 byte for locales where ISO Latin-1 or even ASCII is sufficient.

This multibyte representation is more compact than the wide-character representation. Thus, the multibyte representation is normally used to store data outside of programs. Conversely, it is much easier to process characters of fixed size, so the wide-character representation is usually used inside programs.

Like ISO C, ISO C++ uses the type `wchar_t` to represent wide characters. However in C++, `wchar_t` is a keyword rather than a type definition. Thus, it is possible to overload all functions with this type.

In a multibyte string, the same byte may represent a character or even just a part of the character. During iteration through a multibyte string, each byte is interpreted according to a current "shift state." Depending on the value of the byte and the current shift state, a byte may represent a certain character or a change of the current shift state. A multibyte string always starts in some defined initial shift state. For example, in the initial shift state the bytes may represent ISO Latin-1 characters until an escape character is encountered. The character following the escape character identifies the new shift state. For example, that character may switch to a shift state in which the bytes are interpreted as Arabic characters until the next escape character is encountered.

The class template `codecvt<>` (described in Section 14.4.4, page 720) is used to convert between different character encodings. This class is used mainly by the class `basic_filebuf<>` (see page 627) to convert between internal and external representations. The C++ standard actually makes no assumptions about multibyte character encodings, but it supports the notion of shift states. The members of the `codecvt<>` class support an argument that may be used to store an arbitrary state of a string. They also support a function intended to determine the character sequence used to return to the initial shift state.

14.1.2 Character Traits

The different representations of character sets imply variations that are relevant for the processing of strings and I/O. For example, the value used to represent "end-of-file" or the details of comparing characters may differ for representations.

The string and stream classes are intended to be instantiated with built-in types, especially with `char` and `wchar_t`. The interface of built-in types cannot be changed. Thus, the details on how to deal with aspects that depend on the representation are factored into a separate class, a so-called "traits class." Both the string and stream classes take a traits class as a template argument. This argument defaults to the class `char_traits`, parameterized with the template argument that defines the character type of the string or stream:

```
namespace std {
    template<class charT,
             class traits = char_traits<charT>,
             class Allocator = allocator<charT> >
    class basic_string;
}
```

```
namespace std {
    template <class charT,
              class traits = char_traits<charT> >
    class basic_istream;
    template <class charT,
              class traits = char_traits<charT> >
    class basic_ostream;
    ...
}
```

The character traits have type `char_traits<>`. This type is defined in `<string>` and is parameter-ized for the specific character type:

```
namespace std {
    template <class charT>
    struct char_traits {
        ...
    };
}
```

The traits classes define all fundamental properties of the character type and the corresponding op-erations necessary for the implementation of strings and streams as static components. Table 14.1 lists the members of `char_traits`.

The functions that process strings or character sequences are present for optimization only. They could also be implemented by using the functions that process single characters. For example, `copy()` can be implemented using `assign()`. However, there might be more efficient implementa-tions when dealing with strings.

Note that counts used in the functions are exact counts, not maximum counts. That is, string termination characters within these sequences are ignored.

The last group of functions cares about the special processing of the character that represents end-of-file (EOF). This character extends the character set by an artificial character to indicate spe-cial processing. For some representations, the character type may be insufficient to accommodate this special character because it has to have a value that differs from the values of all "normal" characters of the character set. C established the convention to return a character as `int` instead of as `char` from functions reading characters. This technique was extended in C++. The charac-ter traits define `char_type` as the type to represent all characters, and `int_type` as the type to represent all characters plus EOF. The functions `to_char_type()`, `to_int_type()`, `not_eof()`, and `eq_int_type()` define the corresponding conversions and comparisons. It is possible that `char_type` and `int_type` are identical for some character traits. This can be the case if not all values of `char_type` are necessary to represent characters so that there is a spare value that can be used for end-of-file.

`pos_type` and `off_type` are used to define file positions and offsets (see page 634 for details).

Expression	Meaning
char_type	The character type (that is, the template argument for char_traits)
int_type	A type large enough to represent an additional, otherwise unused value for end-of-file
pos_type	A type used to represent positions in streams
off_type	A type used to represent offsets between positions in streams
state_type	A type used to represent the current state in multibyte streams
assign(*c1*,*c2*)	Assigns character *c2* to *c1*
eq(*c1*,*c2*)	Returns whether the characters *c1* and *c2* are equal
lt(*c1*,*c2*)	Returns whether character *c1* is less than character *c2*
length(*s*)	Returns the length of the string *s*
compare(*s1*,*s2*,*n*)	Compares up to *n* characters of strings *s1* and *s2*
copy(*s1*,*s2*,*n*)	Copies *n* characters of string *s2* to string *s1*
move(*s1*,*s2*,*n*)	Copies *n* characters of string *s2* to string *s1*, where *s1* and *s2* may overlap
assign(*s*,*n*,*c*)	Assigns the character *c* to *n* characters of string *s*
find(*s*,*n*,*c*)	Returns a pointer to the first character in string *s* that is equal to *c*, or returns zero, if there is no such character among the first *n* characters
eof()	Returns the value of end-of-file
to_int_type(*c*)	Converts the character *c* into the corresponding representation as int_type
to_char_type(*i*)	Converts the representation *i* as int_type to a character (the result of converting EOF is undefined)
not_eof(*i*)	Returns the value *i* unless *i* is the value for EOF; in this case an implementation-dependent value different from EOF is returned
eq_int_type(*i1*,*i2*)	Tests the equality of the two characters *i1* and *i2* represented as int_type (that is, the characters may be EOF)

Table 14.1. Character Traits Members

The C++ standard library provides specializations of char_traits<> for types char and wchar_t:

```
namespace std {
    template<> struct char_traits<char>;
    template<> struct char_traits<wchar_t>;
}
```

The specialization for char is usually implemented by using the global string functions of C that are defined in <cstring> or <string.h>. An implementation might look as follows:

```
namespace std {
    template<> struct char_traits<char> {
        // type definitions:
```

```
typedef char        char_type;
typedef int         int_type;
typedef streampos   pos_type;
typedef streamoff   off_type;
typedef mbstate_t   state_type;

// functions:
static void assign(char& c1, const char& c2) {
    c1 = c2;
}
static bool eq(const char& c1, const char& c2) {
    return c1 == c2;
}
static bool lt(const char& c1, const char& c2) {
    return c1 < c2;
}
static size_t length(const char* s) {
    return strlen(s);
}
static int compare(const char* s1, const char* s2, size_t n) {
    return memcmp(s1,s2,n);
}
static char* copy(char* s1, const char* s2, size_t n) {
    return (char*)memcpy(s1,s2,n);
}
static char* move(char* s1, const char* s2, size_t n) {
    return (char*)memmove(s1,s2,n);
}
static char* assign(char* s, size_t n, char c) {
    return (char*)memset(s,c,n);
}
static const char* find(const char* s, size_t n,
                        const char& c) {
    return (const char*)memchr(s,c,n);
}
static int eof() {
    return EOF;
}
static int to_int_type(const char& c) {
```

```
        return (int)(unsigned char)c;
    }
    static char to_char_type(const int& i) {
        return (char)i;
    }
    static int not_eof(const int& i) {
        return i!=EOF ? i : !EOF;
    }
    static bool eq_int_type(const int& i1, const int& i2) {
        return i1 == i2;
    }
  };
}
```

See Section 11.2.14, page 503, for the implementation of a user-defined traits class that lets strings behave in a case-insensitive manner.

14.1.3 Internationalization of Special Characters

One issue in conjunction with character encodings remains: How are special characters such as the newline or the string termination character internationalized? The class `basic_ios` has members `widen()` and `narrow()` that can be used for this purpose. Thus, the newline character in an encoding appropriate for the stream `strm` can be written as follows:

    `strm.widen('\n')`   *// internationalized newline character*

The string termination character in the same encoding can be created like this:

    `strm.widen('\0')`   *// internationalized string termination character*

See the implementation of the `endl` manipulator on page 613 for an example use.

The functions `widen()` and `narrow()` actually use a locale object, more precisely the `ctype` facet of this object. This facet can be used to convert all characters between `char` and some other character representations. It is described in Section 14.4.4, page 716. For example, the following expression converts the character c of type `char` into an object of type `char_type` by using the locale object `loc`[2]:

    `std::use_facet<std::ctype<char_type> >(loc).widen(c)`

The details of the use of locales and their facets are described in the following sections.

---

[2] Note that you have to put a space between the two ">" characters. ">>" would be parsed as shift operator, which would result in a syntax error.

14.2   The Concept of Locales

A common approach to internationalization is to use environments, called *locales*, to encapsulate national or cultural conventions. The C community uses this approach. Thus, in the context of internationalization, a locale is a collection of parameters and functions used to support national or cultural conventions. According to X/Open conventions,[3] the environment variable LANG is used to define the locale to be used. Depending on this locale, different formats for floating-point numbers, dates, monetary values, and so on are used.

The format of the string defining a locale is normally this:

language[_*area*[.*code*]]

language represents the language, such as English or German. *area* is the area, country, or culture where this language is used. It is used, for example, to support different national conventions even if the same language is used in different nations. *code* defines the character encoding to be used. This is mainly important in Asia, where different character encodings are used to represent the same character set.

Table 14.2 presents a selection of typical language strings. However, note that these strings are *not* yet standardized. For example, sometimes the first character of *language* is capitalized. Some implementations deviate from the format mentioned previously and, for example, use english to select an English locale. All in all, the locales that are supported by a system are implementation specific.

For programs, it is normally no problem that these names are not standardized! This is because the locale information is provided by the user in some form. It is common that programs simply read environment variables or some similar database to determine which locales to use. Thus, the burden of finding the correct locale names is put on the users. Only if the program always uses a special locale does the name need to be hard coded in the program. Normally, for this case, the C locale is sufficient, and is guaranteed to be supported by all implementations and to have the name C.

The next section presents the use of different locales in C++ programs. In particular, it introduces *facets* of locales that are used to deal with specific formatting details.

C also provides an approach to handle the problem of character sets with more than 256 characters. This approach is to use the character type wchar_t, a type definition for one of the integral types with language support for wide-character constants and wide-character string literals. However, apart from this, only functions to convert between wide characters and narrow characters are supported. This approach was also incorporated into C++ with the character type wchar_t, which is, unlike the C approach, a distinct type in C++. However, C++ provides more library support than C, because basically everything available for char is also available for wchar_t, and any other type may be used as a character type.

---

[3] POSIX and X/Open are standards for operating system interfaces.

Locale	Meaning
C	Default: ANSI-C conventions (English, 7 bit)
de_DE	German in Germany
de_DE.88591	German in Germany with ISO Latin-1 encoding
de_AT	German in Austria
de_CH	German in Switzerland
en_US	English in the United States
en_GB	English in Great Britain
en_AU	English in Australia
en_CA	English in Canada
fr_FR	French in France
fr_CH	French in Switzerland
fr_CA	French in Canada
ja_JP.jis	Japanese in Japan with *Japanese Industrial Standard (JIS)* encoding
ja_JP.sjis	Japanese in Japan with *Shift JIS* encoding
ja_JP.ujis	Japanese in Japan with *UNIXized JIS* encoding
ja_JP.EUC	Japanese in Japan with *Extended UNIX Code* encoding
ko_KR	Korean in Korea
zh_CN	Chinese in China
zh_TW	Chinese in Taiwan
lt_LN.bit7	ISO Latin, 7 bit
lt_LN.bit8	ISO Latin, 8 bit
POSIX	POSIX conventions (English, 7 bit)

Table 14.2. Selection of Locale Names

14.2.1   Using Locales

Using translations of textual messages is normally not sufficient for true internationalization. For example, different conventions for numeric, monetary, or date formatting also have to be used. In addition, functions manipulating letters should depend on character encoding to ensure the correct handling of all characters that are letters in a given language.

According to the POSIX and X/Open standards, it is already possible in C programs to set a locale. This is done using the function setlocale(). Changing the locale influences the results of character classification and manipulation functions, such as isupper() and toupper(), and the I/O functions, such as printf().

However, the C approach has several limitations. Because the locale is a global property, using more than one locale at the same time (for example, when reading floating-point numbers in English and writing them in German) is either not possible or is possible only with a relatively large effort. Also, locales cannot be extended. They provide only the facilities the implementation chooses to provide. If something the C locales do not provide must also be adapted to national conventions, a different mechanism has to be used to do this. Finally, it is not possible to define new locales to support special cultural conventions.

The C++ standard library addresses all of these problems with an object-oriented approach. First, the details of a locale are encapsulated in an object of type `locale`. Doing this immediately provides the possibility of using multiple locales at the same time. Operations that depend on locales are configured to use a corresponding locale object. For example, a locale object can be installed for each I/O stream, which is then used by the different member functions to adapt to the corresponding conventions. This is demonstrated by the following example:

```
// i18n/loc1.cpp

#include <iostream>
#include <locale>
using namespace std;

int main()
{
    // use classic C locale to read data from standard input
    cin.imbue(locale::classic());

    // use a German locale to write data to standard ouput
    cout.imbue(locale("de_DE"));

    // read and output floating-point values in a loop
    double value;
    while (cin >> value) {
        cout << value << endl;
    }
}
```

The statement

```
    cin.imbue(locale::classic());
```

assigns the "classic" C locale to the standard input channel. For the classic C locale, formatting of numbers and dates, character classification, and so on is handled as it is in original C without any locales. The expression

```
    std::locale::classic()
```

obtains a corresponding object of class `locale`. Using the expression

```
    std::locale("C")
```

instead would yield the same result. This last expression constructs a `locale` object from a given name. The name "C" is a special name, and actually is the only one a C++ implementation is required to support. There is no requirement to support any other locale, although it is assumed that C++ implementations also support other locales.

Correspondingly, the statement

```
cout.imbue (locale("de_DE"));
```

assigns the locale de_DE to the standard output channel. This is, of course, successful only if the system supports this locale. If the name used to construct a locale object is unknown to the implementation, an exception of type runtime_error is thrown.

If everything was successful, input is read according to the classic C conventions and output is written according to the German conventions. The loop thus reads floating-point values in the normal English format, for example

47.11

and prints them using the German format, for example

47,11

Yes, the Germans really use a comma as a "decimal point."

Normally, a program does not predefine a specific locale except when writing and reading data in a fixed format. Instead, the locale is determined using the environment variable LANG. Another possibility is to read the name of the locale to be used. The following program demonstrates this:

```
// i18n/loc2.cpp

#include <iostream>
#include <locale>
#include <string>
#include <cstdlib>
using namespace std;

int main()
{
    // create the default locale from the user's environment
    locale langLocale("");

    // and assign it to the standard ouput channel
    cout.imbue(langLocale);

    // process the name of the locale
    bool isGerman;
    if (langLocale.name() == "de_DE" ||
        langLocale.name() == "de" ||
        langLocale.name() == "german") {
        isGerman = true;
```

```
        }
        else {
            isGerman = false;
        }

        // read locale for the input
        if (isGerman) {
            cout << "Sprachumgebung fuer Eingaben: ";
        }
        else {
            cout << "Locale for input: ";
        }
        string s;
        cin >> s;
        if (!cin) {
            if (isGerman) {
                cerr << "FEHLER beim Einlesen der Sprachumgebung"
                     << endl;
            }
            else {
                cerr << "ERROR while reading the locale" << endl;
            }
            return EXIT_FAILURE;
        }
        locale cinLocale(s.c_str());

        // and assign it to the standard input channel
        cin.imbue(cinLocale);

        // read and output floating-point values in a loop
        double value;
        while (cin >> value) {
            cout << value << endl;
        }
    }
```

In this example, the following statement creates an object of the class locale:

```
    locale langLocale("");
```

Passing an empty string as the name of the locale has a special meaning: The default locale from the user's environment is used (this is often determined by the environment variable LANG). This locale is assigned to the standard input stream with the statement

```
cout.imbue(langLocale);
```

The expression

```
langLocale.name()
```

is used to retrieve the name of the default locale, which is returned as an object of type `string` (see Chapter 11).

The following statements construct a locale from a name read from standard input:

```
string s;
cin >> s;
...
locale cinLocale(s.c_str());
```

To do this, a word is read from the standard input and used as the constructor's argument. If the read fails, the `ios_base::failbit` is set in the input stream, which is checked and handled in this program:

```
if (!cin) {
    if (isGerman) {
        cerr << "FEHLER beim Einlesen der Sprachumgebung"
             << endl;
    }
    else {
        cerr << "ERROR while reading the locale" << endl;
    }
    return EXIT_FAILURE;
}
```

Again, if the string is not a valid value for the construction of a locale, a `runtime_error` exception is thrown.

If a program wants to honor local conventions, it should use corresponding locale objects. The static member function `global()` of the class `locale` can be used to install a global locale object. This object is used as the default value for functions that take an optional locale object as an argument. If the locale object set with the `global()` function has a name, it is also arranged that the C functions dealing with locales react correspondingly. If the locale set has no name, the consequences for the C functions depend on the implementation.

Here is an example of how to set the global locale object depending on the environment in which the program is running:

```
/* create a locale object depending on the program's environment and
 * set it as the global object
```

```
    */
    std::locale::global(std::locale(""));
```

Among other things, this arranges for the corresponding registration for the C functions to be executed. That is, the C functions are influenced as if the following call was made:

```
    std::setlocale(LC_ALL,"")
```

However, setting the global locale does not replace locales already stored in objects. It only modifies the locale object copied when a locale is created with a default constructor. For example, the stream objects store locale objects that are not replaced by a call to `locale::global()`. If you want an existing stream to use a specific locale, you have to tell the stream to use this locale using the `imbue()` function.

The global locale is used if a locale object is created with the default constructor. In this case, the new locale behaves as if it is a copy of the global locale at the time it was constructed. The following three lines install the default locale for the standard streams:

```
    // register global locale object for streams
    std::cin.imbue(std::locale());
    std::cout.imbue(std::locale());
    std::cerr.imbue(std::locale());
```

When using locales in C++, it is important to remember that the C++ locale mechanism is only loosely coupled to the C locale mechanism. There is only one relation to the C locale mechanism: The global C locale is modified if a named C++ locale object is set as the global locale. In general, you should not assume that the C and the C++ functions operate on the same locales.

14.2.2   Locale Facets

The actual dependencies on national conventions are separated into several aspects that are handled by corresponding objects. An object dealing with a specific aspect of internationalization is called a *facet*. A locale object is used as a container of different facets. To access an aspect of a locale, the type of the corresponding facet is used as the index. The type of the facet is passed explicitly as a template argument to the template function `use_facet()`, accessing the desired facet. For example, the expression

```
    std::use_facet<std::numpunct<char> >(loc)
```

accesses the facet type `numpunct` for the character type `char` of the locale object `loc`. Each facet type is defined by a class that defines certain services. For example, the facet type `numpunct` provides services used in conjunction with the formatting of numeric and Boolean values. For example, the following expression returns the string used to represent `true` in the locale `loc`.

```
    std::use_facet<std::numpunct<char> >(loc).truename()
```

Table 14.3 provides an overview over the facets predefined by the C++ standard library. Each facet is associated with a category. These categories are used by some of the constructors of locales to create new locales as the combination of other locales.

Category	Facet Type	Used for
numeric	num_get<>()	Numeric input
	num_put<>()	Numeric output
	numpunct<>()	Symbols used for numeric I/O
time	time_get<>()	Time and date input
	time_put<>()	Time and date output
monetary	money_get<>()	Monetary input
	money_put<>()	Monetary output
	moneypunct<>()	Symbols used for monetary I/O
ctype	ctype<>()	Character information (toupper(), isupper())
	codecvt<>()	Conversion between different character encodings
collate	collate<>()	String collation
messages	messages<>()	Message string retrieval

Table 14.3. Facet Types Predefined by the C++ Standard Library

It is possible to define your own versions of the facets to create specialized locales. The following examples demonstrates how this is done. It defines a facet using German representations of the Boolean values:

```cpp
class germanBoolNames : public std::numpunct_byname<char> {
  public:
    germanBoolNames (const char *name)
      : std::numpunct_byname<char>(name) {
    }
  protected:
    virtual std::string do_truename () const {
        return "wahr";
    }
    virtual std::string do_falsename () const {
        return "falsch";
    }
};
```

The class `germanBoolNames` derives from the class `numpunct_byname`, which is defined by the C++ standard library. This class defines punctuation properties depending on the locale used for numeric formatting. Deriving from `numpunct_byname` instead of from `numpunct` lets you customize the members not overridden explicitly. The values returned from these members still depend on the name used as the argument to the constructor. If the class `numpunct` had been used as the base class, the behavior of the other functions would be fixed. However, the class `germanBoolNames` overrides the two functions used to determine the textual representation of `true` and `false`.

To use this facet in a locale, you need to create a new locale using a special constructor of the class `locale`. This constructor takes a locale object as its first argument and a pointer to a facet as its second argument. The created locale is identical to the first argument except for the facet that is passed as the second argument. This facet is installed in the newly create locale after the first argument is copied:

```
std::locale loc (std::locale(""), new germanBoolNames(""));
```

The `new` expression creates a facet that is installed in the new locale. Thus, it is registered in `loc` to create a variation of `locale("")`. Since locales are immutable, you have to create a new locale object if you want to install a new facet to a locale. This locale object can be used like any other locale object. For example,

```
std::cout.imbue(loc);
std::cout << std::boolalpha << true << std::endl;
```

would have the following output:

```
wahr
```

You also can create a completely new facet. In this case, the function `has_facet()` can be used to determine whether such a new facet is registered for a given locale object.

14.3   Locales in Detail

A C++ locale is an immutable container for facets. It is defined in the `<locale>` header file as follows:

```
namespace std {
    class locale {
    public:
        // global locale objects
        static const locale& classic();              // classic C locale
        static       locale  global(const locale&);  // set global locale

        // internal types and values
        class facet;
        class id;
        typedef int category;
        static const category none, numeric, time, monetary,
                              ctype, collate, messages, all;

        // constructors
        locale() throw();
        explicit locale (const char* name);
```

```
// create locale based on other locales
locale (const locale& loc) throw();
locale (const locale& loc, const char* name, category);
template <class Facet>
  locale (const locale& loc, Facet* fp);
locale (const locale& loc, const locale& loc2, category);

// assignment operator
const locale& operator= (const locale& loc) throw();
template <class Facet>
  locale combine (const locale& loc);

// destructor
~locale() throw();

// name (if any)
basic_string<char> name() const;

// comparisons
bool operator== (const locale& loc) const;
bool operator!= (const locale& loc) const;

// sorting of strings
template <class charT, class Traits, class Allocator>
  bool operator() (
      const basic_string<charT,Traits,Allocator>& s1,
      const basic_string<charT,Traits,Allocator>& s2) const;
};

// facet access
template <class Facet>
  const Facet& use_facet (const locale&);
template <class Facet>
  bool has_facet (const locale&) throw();
}
```

The strange thing about locales is how the objects stored in the container are accessed. A facet in a locale is accessed using the type of the facet as the index. Because each facet exposes a different interface and suits a different purpose, it is desirable to have the access function to locales return a type corresponding to the index. This is exactly what can be done with a type as the index. Using the facet's type as an index has the additional advantage of having a type-safe interface.

Locales are immutable. This means the facets stored in a locale cannot be changed (except when locales are being assigned). Variations of locales are created by combining existing locales and facets to create a new locale. Table 14.4 lists the constructors for locales.

Expression	Effect
`locale()`	Creates a copy of the current global locale
`locale(`*name*`)`	Creates a locale from the string name
`locale(`*loc*`)`	Creates a copy of locale *loc*
`locale(`*loc1,loc2,cat*`)`	Creates a copy of locale *loc1*, with all facets from category *cat* replaced with facets from locale *loc2*
`locale(`*loc,name,cat*`)`	Equivalent to `locale(`*loc*`,locale(`*name*`),`*cat*`)`
`locale(`*loc,fp*`)`	Creates a copy of locale *loc* and installs the facet to which *fp* refers
loc1 `=` *loc2*	Assigns locale *loc2* to locale *loc1*
loc1`.template combine<`*F*`>(`*loc2*`)`	Creates a copy of locale *loc1* but with the facet of type *F* taken from *loc2*

Table 14.4. Constructing Locales

Almost all constructors create a copy of some other locale. Merely copying a locale is considered to be a cheap operation. Basically, it consists of setting a pointer and increasing a reference count. Creating a modified locale is more expensive. In this case, a reference count for each facet stored in the locale has to be adjusted. Although the standard makes no guarantees about such efficient behavior, it is likely that all implementations will be rather efficient for copying locales.

Two of the constructors listed in Table 14.4 take names of locales. The names accepted are not standardized, with the exception of the name C. However, the standard requires that the documentation with the C++ standard library lists the accepted names. It is assumed that most implementations will accept names as outlined in Section 14.2, page 692.

The member function `combine()` needs some explanation because it uses a feature that was implemented in compilers only recently. It is a member function template with an explicitly specified template argument. This means the template argument is not deduced implicitly from an argument because there is no argument from which the type can be deduced. Instead, the template argument is specified explicitly (type F in this case).

The two functions that access facets in a locale object use the same technique (Table 14.5). The major difference is that these two functions are global template functions, thereby making this ugly syntax involving the `template` keyword unnecessary.

The function `use_facet()` returns a reference to a facet. The type of this reference is the type passed explicitly as the template argument. If the locale passed as the argument does not contain a corresponding facet, the function throws a `bad_cast` exception. The function `has_facet()` can be used to test whether a particular facet is present in a given locale.

Expression	Effect
`has_facet<F>(`*loc*`)`	Returns `true` if a facet of type *F* is stored in locale *loc*
`use_facet<F>(`*loc*`)`	Returns a reference to the facet of type *F* stored in locale *loc*

Table 14.5. Accessing Facets

The remaining operations of locales are listed in Table 14.6. The name of a locale is maintained if the locale was constructed from a name, or one or more named locales. However, again, the standard makes no guarantees about the construction of a name resulting from combining two locales. Two locales are considered to be identical if one is a copy of the other or if both locales have the same name. It is natural to consider two objects to be identical if one is a copy of the other. But what about this naming stuff? The idea behind this is basically that the name of the locale reflects the names used to construct the named facets. For example, the locale's name might be constructed by joining the names of the facets in a particular order, separating the individual names by separation characters. Using this scheme it would possible to identify two locale objects as identical if they are constructed by combining the same named facets into locale objects. In other words, the standard basically requires that two locales consisting of the same set of named facets be considered identical. Thus, the names will probably be constructed carefully to support this notion of equality.

Expression	Effect
loc`.name()`	Returns the name of locale *loc* as `string`
loc1 `==` *loc2*	Returns `true` if *loc1* and *loc2* are identical locales
loc1 `!=` *loc2*	Returns `true` if *loc1* and *loc2* are different locales
loc`(`*str1*`,`*str2*`)`	Returns the Boolean result of comparing strings *str1* and *str2* for ordering (whether *str1* is less than *str2*)
`locale::classic()`	Returns `locale("C")`
`locale::global(`*loc*`)`	Installs *loc* as the global locale and returns the previous global locale

Table 14.6. Operations of Locales

The parentheses operator makes it possible to use a locale object as a comparator for strings. This operator uses the string comparison from the `collate` facet to compare the strings passed as the argument for ordering. Thus, it returns whether one string is less than the other string according to the locale object. This is the behavior of an STL function object (see Section 8.1, page 293), so you can use a locale object as a sorting criterion for STL algorithms that operate on strings. For example, a vector of strings can be sorted according to the rules for string collation of the German locale as follows:

```
std::vector<std::string> v;
...
// sort strings according to the German locale
std::sort (v.begin(),v.end(),        // range
           locale("de_DE"));         // sorting criterion
```

14.4 Facets in Detail

The important aspect of locales are the contained facets. All locales are guaranteed to contain certain standard facets. The description of the individual facets in the following subsections provides which instantiations of the corresponding facet are guaranteed. In addition to these facets, an implementation of the C++ standard library may provide additional facets in the locales. What is important is that the user can also install her own facets or replace standard ones.

Section 14.2.2, page 698, discussed how to install a facet in a locale. For example, the class `germanBoolNames` was derived from the class `numpunct_byname<char>`, one of the standard facets, and installed in a locale using the constructor, taking a locale and a facet as arguments. But what do you need to create your own facet? Every class F that conforms to the following two requirements can be used as a facet:

1. F derives publicly from class `locale::facet`. This base class mainly defines some mechanism for reference counting that is used internally by the locale objects. It also declares the copy constructor and the assignment operator to be private, thereby making it infeasible to copy or to assign facets.

2. F has a publicly accessible static member named `id` of type `locale::id`. This member is used to look up a facet in a locale using the facet's type. The whole issue of using a type as the index is to have a type-safe interface. Internally, a normal container with an integer as the index is used to maintain the facets.

The standard facets conform not only to these requirements but also to some special implementation guidelines. Although conforming to these guidelines is not required, doing so is useful. The guidelines are as follows:

1. All member functions are declared to be `const`. This is useful because `use_facet()` returns a reference to a `const` facet. Member functions that are not declared to be `const` can't be invoked.

2. All public functions are nonvirtual and delegate each request to a protected virtual function. The protected function is named like the public one, with the addition of a leading `do_`. For example, `numpunct::truename()` calls `numpunct::do_truename()`. This style is used to avoid hiding member functions when overriding only one of several virtual member functions that has the same name. For example, the class `num_put` has several functions named `put()`. In addition, it gives the programmer of the base class the possibility of adding some extra code in the nonvirtual functions, which is executed even if the virtual function is overridden.

The following description of the standard facets concerns only the public functions. To modify the facet you have always to override the corresponding protected functions. If you define functions with the same interface as the public facet functions, they would only overload them because these functions are not virtual.

For most standard facets, a "_byname" version is defined. This version derives from the standard facet and is used to create an instantiation for a corresponding locale name. For example, the class `numpunct_byname` is used to create the `numpunct` facet for a named locale. For example, a German `numpunct` facet can be created like this:

```
std::numpunct_byname("de_DE")
```

The `_byname` classes are used internally by the locale constructors that take a name as an argument. For each of the standard facets supporting a name, the corresponding `_byname` class is used to construct an instance of the facet.

14.4.1 Numeric Formatting

Numeric formatting converts between the internal representation of numbers and the corresponding textual representations. The iostream operators delegate the actual conversion to the facets of the `locale::numeric` category. This category is formed by three facets:

1. `numpunct`, which handles punctuation symbols used for numeric formatting and parsing
2. `num_put`, which handles numeric formatting
3. `num_get`, which handles numeric parsing

In short, the facet `num_put` does the numeric formatting described for iostreams in Section 13.7, page 615, and `num_get` parses the corresponding strings. Additional flexibility not directly accessible through the interface of the streams is provided by the `numpunct` facet.

Numeric Punctuation

The `numpunct` facet controls the symbol used as the decimal point, the insertion of optional thousands separators, and the strings used for the textual representation of Boolean values. Table 14.7 lists the members of `numpunct`.

Expression	Meaning
`np.decimal_point()`	Returns the character used as the decimal point
`np.thousands_sep()`	Returns the character used as the thousands separator
`np.grouping()`	Returns a `string` describing the positions of the thousands separators
`np.truename()`	Returns the textual representation of `true`
`np.falsename()`	Returns the textual representation of `false`

Table 14.7. Members of the `numpunct` Facet

`numpunct` takes a character type `charT` as the template argument. The characters returned from `decimal_point()` and `thousand_sep()` are of this type, and the functions `truename()` and `falsename()` return a `basic_string<charT>`. The two instantiations `numpunct<char>` and `numpunct<wchar_t>` are required.

Because long numbers are hard to read without intervening characters, the standard facets for numeric formatting and numeric parsing support thousands separators. Often, the digits representing an integer are grouped into triples. For example, one million is written like this:

```
1,000,000
```

Unfortunately, it is not used everywhere exactly like that. For example, in German a period is used instead of a comma. Thus, a German would write one million like this:

```
1.000.000
```

This difference is covered by the `thousands_sep()` member. But this is not sufficient because in some countries digits are not put into triples. For example, in Nepal people would write

```
10.00.000
```

using even different numbers of digits in the groups. This is where the string returned from the function `grouping()` comes in. The number stored at index *i* gives the number of digits in the *i*th group, where counting starts with zero for the rightmost group. If there are fewer characters in the string than groups, the size of the last specified group is repeated. To create unlimited groups, you can use the value `numeric_limits<char>::max()` or, if there is no group at all, the empty string. Table 14.8 lists some examples of the formatting of one million.

String	Result
{ 0 } or "" (the default for grouping())	1000000
{ 3, 0 } or "\3"	1,000,000
{ 3, 2, 3, 0 } or "\3\2\3"	10,00,000
{ 2, CHAR_MAX, 0 }	10000,00

Table 14.8. Examples of Numeric Punctuation of One Million

Note that normal digits are usually not very useful. For example, the string "2" specifies groups of 50 digits for ASCII encoding because the character '2' has the integer value 50 in the ASCII character set.

Numeric Formatting

The `num_put` facet is used for textual formatting of numbers. It is a template class that takes two template arguments: the type `charT` of the characters to be produced and the type `OutIt` of an output iterator to the location at which the produced characters are written. The output iterator defaults to `ostreambuf_iterator<charT>`. The `num_put` facet provides a set of functions, all called `put()` and differing only in the last argument. You can use the facet as follows:

```
std::locale    loc;
OutIt          to = ...;
std::ios_base& fmt = ...;
charT          fill = ...;
T              value = ...;
```

```
// get numeric output facet of the loc locale
const std::num_put<charT,OutIt>& np
  = std::use_facet<std::num_put<charT,OutIt> >(loc);
```

```
// write value with numeric output facet
np.put(to, fmt, fill, value);
```

These statements would produce a textual representation of the value `value` using characters of type `charT` written to the output iterator `to`. The exact format is determined from the formatting flags stored in `fmt`, where the character `fill` is used as a fill character. The `put()` function returns an iterator pointing immediately after the last character written.

The facet `num_put` provides member functions that take objects of types `bool`, `long`, `unsigned long`, `double`, `long double`, and `void*` as the last argument. It does not provide member functions, for example, for `short` or `int`. This is no problem because corresponding values of built-in types are promoted to supported types if necessary.

The standard requires that the two instantiations `num_put<char>` and `num_put<wchar_t>` are stored in each locale (both using the default for the second template argument). In addition, the C++ standard library supports all instantiations that take a character type as the first template argument and an output iterator type as the second. Of course, it is not required that all of these instantiations are stored in each locale because this would be an infinite amount of facets.

Numeric Parsing

The facet `num_get` is used to parse textual representations of numbers. Corresponding to the facet `num_put`, it is a template that takes two template arguments: the character type `charT` and an input iterator type `InIt`, which defaults to `istreambuf_iterator<charT>`. It provides a set of `get()` functions that differ only in the last argument. You can use the facet as follows:[4]

```
std::locale        loc;                     // locale
InIt               beg = ...;               // begin of input sequence
InIt               end = ...;               // end of input sequence
std::ios_base&     fmt = ...;               // stream which defines input format
std::ios_base::iostate err;                 // state after call
T                  value;                   // value after successful call

// get numeric input facet of the loc locale
const std::num_get<charT,InIt>& ng
  = std::use_facet<std::num_get<charT,InIt> >(loc);

// read value with numeric input facet
ng.get(beg, end, fmt, err, value);
```

These statements attempt to parse a numeric value corresponding to the type `T` from the sequence of characters between `beg` and `end`. The format of the expected numeric value is defined by the argument `fmt`. If the parsing fails, `err` is modified to contain the value `ios_base::failbit`. Otherwise, `ios_base::goodbit` is stored in `err` and the parsed value in `value`. The value of `value` is modified only if the parsing is successful. `get()` returns the second parameter (`end`) if the

---

[4] See `http://www.josuttis.com/libbook/examples.html` for a complete example program.

sequence was used completely. Otherwise, it returns an iterator pointing to the first character that could not be parsed as part of the numeric value.

The facet num_get supports functions to read objects of the types bool, long, unsigned short, unsigned int, unsigned long, float, double, long double, and void*. There are some types for which there is no corresponding function in the num_put facet; for example, unsigned short. This is because writing a value of type unsigned short produces the same result as writing a value of type unsigned short promoted to an unsigned long. However, reading a value as type unsigned long and then converting it to unsigned short may yield a different value than reading it as type unsigned short directly.

The standard requires that the two instantiations num_get<char> and num_get<wchar_t> be stored in each locale (both using the default for the second template argument). In addition, the C++ standard library supports all instantiations that take a character type as the first template argument and an input iterator type as the second. As with num_put, not all supported instantiations are required to be present in all locale objects.

14.4.2   Time and Date Formatting

The two facets time_get and time_put in the category time provide services for parsing and formatting times and dates. This is done by the member functions that operate on objects of type tm. This type is defined in the header file <ctime>. The objects are not passed directly; rather, a pointer to them is used as the argument.

Both facets in the time category depend heavily on the behavior of the function strftime() (also defined in the header file <ctime>). This function uses a string with conversion specifiers to produce a string from a tm object. Table 14.9 provides a brief summary of the conversion specifiers. The same conversion specifiers are also used by the time_put facet.

Of course, the exact string produced by strftime() depends on the C locale in effect. The examples in the table are given for the "C" locale.

Time and Date Parsing

The facet time_get is a template that takes a character type charT and an input iterator type InIt as template arguments. The input iterator type defaults to istreambuf_iterator<charT>. Table 14.10 lists the members defined for the time_get facet. All of these members, except date_order(), parse the string and store the results in the tm object pointed to by the argument t. If the string could not be parsed correctly, either an error is reported (for example, by modifying the argument err) or an unspecified value is stored. This means that a time produced by a program can be parsed reliably but user input cannot. With the argument fmt, other facets used during parsing are determined. Whether other flags from fmt have any influence on the parsing is not specified.

All functions return an iterator that has the position immediately after the last character read. The parsing stops if parsing is complete or if an error occurs (for example, because a string could not be parsed as a date).

Specifier	Meaning	Example
%a	Abbreviated weekday	Mon
%A	Full weekday	Monday
%b	Abbreviated month name	Jul
%B	Full month name	July
%c	Locale's preferred date and time representation	Jul 12 21:53:22 1998
%d	Day of the month	12
%H	Hour of the day using a 24-hour clock	21
%I	Hour of the day using a 12-hour clock	9
%j	Day of the year	193
%m	Month as decimal number	7
%M	Minutes	53
%p	Morning or evening (am or pm)	pm
%S	Seconds	22
%U	Week number starting with the first Sunday	28
%W	Week number starting with the first Monday	28
%w	Weekday as a number (Sunday == 0)	0
%x	Locale's preferred date representation	Jul 12 1998
%X	Locale's preferred time representation	21:53:22
%y	The year without the century	98
%Y	The year with the century	1998
%Z	The time zone	MEST
%%	The literal %	%

Table 14.9. Conversion Specifiers for `strftime()`

A function reading the name of a weekday or a month reads both abbreviated names and full names. If the abbreviation is followed by a letter, which would be legal for a full name, the function attempts to read the full name. If this fails, the parsing fails, even though an abbreviated name was already parsed successfully.

Whether a function that is parsing a year allows two-digit years is unspecified. The year that is assumed for a two-digit year, if it is allowed, is also unspecified.

`date_order()` returns the order in which the day, month, and year appear in a date string. This is necessary for some dates because the order cannot be determined from the string representing a date. For example, the first day in February in the year 2003 may be printed either as 3/2/1 or as 1/2/3. Class `time_base`, which is the base class of the facet `time_get`, defines an enumeration called `dateorder` for possible date order values. Table 14.11 lists these values.

The standard requires that the two instantiations `time_get<char>` and `time_get<wchar_t>` are stored in each locale. In addition, the C++ standard library supports all instantiations that take `char` or `wchar_t` as the first template argument, and a corresponding input iterator as the second. All of these instantiations are not required to be stored in each locale object.

Expression	Meaning
tg.get_time(*beg*,*end*,*fmt*,*err*,*t*)	Parses the string between *beg* and *end* as the time produced by the X specifier for strftime()
tg.get_date(*beg*,*end*,*fmt*,*err*,*t*)	Parses the string between *beg* and *end* as the date produced by the x specifier for strftime()
tg.get_weekday(*beg*,*end*,*fmt*,*err*,*t*)	Parses the string between *beg* and *end* as the name of the weekday
tg.get_monthname(*beg*,*end*,*fmt*,*err*,*t*)	Parses the string between *beg* and *end* as the name of the month
tg.get_year(*beg*,*end*,*fmt*,*err*,*t*)	Parses the string between *beg* and *end* as the year
tg.date_order()	Returns the date order used by the facet

Table 14.10. Members of the time_get *Facet*

Value	Meaning
no_order	No particular order (for example, a date may be in Julian format)
dmy	The order is day, month, year
mdy	The order is month, day, year
ymd	The order is year, month, day
ydm	The order is year, day, month

Table 14.11. Members of the Enumeration dateorder

Time and Date Formatting

The facet time_put is used for formatting times and dates. It is a template that takes as arguments a character type charT and an optional output iterator type OutIt. The latter defaults to type ostreambuf_iterator (see page 665).

The facet time_put defines two functions called put(), which are used to convert the date information stored in an object of type tm into a sequence of characters written to an output iterator. Table 14.12 lists the members of the facet time_put.

Expression	Meaning
tp.put(*to*,*fmt*,*fill*,*t*,*cbeg*,*cend*)	Converts according to the string [*cbeg*,*cend*)
tp.put(*to*,*fmt*,*fill*,*t*,*cvt*,*mod*)	Converts using the conversion specifier *cvt*

Table 14.12. Members of the time_put *Facet*

Both functions write their results to the output iterator *to* and return an iterator pointing immediately after the last character produced. The argument *fmt* is of type ios_base and is used to access other facets and potentially additional formatting information. The character *fill* is used when a space character is needed and for filling. The argument *t* points to an object of type `tm` that is storing the date to be formatted.

The version of `put()` that takes two characters as the last two arguments formats the date found in the `tm` object to which *t* refers, interpreting the argument *cvt* like a conversion specifier to `strftime()`. This `put()` function does only one conversion; namely, the one specified by the *cvt* character. This function is called by the other `put()` function for each conversion specifier found. For example, using `'X'` as the conversion specifier results in the time that is stored in `*t` being written to the output iterator. The meaning of the argument *mod* is not defined by the standard. It is intended to be used as a modifier to the conversion as found in several implementations of the `strftime()` function.

The version of `put()` that takes a string defined by the range [*cbeg,cend*) to guide the conversion behaves very much like `strftime()`. It scans the string and writes every character that is not part of a conversion specification to the output iterator *to*. If it encounters a conversion specification introduced by the character %, it extracts an optional modifier and a conversion specifier. The function continues by calling the other version of `put()`, using the conversion specifier and the modifier as the last two arguments. After processing a conversion specification, `put()` continues to scan the string.

Note that this facet is somewhat unusual because it provides a nonvirtual member function; namely, the function `put()`, which uses a string as the conversion specification. This function cannot be overridden in classes derived from `time_put`. Only the other `put()` function can be overridden.

The standard requires that the two instantiations `time_put<char>` and `time_put<wchar_t>` are stored in each locale. In addition, the C++ standard library supports all instantiations that take `char` or `wchar_t` as the first template argument and a corresponding output iterator as the second. There is no guaranteed support for instantiations using a type other than `char` or `wchar_t` as the first template argument. Also, it is not guaranteed that any instantiations other than `time_put<char>` and `time_put<wchar_t>` be stored in locale objects by default.

14.4.3 Monetary Formatting

The category `monetary` consists of the facets `moneypunct`, `money_get`, and `money_put`. The facet `moneypunct` defines the format of monetary values. The other two use this information to format or to parse a monetary value.

Monetary Punctuation

Monetary values are printed differently depending on the context. The formats used in different cultural communities differ widely. Examples of the varying details are the placement of the currency symbol (if present at all), the notation for negative or positive values, the use of national or international currency symbols, and the use of thousands separators. To provide the necessary flexibility, the details of the format are factored into the facet `moneypunct`.

The facet `moneypunct` is a template that takes as arguments a character type `charT` and a Boolean value that defaults to `false`. The Boolean value indicates whether local (`false`) or international (`true`) currency symbols are to be used. Table 14.13 lists the members of the facet `moneypunct`.

Expression	Meaning
`mp.decimal_point()`	Returns a character to be used as the decimal point
`mp.thousands_sep()`	Returns a character to be used as the thousands separator
`mp.grouping()`	Returns a string specifying the placement of the thousands separators
`mp.curr_symbol()`	Returns a string with the currency symbol
`mp.positive_sign()`	Returns a string with the positive sign
`mp.negative_sign()`	Returns a string with the negative sign
`mp.frac_digits()`	Returns the number of fractional digits
`mp.pos_format()`	Returns the format to be used for non-negative values
`mp.neg_format()`	Returns the format to be used for negative values

Table 14.13. Members of the `moneypunct` *Facet*

`moneypunct` derives from the class `money_base`. This base class defines an enumeration called `part`, which is used to form a pattern for monetary values. The class also defines a type called `pattern` (which is actually a type definition for `char[4]`). This type is used to store four values of type `part` that form a pattern describing the layout of a monetary value. Table 14.14 lists the five possible `parts` that can be placed in a pattern.

Value	Meaning
`none`	At this position, spaces may appear but are not required
`space`	At this position, at least one space is required
`sign`	At this position, a sign may appear
`symbol`	At this position, the currency symbol may appear
`value`	At this position, the value appears

Table 14.14. Parts of Monetary Layout Patterns

`moneypunct` defines two functions that return patterns: the function `neg_format()` for negative values and the function `pos_format()` for non-negative values. In a pattern, each of the parts `sign`, `symbol`, and `value` is mandatory, and one of the parts `none` and `space` has to appear. This does not mean, however, that there is really a sign or a currency symbol printed. What is printed at the positions indicated by the parts depends on the values returned from other members of the facet and on the formatting flags passed to the functions for formatting.

Only the value always appears. Of course, it is placed at the position where the part `value` appears in the pattern. The value has exactly `frac_digits()` fractional digits, with `decimal_point()` used as the decimal point (unless there are no fractional digits, in which case no decimal point is used).

When reading monetary values, thousand separators are allowed but not required in the input. When present they are checked for correct placements according to `grouping()`. If `grouping()` is empty, no thousand separators are allowed. The character used for the thousands separator is the one returned from `thousands_sep()`. The rules for the placement of the thousands separators are identical to the rules for numeric formatting (see page 705). When monetary values are printed, thousands separators are always inserted according to the string returned from `grouping()`. When monetary values are read, thousands separators are optional unless the grouping string is empty. The correct placement of thousands separators is checked after all other parsing is successful.

The parts `space` and `none` control the placement of spaces. `space` is used at a position where at least one space is required. During formatting, if `ios_base::internal` is specified in the format flags, fill characters are inserted at the position of the `space` or the `none` part. Of course, filling is done only if the minimum width specified is not used with other characters. The character used as the space character is passed as the argument to the functions for the formatting of monetary values. If the formatted value does not contain a space, `none` can be placed at the last position. `space` and `none` may not appear as the first part in a pattern, and `space` may not be the last part in a pattern.

Signs for monetary values may consist of more than one character. For example, in certain contexts parentheses around a value are used to indicate negative values. At the position where the `sign` part appears in the pattern, the first character of the sign appears. All other characters of the sign appear at the end after all other components. If the string for a sign is empty, no character indicating the sign appears. The character that is to be used as a sign is determined with the function `positive_sign()` for non-negative values and `negative_sign()` for negative values.

At the position of the `symbol` part, the currency symbol appears. The symbol is present only if the formatting flags used during formatting or parsing have the `ios_base::showbase` flag set. The string returned from the function `curr_symbol()` is used as the currency symbol. The currency symbol is a local symbol to be used to indicate the currency if the second template argument is `false` (the default). Otherwise, an international currency symbol is used.

Table 14.15 illustrates all of this, using the value $-1234.56 as an example. Of course, this means that `frac_digits()` returns 2. In addition, a width of 0 is always used.

The standard requires that the instantiations `moneypunct<char>`, `moneypunct<wchar_t>`, `moneypunct<char,true>`, and `moneypunct<wchar_t,true>` are stored in each locale. The C++ standard library does not support any other instantiation.

Monetary Formatting

The facet `money_put` is used to format monetary values. It is a template that takes a character type `charT` as the first template argument and an output iterator `OutIt` as the second. The output iterator defaults to `ostreambuf_iterator<charT>`. The two member functions `put()` produce a sequence of characters corresponding to the format specified by a `moneypunct` facet. The value to

Pattern	Sign	Result
symbol none sign value		$1234.56
symbol none sign value	–	$-1234.56
symbol space sign value	–	$ -1234.56
symbol space sign value	()	$ (1234.56)
sign symbol space value	()	($ 1234.56)
sign value space symbol	()	(1234.56 $)
symbol space value sign	–	$ 1234.56-
sign value space symbol	–	-1234.56 $
sign value none symbol	–	-1234.56$

Table 14.15. Examples of Using the Monetary Pattern

be formatted is either passed as type `long double` or as type `basic_string<charT>`. You can use the facet as follows:

```
// get monetary output facet of the loc locale
const std::money_put<charT,OutIt>& mp
  = std::use_facet<std::money_put<charT,OutIt> >(loc);
```

```
// write value with monetary output facet
mp.put(to, intl, fmt, fill, value);
```

The argument `to` is an output iterator of type `OutIt` to which the formatted string is written. `put()` returns an object of this type pointing immediately after the last character produced. The argument `intl` indicates whether a local or an international currency symbol is to be used. `fmt` is used to determine formatting flags, such as the width to be used and the `moneypunct` facet defining the format of the value to be printed. Where a space character has to appear, the character `fill` is inserted.

The argument `value` has type `long double` or type `basic_string<charT>`. This is the value that is formatted. If the argument is a string, this string may consist only of decimal digits with an optional leading minus sign. If the first character of the string is a minus sign, the value is formatted as a negative value. After it is determined that the value is negative, the minus sign is discarded. The number of fractional digits in the string is determined from the member function `frac_digits()` of the `moneypunct` facet.

The standard requires that the two instantiations `money_put<char>` and `money_put<wchar_t>` are stored in each locale. In addition, the C++ standard library supports all instantiations that take `char` or `wchar_t` as the first template argument and a corresponding output iterator as the second. All of these instantiations are not required to be stored in each locale object.

Monetary Parsing

The facet `money_get` is used for parsing of monetary values. It is a template class that takes a character type `charT` as the first template argument and an input iterator type `InIt` as the second. The second template argument defaults to `istreambuf_iterator<charT>`. This class defines two member functions called `get()` that try to parse a character and, if the parse is successful, store the result in a value of type `long double` or of type `basic_string<charT>`. You can use the facet as follows:

```
// get monetary input facet of the loc locale
const std::money_get<charT,InIt>& mg
  = std::use_facet<std::money_get<charT,InIt> >(loc);

// read value with monetary input facet
mg.get(beg, end, intl, fmt, err, val);
```

The character sequence to be parsed is defined by the sequence between `beg` and `end`. The parsing stops as soon as either all elements of the used pattern are read or an error is encountered. If an error is encountered, the `ios_base::failbit` is set in `err` and nothing is stored in `val`. If parsing is successful, the result is stored in the value of types `long double` or `basic_string` that is passed by reference as argument `val`.

The argument `intl` is a Boolean value that selects a local or an international currency string. The `moneypunct` facet defining the format of the value to be parsed is retrieved using the locale object imbued by the argument `fmt`. For parsing a monetary value, the pattern returned from the member `neg_format()` of the `moneypunct` facet is always used.

At the position of `none` or `space`, the function that is parsing a monetary value consumes all available space, unless `none` is the last part in a pattern. Trailing spaces are not skipped. The `get()` functions return an iterator that points after the last character that was consumed.

The standard requires that the two instantiations `money_get<char>` and `money_get<wchar_t>` be stored in each locale. In addition, the C++ standard library supports all instantiations that take `char` or `wchar_t` as the first template argument and a corresponding input iterator as the second. All of these instantiations are not required to be stored in each locale object.

14.4.4 Character Classification and Conversion

The C++ standard library defines two facets to deal with characters: `ctype` and `codecvt`. Both belong to the category `locale::ctype`. The facet `ctype` is used mainly for character classification, such as testing whether a character is a letter. It also provides methods for conversion between lowercase and uppercase letters and for conversion between `char` and the character type for which the facet is instantiated. The facet `codecvt` is used to convert characters between different encodings and is used mainly by `basic_filebuf` to convert between external and internal representations.

Character Classification

The facet `ctype` is a template class parameterized with a character type. Three kinds of functions are provided by the class `ctype<charT>`:

1. Functions to convert between `char` and `charT`
2. Functions for character classification
3. Functions for conversion between uppercase and lowercase letters

Table 14.16 lists the members defined for the facet `ctype`.

Expression	Effect
`ct.is(`*m*,*c*`)`	Tests whether the character *c* matches the mask *m*
`ct.is(`*beg*,*end*,*vec*`)`	For each character in the range between *beg* and *end*, places a mask matched by the character in the corresponding location of *vec*
`ct.scan_is(`*m*,*beg*,*end*`)`	Returns a pointer to the first character in the range between *beg* and *end* that matches the mask *m* or *end* if there is no such character
`ct.scan_not(`*m*,*beg*,*end*`)`	Returns a pointer to the first character in the range between *beg* and *end* that does not match the mask *m* or *end* if all characters match the mask
`ct.toupper(`*c*`)`	Returns an uppercase letter corresponding to *c* if there is such a letter; otherwise *c* is returned
`ct.toupper(`*beg*,*end*`)`	Converts each letter in the range between *beg* and *end* by replacing the letter with the result of `toupper()`
`ct.tolower(`*c*`)`	Returns a lowercase letter corresponding to *c* if there is such a letter; otherwise *c* is returned
`ct.tolower(`*beg*,*end*`)`	Converts each letter in the range between *beg* and *end* by replacing the letter with the result of `tolower()`
`ct.widen(`*c*`)`	Returns the `char` converted to `charT`
`ct.widen(`*beg*,*end*,*dest*`)`	For each character in the range between *beg* and *end*, places the result of `widen()` at the corresponding location in *dest*
`ct.narrow(`*c*,*default*`)`	Returns the `charT` *c* converted to `char`, or the `char` *default* if there is no suitable character
`ct.narrow(`*beg*,*end*,*default*,*dest*`)`	For each character in the range between *beg* and *end*, places the result of `narrow()` at the corresponding location in *dest*

Table 14.16. Services Defined by the `ctype<charT>` Facet

The function `is(`*beg*,*end*,*vec*`)` is used to store a set of masks in an array. For each of the characters in the range between *beg* and *end*, a mask with the attributes corresponding to the character is stored in the array pointed to by *vec*. This is useful to avoid virtual function calls for the classification of characters if there are lots of characters to be classified.

The function `widen()` can be used to convert a character of type `char` from the native character set to the corresponding character in the character set used by a locale. Thus, it makes sense to widen a character even if the result is also of type `char`. For the opposite direction, the function `narrow()` can be used to convert a character from the character set used by the locale to a corresponding `char` in the native character set, provided there is such a `char`. For example, the following code converts the decimal digits from `char` to `wchar_t`:

```
std::locale loc;
char narrow[] = "0123456789";
wchar_t wide[10];
```

```
std::use_facet<std::ctype<wchar_t> >(loc).widen(narrow, narrow+10,
                                                              wide);
```

Class `ctype` derives from the class `ctype_base`. This class is used only to define an enumeration called `mask`. This enumeration defines values that can be combined to form a bitmask used for testing character properties. The values defined in `ctype_base` are shown in Table 14.17. The functions for character classification all take a bitmask as an argument, which is formed by combinations of the values defined in `ctype_base`. To create bitmasks as needed, you can use the operators for bit manipulation (`|`, `&`, `^`, and `~`). A character matches this mask if it is any of the characters identified by the mask.

Value	Meaning
`ctype_base::alnum`	Tests for letters and digits (equivalent to `alpha|digit`)
`ctype_base::alpha`	Tests for letters
`ctype_base::cntrl`	Tests for control characters
`ctype_base::digit`	Tests for decimal digits
`ctype_base::graph`	Tests for punctuation characters, letters, and digits (equivalent to `alnum|punct`)
`ctype_base::lower`	Tests for lowercase letters
`ctype_base::print`	Tests for printable characters
`ctype_base::punct`	Tests for punctuation characters
`ctype_base::space`	Tests for space characters
`ctype_base::upper`	Tests for uppercase letters
`ctype_base::xdigit`	Tests for hexadecimal digits

Table 14.17. Character Mask Values Used by `ctype`

Specialization of `ctype<>` for Type `char`

For better performance of the character classification functions, the facet `ctype` is specialized for the character type `char`. This specialization does not delegate the functions dealing with character classification (`is()`, `scan_is()`, and `scan_not()`) to corresponding virtual functions. Instead, these functions are implemented inline using a table lookup. For this case additional members are provided (Table 14.18).

Expression	Effect
`ctype<char>::table_size`	Returns the size of the table (>=256)
`ctype<char>::classic_table()`	Returns the table for the "classic" C locale
`ctype<char>(table,del=false)`	Creates the facet with table *table*
`ct.table()`	Returns the current table of facet `ct`

Table 14.18. Additional Members of `ctype<char>`

Manipulating the behavior of these functions for specific locales is done with a corresponding table of masks that is passed as a constructor argument:

```
// create and initialize the table
std::ctype_base::mask mytable[std::ctype<char>::table_size] = {
    ...
};

// use the table for the ctype<char> facet ct
std::ctype<char> ct(mytable,false);
```

This code constructs a `ctype<char>` facet that uses the table `mytable` to determine the character class of a character. More precisely, the character class of the character c is determined by

```
mytable[static_cast<unsigned char>(c)]
```

The static member `table_size` is a constant defined by the library implementation and gives the size of the lookup table. This size is at least 256 characters. The second optional argument to the constructor of `ctype<char>` indicates whether the table should be deleted if the facet is destroyed. If it is `true`, the table passed to the constructor is released by using `delete[]` when the facet is no longer needed.

The member function `table()` is a protected member function that returns the table that is passed as the first argument to the constructor. The static protected member function `classic_table()` returns the table that is used for character classification in the classic C locale.

Global Convenience Functions for Character Classification

Convenient use of the `ctype` facets is provided by predefined global functions. Table 14.19 lists all of the global functions.

Function	Effect
`isalnum(c, loc)`	Returns whether *c* is a letter or a digit (equivalent to `isalpha()&&isdigit()`)
`isalpha(c, loc)`	Returns whether *c* is a letter
`iscntrl(c, loc)`	Returns whether *c* is a control character
`isdigit(c, loc)`	Returns whether *c* is a digit
`isgraph(c, loc)`	Returns whether *c* is a printable, nonspace character (equivalent to `isalnum()&&ispunct()`)
`islower(c, loc)`	Returns whether *c* is a lowercase letter
`isprint(c, loc)`	Returns whether *c* is a printable character (including whitespaces)
`ispunct(c, loc)`	Returns whether *c* is a punctuation character (that is, it is printable, but it is not a space, digit, or letter)
`isspace(c, loc)`	Returns whether *c* is a space character
`isupper(c, loc)`	Returns whether *c* is an uppercase letter
`isxdigit(c, loc)`	Returns whether *c* is a hexadecimal digit
`tolower(c, loc)`	Converts *c* from an uppercase letter to a lowercase letter
`toupper(c, loc)`	Converts *c* from a lowercase letter to an uppercase letter

Table 14.19. Global Convenience Functions for Character Classification

For example, the following expression determines whether the character c is a lowercase letter in the locale `loc`:

```
std::islower(c,loc)
```

It returns a corresponding value of type `bool`.

The following expression returns the character c converted to an uppercase letter, if c is a lowercase letter in the locale `loc`:

```
std::toupper(c,loc)
```

If c is not a lowercase letter, the first argument is returned unmodified.

The expression

```
std::islower(c,loc)
```

is equivalent to the following expression:

```
std::use_facet<std::ctype<char> >(loc).is(std::ctype_base::lower,c)
```

This expression calls the member function `is()` of the facet `ctype<char>`. `is()` determines whether the character c fulfills any of the character properties that are passed as the bitmask in the first argument. The values for the bitmask are defined in the class `ctype_base`. See page 502 and page 669 for examples of the use of these convenience functions.

The global convenience functions for character classification correspond to C functions that have the same name but only the first argument. They are defined in `<cctype>` and `<ctype.h>`, and always use the current global C locale.[5] Their use is even more convenient:

```
if (std::isdigit(c)) {
    ...
}
```

However, by using them you can't use different locales in the same program. Also, you can't use a user-defined `ctype` facet using the C function. See page 497 for an example that demonstrates how to use these C functions to convert all characters of a string to uppercase letters.

It is important to note that the C++ convenience functions should not be used in code sections where performance is crucial. It is much faster to obtain the corresponding facet from the locale and use the functions on this object directly. If a lot of characters are to be classified according to the same locale, this can be improved even more, at least for non-`char` characters. The function is(*beg*,*end*,*vec*) can be used to determine the masks for typical characters: This function determines for each character in the range [*beg*,*end*) a mask that describes the properties of the character. The resulting mask is stored in *vec* at the position corresponding to the character's position. This vector can then be used for fast lookup of the characters.

Character Encoding Conversion

The facet `codecvt` is used to convert between internal and external character encoding. For example, it can be used to convert between Unicode and EUC (Extended UNIX Code), provided the implementation of the C++ standard library supports a corresponding facet.

This facet is used by the class `basic_filebuf` to convert between the internal representation and the representation stored in a file. The class `basic_filebuf<charT,traits>` (see page 627) uses the instantiation `codecvt<charT,char,typename traits::state_type>` to do so. The facet used is taken from the locale stored with `basic_filebuf`. This is the major application of the `codecvt` facet. Only rarely is it necessary to use this facet directly.

In Section 14.1, page 686, some basics of character encodings are introduced. To understand `codecvt`, you need to know that there are two approaches for the encoding of characters: One is character encodings that use a fixed number of bytes for each character (wide-character representation), and the other is character encodings that use a varying number of bytes per character (multibyte representation).

It is also necessary to know that multibyte representations use so-called *shift states* for space efficient representation of characters. The correct interpretation of a byte is possible only with the correct shift state at this position. This in turn can be determined only by walking through the whole sequence of multibyte characters (see Section 14.1, page 686, for more details).

The `codecvt<>` facet takes three template arguments:

---

[5] This locale is only identical to the global C++ locale if the last call to `locale::global()` was with a named locale and if there was no call to `setlocale()` since then. Otherwise, the locale used by the C functions is different from the global C++ locale.

1. The character type `internT` used for an internal representation
2. The type `externT` used to represent an external representation
3. The type `stateT` used to represent an intermediate state during the conversion

The intermediate state may consist of incomplete wide characters or the current shift state. The C++ standard makes no restriction about what is stored in the objects representing the state.

The internal representation always uses a representation with a fixed number of bytes per character. Mainly the two types `char` and `wchar_t` are intended to be used within a program. The external representation may be a representation that uses a fixed size or a multibyte representation. When a multibyte representation is used, the second template argument is the type used to represent the basic units of the multibyte encoding. Each multibyte character is stored in one or more objects of this type. Normally, the type `char` is used for this.

The third argument is the type used to represent the current state of the conversion. It is necessary, for example, if one of the character encodings is a multibyte encoding. In this case, the processing of a multibyte character might be terminated because the source buffer is drained or the destination buffer is full while one character is being processed. If this happens, the current state of the conversion is stored in an object of this type.

Similar to the other facets, the standard requires support for only very few conversions. Only the following two instantiations are supported by the C++ standard library:

1. `codecvt<char,char,mbstate_t>`, which converts the native character set to itself (this is actually a degenerated version of the `codecvt` facet)
2. `codecvt<wchar_t,char,mbstate_t>`, which converts between the native tiny character set (that is, `char`) and the native wide-character set (that is, `wchar_t`)

The C++ standard does not specify the exact semantics of the second conversion. The only natural thing to do, however, is to split each `wchar_t` into `sizeof(wchar_t)` objects of type `char` for the conversion from `wchar_t` to `char`, and to assemble a `wchar_t` from the same amount of `char`s when converting in the opposite direction. Note that this conversion is very different from the conversion between `char` and `wchar_t` done by the `widen()` and `narrow()` member functions of the `ctype` facet: While the `codecvt` functions use the bits of multiple `char`s to form one `wchar_t` (or vice versa), the `ctype` functions convert a character in one encoding to the corresponding character in another encoding (if there is such a character).

Like the `ctype` facet, `codecvt` derives from a base class used to define an enumeration type. This class is named `codecvt_base`, and it defines an enumeration called `result`. The values of this enumeration are used to indicate the results of `codecvt`'s members. The exact meanings of the values depend on the member function used. Table 14.20 lists the member functions of the `codecvt` facet.

The function `in()` converts an external representation to an internal representation. The argument *s* is a reference to a `stateT`. At the beginning, this argument represents the shift state used when the conversion is started. At the end, the final shift state is stored there. The shift state passed in can differ from the initial state if the input buffer to be converted is not the first buffer being converted. The arguments *fb* (from begin) and *fe* (from end) are of type `const internT*`, and represent the beginning and the end of the input buffer. The arguments *tb* (to begin) and *te* (to end) are of type `externT*`, and represent the beginning and the end of the output buffer. The arguments *fn*

Expression	Meaning
`cvt.in(`*s*`,`*fb*`,`*fe*`,`*fn*`,`*tb*`,`*te*`,`*tn*`)`	Converts external representation to internal representation
`cvt.out(`*s*`,`*fb*`,`*fe*`,`*fn*`,`*tb*`,`*te*`,`*tn*`)`	Converts internal representation to external representation
`cvt.unshift(`*s*`,`*tb*`,`*te*`,`*tn*`)`	Writes escape sequence to switch to initial shift state
`cvt.encoding()`	Returns information about the external encoding
`cvt.always_noconv()`	Returns `true` if no conversion will ever be done
`cvt.length(`*s*`,`*fb*`,`*fe*`,`*max*`)`	Returns the number of `externT`s from the sequence between *fb* and *fe* to produce *max* internal characters
`cvt.max_length()`	Returns the maximum number of `externT`s necessary to produce one `internT`

Table 14.20. Members of the `codecvt` *Facet*

(from next, of type `const externT*&`) and *tn* (to next, of type `internT*&`) are references used to return the end of the sequence converted in the input buffer and the output buffer respectively. Either buffer may reach the end before the other buffer reaches the end. The function returns a value of type `codecvt_base::result`, as indicated in Table 14.21.

Value	Meaning
`ok`	All source characters were converted successfully
`partial`	Not all source characters were converted, or more characters are needed to produce a destination character
`error`	A source character was encountered that cannot be converted
`noconv`	No conversion was necessary

Table 14.21. Return Values of the Conversion Functions

If `ok` is returned the function made some progress. If `fn == fe` holds, this means that the whole input buffer was processed and the sequence between *tb* and *tn* contains the result of the conversion. The characters in this sequence represent the characters from the input sequence, potentially with a finished character from a previous conversion. If the argument *s* passed to `in()` was not the initial state, a partial character from a previous conversion that was not completed could have been stored there.

If `partial` is returned, either the output buffer was full before the input buffer could be drained or the input buffer was drained when a character was not yet complete (for example, because the last byte in the input sequence was part of an escape sequence switching between shift states). If *fe*==*fn*, the input buffer was drained. In this case, the sequence between *tb* and *tn* contains all characters that were converted completely but the input sequence terminated with a partially converted character. The necessary information to complete this character's conversion during a subsequent conversion is stored in the shift state *s*. If *fe*!=*fn*, the input buffer was not completely drained. In this case, *te*==*tn* holds; thus, the output buffer is full. The next time the conversion is continued, it should start with *fn*.

The return value `noconv` indicates a special situation. That is, no conversion was necessary to convert the external representation to the internal representation. In this case, *fn* is set to *fb* and *tn* is set to *tb*. Nothing is stored in the destination sequence because everything is already stored in the input sequence.

If `error` is returned, that means a source character that could not be converted was encountered. There are several reasons why this can happen. For example, the destination character set has no representation for a corresponding character, or the input sequence ends up with an illegal shift state. The C++ standard does not define any method that can be used to determine the cause of the error more precisely.

The function `out()` is equivalent to the function `in()`, except that it converts in the opposite direction. That is, it converts an internal representation to an external representation. The meanings of the arguments and the values returned are the same; only the types of the arguments are swapped. That is, *tb* and *te* now have the type `const internT*`, and *fb* and *fe* now have the type `const externT*`. The same applies to *fn* and *tn*.

The function `unshift()` inserts characters necessary to complete a sequence when the current state of the conversion is passed as the argument *s*. This normally means that a shift state is switched to the initial switch state. Only the external representation is terminated. Thus, the arguments *tb* and *tf* are of type `externT*`, and *tn* is of type `externT&*`. The sequence between *tb* and *te* defines the output buffer in which the characters are stored. The end of the result sequence is stored in *tn*. `unshift()` returns a value as shown in Table 14.22.

Value	Meaning
ok	The sequence was completed successfully
partial	More characters need to be stored to complete the sequence
error	The state is invalid
noconv	No character was needed to complete the sequence

Table 14.22. Return Values of the Function `unshift()`

The function `encoding()` returns some information about the encoding of the external representation. If `encoding()` returns −1, the conversion is state dependent. If `encoding()` returns 0, the number of `externT`s needed to produce an internal character is not constant. Otherwise, the number of `externT`s needed to produce an `internT` is returned. This information can be used to provide appropriate buffer sizes.

The function `always_noconv()` returns `true` if the functions `in()` and `out()` never perform a conversion. For example, the standard implementation of `codecvt<char, char, mbstate_t>` does no conversion, and thus, `always_noconv()` returns `true` for this facet. However, this only holds for the `codecvt` facet from the "C" locale. Other instances of this facet may actually do a conversion.

The function `length()` returns the number of `externT`s from the sequence between *fb* and *fe* necessary to produce *max* characters of type `internT`. If there are fewer than *max* complete `internT` characters in the sequence between *fb* and *fe*, the number of `externT`s used to produce a maximum number of `internT`s from the sequence is returned.

14.4.5 String Collation

The facet `collate` handles differences between conventions for the sorting of strings. For example, in German the letter "ü" is treated as being equivalent to the letter "u" or to the letters "ue" for the purpose of sorting strings. For other languages, this letter is not even a letter, and it is treated as a special character, when it is treated at all. Other languages use slightly different sorting rules for certain character sequences. The `collate` facet can be used to provide a sorting of strings that is familiar to the user. Table 14.23 lists the member functions of this facet. In this table, `col` is an instantiation of `collate`, and the arguments passed to the functions are iterators that are used to define strings.

Expression	Meaning
`col.compare`(*beg1*,*end1*,*beg2*,*end2*)	Returns 1 if the first string is greater than the second 0 if both strings are equal −1 if the first string is smaller than the second
`col.transform`(*beg*,*end*)	Returns a string to be compared with other transformed strings
`col.hash`(*beg*,*end*)	Returns a hash value (of type `long`) for the string

Table 14.23. Members of the `collate<>` *Facet*

The `collate` facet is a class template that takes a character type `charT` as its template argument. The strings passed to `collate`'s members are specified using iterators of type `const charT*`. This is somewhat unfortunate because there is no guarantee that the iterators used by the type `basic_string<charT>` are also pointers. Thus, strings have to be compared using something like this:

```
locale loc;
string s1, s2;
...
// get collate facet of the loc locale
const std::collate<charT>& col
  = std::use_facet<std::collate<charT> >(loc);

// compare strings by using the collate facet
int result = col.compare(s1.data(), s1.data()+s1.size(),
                         s2.data(), s2.data()+s2.size());
```

```
if (result == 0) {
    // s1 and s2 are equal
    ...
}
```

The reason for this limitation is that you cannot predict which iterator types are necessary. It would be necessary to have collation facets for the pointer type and for an infinite amount of iterator types.

Of course, here the special convenience function of `locale` can be used to compare strings (see page 703):

```
int result = loc(s1,s2);
```

But this works only for the `compare()` member function. There are no convenient functions defined by the C++ standard library for the other two members of `collate`.

The `transform()` function returns an object of type `basic_string<charT>`. The lexicographical order of strings returned from `transform()` is the same as the order of the original strings using `collate()`. This ordering can be used for better performance if one string has to be compared with many other strings. Determining the lexicographical order of strings can be much faster than using `collate()`. This is because the national sorting rules can be relatively complex.

The C++ standard library mandates support only for the two instantiations `collate<char>` and `collate<wchar_t>`. For other character types, users must write their own specializations, potentially using the standard instantiations.

14.4.6 Internationalized Messages

The `messages` facet is used to retrieve internationalized messages from a catalog of messages. This facet is intended primarily to provide a service similar to that of the function `perror()`. This function is used in POSIX systems to print a system error message for an error number stored in the global variable `errno`. Of course, the service provided by `messages` is more flexible. Unfortunately, it is not defined very precisely.

The `messages` facet is a template class that takes a character type `charT` as its template argument. The strings returned from this facet are of type `basic_string<charT>`. The basic use of this facet consists of opening a catalog, retrieving messages, and then closing the catalog. The class `messages` derives from a class `messages_base`, which defines a type `catalog` (actually, it is a type definition for `int`). An object of this type is used to identify the catalog on which the members of `messages` operate. Table 14.24 lists the member functions of the `messages` facet.

The name passed as the argument to the `open()` function identifies the catalog in which the message strings are stored. This can be, for example, the name of a file. The *loc* argument identifies a `locale` object that is used to access a `ctype` facet. This facet is used to convert the message to the desired character type.

The exact semantics of the `get()` member are not defined. An implementation for POSIX systems could, for example, return the string corresponding to the error message for error *msgid*, but this behavior is not required by the standard. The *set* argument is intended to create a substructure

Expression	Meaning
msg.open(*name*,*loc*)	Opens a catalog and returns a corresponding ID
msg.get(*cat*,*set*,*msgid*,*def*)	Returns the message with ID *msgid* from catalog *cat*; if there is no such message, *def* is returned instead
msg.close(*cat*)	Closes the catalog *cat*

Table 14.24. Members of the messages<> *Facet*

within the messages. For example, it might be used to distinguish between system errors and errors of the C++ standard library.

When a message catalog is no longer needed, it can be released using the close() function. Although the interface using open() and close() suggests that the messages are retrieved from a file as needed, this is by no means required. Actually, it is more likely that open() reads a file and stores the messages in memory. A later call to close() would then release this memory.

The standard requires that the two instantiations messages<char> and messages<wchar_t> be stored in each locale. The C++ standard library does not support any other instantiations.

Chapter 15

Allocators

Allocators were introduced in Section 3.4, page 31. They represent a special memory model and are an abstraction used to translate the *need* to use memory into a raw *call* for memory. This chapter describes allocators in detail.

15.1 Using Allocators as an Application Programmer

For the application programmer, using different allocators should be no problem. You simply have to pass the allocator as a template argument. For example, the following statements create different containers and strings using the special allocator `MyAlloc<>`:

```
// a vector with special allocator
std::vector<int,MyAlloc<int> > v;
```

```
// an int/float map with special allocator
std::map<int,float,less<int>,
        MyAlloc<std::pair<const int,float> > > m;
```

```
// a string with special allocator
std::basic_string<char,std::char_traits<char>,MyAlloc<char> > s;
```

If you use your own allocator, it probably is a good idea to make some type definitions. For example:

```
// special string type that uses special allocator
typedef std::basic_string<char,std::char_traits<char>,
                          MyAlloc<char> > xstring;
```

```
// special string/string map type that uses special allocator
typedef std::map<xstring,xstring,less<xstring>,
                 MyAlloc<std::pair<const xstring,xstring> > > xmap;
```

// create object of this type
```
xmap mymap;
```
When you use objects with other than the default allocator, you'll see no difference. However, beware that you don't mix elements with different allocators; otherwise, the behavior is undefined. You can check whether two allocators use the same memory model by using operator ==. If it returns `true`, you can deallocate storage allocated from one allocator via the other. To access the allocator, all types that are parameterized by an allocator provide the member function `get_allocator()`. For example:
```
if (mymap.get_allocator() == s.get_allocator()) {
```
     // OK, `mymap` *and* s *use the same or interchangeable allocators*
```
    ...
}
```

15.2   Using Allocators as a Library Programmer

This section describes the use of allocators from the viewpoint of people who use allocators to implement containers and other components that are able to handle different allocators. This section is based, with permission, partly on Section 19.4 of Bjarne Stroustrup's *The C++ Programming Language*, 3rd edition.

Allocators provide an interface to allocate, create, destroy, and deallocate objects (Table 15.1). With allocators, containers and algorithms can be parameterized by the way the elements are stored. For example, you could implement allocators that use shared memory or that map the elements to a persistent database.

Expression	Effect
a.allocate(num)	Allocates memory for num elements
a.construct(p,val)	Initializes the element to which p refers with val
a.destroy(p)	Destroys the element to which p refers
a.deallocate(p,num)	Deallocates memory for num elements to which p refers

Table 15.1. Fundamental Allocator Operations

As an example, let's look at a naive implementation of a vector. A vector gets its allocator as a template or a constructor argument and stores it somewhere internally:
```
namespace std {
    template <class T,
              class Allocator = allocator<T> >
    class vector {
        ...
```

```
    private:
      Allocator alloc;      // allocator
      T*        elems;      // array of elements
      size_type numElems;   // number of elements
      size_type sizeElems;  // size of memory for the elements
      ...

    public:
      // constructors
      explicit vector(const Allocator& = Allocator());
      explicit vector(size_type num, const T& val = T(),
                      const Allocator& = Allocator());
      template <class InputIterator>
      vector(InputIterator beg, InputIterator end,
             const Allocator& = Allocator());
      vector(const vector<T,Allocator>& v);
      ...
  };
}
```

The second constructor that initializes the vector by num elements of value val could be implemented as follows:

```
namespace std {
    template <class T, class Allocator>
    vector<T,Allocator>::vector(size_type num, const T& val,
                                const Allocator& a)
     : alloc(a)      // initialize allocator
    {
        // allocate memory
        sizeElems = numElems = num;
        elems = alloc.allocate(num);

        // initialize elements
        for (size_type i=0; i<num; ++i) {
            // initialize ith element
            alloc.construct(&elems[i],val);
        }
    }
}
```

Expression	Effect
uninitialized_fill(beg,end,val)	Initializes [beg,end) with val
uninitialized_fill_n(beg,num,val)	Initializes num elements starting from beg with val
uninitialized_copy(beg,end,mem)	Initialize elements starting from mem with the elements of [beg,end)

Table 15.2. Convenience Functions for Uninitialized Memory

However, for the initialization of uninitialized memory the C++ standard library provides some convenience functions (Table 15.2). Using these functions, the implementation of the constructor becomes even simpler:

```
namespace std {
    template <class T, class Allocator>
    vector<T,Allocator>::vector(size_type num, const T& val,
                                        const Allocator& a)
     : alloc(a)      // initialize allocator
    {
        // allocate memory
        sizeElems = numElems = num;
        elems = alloc.allocate(num);

        // initialize elements
        uninitialized_fill_n(elems, num, val);
    }
}
```

The member function `reserve()`, which reserves more memory without changing the number of elements (see page 149), could be implemented as follows:

```
namespace std {
    template <class T, class Allocator>
    void vector<T,Allocator>::reserve(size_type size)
    {
        // reserve() never shrinks the memory
        if (size <= sizeElems) {
            return;
        }

        // allocate new memory for size elements
        T* newmem = alloc.allocate(size);
```

```
// copy old elements into new memory
uninitialized_copy(elems,elems+numElems,newmem);

// destroy old elements
for (size_type i=0; i<numElems; ++i) {
    alloc.destroy(&elems[i]);
}

// deallocate old memory
alloc.deallocate(elems,sizeElems);

// so, now we have our elements in the new memory
sizeElems = size;
elems = newmem;
    }
}
```

Raw Storage Iterators

In addition, class `raw_storage_iterator` is provided to iterate over uninitialized memory to initialize it. Therefore, you can use any algorithms with a `raw_storage_iterator` to initialize memory with the values that are the result of that algorithm.

For example, the following statement initializes the storage to which `elems` refers by the values in range [x.begin(),x.end()):

```
copy (x.begin(), x.end(),                          // source
        raw_storage_iterator<T*,T>(elems));        // destination
```

The first template argument (T*, here) has to be an output iterator for the type of the elements. The second template argument (T, here) has to be the type of the elements.

Temporary Buffers

In code you might also find the `get_temporary_buffer()` and `return_temporary_buffer()`. They are provided to handle uninitialized memory that is provided for short, temporary use inside a function. Note that `get_temporary_buffer()` might return less memory than expected. Therefore, `get_temporary_buffer()` returns a pair containing the address of the memory and the size of the memory (in element units). Here is an example of how to use it:

```
void f()
{
    // allocate memory for num elements of type MyType
    pair<MyType*,std::ptrdiff_t> p
      = get_temporary_buffer<MyType>(num);
```

```
if (p.second == 0) {
    // could not allocate any memory for elements
    ...
}
else if (p.second < num) {
    // could not allocate enough memory for num elements
    // however, don't forget to deallocate it
    ...
}

// do your processing
...

// free temporarily allocated memory, if any
if (p.first != 0) {
    return_temporary_buffer(p.first);
}
}
```

However, it is rather complicated to write exception-safe code with `get_temporary_buffer()` and `return_temporary_buffer()`, so they are usually no longer used in library implementations.

15.3   The Default Allocator

The default allocator is declared as follows:

```
namespace std {
    template <class T>
    class allocator {
      public:
        // type definitions
        typedef size_t     size_type;
        typedef ptrdiff_t  difference_type;
        typedef T*         pointer;
        typedef const T*   const_pointer;
        typedef T&         reference;
        typedef const T&   const_reference;
        typedef T          value_type;

        // rebind allocator to type U
```

```
template <class U>
struct rebind {
    typedef allocator<U> other;
};

// return address of values
pointer        address(reference value) const;
const_pointer address(const_reference value) const;

// constructors and destructor
allocator() throw();
allocator(const allocator&) throw();
template <class U>
  allocator(const allocator<U>&) throw();
~allocator() throw();

// return maximum number of elements that can be allocated
size_type max_size() const throw();

// allocate but don't initialize num elements of type T
pointer allocate(size_type num,
                    allocator<void>::const_pointer hint = 0);

// initialize elements of allocated storage p with value value
void construct(pointer p, const T& value);

// delete elements of initialized storage p
void destroy(pointer p);

// deallocate storage p of deleted elements
void deallocate(pointer p, size_type num);
};
}
```

The default allocator uses the global operators new and delete to allocate and deallocate memory. Thus, allocate() may throw a bad_alloc exception. However, the default allocator may be optimized by reusing deallocated memory or by allocating more memory than needed to save time in additional allocations. So, the exact moments when operator new and operator delete are called are unspecified. See page 735 for a possible implementation of the default allocator.

There is a strange definition of a template structure inside the allocator, called `rebind`. This template structure provides the ability that any allocator may allocate storage of another type indirectly. For example, if `Allocator` is an allocator type, then

```
Allocator::rebind<T2>::other
```

is the type of the same allocator specialized for elements of type T2.

`rebind<>` is useful if you implement a container and you have to allocate memory for a type that differs from the element's type. For example, to implement a deque you typically need memory for arrays that manage blocks of elements (see the typical implementation of a `deque` on page 160). Thus, you need an allocator to allocate arrays of pointers to elements:

```
namespace std {
    template <class T,
              class Allocator = allocator<T> >
    class deque {
        ...
      private:
        // rebind allocator for type T*
        typedef typename Allocator::rebind<T*>::other PtrAllocator;

        Allocator     alloc;        // allocator for values of type T
        PtrAllocator  block_alloc;  // allocator for values of type T*
        T**           elems;        // array of blocks of elements
        ...
    };
}
```

To manage the elements of a deque you have to have one allocator to handle arrays/blocks of elements and another allocator to handle the array of element blocks. The latter has type `PtrAllocator`, which is the same allocator as for the elements. By using `rebind<>` the Allocator for the elements (`Allocator`) is bound to the type of an array of elements (T*).

The default allocator has the following specialization for type `void`:

```
namespace std {
    template <>
    class allocator<void> {
      public:
        typedef void*       pointer;
        typedef const void* const_pointer;
        typedef void        value_type;
        template <class U>
        struct rebind {
            typedef allocator<U> other;
```

```
            };
        };
    }
```

15.4   A User-Defined Allocator

Writing your own allocator is not very hard. The most important issue is how you allocate or deallocate the storage. The rest is more or less obvious. As an example, let's look at a naive implementation of the default allocator:

```
// util/defalloc.hpp

namespace std {
    template <class T>
    class allocator {
      public:
        // type definitions
        typedef size_t     size_type;
        typedef ptrdiff_t  difference_type;
        typedef T*         pointer;
        typedef const T*   const_pointer;
        typedef T&         reference;
        typedef const T&   const_reference;
        typedef T          value_type;

        // rebind allocator to type U
        template <class U>
        struct rebind {
            typedef allocator<U> other;
        };

        // return address of values
        pointer address (reference value) const {
            return &value;
        }
        const_pointer address (const_reference value) const {
            return &value;
        }
```

```cpp
/* constructors and destructor
 * - nothing to do because the allocator has no state
 */
allocator() throw() {
}
allocator(const allocator&) throw() {
}
template <class U>
  allocator (const allocator<U>&) throw() {
}
~allocator() throw() {
}


// return maximum number of elements that can be allocated
size_type max_size () const throw() {
    // for numeric_limits see Section 4.3, page 59
    return numeric_limits<size_t>::max() / sizeof(T);
}


// allocate but don't initialize num elements of type T
pointer allocate (size_type num,
                    allocator<void>::const_pointer hint = 0) {
    // allocate memory with global new
    return (pointer)(::operator new(num*sizeof(T)));
}


// initialize elements of allocated storage p with value value
void construct (pointer p, const T& value) {
    // initialize memory with placement new
    new((void*)p)T(value);
}


// destroy elements of initialized storage p
void destroy (pointer p) {
    // destroy objects by calling their destructor
    p->~T();
}


// deallocate storage p of deleted elements
```

```
        void deallocate (pointer p, size_type num) {
            // deallocate memory with global delete
            ::operator delete((void*)p);
        }
    };

    // return that all specializations of this allocator are interchangeable
    template <class T1, class T2>
    bool operator== (const allocator<T1>&,
                     const allocator<T2>&) throw() {
        return true;
    }
    template <class T1, class T2>
    bool operator!= (const allocator<T1>&,
                     const allocator<T2>&) throw() {
        return false;
    }
}
```

Using this base implementation you should find it no problem to implement your own allocator. Typically, the only things that differ from this implementation are `max_size()`, `allocate()`, and `deallocate()`. In these three functions, you program your own policy of memory allocation, such as reusing memory instead of freeing it immediately, using shared memory, or mapping the memory to a segment of an object-oriented database.

See `http://www.josuttis.com/libbook/examples.html` for additional examples.

15.5 Allocators in Detail

According to the specified requirements, allocators have to provide the following types and operations. There are special requirements for allocators that can be used by the standard containers. Allocators that are not provided for the standard containers may have less requirements.

15.5.1 Type Definitions

***allocator*::value_type**
- The type of the elements.
- It is equivalent to T for `allocator<T>`.

allocator : : **size_type**
- The type for unsigned integral values that can represent the size of the largest object in the allocation model.
- To be usable by the standard containers, this type must be equivalent to `size_t`.

allocator : : **difference_type**
- The type for signed integral values that can represent the difference between any two pointers in the allocation model.
- To be usable by the standard containers, this type must be equivalent to `ptrdiff_t`.

allocator : : **pointer**
- The type of a pointer to the element type.
- To be usable by the standard containers, this type must be equivalent to `T*` for `allocator<T>`.

allocator : : **const_pointer**
- The type of a constant pointer to the element type.
- To be usable by the standard containers, this type must be equivalent to `const T*` for `allocator<T>`.

allocator : : **reference**
- The type of a reference to the element type.
- It is equivalent to `T&` for `allocator<T>`.

allocator : : **const_reference**
- The type of a constant reference to the element type.
- It is equivalent to `const T&` for `allocator<T>`.

allocator : : **rebind**
- A template structure that provides the ability that any allocator may allocate storage of another type indirectly.
- It has to be declared as follows:
```
    template <class T>
    class allocator {
      public:
        template <class U>
        struct rebind {
            typedef allocator<U> other;
        };
        ...
    }
```
- See page 734 for an explanation of the purpose of `rebind`.

15.5.2   Operations

allocator::**allocator** ()

- The default constructor.
- Creates an allocator object.

allocator::**allocator** (const allocator& a)

- The copy constructor.
- Copies an allocator object so that storage allocated from the original and from the copy can be deallocated via the other.

allocator::~**allocator** ()

- The destructor.
- Destroys an allocator object.

pointer *allocator*::**address** (reference *value*)

const_pointer *allocator*::**address** (const_reference *value*)

- The first form returns a nonconstant pointer to the nonconstant *value*.
- The second form returns a constant pointer to the constant *value*.

size_type *allocator*::**max_size** ()

- Returns the largest value that can be passed meaningfully to allocate() to allocate storage.

pointer *allocator*::**allocate** (size_type *num*)

pointer *allocator*::**allocate** (size_type *num*, allocator<void>::const_pointer *hint*)

- Both forms return storage for *num* elements of type T.
- The elements are not constructed/initialized (no constructors are called).
- The optional second argument has an implementation-specific meaning. For example, it may be used by an implementation to help improve performance.

void *allocator*::**deallocate** (pointer *p*, size_type *num*)

- Frees the storage to which *p* refers.
- The storage of *p* has to be allocated by allocate() of the same or an equal allocator.
- *p* must not be NULL or 0.
- The elements have to have been destroyed already.

void *allocator*::**construct** (pointer *p*, const T& *value*)

- Initializes the storage of one element to which *p* refers with *value*.
- It is equivalent to new((void*)*p*)T(*value*).

void *allocator*::**destroy** (pointer *p*)

- Destroys the object to which *p* refers without deallocating the storage.
- Simply calls the destructor for the object.
- It is equivalent to ((T*)*p*)->~T().

bool **operator ==** (const *allocator*& *a1*, const *allocator*& *a2*)

- Returns true if allocators *a1* and *a2* are interchangeable.
- Two allocators are interchangeable if storage allocated from each can be deallocated via the other.
- To be usable by the standard containers, allocators of the same type are required to be interchangeable. So, this function should always return true.

bool **operator !=** (const *allocator*& *a1*, const *allocator*& *a2*)

- Returns true if two allocators are not interchangeable.
- It is equivalent to !(*a1* == *a2*).
- To be usable by the standard containers, allocators of the same type are required to be interchangeable. So, this function should always return false.

15.6   Utilities for Uninitialized Memory in Detail

This section describes the auxiliary functions for uninitialized memory in detail. The exemplary exception safe implementation of these functions is based with permission on code by Greg Colvin.

void **uninitialized_fill** (ForwardIterator *beg*, ForwardIterator *end*,
                            const T& *value*)

- Initializes the elements in the range [*beg*,*end*) with *value*.
- This function either succeeds or has no effect.
- This function usually is implemented as follows:
```
namespace std {
    template <class ForwIter, class T>
    void uninitialized_fill(ForwIter beg, ForwIter end,
                            const T& value)
    {
        typedef typename iterator_traits<ForwIter>::value_type VT;
        ForwIter save(beg);
        try {
            for (; beg!=end; ++beg) {
                new (static_cast<void*>(&*beg))VT(value);
            }
        }
```

```
                catch (...) {
                    for (; save!=beg; ++save) {
                        save->~VT();
                    }
                    throw;
                }
            }
        }
```

void **uninitialized_fill_n** (ForwardIterator *beg*, Size *num*, const T& *value*)

- initializes *num* elements starting from *beg* with *value*.
- This function either succeeds or has no effect.
- This function usually is implemented as follows:

```
    namespace std {
        template <class ForwIter, class Size, class T>
        void uninitialized_fill_n (ForwIter beg, Size num,
                                   const T& value)
        {
            typedef typename iterator_traits<ForwIter>::value_type VT;
            ForwIter save(beg);
            try {
                for (; num--; ++beg) {
                    new (static_cast<void*>(&*beg))VT(value);
                }
            }
            catch (...) {
                for (; save!=beg; ++save) {
                    save->~VT();
                }
                throw;
            }
        }
    }
```

- See page 730 for an example of the use of uninitialized_fill_n().

ForwardIterator **uninitialized_copy** (InputIterator *sourceBeg*,
                                        InputIterator *sourceEnd*,
                                        ForwardIterator *destBeg*)

- Initializes the memory starting at *destBeg* with the elements in the range [*sourceBeg*,*sourceEnd*).
- The function either succeeds or has no effect.
- The function usually is implemented as follows:

```
namespace std {
    template <class InputIter, class ForwIter>
    ForwIter uninitialized_copy(InputIter beg, InputIter end,
                                ForwIter dest)
    {
        typedef typename iterator_traits<ForwIter>::value_type VT;
        ForwIter save(dest);
        try {
            for (; beg!=end; ++beg,++dest) {
                new (static_cast<void*>(&*dest))VT(*beg);
            }
            return dest;
        }
        catch (...) {
            for (; save!=dest; ++save) {
                save->~VT();
            }
            throw;
        }
    }
}
```

- See page 730 for an example of the use of uninitialized_copy().

Internet Resources

The Internet is a huge source of information regarding the topic of this book. Here is a list of my recommendations of sites where you could find additional, relevant information.

Where You Can Get the Standard

The American National Standards Institute (ANSI) sells the C++ standard in the United States. At the time this book was written, you could get the C++ standard at the Electronics Standard Store of ANSI for $18 (US) at the following site:

```
http://www.ansi.org/
```

Newsgroups

The following newsgroups discuss C++, the standard, and the C++ standard library:

- General aspects of C++ (unmoderated)
    ```
    comp.lang.c++
    ```
- General aspects of C++ (moderated)
    ```
    comp.lang.c++.moderated
    ```
- Aspects of the C++ standard (moderated)
    ```
    comp.std.c++
    ```
    For more information about this newsgroup see
    ```
    http://www.jamesd.demon.co.uk/csc/faq.html
    ```

Internet Addresses/URLs

This section lists links that provide additional related informations regarding the C++ standard library and the STL. However, books might have a longer life than Internet sites, and the links listed here may be not valid in the future. Therefore, I will provide the actual list of links for this book at the following site (and I expect my site to be stable):

```
http://www.josuttis.com/libbook/
```

The following links refer to issues of the whole C++ standard library:
- FAQs (frequently asked questions) about the standardization of C++:
    ```
    http://www.jamesd.demon.co.uk/csc/faq.html
    ```
- The official home page of ISO working group for the standardization of C++
    ```
    http://www.open-std.org/jtc1/sc22/wg21
    ```
- The Dinkum C++ Library Reference
    ```
    http://www.dinkumware.com/refxcpp.html
    ```
- The C++ standard library implementation for the EGCS C++ compiler
    ```
    http://sourceware.cygnus.com/libstdc++/
    ```
- The EGCS C++ compiler
    ```
    http://egcs.cygnus.com/
    ```
- The Boost repository for free, peer-reviewed C++ libraries
    ```
    http://www.boost.org/
    ```
- Blitz++, a C++ class library for scientific computing
    ```
    http://www.oonumerics.org/blitz/
    ```

The following links refer to issues of the STL:
- The freely available STL implementation by SGI
    ```
    http://www.sgi.com/Technology/STL/
    ```
- STLport for several platforms
    ```
    http://www.stlport.org/
    ```
- Mumit's STL Newbie Guide
    ```
    http://www.xraylith.wisc.edu/~khan/software/stl/STL.newbie.html
    ```
- David Musser's STL site
    ```
    http://www.cs.rpi.edu/~musser/stl.html
    ```
- STL FAQs
    ```
    ftp://butler.hpl.hp.com/stl/stl.faq
    ```
- Safe STL by Cay Horstmann
    ```
    http://www.horstmann.com/safestl.html
    ```
- Warren Young's STL Resource List
    ```
    http://www.cyberport.com/~tangent/programming/stl/resources.html
    ```

Bibliography

The following bibliography lists the books and sources that were mentioned, adopted, or cited in this book and lists books that give additional details. Note that this is not a comprehensive list of books. It is my personal list of books regarding this topic.

Matthew H. Austern
Generic Programming and the STL
Using and Extending the C++ Standard Template Library
Addison-Wesley, Reading, MA, 1998

Ulrich Breymann
Komponenten entwerfen mit der STL
Addison-Wesley, Bonn, Germany, 1999

Bernd Eggink
Die C++ iostreams–Library
Hanser Verlag, München, Germany, 1995

Margaret A. Ellis, Bjarne Stroustrup
The Annotated C++ Reference Manual (ARM)
Addison-Wesley, Reading, MA, 1990

Graham Glass, Brett Schuchert
The STL <Primer>
Prentice-Hall, Englewood Cliffs, NJ, 1996

ISO
Information Technology — Programming Languages — C++
Document Number ISO/IEC 14882-1998
ISO/IEC, 1998

Scott Meyers
More Effective C++
35 New Ways to Improve Your Programs and Designs
Addison-Wesley, Reading, MA, 1996

David R. Musser, Atul Saini
STL Tutorial and Reference Guide
C++ Programming with the Standard Template Library
Addison-Wesley, Reading, MA, 1996

Mark Nelson
C++ Programmer's Guide to the Standard Template Library
IDG Books Worldwide, Foster City, CA, 1995

ObjectSpace
Systems<Toolkit> UNIX Reference Manual
ObjectSpace, 1995

P. J. Plauger
The Draft Standard C++ Library
Prentice Hall, Englewood Cliffs, NJ, 1995

Bjarne Stroustrup
The C++ Programming Language, 3rd edition
Addison-Wesley, Reading, MA, 1997

Bjarne Stroustrup
The Design and Evolution of C++
Addison-Wesley, Reading, MA, 1994

Steve Teale
C++ IOStreams Handbook
Addison-Wesley, Reading, MA, 1993

Index

~ 599
   for valarrays **573**
! 601
   for valarrays **573**
!=
   derived from == **69**
   for allocators **740**
   for complex 537, **545**
   for containers **145**, **234**
   for deques **162**
   for iterators 83, **252**
   for lists **168**
   for locales 700, **703**
   for maps **198**
   for multimaps **198**
   for multisets **179**
   for pairs 34
   for queues **449**
   for sets **179**
   for stacks **440**
   for strings **511**
   for valarrays **573**
   for vectors **151**
%
   for valarrays **573**
%=
   for valarrays **574**
& 599

   for bitsets **467**
   for valarrays **573**
&&
   for valarrays **573**
&=
   for valarrays **574**
()
   as operator **125**
   for locales **703**
*
   for auto_ptrs **54**
   for complex 538, **544**
   for iterators 83, **252**
   for valarrays **573**
*=
   for complex 538
   for valarrays **574**
+
   for complex 538, **544**
   for iterators **255**
   for strings 492, **524**
   for valarrays **573**
++ **86**
   for iterators 83, **252**, **258**
   for vector iterators **258**
   problem **258**
+=
   for complex 538

for iterators **255**
for strings **490**, **515**
for valarrays **574**

-

for complex 538, **544**
for iterators **255**
for valarrays **573**

-- **86**

for iterators **255**, **258**
for vector iterators **258**
problem **258**

-=

for complex 538
for iterators **255**
for valarrays **574**

->

for auto_ptrs **54**
for iterators 91, **252**

/

for complex 538, **544**
for valarrays **573**

/=

for complex 538
for valarrays **574**

<

for complex 538
for containers **145**, **234**
for deques **162**
for iterators **255**
for lists **168**
for maps **198**
for multimaps **198**
for multisets **179**
for pairs 34
for queues **449**
for sets **179**
for stacks **440**
for strings **511**

for valarrays **573**
for vectors **151**

<< **593**, 652

conventions **662**
for bitsets *462*, **468**
for complex *532*, 539, **544**
for stream buffers 597, 683
for strings 492, **524**
for valarrays **573**

<<=

for valarrays **574**

<=

derived from < **69**
for containers **145**, **234**
for deques **162**
for iterators **255**
for lists **168**
for maps **198**
for multimaps **198**
for multisets **179**
for pairs 34
for queues **449**
for sets **179**
for stacks **440**
for strings **511**
for valarrays **573**
for vectors **151**

=

for deques **163**
for iterators 83
for lists **168**
for strings **489**
for vectors **151**

==

for allocators 728, **740**
for complex 537, **545**
for containers **145**, **234**
for deques **162**

for iterators   83, **252**
for lists   **168**
for locales   700, **703**
for maps   **198**
for multimaps   **198**
for multisets   **179**
for pairs   34
for queues   **449**
for sets   **179**
for stacks   **440**
for strings   **511**
for valarrays   **573**
for vectors   **151**

>

derived from <   **69**
for containers   **145, 234**
for deques   **162**
for iterators   **255**
for lists   **168**
for maps   **198**
for multimaps   **198**
for multisets   **179**
for pairs   34
for queues   **449**
for sets   **179**
for stacks   **440**
for strings   **511**
for valarrays   **573**
for vectors   **151**

>=

derived from <   **69**
for containers   **145, 234**
for deques   **162**
for iterators   **255**
for lists   **168**
for maps   **198**
for multimaps   **198**

for multisets   **179**
for pairs   34
for queues   **449**
for sets   **179**
for stacks   **440**
for strings   **511**
for valarrays   **573**
for vectors   **151**

>>   **594**, 652

conventions   **662**
for bitsets   **468**
for `complex`   *532*, 539, **544**
for stream buffers   683
for strings   492, **524**
for valarrays   **573**

>>=

for valarrays   **574**

[]

for deques   **162**
for iterators   **255**
for maps   92, **205**
for vectors   **152**

^

for bitsets   **468**
for valarrays   **573**

^=

for valarrays   **574**

| **632**

for bitsets   **468**
for valarrays   **573**

|=

for valarrays   **574**

||

for valarrays   **573**

A

abort() **72**
abs() *121*
    for complex   536, **543**
    for valarrays   **574**
    global function   582
absolute to relative values   331, 431
accumulate()   **425**
acos()
    for valarrays   **575**
    global function   581
adapter
    for containers   **435**
    for functions
        see function adapter
    for member functions
        see member function adapter
address
    input   596
    output   596
address()
    for allocators   **739**
address of the author   **6**
adjacent_difference()   **431**, *432*
adjacent_find()   **354**
adjustfield   **618**
adjustment   618
advance()   **259**, *282*, *389*
<algo.h>   321, 425
algorithm   74, **94**, **321**
    absolute to relative values   331, 431
    accumulate()   **425**
    adjacent_difference()   **431**
    adjacent_find()   **354**
    auxiliary functions   **332**
    binary_search()   **410**
    call element member function   **307**
    change order of elements   **386**

comparing   **356**
complexity   **21**
copy()   **271**, **363**
copy and modify elements   **367**
copy_backward()   **363**
copy elements   **363**
count()   **338**
count_if()   **338**
counting elements   **338**
destination   **111**
equal()   **356**, *499*
equal_range()   **415**
fill()   **372**
fill_n()   **372**
find()   **341**
find_end()   **350**
find_first_of()   **352**
find_if()   *121*, **341**
for_each()   *300*, **334**
for sorted ranges   330, **409**
function as argument   **119**
generate()   **373**
generate_n()   **373**
header file   **321**
heap   **406**
includes()   **411**
inner_product()   **427**
inplace_merge()   **423**
intersection   **419**
lexicographical_compare()   **360**
lower_bound()   **413**
make_heap()   **406**
manipulating   **111**
max_element()   **340**
maximum   **339**
merge()   **416**

min_element() **339**
minimum **339**
mismatch() **358**
modify elements **372**
modifying **111**, 325, **363**
multiple ranges **101**
mutating 327, **386**
next_permutation() **391**
nonmodifying 323, **338**
nth_element() **404**
numeric 331, **425**
overview **322**
partial_sort() **400**
partial_sort_copy() **402**
partial_sum() **429**
partition() **395**
pop_heap() **407**
prev_permutation() **391**
push_heap() **406**
random_shuffle() **393**
ranges **97**
relative to absolute values 331, 429
remove() **378**
remove_copy() **380**
remove_copy_if() **380**
remove_if() **378**
removing 326, **378**
removing duplicates **381**
removing elements **111**
replace() **375**
replace_copy() **376**
replace_copy_if() **376**
replace_if() **375**
replacing elements **375**
result 298
reverse() **386**
reverse_copy() **386**
rotate() **388**

rotate_copy() **389**
search() **347**, *499*
searching elements 324, **341**
search_n() **344**
set complement **421**
set difference **420**
set_difference() **420**
set_intersection() **419**
set_symmetric_difference()
    420, 421
set_union() **418**
sort() **397**
sort_heap() **407**
sorting **328, 397**
stable_partition() **395**
stable_sort() **397**
suffix _copy 323
suffix _if 323
swapping **370**
swap_ranges() **370**
transform() *120, 131*, **367, 368,**
    497
transform elements **367**
union elements **418**
unique() **381**
unique_copy() **384**
upper_bound() **413**
user-defined 285
<algorithm> 33, 66, 96, **321**
algostuff.hpp **332**
alias free 547
allocate()
    for allocators **728, 739**
allocator **31, 727**
    != **740**
    == 728, **740**
    address() **739**
    allocate() 728, **739**

`const_pointer` **738**
`const_reference` **738**
`construct()` 728, **739**
constructor **739**
`deallocate()` 728, **739**
default 32, **732**
`destroy()` 728, **740**
destructor **739**
`difference_type` **738**
`get_allocator()` **728**
`max_size()` **739**
`pointer` **738**
`rebind` 734, **738**
`reference` **738**
`size_type` **738**
usage **727**
user-defined 735
`value_type` **737**
`allocator_type`
    for containers **231, 247**
    for strings **526**
`alnum`
    for `ctype_base` 717
`alpha`
    for `ctype_base` 717
`always_noconv()`
    for `codecvt` facet **721**
ambiguous
    numeric functions **581**
amortized complexity 22
antisymmetric 176
`any()`
    for bitsets **464**
app flag **631**
`append()`
    for strings **490, 515, 516**
`apply()`
    for valarrays **572**

`arg()`
    for complex 536, **543**
`argc` 21, *633*
`argument_type` 310
`argv` 21, *633*
arithmetic
    of iterators 255
array
    associative **92, 205**
    as STL container **218**
    container **155**
    wrapper **219**
`asin()`
    for valarrays **575**
    global function 581
`assign()`
    for `char_traits` **689**
    for containers **236, 237**
    for deques **163**
    for lists **168**
    for strings **489, 514**
    for vectors **151**
assignable 135
assignment
    for containers 147
    for deques **163**
    for iterators 83
    for lists **168**
    for vectors **151**
associative array **92, 205**, *207*
associative container **75**
    manipulating access **115**
    sorting criterion 538
    user-defined inserter **288**
`at()`
    for containers **237**
    for deques 162, **237**

for strings **513**
for vectors **152, 237**
`atan()`
for valarrays **575**
global function 581
`atan2()`
for valarrays **575**
global function 581
ate flag **631**
`atexit()` **72**
author **6**
auto pointer
see auto_ptr
`auto_ptr` **38**
`*` **54**
`->` **54**
`=` **41**
assignment operator **41**
constructor **52, 53**
conversions **55**
destructor **53**
`element_type` **52**
`get()` **54**
header file **51**
implementation **56**
initialization **40**
`release()` **54**
`reset()` **54**
`auto_ptr_ref` 51, **55**

B

`back()`
for containers **238**
for deques **162**
for lists **168**
for queues **449**
for vectors **152**
back inserter 106, **272**

`back_inserter` **106, 272**
`bad()`
for streams 598
`bad_alloc` **25, 26**
`badbit` **597**
`bad_cast` **25, 26**
`bad_exception` **25, 26**
`bad_typeid` **25, 26**
`base()` **269**
`basefield` **621**
`basic_filebuf` **627**, 643
for streams 643
`basic_fstream` **627**
basic guarantee 139
`basic_ifstream` **627**
`basic_ios` **588**
`basic_istream` **588**
see input stream
`basic_istringstream` **645**
`basic_ofstream` **627**
`basic_ostream` **588**
see output stream
`basic_ostringstream` **645**
`basic_streambuf` 588, **668**
see output buffer and input buffer
`basic_string` **471**
see string
`basic_stringbuf` **645**
`basic_stringstream` **645**
`beg` **635**
`begin()`
for containers 83, **145, 239**
for deques **162**
for lists **169**
for maps **200**
for multimaps **200**
for multisets **182**
for sets **182**

for strings   *497*, **525**
for vectors   **153**
bibliography   **745**
bidirectional iterator   93, **255**
    distance   261
    step backward   259
    step forward   259
bidirectional_iterator   288
Big-O notation   **21**
binary flag   **631**
binary_function   **310**
binary predicate   **123**
binary representation   **462**
binary_search()   **410**
bind1st   **306**, *311*
bind2nd   *132*, **133**, **306**, *311*, *338*
bitfield
    with dynamic size   **158**
        see vector<bool>
    with static size   **460**
        see bitset
bitset   **460**
    &   **467**
    <<   *462*, **468**
    >>   **468**
    ^   **468**
    | **468**
    any()   **464**
    binary representation   *462*
    constructor   **463**, **464**
    count()   **464**
    examples   **460**
    flip()   **465**, **466**
    header file   **460**
    input   **468**
    none()   **464**
    output   **468**
    reference   **467**

reset()   **465**
set()   **465**
size()   **464**
test()   **465**
to_string()   **468**
to_ulong()   *462*, **468**
<bitset>   **460**
BLAS   **548**
Blitz   547, **744**
books   **745**
bool
    input   **595**, **617**
    input format   **617**
    numeric limits   60
    output   **595**, **617**
    output format   **617**
bool type   **18**
boolalpha flag   **617**
boolalpha manipulator   **617**
Boolean conditions
    in loops   **600**
    of streams   **600**
Boolean vector   **158**
Boost   225, 313, **744**
buffer
    see output buffer and input buffer

C

"C" locale   694
callback
    for streams   **661**
capacity
    of strings   **485**
    of vectors   **149**
capacity()
    for containers   **233**
    for strings   486, **510**
    for vectors   149

carray **219**

catalog

    for `message_base` **725**

category

    of container iterators   239

    of iterators   93, **251**

category

    for locales   700

`<cctype>`   720

`ceil()`

    global function   581

`cerr`   **585**, 592

    redirecting   **641**

`<cfloat>`   59, 60

`char`

    classification   **716**

    input   595

    numeric limits   60

`char*`

    input   596

`char*` stream   **649**

    `freeze()`   650

    `str()`   650

character

    classification   **716**

    encoding conversion   **720**

    traits   *504*, **687**

`char_traits`   *479, 590*, **687**

    `assign()`   **689**

    `char_type`   **689**

    `compare()`   *504*, **689**

    `copy()`   **689**

    `eof()`   **689**

    `eq()`   *504*, **689**

    `eq_int_type()`   **689**

    `find()`   *504*, **689**

    `int_type`   **689**

    `length()`   **689**

`lt()`   *504*, **689**

`move()`   **689**

`not_eof()`   **689**

`off_type`   **689**

`pos_type`   **689**

`state_type`   **689**

`to_char_type()`   **689**

`to_int_type()`   **689**

`char_type`

    for `char_traits`   **689**

`cin`   **585**, 592

    redirecting   **641**

class

    `auto_ptr`   **38**

    `bad_alloc`   **25**

    `bad_cast`   **25**

    `bad_exception`   **25**

    `bad_typeid`   **25**

    `basic_filebuf`   **627**, 643

    `basic_fstream`   **627**

    `basic_ifstream`   **627**

    `basic_ios`   **588**

    `basic_istream`   **588**

    `basic_istringstream`   **645**

    `basic_ofstream`   **627**

    `basic_ostream`   **588**

    `basic_ostringstream`   **645**

    `basic_streambuf`   588, **668**

    `basic_string`   **471**

    `basic_stringbuf`   **645**

    `basic_stringstream`   **645**

    `bitset`   **460**

      see bitset

    `carray`   **219**

    `codecvt`   **720**

    `codecvt_base`   **721**

    `collate`   **724**

    `complex`   **529**

ctype **716**
ctype_base **717**
deque
  see deque
domain_error **25**
exception **25**
facet 700
failure 25, **602**
filebuf **627**, 643
fpos **634**
fstream **627**
gslice **560, 577**
gslice_array **561, 577**
hash_map **221**
hash_multimap **221**
hash_multiset **221**
hash_set **221**
ifstream **627, 629**
indirect_array **567**
invalid_argument **25**
I/O functions **652**
ios **590**
ios_base **588**
ios_base::failure 25, **602**
iostream **591**
iostream_withassign 591
istream **584, 591**
istreambuf_iterator **665**
istream_withassign 591
istringstream **645**
istrstream **649**
iterator 288
length_error **25**
list
  see list
locale 694
logic_error **25**

map
  see map
mask_array **564**
message_base **725**
messages **725**
money_base **712**
money_get **715**
moneypunct **711**
money_put **713**
multimap
  see multimap
multiset
  see multiset
numeric_limits **59**
num_get **707**
numpunct **705**
num_put **706**
ofstream **627, 629**
ostream **585, 591**
ostreambuf_iterator **665**
ostream_withassign 591
ostringstream **645**
ostrstream **649**
out_of_range **25**
overflow_error **25**
priority_queue **453**
queue **444**
range_error **25**
runtime_error **25**
sentry **658**
set
  see set
slice **555, 575**
slice_array **556, 575**
stack **435**
streambuf 590, **668**
string **471**
stringbuf **645**

`stringstream` **645**
`strstream` **649**
`strstreambuf` **649**
`time_base` **709**
`time_get` **708**
`time_put` **710**
`underflow_error` **25**
`valarray` **547**
`vector`
  see vector
`wfilebuf` **627**
`wfstream` **627**
`wifstream` **627**
`wios` **590**
`wiostream` **591**
`wistream` **591**
`wistringstream` **645**
`wofstream` **627**
`wostream` **591**
`wostringstream` **645**
`wstreambuf` **590, 668**
`wstring` **471**
`wstringbuf` **645**
`wstringstream` **645**
class hierarchy
  of exceptions **25**
  of file stream classes **627**
  of stream classes **588**
  of string stream classes **645**
`classic()`
  for locales *694*, 700, **703**
`classic_table()`
  for ctype facet **718**
`clear()`
  for containers **145, 244**
  for deques **163**
  for lists **170**
  for maps **202**

  for multimaps **202**
  for multisets **183**
  for sets **183**
  for streams **598,** *599, 633, 636*
  for strings **490, 518**
  for vectors **154**
`<climits>` 59, 60
`clog` **585**
`close()`
  for `messages` facet **725**
  for streams **633**
`<cmath>` **581**
`cntrl`
  for `ctype_base` **717**
`codecvt` facet **720**
  `always_noconv()` **721**
  `encoding()` **721**
  `in()` **721**
  `length()` **721**
  `max_length()` **721**
  `out()` **721**
  `unshift()` **721**
`codecvt_base` **721**
  `error` 722
  `noconv` 722
  `ok` 722
  `partial` 722
  `result` **722**
`collate` facet **724**
  `compare()` **724**
  `hash()` **724**
  `transform()` **724**
`collate` locale category **724**
collection 73
  of collections *360*
`combine()`
  for locales **700, 702**
command-line arguments **21, 633**

commit-or-rollback **139**

compare

    lexicographical **360**

    ranges **356**

compare()

    for char_traits *504*, **689**

    for collate facet **724**

    for strings **511, 512**

comparison operators **69**

    for containers 147

compiler requirements 9

complementary set **421**

complex **529**

    != 537, **545**

    * 538, **544**

    *= 538

    + 538, **544**

    += 538

    - 538, **544**

    -= 538

    / 538, **544**

    /= 538

    < 538

    << *532*, 539, **544**

    == 537, **545**

    >> *532*, 539, **544**

    abs() 536, **543**

    and associative containers **537**, 538

    arg() 536, **543**

    conj() 533, **541**

    constructor 533, **541**

    cos() 540, **546**

    cosh() 540, **546**

    examples **530**

    exp() 540, **545**

    header file **529**

    imag() 536, **543**

    I/O *532*, **539**, 544

log() 540, **545**

log10() 540, **545**

norm() 536, **543**

polar() 533, **541**

pow() 540, **545**

read *532*, 544

reading **539**

real() 536, **543**

sin() 540, **546**

sinh() 540, **546**

sqrt() 540, **545**

tan() 540, **546**

tanh() 540, **546**

type conversions 534

value_type **541**

write *532*, 544

writing **539**

<complex> **529**

complexity **21**

    amortized 22

compose1 **314**

compose1 **313**

compose2 **316**

compose2 **313**

compose_f_gx 313, **314**

compose_f_gx_hx 313, **316**

compose_f_gx_hy 313, **318**

compose_f_gxy **313**

compose function object **313**

compressing whitespaces *385*

conditions

    in loops **600**

conj()

    for complex 533, **541**

constant

    EXIT_FAILURE **72**

    EXIT_SUCCESS **72**

    NULL **71**

constant complexity   **21**
const_cast   20
const_iterator
   for containers   85, **230**
   for strings   **508**
const_mem_fun1_ref_t   309
const_mem_fun1_t   309
const_mem_fun_ref_t   309
const_mem_fun_t   309
const_pointer
   for allocators   **738**
   for strings   **508**
const_reference
   for allocators   **738**
   for containers   **230**
   for strings   **507**
const_reverse_iterator
   for containers   **230**
   for strings   **508**
construct()
   for allocators   728, **739**
constructor
   as template   **13**
   for allocators   **739**
   for auto_ptrs   **52, 53**
   for bitsets   **463, 464**
   for complex   533, **541**
   for containers   **231, 232, 247**
   for deques   **162**
   for lists   **167**
   for locales   700, **702**
   for maps   **196**
   for multimaps   **196**
   for multisets   **177**, *189*
   for pairs   **34**
   for priority queues   **458, 459**
   for queues   **448**
   for sets   **177**

for stacks   **440**
for strings   *501*, **508, 509**
for valarrays   **548, 570**
for vectors   **150**
contact with the author   **5**
container   73, **75, 143, 435**
   !=   **145, 234**
   <   **145, 234**
   <=   **145, 234**
   ==   **145, 234**
   >   **145, 234**
   >=   **145, 234**
   adapters   **435**
   allocator_type   **231, 247**
   assign()   **236, 237**
   assignment   147
   at()   **237**
   back()   **238**
   begin()   83, **145, 239**
   call member function for elements
      134, 307
   capacity()   **233**
   clear()   **145, 244**
   comparison   **226**
   comparison operators   147
   const_iterator   85, **230**
   const_reference   **230**
   const_reverse_iterator   **230**
   constructor   **231, 232, 247**
   count()   **234**
   deque
     see deque
   destructor   **231, 232**
   difference_type   **231**
   element requirements   **134**
   empty()   **145**, 146, **233**
   end()   83, **145, 239**
   equal_range()   **236**

erase() 242, 243
exceptions handling overview 248
find() 235
front() 238
get_allocator() 247
initialization 144
insert() 240, 241
iterator 85
iterator 230
iterator category 239
key_comp() 236
key_compare 231
key_type 231
list
   see list
lower_bound() 235
map
   see map
mapped_type 231
max_size() 145, 146, 233
multimap
   see multimap
multiset
   see multiset
of containers 360
ordinary arrays 218
pop_back() 243
pop_front() 243
print elements 118
push_back() 241
push_front() 241
rbegin() 109, 145, 239
reference 230
reference counting 222
reference semantics 135
rend() 109, 145, 240
reserve() 233
resize() 244, 248

reverse_iterator 230
set
   see set
size() 145, 146, 233
size operations 146
size_type 231
swap() 140, 145, 147, 237
swapping 147
upper_bound() 235
user-defined 217
value_comp() 236
value_compare 231
value semantics 135
value_type 230
vector
   see vector
container_type
   for priority queues 458
   for queues 448
   for stacks 439
conversion
   absolute to relative values 331, 431
   between character encodings 720
   relative to absolute values 331, 429
copy()
   algorithm 363
   algorithm implementation 271
   for char_traits 689
   for strings 484, 513
copyable 134
copy and modify elements 367
copy and replace elements 376
copy_backward() 363
copy constructor
   as template 13, 35
copyfmt()
   for streams 615, 616, 641, 653, 661
copyfmt_event 661

copying elements **363**

cos()

    for complex   540, **546**

    for valarrays   **575**

    global function   581

cosh()

    for complex   540, **546**

    for valarrays   **575**

    global function   581

count()   **338**

    for bitsets   **464**

    for containers   **234**

    for maps   198

    for multimaps   198

    for multisets   180

    for sets   180

CountedPtr   **222**

count_if()   **338**

counting elements   **338**

cout   **585**, 592

    redirecting   **641**

cshift()

    for valarrays   **572**

<cstddef>   **71**

<cstdlib>   **71**, **581**

c_str()

    for strings   484, **513**, *629*

C-string   471

<cstring>   689

<ctime>   708

ctype facet   **716**

    classic_table()   **718**

    is()   **716**

    narrow()   **716**

    scan_is()   **716**

    scan_not()   **716**

    table()   **718**

    table_size   **718**

    tolower()   **716**

    toupper()   **716**

    widen()   **716**

ctype locale category   **715**

ctype_base   **717**

    alnum   717

    alpha   717

    cntrl   717

    digit   717

    graph   717

    lower   717

    mask   **717**

    print   717

    punct   717

    space   717

    upper   717

    xdigit   717

<ctype.h>   720

cur   **635**

curr_symbol()

    for moneypunct facet   **712**

D

data()

    for strings   484, **513**

data type

    see type

dateorder

    for time_base   **709**

date_order()

    for time_get facet   **708**

deallocate()

    for allocators   728, **739**

dec flag   **621**

dec manipulator   **622**

decimal_point()

    for moneypunct facet   **712**

    for numpunct facet   **705**

decimal representation   621
default
    allocator   32, **732**
    template parameter   **10**
denorm_absent   64
denorm_indeterminate   64
denorm_min()
    for numeric limits   62
denorm_present   64
deque   **160**, *164*
    see container
    !=   **162**
    <   **162**
    <=   **162**
    =   **163**
    ==   **162**
    >   **162**
    >=   **162**
    []   **162**
    assign()   **163**
    assignment   **163**
    at()   **162**
    back()   **162**
    begin()   **162**
    clear()   **163**
    constructor   **162**
    empty()   **162**
    end()   **162**
    erase()   **163**
    exception handling   **164**
    front()   **162**
    header file   **160**
    insert()   **163**
    max_size()   **162**
    member functions   **162**
    operations   **162**
    pop_back()   **163**
    pop_front()   **163**

    push_back()   **163**
    push_front()   **163**
    rbegin()   **162**
    rend()   **162**
    resize()   **163**
    size()   **162**
    subscript operator   **162**
    swap()   **163**
<deque>   **160**
<deque.h>   160
destination of algorithms   **111**
destroy()
    for allocators   728, **740**
destroyable   135
destructor
    for allocators   **739**
    for auto_ptrs   **53**
    for containers   **231**, **232**
    for lists   **167**
    for locales   700
    for maps   **196**
    for multimaps   **196**
    for multisets   **177**
    for sets   **177**
    for strings   **509**
    for valarrays   **570**
    for vectors   **150**
dictionary   *209*
difference of two sets   **420**
difference_type
    for allocators   **738**
    for containers   **231**
    for strings   **507**
digit
    for ctype_base   717
digits
    for numeric limits   61, *462*

`digits10`
    for numeric limits   61
`distance()`   **261**, **287**
`div()`
    global function   582
`divides`   **305**
dmy date order   710
`domain_error`   **25**, **28**
`double`
    numeric limits   60
duplicates removing   **381**
dynamic array container   **155**
`dynamic_cast`   19, 26

E

`eback()`
    for input buffers   **676**
EGCS   5, 744
`egptr()`
    for input buffers   **676**
element access
    for lists   **168**
    for vectors   **152**
`element_type`
    for `auto_ptrs`   **52**
email   **5**
`empty()`
    for containers   **145**, 146, **233**
    for deques   **162**
    for lists   **168**
    for maps   **198**
    for multimaps   **198**
    for multisets   **179**
    for priority queues   **459**
    for queues   **449**
    for sets   **179**
    for stacks   **440**

    for strings   485, **510**
    for vectors   **151**
empty range   84
encoding
    conversion   **720**
`encoding()`
    for `codecvt` facet   **721**
end   **635**
`end()`
    for containers   83, **145**, **239**
    for deques   **162**
    for lists   **169**
    for maps   **200**
    for multimaps   **200**
    for multisets   **182**
    for sets   **182**
    for strings   *497*, **525**
    for vectors   **153**
`endl` manipulator   **586**, 587, **612**, 683
end-of-file   **590**
end-of-stream iterator   108, **280**
`ends` manipulator   587, 612, *650*
environment variable
    `LANG`   **692**
EOF   590, 597
    internationalized   689
`eof()`
    for `char_traits`   **689**
    for streams   598
`eofbit`   **597**
`epptr()`
    for output buffers   **668**
`epsilon()`
    for numeric limits   61
`eq()`
    for `char_traits`   *504*, **689**
`eq_int_type()`
    for `char_traits`   **689**

equal()   **356**, *499*
    for `istreambuf_iterator`   **666**
`equal_range()`   **415**
    for containers   **236**
    for maps   198
    for multimaps   198
    for multisets   *180*
    for sets   *180*
`equal_to`   *132*, **305**, *319*
`erase()`
    for containers   **185, 242, 243**
    for deques   **163**
    for lists   **170**
    for maps   202
    for multimaps   202
    for multisets   182, *189*
    for sets   182, *186*
    for strings   491, *501*, **518**
    for vectors   **154**
`erase_event`   661
`error`
    for `codecvt_base`   722
error handling   **25**
    in the STL   **137**
even element   306
`event`   661
`event_callback`   661
example code   **5**
    auxiliary functions   **332**
exception   **29**
    `bad_alloc`   **25**
    `bad_cast`   **25**
    `bad_exception`   **25**
    `bad_typeid`   **25**
    classes   **25**
    declaration   **16**
    deriving   **30**
    `domain_error`   **25**

`exception`   **25**
    `failure`   25
    header files   **28**
    `invalid_argument`   **25**
    `ios_base::failure`   25, **602**
    `length_error`   **25**
    `logic_error`   **25**
    members   **28**
    `out_of_range`   **25**
    `overflow_error`   **25**
    `range_error`   **25**
    `runtime_error`   **25**
    specification   **16**, 26
    `throw`   **16**
    `underflow_error`   **25**
    user-defined   **29**, *441*, *450*
    `what()`   **28**, *29*
`exception`   **25**
`<exception>`   **28**
exception handling   15, 25
    `auto_ptr`   **38**
    for deques   **164**
    for lists   **172**
    for maps   **207**
    for multimaps   **207**
    for multisets   **185**
    for sets   **185**
    for vectors   **155**
    in the STL   **139, 248**
`exceptions()`
    for streams   602
exception safety   **139**
exception specification   **16**, 26
`exit()`   **72**
`EXIT_FAILURE` constant   **72**
`EXIT_SUCCESS` constant   **72**
`exp()`
    for `complex`   540, **545**

for valarrays **575**
global function 581
`explicit` **18**
`export` 10
extending STL **141**
extractor
for streams 586, 593

F

`fabs()`
global function 581
facet **698, 704**
`codecvt` **720**
`collate` **724**
`ctype` **716**
for character classification **716**
for character encoding conversion **720**
for date formatting **708**
for internationalized messages **725**
for monetary formatting **711**
for numeric formatting **705**
for string collation **724**
for time formatting **708**
id 704
`messages` **725**
`money_get` **715**
`moneypunct` **711**
`money_put` **713**
`num_get` **707**
`numpunct` **705**
`num_put` **706**
`time_get` **708**
`time_put` **710**
type 700
`fail()`
for streams 598
`failbit` **597**

`failed()`
for `ostreambuf_iterator` **666**
`failure` 25, **602**
`false` **18**
`falsename()`
for `numpunct` facet **705**
feedback to the author **5**
field width 618
file **627**
access **627**, *629*
opening **627**
positioning **634**
read and write 643
`filebuf` **627**, 643
file descriptor 637, 672
`fill()` **372**
for streams 618
for valarrays **571**
fill character 618
`fill_n()` **372**
filter 601, 611
`find()`
algorithm **341**
finding subrange 99
for `char_traits` *504*, **689**
for containers **235**
for maps **198**
for multimaps **198**
for multisets 180, *189*
for sets 180, *186*
for strings **520, 521**
return value 99
`find_end()` **350**
`find_first_not_of()`
for strings **522**
`find_first_of()`
algorithm **352**
for strings **522**

`find_if()`   *121, 211,* **341**

finding algorithms   324, **341**

`find_last_not_of()`

   for strings   **523**

`find_last_of()`

   for strings   **523**

find limit   343

`first`

   for pairs   34

`first_argument_type`   310

`first_type`

   for pairs   34

`fixed` flag   **623**

`fixed` manipulator   **625**

`flags()`   *539*

   for streams   615, **616**

`flip()`

   for bitsets   **465, 466**

   for `vector<bool>::reference`
      158, 159

`float`

   numeric limits   60

`float_denorm_style`   **63**

`floatfield`   **623**

`<float.h>`   59, 60

floating-point I/O formats   623

`float_round_style`   **63**

`floor()`

   global function   581

`flush()`

   for output streams   **611**

`flush` manipulator   587, 612, 683

`fmod()`

   global function   581

`for_each()`   *300,* **334**

   return value   **300**

   versus `transform()`   **325**

format flags   **615**

formatted I/O   **615**

formatting

   of `bool`   595, **617**

   of floating-point values   623

forward iterator   **254**

   distance   261

   step forward   259

   versus output iterator   254

`forward_iterator`   288

`fpos`   **634**

`frac_digits()`

   for `moneypunct` facet   **712**

`freeze()`   650, *651*

`frexp()`

   global function   581

`front()`

   for containers   **238**

   for deques   **162**

   for lists   **168**

   for queues   **449**

   for vectors   **152**

front inserter   106, **274**

`front_inserter`   **106**, 272

`fstream`   **627**

`<fstream>`   **628**

function

   as argument   **119**

   as sorting criterion   **123**

function adapter   132, **306**

   `bind1st`   **306**, *311*

   `bind2nd`   **306**, *311*

   `compose1`   **314**

   `compose1`   **313**

   `compose2`   **316**

   `compose2`   **313**

   `compose_f_gx`   **313, 314**

   `compose_f_gx_hx`   **313, 316**

   `compose_f_gx_hy`   **313, 318**

    compose_f_gxy **313**
    mem_fun **307**
    mem_fun_ref **307**
    not1 **306**
    not2 **306**
    ptr_fun **310**
<functional> **305**, 306, 321
functional composition 134, **313**
<function.h> 305, 321
function object **124**, *213*, **293**
    as sorting criterion **294**
    bind1st **306**, *311*
    bind2nd **306**, *311*
    compose1 **314**
    compose1 **313**
    compose2 **316**
    compose2 **313**
    compose_f_gx **313**, **314**
    compose_f_gx_hx **313**, **316**
    compose_f_gx_hy **313**, **318**
    compose_f_gxy **313**
    divides **305**
    equal_to **305**
    greater **305**
    greater_equal **305**
    header file **305**
    less **305**
    less_equal **305**
    logical_and **305**
    logical_not **305**
    logical_or **305**
    mem_fun **307**, **308**
    mem_fun_ref **307**
    minus **305**
    modulus **305**
    multiplies **305**
    negate **305**
    not1 **306**

    not2 **306**
    not_equal_to **305**
    plus **305**
    predefined **131**
    ptr_fun **310**
    state **296**
    times **305**
    user-defined **310**
functor **124**, **293**

G

gcount()
    for input streams **609**
general inserter **275**
general slice **560**
    see gslice
generate() **373**
generate_n() **373**
get()
    for auto_ptrs **54**
    for input streams **608**, *629*
    for messages facet **725**
    for money_get facet **715**
    for num_get facet **707**
get_allocator() **728**
    for containers **247**
    for strings **526**
get buffer **676**
    iterator **666**
get_date()
    for time_get facet **708**
getline()
    for input streams **608**
    for strings 493, **525**
getloc()
    for stream buffers **664**, *669*
    for streams **626**

get_monthname()
    for time_get facet   **708**
get_temporary_buffer()   731
get_time()
    for time_get facet   **708**
get_weekday()
    for time_get facet   **708**
get_year()
    for time_get facet   **708**
global()
    for locales   697, 700, **703**
good()   601
    for streams   598
goodbit   **597**
gptr()
    for input buffers   **676**
graph
    for ctype_base   717
greater   *186*, **305**, *338*
greater_equal   **305**
grouping()
    for moneypunct facet   **712**
    for numpunct facet   **705**
gslice   **560**, **577**
    constructor   **577**
    size()   **577**
    start()   **577**
    stride()   **577**
gslice_array   **561**, **577**

H

half-open range   84, **97**
hardfail   **598**
has_denorm
    for numeric limits   62, **63**
has_denorm_loss
    for numeric limits   62

has_facet()
    for locales   700, **702**
hash()
    for collate facet   **724**
hash_map   **221**
hash_multimap   **221**
hash_multiset   **221**
hash_set   **221**
hash table   **221**
has_infinity
    for numeric limits   61
has_quiet_NaN
    for numeric limits   61
has_signaling_NaN
    for numeric limits   61
header file   **24**
    "algostuff.hpp"   **332**
    <algo.h>   321, 425
    <algorithm>   33, 66, 96, **321**
    <bitset>   **460**
    <cctype>   720
    <cfloat>   59, 60
    <climits>   59, 60
    <cmath>   **581**
    <complex>   **529**
    <cstddef>   **71**
    <cstdlib>   **71**, **581**
    <cstring>   689
    <ctime>   708
    <ctype.h>   720
    <deque>   **160**
    <deque.h>   160
    <exception>   **28**
    extension   24
    <float.h>   59, 60
    for algorithms   **321**
    for auto_ptrs   **51**
    for bitsets   **460**

for `complex` **529**
for `deques` **160**
for exceptions **28**
for function objects **305**
for I/O **592**
for lists **166**
for maps **194**
for multimaps **194**
for multisets **175**
for priority queues **454**
for queues **444**
for sets **175**
for stacks **435**
for streams **592**
for strings **479**
for valarrays **547**
for vectors **148**
`<fstream>` **628**
`<functional>` **305**, 306, 321
`<function.h>` 305, 321
`<iomanip>` **614**
`<ios>` 28, 607
`<iosfwd>` **592**
`<iostream>` **592**, 681
`<iostream.h>` 25
`<istream>` **592**
`<iterator>` **251, 665**
`<iterator.h>` 251
`<limits>` **60**
`<limits.h>` 59, 60
`<list>` **166**
`<list.h>` 166
`<locale>` **700**
`<map>` **194**
`<map.h>` 194
`<memory>` 51
`<multimap.h>` 194
`<multiset.h>` 175

`<new>` 28
`<numeric>` **321, 425**
`<ostream>` **592**
`<queue>` **444, 454**
`<Queue.hpp>` 450
`<set>` **175**
`<set.h>` 175
`<sstream>` **646**
`<stack>` **435**
`<stack.h>` 435, 444, 454
`<Stack.hpp>` 441
`<stddef.h>` 71
`<stdexcept>` **28**
`<stdlib.h>` 71
`<streambuf>` **592**
`<string>` **479, 688**
`<string.h>` 689
`<strstream>` **649**
`<typeinfo>` 28
`<utility>` 33, 34, 69
`<valarray>` **547**
`<vector>` **148**
`<vector.h>` 148
heap algorithms **406**
heapsort **329**, 406
hex flag **621**
hex manipulator **622**
hexadecimal representation 621

I

`i18n`
    see internationalization
`id`
    for locales 700
`ifstream` **627, 629**
`ignore()`
    for input streams *532*, **609**, *614*
    for streams *614*

imag()
    for complex   536, **543**
imbue()   *539*, 694
    for streams   626, *694*
imbue_event   661
implementation
    of manipulators   **614**
in()
    for codecvt facet   **721**
in flag   **631**
in_avail()
    for input buffers   **663**
include file
    see header file
includes()   **411**
increment
    for iterators   83
index of the book   **747**
index operator
    for iterators   **255**
    for maps   92, **205**
indirect array   **567**
indirect_array   **567**, 579
infinity()
    for numeric limits   61
initialize
    a container   **144**
inner_product()   **427**
inplace_merge()   **423**
input   **583**
    see input stream and stream
    defining numeric bases   621
    field width   620
    hexadecimal   621
    line-by-line   **493**
    octal   621
    of addresses   596
    of bitsets   **468**

    of bool   **595**, 617
    of char   595
    of char*   596
    of complex   532, **539**, 544
    of objects in a loop   600
    of strings   **492**, **524**, 620
    of void*   596
    of wchar_t   595
    operator >>   **594**
    redirecting   **641**
    skip input   282
    standard functions   **607**
input buffer   **676**
    eback()   **676**
    egptr()   **676**
    gptr()   **676**
    in_avail()   **663**
    iterator   **666**
    pbackfail()   **677**
    sbumpc()   **663**, **676**
    setg()   **677**
    sgetc()   **663**, **676**
    sgetn()   **663**, **677**
    snextc()   **663**
    sputbackc()   **663**, **676**
    sungetc()   **663**, **676**
    uflow()   **676**
    underflow()   **676**
    xsgetn()   **677**
input iterator   **252**
    distance   261
    step forward   259
input_iterator   288
input stream
    buffer iterators   **665**
    buffers   **663**
    gcount()   **609**
    get()   **608**

getline() **608**

ignore() *532*, **609**, *614*

iterator   107, **280**

member functions   **607**

peek()   **609**

putback()   **609**

read()   **608**

readsome()   **609**

sentry   **658**

unget()   **609**

insert()

    called by inserters   272

    for containers   **240**, **241**

    for deques   **163**

    for lists   **170**

    for maps   202, **203**

    for multimaps   202, **203**

    for multisets   182, **183**, *184*, *189*

    for sets   182, **183**, *184*, *186*

    for strings   491, **516**, **517**

    for vectors   **154**

INSERT_ELEMENTS()   **332**

inserter   104, **106**, **271**, **272**, **275**

    for streams   586, 593

    user-defined   **288**

insert iterator   104, **271**

int

    numeric limits   60

internal flag   **618**

internal manipulator   **619**

internationalization   **685**

    of EOF   689

    of I/O   **625**

    of special characters   691

Internet   5, **743**

intersection   **419**

introsort   **329**

intrusive approach   217

int_type

    for char_traits   **689**

invalid_argument   **25**, **27**

invasive approach   217

I/O   **583**

    see input, output, and stream

    binary representation   **462**

    classes   **588**

    file access   **627**

    filter framework   601, 611

    for classes   **652**

    for complex   *532*, **539**, 544

    formatted   **615**

    header files   **592**

    in C++   *587*

    internationalization   **625**

    manipulators   **586**, **612**

    operators   593

    overloading operators   **652**

    redirecting standard streams   **641**

    user-defined stream buffers   668

    with C++   *611*

    with streams   *587*

<iomanip>   **614**

ios

    see stream

ios   **590**

<ios>   28, 607

ios_base   **588**

    see stream

ios_base::failure   25, 28, **602**

<iosfwd>   **592**

iostream   **591**

<iostream>   **592**, 681

<iostream.h>   25

iostream_withassign   591

ipfx()   658

irreflexive   176

is()
    for ctype facet   **716**
isalnum()   **719**
isalpha()   **719**
is_bounded
    for numeric limits   61
iscntrl()   **719**
isdigit()   **719**
is_exact
    for numeric limits   61
isfx()   658
isgraph()   **719**
is_iec559
    for numeric limits   61
is_integer
    for numeric limits   61
islower()   **719**
is_modulo
    for numeric limits   61
is_open()
    for streams   633
isprint()   **719**
ispunct()   **719**
is_signed
    for numeric limits   61
isspace()   *502*, **719**
is_specialized
    for numeric limits   61
istream
    see input stream and stream
istream   **584**, **591**
<istream>   **592**
istreambuf_iterator   **665**, **666**
    equal()   **666**
istream iterator   107, **280**
    end-of-stream   108, **280**
    skip input   282
istream_withassign   591

istringstream   **645**
istrstream   **649**
isupper()   **719**
isxdigit()   **719**
iterator   74, **83**, **251**
    !=   83, **252**
    *   83, **252**
    +   **255**
    ++   83, **86**, **252**, **258**
    +=   **255**
    += versus advance()   260
    -   **255**
    --   **86**, **255**, **258**
    -=   **255**
    ->   91, **252**
    <   **255**
    <=   **255**
    =   83
    ==   83, **252**
    >   **255**
    >=   **255**
    []   **255**
    adapters   104, **264**
    advance()   259, *389*
    arithmetic   255
    assignment   83
    auxiliary functions   **259**
    back_inserter   **106**, **272**
    back inserters   **272**
    bidirectional   93, **255**
    categories   93, **251**
    check order   99
    convert into reverse iterator   **265**
    distance()   261
    end-of-stream   108, **280**
    for containers   85
    for lists   **169**
    for maps   **200**

for multimaps   **200**
for multisets   **182**, *189*
for sets   **182**
for stream buffers   **665**
for streams   107, **277**, *282*
for strings   **497**
for vectors   **153**
forward   **254**
`front_inserter`   **106**, 272
front inserters   **274**
general inserters   **275**
increment   83
input   **252**
inserter   **106**, **272**
inserters   104, **275**
iterator tags   **283**
iterator traits   **283**
`iter_swap()`   263
output   **253**
past-the-end   83
random access   93, **255**
ranges   84
`raw_storage_iterator`   **731**
reverse   109, **264**
step forward   259
swapping values   263
user-defined   **288**
`iterator`   288
for containers   **230**
for strings   **508**
`<iterator>`   **251**, **665**
iterator adapter   104, **264**
for streams   107, **277**
inserter   **271**
inserters   104
reverse   109
user-defined   **288**
`<iterator.h>`   251

iterator tag   **283**
iterator traits   **283**
for pointers   285
`iter_swap()`   **263**
`iword()`
for streams   659

K

`key_comp()`
for containers   **236**
`key_compare`
for containers   **231**
`key_type`
for containers   **231**
Koenig lookup   17

L

`labs()`
global function   582
`LANG` environment variable   **692**
language features   9
lazy evaluation with valarrays   554
`ldexp()`
global function   581
`ldiv()`
global function   582
`left` flag   **618**
`left` manipulator   **619**
`length()`
for `char_traits`   **689**
for `codecvt` facet   **721**
for strings   485, **510**
for valarrays   **571**
`length_error`   25, 27
`less`   *132*, **305**, *375*, *379*
`less_equal`   **305**
`lexicographical_compare()`   **360**
lexicographical comparison   **360**

`<limits>` **60**
`<limits.h>` 59, 60
limits of types **59**
linear complexity **21**
line-by-line input **493**
list **166**, *172*
    see container
    `!=` **168**
    `<` **168**
    `<=` **168**
    `=` **168**
    `==` **168**
    `>` **168**
    `>=` **168**
    `assign()` **168**
    assignment **168**
    `back()` **168**
    `begin()` **169**
    `clear()` **170**
    constructor **167**
    destructor **167**
    element access **168**
    `empty()` **168**
    `end()` **169**
    `erase()` **170**
    exception handling **172**
    `front()` **168**
    header file **166**
    `insert()` **170**
    iterators **169**
    `max_size()` **168**
    member functions **167**
    `merge()` *172*, **246**
    operations **167**
    `pop_back()` **170**
    `pop_front()` **170**
    `push_back()` **170**, *172*
    `push_front()` **170**, *172*
    `rbegin()` **169**
    `remove()` **169**, *170*, **242**
    `remove_if()` **169**, **242**
    removing elements **169**
    `rend()` **169**
    `resize()` **170**
    `reverse()` **246**
    `size()` **168**
    `sort()` *172*, **245**
    special member functions 244
    `splice()` *172*, **245**
    splice functions 171
    `swap()` **168**
    `unique()` *172*, **244**
`<list>` **166**
`<list.h>` 166
literal of type string 471
literature **745**
locale **692**
    `!=` 700, **703**
    `()` **703**
    `==` 700, **703**
    as sorting criterion 703
    `"C"` 694
    `category` 700
    class 694
    `classic()` *694*, 700, **703**
    `collate` category **724**
    `combine()` 700, **702**
    constructor 700, **702**
    `ctype` category **715**
    default constructor 698
    destructor 700
    `facet` 700
    facets **698**, **704**
    `global()` 697, 700, **703**
    `has_facet()` 700, **702**
    `id` 700, 704

imbue() a stream   694
messages category   **725**
monetary category   **711**
name()   697, 700, **703**
numeric category   **705**
string collation   **724**
string comparisons   **703**
time category   **708**
type   694
use_facet()   700, **702**
<locale>   **700**
log()
    for complex   540, **545**
    for valarrays   **575**
    global function   581
log10()
    for complex   540, **545**
    for valarrays   **575**
    global function   581
logarithmic complexity   **21**
logical_and   **305**, *317*
logical_not   **305**
logical_or   **305**
logic_error   **25**, **27**
long
    numeric limits   60
loop
    condition   **600**
    for reading objects   600
lower
    for ctype_base   717
lower_bound()   **413**
    for containers   **235**
    for maps   198
    for multimaps   198
    for multisets   *180*
    for sets   *180*
lower string characters   497

lt()
    for char_traits   *504*, **689**
lvalue   **55**

M

main()   **21**
make_heap()   *329*, **406**, *407*, *456*
make_pair()
    for pairs   34, **36**, *203*
manipulator   **586**, **612**
    boolalpha   **617**
    dec   **622**
    endl   **586**, 587, **612**, 683
    ends   587, 612, *650*
    fixed   **625**
    flush   587, 612, 683
    hex   **622**
    implementing   **614**
    internal   **619**
    left   **619**
    mechanism   **612**
    noboolalpha   **617**
    noshowbase   **623**
    noshowpoint   **625**
    noshowpos   **621**
    noskipws   **626**, *684*
    nounitbuf   **626**
    nouppercase   **621**
    oct   **622**
    resetiosflags()   **616**
    right   **619**
    scientific   **625**
    setfill()   **619**
    setiosflags()   **616**
    setprecision()   **625**
    setw()   596, **619**, *629*
    showbase   **623**
    showpoint   **625**

showpos **621**

skipws **626**

unitbuf **626**

uppercase **621**

user-defined **614**

ws 587, 612

map *91*, **194**, *207*, *211*, *213*

  see container

  != **198**

  < **198**

  <= **198**

  == **198**

  > **198**

  >= **198**

  [] 92, **205**

  as associative array **92**, **205**

  begin() **200**

  clear() **202**

  constructors **196**

  count() 198

  destructor **196**

  empty() **198**

  end() **200**

  equal_range() 198

  erase() 202

  exception handling **207**

  find() **198**

  header file **194**

  index operator 92, **205**

  insert() 202, **203**

  iterators **200**

  lower_bound() 198

  manipulating access **115**

  max_size() **198**

  member functions **196**

  operations **196**

  rbegin() **200**

  removing elements **204**

rend() **200**

replace key **201**

size() **198**

sorting criterion 195, 197, *213*

subscript 92

subscript operator **205**

swap() **199**

upper_bound() 198

user-defined inserter **288**

<map> **194**

<map.h> 194

mapped_type

  for containers **231**

mask

  for ctype_base **717**

mask_array **564**, **578**

max() **66**

  for numeric limits 61, *614*

  for valarrays **571**

max_element() **340**

max_exponent

  for numeric limits 61

max_exponent10

  for numeric limits 61

maximum

  of elements **339**

  of two values **66**

  of types **64**

  value of numeric types **59**

max_length()

  for codecvt facet **721**

max_size()

  for allocators **739**

  for containers 145, 146, **233**

  for deques **162**

  for lists **168**

  for maps **198**

  for multimaps **198**

for multisets **179**
for sets **179**
for strings 486, **510**
for vectors **151**
mdy date order 710
member
as sorting criterion **123**
member function
as template **11**
member function adapter **307**
mem_fun **308**
mem_fun_ref **307**
member template **11**
memchr() 689
memcmp() 689
memcpy() *678*, 689
mem_fun **307**, **308**
mem_fun1_ref_t 309
mem_fun1_t 309
mem_fun_ref **307**
mem_fun_ref_t 309
mem_fun_t 309
memmove() 689
<memory> 51
memory leak 38
memset() 689
merge() **416**
for lists *172*, **246**
message_base **725**
catalog **725**
messages facet **725**
close() **725**
get() **725**
open() **725**
messages locale category **725**
min() **66**
for numeric limits 61
for valarrays **571**

min_element() **339**
min_exponent
for numeric limits 61
min_exponent10
for numeric limits 61
minimum
of elements **339**
of two values **66**
of types **64**
value of numeric types **59**
minus **305**
mirror elements 370
mismatch() **358**
modf()
global function 581
modifying algorithms 325, **363**
modifying elements **325**, **363**
modulus **305**, *306*, *377*
monetary locale category **711**
money_base **712**
none 712
part 712
pattern 712
sign 712
space 712
symbol 712
value 712
money_get facet **715**
get() **715**
moneypunct facet **711**
curr_symbol() **712**
decimal_point() **712**
frac_digits() **712**
grouping() **712**
negative_sign() **712**
neg_format() **712**
pos_format() **712**

    `positive_sign()`   **712**
    `thousands_sep()`   **712**
`money_put` facet   **713**
    `put()`   **714**
`move()`
    for `char_traits`   **689**
multibyte format   **686**
multimap   **194**, *209*
    see container
    `!=`   **198**
    `<`   **198**
    `<=`   **198**
    `==`   **198**
    `>`   **198**
    `>=`   **198**
    `begin()`   **200**
    `clear()`   **202**
    constructors   **196**
    `count()`   198
    destructor   **196**
    `empty()`   **198**
    `end()`   **200**
    `equal_range()`   198
    `erase()`   202
    exception handling   **207**
    `find()`   **198**
    header file   **194**
    `insert()`   202, **203**
    iterators   **200**
    `lower_bound()`   198
    manipulating access   **115**
    `max_size()`   **198**
    member functions   **196**
    operations   **196**
    `rbegin()`   **200**
    removing elements   **204**
    `rend()`   **200**
    replace key   **201**

    `size()`   **198**
    sorting criterion   195, 197, *213*
    `swap()`   **199**
    `upper_bound()`   198
    user-defined inserter   **288**
`<multimap.h>`   194
`multiplies`   *132*, **305**, *367*
multiset   **175**, *189*
    see container
    `!=`   **179**
    `<`   **179**
    `<=`   **179**
    `==`   **179**
    `>`   **179**
    `>=`   **179**
    `begin()`   **182**
    `clear()`   **183**
    constructor   *189*
    constructors   **177**
    `count()`   180
    destructor   **177**
    `empty()`   **179**
    `end()`   **182**
    `equal_range()`   *180*
    `erase()`   182, *189*
    exception handling   **185**
    `find()`   180, *189*
    header file   **175**
    `insert()`   182, **183**, *184*, *189*
    iterator   *189*
    iterators   **182**
    `lower_bound()`   *180*
    manipulating access   **115**
    `max_size()`   **179**
    member functions   **177**
    operations   **177**
    `rbegin()`   **182**
    `rend()`   **182**

size() **179**
sorting criterion   176, 178, *191*
swap() **182**
upper_bound() *180*
user-defined inserter **288**
<multiset.h> 175
mutating algorithms   327, **386**

N

name()
    for locales   697, 700, **703**
namespace **16**
    Koenig lookup   17
    rel_ops **69**
    std **23**
    using declaration **17**, *23*
    using directive **17**, *24*
narrow()
    for ctype facet **716**
    for streams   626
narrow stream   585
negate **305**
negative_sign()
    for moneypunct facet **712**
neg_format()
    for moneypunct facet **712**
nested class
    as template **14**
new   26
    and auto_ptr **39**
<new> 28
newline
    internationalized   691
newsgroups **743**
next_permutation() **391**
n-log-n complexity **21**
noboolalpha manipulator **617**

noconv
    for codecvt_base   722
nocreate flag **632**
none()
    for bitsets **464**
none monetary pattern   712
nonmodifying algorithms   323, **338**
no-op   98
no_order date order   710
noreplace flag **632**
norm()
    for complex   536, **543**
noshowbase manipulator **623**
noshowpoint manipulator **625**
noshowpos manipulator **621**
noskipws manipulator **626**, *684*
not1 **306**, *343*
not2 **306**
not_eof()
    for char_traits **689**
not_equal_to **305**
nounitbuf manipulator **626**
nouppercase manipulator **621**
npos
    for strings **474**, **495**, 508
nth_element() **404**
    versus partition()   330
NULL **71**
    and strings   484
number of elements **338**
numeric
    algorithms   331, **425**
    base   621
    formatting   620, **705**
    global functions **581**
    libraries **529**
    limits **59**
<numeric> **321**, **425**

numeric locale category **705**
numeric_limits **59**, *462*, *614*
num_get facet **707**
    get() **707**
numpunct facet **705**
    decimal_point() **705**
    falsename() **705**
    grouping() **705**
    thousands_sep() **705**
    truename() **705**
num_put facet **706**
    put() **706**

O

oct flag **621**
oct manipulator **622**
octal representation 621
odd element 306
offsetof() **71**
off_type
    for char_traits **689**
    for streams **635**
ofstream **627**, **629**
ok
    for codecvt_base 722
O(n) **21**
open()
    for messages facet **725**
    for streams 633, **634**
Open Closed Principle **217**
openmode
    for streams 631
operator
    -> for iterators 91
    const_cast 20
    dynamic_cast 19, 26
    for I/O 593
    for type conversion **19**

    reinterpret_cast 20
    static_cast 19
    typeid 26
    ! 601
    & 599
    << **593**, 652
    >> **594**, 652
    | **632**
    ~ 599
opfx() 658
ordered collection 75
order of elements change **386**
osfx() 658
ostream
    see output stream and stream
ostream **585**, **591**
<ostream> **592**
ostreambuf_iterator **665**, **666**
    failed() **666**
ostream iterator 107, **278**
ostream_withassign 591
ostringstream **645**
ostrstream **649**
out()
    for codecvt facet **721**
out flag **631**
out_of_range 25, **28**
output **583**
    see output stream and stream
    adjustment 618
    defining floating-point notation 623
    field width 618
    fill character 618
    hexadecimal 621
    numeric bases 621
    octal 621
    of addresses 596
    of bitsets **468**

of `bool` **595**, 617
of `complex` *532*, **539**, 544
of numeric values   620
of strings   **492**, **524**
of `void*`   596
operator `<<`   **593**
positive sign   620
redirecting   **641**
signs   620
standard functions   **610**
output buffer   **668**
    `epptr()`   **668**
    iterator   **665**
    `overflow()`   **669**
    `pbase()`   **668**
    `pbump()`   **675**
    `pptr()`   **668**
    `seekoff()`   676
    `seekpos()`   676
    `setp()`   **673**
    `sputc()`   **663**, **668**
    `sputn()`   **663**, **669**
    `sync()`   **675**
    `xsputn()`   **669**
output iterator   **253**
    versus forward iterator   254
`output_iterator`   288
output stream
    buffer iterators   **665**
    buffers   **663**
    `flush()`   **611**
    iterator   107, **278**
    member functions   **610**
    `put()`   **610**
    `sentry`   **658**
    `write()`   **610**, *658*
`overflow()`   *669*
    for output buffers   **669**

`overflow_error`   **25**, **28**
overloading
    of I/O operators   **652**
    with functions as parameter   612

P

`pair`   **33**, *184*
    `!=`   34
    `<`   34
    `<=`   34
    `==`   34
    `>`   34
    `>=`   34
    constructor   34
    `first`   34
    `first_type`   34
    `make_pair()`   34, **36**, *203*
    `second`   34
    `second_type`   34
part
    for `money_base`   **712**
partial
    for `codecvt_base`   722
`partial_sort()`   *329*, **400**
`partial_sort_copy()`   **402**
`partial_sum()`   **429**, *432*
`partition()`   **395**
    versus `nth_element()`   330
past-the-end iterator   83
pattern
    for `money_base`   **712**
`pbackfail()`
    for input buffers   **677**
`pbase()`
    for output buffers   **668**
`pbump()`
    for output buffers   **675**

peek()
   for input streams **609**
performance **21**
   of streams **681**
perror() 725
plus **305**, *336*, *431*
POD 156
pointer
   auto_ptr **38**
   input 596
   iterator traits 285
   NULL **71**
   output 596
pointer
   for allocators **738**
   for strings **508**
polar()
   for complex 533, **541**
pop()
   for priority queues **459**
   for queues **449**
   for stacks **440**
pop_back()
   for containers **243**
   for deques **163**
   for lists **170**
   for vectors **154**
pop_front()
   for containers **243**
   for deques **163**
   for lists **170**
pop_heap() **407**, *456*
pos_format()
   for moneypunct facet **712**
positioning
   in files **634**
positive_sign()
   for moneypunct facet **712**

pos_type
   for char_traits **689**
   for streams **634**
pow()
   for complex 540, **545**
   for valarrays **574**, **575**
   global function *311*, 581
pptr()
   for output buffers **668**
precision() *539*
   for streams 623
predicate **121**, **302**, 322
   binary **123**
   unary **121**
prev_permutation() **391**
print
   for ctype_base 717
PRINT_ELEMENTS() **118**, **332**
printing
   see output
priority queue **453**
   constructor **458**, **459**
   container_type **458**
   empty() **459**
   header file **454**
   pop() **459**
   push() **459**
   size() **459**
   size_type **458**
   top() **459**
   value_type **457**
priority_queue **453**
proxy
   for bitsets 466
   for vector<bool> 158
ptrdiff_t type **71**
ptr_fun **310**, *319*

`pubimbue()`
    for stream buffers   **664**
`pubseekoff()`
    for stream buffers   **664**
`pubseekpos()`
    for stream buffers   **664**
`pubsetbuf()`
    for stream buffers   **664**
`punct`
    for `ctype_base`   717
pure abstraction   94
`push()`
    for priority queues   **459**
    for queues   **449**
    for stacks   **440**
`push_back()`
    called by inserters   272
    for containers   **241**
    for deques   **163**
    for lists   **170**, *172*
    for strings   **490**, **516**
    for vectors   **154**
`push_front()`
    called by inserters   272
    for containers   **241**
    for deques   **163**
    for lists   **170**, *172*
`push_heap()`   **406**, *407*, *456*
`put()`
    for `money_put` facet   **714**
    for `num_put` facet   **706**
    for output streams   **610**, *629*
    for `time_put` facet   **710**
`putback()`
    for input streams   **609**
put buffer   **668**
    iterator   **665**
`putchar()`   *669*

`pword()`
    for streams   659

Q

quadratic complexity   **21**
queue
    `!=`   **449**
    `<`   **449**
    `<=`   **449**
    `==`   **449**
    `>`   **449**
    `>=`   **449**
    `back()`   **449**
    constructor   **448**
    `container_type`   **448**
    `empty()`   **449**
    `front()`   **449**
    header file   **444**
    `pop()`   **449**
    `push()`   **449**
    `size()`   **448**
    `size_type`   **448**
    user-defined version   **450**
    `value_type`   **448**
queue   **444**
`<queue>`   **444**, **454**
`<Queue.hpp>`   450
quicksort   **328**
`quiet_NaN()`
    for numeric limits   61

R

`radix`
    for numeric limits   61
`rand()`   *374*
    global function   582
random access   76
    to files   **634**

random access iterator   93, **255**
   distance   261
   step backward   259
   step forward   259
`random_access_iterator`   288
`random_shuffle()`   **393**
range   **97**
   change order of elements   **386**
   comparing   **356**
   copy   **363**
   copy and modify elements   **367**
   counting elements   **338**
   empty   84
   for iterators   84
   half-open   **97**
   in algorithms   **97**
   maximum   **339**
   minimum   **339**
   modify elements   **372**
   modifying   **363**
   multiple   **101**
   mutating   **386**
   notation   **97**
   numeric processing   **425**
   of values   **59**
   removing duplicates   **381**
   removing elements   **111**, **378**
   replacing elements   **375**
   searching elements   324, **341**
   sorting   **397**
   swapping elements   **370**
   transform elements   **367**
   valid   **97**, 99
`range_error`   25, **28**
`raw_storage_iterator`   **731**
`rbegin()`   109, **265**, 269
   for containers   **145**, **239**
   for deques   **162**

   for lists   **169**
   for maps   **200**
   for multimaps   **200**
   for multisets   **182**
   for sets   **182**
   for strings   **526**
   for vectors   **153**
`rdbuf()`
   for streams   *636*, **639**, *641*, **683**
`rdstate()`   *599*
   for streams   598
reachable   **97**
`read()`
   for input streams   **608**
   global function   *678*
reading
   see input
`readsome()`
   for input streams   **609**
`real()`
   for `complex`   536, **543**
reallocation
   for strings   486
   for vectors   149
`rebind`
   for allocators   **734**, **738**
red-black tree   **176**
redirecting
   streams   **641**
`reference`
   for allocators   **738**
   for bitsets   **467**
   for containers   **230**
   for strings   **507**
   for `vector<bool>`   159
reference counting
   for containers   **222**
   for strings   506

reference semantics
    of container elements **135**
register_callback()
    for streams 661
reinterpret_cast 20
relative to absolute values 331, 429
release()
    for auto_ptrs **54**
rel_ops **69**
remove() **378**
    for lists **169**, *170*, **242**
remove_copy() **380**
remove_copy_if() **380**
remove_if() **302**, **378**
    for lists **169**, **242**
removing algorithms 326, **378**
removing duplicates **381**
removing elements **111**, 326
rend() 109, **265**, 269
    for containers **145**, **240**
    for deques **162**
    for lists **169**
    for maps **200**
    for multimaps **200**
    for multisets **182**
    for sets **182**
    for strings **526**
    for vectors **153**
replace() **375**
    for strings 491, *501*, **519**, **520**
replace and copy elements **376**
replace_copy() **376**
replace_copy_if() **376**
replace_if() **375**
representation
    binary 462
    decimal 621

    hexadecimal 621
    octal 621
requirements
    for container elements **134**
    for sorting criteria **176**
    for the compiler 9
reserve()
    for containers **233**
    for strings **486**, 488, **510**
    for vectors **149**
reset()
    for auto_ptrs **54**
    for bitsets **465**
resetiosflags() manipulator **616**
resize()
    for containers **244**, 248
    for deques **163**
    for lists **170**
    for strings 491, **518**
    for valarrays **571**
    for vectors **154**
resource leak 38
result
    for codecvt_base **722**
result_type 310
return_temporary_buffer() 731
reverse() **386**
    for lists **246**
    for strings *501*
reverse_copy() **386**
reverse iterator 109, **264**
    base() **269**
    convert into iterator **269**
reverse_iterator
    for containers **230**
    for strings **508**
rfind()
    for strings **520**, **521**

right flag **618**
right manipulator **619**
rotate() **388**
rotate_copy() **389**
round_error()
    for numeric limits 61
round_indeterminate 64
round_style
    for numeric limits 61, **63**
round_to_nearest 64
round_toward_infinity 64
round_toward_neg_infinity 64
round_toward_zero 64
runtime_error **25, 28**
rvalue **55**

S

safe STL **138**
sbumpc()
    for input buffers **663**, 676
scan_is()
    for ctype facet **716**
scan_not()
    for ctype facet **716**
scientific flag **623**
scientific manipulator **625**
search() **347**, *499*
searching algorithms 324, **341**
search_n() **344**
search_n_if() 346
second
    for pairs 34
second_argument_type 310
second_type
    for pairs 34
seekdir **635**
seekg()
    for streams 634, *636*, 644

seekoff()
    for output buffers 676
seekp() *651*
    for streams 634, 644
seekpos()
    for output buffers 676
self-defined
    see user-defined
sentry **658**
sequence
    see range
sequence container **75**
set *87*, **175**, *186*
    see container
    != **179**
    < **179**
    <= **179**
    == **179**
    > **179**
    >= **179**
    begin() **182**
    clear() **183**
    constructors **177**, *186*
    count() 180
    destructor **177**
    empty() **179**
    end() **182**
    equal_range() *180*
    erase() 182, *186*
    exception handling **185**
    find() 180, *186*
    header file **175**
    insert() 182, **183**, *184*, *186*
    insert elements **183**
    iterators **182**, *186*
    lower_bound() *180*
    manipulating access **115**
    max_size() **179**

member functions   **177**
operations   **177**
rbegin()   **182**
rend()   **182**
size()   **179**
sorting criterion   176, 178, *191*
swap()   **182**
upper_bound()   *180*
user-defined inserter   **288**
user-defined sorting criterion   *294*
set()
　for bitsets   **465**
<set>   175
set_difference()   **420**
setf()
　for streams   **615**
setfill() manipulator   **619**
setg()   *678*
　for input buffers   **677**
<set.h>   175
set_intersection()   **419**
setiosflags() manipulator   **616**
setlocale()   693
setp()
　for output buffers   **673**
setprecision() manipulator   **625**
setstate()
　for streams   598
set_symmetric_difference()   **420,**
　　421
set_union()   **418**
setw() manipulator   596, **619**, *629*
sgetc()
　for input buffers   **663, 676**
sgetn()
　for input buffers   **663, 677**
shift()
　for valarrays   **572**

short
　numeric limits   60
showbase flag   **622**
showbase manipulator   **623**
showpoint flag   **624**
showpoint manipulator   **625**
showpos flag   **620**
showpos manipulator   **621**
sign monetary pattern   712
signaling_NaN()
　for numeric limits   61
sin()
　for complex   540, **546**
　for valarrays   **575**
　global function   581
sinh()
　for complex   540, **546**
　for valarrays   **575**
　global function   581
size
　of containers   **146**
　of strings   **485**
　of vectors   **149**
size()
　for bitsets   **464**
　for containers   **145**, 146, **233**
　for deques   **162**
　for lists   **168**
　for maps   **198**
　for multimaps   **198**
　for multisets   **179**
　for priority queues   **459**
　for queues   **448**
　for sets   **179**
　for stacks   **440**
　for strings   485, **510**
　for valarray gslice   **577**
　for valarrays   **571**

for valarray `slice` **576**
for vectors **151**
`size_t` type **71**
`size_type` 474
for allocators **738**
for containers **231**
for priority queues **458**
for queues **448**
for stacks **439**
for strings 495, **507**
`skipws` flag **625**
`skipws` manipulator **626**
`slice` **555, 575**
constructor **576**
`size()` **576**
`start()` **576**
`stride()` **576**
`slice_array` **556, 575**
smart pointer
`auto_ptr` **38**
for reference counting **222**
`snextc()`
for input buffers **663**
sort
elements 328
`sort()` *123, 328,* **397**
for lists *172,* **245**
versus `stable_sort()` 398
sorted collection 75
sorted range **409**
`sort_heap()` *329,* **407**
sorting algorithms **328, 397**
sorting criterion
as constructor parameter 178, 197
as template parameter 178, 197
at runtime *191, 213*
for maps 195, 197, *213*
for multimaps 195, 197, *213*

for multisets 176, 178, *191*
for sets 176, 178, *191*
for strings **213**, 499
function **123**
function object **294**
locale as 703
requirements **176**
user-defined **123**, *294*
sorting elements **397**
space
compressing *385*
space
for `ctype_base` 717
space monetary pattern 712
special characters
internationalized 691
`splice()`
for lists *172,* **245**
`sputbackc()`
for input buffers **663, 676**
`sputc()`
for output buffers **663, 668**
`sputn()`
for output buffers **663, 669**
`sqrt()`
for `complex` 540, **545**
for valarrays **575**
global function 581
`srand()`
global function 582
`<sstream>` **646**
`stable_partition()` **395**
`stable_sort()` *329,* **397**
versus `sort()` 398
stack **435**
`!=` **440**
`<` **440**
`<=` **440**

== **440**

> **440**

>= **440**

constructor **440**

container_type **439**

empty() **440**

header file **435**

pop() **440**

push() **440**

size() **440**

size_type **439**

top() **440**

user-defined version **441**

value_type **439**

<stack> **435**

<stack.h> 435, 444, 454

<Stack.hpp> 441

stack unwinding 15

standard error channel 585

    redirecting **641**

standard input channel 585

    redirecting **641**

standard operators

    for I/O 593

standard output channel 585

    redirecting **641**

standard template library **73**

    see STL

start()

    for valarray gslice **577**

    for valarray slice **576**

state

    of function objects **296**

    of streams **597**

state_type

    for char_traits **689**

static array container **155**

static_cast 19

std namespace **23**

<stddef.h> 71

stderr 585

<stdexcept> **28**

stdin 585

<stdlib.h> 71

stdout 585

STL **73**

    algorithms 74, **94**, 111, **321**

    commit-or-rollback **139**

    container adapters **435**

    containers 73, **75**, **143**

    element requirements **134**

    error handling **137**

    exceptions handling **139**, 248

    extending **141**

    function objects **124**, **293**

    functor **293**

    functors **124**

    introduction **73**

    iterator adapters 104, **264**

    iterators 74, **83**, **251**

    manipulating algorithms **111**

    predicates **121**, 322

    priority queues **453**

    problems **136**

    queues **444**

    ranges **97**

    safe STL **138**

    stacks **435**

    transaction safe **139**

str() *539*, 650

    for string streams **647**

stream **583**, *587*

    << conventions **662**

    >> conventions **662**

    adjustfield **618**

    adjustment 618

app flag **631**
ate flag **631**
bad() 598
badbit **597**
basefield **621**
basic_filebuf 643
beg **635**
binary flag **631**
boolalpha flag **617**
boolalpha manipulator **617**
buffer iterators **665**
buffers **663, 668**
callback **661**
character traits **687**
classes **588**
clear() 598, *633, 636*
close() 633
connecting 637
copyfmt() 615, **616**, *641, 653*, **661**
copyfmt_event 661
cur **635**
dec flag **621**
dec manipulator **622**
defining floating-point notation 623
end **635**
endl manipulator **586**, 587, **612**, 683
end-of-file **590**
ends *650*
ends manipulator 587, 612
EOF 590
eof() 598
eofbit **597**
erase_event 661
event 661
event_callback 661
examples 611
exceptions() 602
fail() 598

failbit **597**
failure **602**
field width 618
file access **627**
filebuf 643
fill() 618
fill character 618
fixed flag **623**
fixed manipulator **625**
flags() 615, **616**
floatfield **623**
flush manipulator 587, 612, 683
for char* **649**
for file descriptors 637, 672
format flags **615**
formatting **615**
formatting of bool 595, **617**
fpos **634**
freeze() 650
getloc() 626
good() 598
goodbit **597**
hardfail **598**
header files **592**
hex flag **621**
hex manipulator **622**
hexadecimal 621
ignore() *614*
imbue() 626, 694
imbue_event 661
in flag **631**
input buffers **676**
input functions **607**
internal flag **618**
internal manipulator **619**
internationalization **625**
is_open() 633
iterators **277**

iword()   659
left flag   **618**
left manipulator   **619**
manipulators   **586, 612**
member functions   **607**
narrow()   626
noboolalpha manipulator   **617**
nocreate flag   **632**
noreplace flag   **632**
noshowbase manipulator   **623**
noshowpoint manipulator   **625**
noshowpos manipulator   **621**
noskipws manipulator   **626**, *684*
nounitbuf manipulator   **626**
nouppercase manipulator   **621**
numeric bases   621
oct flag   **621**
oct manipulator   **622**
octal   621
off_type   **635**
open()   633, **634**
openmode   631
operator !   600
operator bool   600
operator void*   600
out flag   **631**
output buffers   **668**
output functions   **610**
performance   **681**
positioning   **634**
pos_type   **634**
precision()   623
pword()   659
rdbuf()   *636*, **639, 683**
rdstate()   598
read and write   643
read and write position   **644**
redirecting standard streams   **641**

register_callback()   661
resetiosflags() manipulator   **616**
right flag   **618**
right manipulator   **619**
scientific flag   **623**
scientific manipulator   **625**
seekg()   634, *636*, 644
seekp()   634, 644
sentry   **658**
setf()   **615**
setfill() manipulator   **619**
setiosflags() manipulator   **616**
setprecision() manipulator   **625**
setstate()   598
setw()   *629*
setw() manipulator   596, **619**
showbase flag   **622**
showbase manipulator   **623**
showpoint flag   **624**
showpoint manipulator   **625**
showpos flag   **620**
showpos manipulator   **621**
skipws flag   **625**
skipws manipulator   **626**
state   **597**
state and open()   **634**
str()   650
strings   **645**
synchronize streams   **637**
synchronize with C   **682**
sync_with_stdio()   **682**
tellg()   634
tellp()   634
testing the state   **600**
tie()   **637**, 638
trunc flag   **631**
unitbuf   **683**
unitbuf flag   **625**

unitbuf manipulator **626**
unsetf() **615**
uppercase flag **620**
uppercase manipulator **621**
user-defined buffers 668
widen() 626
width() 618, *653*
ws manipulator 587, 612
xalloc() 659
streambuf 590, **668**
    see stream buffer
`<streambuf>` **592**
stream buffer **663**
    see output buffer and input buffer
    `<<` 597, 683
    `>>` 683
    for file descriptors 637, 672
    getloc() **664**
    pubimbue() **664**
    pubseekoff() **664**
    pubseekpos() **664**
    pubsetbuf() **664**
    user-defined 668
stream iterator 107, **277**, *282*
    end-of-stream 108, **280**
    skip input 282
streamoff **635**
streampos **634**
streamsize **607**
strftime() 708
strict weak ordering **176**
stride()
    for valarray gslice **577**
    for valarray slice **576**
string **471**
    != **511**
    + 492, **524**
    += **490**, **515**

`<` **511**
`<<` 492, **524**
`<=` **511**
= **489**
== **511**
`>` **511**
`>=` **511**
`>>` 492, **524**
allocator_type **526**
and NULL 484
and vectors 155
append() **490, 515, 516**
assign() **489**, **514**
at() **513**
automatic type conversions 484
begin() *497*, **525**
capacity **485**
capacity() 486, **510**
char* stream **649**
character traits 503, **687**
clear() 490, **518**
compare() **511, 512**
compare case-insensitive *213*
comparisons 488
concatenation 492
const_iterator **508**
const_pointer **508**
const_reference **507**
const_reverse_iterator **508**
constructor *501*, **508, 509**
converting index into iterator 500
converting into char* 484, 513, *629*
converting iterator into index 500
copy() 484, **513**
c_str() 484, **513**, *629*
data() 484, **513**
destructor **509**
difference_type **507**

empty() 485, **510**
end() *497*, **525**
erase() 491, *501*, **518**
find() **520**, **521**
find_first_not_of() **522**
find_first_of() **522**
find_last_not_of() **523**
find_last_of() **523**
get_allocator() **526**
getline() 493, **525**
header file **479**
index to iterator conversion 500
input **492**, **524**, 596, 620
insert() 491, **516**, **517**
internationalization 503
iterator **508**
iterator operator ++ **258**
iterator operator -- **258**
iterators **497**
iterator to index conversion 500
length() 485, **510**
literal 471
locale dependent collations **724**
locale dependent comparisons 489
lower characters 497
max_size() 486, **510**
not case-sensitive 499
npos **474**, **495**, 508
output **492**, **524**
pointer **508**
push_back() **490**, **516**
rbegin() **526**
reallocation 486
reference **507**
rend() **526**
replace() 491, *501*, **519**, **520**
reserve() **486**, 488, **510**
resize() 491, **518**

reverse() *501*
reverse_iterator **508**
rfind() **520**, **521**
search functions 493
size **485**
size() 485, **510**
size_type 495, **507**
sorting criterion **213**, 499
str() *653*
stream functions **645**
substr() 492, **524**
substrings 492
swap() **490**, **515**
traits_type **507**
upper characters 497
value_type **507**
string **471**
<string> **479**, **688**
stringbuf **645**
<string.h> 689
string::npos **474**, **495**
stringstream **645**
string streams **645**
    str() **647**
string termination character
    internationalized 691
strlen() 689
strstream **649**
<strstream> **649**
strstreambuf **649**
subscript operator
    for deques **162**
    for maps 92, **205**
    for vectors **152**
substr()
    for strings 492, **524**

suffix
    `_copy` 323
    `_if` 323
`sum()`
    for valarrays **572**
`sungetc()`
    for input buffers **663**, **676**
`swap()` **67**
    for containers *140*, **145**, 147, **237**
    for deques **163**
    for lists **168**
    for maps **199**
    for multimaps **199**
    for multisets **182**
    for sets **182**
    for strings **490**, **515**
    for vectors 149, **151**
swapping
    for containers 147
    iterator values 263
    two values **67**
swapping elements **370**
`swap_ranges()` **370**
symbol monetary pattern 712
`sync()` 658
    for output buffers **675**
`sync_with_stdio()`
    for streams **682**

T

`table()`
    for `ctype` facet **718**
`table_size`
    for `ctype` facet **718**
tags
    for iterators **283**
`tan()`
    for `complex` 540, **546**

    for valarrays **575**
    global function 581
`tanh()`
    for `complex` 540, **546**
    for valarrays **575**
    global function 581
`tellg()`
    for streams 634
`tellp()`
    for streams 634
template **9**
    constructor **13**
    copy constructor *35*
    default parameter **10**
    member templates **11**
    nested class **14**
    nontype parameters **10**
    `typename` **11**
`test()`
    for bitsets **465**
`thousands_sep()`
    for `moneypunct` facet **712**
    for `numpunct` facet **705**
`throw` **16**, *441*, *450*
throw specification **16**
`tie()`
    for streams **637**, 638
time locale category **708**
`time_base` **709**
    `dateorder` **709**
    `dmy` 710
    `mdy` 710
    `no_order` 710
    `ydm` 710
    `ymd` 710
`time_get` facet **708**
    `date_order()` **708**
    `get_date()` **708**

get_monthname() **708**

get_time() **708**

get_weekday() **708**

get_year() **708**

time_put facet **710**

put() **710**

times **305**

tinyness_before

for numeric limits 62

to_char_type()

for char_traits **689**

to_int_type()

for char_traits **689**

tolower() *497*, **719**

for ctype facet **716**

top()

for priority queues **459**

for stacks **440**

to_string()

for bitsets **468**

to_ulong() *462*

for bitsets **468**

toupper() *497*, *669*, **719**

for ctype facet **716**

traits

for characters *504*, **687**

for iterators **283**

traits_type

for strings **507**

transaction safe **139**

transform() *120*, *131*, **367**, **368**, *497*

for collate facet **724**

versus for_each() **325**

transform elements **367**

transitive 176

traps

for numeric limits 62

true **18**

truename()

for numpunct facet **705**

trunc flag **631**

type

bool **18**

ptrdiff_t **71**

size_t **71**

wchar_t 687, **692**

type conversion **19**

typeid 26

<typeinfo> 28

typename **11**

U

uflow()

for input buffers **676**

unary_function **310**

unary predicate **121**

underflow()

for input buffers **676**

underflow_error **25**, **28**

unexpected() 26

unget()

for input streams **609**

uninitialized_copy() *730*, **742**

uninitialized_fill() 730, **740**

uninitialized_fill_n() *730*, **741**

union set **418**

unique() **381**

for lists *172*, **244**

unique_copy() **384**

unitbuf **683**

unitbuf flag **625**

unitbuf manipulator **626**

unsetf()

for streams **615**

unshift()

for codecvt facet **721**

upper
    for `ctype_base`   717
`upper_bound()`   **413**
    for containers   **235**
    for maps   198
    for multimaps   198
    for multisets   *180*
    for sets   *180*
uppercase flag   **620**
uppercase manipulator   **621**
upper string characters   497
URLs   **743**
`use_facet()`   698
    for locales   700, **702**
user-defined
    algorithm   285
    allocator   735
    container   **217**
    exception   *441, 450*
    function object   **310**
    inserter   **288**
    iterator   **288**
    iterator adapter   **288**
    manipulators   **614**
    sorting criterion   **123**, *294*
    stream buffers   668
using declaration   **17**, *23*
using directive   **17**, *24*
utilities   **33**
`<utility>`   33, 34, 69

V

valarray   **547**
    `~`   **573**
    `!`   **573**
    `!=`   **573**
    `%`   **573**
    `%=`   **574**
    `&`   **573**
    `&&`   **573**
    `&=`   **574**
    `*`   **573**
    `*=`   **574**
    `+`   **573**
    `+=`   **574**
    `-`   **573**
    `-=`   **574**
    `/`   **573**
    `/=`   **574**
    `<`   **573**
    `<<`   **573**
    `<<=`   **574**
    `<=`   **573**
    `==`   **573**
    `>`   **573**
    `>=`   **573**
    `>>`   **573**
    `>>=`   **574**
    `^`   **573**
    `^=`   **574**
    `|`   **573**
    `|=`   **574**
    `||`   **573**
    `abs()`   **574**
    `acos()`   **575**
    `apply()`   **572**
    `asin()`   **575**
    `atan()`   **575**
    `atan2()`   **575**
    constructor   **548, 570**
    `cos()`   **575**
    `cosh()`   **575**
    `cshift()`   **572**
    destructor   **570**
    `exp()`   **575**
    `fill()`   **571**

gslice **560**
gslice_array **561**
header file **547**
indirect array **567**
indirect_array **567**
lazy evaluation 554
length() **571**
log() **575**
log10() **575**
mask_array **564**
max() **571**
min() **571**
pow() **574, 575**
resize() **571**
shift() **572**
sin() **575**
sinh() **575**
size() **571**
slice **555**
slice_array **556**
sqrt() **575**
sum() **572**
tan() **575**
tanh() **575**
type conversions 554
valarray **547**
<valarray> **547**
valid range **97**, 99
value monetary pattern 712
value_comp()
    for containers **236**
value_compare
    for containers **231**
value pair **33**
value semantics
    of container elements **135**
value_type
    for allocators **737**

for complex **541**
for containers **230**
for insert() **203**
for priority queues **457**
for queues **448**
for stacks **439**
for strings **507**
vector **148**, *156*
    see container
    != **151**
    < **151**
    <= **151**
    = **151**
    == **151**
    > **151**
    >= **151**
    [] **152**
    and strings 155
    as dynamic array **155**
    assign() **151**
    assignment **151**
    at() **152**
    back() **152**
    begin() **153**
    capacity **149**
    capacity() 149
    clear() **154**
    constructor **150**
    constructor 729
    contiguity of elements **155**
    destructor **150**
    element access **152**
    empty() **151**
    end() **153**
    erase() **154**
    exception handling **155**
    for bool **158**
    front() **152**

header file **148**
insert() **154**
iterator operator ++ **258**
iterator operator -- **258**
iterators **153**
max_size() **151**
member functions **150**
operations **150**
pop_back() **154**
push_back() **154**
rbegin() **153**
reallocation 149
removing elements 153
rend() **153**
reserve() **149**, 730
resize() **154**
shrink capacity 149
size **149**
size() **151**
subscript operator **152**
swap() 149, **151**
<vector> **148**
vector<bool> **158**
flip() **158**, 159
reference 159
<vector.h> 148
void*
input 596
output 596

W

wcerr **592**
wchar_t
input 595
numeric limits 60
wchar_t type 687, **692**
wcin **592**

wclog **592**
wcout **592**
Web site **5**
wfilebuf **627**
wfstream **627**
what() **28**, *29*
whitespace
compressing *385*
wide-character format **686**
widen()
for ctype facet **716**
for streams 626
width()
for streams 618, *653*
wifstream **627**
wios **590**
wiostream **591**
wistream **591**
wistringstream **645**
wofstream **627**
wostream **591**
wostringstream **645**
wrapper
for arrays **219**
write()
for output streams **610**, *658*
global function *672*, *673*
writing
see output
ws manipulator 587, 612
wstreambuf 590, **668**
see output buffer and input buffer
wstreampos **634**
wstring **471**
see string
wstringbuf **645**
wstringstream **645**

X

`xalloc()`
    for streams   659
`xdigit`
    for `ctype_base`   717
`xsgetn()`
    for input buffers   **677**

`xsputn()`
    for output buffers   **669**

Y

ydm date order   710
ymd date order   710

Register Your Book

at informit.com/register

You may be eligible to receive:

- Advance notice of forthcoming editions of the book
- Related book recommendations
- Chapter excerpts and supplements of forthcoming titles
- Information about special contests and promotions throughout the year
- Notices and reminders about author appearances, tradeshows, and online chats with special guests

Contact us

If you are interested in writing a book or reviewing manuscripts prior to publication, please write to us at:

Editorial Department
Addison-Wesley Professional
75 Arlington Street, Suite 300
Boston, MA 02116 USA
Email: AWPro@aw.com

Visit us on the Web: informit.com/aw